IS 13968-1   10/25/02

C0-ALP-231

Syntactic Heads and Word Formation

Recent Titles in
OXFORD STUDIES IN COMPARATIVE SYNTAX
Richard Kayne, *General Editor*

Syntactic Heads and Word Formation

Marit Julien

OXFORD
UNIVERSITY PRESS

2002

OXFORD
UNIVERSITY PRESS

Oxford   New York
Auckland   Bangkok   Buenos Aires   Cape Town   Chennai
Dar es Salaam   Delhi   Hong Kong   Istanbul   Karachi   Kolkata
Kuala Lumpur   Madrid   Melbourne   Mexico City   Mumbai   Nairobi
São Paulo   Shanghai   Singapore   Taipei   Tokyo   Toronto

and an associated company in Berlin

Copyright © 2002 by Oxford University Press, Inc.

Published by Oxford University Press, Inc.
198 Madison Avenue, New York, New York 10016

www.oup.com

Oxford is a registered trademark of Oxford University Press

All rights reserved. No part of this publication may be reproduced,
stored in a retrieval system, or transmitted, in any form or by any means,
electronic, mechanical, photocopying, recording, or otherwise,
without the prior permission of Oxford University Press.

Library of Congress Cataloging-in-Publication Data
Julien, Marit.
Syntactic heads and word formation / Marit Julien.
p. cm.—(Oxford studies in comparative syntax)
Includes bibliographical references and index.
ISBN 0-19-514950-5; ISBN 0-19-514951-3 (pbk.)
1. Grammar, Comparative and general—Verb. 2. Order (Grammar). 3. Grammar, Comparative and
general—Morphology. 4. Grammar, Comparative and general—Syntax. I. Title. II. Series.
P281 .J85 2002
415—dc21   2001050092

P
281
.J85
2002

2 4 6 8 9 7 5 3 1

Printed in the United States of America
on acid-free paper

Acknowledgments

The study presented here owes a lot to two people in particular. First, to Tarald Taraldsen, who was my supervisor throughout this and previous projects. He always had insightful comments, he was always able to detect the weak points of my argumentation, and he was always quite enthusiastic about what I was doing. I am not sure what would have become of the enterprise without his guidance and support.

Second, to Helge Leirvik, my best friend, who was always there to cheer me up when I was not too optimistic. Over the years, he has patiently listened to me talking about linguistics and often even managed to look interested. I am very grateful for his company.

I would also like to thank the members of my doctoral committee: Mark Baker, who also provided some useful suggestions at the beginning of the project; Anders Holmberg, who has influenced my thinking considerably; and Gunlög Josefsson, whose remarks at the final stage were very helpful.

Thanks to Guglielmo Cinque and an anonymous reviewer for very useful comments on the manuscript, and to Lars-Olof Delsing, who gave some good advice at the very beginning of my writing.

Thanks to everyone in the linguistics department in Tromsø, and to the linguists and staff at HIL in Leiden, who welcomed me there when I felt the need to get away from the subarctic for a while. Special thanks to Hans Bennis for encouragement and to Sjef Barbiers for asking a very important question.

Thanks to the staff at the University Library in Tromsø, who managed to get me descriptions of so many little-known languages from all over the world. I very much appreciate their effort. I also appreciate the fact that interlibrary loans are still free here in Tromsø. For the sake of the advancement of knowledge, I hope this never will change.

Finally, I thank the Research Council of Norway for financing the study (grant no. 110928/520). I am very grateful for the chance I was given to work on the problems of wordhood for so long almost without interruption. It has been a luxury.

Contents

Syntactic Heads and Word Formation

Introduction: An Overview of the Work

The topic of this book is the formation of morphologically complex words. That is, it deals with the mechanisms of grammar that may cause two or more of the minimal meaningful elements of language—the morphemes—to be combined into one single word. The claim that will be developed in much more detail in the following chapters is that word formation is mainly a matter of syntax. That is, the basic building blocks of syntax are individual morphemes, not words, and it is the syntax that determines the order of morphemes within each complex word, in very much the same way as it determines the order of words in phrases and sentences.

But notably, I also argue that the notion of 'word' itself cannot be defined in syntactic terms. Rather, it appears that the only criteria that can be used to detect the words in any string of speech are distributional ones. Thus, for speakers as well as for linguists, a word is a morpheme sequence that shows cohesion internally and has independent distribution externally.

If words are characterized by their distributional properties, it follows that it is not necessarily correct to associate the word with one particular type of syntactic constituent, such as $X°$. A necessary condition for two morphemes to form a word is that they are linearly adjacent and that this adjacency is a recurrent pattern in the language in question. My claim is that this is also a sufficient condition: when two morphemes regularly appear immediately adjacent to each other, the two morphemes will tend to be seen as one grammatical word.

Now if a morpheme X precedes a morpheme Y and there is a word XY, there are at least three different syntactic relations that may obtain between the syntactic nodes X and Y. The two nodes may be contained in a complex syntactic head, or X may be the final element of a constituent in Spec-YP, or Y may be the head of the complement of XP, provided that there is no phonologically realized material in the specifier position of that complement. But if morphemes may combine into words in any of these three configurations, it follows that grammar does not have at its disposal any operations that specifically form words. On this view, words are *perceived* rather than *formed*. That is, the word in the nonphonological sense is an epiphenomenon that really has no status in grammar.

In this work, the predictions concerning morpheme ordering that follow from the approach just sketched are tested against the patterns of verbal inflection found in a broad sample of languages drawn from all over the world. The conclusion is that the predictions are borne out to a considerable degree. Even if this does not prove that the syntactic approach is correct, it certainly suggests that the syntactic approach is the more adequate one, since it requires fewer auxiliary assumptions than competing lexical theories.

The study is greatly inspired by the Distributed Morphology approach of Halle and Marantz (1993, 1994). The theory that I develop, however, makes use of a smaller set of word-forming tools than Distributed Morphology does. First, I do not recognize the operation referred to by Halle and Marantz as morphological merger, which is the operation whereby structurally adjacent heads can be joined under a zero level node even in the absence of head movement; second, I do not allow the actual order of morphemes to be attributed to the properties of individual affixes. Instead, in my theory the surface order of morphemes is a direct consequence of syntax.

The work is organized as follows. Chapter 1 is a general introduction to the field of inquiry that I will be concerned with and to the theoretical framework that I am going to assume. I begin with a brief recapitulation of the history of lexicalist and nonlexicalist approaches to word formation within the generative tradition. After that I give an outline of the model of grammar on which the study is based. This model is characterized by the assumptions that syntactic structures are built from abstract morphemes and that the phonological shape of these morphemes is only determined at Spell-Out—that is, at a stage where the base-generated morpheme order, and even the number of morphemes, may have been altered by subsequent syntactic operations.

I then go on to deal with various definitions of the concept 'word'. The conclusion of this discussion is that 'word' in a nonphonological sense is a label for morpheme strings that share certain distributional properties. Apart from this, the concept 'word' is of very little relevance to grammar.

In the final section of chapter 1 I present some results from a survey I have conducted of verbal morphology and word order in a sample of 530 languages, representing 280 genera from all over the world. It appears, for example, that if the tense markers of natural languages are classified according to their realization relative to the verb stem—as prefix, suffix, free preposed marker, or free postposed marker—one sees that these types are not evenly distributed across languages. Not only are certain types of tense markers generally preferred over others but also there are observable correlations between certain tense marker types and certain word orders within the clause. It is these interdependencies that are explored in more depth in the remainder of the work.

The topic of chapter 2 is head-to-head movement, a process which is widely assumed to be a word-forming one. However, there are still quite a few questions pertaining to head movement that have not been conclusively answered. The first problem that I take up in chapter 2 is the trigger for head movement. In the checking theory of Chomsky (1993, 1995), where words come fully inflected from the lexicon, the only trigger for movement is the need to check the features of the moving element and of the attractor. In theories that deal more explicitly with word formation, be it in syntax or in a syntax-like component of the lexicon, the concept of *morphological subcategorization* has played a central part. Thus, it is often assumed that if a lexical root adjoins to an inflectional marker, it is because the inflectional marker subcategorizes morphologically for an element of that particular lexical class. Conversely, in the apparently exceptional cases where root and inflection marker do not combine morphologically, although one would expect them to do so, many theorists have proposed that it is because the root does not meet the morphological subcategorization requirements of the inflectional marker and that these requirements may then trigger the insertion of auxiliaries in such constructions.

I propose instead that head movement is triggered by a strong head feature in the attracting head. That is, if a head has a strong head feature it will attract the next head down. However, the derivation will crash if the complement feature of the attractor is not checked. Hence, the head movement operation is only successful if the head of the complement satisfies both the head feature and the complement feature of the attracting head. That is, for any given X°, its complement feature will ensure that the complement of X° is of the right category. Now if X° always has a complement of the category YP, and the head Y° of that complement is always attracted to X°, the consequence is that X° in all its occurrences forms a complex head with a Y°. Hence, X° will have the appearance of an affix. In this way, the concept of morphological subcategorization is reformulated in syntactic terms.

While the concept of feature checking is thus retained, my proposal differs from that of Chomsky (1993, 1995) in that I argue that words do not come fully inflected from the lexicon but, instead, morphemes are inserted separately into syntactic structures, so that syntactic movement may have morphological consequences.

The next topic of chapter 2 is excorporation. The question of excorporation is crucial to a theory like the one I am developing here, since if excorporation is possible—if a head may move through another head—two heads need not be adjacent at Spell-Out even if they constitute a complex head at an earlier stage of the derivation. Then the connection between head movement and word formation becomes rather loose. After taking both theoretical and empirical arguments into consideration, I conclude that excorporation is not possible and that the morpheme order inside a word formed by head movement is tightly conditioned by the underlying sequence of heads.

I then go on to deal with 'morphological merger', an operation which has been proposed in order to account for certain cases of word formation where head movement is claimed to be absent. My conclusion is that it would be better to refrain from assuming this operation. After that, chapter 2 is rounded off with a discussion of the word properties of complex syntactic heads.

In chapter 3 I turn to a discussion of head-final languages. The analysis I propose of the syntax of these languages is based on the suggestion in Kayne (1994) that head-final order combined with suffixing and agglutinating morphology might be the result of successive movements of complements to specifier positions or, more precisely, of the complement of every head H in IP to the Spec of HP. In my analysis, this movement is triggered by the complement-selectional features of the complement-taking heads in IP, which take effect in the absence of strong head features and strong features triggering argument raising.

In addition, I show that head-final languages tend to make extensive use of movement to the CP-domain. This latter type of movement is what lies behind the dislocation phenomena traditionally referred to as 'scrambling'. My claim is that movement to the CP-domain, which can have profound consequences for the ordering of clausal constituents, is triggered by discourse-related features.

Chapter 4 deals with prefixed verbal inflectional markers. I argue that since neither the head movement analysis nor the movement-to-Spec analysis can be extended to these markers, it must be the case that when an inflectional marker is prefixed to a verb root, the inflectional marker and the verb root represent syntactic heads that have not been moved with respect to each other. That is, the prefix is simply the spellout of a head that is in a higher position than the root it combines with. Such an element can be seen as part of the verbal word if it regularly appears in front of the verb and if it cannot be separated from the verb by phrasal constituents. We then have a complex word which is not the outcome of any particular operation but just the consequence of the distributional properties of the morpheme string that makes up the word.

While chapters 2 through 4 are thus concerned with the question of how individual inflectional markers come to precede or follow the verb, chapter 5 is an attempt at giving an overview of the distribution within clauses of the verb root and of verbal inflectional markers. The positioning of verbal markers in different word orders is discussed along with the relative ordering of various inflectional markers—in particular tense and aspect markers. It appears that the patterns that we find can all be derived syntactically from a uniform base order and that data which have been pointed to as counterevidence of the syntactic approach to word formation also allow analyses that are not in conflict with the view that word formation is syntactic.

However, while the syntactic approach to word formation implies that individual morphemes are associated with separate syntactic heads, a brief examination of agreement markers reveals that agreement markers must be analyzed differently from other verbal inflectional markers. There is much more variation to be found cross-linguistically in the distribution of agreement markers than what I have shown to be the case with markers of other categories. Together with the insight that agreement markers are also different from other inflectional markers in that they have no independent content, this leads to the conclusion that agreement markers do not in themselves represent syntactic heads but, instead, agreement markers spell out features that are added to heads whose basic content is something else.

In the last main chapter, chapter 6, I raise the question of whether grammar has a separate morphology module. If complex words are formed in syntax, one might think that there is nothing left for such a module to do. However, there are cases where the relation between the morphemes in the surface order and the underlying sequence of syntactic heads is not as straightforward as the discussion in the preceding chapters has suggested. The relevant phenomena, which might be taken to be the workings of morphology, are discontinuous marking, fused marking, allomorphy, and syncretism.

Concerning discontinuous marking, I argue that it does not really exist; what we have instead is two markers that combine to give a particular meaning. As for fused marking, it is the process whereby two sister nodes coalesce, leaving only one terminal that will be spelled out by one single lexical item. This can be seen as an essentially syntactic operation, which is ultimately contingent on the contents of the lexicon.

Allomorphy and syncretism, by contrast, cannot be explained solely with reference to syntax and/or phonology. Thus, it appears that these two phenomena are truly of a morphological nature. But crucially, allomorphy and syncretism do not only have relevance inside complex words; these phenomena can also be found with free morphemes. Hence, if this is morphology, morphology deals with the shape of individual morphemes and not with the formation of words. We can thus retain the idea that the status of a given morpheme as free or bound, as well as its position relatively to the lexical element that it combines with, are decided by syntax alone.

Finally, I would like to add a comment concerning the linguistic examples given in this book. As the reader will notice, I present examples of sentences, phrases, and words from many different languages. Some examples have a form that is not in accordance with the capitalization and punctuation conventions of English. The reason is that these examples are from languages that do not use the Latin alphabet or have no official orthography at all. In either case, the examples reflect the pronunciation of the language rather than the orthography. I feel that it would then be misleading to add capitals and punctuation as if it were an example of the written language. It also sometimes happens that an upper case letter represents a different sound than a lower case letter, as in the Hua examples on page 273–274. Consequently, I have rendered all examples exactly as they are given in my source.

1

On Syntax and Complex Words

1.1 Overview

The last decades have witnessed the development of two competing lines of thinking about morphology and its relation to syntax. The schism stems from the trivial observation that morphology and syntax are seemingly separate domains of grammar which still to some extent must interact. For example, only words that carry certain morphosyntactic features will be acceptable in any given syntactic position. For a strict lexicalist, this is as far as the interaction goes (see, e.g., Di Sciullo & Williams 1987, Anderson 1992). On this view, the individual grammatical morphemes are related to syntactic structure only indirectly, in that they supply the features that the word must have in order to be licit in the position that it occupies in syntax. The particular realization of various features within the word form will then have to be accounted for by rules and principles that apply specifically to morphology.

On another interpretation, the relation between morphological markers and syntactic positions is a rather direct one. The basis of this view, which I will call the *syntactic* approach to morphology, is the idea that individual morphemes can have their own syntactic representation, as tense markers were assumed to have already in early generative syntax. This approach has been further elaborated in a number of works, in particular Baker (1988a), Halle and Marantz (1993, 1994), and Marantz (1997, 2001).

In order to provide an appropriate historical backdrop for the discussion that follows, the next section of this chapter, section 1.2, sketches the development of the lexicalist approach to word formation within generative grammar and of the competing syntactic view.

In section 1.3 I present the model of grammar that I am assuming and defending in this work; a model in which all types of morpheme collocations—that is, clauses as well as complex words—are the products of syntax.

In section 1.4 I turn to a discussion of the concept 'word'. This discussion is necessary in the present context, since only when we have made clear exactly what it means to be a word will we be able to state precisely what is meant by a 'word-forming process'. In particular, I show in this section that while the phonological word seems to be a well-defined concept that clearly has a place in grammatical theory, the notion of 'grammatical' word is a much more elusive one, which cannot be unambiguously defined except in distributional terms. My conclusion is that 'grammatical word' is a distributional concept and that the fact that two or more morphemes constitute a complex word does not tell us anything about the syntactic structural relations between the morphemes in question. I then go on to consider some structural configurations of morphemes that might allow the morphemes in question to form a complex word.

Finally, in section 1.5 I present some of the results from a survey I have conducted on verbal morphology. Unlike most earlier investigators, I have looked at both free and bound grammatical markers, since only by doing so can we get the full picture of how verb roots are positioned relative to the grammatical markers. I have also used a large sample, with languages from all parts of the world, and in order to avoid genetic and areal bias, I have followed Dryer (1992) and grouped the languages into genera and geographical areas. The material presented in section 1.5 will be discussed at various points in the chapters that follow.

1.2 The lexicalist controversy

Although its roots reach even further back, the story that will concern us here starts with the early generativists and more precisely with Chomsky (1957). In this work, the syntactic analysis of word formation was introduced with the suggestion that verbal affixes enter syntax independently of the verb itself, so that the underlying structure of an expression like (1a) is (1b).

(1) *English*
  a. John ate an apple.
  b. John PAST+eat an apple

The general idea of this analysis was to become a standard assumption in generative syntax for the next decades, although the details of the mechanism that joins the verb stem and the affix have been understood in various ways over the years. Moreover, Chomsky (1957) extended the syntactic analysis into the derivational domain, as he argued that complex nominals are formed from sentences by transformation rules essentially similar to the rules that convert base sentences to derived sentences (a view that was developed in detail by Lees 1960). Taken together these two proposals implied that the basic building blocks of syntax are morphemes and not necessarily entire words and, consequently, that the transformations that alter the order of these atoms can plausibly have both morphological and syntactic effects.

A further elaboration of the syntactic approach was presented in Chomsky (1981). Here verbal inflectional morphology was, as before, taken to be generated in the INFL° head which is outside of VP. However, it was assumed that the affixes are joined to the verb inside VP at S-structure. To account for this a rule of *affix lowering* was postulated, which "assigns the elements of INFL to the initial verbal element of VP" (Chomsky 1981:256). The application of the rule was parameterized, the options being that it applies in syntax or at PF. If the rule applies in the PF component, it is a morphological rule. In other words, this is a rule that can operate on both sides of the morphology/syntax interface, and it indicates that syntax and morphology must be closely connected.

The concept of affix lowering was entertained in many works to follow. One main reason for this was that it provided a feasible explanation for the syntactic behavior of English main verbs, as can be seen, for example, in Pollock (1989), an article that focuses on ordering contrasts between French and English as exemplified in (2).

(2) *English/French*
   a.   John often kisses Mary.
   b. * John kisses often Mary.
   c. * Jean souvent embrasse Marie.
   d.   Jean embrasse souvent Marie.

The clauses in (2) show that whereas an English nonauxiliary finite verb must follow an adverb like *often*, its French counterpart obligatory precedes adverbs of this type. Given the assumption that the adverbs are adjoined to VP, the conclusion follows that English main verbs stay inside VP while French main verbs have to move out—that is, raise to some higher functional head where they pick up inflectional markers. The derivation of the French verb forms is thus straightforward. The fact that English verbs also carry inflection is taken to be a consequence of affixes generated in INFL° lowering and attaching to the V° head. The last stage in this particular line of thought was the additional suggestion of Chomsky (1991) that the ECP-violating downward movement of an X° is repaired by subsequent LF-raising of the V-INFL complex.

While the syntactic analysis of inflectional morphology stood its ground, views began to differ concerning the applicability of this type of analysis to derivational morphology. A seminal work was Chomsky's (1970) "Remarks on Nominalization." Chomsky's contention was that derived nominals differ in several important respects from, for example, gerundive nominals, which presumably are transformationally related to clauses. He then introduced what he termed the 'lexicalist' position, stating that at least some of the relations that had for some time been viewed as transformational belonged instead in the lexicon.[1] Consequently, a firm line was drawn between "inflectional morphology, part of syntax proper, and strictly derivational morphology, part of the lexicon" (Chomsky 1991:421). In other words, whereas the overt markers of inflectional categories are now taken to be attached to the root by operations that are truly syntactic, the types of complex word formation traditionally referred to as 'derivation' are relegated to the lexicon; that is, it is assumed that these operations must be completed before the word is inserted into a syntactic phrase marker.

However, the lexicalist view on derivational morphology has not yet won out. A very influential articulation of a competing view is found in Baker (1988a), where it is demonstrated rather convincingly that the syntactic properties of complex words are often better understood if the words are seen as formed by syntactic operations. This work thus harks back to the aforementioned Lees (1960), and it also builds on more recent contributions such as that of Aissen (1979) on verb raising and several studies of noun incorporation. Following this line of investigation, Baker was able to analyze a range of constructions—from verbal derivational categories such as causatives, passives, and benefactives to noun incorporation structures—as the results of syntactic head movement operations.

If Baker's proposal is considered together with the verb-raising analysis of inflection, a conception of morphology emerges according to which both inflectional and derivational word formation may be interpreted in terms of syntax. That is, we might conceive of a general and complete theory of complex words based on the idea that every morphological element is also a syntactic element and that the internal structure of words can be accounted for by the right syntactic theory. One attempt to formulate such a theory is the so-called Distributed Morphology of Halle and Marantz (1993, 1994), with further elaboration in Halle (1997) and Marantz (1997, 2001). The present work is greatly inspired by their approach, even if explicit reference to their articles is relatively scarce in the following chapters.

Lately, a revival of the other side of the lexicalist controversy has also taken place. Recall that the original formulation, in Chomsky (1970), of what has come to be known as the Lexicalist Hypothesis was a relatively weak one, since it allowed for the possibility that *inflectional* word formation might be accounted for in a transformationalist framework. Stronger versions have later been formulated, some in effect claiming that the internal structure of words is never visible to or manipulated by syntax (see, e.g., Lapointe 1980, Selkirk 1982, Di Sciullo & Williams 1987, Anderson 1992). Even more recently, a strong lexicalist standpoint has made its way into the mainstream of syntactic theory, in the form of the checking approach to morphology introduced in Chomsky (1993), mainly on the basis of the word order in English and further developed in Chomsky (1995). According to checking theory, words enter syntax as fully inflected forms, and the only purpose of syntactic movement is to sanction the features that are present in each lexical item.

1.3 An outline of the model

Of the models of morphology that have been developed so far, there are several which in many cases will give a correct result; that is, which will allow for the creation of the word forms that are actually attested. As long as descriptive adequacy is what one is after, it does not matter so much what one's general view on morphology is; one might see it either as being primarily the putting together of the pieces that make up the words or as the application of various processes onto stems, which are then the true raw material of morphology. Many morphological data can be made to fit both into morpheme-based lexical theories like those of, for example, Selkirk (1982), Di Sciullo and Williams (1987), or Lieber (1992) or into a process-based one, such as Anderson (1992) and Aronoff (1994).

However, there exist complex word forms whose syntactic properties cannot easily be made to follow from a lexical analysis. The most comprehensive treatment to date of such word forms is Baker (1988a); further examples are found in many places in the literature. These forms could be seen as compelling evidence in favor of a syntactic approach to morphology. It can further be argued that even in cases where a syntactic analysis is not forced by the raw facts, such an analysis nevertheless yields the simplest and most principled account of the word forms in question. Hence, the syntactic approach is preferable because it is superior when it comes to explanatory adequacy. Then, once the view is taken that complex words can be formed in syntax, it follows that the elements that words are made of must be allowed to have their own lexical and syntactic representation. Consequently, word formation must be basically concatenative, and so the process model is in principle unavailable.

The model of word formation that will be defended in this work is based on two fundamental assumptions: first, that all morphemes are listed separately in the lexicon and, second, that they are inserted separately into syntactic structures. The term *morpheme* is used here in a sense which is closely related to that of Bloomfield (1933:161), who defines the morpheme as "a linguistic form which bears no partial phonetic-semantic resemblance to any other form."[2] That is, for Bloomfield a morpheme is a minimal unique pairing of specific form with specific meaning. In the present model, individual morphemes also have syntactic properties, so that they correctly should be thought of as having a tripartite structure, made up of phonological, syntactic, and semantic features (cf. Halle & Marantz 1993, 1994).[3] For the phonological part of a morpheme I will also use the term *marker*. In most cases the marker consists of segments, but there are also morphemes whose phonological representations are tones and other nonsegmental devices.[4]

Concerning the insertion of morphemes into syntactic structures or, more precisely, into syntactic terminal nodes, I assume that it takes place after the building of syntactic structures has been completed and also after other processes have applied that operate on terminals in certain ways, so that the set of terminal nodes that are subject to lexical insertion is not necessarily identical to the set of terminal nodes that the syntactic representation was originally built from (an example of such a process is the fusion of two nodes into one). In other words, I adopt the idea of Late Insertion which already has been proposed by Halle and Marantz (1993, 1994), among others. The model of grammar I have in mind is shown in (3).

Prior to Lexical Insertion, the terminal nodes of syntax consist of morphosyntactic and semantic features only. At the point of Lexical Insertion, the terminals are provided with phonological features, supplied by morphemes from the lexicon. The criterion for inserting a morpheme in a given terminal node is that its features are nondistinct from the features of that node (Halle & Marantz 1993). From the resulting feature complexes, the features that are relevant at PF are mapped to PF, and the features that are relevant at LF are handed over to LF.

(3)

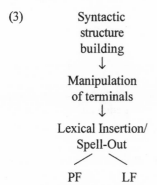

Syntactic
structure
building
↓
Manipulation
of terminals
↓
Lexical Insertion/
Spell-Out

PF   LF

The reason for associating Lexical Insertion with the Spell-Out procedure is of course that Lexical Insertion introduces phonological features, so that the mapping to PF is triggered. The motivation for proposing that the very same structure which is mapped to PF also maps to LF is perhaps less obvious. What lies behind this proposal is the idea that Lexical Insertion is an all-in-one operation, whereby morphemes must map their phonological, syntactic, and semantic features simultaneously for the insertion to be successful. It is further justified by the fact that although morphemes are inserted into the derivation one by one, there are many cases where a sequence of morphemes can have a noncompositional interpretation. But if a sequence of morphemes has a non-compositional meaning, the sequence must be listed in the lexicon along with its meaning. Thus, we must allow for the existence of morphologically complex lexical entries, or morphologically complex *listemes*, in the terminology of Di Sciullo and Williams (1987), and for the redundancy that follows from this: many morphemes will have multiple occurrences in the lexicon since they will be listed once as single morphemes and appear in addition as a part of one or more complex listemes. Some of these complex listemes will have an idiosyncratic meaning, whereas others are fully transparent but listed simply because they occur frequently (see Jackendoff 1997 for a detailed argumentation for this conception of the lexicon). It should now be clear why LF must have access to the level of derivation where insertion takes place: when the individual morphemes which make up a complex listeme with idiosyncratic meaning are inserted into the syntactic phrase marker, they are also matched with the meaning of the entry as a whole, and it is this meaning which must be handed over to LF.

The idea that there is one single structure which is read off by both PF and LF—the Single Output hypothesis—is also defended in Groat and O'Neil

(1996) but for different reasons. My proposal is compatible with theirs, except that where they see covert movement as movement which does not bring phonological features along, a Late Insertion approach like mine will have to assume a copy theory of movement (Chomsky 1995, 1998) and then say that 'covert movement' of an element means that the corresponding lexical item is not inserted in the highest copy, but in a lower copy of the same element. It may still be possible for LF to target a higher copy. Even if PF and LF read off the same structure, the two interfaces need not target the same copy of every element in that structure.[5]

In the phonological half of the interpretation procedure, morphemes are parsed into phonological constituents and given their final shape. But notably, in addition to the grouping together of morphemes which results from the phonological parsing, it also often happens that a sequence of two or more morphemes is perceived as forming a (grammatical) word. From the assumptions stated above, one point is clear: a morphologically complex word cannot be a simplex $X°$. If each morpheme occupies a syntactic terminal node, then every complex word must be composed of more than one of these nodes. The leitmotif of the present study is thus the following question: when a string of morphemes has the appearance of a word, which possibilities are there for the internal organization of that string? Put differently, we will be investigating the configurations of terminal nodes that may cause a sequence of nodes to be perceived as a word.

Note that it does not necessarily follow from this model that every complex word form should be segmentable into morphemes, all of which express one and only one semantic feature. Various types of deviation from the purely agglutinative pattern result from the processes that may apply in the course of the derivation. For example, two terminal nodes may fuse so that their combined feature content will be realized by one single marker. Still, I would like to point out that my model does capture the fact that agglutinating morphology seems to be the default type. This can be seen from my survey of tense and aspect morphology in the world's languages, which will be presented below, in section 1.5.

Of the 530 languages represented in that survey, the vast majority have tense or aspect morphemes whose phonological representation are segmental (in the traditional sense)[6] and formally separate from the verb stem. A few languages have not grammaticalized tense or aspect at all (or at least no tense or aspect markers can be identified from the sources I have consulted). In some languages, such as the Germanic ones, the agglutinative pattern coexists with stem alternations. But the only languages in my survey where the formal exponents of tense/aspect are never in temporal sequence with the verb stem are the Semitic ones and the Adamawa-Ubangi language Linda.

Concerning the Semitic languages, it has been shown rather convincingly in the autosegmental approach of McCarthy (1982) that the tense morphemes of these languages are structurally separate from the verbal root although tense marker and verbal root are pronounced simultaneously, so that they are not separate in the linear order. The same point can be made for Linda, where various aspects are expressed as tones, sometimes in combination with redupli-cation (Cloarec 1972). Both tone changes and reduplication can be seen as expansions of the stem; that is, as in principle affixing operations whereby certain phonological elements are combined with the stem (for a treatment of reduplication along these lines, see Marantz 1982, McCarthy & Prince 1986; for an analysis of tones as morphemes, see Pulleyblank 1986). That is, nonlinear morphology of the Semitic root-and-pattern type, as well as tone alternations and the like, can be seen as the result of not imposing a linear order on syntactic terminals but instead of associating them with different tiers or planes.

It follows that none of the 530 languages in my survey expresses tense primarily by means of nonconcatenative processes.[7] This fact suggests that the morphological patterns that are habitually pointed to as being problematic for a morpheme-based approach, such as inflection by root alternation, are not the basic ones. The normal way of expressing a grammatical category such as tense is to have a tense morpheme which is either pronounced as a separate word or else realized as an expansion of the verb stem.

If we now relate this to the standard assumption that the category of tense is also represented as a syntactic head, it seems obvious that the simplest grammar would be one where the tense morpheme is generated directly in the tense head, as in the approach I am endorsing. Compared to this there is an unattractive redundancy in lexicalist approaches to morphology, where syntax is denied access to the constituents of words. In order to produce the forms that we actually see, lexicalist approaches have to make morphology mimic syntax and thus build the same structure twice: once inside the word and once in syntax. Alternatively, in word-based theories such as Anderson (1992), the syntactic structure is duplicated at a separate level of morphological representation. As pointed out by Drijkoningen (1994), if grammars are ruled by economy considerations, the lexicalist model cannot be the correct one.

For these reasons, among others, I believe that the syntactic approach to morphology is on the right track, since it captures directly what is typical and regular in word formation—namely, affixation. To put it differently, the syntactic approach gives a correct perspective on the regularities and irregularities of word formation in that it pays more attention to what normally happens and is not led astray by the existence of other patterns. For such aberrant cases as the Germanic strong verb conjugation, one would have to assume that some additional operation applies—for example, that T° and V° are fused, so that one lexical element can spell out V° and T° simultaneously, or else that a special allomorph of the root is combined with a null affix, as in Halle and Marantz (1993). Either analysis would correctly predict that stem alternation as the sole expression of an inflectional feature is a marginal phenomenon (notably, in the Germanic languages, weak verb conjugation is productive, whereas strong verb conjugation is generally not).[8]

But before I go on to discuss in more detail the word-forming mechanisms of syntax, I will now provide a clarification of what exactly is the content of the concept 'word'.

1.4 The concept of 'word'

Of all linguistic entities, the word is perhaps the hardest one to define.[9] In Bussmann (1996:521) the situation is aptly characterized as follows: even though 'word' is a "term used intuitively in everyday language for a basic element of language, numerous linguistic attempts at defining the concept are not uniform and remain controversial."

Within linguistics the lack of precision of the term 'word' is to some degree acknowledged, and, consequently, more specific terms are often employed to convey its various meanings. Some of these specific terms have a clear definition, while others are still not precise enough to be of any help in delimiting a coherent class of elements. In the following, we will take a closer look at some of these terms.

First, 'word' may be taken to mean 'lexeme': an element that is represented in the lexicon. However, the property of being listed may be ascribed to words, phrases, and even sentences and also, depending on one's view of morphology, to individual morphemes. Since the set of lexemes (or *listemes*) cross-cuts the sets of grammatical units in this way, the notion of lexeme can be left aside as having no implications for the reference of any other senses of 'word'. (See Di Sciullo & Williams 1987 for a detailed discussion of listedness.)

Another clearly distinguishable meaning of 'word' is that of *phonological* word, which very roughly can be characterized as a chunk of phonological material big enough to be pronounced in isolation. The phonological word will be dealt with in 1.4.1 below.

If we put aside these two meanings of 'word', the lexical word and the phonological word, we are left with what is sometimes referred to as the 'grammatical' word: the word as seen from a morphological or a syntactic point of view. The problem with the concept of 'grammatical word' is that the criteria by which words, in a nonlexical and nonphonological sense, can be unambiguously identified, are not so easily stated. This is discussed in 1.4.2, and the conclusion is that the 'grammatical' word is a distributional concept and not really a grammatical one.

In 1.4.3, I round off this preliminary investigation into wordhood by presenting some syntactic configurations that might be able to give morpheme sequence the distribution that is characteristic of 'grammatical' words.

1.4.1   The phonological word
Since the introduction of the prosodic hierarchy, the phonological word is properly characterized as the prosodic constituent that immediately dominates the foot and that is identified as the domain of primary stress placement and of various other phonological processes. The phonological words are themselves the building blocks either of clitic groups or of phonological phrases, a matter which we will return to shortly.

For the present purpose we will concentrate on the relation of phonological words to morphological and syntactic constituents. Our point of departure will be the very detailed and influential treatment of prosodic domains found in Nespor and Vogel (1986). Nespor and Vogel (hereafter N&V) begin their discussion of the phonological word by noting that it is the lowest constituent of the prosodic hierarchy that can be constructed with reference to nonphonological information. In particular, the phonological word represents the interaction between phonology and morphology in that a phonological word either corresponds to a morphological word or is constructed on the basis of information on the internal structure of morphological words. By 'morphological word' is meant a (possibly compound) stem plus all affixes associated with it. N&V offer Modern Greek and Classical Latin as examples of languages where phonological words coincide with morphological words. Consider first the Greek words in (4).

(4) *Greek* (Nespor & Vogel 1986:111, 113)
    a. συμ–πίν ω   [simbíno]$_\omega$ < [sin+pinó]
        with-drink.PRES.1s
        'I drink in company'

    b. καντ–ίλα [kandíla]$_\omega$ c. ξυλο–θιμονιά [ksiloθimonyá]$_\omega$
        lamp-DIM   wood-stack
        'small lamp'   'wood stack'

We have here evidence that in Greek, prefixes (4a) and suffixes (4b) are included in a phonological word with the lexical stem they attach to and the two members of a compound are included in the same ω (4c). Each of the strings has one and only one stressed syllable, and further, the processes of Nasal Assimilation and Stop Voicing (i.e., voicing of a stop when it is preceded by a nasal), which both apply obligatorily only within ω, also apply here (Nasal Assimilation in (4a), Stop Voicing in (4ab)).

    In Latin, main stress assignment applied in a similar way to simple, derived, and compound words, as shown in (5).

(5) *Latin* (Nespor & Vogel 1986:115)
    a. stratēgus   b. stomachōsus   c. vivi-rádix
        'chief'   stomach-ADJ   alive-root
                        'irritated'   'offshoot'

In all the examples in (5), the heavy penultimate syllable attracts main stress, a fact which indicates that each string is a phonological word.

    According to N&V the phonological words shown above correspond not only to morphological words but also to terminal nodes of syntax. This claim appears to be rather weakly grounded. It is based on the assumption that a (possibly compound) stem plus derivational and inflectional affixes constitute one single syntactic terminal. Since this is also the maximal extension of the phonological word, on N&V's account, it follows that the phonological word cannot exceed the syntactic terminal element. N&V thus take for granted that the units traditionally viewed as morphological words cannot be made up of more than one $X°$. As will be clear by now, this is precisely what is being questioned in the present study.

N&V hold, however, that phonological words are not necessarily congruent with morphological/syntactic constituents. In many languages, a morphological word as defined above may contain more than one ω. This is the case in Turkish and Hungarian, as (6)–(7) show.

(6) *Turkish* (Nespor & Vogel 1986:120f)
   a. çáy evì   b.   bu-gün
    tea house   this-day
                 'today'

(7) *Hungarian* (Nespor & Vogel 1986:123)
   a. [könyv]$_\omega$ [tár]$_\omega$ b.   [lát]$_\omega$ [kép-unk]$_\omega$
    book   collection   sight-image-1pPOSS
    'library'   'our view'

Since it can be shown that rules of primary stress placement and vowel harmony in these languages have ω as their domain, it follows that each of the strings given above must consist of two ω's. (For details, the reader is referred to Nespor & Vogel 1986.) It is worth noting that in (7b), which is a possessive form of the compound *látkép* 'view', the second ω does not correspond to any nonphonological constituent. The principled non-isomorphism of the prosodic hierarchy on one hand and the morphological-syntactic hierarchy on the other, repeatedly emphasized by N&V, is thus demonstrated.

Nespor and Vogel's contention that in spite of the relative independence of the two domains of grammar, phonological words cannot be constructed across $X°$-boundaries, is closely tied to their argumentation that clitics, which are generally recognized as syntactic elements,[10] never form a phonological word with their host. They claim instead that a clitic is a separate ω and that the clitic and its host constitute a prosodic unit called a *clitic group*. One reason for postulating the clitic group is the observation that sequences of clitic plus host sometimes show the characteristics of phonological words and sometimes that of phonological phrases. Since clitics thus cannot be unambiguously associated either with affixes or with full words, a separate prosodic constituent is proposed in order to accommodate clitics into prosodic structure.

As examples of languages where clitics are often claimed to be word-internal, N&V mention Classical Latin and Demotic Greek. In both of these languages, the addition of a clitic to a word produces a new stress pattern, as shown in (8) and (9).

(8) *Latin* (Nespor & Vogel 1986:146)
    a. vírum   b.   virúm-que
       man.ACC   man.ACC-and

(9) *Greek* (Nespor & Vogel 1986:147)
    a. o   άνθρωποσ [o ánθropos]
       'the person'

    b. o   άνθρωπόσ μασ [o ánθropòs mas]
       the person   our
       'our person'

As examples of alleged word-external clitics, N&V offer the following:

(10) *Spanish* (Nespor & Vogel 1986:146)
     dá-ndo-nos-los
     give-PROG-us.DAT-them
     'giving them to us'

(11) *Turkish* (Nespor & Vogel 1986:146)
     ali-yor-lár-sa
     take-PRES-3p-if
     'if they had caught it'

Each of the strings in (10) and (11) must be more than one ω, since in Spanish, stress cannot fall on the fourth-to-last syllable, and in Turkish, even for suffixed words the norm is final stress. The stress patterns in (10) and (11) thus show that the clitics (*nos, los, sa*) must be in a separate stress domain from the stem.

Consideration of these and similar facts has led many to conclude that when a clitic is added to a word, the result is either a phonological word or a phonological phrase (see, e.g., Booij 1983, 1996, Zwicky 1985a). This is challenged by N&V, who add to their defense of the clitic group by claiming that certain phonological phenomena are characteristic only of the group consisting of word plus clitic(s).

The data they present to support this are not altogether convincing, however. They start by examining Italian clitic pronouns, which can be shown not to form a ω with their host. For example, the rule of intervocalic *s*-voicing applies inside words but not across the juncture between a clitic and a word. This is illustrated in (12).

(12) *Italian* (Nespor & Vogel 1986)
    a. lo   [s]alut-o (*[z])   b.   a[z]ola
       him   greet-PRES.1s   'button hole'
       'I greet him'

Further, as (13a) illustrates, the combination of clitic and host provides the appropriate environment for Raddoppiamento Sintattico, a phonological process found in Italian which in certain cases lengthens the initial consonant of words. Raddoppiamento Sintattico also applies to sequences of independent words, as shown in (13b).

(13) *Italian*   (Nespor & Vogel 1986)
  a. da-[m:]i   b.   metá [f:]arfalle
      'give-me'   'half (a) butterfly'

If the two processes shown above are used as diagnostic tools, the Italian clitic pronouns are separate phonological words. N&V are nevertheless reluctant to grant them the status of independent elements, since clitics are, as N&V note, phonologically dependent in a way that other words are not; specifically, clitics may never occur alone or receive contrastive stress. Because of this, and because of the ambiguous behavior of clitics demonstrated in (8)–(11), N&V conclude that clitics must have a special place in phonological theory.

If the original postulation of the clitic group in Hayes (1989)[11] is correct, clitics must share this place with all function words—for Hayes, any function word will be included in a clitic group with the content word that is closest to it structurally. At the same time, clitics often share characteristics with elements that are parts of compounds. For example, in compounds we also find constituents that are word-like but never occur in isolation, no matter what their prosodical status might be (so-called cranberry morphs). Furthermore, in Italian, the two parts of a compound behave as separate words with respect to intervocalic *s*-voicing and Raddoppiamento Sintattico, as shown below:

(14) *Italian*   (Monachesi 1996:93)
  a. tocca-[s]ana   b.   blù [n:]otte
      touch-sound   blue night
      'cure all'   'dark blue'

It appears that the place of clitics in the prosodic hierarchy need not be so special after all. In fact, there is no a priori reason to believe that all clitics should have the same phonological properties. Even if they are all phonologically deficient, their deficiency may still be a matter of degree. Thus, while some clitics may be analyzed as words phonologically (see, e.g., Monachesi 1995, 1996), there are also many examples of clitics that enter into phonological word formation in the same way as affixes. Anderson (1992) claims that this is the case in Kwakwala. As (15) illustrates, in Kwakwala, the articles, possessives, and case markers that syntactically belong with the noun that follows them in the linear order are phonologically included in the word that precedes them. These elements can therefore not be seen as inflectional affixes but rather as word-internal clitics.

(15) *Kwakwala*   (Anderson 1992:18)

nanaqəsil-ida   iʔgəl'wat-i   əliwinux̣ʷa-s-is   mestuwi   la-x̣a
guides-ART.S   expert-DEM   hunter-INSTR-his   harpoon   P-ART.O
migʷat-i
seal-DEM
'An expert hunter guides the seal with his harpoon.'

Another relevant example is Zoque, where the ergative case marker, which is positioned after the noun phrase it modifies, forms a phonological word with whichever element comes last in that noun phrase:

(16) *Zoque*   (Faarlund 1997)

a. te'   che'-bü   xha'e-'is   mya'ü-bya   tüp
   DET   little-REL   girl-ERG   sell-INCMPL fruit
   'The little girl is selling fruit.'

b. te'   xha'e   che'-bü-'is   mya'ü-bya   tüp
   DET   girl   little-REL-ERG   sell-INCMPL fruit
   'The little girl is selling fruit.'

c. te'   püt   kyud-u-bü-'is   te'   tüp   ka'-u
   DET   man eat-COMPL-REL-ERG DET fruit die-COMPL
   'The man who ate the fruit died.'

The main criterion for analyzing the chunks containing a lexical stem and the ergative marker as one phonological word is that they behave as such with respect to stress placement: in accordance with the rule in Zoque they have penultimate stress (Jan Terje Faarlund, personal communication).

A similar argumentation is presented in Selkirk and Shen (1990). Selkirk and Shen claim that in Shanghai Chinese functional elements form a phonological word with a preceding lexical item. This claim is based on the assumption that the phonological word is the domain of certain processes that affect the distribution of tones. To get an idea of how these processes work, we will first look at the realization of tone in compounds, which correspond to single phonological words. As (17) illustrates, in compounds the lexical tone is removed from all but the leftmost morpheme. The tone contour of this morpheme is then distributed over the first two syllables of the compound. Any remaining syllables are assigned low tone by default, as in (17b).

(17) *Shanghai Chinese*   (Selkirk & Shen 1990)

a. HL   MH   H L
   thi   tshi   >   thitshi
   'sky'   'air, gas'   'weather'

    b. MH   HL   LH   M H   L
       sou   foN dziN > soufoNdziN
       'hand' 'wind' 'organ'   'accordion'

Crucially, sequences made up of a lexical item and one or more following function words are treated in the same way as compounds with respect to tone:

(18) *Shanghai Chinese* (Selkirk & Shen 1990)
    a. LH   MH LH   LH   (L H L   L)
       'mo   ku 'noN 'va > 'mo ku 'noN 'va
       'scold' ASP 2s   Q   '(Has someone) scolded you?'

    b. MH   MH LH HL   (M H) (L H)
       tsou   taw 'noetsiN > tsou taw 'noetsiN
       'walk'   'to' 'Nanjing' 'walk to Nanjing'

    c. MH   LH   LH MH   (M H) (L H)
       taN   'ngu 'njitsz > taN 'ngu 'njitsz
       'hit'   1s   'son'   'hit my son'

    d. MH   MH   HL   LH   (M H L) (LH)
       taw   ?iq   pe   'zo > taw ?iq pe 'zo
       'pour' QUANT CLASS 'tea' 'pour a cup of tea'

In the above examples, the extension of each phonological word is indicated by the parentheses in the tone row. It appears that the construction of these phonological words, contrary to what is claimed by Nespor and Vogel (1986) and Hayes (1989), is not necessarily dependent on (syntactic) structural relations. According to the aforementioned authors, a functional element ('clitic' in their terms) will attach phonologically to the potential host that is closest to it structurally—that is, the lexical element with which it shares the highest number of dominating nodes.[12] In (18a) this holds trivially, since the whole construction contains only one lexical element. In (18b), however, the theories referred to above would predict that the preposition should attach to the noun that follows it, since together the two elements form a PP. But we see that, instead, the preposition forms a ω with the verb that precedes it. Similarly, in (18c) the pronoun belongs with the noun syntactically but with the verb prosodically, and in (18d) the function words in the DP attach to the verb and not to the noun.

    These facts might lead to the belief that c-command is the relevant structural relation for phonological word formation, since in all the examples in (18) the verb presumably c-commands everything to its right.[13] However, if a wider range of data is considered, it becomes evident that phonological words in Shanghai Chinese are built without any reference to structural relations. Consider example (19), where the particle *'geq*, which marks all complements of nouns and must be taken to head these complements, combines with a PP to form a modifier of the nominal head *'lu* 'way'. Since the noun *'noetsiN* is embedded in this PP, it cannot possibly c-command the particle. Instead the particle c-commands the noun. Nevertheless these two elements form a single phonological word.

(19) *Shanghai Chinese* (Selkirk & Shen 1990)

MH	MH	LH	HL	LH	LH		(MH)	(MH)	(L H L)	(LH)
tsou	taw	'noetsiN	'geq	'lu	>		tsou	taw	'noetsiN 'geq	'lu
							[_{VP}	[_{DP}		]]
'walk'	'to'	'Nanjing'	PRT	'way'				'take the way to Nanjing'		

We thus have evidence that when a functional element and a lexical element together form a phonological word, the c-command relation between them may go in either direction. If we now turn to the phrase in (20), we get a clear indication that c-command is not at all relevant for the organization of syntactic terminals into phonological words.

(20) *Shanghai Chinese* (Selkirk & Shen 1990)

LH	LH		(LH)	(LH)
'zaw	'mo	>	'zaw	'mo
'toward'	'horse'		'toward the horse'	

In this example, a preposition and its nominal complement belong to different phonological words even though they are closely related syntactically. The reason for this is that the elements are in the wrong order. We have seen, in (18b), that a preposition may form a ω with a lexical element that precedes it. It cannot form a ω with a lexical element that follows it, however, since in this language, the left edge of any ω must coincide with the left edge of a lexical item (N, A or V). This means that in the construction of phonological words in Shanghai Chinese, reference is made solely to edges of constituents and to linear order. Structural relations as such are of no importance.

The relevance of edges is also seen from the fact that contrary to what we would expect from what has hitherto been said, the preposition in (19) is not included in a phonological word with the verb that precedes it. This is due to the fact that, as indicated in the third line of the example, the preposition is the leftmost element of a complex DP. Since this DP forms a separate phonological phrase, a phonological phrase boundary falls between the verb and the preposition. Formation of phonological words across this boundary is necessarily blocked, since any phonological word must be exhaustively dominated by only one phonological phrase.

In sum, Selkirk and Shen's treatment of phonological words in Shanghai Chinese shows that, in this language, items with an independent syntactic realization are routinely combined into phonological words. The only limitations to the word-building process have to do with constituent boundaries in syntax and with the parsing requirements of the prosodic hierarchy itself.

In Finnish, phonological words can be identified as the domain of vowel harmony, whereby rounded vowels must agree with respect to the feature [±BACK]. Vowel harmony applies to combinations of stem and suffixes, as illustrated in (21), but not to compounds or to phrases, as shown in (22).

(21) *Finnish* (Karlsson 1991)

    a. pöydä-llä
       table-ADESS
       'on the table'

    b. kadu-lla
       street-ADESS
       'in the street'

    c. poika-mainen
       boy-ADJ
       'boyish'

    d. tyttö-mäinen
       girl-ADJ
       'girlish'

(22) *Finnish*

    a. pää-kaupunki
       head-city
       'capital'

    b. Salo-n   lähe-llä
       Salo-GEN near-ADESS
       'near Salo'

Interestingly, the Finnish particle clitics undergo vowel harmony (for a detailed discussion of these clitics, see Nevis 1988a). One such clitic is the interrogative marker *-ko/-kö*, which is preceded by the finite verb or alternatively by the topic:

(23) *Finnish* (Karlsson 1991)

    a. Tule-t-ko?
       come-2s-Q
       'Are you coming?'

    b. Sinä-kö   sen   te-i-t?
       you-Q   it   do-PAST-2s
       'Was it you who did it?'

These data suggest that the Finnish interrogative marker is integrated in the host word phonologically, notwithstanding the fact that its distribution is clearly syntactic.[14]

Still another piece of evidence that an element with an independent syntactic distribution may be a subpart of a phonological word is found in Norwegian. In this language, certain pronouns occur in two forms, one weak and one strong. The weak pronouns are syntactically similar to the strong ones except in their ability to undergo object shift (see, e.g., Holmberg & Platzack 1995). There is no doubt that both types of pronouns are independent syntactic elements. For example, both weak and strong pronouns may function as subjects, as shown in (24), or as objects, as in (25).

(24) *Norwegian*

    a. Det   har   han.
       that has   he
       'So he has.'

    b. Det   har-n.
       that has-he
       'So he has.'

(25) *Norwegian*

a. Vi har   han.
   we have him
   'We have him.'

b. Vi har-n.
   we have-him
   'We have him.'

Due to the phonological dependency of the weak pronoun, however, it cannot be sentence initial; it will have to be preceded by some element—for example, a complementizer. This is illustrated in (26).

(26) *Norwegian*

a. Han bodde i London.
   'He lived in London.'

b. * n bodde i London

c. Da-n bodde i London.
   'When-he lived in London.'

An interesting fact about the weak pronoun *-n* is that it is affected by the internal sandhi rule of retroflexation. In most Norwegian dialects, a sequence of /r/ and a coronal is realized as a retroflex with the articulation mode of the coronal (see Kristoffersen 2000). We thus have the following:

(27) *Norwegian*

a. sur   [sʉːr]
   'sour'

b. sur-t   [sʉːtʰ]
   'sour-NEUT'

Retroflexation occurs both within words and across word boundaries, but only within phonological words is it obligatory; compare (28a,b,c) with (28d).

(28) *Norwegian*

a. barn   ['baːɳ] *['baːrn]
   'child'

b. bar-n   ['baːɳ] *['baːrn]
   bar-DEF.SG
   'the bar'

c. leser-ne   [²leːsənə] *[²leːsərnə]
   reader-DEF.PL
   'the readers'

d. for Nils [fɔ'ɳils] ~ [fɔr'nils]
   'for Nils'

Retroflexation is also optional in compounds, as shown in (29a). It is obligatory, however, when a word combines with a weak pronoun, as (29b) shows.[15]

(29) *Norwegian*

a. vinter-natt   [²vintə,ɳatʰ] ~ [²vintər,natʰ]
   winter-night
   'winter's night'

    b. har-n   ['hɑːn̩] *['hɑːrn]
        'has-he/him'

We see here that the verb and the weak pronoun in (29b) are more closely tied together phonologically than are the two parts of the compound in (29a). The string in (29b) is clearly one ω, and it obviously has internal syntactic structure.

    When the weak pronoun *-n* cannot be included in a syllable of its host, it is realized as a separate syllable. But notably, it can never be the head of a foot:

(30) *Norwegian*
    a. mot-n ['muːtn̩]   b.   bak-n ['bɑːkən]
        'against-him'   'behind-him'

This means that *-n* not only forms a phonological word with its host; its prosodic deficiency is such that it is always included in a foot with a part of the word it attaches to phonologically. The weak pronoun is thus a syntactic element which is considerably more deeply embedded in prosodic structure than theories such as that of Nespor and Vogel (1986) allow for.

    When taken together, the data that have been presented in this subsection suggest that the elements referred to as clitics do not constitute a coherent class phonologically. Even Nespor and Vogel (1986:149) acknowledge this when they state that "whether or not an element is a clitic should be decided on non-phonological criteria." This means that 'clitic' is for them not primarily a phonological concept. The problem with this is that clitics cannot be defined on purely syntactic criteria, either, since their syntactic behavior is shared by non-clitics as well. That is, there are simple clitics, which have the syntactic distribution of ordinary syntactic elements, and there are special clitics, with idiosyncratic syntactic distribution; but notably such idiosyncratic distribution is also found with elements that are word-like phonologically. As Anderson (1992:209) points out: "Prosodic dependence can be found either with or without special placement, and vice versa." In order to distinguish clitics from, on the one hand, ordinary affixes and, on the other hand, full words, we might therefore say that a clitic is a prosodically deficient element whose distribution is clearly determined by syntax. (See also Zwicky & Pullum 1983 and Zwicky 1985a.) As we have seen, such an element can be a subconstituent of a word phonologically. But, because of its distribution, it is generally not considered to be involved in word formation proper. Rather, the issue of word formation is in most cases restricted to the combination of roots with elements that are not so obviously of a syntactic nature. It is these combinations that are commonly referred to as 'grammatical words'. The content of the notion 'grammatical word' is the topic of the next subsection.

1.4.2 The 'grammatical' word

The expression 'grammatical word' is used here, like elsewhere in the literature, as a convenient term for the word in a nonphonological sense. This use is not strictly correct, of course, since phonology is also a part of grammar. Nevertheless, I will employ the term to denote the word as seen from a morphological and/or syntactic perspective.

It was noted in the introduction to this section that although most speakers have an intuitive idea of what constitutes a word in his or her language, it is not so easy to come up with a universal definition of 'word'—that is, of the *grammatical* word. Most attempts at doing so list a collocation of properties which are claimed to be typical of words, but at the same time these descriptions tend to beg the question of what a word really is. For example, Anderson (1992:17) states that apart from being phonological units or lexemes, words can be characterized as "the irreducible terminal elements of syntactic structure [and] as the domain of principles regulating the appearance of morphological material." Unfortunately, the claim that words are equivalent to syntactic terminals is theory-dependent and highly debatable, and defining them as the domain of morphology is necessarily circular, since 'morphological material' must mean whatever appears inside words. Neither of these criteria will be a reliable guide to the identification of words. Nevertheless similar conceptions of wordhood are frequently encountered in the literature.

In addition to the syntactic and morphological properties already mentioned, words are often claimed to have the semantic property of being referentially opaque (see, e.g., Di Sciullo & Williams 1987, Spencer 1991). To take Spencer's example, the element *tea* in *teapot* cannot be referred to by a pronoun, as shown in (31).

(31) * He took the tea$_i$pot and poured it$_i$ into the cup.

It appears however that the opacity illustrated here is typical of languages with limited word-building resources and certainly does not hold universally. In a highly synthetic language like Greenlandic, for example, it is perfectly natural for an incorporated noun, as in (32a), to be subsequently referred to by agreement suffixes (or by empty pronominals) as in (32b).

(32) *Greenlandic* (Sadock 1980:311)
    a. Suulut   timmisartu-lior-poq.
        Søren.ABS   aeroplane-make-IND.3s
        'Søren made an airplane.'

    b. Sulu-usa-qar-poq   aquute-qar-llu-ni-lu.
        wing-like-have-IND.3s rudder-have-CTMP-4s-and
        'It has wings and a rudder.'

In short, this sequence of sentences shows that in Greenlandic "an incorporated object establishes a discourse referent just as well as an independent indefinite NP" (Sadock 1980:311; see also the additional examples given in Sadock 1986).[16]

The contrast between compounds in languages like English on one hand and complex words in languages with regular noun incorporation on the other is commented on by Baker (1988a:78–81), who notes that whereas in English, N-V combinations are necessarily deverbal (*truck-driver, man-watching*), in languages traditionally termed polysynthetic similar combinations regularly appear as main verbs, with a normal predicative function. The fact that elements inside those verbs can be fully referential is explained by Baker as a consequence of the syntactic nature of the word formation in question. That is, in a construction like (32a) it is possible for the verbal word to have both a referential and a predicative function just because these functions are fulfilled by separate elements inside the word—elements that are separate syntactic heads at an earlier stage of the derivation.

The referential opacity of English words is also discussed by Sproat (1985, 1988), who argues that the reason one cannot generally refer anaphorically to an element that is contained within a word is the fact that only maximal projections can have a reference. In English, coreference between an anaphor and an element inside a word is disfavored since elements inside words are not maximal projections. However, Sproat also notes that it is possible to violate the requirement that both members of an anaphoric relation must be maximal projections, so that patterns such as (33a) are marginally acceptable.

(33) *English* (Sproat 1988:299)
    a.   McCarthy$_i$ites are now puzzled by him$_i$.
    b. * He$_i$ distrusts McCarthy$_i$ites.

The anaphoric islandhood of words is thus not absolute.[17] Further, (33a) can be compared to the completely ungrammatical (33b), where the indicated coreference would violate the Condition C of Binding Theory. It appears that when parts of words are allowed to refer, they are subject to the same conditions of Binding Theory that restrict coreference between ordinary syntactic elements—in other words: word-internal elements are in this respect treated by syntax in the same way as full word categories.[18]

It should be obvious from these considerations that referential opacity is not a reliable criterion for wordhood. It can be retained as such by denying constituents with internal referring elements the status of grammatical words, as Di Sciullo and Williams (1987:107) in effect do when they maintain that if an alleged word is composed of syntactically accessible parts, it is not a syntactic atom or a morphological object (which in their theory are the essential properties of syntactic and morphological words, respectively), but merely a phonological word. But again the argumentation is circular, saying that since a grammatical word contains no syntactically accessible parts, elements that do are not grammatical words. This is an example of what Sproat (1988) points out: that once a hypothesis of lexical integrity is stipulated, it follows trivially that reference into a word is ruled out.

The inadequacy of the criteria mentioned above comes into full light if we try to use them to determine the status of elements that may or may not be separate words. As an example, consider the Mandarin Chinese aspectual markers shown in (34)–(35).

(34) *Mandarin Chinese* (Zheng 1994)
    wo   du   le   zhe ben   shu
    I   read PERF this CLASS book
    'I have read this book.'

(35) *Mandarin Chinese* (Norman 1988:163)
    wo   kan-le   neibenr   shu
    I   read-PERF that   book
    'I read that book.'

In Mandarin Chinese there are three aspect markers that appear in postverbal position. These are the perfective *le,* the progressive *zhe,* and the experiential *gou.* In some works on Chinese, these aspect markers are written as separate words, as in (34). In other works, they are written as suffixes on the verb, as in (35). So how do we know whether they belong to the verbal word or not? It appears that the lexicalist criteria for wordhood are of little help in this matter, since they only apply after the decision has been made. If the combination of verb and aspect marker is seen as one word, it follows, on the lexicalist view, that the positioning of the aspect marker is determined by morphological principles. If, on the other hand, the aspect marker is seen as an independent grammatical word, its position must be determined by syntax. Similarly, if verb plus aspect marker is one word, the lexicalist hypothesis states that this word must be an indivisible syntactic element. If the aspect marker is seen instead as a separate word, the lexicalist view will allow it to have its own syntactic representation. As for the referential opacity criterion, it is not relevant here, since the aspect marker will not in any case be able to have a reference apart from its grammatical function.

Trivial as all this may seem, it illustrates my point that one needs criteria for wordhood that are independent of one's theory of how morphology and syntax work and interact and of one's ideas of how words ought to behave. Instead of listing the properties that are ascribed to words by this or that theory, we ought to ask what it is that leads us to interpret certain strings as words in the first place.

One answer to the problem of identifying words was given by Bloomfield (1933:178–181), who stated that a word is a free form which does not consist entirely of (two or more) lesser free forms; that is, a word is a *minimal free form.* The word is thus the smallest unit that may appear in isolation.

Let us now try to apply this criterion to the Greenlandic clause in (32b), repeated below as (36).

(36) *Greenlandic* (= ex. (32b), ch. 1)
Sulu-usa-qar-poq   aquute-qar-llu-ni-lu.
wing-like-have-IND.3s   rudder-have-CTMP-4s-and
'It has wings and a rudder.'

It can be shown that the first word is *suluusaqarpoq*, as indicated by the orthographic spacing. This string consists of four elements, neither of which is able to stand on its own. First, the initial element *sulu-*, which is a nominal root meaning 'wing', is never realized in this form in isolation (except in metalinguistic discourse, as in this sentence).[19] For example, in its most unmarked form, the absolutive, it will have the suffix *-k* so that the full form will be *suluk*. In the present case the suffix *-usa* is added, so that a derived nominal is created with the meaning 'wing-like object'. However, the derived stem *suluusa-* never occurs in isolation in this form; in the absolutive it will surface as *suluusaq*. The third element is the verbal root *-qar-*, which must always be preceded by some nominal element. But even with this nominal element in place, the string *suluusaqar-* 'to have (the like of) wings' is incomplete and must be combined with some verbal inflectional ending. The inflection marker itself is also unable to stand alone, of course, and it follows that *suluusaqarpoq* 'it has wings' is the minimal form that can be uttered in isolation. That is, this complex form, but none of its parts, is a word.[20]

Considering the remainder of the clause in (36), it starts with an element *aquut* which is also able to occur in isolation, since it is identical to the absolutive form of the nominal meaning 'rudder'. In this particular construction, however, it should not be viewed as an independent word, since without this nominal stem the elements that follow is not a complete utterance. Thus, the second minimal free form that can be isolated from the string of morphemes is *aquuteqarlluni* 'it has a rudder'.[21]

Now only the final element *-lu* is not accounted for. It is clear that *-lu* cannot occur in isolation, so on this criterion it is not a word. It follows from Bloomfield's definition that when *-lu* is attached to a word, the resulting combination must also be a word, since its immediate constituents are not free forms, but instead one free and one bound form. In this respect the combination of *-lu* and a preceding word is similar to the combination of the nominal stem *aquut* and the complex *-qarlluni*. Even if *-qarlluni* in this example is attached to a potential free form, *-qarlluni* is not a word since it cannot be realized without a preceding stem. This means that an element that attaches to words is not necessarily itself a word.

There is an important difference between *-lu* and the complex *-qarlluni*, however. Whereas the latter in principle attaches to nominal stems, so that it can be said to attach to a word only when some free form of the noun happens to be identical with the stem, *-lu* combines with complex forms of various classes:

(37) *Greenlandic* (Fortescue 1984:120–121)

    a. Ippasaq tikip-put aqagu-lu ikinnguta-at tiki-ssa-pput.
       yesterday arrive-IND.3p tomorrow-and friends-3p arrive-FUT-IND.3p
       'They arrived yesterday and their friends will arrive tomorrow.'

    b. Isir-puq ingil-lu-ni-lu.
       come.in-IND.3s sit.down-CTMP-4s-and
       'She came in and sat down.'

    c. Pilirtuttumik irrui-vuq ini-mi-nul-lu
       quickly wash.up-IND.3s room-4s.REFL-ALL-and
       majuar-lu-ni.
       go.up-CTMP-4s
       'He washed up quickly and went up to his room.'

In the above examples, -*lu* is combined with an adverb in (37a), with a verb in (37b), and with a noun in (37c). Each of the strings that -*lu* attaches to has the form of a full word, consisting of a stem and appropriate inflectional markers.

The ability to combine with words, while at the same time not occurring in isolation, are properties that clitics like -*lu* share with many elements that are generally considered to be words—that is, *function* words. The problem that function words pose for the definition of 'word' is noted by Bloomfield (1933), who takes the English article *the* as an example. *The* is rarely spoken in isolation. However, as Bloomfield points out, *the* has the same distribution as the elements *this* and *that*, which are fully acceptable as utterances. Because of this parallelism, illustrated in (38) (my examples), which I will refer to as the *substitution* criterion, Bloomfield concludes that *the* should also be classified as a word.

(38) *English*

    a. this linguist   ~   this famous linguist
    b. that linguist   ~   that famous linguist
    c. the linguist   ~   the famous linguist

Bloomfield further advances a similar argumentation in favor of treating a clitic as a word whenever the clitic has a full word alternant, as in the case of the simple clitics in English and the pronominal clitics in Romance. "In view of the total structure of the language," as Bloomfield phrases it (1933:179), all these elements have the status of words.

Returning to -*lu*, it appears that this element can only be replaced by other clitics with a similar coordinating function,[22] as in the following examples:

(39) *Greenlandic* (Fortescue 1984:121–122)
  a. Illu-at kusanar-puq   kial-lu-ni-lu.
    house-3p be.pretty-IND.3s be.warm-CTMP-4s-and
    'Their house is pretty and (it is) warm.'

  b. Qimmiq taanna nakuarsu-vuq saamasuu-llu-ni-li.
    dog   that be.strong-IND.3s be.gentle-CTMP-4s-but
    'That dog is strong but (it is) gentle.'

(40) *Greenlandic* (Fortescue 1984:127)
  a. palasi(-lu) niuirtur-lu
    priest-and shopkeeper-and
    '(both) the priest and the shopkeeper'

  b. palasi(-luunniit) niuirtur-luunniit
    priest-or   shopkeeper-or
    'either the priest or the shopkeeper'

Because of the fact that -*lu* is a dependent element that occurs in the same positions as other dependent elements, we would tend to conclude that it is not a word, but a bound marker.

Some observations that can be taken to bear on the present problem are found in another vintage text. Boas (1911:30) suggests that *freedom of position* is a necessary part of the definition of the word: "Whenever a certain phonetic group appears in a variety of positions in a sentence, and always in the same form, without any, or at least without material, modifications, we readily recognize its individuality, and in an analysis of the language we are inclined to consider it as a separate word." Boas is thus willing to grant the status of word even to elements that are phonologically weak, given that their position relative to other elements of the clause is not entirely fixed.

If we consider -*lu* again with this in mind, we see from the above examples that its position is free in the sense that it is not defined relatively to any other element of the clause, such as subject or verb. But it is fixed in the sense that -*lu* always follows the first constituent of the second conjunct, whatever this constituent may be (see Fortescue 1984 p. 120, p. 126).[23] In other words, -*lu* is one of the second position clitics, which is a well-known type of special clitic.[24] Boas (1911:32), discussing similar "weak phonetic groups which have a definite position," notes that "it seems entirely arbitrary whether these phonetic groups are considered as separate words." The important fact about clitics is that they are treated as independent elements by syntax and at the same time they are prosodically deficient. Whether one wants to count such elements as (grammatical) words or not is ultimately a matter of taste.

Now it is time to go back to the Mandarin Chinese aspect markers presented in (34)–(35) and look at them in the light of the criteria discussed above. It can be shown that these markers are always strictly adjacent to the verb[25] and that they can never appear in isolation, although the verb can—for example, in answers, as in (41b). The aspect marker must minimally be accompanied by a verb to make an utterance, as in (42b).[26]

(41) *Mandarin Chinese*

    a. ni   lai   ma   b.   lai

       2s come Q   come

       'Are you coming?'   'Yes.'

(42) *Mandarin Chinese* (Li & Thompson 1981:90)

    a. júzi   huài   le   ma?   b. huài   le

       orange spoiled PERF Q   spoiled PERF

       'Are the oranges spoiled?'   'Yes.'

The complex consisting of a verb and an aspect marker has a relative freedom of position within the clause. It can, for example precede the subject, as (43a), or follow both the subject and an adverbial, as in (43b).

(43) *Mandarin Chinese* (Li & Thompson 1981:91)

    a. jin-lai-le   yi-ge   ren

       enter-come-PERF one-CLASS person

       'A person came in.'

    b. wo zai nali   zhu-le   liang-ge   yue

       I   at   there live-PERF two-CLASS month

       'I lived there for two months.'

This means that both on the minimal free form criterion and on the freedom of position criterion it is the verb and the aspect marker together that show the behavior of a word, and not the aspect marker alone. As for the substitution criterion, it appears that an aspect marker can only be replaced by another aspect marker. The logical conclusion is that the aspect marker is not a separate word but instead it forms a word with the verb that it is adjacent to.

When the aspect markers are nevertheless sometimes written as separate words it probably has to do with the fact that they are written as separate characters in the Chinese script. The influence of the Chinese writing system on the recognition of words in the language is commented on by Li and Thompson (1981:13–14). Li and Thompson notice that the claim that modern Chinese dialects are monosyllabic must arise from the assumption that each character of the writing system represents a word. This assumption is, as they point out, not very well grounded. On a closer analysis, Mandarin in particular has a very large number of polysyllabic words. Concerning the aspect markers, there is thus no a priori reason to regard them as independent words. The tendency to do so must have more to do with convention than with the grammatical characteristics of these markers.

The preceding paragraphs were aimed at drawing the demarcation line between bound forms and words. To complete the discussion of wordhood it is also necessary to look at the difference between words and phrases. Again, we will turn to Bloomfield (1933), who observes that besides the ability to occur in isolation and/or be substituted for other elements that have this ability (in addition to freedom of position, which he does not mention), there is another criterion for wordhood, namely *indivisibility*, which distinguishes phrases from compounds and phrasal words. More precisely, even if both words and phrases can be built from words, with phrases it is normally the case that they can be broken up by additional words and phrases, whereas words that consist of words cannot be interrupted in this way. This is shown by the contrast between the phrase in (44) and the compound in (45) and between the phrase in (46) and the phrasal word in (47).

(44) *English*
    a.   a black bird
    b.   a black and beautiful bird

(45) *English*
    a.   a blackbird
    b. * a black-and-beautiful-bird

(46) *English*
    a.   a jack in the box
    b.   a jack in the little box

(47) *English*
    a.   a jack-in-the-box
    b. * a jack-in-the-little-box

Compounds and phrasal words are thus examples of words that are not minimal free forms. The reason for counting them as words is that they share with words the indivisibility demonstrated above, and they also show the syntactic behavior of noncompound words—that is, of simplex stems. To borrow another example from Bloomfield, as a phrase *devil-may-care* would be a combination of a subject and two verbs, but as a word it is an adjective with the syntactic distribution of ordinary adjectives, as illustrated in (48).

(48) *English*
    a devil-may-care taxi driver

These considerations have relevance for a case discussed by Boas (1911). In Pawnee a nominal free form can be inserted into a string that is normally taken to be a verb; see (49c).

(49) *Pawnee* (Boas 1911:31)

a.	tā-t-u-kᵘt	b.	rīks	c.	tā-t-u-rīks-kᵘt
	IND-1s-BEN-cut		'arrow'		IND-1s-BEN-arrow-cut
	'I have cut it for you.'				'I have cut your arrow.'

This is an example of noun incorporation, of course, the process that has caused so much debate over the years. Now we have in (49c) is a combination of two potentially free forms, where, moreover, one of them actually interrupts the other. On a strict interpretation of the criteria of minimality and indivisibility, (49c) must therefore be a phrase. However, Boas notes, regardless of its internal structure this string behaves like an ordinary verb of the language. It is inflected like a verb and it has the distribution of a verb. It should be added that the incorporation of nominals into the verb is fairly restricted; the incorporated element must be a stem, not a phrase, and it must also be either the object of a transitive verb or the subject of an intransitive verb (Parks 1976).

Finally note that on the indivisibility criterion it is clear that the article *the* should be considered a word, since it may be separated from the head noun by intervening phrasal material. The syntactic nature of its distribution is thus not questionable.

Let us now summarize what we have found to be the characteristics of the grammatical word, trying to home in on an adequate definition. First, two properties that distinguish grammatical words from smaller elements are the ability to occur in isolation and the relative freedom of position within the phrase or the clause. If a string of one or more morphemes has either of these properties, it is minimally a grammatical word. Further, a grammatical word cannot be freely interrupted by other free forms. A string that can be interrupted by words or phrases is a phrase, unless there are very specific restrictions on the inserted material and the resulting complex behaves as a word on other relevant tests. Of these criteria, the necessary and crucial ones appear to be (relative) freedom of position (or *independent distribution*) and indivisibility (or *internal cohesion*), since forms that meet these two criteria tend to be regarded as words whether or not they are minimal free forms. To this we might add the observation that the order of elements inside words tend to be fixed, and if alternative orders are possible, any change of order generally correlates with a change in cognitive meaning, whereas within phrases, permutations often have discourse functional effects.

The set of criteria listed above would presumably enable us to detect the grammatical words in any string of speech. But notice that they do not tell us anything about the mechanisms of grammar that have formed these words. In particular, it does not follow that a word must be a single terminal of syntax, impenetrable to all syntactic operations. The criteria by which grammatical words are identified only serve to pick out the substrings of speech that share certain distributional properties—properties that are compatible with various theories of word construction. To use a paraphrase: we can see that a word has internal cohesion and independent distribution, but we cannot see directly how it came to have those properties.[27]

Accordingly, my working hypothesis in the following will be that 'word' in the nonphonological sense is a distributional concept. That is, if a given string of morphemes is regarded as a word, it simply means that the morphemes in question regularly appear adjacent to each other and in a certain order. The reason the morphemes show such behavior is to be found in their syntax. But notably, the structural relation between the morphemes is not directly relevant for the word status of the string; it only matters insofar as some structural arrangements of morphemes may result in independent distribution and internal cohesion, whereas others may not.

Crucially, if wordhood cannot be associated with any particular structural morpheme configuration, it follows that grammar cannot have at its disposal any specific word-forming devices. If a word is just the accidental outcome of the manipulation of morphemes that takes place in syntax, it must be the case that words come into being in our perception; that is, words are *perceived* rather than *formed*. Hence, the correct formulation of the question that I will focus on in this work is not 'how are complex words formed?' but instead 'how can two or more morphemes, each of which a syntactic terminal, come to be perceived as one single word?'

1.4.3   The syntax of words
I will now start from the assumption that morphological constituents are also minimal elements of syntax, namely syntactic heads, and then try to consider how these basic elements could possibly come to be combined into words. Since what mechanisms one will claim to be operating on syntactic primes is of course dependent on one's conception of syntax in general, it should be noted that I will adopt the theory of Kayne (1994), according to which syntax is subject to the following restrictions:

(50) *Restrictions on syntax*   (after Kayne 1994)
    a. Nodes are binary branching or nonbranching.
    b. Asymmetric c-command maps into linear precedence.
    c. Syntactic movement is always to the left.
    d. Adjunction is always to the left.

To the syntactic requirements in (50) must be added the obvious requirement that if two or more morphemes, syntactically represented as heads, are realized as constituents of one single word, the heads in question must be *adjacent* in some sense that will have to be specified. With this much settled, we can imagine a limited range of syntactic configurations that would allow two heads, $X°$ and $Y°$, to form a word XY.

First, $X°$ and $Y°$ could be included in a complex $X°$—that is, in a complex syntactic head. The complex syntactic head could be formed by head movement, as indicated in (51a), or it could be base generated. Next, $X°$ could be the final element of a constituent in the Spec of Y°, as in (51b), or as a third option, Y° could be the head of the complement of X°, as in (51c).

(51)

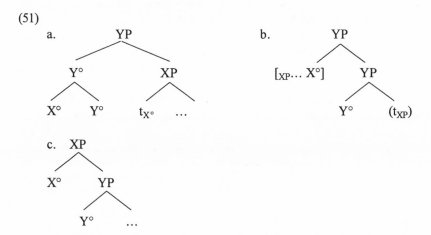

Each of these configurations is likely to cause X and Y to be contiguous with some regularity. In the case of head movement, it is always the next head down that will be attracted to any given head, according to the Head Movement Constraint of Travis (1984). Further, whether or not there is head movement at all is assumed to be dependent on the features of the attracting head. Now if there is no variation in the strength of the features of the attracting head Y°, and no variation with respect to the category of the complement of Y°, the consequence is that Y° always attracts a head of one specific type. Accordingly, a morpheme of type Y will always appear in the combination XY.

The idea that the morphemes X and Y can also form a word in the configuration depicted in (51b) is a more controversial claim. It has been proposed earlier to be the underlying structure of clitic constructions (see, e.g., the analysis of the Scandinavian possessive -*s* in Delsing 1993) but to my knowledge, it was first suggested for affixing in Kayne (1994:52–54). Kayne proposes that a morpheme sequence XY within a word can be produced by moving a head-final XP, the complement of Y°, to the specifier position of YP. If the category of XP is fixed, and XP is always head-final, and movement of XP to the specifier of YP is obligatory, then the sequence XY will be a recurring pattern and possibly be perceived as a word. Further, if complementation is uniformly to the right, then the head finality of XP must be a result of the complement of X° having moved to the left of X°, possibly to Spec-XP. The word-forming process outlined here thus requires that all complements be moved to the left of their selecting heads. The specifier-head relation is therefore most likely to give rise to word formation only in strongly head-final languages, as Kayne points out.

In the configuration in (51c), where linearly contiguous heads surface in the positions where they are base-generated, it is generally not assumed that the heads can form a complex word, either. But if there is no variation in the

category of X° and Y°, and no movement of YP or of its head Y°, and no
phonologically overt material in Spec-YP, the sequence XY would again have
the distribution that is typical of words. Consequently, it is possible that the
two heads may be perceived as one word also in this case.

The morpheme configurations in (51) will be discussed in much detail in the
following chapters. Head movement is the topic of chapter 2, while chapter 3
deals with the specifier-head relation and chapter 4 with the morphological
relations between heads in their base order.

The question now is whether there are other syntactic relations that can be
input to the formation of a word XY. As already mentioned, a natural requirement is that X° and Y° must be linearly adjacent. Then, in addition to the
structures sketched above, we can think of various configurations where Y° is
the initial element of the complement of X°, as in (52).

(52)

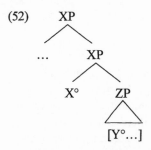

For X° and Y° to enter into regular word formation in this configuration, the
category of each element must be to some degree fixed. If the complement of X°
can belong to any of various categories and/or have many different internal
structures, so that elements of different types can be in the position of Y°, then
X° and Y° are not very likely to combine morphologically.

There are several subcases of (52) that might be considered. One possibility
is illustrated by certain Romance prepositions, such as in the following Italian
examples:

(53) *Italian*

    a. *di lo studente   a'. de-llo studente
       'of the student'   'of-the student'

    b. Sono   di   Londra.   b'. * Sono de-llondra.
       '(I) am   from London.'

In (53a') the preposition *di* forms a word with the initial constituent of its
complement, the definite article *lo*. However, since the preposition can have
complements that are not introduced by an article, as in (53b), the process that
has applied in (53a') is not interpreted as a regular morphological one. The
example (53b) shows that it is not a regular phonological process, either, since
the phonological environment of (53a) is also found in (53b), where the process

does not apply. In short, these data indicate that word formation on the basis of (52) will tend to be sporadic.

Note also that (53a') can be analyzed as an instantiation of (51c) if the article is seen as the D° head of the DP that is the complement of the preposition. In any case, the sequence consisting of the preposition and the article is not regular enough to be conceived of as one word outside of phonology.

Now consider a case where Y° is the initial element of the complement of X° without being the head of this complement. As indicated in (54), Y° must then be the initial element of the specifier of the complement of X°. This means that the relation between X° and Y° is a rather indirect one.

(54)

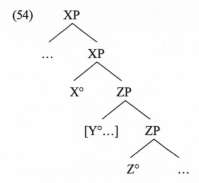

When we ask whether this configuration can feed word formation at all, it is important to keep in mind the distinction between, on one hand, structures that can be a diachronic source of morphological patterns and, on the other hand, structures that can be input to word formation synchronically. It is a well-known fact that many affixes have started out as separate words historically. A necessary condition for one word to develop into an affix on another word is that the two words must regularly occur linearly adjacent to each other. Their structural relation is of less importance in this respect. The X° and Y° of (54) can thus perfectly well represent two separate words that will *later* enter into a morphological relationship.

Comrie (1980) describes a development of this kind that has taken place in some of the Mongolian languages. The original pattern is still found in modern Khalkha; in this language the subject may either precede or follow the verb, as shown in (55). In the latter case the subject is defocused and unstressed (Comrie 1980).

(55) *Khalkha* (Comrie 1980:91)

a.	bi	med-ne		b.	med-ne	bi
	I	know-PRES			know-PRES	I

In a construction like (55b) the subject must occupy a Spec position below the inflected verb; in other words, (55b) is an instantiation of (54), with the verb as X° and the postverbal pronominal subject as Y°.[28]

The alternation illustrated in (55) was also found in Classical Mongolian. Today, the postverbal pronominal subject has developed into an ordinary subject agreement marker in some of the Mongolian languages, such as Buryat:

(56) *Buryat* (Comrie 1980:91)
    a. (bi) jaba-na-b   b. * (bi) jaba-na
        I   go-PRES-1s
        'I am going.'

As (56) demonstrates, the subject agreement marker is now obligatory in Buryat. The fact that it can co-occur with a pronominal subject indicates that it is no longer a pronominal element in itself; rather, it has been reanalyzed as the realization of the functional category that hosts subject agreement. But then the structural relation between the morphemes in (56a) must be different from the relation between the cognate morphemes in (55b). In (56a), the agreement marker must be located in a head belonging to the extended projection of the verb, in the sense of Grimshaw (1991, 1997), and the operation that gives the surface order as output is either head movement of the verb into its functional domain or phrasal movement of VP to Spec-TP and possibly of TP to a higher head. This means that the actual structure underlying the complex word in (56a) is either (51a) or (51b), not (52) or (54).

This example suggests that although in a structure like (54) the development of a morphological relationship between $X°$ and $Y°$ may be triggered, a different underlying syntactic structure will be postulated once the morphological relationship has been established. It is interesting to note, though, an analysis proposed in Pearson (2000) of a class of languages where the word order is exactly the opposite of what has now come to be seen as the universal base order. In these languages, direct objects precede indirect objects, and adverbs also occur in the inverse order compared to the order argued for in Cinque (1999). One of Pearson's examples is Malagasy:

(57) *Malagasy* (Pearson 2000)
    Na-nolotra   ny   dite ny   vahiny ny   zazavavy.
    PAST-offer   ART tea   ART guest   ART girl
    'The girl offered the guests the tea.'

Following the suggestion of Pearson (2000), we might say that the surface word order in (57) is created by moving the arguments out of VP, the remnant VP over the direct object, the XP containing the VP and the direct object over the indirect object; and, finally, the XP containing the VP, the direct object, and the indirect object to the left of the subject. Since $V°$ is now the only overt element in VP, it follows that the verb will be the leftmost element of the XP that moves across the subject, presumably to a Spec position below $T°$. If this is correct, (57) is an example of a head (the tense marker) forming a word with the initial element of a phrase in the Spec immediately below. The reason this is possible in Malagasy is then probably that every clause is derived in this way, so that the verb regularly is linearly adjacent to the tense marker. The two elements together will therefore tend to be perceived as one word.[29]

1.5 A survey of word order and morpheme order

I will now present some results from a survey I have done of the ordering of verb roots and inflectional morphemes in languages with different word orders. Notably, if every morpheme represents a syntactic node, and if syntax is restricted in the way I have already suggested, there are some arrangements of morphemes we would expect to see while others are predicted not to be derivable. Thus, it becomes essential to check what the facts are in the languages of the world. Moreover, most typological investigations of morpheme order have concentrated on the morpheme order within words. In a syntactic approach like mine, the ordering of free inflectional morphemes is just as relevant. For these reasons, it seemed necessary to start the investigation by collecting information about a relatively large number of languages.

The reason I have restricted the investigation to verb morphology is that only in this domain do we have a clear and widely accepted conception of the syntactic structure associated with various morphological categories. I have concentrated on the relation between tense markers and verbal roots, since the category of tense is found in a majority of languages, even in those that have very little verb morphology. There is also a certain consensus that tense projects a functional category of its own, so that in most or all languages the clausal projections will include the following elements:

(58)

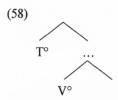

That is, the X° and Y° of (51) may have the values T° and V°. Accordingly, we would expect tense morphemes to pattern in certain ways relative to the verb root. The purpose of the survey was to show whether our predictions are actually borne out.

The survey is based on a sample consisting of 530 languages from all over the world. In order to avoid genetic bias, the languages are grouped into 280 *genera*, which are genetic units with such a high degree of internal similarity that the validity of the unit is uncontroversial (see Dryer 1992). Or, in the words of Nichols (1990:477), who employs the term *family* for what is here called genus: "The family can be defined as the depth within which regular sound correspondences are numerous and genetic relatedness is clear, even self-evident."

To mention a few, the major branches of Indo-European—Celtic, Germanic, Romance, Slavic, Indic, and others—are genera. As the languages of any one genus are so closely related to each other, the occurrence of a typological trait in several languages belonging to one and the same genus should be seen as only one instantiation of this trait.[30] For example, in determining whether tense suffixes are generally preferred over tense prefixes in natural language, the 100 or so Pama-Nyungan languages, which all have tense suffixes, should not be allowed to outweigh Tiwi, a language with tense prefixes, since the Pama-Nyungan pattern is the result of one single line of development, just as the Tiwi prefix is. Thus, it seems clear that we get a more correct result if we count genera instead of languages.

In the identification of genera worldwide I have, with a few minor exceptions (see appendix 2), followed Dryer (1992), who has conducted a survey with a purpose somewhat different from mine but with what seems to be a sound methodology. I also follow Dryer (1992) in dividing the world into six large geographical areas: Africa, Eurasia, Southeast Asia and Oceania, Australia and New Guinea, North America, and South America. In addition, I have included a number of creole languages, which I have treated as a separate 'area'. Frequencies of ordering patterns are calculated for each area. In this way, large-scale areal phenomena can be controlled for; they will show up as differences among areas with respect to dominant patterns. (See Dryer 1989, 1992, for a more detailed discussion of the sampling methodology.)

The survey was carried out by looking at the sample of languages described above and trying to establish, for each language, the unmarked order of the main elements of the clause (subject, object, verb), as well as the arrangement of morphological elements within the finite verb. The variables that have been used for statistical purposes are, first, whether the language is verb-initial, verb-medial, or verb-final (I have thus abstracted away from the relative order of arguments); and second, whether the tense marker is (a) an affix or a free morpheme and (b) preceding or following the verb root.[31] The counting, however, was done on the genus level, such that if only one order is found within a genus, this genus is registered only once. If, on the other hand, two or more orders are represented within one single genus, this genus is included in all relevant groups.

For the sake of getting a more complete overview, I have counted free tense markers as well as bound ones. In this way the frequency of prefixed tense markers vs. suffixed tense markers can be calculated relative to *all* tense markers. I have also noted whether the free marker precedes or follows the verb. Notably, I do not distinguish between free inflected tense markers and free *un*inflected tense markers. In my view, both types can be realizations of the tense head; the difference between the two types is minimally that the former, but not the latter, are combined with agreement markers.[32]

Finally, in the case of languages that have no obvious tense marker, I have recorded the distribution of aspect markers instead, since in the absence of tense markers, it is aspect markers that represent grammaticalized temporal relations.

The relative frequencies of the various realizations of tense/aspect in Africa, the first geographical area to be dealt with here, are shown in table 1.1. The boxes in the main body of the table represent the 12 logically possible combinations of verb position and realization of the tense/aspect marker relative to the verb. To the right I sum up the numbers of genera with each verb position, and in the bottom row, the overall frequencies of each type of tense/aspect marker. All percentages are calculated relative to the total number of genera from this area represented in the survey, given in the bottom right corner, since it is too early at this stage to decide whether to calculate the frequencies of marker types within each word order type (i.e., horizontally) or the frequencies of word order types relative to the realization of the tense/aspect marker (i.e., vertically). I therefore just give the frequency of each combination of marker type and word order.

We see that in Africa, tense suffixes are far more frequent than tense prefixes (59% vs. 35%). Only in verb-initial languages are prefixes more frequent than suffixes. Still, Africa has the highest prefix frequency of all areas. Also note that verb-initial languages very rarely have free preposed markers. In verb-medial languages, by contrast, a free preposed marker is the preferred realization of the tense morpheme, closely followed by suffixes and prefixes. More than half of all genera with verb-final languages have tense suffixes; conversely, most languages with tense suffixes are verb-final.

TABLE 1.1 — **AFRICA**
Language genera according to basic word order and realization of tense (or aspect) marker. Note that the Semitic languages of Southwest Asia are included in this area.

Word order	T(A)+V		V+T(A)		T(A) V[a]		V T(A)[b]		Total	
	No.	%	No.	%	No.	%	No.	%	No.	%
V-initial	5	10	1	2	1	2	1	2	8	16
V-medial	12	24	12	24	14	29	6	12	29	59
V-final	5	10	16	33	9	18	2	4	25	51
All orders	17	35	29	59	21	43	8	16	$N = 49$	

Since the counting is based on genera, the figures in the body of the table do not add up to the figures given in the rightmost row and in the bottom line. For example, the column to the left (T(A)+V) shows that tense (or aspect) prefixes are found together with verb-initial order in 5 genera, the combination of tense (or aspect) prefixes and verb-medial order is found in 12 genera, whereas 5 genera contain languages that are both prefixing and verb-final. The bottom line indicates that prefixes are found in a total of 17 genera. Some of these genera must therefore contain more than one combination with respect to word order and realization of tense marker.

[a] This type includes all languages where a free tense/aspect marker precedes the verb, whether or not this marker is adjacent to the verb.

[b] This type includes all languages where a free tense/aspect marker follows the verb, whether or not this marker is adjacent to the verb.

TABLE 1.2 — **EURASIA**

Language genera according to basic word order and realization of tense (or aspect) marker. See table 1.1 for an explanation of the computation. The area includes Europe and Asia except Southeast Asia.

Word order	T(A)+V No. %	V+T(A) No. %	T(A) V No. %	V T(A) No. %	Total No. %
V-initial		1 2			1 3
V-medial	1 3	12 36			12 36
V-final	3 9	23 70		1 3	24 73
Uncertain		1 3			1 3
All orders	2 6	33 100		1 3	*N* = 33

An empty cell means that there is no language of the relevant type in my material.

If we turn to the next major area, Eurasia (table 1.2), we see that here suffixed tense markers are found in all genera and that only a few genera display other realizations in addition. At the same time, SOV is the dominating pattern, regardless of the realization of tense.

In Southeast Asia and Oceania (table 1.3) most genera have free tense markers, which in most cases precede the verb. The most frequent combinations involving affixes are suffix and verb-final order, followed by prefix and verb-initial order.

TABLE 1.3 — **SOUTHEAST ASIA AND OCEANIA**

Language genera according to basic word order and realization of tense (or aspect) marker. See table 1.1 for an explanation of the computation. The area includes Sino-Tibetan, Thai, Mon-Khmer, and Oceanic languages.

Word order	T(A)+V No. %	V+T(A) No. %	T(A) V No. %	V T(A) No. %	Total No. %
V-initial	3 14		2 9	2 9	5 23
V-medial	2 9	2 9	14 64	3 14	15 68
V-final	2 9	4 18			5 23
Uncertain			1 5		1 5
All orders	6 27	6 27	15 68	5 23	*N* = 22

An empty cell means that there is no language of the relevant type in my material.

TABLE 1.4 — **AUSTRALIA AND NEW GUINEA**
Language genera according to basic word order and realization of tense (or aspect) marker. See table 1.1 for an explanation of the computation. Note that the Austronesian languages of New Guinea are not included here, they belong to Southeast Asia and Oceania.

Word order	T(A)+V		V+T(A)		T(A) V		V T(A)		Total	
	No.	%	No.	%	No.	%	No.	%	No.	%
V-medial	1	2	4	9	3	7	1	2	8	19
V-final	1	2	22	51	3	7	3	7	26	60
Uncertain	2	5	17	40	1	2	3	7	21	49
All orders	4	9	35	81	6	14	6	14	\(N = 43\)	

In the fourth major area, Australia and New Guinea (table 1.4), we see that tense suffixes are almost as dominating as in Eurasia and that tense prefixes are relatively rare.

A complicating factor here is that in nearly half of all genera there are languages for which it has not been possible to identify an unmarked word order. Either the sources give no information at all on this topic, or else we are told that the word order is "free", meaning that any permutation of subject, object, and verb is grammatical.[33] If we look only at languages for which a basic word order has been stated, we see that 26 genera have verb-final languages whereas verb-medial orders are found in 8 genera—that is, the order is SOV in 3 out of 4 genera. In all orders, however, suffixation is clearly the preferred way of expressing tense.

Next, we turn to North America (table 1.5), where we again encounter the problem that the word order of many languages has been labeled "uncertain"; that is, it is unknown or else said to be "free"—in fact, this is the most frequent of all orders. But also here we see that even though many languages have tense prefixes, tense suffixes are even more frequent—73% of all genera contain languages with this property. The most frequent combinations of all are tense suffixes and verb-final order and tense suffixes and "uncertain" word order. Also note that there is a weak correlation between verb-initial order and tense prefixes, just like we saw in Africa and in Southeast Asia and Oceania.

TABLE 1.5 — **NORTH AMERICA**
Language genera according to basic word order and realization of tense (or aspect) marker. See table 1.1 for an explanation of the computation. The area includes Mexico and the Aztecan and Mayan languages of Central America.

Word order	T(A)+V		V+T(A)		T(A) V		V T(A)		Total	
	No.	%	No.	%	No.	%	No.	%	No.	%
V-initial	8	11	9	12	5	7	1	1	18	25
V-medial	6	8	10	14	4	5			16	22
V-final	5	7	25	34	1	1	3	4	28	38
Uncertain	10	14	24	33			2	3	32	44
All orders	24	33	53	73	9	12	6	8	*N* = 73	

An empty cell means that there is no language of the relevant type in my material.

In South America, by contrast, tense prefixes are found in only four genera (table 1.6). A few genera have free tense or aspect markers (six genera altogether—some of these have both preposed and postposed markers), but the great majority (86%) of all genera are suffixing. At the same time, verb-final orders are found in more than half of the genera. Further, the frequency of "uncertain" word order, both overall and among languages with tense suffixes, is relatively high, but not as high as in Australia and New Guinea and North America.

TABLE 1.6 — **SOUTH AMERICA**
Language genera according to basic word order and realization of tense (or aspect) marker. See table 1.1 for an explanation of the computation. The area includes Central America, except Aztecan and Mayan languages.

Word order	T(A)+V		V+T(A)		T(A) V		V T(A)		Total	
	No.	%	No.	%	No.	%	No.	%	No.	%
V-initial			3	6					4	8
V-medial	1	2	12	24					12	24
V-final	2	4	24	47	2	4	4	8	29	57
Uncertain	1	2	11	22	1	2	2	4	14	27
All orders	4	8	44	86	3	6	6	12	*N* = 51	

An empty cell means that there is no language of the relevant type in my material.

I have also included a group of languages which are not represented in the sample of Dryer (1992), namely creoles. Creoles are particularly interesting on the assumption that they reflect UG more directly than languages with a longer linguistic history (which admittedly is not an uncontroversial claim, but see Bickerton 1981, 1984, 1990). Since creoles do not naturally fall into genetic groupings, I have instead classified them according to lexifier language and geographical area; this classification gives 9 groups altogether.[34]

As table 1.7 shows, there is little variation among creole languages. All creole groups include languages where free tense and/or aspect markers precede the verb, and where the order of clausal constituents is S T/A V O. In addition, there is Sranan, which in one analysis (Voorhoeve 1957) has a prefixed aspect marker; Cape Verdean and Kituba, which have a suffixed marker of anterior tense in addition to the free preposed tense markers; Kriyol, where the free tense marker follows the verb; and Afrikaans, where the order S Past O V alternates with SVO.

Finally, the distribution of morphological patterns and word order patterns across the world is summed up in table 1.8, which shows, for each combination of word order and tense marking type, the total number of genera with this combination and the percentage of genera with this type relative to the total number of genera represented in the survey.

We see that the preferred realization of tense, found in 72% of all genera, is as a verbal suffix. This reflects the fact that verb+tense suffix is the most frequent pattern in all areas or groups except in Southeast Asia and Oceania and in creoles. In these latter groups most languages have a free tense marker preceding the verb. The free preposed marker is the second most frequent of all patterns; even so, being represented in 23% of all genera, it is significantly less frequent than suffixes. Tense prefixes are found in only 21% of all genera, whereas the least common of all tense marker realizations is a free marker following the verb, with an overall frequency of 12%.

If the realization of the tense marker is viewed in relation to word order, it appears that in verb-initial languages, prefixing is slightly more frequent than

TABLE 1.7 — **CREOLES**
Creole groups according to basic word order and realization of tense (or aspect) marker. See table 1.1 for an explanation of the computation.

Word order	T(A)+V		V+T(A)		T(A) V		V T(A)		Total	
	No.	%	No.	%	No.	%	No.	%	No.	%
V-medial	1	11	2	22	9	100	1	11	9	100
V-final					1	11			1	11
All orders	1	11	2	22	9	100	1	11	$N = 9$	

An empty cell means that there is no language of the relevant type in my material.

TABLE 1.8 — **THE WORLD**
Language genera according to basic word order and realization of tense (or aspect) marker. The 9 creole groups of table 1.7 are included.

Word order	T(A)+V		V+T(A)		T(A) V		V T(A)		Total	
	No.	%	No.	%	No.	%	No.	%	No.	%
V-initial	16	6	14	5	8	3	5	2	36	13
V-medial	24	9	54	19	44	16	13	5	101	36
V-final	18	6	114	41	16	6	13	5	138	49
Uncertain	13	5	53	19	3	1	7	3	69	25
All orders	60	21	202	72	63	23	33	12	$N = 280$	

suffixing. In addition, a number of verb-initial languages have free preposed markers.

In verb-medial languages, most tense markers are suffixed, but the combination of SVO and a free preposed tense-marker is also rather frequent. However, if we compare the occurrence of prefixes in verb-initial and verb-medial languages, we see that relatively few verb-medial languages have tense prefixes (the fact that the combination of tense prefix and verb-medial order is nevertheless more frequent than tense prefix and verb-initial order is due to the high overall number of verb-medial languages).

In verb-final languages, suffixes are overwhelmingly dominating, being more than twice as frequent as all other patterns taken together.[35] We also see that there are relatively few free postposed tense markers in this group. Preposed markers, on the other hand, are free nearly as often as they are affixed.

In short, the tables presented here show that if the tense markers of natural languages are classified according to their realization relative to the verb stem, then it is clear that the four classes of prefix, suffix, free preposed marker, and free postposed marker are not evenly distributed across languages.[36] We see that not only are certain types of tense markers generally preferred over others, but there are also observable correlations between certain tense marker types and certain word orders within the clause. These statistical tendencies indicate that the realization of tense in a given language does not depend on mere chance. Rather, the choice of tense marker must be influenced, although not wholly determined, by other aspects of grammar, such as sentential syntax. It is these interdependencies that will be explored in more depth in the following chapters.

Notes

1. But see Marantz (1997) for an updated reading of "Remarks on Nominalization" in the light of Bare Phrase Structure (Chomsky 1995).

2. I am aware that some readers will probably have objections to this terminology, claiming that 'morpheme' is the term for an abstract meaning unit which is realized by *morphs*. (See, e.g., Bauer 1988, Aronoff 1994). However, the practice I adopt is a fairly well-established one; a process of semantic drift has taken place (see Matthews 1991:107) which I do not see it as my obligation to reverse. And besides, since I will focus here on word structure and not on allomorphic variation, when I talk about 'morpheme order' it does not make much difference which sense of 'morpheme' is intended.

3. The fact that each of the parts of a morpheme may be zero, as morphemes may be phonologically empty, meaningless, or lacking a syntactic category (but not all at the same time) does not alter the overall picture.

4. In this I depart from Bloomfield (1933:161), who says that "[A] morpheme . . . consists of one or more phonemes." No such requirement follows, however, from his definition of morpheme per se.

5. It has been proposed that 'covert movement' does not exist. If this is true, it must be the case that both LF and PF always target the highest copy. See, e.g., Kayne (1998) for a defense of this view. Also note, by the way, that if 'covert movement' is taken to be *feature* movement, as in the approach sketched in chapter 4 of Chomsky (1995), one need not stipulate that feature movement must take place after Spell-Out; the result would be the same if the (nonphonological) features have already moved when the structure is handed over to PF. Thus, this version of minimalism could be compatible with the Single Output hypothesis. The idea that feature movement takes place before Spell-Out is also defended in Roberts (1998).

6. In more recent works, the term 'segment' is used not only for those elements of a phonological representation which are linearly separate (and which traditionally are called segments), but also for other minimal units of the representation. See, e.g., Goldsmith (1990:9–10).

7. At first blush, Classical Tibetan might appear to be the exception. For example, Jäschke (1954) and Hodge (1990) report that verbal inflection in the classical language was expressed formally as alternations in the verbal root. However, Beyer (1992) shows that the four stem types (present, past, future, and imperative) can be analyzed as the combination of an abstract root and certain prefixed or suffixed consonants. In addition to the affixes, vowel rounding sometimes occurred. In the course of time, the old affixing system was lost, so that in the modern language, different stems are distinguished only by their tone patterns and by the vowel being higher in the present stem than elsewhere. In fact, many verbs show no alternation at all. Consequently, new suffixes have developed as the principal exponents of tense (see Jäschke 1954, Goldstein & Nornang 1970), a fact that neatly illustrates my claim that affixing is the default morphological operation.

8. Geert Booij (personal communication) informs me that in Dutch, the strong verb pattern can sometimes be extended to new verbs. Nevertheless, new verbs are normally weak, and it is clear that even in Dutch, weak conjugation is the dominant pattern.

9. Witness, for example, the fact that Juilland and Roceric (1972) list 132 references on the linguistic concept of 'word'.

10. For a syntactic treatment of (Romance) clitic placement, see, e.g., Kayne (1991, 1994), Sportiche (1996), Manzini and Savoia (1998). For a different approach, see, e.g., Anderson (1992, 1996).

11. The paper published as Hayes (1989) actually predates Nespor and Vogel (1986); it was presented at a conference on metrical theory held at Stanford University in 1984 and is referred to by Nespor and Vogel.

12. Unfortunately, the term 'lexical element' is ambiguous: it may mean 'an element that is listed in the lexicon' or 'a member of one of the major, substantive categories N, A, V, (and possibly P)'. Even if it would be better to have a different term for the second meaning, I will follow common practice and use 'lexical element' in this sense. I will try to avoid confusion by using 'lexical item' or 'lexical entry' to refer to the contents of the lexicon.

13. There might be a certain doubt considering the c-command relations of (18a). On a very plausible analysis, the verb has adjoined to the Asp head (Zheng 1994). The syntactic structure shown in (i) can then be proposed for (18a) (irrelevant details are omitted).

(i)

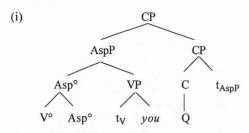

If segments are exempted from the c-command relation, the verb in (i) will c-command the aspect marker and the object. If the aspect phrase is really in Spec-CP, as depicted here, the question marker in C is not c-commanded by the verbal head. See the discussion of c-command in Kayne (1994).

14. In Holmberg (1998a) the question marker *-kO* is analyzed as a realization of the C° head, for which a phonological host is provided either by head moving the verb to C° or by moving a (focused) phrase to Spec-CP. Alternatively, *-kO* could be analyzed as a realization of the Foc° head of Rizzi (1997).

15. Kristoffersen (2000) claims that retroflexation is also obligatory in compounds. It is probably true that in colloquial speech, there will almost always be retroflexation in compounds. However, there is a clear contrast between compounds on one hand and roots, inflected words, and sequences including the weak pronoun *-n* on the other, in that compounds can be pronounced without retroflexation while this is ungrammatical in the other cases.

16. Denny (1989) objects to this conclusion, claiming that the examples cited by Sadock (1980, 1986) result from Danish influence. Concerning nouns which are incorporated into the verbs *-taar-* 'get' and *-gar-* 'have', as in the following example, he has a different proposal.

(i) *Greenlandic* (Denny 1989:239)
Erner-taar-put,   atser-lu-gu-lu   Mala-mik.
son-get-IND.3p   call-CTMP-3O-and   Mala-INSTR
'They got a son, and they called him Mala.'

Denying that Greenlandic incorporated nouns have independent syntactic function, Denny claims that in this case, it is the derived verb that has the property of introducing the discourse referent. Unfortunately, I do not see how this can mean that the incorporated noun does not represent this referent in syntax.

17. This observation surely casts doubt on the following passage from Di Sciullo and Williams (1987:53): "So two unrelated ways of dividing up the universe of linguistic objects converge: those that share the formal property of being head-final share the further property of being syntactically opaque, and only those. We feel that this convergence gives the notion 'word' its surest content."

It appears that neither of their criteria for wordhood has empirical support. First, it is possible for elements inside words to be syntactically active; second, examples of left-headed morphology are not unheard of. Some of these examples can be made to fit Di Sciullo and Williams's definition with the help of their notion of Relativized Head, according to which the head with respect to a given feature is the rightmost element marked for this feature. Of course, if a given feature appears only once within the word, the element that carries this feature will always be the rightmost element marked for this feature, even if it should be the first of several prefixes, for example. But then the rightheadedness constraint might as well be reformulated as a leftheadedness constraint, while neither will have very much empirical content. Besides, genuine counterevidence to the claim that words are head-final can be found. In some languages, for example, the first element will be the head in N-N compounds. If both nouns have the same features, then the head must be identified only on the basis of its position to the left. (For examples, see, e.g., Lieber 1992.)

18. A similar argument is advanced in Lieber (1992). See also Drijkoningen (1994), where it is argued that the referential islandhood of (many) constituents of words is compatible with a syntactic approach to word formation if it is seen as a consequence of the computation of complex words at LF.

19. For grammatical information on Greenlandic I have relied on Fortescue (1984) and Berthelsen et al. (1977).

20. A similar argumentation is found in Boas (1911:30–31). See also the discussion of Greenlandic words in Sadock (1980:302–303).

21. The contemporative mood indicates that this must be a subordinate clause; the fourth person marking indicates that its subject is coreferential with the matrix subject (see Fortescue 1984).

22. Whereas various clitics serve to mark conjunction structures, as shown, subordination relations between clauses are as a rule shown by the presence of some subordinate mood on the embedded verb, sometimes in combination with certain derivational markers. See Fortescue (1984).

23. It can also be copied on the first conjunct for emphasis, as indicated in (40a).

24. For a discussion of special clitic positioning, see, e.g., Klavans (1985), Zwicky (1985a), Anderson (1992).

25. Mandarin Chinese has another particle *le*, which appears at the right periphery at the sentence and therefore is not always adjacent to the verb. Li and Thompson (1981) gloss this particle as C(urrently) R(elevant) S(tate), as opposed to the perfective *le* shown in (34), (35), (42), and (43). An example of the CRS-marker *le* is given in (i). Notably, the two *le* particles may co-occur, as in (ii). It is important to bear in mind that what is said in the text refers only to the perfect particle *le*.

(i) *Mandarin Chinese*   (Li & Thompson 1981:239)
    tā   mǎ   fángzi   le   ma?
    3s   buy   house   CRS   Q
    'Did she buy a house?'

(ii) *Mandarin Chinese*   (Li & Thompson 1981:244)
    wǒ   hē   le   sān   bēi   kāfēi   le
    I   drink   PERF   three   cup   coffee   CRS
    'I have drunk three cups of coffee.'

26. Thanks to Ove Lorentz for helping me with some of the Mandarin Chinese examples.

27. Cf. Di Sciullo and Williams (1987:48): "The rules of syntax can see that a word has such and such properties, but they cannot see how it came to have those properties."

28. More precisely, X° is the tense head, which is immediately preceded by the verb root. Either the verb root has head-moved to T° or else VP has moved to Spec-TP, as proposed for head-final languages in chapter 3. On the latter analysis, (55b) probably has the same structure as the constructions with postverbal elements known from Turkish and other head-final languages, analyzed in chapter 3 as the result of movement operations which are triggered by discourse-related features and which cause the IP and the subject to end up in Spec-positions in the CP-domain.

29. But see the alternative analysis of Malagasy in Rackowski and Travis (2000).

30. See also chapter 8 in Greenberg (1963).

31. Infixes are classified as either prefixes or suffixes, depending on whether they target the left or the right edge of the root. See McCarthy and Prince (1993b).

32. That is, I assume no principled contrast between the following constructions:

(i) *Bambara*   (Kastenholz 1989:86)
    à   ná   sà
    he   FUT   die
    'He will die.'

(ii) *Sengoi*   (Means et al. 1986)
    ke   ki-ha   muit
    3s   3s-FUT   enter
    'She will enter.'

In my opinion, the presence or absence of person inflection on the tense/aspect marker does not necessarily bear on the syntactic status of this marker.

In Dryer's (1992) terms, the tense marker in (i) is a particle, whereas the tense marker in (ii) is an auxiliary. Interestingly, Dryer finds a statistical difference in the position of the two types of elements: whereas T/A particles tend to precede the verb in both VO and OV languages, T/A auxiliaries normally precede the verb in VO languages but follow the verb in OV languages.

A possible explanation for this contrast is that uninflected tense markers are the realizations of T° heads to which the verb has not moved, whereas what Dryer calls auxiliaries are often V°+T° combinations. The 'auxiliaries' are typically not obligatory, and when they occur, they are in the position which would otherwise be occupied by the finite verb, while the main verb shows up in some nonfinite form. The fact that the nonfinite verb must precede the auxiliary in many SOV languages can be taken as support for Kayne's (1994) proposal that in head-final languages, complements must move across their selecting heads (see the discussion of head-final languages in chapter 3).

33. There is reason to suspect that even in languages where any order of verb and arguments is allowed, one order is the basic one which will be used unless discourse functional considerations calls for a different order.

For example, in his work on the Australian language Pitta-Pitta, Blake (1979:213) notes that the orders SOV, SVO, and VSO all occur; he then adds that "the topic precedes the comment but a focused element is commonly brought to the beginning of the sentence. . . . It is this principle that produces most of the apparent freedom of word order." The fact that SOV is a common pattern in elicited sentences (Blake 1979:214) may indicate that this is the unmarked order in Pitta-Pitta.

Similarly, in a discussion of word order in Dyirbal, Dixon (1972:291) starts out by saying that "word order is exceptionally free in Dyirbal." He goes on to list a number of ordering preferences, among these the tendency for a nominative DP to precede an ergative DP which, in turn, precedes the verb; that is, the preferred order in transitive clauses is OSV. Finally, he adds the observation that "the relative ordering 'preferences' listed above are more likely to be adhered to if ambiguity would otherwise result." Now this is a clear indication that OSV is in fact the unmarked order, the order that one sticks to in cases where order is the only indication of sentential functions.

34. The groups are: (1) English-based, Caribbean; (2) English-based, West African; (3) English-based, Oceanic; (4) French-based, Caribbean; (5) French-based, Indian Ocean; (6) Dutch-based; (7) Portuguese-based; (8) Spanish-based; (9) Others (see appendix 2).

35. This tendency was also noted by Greenberg (1966). Of the 12 exclusively suffixing languages in his sample, 10 were verb final. In Hawkins and Gilligan (1988:224) the correlation between verb finality and tense suffixes in particular is stated as follows (universal 14): "If a language has SOV, Tense affixes on V (if any) are suffixed with greater than chance frequency."

36. There exists of course also a fifth type of tense marking, in that tense can be realized as modification of the verbal stem. However, as noted in section 1.3, very few languages have stem alternations as their principal or only way of expressing tense. In my sample, only the Semitic languages represent this type. Likewise, whereas a number of languages have aspectual categories realized on the verb stem, in the form of tone patterns or other stem alternations, these markings in most cases combine with or alternate with temporal and/or aspectual affixes.

In the framework adopted here, nonsegmental markings of tense (or aspect) indicate that the T° (or A°) head has fused with the V° head. The topic of fused markers will be dealt with in section 6.2.2.

2

Head Movement and Complex Heads

2.1 Overview

The topic of this chapter is head movement and the formation of complex heads. Of the syntactic processes and configurations claimed in section 1.4.3 to give rise to complex words, head movement is far more widely recognized than the others. The syntactic process of head movement, whereby a syntactic head moves and adjoins to the next higher head, obeying the HMC of Travis (1984), is a well-established element of current syntactic analyses. It is also often assumed to feed word formation.

Now if syntax is restricted in the way summarized in example (50), ch. 1, it must be the case that head movement is always leftward and that the moving head invariably ends up to the left of the head it adjoins to. The movement operation can be repeated, so that the newly formed complex head is further moved and left-adjoined to a third head. The morphological outcome of each step is that a suffix is added to the word form that has already been built up. I assume here that excorporation is not an option; this assumption is discussed in section 2.3. This means that if the heads X°, Y° and Z° are arranged syntactically as in (1a), the combination of these categories into one word by head-to-head movement can only give the constituent order shown in (1b). Other orders, such as those illustrated in (1c)–(1e), should not be derivable at all from the initial configuration in (1a).

(1)

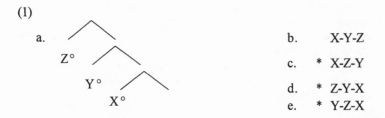

a.		b.		X-Y-Z
	Z°	c.	*	X-Z-Y
	Y°	d.	*	Z-Y-X
	X°	e.	*	Y-Z-X

The consequence of iterated head movement is thus that infinitely complex words can be built up; inside those words the order of morphemes will be exactly the opposite of the order of the corresponding syntactic heads in the base structure. This conforms to what has come to be the usual interpretation of the

Mirror Principle of Baker (1985, 1988a). I will refer to it as the Generalized Mirror Principle (GMP).

There are many examples to be found in the languages of the world that seem to corroborate the GMP. Below I present some complex verbal words that can all be argued to be derived by successive incorporation of verbal heads.

(2) *Fulfulde* (Fagerli 1994:51)
Hayatu dar-t-in-an-i   yam njamndi.
Hayatu stand-REP-CAUS-BEN-VAP   me metal
'Hayatu redressed the metal piece for me.'

(3) *Northern Saami* (see Nickel 1990:49)
Mii   veahkeh-eažža-i-met da-i-d   olbmu-i-d.
1p.NOM help-POT-PAST-1p   that-PL-ACC person-PL-ACC
'We might (have) helped those people.'

(4) *Kashmiri* (Wali & Koul 1997:214)
bɪ   d'a:v-ɪna:v-an   su   mohna-s   kita:b
I   give-CAUS-FUT he   Mohan-DAT book
'I will make him give a book to Mohan.'

(5) *Guajira* (Olza Zubiri & Jusay 1978)
Ant-irr-e-chi   taya   kattaluota-kalü.
arrive-CAUS-FUT-MASC.SG 1s.MASC letter-FEM.SG.DEF
'I will make the letter arrive.'

However, since the Mirror Principle is strictly only a descriptive characterization of the output of grammar, one can conceive of more than one way in which the relevant surface structures can be derived. The syntactic incorporation analysis suggested above is not necessarily the only possibility. An alternative lexicalist interpretation is proposed, for example, in Chomsky (1995:195–196). Still, the syntactic approach seems to have its advantages, and it is certainly worth exploring to its full depth. In particular, while the order of suffixes seen above follows directly in a model where words can be built up by head movement, in a lexicalist analysis some additional mechanism would have to be stipulated which ensures that morphemes are added in an order that corresponds to the order of heads in the syntactic structure that the word is inserted into. Otherwise, the regularities that can be observed must either be ignored or considered purely accidental.

Even if we thus assume that words can be formed by head movement, there are still many problems that need to be addressed before we have a full understanding of head movement as a word-forming process. In the following, some of these problems will be dealt with.

In section 2.2 I address the question of what is the driving force behind head movement. The idea I am defending is that a word-forming head movement operation is not a consequence of morphological subcategorizational properties; instead, it is triggered by the presence of a strong head feature in the attracting head. Since it is always the head of the complement that is attracted, and since the categorial feature of the complement of the attracting head will necessarily be checked simultaneously, the operation is only successful if the head of the complement is of the right type. It follows that there is no need to specify the category that the head will attach to morphologically.

The topic of section 2.3 is excorporation, or the possibility of moving a head through another head. I conclude, after having examined a number of apparent counterexamples, that excorporation does not seem to be an operation that languages make use of and that a complex head formed by head movement will necessarily behave as a word, its internal morpheme order mirroring the base-generated order of the heads involved.

In section 2.4 I deal with a word-forming mechanism that has been proposed as an alternative to head movement—namely, morphological merger. I argue that there are several problems with assuming such a process, and that it is not necessarily needed to account for the morphological patterns that we see in the world's languages.

Finally, my findings concerning head movement and the word-building properties of this process are summed up in section 2.5.

2.2 The trigger of head movement

I begin the discussion of head movement as a word-forming process by considering the Northern Saami constructions shown in (6).[1] In (6a), an affirmative clause, the verb root has a suffixed tense marker followed by a suffixed subject agreement marker. In (6b), a negated clause, tense is still marked on the main verb, while the subject agreement marker is attached to the negation, which precedes the main verb.

(6) *Northern Saami*
  a. Mu-n   vástid-i-n   oanehaččat.
      I-NOM   answer-PAST-1s   briefly
      'I answered briefly.'

  b. Mu-n   i-n   vástid-án.
      I-NOM   NEG-1s   answer-PAST.PTC
      'I did not answer.'

Since subject agreement always co-occurs with finiteness, one might reasonably guess that it is the finite head which hosts subject agreement (see Rizzi 1997, Platzack 1998). The morpheme order in (6b) suggests that the polarity head is generated below the Fin° head and moved to Fin°. Further, I assume that in (6a) there is an affirmative polarity head which is phonologically zero—after all, (6a) is not *unmarked* with respect to polarity; it is clearly affirmative.[2] My proposal is that the complex verbal words in (6) are formed by head movement and that the syntactic structure of (6a) and (6b) is as shown in (7a) and (7b), respectively (with irrelevant heads left out).

(7)

a.

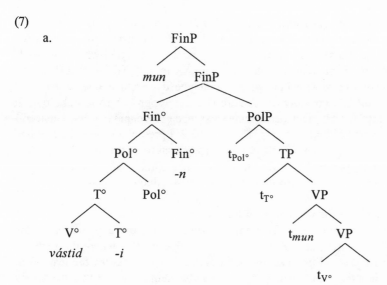

b.

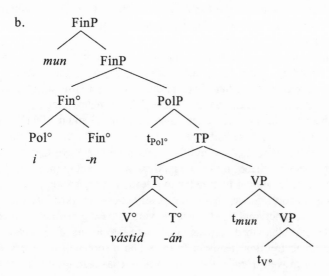

It is a trivial fact that some but not all languages exhibit word forms that may be analyzed as the outcome of head movement. For example, it seems clear that in (8) there has been no movement at all. The subject agreement marker and the tense marker are spelled out as separate words preceding the verb, which may well be realized in situ.

(8)   *Tinrin*   (Osumi 1995:179)
      nrâ   hava   tròa   âwù   sêêdre
      3s   N.PAST   arrive   yesterday evening
      'He only arrived last night.'

The crucial but very simple question that I try to answer in this section is the following: What exactly is the difference between a construction where each syntactic head is a separate word, as in (8), and a construction where the heads are combined, by movement, into one word, as in (6)? To put it differently: What is the driving force behind word-building head movement operations?

I first, in 2.2.1, consider the feature checking approach to morphology of Chomsky (1993, 1995) and also a suggestion made in Koopman (1994) concerning the licensing of lexical heads. Then, in 2.2.2, I present a proposal according to which head movement is driven by a strong feature of the host that induces the host to incorporate the head of its complement. On this approach, the notion of morphological subcategorization is rendered superfluous.

2.2.1 Checking theory and head movement
On the checking approach of Chomsky (1993, 1995) the explanation of the contrast between (6a) and (8) above would be that in (6a), where the verb has moved overtly to the Fin° head, the features of Fin° (and possibly the features of T°) must be strong, thus triggering overt movement of V° so that the strong features can be checked off before the derivation reaches PF. In (8), by contrast, the features of T° and Fin° are weak, so that they will not be checked until LF, and the verb does not have to move overtly.

Notably, it is assumed in the checking approach that the inflectional markers are joined with the verbal root before the verb is merged, so that subsequent movement has no effect on the actual shape of the verbal word—it only serves to check that it has the appropriate feature makeup. This means that there is no causal relation between the absence of head movement in (8) and the fact that the tense and agreement markers are not attached to the verb. On the checking approach, an element that is spelled out in its base position may nevertheless carry affixes. In short, checking theory makes no prediction at all about morphology.

In contrast to this, the model I am defending leads to very strong predictions about morphological form. Since I assume that inflectional markers are inserted in the corresponding functional heads, that the verb is base generated as a bare root, and that the complex word may actually come into existence as heads are successively adjoined to other heads, it follows that a root will not carry any affixes if it has not moved. Hence, the verb form in (6a) could not exist in the absence of movement.

It could still be maintained, however, that the movement of the verb is triggered by inflectional features, as claimed by Chomsky (1993, 1995). Only a minor revision of the checking theory is necessary to incorporate this idea in a framework where words are built in syntax: the overt inflectional markers must be seen as reflexes of the features of the inflectional heads and not of the features of the verb itself. We can then assume that the verb moves in (6a) because its features must be checked off against strong features of T° and Fin° and that in (8), the relevant features are weak so that the verb stays in VP.

The move I have just suggested would work for examples like (6a), where a root is combined with elements belonging to its own functional domain. However, still another revision of the checking theory would be necessary in order to extend this analysis to derivational word formation. Consider the following examples:

(9) *Northern Saami*
    Mu-n   máhca-h-i-n   reivve.
    I.NOM return-CAUS-PAST-1s letter.SG.ACC
    'I returned the letter.'

(10) *Tiwi* (Osborne 1974:32)
    ŋə-rə-əŋəpuɳantə-aŋkələwiɳi
    1s-PAST-dugong-see
    'I saw the dugong.'

The complex verbs in (9) and (10) can both plausibly be analyzed as resulting from a lexical root having moved into a higher verb. In (9), we have V-to-V movement (the verb *máhca-* 'return' has moved into the causative verb), and in (10) we have N-to-V movement (the noun *dugong* has moved into the verb *aŋkələwiɳi* 'see'). If both these movements are triggered by the need to check off some strong feature of the host head, it cannot be that the strong/weak distinction is relevant only to features that reside in inflectional heads. Rather, lexical elements must also be allowed to have a strong feature that triggers overt movement of a lower head.

A suggestion concerning cases like (9) and (10) is given in Koopman (1994). She proposes that lexical heads in general move to appropriate licensing heads to have their lexical properties satisfied. For example, V° is licensed by moving to T°. If a V° is not dominated by a T° of its own it can only get licensed by moving to a higher V° with a full T (and C) specification. However, since Koopman also assumes that head movement operations can be overt or covert, her proposal has little to say about affixation. Nevertheless, for causative verbs Koopman proposes that they universally trigger S-structure incorporation, but of the lower I°, not of V°.[3] Overt V-to-V movement is seen only if the lower V° has moved to the lower I° before the lower I° moves. The existence of morphological causatives is therefore, according to Koopman, a diagnostic criterion for (overt) V-to-I movement. In other words, if a language has both a causative verb and overt V-to-I movement, the causative verb will be an affix.

However plausible Koopman's analysis may be, it is not clear how it would account for the existence of affixal lexical categories other than causative verbs. Although Koopman claims, for example, that the N° heads of arguments must move to the argument-taking V°, she does not discuss why this must sometimes take place overtly, yielding incorporated structures like the one in (10).

It interesting to note, though, that whereas the overall idea of Koopman's (1994) proposal is that head movement is driven by properties of the incorporee, in the only example of overt affixation that she mentions, the need for overt movement is taken to be a consequence of properties of the host head: the causative verb is said to be defective, so that it cannot project a well-formed syntactic structure unless some other head incorporates into it (Koopman 1994:282). Koopman's proposal concerning causatives is reminiscent of the traditional view that the organization of morphemes in constructions like (9) and (10) is a consequence of certain elements being affixes, which means that they must attach to some root or stem. In the next section I look more closely at the very notion of affixhood, which occurs so frequently in the literature but very rarely gets an explanation that goes beyond the purely descriptive level.

2.2.2   The notion of affixhood

Descriptively, affixes are selective with respect to the base that they attach to, in contrast to clitics, which attach (phonologically) to bases of various types, apparent restrictions being a consequence of the syntactic environment of a given clitic. In an attempt to understand the property of being an affix, I will first take another look at clitics, as exemplified by the Northern Saami question marker, shown in (11).

(11) *Northern Saami*
    a. Ovddit   beaivvi-go   lea-t   boaht-án   Oslo-s?
        previous day   Q   be-PRES.2s   come-PAST.PTC   Oslo-LOC
        'Was it the day before yesterday that you came from Oslo?'

    b. Boađ-át   -go   mielde?
        come-PRES.2s   Q   along
        'Are you coming along?'

I will assume that the question marker *go* spells out the [Q] feature of a polarity question Foc° in the CP-domain (see Rizzi 1997).[4] This [Q] feature is strong, so that it needs to be checked overtly by moving a [Q]-marked element to the checking domain of Foc°. This requirement can be satisfied either by moving a phrase to Spec-FocP, as in (11a), or by moving the verb to Foc°, as in (11b). The first option applies if a constituent of the clause is focused; such a focused constituent is always assigned the [Q] feature in polarity questions. The second option is the default solution: if no phrasal constituent is focused, the [Q] feature is assigned to the polarity head, which is included in the finite verb (see 7a).

In the case of head movement, the operation applies only to verbs and is strictly local—the complex verbal word in (11b) has raised from the head position immediately below Foc°. In the case of phrasal movement, by contrast,

the operation need not be local; any [Q]-marked XP in the complement of Foc°
will be attracted to Spec-FocP, regardless of how deeply embedded it is and
regardless of its category. Consider the declarative counterparts of (11ab), given
in (12ab).

(12) *Northern Saami*
 a. (Mu-n)   lea-n   boaht-án   Oslo-s   ovddit   beaivvi.
      I-NOM   be-PRES.1s   come-PAST.PTC Oslo-LOC   previous day
      'I came from Oslo the day before yesterday.'

 b. Boađ-án   mielde.
      come-PRES.1s along
      'I am coming along.'

As we see, the temporal adverbial *ovddit beaivi* 'the day before yesterday' is the
last constituent of the declarative clause. Hence, it must cross all other constituents on its way to Spec-FocP. This shows that the [Q] feature can attract at a
distance.

An affix is different from the clitic just presented in that it normally attaches
to elements of a specific type. This has customarily been taken to mean that
affixes place a more specific requirement on elements that they will attach to.
The first technical formulation of the selectional properties of affixes appeared in
Lieber (1981). In her theory, affixes are lexical elements that, unlike free
morphemes, have a so-called *morphological subcategorization frame* as a part of
their lexical entries, which determines the lexical category of the elements that
the affix can combine with. The morphological subcategorization frame, which
in Lieber's theory is the only property that sets affixes off from other elements,
is specified along with the category membership of the affix itself, so that a
lexical entry for an affix will contain, among other things, information of the
following form:

(13) $[_X \text{Aff} [_Y \underline{\quad}]]$

In (13), the affix has the properties of attaching to an element of category Y and
producing an element of category X.

The idea that it is the morphological subcategorization properties of a given
element which determine the morphological distribution of that element has had
a considerable impact on later theorizing. Baker (1988a) proposed that S-
structure is the syntactic level at which the subcategorization frames of affixes
are satisfied. The relevant requirement was formally expressed as the Stray Affix
Filter:

(14) *Stray Affix Filter* (Baker 1988a:140)
     *X if X is a lexical item whose morphological subcategorization frame is
     not satisfied at S-structure.

Baker's reason for stating that morphological subcategorization applies at S-structure is obvious: in a theory that assumes that affixes are syntactically similar to free words, so that they may head phrases, take arguments, and so on, it follows that an affix must be base-generated in the position required by its syntactic properties. But since it cannot surface unattached, it must be combined with an appropriate host in the course of the derivation. In current terms one would say that this must be accomplished before Spell-Out.[5]

In Rizzi and Roberts (1989) and Roberts (1991) morphological subcategorization is given a syntactic interpretation in that affixal elements are assumed to have a projection level below $X°$—that is, to be X^{-1} elements—and to create a syntactic slot into which an $X°$ of the specified type is substituted. The configuration after substitution, which satisfies the morphological subcategorizational properties of X^{-1}, is shown in (15) (which is identical to Roberts's (6a) except that I have switched the incorporee to the left of the host).

(15)

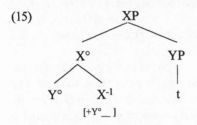

The notion of morphological subcategorization is somewhat unsatisfactory, though. It does little more than restate the fact that the affixal element always occurs with a host element of a certain type.[6] Moreover, one could ask whether it is not wholly redundant in a theory where affixation is taken to be the result of syntactic operations. For example, if a head triggers head movement by attracting another head, it will necessarily be the next head down, the head of the complement, that is attracted.[7] If the category of the complement is fixed by independent principles, the consequence will be that a given affixal head will always attract heads of a certain category. Thus, it may be sufficient to say of an affixal category that it attracts a head, since in any configuration, general syntactic principles, including restrictions on head movement, will do the rest.

As for the question of what may cause a head to attract another head, I will adopt the suggestion made above that a head that attracts another head has a strong head feature: more precisely, I assume that the relevant features are categorial features and that they can be found in both functional and lexical heads.

I will also assume that in addition to categorial and other features, every head that takes a complement has a complement selectional feature, or c-feature, which specifies the category of the complement of the head (see Svenonius 1994a and Holmberg 2000a). The c-feature is uninterpretable in the sense of Chomsky (1995), which means that it needs to be matched against the relevant feature of the complement, by movement of the relevant feature of the complement to the checking domain of the selecting head. I will refer to this operation as c-checking.

Now if a head has a strong head feature, for example a V-feature, it will attract the next head down if that head has a V-feature. However, the derivation will crash if the c-feature of the attractor is not also checked. Hence, the head movement operation is only successful if the head of the complement satisfies both the categorial feature and the c-feature of the attracting head. Now if a given $X°$ always occurs with a complement, and the head of that complement is always attracted to $X°$, the c-feature of $X°$ will ensure that $X°$ invariably forms a complex head with a head of a certain category. Hence, $X°$ will have the appearance of an affix.

Note, by the way, that if the attracting head is lexical, its attracting head feature will have the same target as its c-feature. For example, in the case of the affixal verb in (10) there must be a nominal feature that serves to attract the object, so that it forms a complex head with the verb (as argued in Baker 1988a and 1996, in some languages this is one way to license the object). If the attracting head is functional, on the other hand, we may be talking of two different targets. Thus, if we assume that the head encoding subject agreement in (6a) has a PolP complement, this must be dictated by its c-feature. The actual head movement, however, is probably triggered by a strong V-feature which is present in all the functional heads of IP. Consequently, there is head movement all the way from $V°$ upward, so that all the verbal markers end up as suffixes on the verb.

It seems clear that having both an operation of complement selection, determined by subcategorizational properties, and a subsequent operation of c-checking is redundant. Instead, one might propose that c-checking is how complement selection is carried out technically. This means that the relation between a head and its complement is referred to only once in a derivation.

Concerning the actual form of the c-checking movement operation, Holmberg (2000a) proposes that there are three options, as listed under (16).

(16) *Checking of c-selectional features (c-checking)*
  A selectional feature of a head $Y°$ selecting a complement XP may be checked
  a. by movement of the X feature to $Y°$
  b. by head movement of $X°$ to $Y°$
  c. by movement of XP to the Spec of YP

As we see, options (16b) and (16c) involve overt movement. The XP-movement solution will be discussed in chapter 3. What I want to propose concerning the head movement solution is that although c-features can be checked by head movement, this movement must be triggered by some other feature, so that the c-feature is checked as a 'free rider' (Chomsky 1995). In other words, a c-feature alone is never able to extract the head out of its complement. Instead, as we will see in chapter 3, a strong c-feature will trigger movement of the complement as whole.

As for the feature movement option, it is likely that this is what allows the formation of structures like (8) above, where each head is spelled out in its base position and there is no overt movement.

In this chapter, we concentrate on cases where head movement applies. I will now go on to show that triggering overt movement is not necessarily a property of categories as such, but rather of individual morphemes, where 'morpheme' refers to a feature bundle that constitutes a syntactic terminal node prior to the insertion of lexical material.

We have already seen that in Northern Saami, the markers of tense and subject agreement are suffixed to the verb stem in affirmative clauses, while in the corresponding negative clause it is the negative marker that is combined with subject agreement. The facts are similar in other Finnic languages, except that in some of them it is the negation and not the main verb that is marked for tense (see Trosterud 1994). As shown in (7a), the affirmative polarity heads attracts $T°$ and is itself attracted by $Fin°$. In (7b), by contrast, the negative polarity head does not attract $T°$, so that the complex $V°+T°$ head is stranded in $T°$.[8] That is, a [–NEG] polarity head has a strong V-feature, which triggers movement of the $V°+T°$ head, whereas a [+NEG] polarity head does not.

One might assume that one reason for this contrast is that a [+NEG] polarity head has its own phonological realization, whereas a [–NEG] polarity head can only get a phonological realization by attracting some other head. However, if we consider Finnish, which is closely related to Saami, it appears that this is not the correct generalization of the contrast shown in (7ab). In passive verbs in Finnish, there is an overt realization of [–NEG] polarity, which shows up as the outermost suffix on the verb (Mitchell 1991). In the corresponding negative, the polarity marker is separated from the verb:

(17) *Finnish* (Mitchell 1991:375)
    a. Talo   maala-ta-an.
        house   paint-PASS-AFF
        'The house is being painted.'

    b. Talo-a   e-i   maala-ta.
        house-PART   NEG-3s   paint-PASS
        'The house is not being painted.'

On the basis of (17), we must conclude, for the Finnic languages, that a polarity head with the feature [–NEG] will attract the head of its complement, whereas a polarity head with the feature [+NEG] will not. Thus, the property of affixhood is connected to individual features and not to categories; in Finnic, it is only *negative* polarity heads that forces the head of the complement of $Pol°$ to raise overtly into the checking domain of $Pol°$.[9]

A similar case can be made for Bambara. Bambara has fused markers of polarity and tense, which are suffixed to the verb or appear in front of it depending on the feature content of the marker. This is seen in the following two examples, which both are in the past tense but differ with respect to polarity.

(18) *Bambara* (Kastenholz 1989:66–67)

a.	màsakE	wúli-la		b.	ù má	wúli
	chief	rise-PAST.AFF			3p PAST.NEG	rise
	'The chief stood up.'				'They did not stand up.'	

As we see, the affirmative past head triggers verb movement, whereas the negative past head does not. Strikingly, this is exactly the same contrast as we saw in Finnish. It remains to see whether it holds generally that, if a language has polarity markers with different morphological properties, it will be the affirmative marker that is affixed.

In contrast to the claim put forth here that a head with a strong head feature will always attract the next head down, it has been claimed that head movement is sometimes blocked for morphological reasons. What I have in mind is constructions with the so-called 'aspectual' auxiliaries 'be' and 'have', as exemplified in (19).

(19) *English*
  a. The cat is playing with the mouse.
  b. The cat has caught the mouse.

The traditional analysis of these constructions says that the auxiliaries are inserted in order to save an affixal element, the tense marker, which would otherwise be left unattached as the main verb is combined with an element whose features are incompatible with the morphological selection properties of T°. However, in Julien (2001) I argue that constructions with the auxiliaries 'be' and 'have' are in fact biclausal, with a finite auxiliary as the V° of the matrix clause and a nonfinite main verb as the V° of the embedded clause. The presence of the auxiliaries thus has nothing to do with morphological form. Affixal heads have their properties satisfied by attracting the next head down in these constructions as elsewhere.

To sum up the discussion of affixes, an affix is the phonological realization of a syntactic head containing a strong feature that triggers overt movement of the head of its complement, or, as we will see in the next chapter, of the whole complement. Of course, this is not the ultimate explanation of affixhood; one can still ask why the relevant feature is strong in some cases but not in others. Nevertheless, I think we have made some progress in that we have dispensed with the notion of 'morphological subcategorization', which was shown to be redundant as long as the category of the complement of a given head is determined by other principles.

2.3 Excorporation

In the preceding discussion of head movement I have assumed that one cannot *excorporate*—that is, move an element out of a complex head. Indeed, it usually seems to be the case that once a complex head is formed, it can only move on as a whole. For example, in verb-raising constructions, it is not possible for the verb to move through T° and not carry T° along. Thus, as noted in Roberts (1991), it is strongly ungrammatical to move an auxiliary to C° leaving T° behind, as in (20a). Roberts does not mention the possibility that the ungrammaticality of (20a) might be due to the insertion of *do* in the position of the trace of the auxiliary. But notably, the construction is just as bad without *do*-insertion, as shown in (20b).

(20) *English*
    a. * Have John does gone?
    b. * Have John's gone?

And regardless of the complexities of the English auxiliary system, an effect similar to that illustrated in (20a,b) is also found in Norwegian, where both auxiliaries and full verbs move to C° in root clauses (I here abstract away from the finer structure of the CP-domain; see Rizzi 1997). A verb moving to C° must carry T° with it, as illustrated in (21).

(21) *Norwegian*
    a. Komm-er   du   i morgen?
        come-PRES you tomorrow
        'Are you coming tomorrow?'

    b.* Kom du -er   i morgen?
        come you PRES   tomorrow

    c. Ha-r   noen gitt   katt-ene   mat?
        have-PRES anyone given   cat-PL.DEF food
        'Has anyone fed the cats?'

    d.* Ha   noen gi-r   katt-ene   mat?
        have.INF anyone give-PRES cat-PL.DEF food

In fact, constructions like (21b) and (21d) are so blatantly ungrammatical that one can hardly imagine any language learner making mistakes of this kind. But if a head could skip another head or move through it as it moved upward, it would be possible to derive all of the ungrammatical examples above. The facts being what they are, both skipping a head and moving through it must be ruled out by very strong constraints.

In this section, I first, in 2.3.1, deal with the theory of excorporation in more detail; then in 2.3.2 I turn to an empirical discussion based on data from the survey referred to in section 1.5. Some final remarks concerning excorporation follow in 2.3.3.

2.3.1   The theory of excorporation

A number of different proposals have been put forth concerning the possibility or impossibility of excorporation, or head movement through a head. Baker (1988a:73) simply assumes that there is a ban on having traces inside words— that is, on having an $X°$ dominate a trace *plus something else*. This restriction would effectively prevent excorporation, but nevertheless Baker's suggestion essentially merely restates the fact that there is no movement of a subpart of a head.

Lieber (1992:146) chooses a somewhat different tack, stating that movement of an affix out of a word will violate the subcategorization frame of that affix, and movement of a free morpheme out of a word will invariably violate the ECP. Hence, movement of elements out of words is impossible. Lieber's hypothetical examples, however, appear to be rather arbitrarily chosen, so that it is not obvious that her arguments will extend to all instances of excorporation. Her example of excorporation of a free morpheme is a case where a part of an N-N compound moves out. She argues that since the complex $N°$ is not L-marked (only NP is), $N°$ will always be a barrier to government, and any movement out of $N°$ is prohibited.[10] Strikingly, this would seemingly also suffice to rule out her example of affix excorporation, the movement of the *-er* morpheme out of *driver*, which is claimed to violate the subcategorization frame of *-er*.

Notably, Lieber's example of affix excorporation also means moving out the projecting element, the host head. Concerning this kind of operation, Kayne (1994) observes that if c-command is restricted to categories, it follows that a head to which another element has adjoined cannot be moved: the host head will count as a segment, and since segments are not available to c-command, traces of segments cannot be antecedent-governed. Thus, movement of a host is out for structural reasons, and there is no need to make reference to subcategorization properties.

Kayne does not exclude the possibility that the *adjoined* element may move on further, though (Kayne 1994:134 n. 6). The question of whether successive cyclic head movement is possible is discussed in more depth in Roberts (1991), and we will look here at the details of Roberts's treatment. Roberts builds on an idea from Rizzi and Roberts (1989) that head-to-head movement may be either substitution or adjunction. As mentioned in section 2.2.2, Roberts assumes that in cases where head movement has word-building effects, the morphological subcategorization properties of the incorporation host create a structural slot into which the incorporee is substituted. In addition, the host is taken to be an X^{-1}. The resulting structure, shown in (14), is repeated here as (22).

(22)

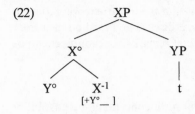

In a configuration like (22), Roberts claims, $Y°$ cannot move on so as to strand X^{-1}. If, for example, $Y° = V°$ and $X^{-1} = I^{-1}$, and $V°$ moves to $C°$ alone, we get the following:

(23)

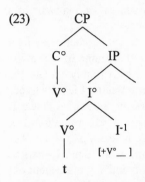

In Roberts's approach, I^{-1} is the ultimate head of IP and dissimilar from its projection $I°$. But then, he notes, I^{-1} counts as an intervening governor for the trace of $V°$, with the consequence that the trace cannot be antecedent-governed. Therefore, $V°$ cannot move out of $I°$, and, more generally, there can be no excorporation out of selected slots.

Roberts's proposal (inspired by Selkirk 1982) that incorporation hosts are of a bar level below $X°$ is not unproblematic. First, if X^{-1} alone is the head in (22), so that X^{-1} and $X°$ are not segments of the same category, then incorporation should not be possible in the first place, since after incorporation $Y°$ would be dominated by $X°$ and therefore not able to c-command its trace. To get around this unwanted consequence, Roberts (1991:215) adds the stipulation that "any index possessed by an incorporee percolates to the complex formed after incorporation; this ensures that the trace in the base position is antecedent-governed." Clearly, the idea of index percolating cannot be extended to other types of movement, so it would be better to do without it here as well. Second, in a configuration like (22) the *host*, X^{-1}, should be able to leave $X°$ as far as only structure is considered. If X^{-1} is able to c-command from its landing site in the same way as $Y°$ is assumed to do in (22), there will be no violation of the ECP.

In a theory where movement is always upward and to the left, excorporation of the host would be expected to be vacuous with respect to the order of heads. If, for example, $V°$ moves to $T°$ and $T°$ moves on, the only effect is that each head ends up higher than its base position. The relative order of $T°$ and $V°$ is not affected. The question is now how the movement of V° would be detected by the language learner. In a model where certain adverbials are adjoined to VP, the position of V° relative to these would show whether V° has moved or not, but, as Cinque (1999) demonstrates, this understanding of adverbial placement is probably too simplistic. If, as Cinque proposes, the adverbials that precede VP are generated as specifiers of separate heads, then a verb may have moved out of VP even if it follows a clause-medial adverbial, and the relative position of verb and adverbial is not necessarily an indicator of verb movement.

More generally, head movement followed by host excorporation would lead to an upward shift of the sequence of heads. This kind of operation, I suspect, would hardly be detectable and would thus not be passed on from one generation to another. Hence, I am inclined to believe that the operation does not exist, and I will assume that all instances of head movement create structures like (24), which is the structure Roberts (1991) reserves for nonselected head movement:

(24)

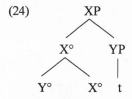

As far as the host is concerned, it cannot excorporate if c-command is restricted to categories.[11] Movement of the adjoined head, though, might still be possible. In (24), the X° sister of Y° is not a head; it is only a segment, and it cannot block antecedent government of the trace of Y°. Therefore, Roberts (1991) concludes, in this case Y° will be able to excorporate from X°.[12]

But note that if the proposal is correct, as put forth in section 2.2.2, that a head movement operation is licit only if the attracted head matches the c-feature of the attracting head, movement of Y° to a higher head will inevitably crash. Thus, in a converging derivation, any head movement operation targeting the head of XP must move X° itself. If the lower X° cannot move because it is a segment, the only remaining option is to move the complex head [X° Y° X°]. This would mean that a complex head can only move on as a whole, and there is no excorporation.

2.3.2 The facts of excorporation
Before we take this theoretical discussion any further, it might be useful to consider what consequences excorporation, or successive cyclic head movement, would be expected to have, so that we can see whether these consequences are actually attested in real languages. If successive cyclic head movement is allowed, it should, for example, be possible for the verb to move past one or more of the heads in its inflectional domain. In the model I assume here, where the functional categories associated with the verb are invariably generated to the left of V°, any occurrence of verbal functional elements to the right of V° must

be the result of movement. As we have already seen, it often happens that the verb moves, successively picking up functional elements as suffixes, so that the moving head gets more complex with each step. What we must look for as evidence for excorporation is cases where the verb precedes a non-bound functional element; that is, cases where the verb has moved past a functional head without ending up in a local relation to that head.

Turning now to the survey which was presented in section 1.5, we see that the least frequent realization of tense and aspect markers is as free markers following the verb. This pattern is found in only 33 genera.[13] Moreover, in 20 of these cases the relevant marker is not only following the verb, it follows the whole VP. Two examples will illustrate this:

(25) *Logbara* (Tucker & Bryan 1966:46; Nigel Fabb, personal communication)
    má-ɔmvɛ mvá   rá
    I-call   child   COMPL
    'I called the child.'

(26) *Coahuiltec* (Troike 1981:666)
    xawu: pil'in xa-ta:m tače:-t mami:k-k'ay am   e:?
    man   other   2-breast DEM-3 3S/2O-touch PAST Q
    'Has another man touched your breasts?'

Notably, the surface order in (25) and (26) could be derived by movement of VP to the left of $T°$, and there is no need to postulate that $V°$ has head-moved through $T°$. In (26), there must have been further movement of TP to the left of the question marker, which presumably is generated higher up than $T°$.

A hint that constructions of the type shown above actually do result from XP-movement is found in Voorhoeve (1975), in a brief discussion of Kimaghama, a language of the New Guinean group Kolopom. An example of constituent order in Kimaghama is given as follows:

(27) *Kimaghama* (Voorhoeve 1975:365)
    nö nie awra   aghatj
    he me beat   FUT
    'He will beat me.'

Voorhoeve (1975:365) adds the observation that "tense markers precede it [the verb] in question sentences containing a question word." Further details of the question word constructions are not given, but we can reasonably guess that if the verb does not precede the tense marker if a question word is present, it might be because the verb and the question word compete for the same position in front of the tense marker. More precisely, since *wh*-movement normally is XP-movement, it is possible that the *wh*-XP prevents the VP from moving to the front of the tense marker. Voorhoeve's observation might therefore be taken as support for the idea that where the verb as well as its arguments precede the tense marker, what we have is VP-movement and not head movement.[14] This means that 20 of the 33 genera where V T order is found can be ignored in our search for examples of excorporation.[15]

Of the remaining 12 genera, an additional 5 may be left out of consideration due to lack of detailed information on word order. The genera I have in mind are Nicobarese, Timor-Alor-Pantar, Wintun, Taracahitic, and Tucanoan. It is not clear from the available sources whether the languages with V T order in these genera should be grouped with the VP-moving languages just discussed. Since this possibility cannot be excluded, and since, in any case, there is nothing which a more detailed discussion of the languages in question could be based on, I will leave them aside.[16]

After 25 genera now have been eliminated, we are left with the following 8 suspects: Kuliak (represented in my survey by Ik), Bongo-Bagirmi (represented by Baka), Karen (represented by Moulmein Sgaw), Polynesian (the language in question is Maori), West Barkly (represented by Wambaya), Daly (represented by Ngankikurungkurr), Pimic (Northern Tepehuan, Tohono O'odham), and Portuguese-based creoles (represented by Kriyol). In all of these genera, one or more languages are reported to have tense marking elements that follow, or may follow, the verb, without there being any clear evidence that the V T order is derived by XP-movement. In the following, I will look more closely at some of the relevant languages.

In Ik, Wambaya, and the Pimic languages Northern Tepehuan and Tohono O'odham, the tense marker is an enclitic, which means that it always must be preceded by some element. In Ik, for example, the pattern found in root clauses is that the tense marker is preceded by the verb, to which subject agreement is adjoined:

(28) *Ik* (Serzisko 1992:48)
     en-ata be   ceki-a   saatso
     see-3p PAST woman-ACC yesterday
     'They saw the woman yesterday.'

In embedded clauses, by contrast, the tense marker will be preceded only by the subjunction, as shown below:

(29) *Ik* (Serzisko 1992:49)
     na   be   ceki-a   en-ie   wici-a   ...
     when PAST woman-ACC see-SUBJC children-ACC
     'When the woman saw the children...'

In (29), the verb has apparently adjoined to a mood head, hence the subjunctive suffix. Since the tense marker already has a base-generated element in front of it,[17] there is no need for the verb to move higher than mood.[18] In (28), on the other hand, the situation is different. According to Serzisko (1992), the tense marker is a second position clitic and triggers movement of the verbal word, which includes the agreement marker, to the front of the clause.

Whatever the details are, it appears that verb movement in Ik is similar to the Long Head Movement (LHM) found in Romance and Slavic languages and in Breton (see Borsley et al. 1996 for an overview). In these languages, a nonfinite verb may, in order to save one or more clitics, move to the front of the clause across other heads of the verbal extended projection, thereby seemingly violating the HMC. Some examples will illustrate this:

(30) *(European) Portuguese* (Roberts 1994:213)
Seguir-te-ei   por toda a   parte.
follow-you-will.1s by   all   the   part
'I will follow you everywhere.'

(31) *Bulgarian* (Rivero 1994:65)
Pročel săm   kniga-ta.
read   have.1s   book-the
'I have read the book.'

Various analyses have been proposed of the LHM. Roberts (1994) suggests that just as there is L-related and non-L-related XP-movement (or A- and A'-movement), there are also two types of head movement. LHM, he proposes, is an example of non-L-related head movement, and therefore the L-related heads that intervene between the landing position of the verb (which he takes to be C°) and the position from where it starts do not count as possible landing sites. It follows that the verb does not move *through* T° or other heads in these cases, it just skips over them. (Similar proposals are found in Roberts 1993 and Rivero 1994.)

Toyoshima (1997) proposes that LHM is movement to Spec—a proposal that makes sense considering that this movement operation apparently is triggered by some property of the head in second position. If the nonfinite verb in constructions like (30)–(31) moves to satisfy some property of the finite verb, we would expect a local relation to be established between these two elements as a result of the movement; hence, the Spec of the triggering head is a more plausible landing site than any higher position. (Other facts also speak in favor of such an analysis. For details, see Toyoshima 1997.) As for the exact nature of the trigger of LHM, Toyoshima (1997) relates it to the EPP, and so does Holmberg (2000b) in his analysis of Stylistic Fronting, exemplified in the relative clause in (32).

(32) *Icelandic* (Holmberg 2000b:446)
Hver   held-ur   þú   að   stol-ið   haf-i   hjól-inu?
who.NOM   think-PRES.2s   you   that steal-PTC have-SUBJC   bike-DEF
'Who do you think has stolen the bike?'

As we see, Stylistic Fronting is similar to LHM in that it can move a participle across the finite verb. Holmberg suggests that the EPP, formalized in Chomsky (1995) as a strong D-feature, consists of two features: a D-feature and a feature that requires Spec-IP to be filled by an element that has phonological realization. He proposes that in Stylistic Fronting, only phonological features move, in order to check the latter feature. In a model where movement is copying, we would say that the highest copy of *stolið* 'stolen' in (33) is inserted because its phonological features are needed there.

I will not take the speculations on LHM/Stylistic Fronting any further here; I will merely note that whatever will be the ultimate analysis of these phenomena, we expect the analysis to be valid for Ik as well. Accordingly, there is no reason to assume that the V T order in Ik is evidence of excorporation.

In Wambaya, the second-position clitic encodes subject and object agreement in addition to tense, and it can also encode mood and aspect (Nordlinger 1995). The element preceding the clitic may be the verb, as in (33), but other elements can also occur in this position, as in (34) and (35).

(33) *Wambaya* (Nordlinger 1995:228)
Ngaj-ba   ngu-ny-u.
see-FUT   1sS-2O-FUT
'I will see you.'

(34) *Wambaya* (Nordlinger 1995:235)
Alanga g-a   yarru-Ø.
girl   3sS-PAST go-NONFUT
'The girl went.'

(35) *Wambaya* (Nordlinger 1995:229)
Guyala gunu-ny-udi   ngaj-bi.
NEG   3sMASC.S-2O-IRR.PRES   see-NONFUT
'He isn't looking at you.'

Thus, although the data presented in Nordlinger (1995) are rather sparse, we may conclude from the above examples that Wambaya, just like Ik, possesses a head movement process which is comparable to LHM. (The main topic of Nordlinger's article is the double occurrence of tense marking which also can be seen above. I will return to this in section 5.4.1.)

A similar state of facts obtains in some of the Pimic languages. The examples I show here are from Tohono O'odham, also known as Papago. This language has a so-called auxiliary that encodes speech act modality (imperative vs. nonimperative), subject agreement, tense, and evidential mood, in that order. According to Saxton (1982:109), the auxiliary is "postposed to the clause-initial constituent." That is, the auxiliary can be preceded by exactly one constituent.[19] The category of this constituent is subject to considerable variation. It can be a modal, as in (36); the negation, as in (37); a locative element, as in (38); a focused argument, as in (39); or the verb, as in (40).

(36)   *Tohono O'odham*   (Saxton 1982:109)
    čum   o   pi miḍ g čioj
    CONA NONIMP NEG run ART man
    'The man is trying not to run.'

(37)   *Tohono O'odham*   (Saxton 1982:109)
    pi   o   miḍ g čioj
    NEG NONIMP run ART man
    'The man isn't running.'

(38)   *Tohono O'odham*   (Saxton 1982:123)
    am a-ḍ   kii g ki-kil
    LOC NONIMP-REM.PAST live ART old.men(REDUP)
    'The oldtimers used to live there.'

(39)   *Tohono O'odham*   (Saxton 1982:123)
    hig a-n-t   wa'i   ñii
    that NONIMP-1sS-CTMP only   see.PERF
    'That's the only one I saw.'

(40)   *Tohono O'odham*   (Saxton 1982:109)
    maak a-ñ   g   gogs g   čuukhug
    give NONIMP-1sS ART dog   ART meat
    'I'm giving the dog meat.'

The last example above indicates that Tohono O'odham has recourse to an operation that is strongly reminiscent of LHM.[20] Notably, this operation never targets the elements that are closest to the speech act marker in the linear order—namely, the subject agreement marker, the tense marker, and the evidential marker. If we assume that at least the speech act marker, the tense marker, and the evidential marker represent syntactic heads, this means that, contrary to what one might expect, the operation does not apply to the highest heads below the triggering one. If we look at the category of the elements that may be moved to the first position, it could in fact be argued that these elements are not X°s; rather, movement to the initial position is movement from Spec to Spec.[21] The problem is then the cases where the verb moves to the first position, as in (40). If this is also phrasal movement, it must be a remnant VP that is moved, since the arguments of the verb are left behind.

I conclude that in Ik, Wambaya, and Pimic, the order V T is derived by a movement operation that is similar to LHM. It is possible that this is an XP-movement operation, so that it cannot be taken as support for the idea that excorporation or, alternatively, movement of a head across another head, is possible. As already mentioned, it has been proposed that the landing site in LHM is a Spec position (Toyoshima 1997). Thus, LHM and similar operations are not necessarily relevant to our discussion of complex heads. The fact that LHM can cause a verb to precede a tense marker without forming a word with that tense marker should not be taken as evidence that verbs in general can head-move across tense heads. In the search for possible cases of this, we must turn instead to the languages that have or can have a V T order that is not derived by XP-movement or by anything similar to LHM.

I will concentrate here on two of the languages mentioned earlier—namely, Ngankikurungkurr and Baka—starting with Ngankikurungkurr. In this language, as in many other Australian languages, verbal inflectional markers are attached to an auxiliary that encodes the semantic type of the main verb. I start the discussion by presenting some Ngankikurungkurr clauses:

(41) *Ngankikurungkurr* (Hoddinott & Kofod 1988:115)

A-wuni	fagarri	w-irri-n-ggu		lalirr	kana	miyi.
CLASS-DEM	two	3NS.PERF-AUX-PRES-DU[22]		eat	PUNC	food

'The two of them are eating the food now.'

(42) *Ngankikurungkurr* (Hoddinott & Kofod 1988:118)

W-arra-ni		fititit	tye	kana	gangki-pefi.
3NS.PERF-AUX-PAST		rise.REDUP	PAST	PUNC	sky-ALL

'They rose into the air then.'

(43) *Ngankikurungkurr* (Hoddinott & Kofod 1988:120)

Waytpala	wa-wulmen	w-a		ngindi	du	ngini
white.man	CLASS-old.man	3sPERF-AUX.FUT		1sDO	show	FUT

ngirrgifiriny.
spring

'The old white man will/wants to show me the spring.'

(44) *Ngankikurungkurr* (Hoddinott & Kofod 1988:129)

Nem	minta	yedi		wapup	peyi	ngan kuderri.
3sMASC	NEG	3sPERF.AUX.PAST		sit.down	there	REL billabong

'He did not live there at the billabong.'

These examples taken together give an idea of the ordering of clause elements in Ngankikurungkurr. Note that arguments and adverbials may precede or follow the verbal complex and that the subject usually precedes the object (see Hoddinott & Kofod 1988, p. 70, p. 203 and elsewhere for details). The negation *minta* can follow a preverbal argument, as in (44), or precede it (Hoddinott & Kofod 1988:128). The first element of the verbal complex, if we ignore the negation, is normally the auxiliary,[23] then follow the object agreement marker (which is zero for a 3s direct object),[24] the main verb, and finally, various particles which express tense, mood and aspect (see Hoddinott & Kofod 1988).

In the following I concentrate on the tense, mood, and aspect (TMA) particles, of which *kana* (for punctual or immediate future), *tye* (for past), and *ngini* (for future) are represented in the previous examples. As shown earlier, these markers may intervene between the verb and its complement. If they are to be identified with functional heads, they seem to pose a problem for our theory: we must then apparently assume that the verb has head-moved through or across them. However, as we will see, other solutions might also be available.

First there is the fact that tense is also indicated in the auxiliary. This could be taken to mean that the tense marker of the auxiliary and the tense particle represent different heads—as argued in Cinque (1999) and Julien (2001), clauses contain more than one temporal head. We would then expect the tense elements to yield a compositional reading, with one marker embedded under the other, so that the higher of them denotes an absolute tense and the lower denotes a relative tense. This does not seem to be borne out, however. For example, if the two past markers in (42) were combined in the manner just suggested, we would have a past in the past, semantically equivalent to the English 'had risen'. In (43), we would have a future in the future, corresponding to 'will be going to show'. But there is no indication that this is the actual reading. Instead, it appears that in the above examples, one single tense is redundantly represented both in the auxiliary and in the particle. A possible analysis of this would be that the marker on the auxiliary represents the tense head itself, whereas the particle is a temporal adverbial.

The following example seems to be different, though. Apparently, the past tense of the particle takes scope over the present tense of the auxiliary, so that we get a present-in-the-past reading which is rendered in English as the past progressive:

(45) *Ngankikurungkurr*   (Hoddinott & Kofod 1988:206)
    Kagu   wu-ningki   e-fengku   w-ursi   nginti
    CLASS DEM-ERG   CLASS-snake 3sPERF-AUX.PRES 1sIO
    tyerr-kukuduk   tye.
    mouth-drink.CONT[25]   PAST
    'The snake was putting his tongue in and out at me.'

If the past tense particle takes scope over the auxiliary, it is likely that the past particle represents a higher temporal head and the marking of the auxiliary represents a lower temporal head. The surface order of (45) could then be derived by moving the complement of the particle to the left, by an instance of phrasal movement. It would be interesting to know if other surface orders are possible, but, unfortunately, this example is not at all commented on in Hoddinott and Kofod (1988).

Another example where the temporal particle apparently takes scope over the tense marking of the auxiliary is given in (46), where the past marker *tye* is combined with an auxiliary in the future tense to yield a future-in-the-past reading.

(46) *Ngankikurungkurr* (Hoddinott & Kofod 1988:123)
Ng-irri-gu yerrakul tye kultyinimbi.
1NS-AUX.FUT-DU talk PAST yesterday
'We (two) were going to talk yesterday (but didn't).'

Again, we have to conclude, on the basis of the scope relations, that the past particle must originate in a higher position than the tense marker of the auxiliary. Consequently, both the auxiliary and the verb must have moved across the past particle—in other words, we have phrasal movement instead of head movement. The adverbial 'yesterday' must then be in a position that is higher than the base position of the moved constituent. This can be achieved either by generating the adverbial higher than the auxiliary or by moving it before the phrase containing the auxiliary and the verb is extracted.

According to Hoddinott and Kofod (1988:123), the construction in (46) is mostly used to express unfulfilled desires and intentions of the past. For them, this is due to the auxiliary marking glossed as 'future' being an irrealis marker (Hoddinott & Kofod 1988:120). The following example seems to corroborate this analysis:

(47) *Ngankikurungkurr* (Hoddinott & Kofod 1988:128)
Minta ng-a nyi tipek tye.
NEG 1s-AUX.FUT 2sDO follow PAST
'I did not follow you.'

Here the indicated reading would follow if the auxiliary is marked for irrealis while the past tense is supplied by the particle *tye*. The same holds true of (46). And in (43), the future marking on the auxiliary is combined with a future tense particle, and again, the proposal that auxiliary 'future' is irrealis seems to be a plausible one.

There are still problems, however. If the auxiliary in (47) really has an irrealis marking, we would expect this marking to show up in all negated clauses. But in (44) above, the negation is combined with past tense marking on the auxiliary. Thus, the precise content of the Ngankikurungkurr auxiliary markings is clearly in need of further investigations.

The picture is further complicated if we consider example (48), where, according to Hoddinott and Kofod (1988:123), the future particle *ngini* is used together with the past particle *tye* in order to indicate 'unsuccessful attempted action'.

(48) *Ngankikurungkurr* (Hoddinott & Kofod 1988:123)
Ng-irs-e bang ngini tye luruty.
1s-AUX-FUT poke FUT PAST strong
'I tried to pull strongly.'

But if the marking of the auxiliary is irrealis, it must be a very significant part of this construction, signaling that the action was unaccomplished. The conative element is probably supplied by the future particle. As indicated in (43) above, *ngini* can signal volition as well as future.

As for *tye*, the following example shows that a past tense reading is available even without *tye*. With *tye* omitted, one gets a habitual/continuous reading or one where the action is not completed (Hoddinott & Kofod 1988:118).

(49) *Ngankikurungkurr* (Hoddinott & Kofod 1988:118)

Mada	wetimbi	a-ngalifin	fagarri	w-adde	wapua
long	ago	CLASS-lizard	two	3PERF-AUX.PAST.DU	dwell

weripefi-nide.
cave-LOC
'A long time ago two shaky-paw lizards used to live in a cave.'

This suggests that *tye* serves to express the completion of an action. But then *tye* is like the 'future' marker *ngini* in that it cannot be a pure tense marker. As a matter of fact, it seems to be the case that the so-called tense particles are in general not necessary for the tense interpretation of clauses. Instead, it is the marking on the auxiliary that is the obligatory realization of tense in this language, and it is probably this marker, if any, that should rightly be identified with a tense head.

Regardless of what the ultimate analysis will be of the content of the TMA particles in Ngankikurungkurr, however, there are certain facts suggesting that they should probably not be analyzed as the direct reflexes of inflectional heads at all but instead as adverbial elements of various types. First, the TMA particles do not occur in a fixed relative order, as the following examples show:

(50) *Ngankikurungkurr* (Hoddinott & Kofod 1988:116)

a.
D-ang-im	fi-rsul	kana	pefi.
3sPERF-AUX-PRES	CAUS-rise	PUNC	ALL

'It is almost sunrise now'

b.
Ng-aga-nim	tu	pefi	kana.
1s-AUX-PRES	sleep	ALL	PUNC

'I was almost asleep.'[26]

(51) *Ngankikurungkurr* (Hoddinott & Kofod 1988:119)

a.
D-em-e	baty	pagu	tye	a-ngantyamu.
3sPERF-AUX-PAST	have	TSA	PAST	CLASS-turkey

'He brought the turkey here.'

b.
Miyi	kinyi	ngayi	ng-aganty-i	tye	pagu.[27]
plant.food	DEM	1s	1s-AUX-PAST	PAST	TSA

'I brought this food here.'

Further, whereas the TMA markers often follow the verb, it is also possible for them to precede both the main verb and the auxiliary:

(52) *Ngankikurungkurr* (Hoddinott & Kofod 1988:118)

Ye-ningan	kana	ng-iting-e	madiwirri	walamara.
CLASS-that.one	PUNC	1NS-AUX-PAST	laugh	dance (of women)

'We (women) were laughing and dancing.'

(53) *Ngankikurungkurr* (Hoddinott & Kofod 1988:130)

Minta	nana	g-an-i	fel.
NEG	POT	3sIMPF-AUX-FUT	dive

'He cannot swim / He must not dive.'

This freedom of position would be hard to explain if the TMA particles in Ngankikurungkurr were really the realizations of inflectional heads.

Moreover, Hoddinott and Kofod (1988) give at least one example where *tye* appears twice in the same clause. This example is shown in (54).

(54) *Ngankikurungkurr* (Hoddinott & Kofod 1988:39)

Angku	ngayi	mirsi	y-en-im	wa-weti-ningki
grandfather	1s	die	3sPERF-AUX-PRES	CLASS-little-when[28]
deti	tye	ng-agadi	tye.	
still	PAST	1s-AUX-PAST	PAST	

'My grandfather died when I was still a little boy.'

One might suggest here that the first *tye* belongs to the temporal clause and the second *tye* belongs to the matrix clause. However, since Ngankikurungkurr makes very limited use of embedding structures—the normal way to combine clauses is by juxtaposition (see Hoddinott & Kofod 1988:217–219)—this is not very likely to be the correct analysis. Instead, it seems that both occurrences of *tye* go with the last verb, so that in addition to the past marking of the verb itself, there is also double marking of past in the particle system—a situation we would not expect to see if all instances of PAST are realizations of T° heads.

To conclude the discussion so far, we have seen that the distribution of the Ngankikurungkurr TMA markers casts doubt on the claim that they are the realizations of functional heads. This doubt is strengthened if we consider the shape of these markers. It appears that most, if not all, of the elements that can occur in what Hoddinott and Kofod (1988) refer to as the "the t/m/a slot" may also occupy other positions and modify constituents other than the verb. In the words of Hoddinott and Kofod (1988:107), most TMA markers "also occur as case markers in the noun phrase or act as free adverbs or both." We have already seen the double function of one of these elements: in (42) the allative marker *pefi* is attached to a nominal, whereas in (50a,b) it modifies a verb. Similar examples can be found for other TMA markers. It is a striking fact that the markers retain the same basic meaning in all their uses. For example, *pefi* means something like 'in the direction of' regardless of whether it combines with a noun or with a verb. This suggests that there is only one element *pefi*, which is not the realization of an aspect or mood head but instead rather like an adposition.

Hoddinott and Kofod (1988) sometimes hesitate to link together the various uses of the TMA/case markers. For example, for the future marker *ngini*, they say (p. 121) that it is "homophonous with the purposive clitic." Nevertheless, in their discussion of the purposive marker, they claim that it "is also the future marker in the indicative mood of the verb" (p. 83). Then they point out that "both uses of the modifier share the same general semantic meaning." An example of the 'purposive' marker attached to a nominal is shown below:

(55) *Ngankikurungkurr*   (Hoddinott & Kofod 1988:83)
    Kanbi   ng-errb-e   gerrgirr   yawul-ngini.
    bamboo   1NS-AUX-PAST   cut   spear-PURP
    'We cut some bamboo for spears.'

Interestingly, Hoddinott and Kofod note (p. 121) that if a clause with a purposively marked nominal refers to the future, then *ngini* can be omitted from the V-related position. This strongly suggests that the purposive and the future marker are one and the same, since one of them may substitute for the other.

More generally, I think we can rather safely conclude that the elements that may modify verbs in Ngankikurungkurr are not really tense, aspect, or mood markers at all; they probably belong to categories (adverbials, adpositions etc.) that can readily be combined with nouns or with verbs. This means that in the cases where these markers follow the verb, there is no need to say that the verb has crossed over or moved through the functional heads of its own extended projection, and, consequently, Ngankikurungkurr poses no real problem for our theory.

Turning now to Baka, we first notice that in this language, the past tenses (immediate, near, and remote past) are expressed by means of verbal suffixes, as illustrated by the following examples.

(56) *Baka*   (Kilian-Hatz 1995:244)
    ʔé   jò-ɛ   sɔ   dàdì.
    3s.HUM IMPF.eat-IMM.PAST meat much
    'He ate a lot of meat.'

(57) *Baka*   (Kilian-Hatz 1995:244)
    ma à   ka-ngi   tɛ mò bìtì dàdì.
    1s PERF separate-N.PAST ABL 2s night many
    'I have been away from you for many days.'

(58) *Baka* (Kilian-Hatz 1995:209)

nɔɔ̀	tie	wó	mɛ̀ɛ̀-lo	jókò	ʔèe.
other	time	3p	IMPF.make-REM.PAST	good	thing

'In earlier times they made good things.'

The aspect markers precede the verb, except that in the past tenses, the imperfective marker loses its phonemes and leaves only its low tone, which appears on the verb (Kilian-Hatz 1995:43). The nonpast realization of the imperfective is shown in (59) for comparison.

(59) *Baka* (Kilian-Hatz 1995:188)

ma	6à	mɛ̀ɛ̀	bèlà.
1s	IMPF	do	work

'I am working.'

The Baka examples cited so far seem to pose no problems for our theory as far as the relative position of verb and tense markers is considered—apparently, what we see is a perfectly ordinary case of verb movement leading to suffixing. The analysis of the future markers, however, is less straightforward. (The present tense marker is zero, so there won't be much to say about it.) Below, I first present some examples with *là*, the marker of near future. As we see, this element follows the verb without necessarily being adjacent to it:

(60) *Baka* (Kilian-Hatz 1995:110–111)

a.

gbényi	ʔ-á	kɔtɔ̀	là	à	dukpe.
perhaps	3s.HUM-PERF	come	N.FUT	in	morning

'Perhaps he will come tomorrow.'

b.

ʔé	mu	ɛ	là	ode.
3s.HUM	see	3sO	N.FUT	NEG

'He will not see her/him/it.'

We might guess from the above examples that the future marker is a suffix after all, and that in (60b), both the pronoun and the future marker are attached to the verb by head movement (of the verb). This hypothesis would not hold, however, in light of (61a), where a full DP object intervenes between the verb and the future marker. On the other hand, because of (61b) and (62), where the object stays behind, we cannot say that there is VP-movement across the future marker, either. So if the future marker is the realization of a functional head, we would have to say that the verb moves across it or through it.

(61) *Baka* (Kilian-Hatz 1995:195)

a.

ma	jo	sɔ	là	bike	ode.
1s	eat	meat	N.FUT	D.FUT	NEG

'I won't eat any meat (for the next few days).'

b. ma bɔmɔ̀ là   ndɔ   bike   ode.
   1s buy   N.FUT   plantains D.FUT   NEG
   'I won't buy any plantains.'

(62) *Baka* (Kilian-Hatz 1995:111)
     kɔ̀e ma jo là   ndɔ́   ode.
     FUT 1s eat N.FUT   plantains NEG
     'I won't eat any plantains.'

In addition to the variable order of object and future marker, however, the above examples demonstrate another surprising feature of the future markers in Baka—namely, the possibility of combining two future markers in one clause. In (61ab), the near future marker *là* is combined with the distant future marker *bike*, and in (62), it is combined with *kɔ̀e*, the general future marker.

It turns out that any two future markers may co-occur, and there is no indication that we get a future-in-the-future reading, as we would expect when two future tenses are combined. Example (63) shows the combination of the general future marker and the distant future marker (*kɔ̀e* and *kɔ̀mbɛ* are alternative realizations of the same element).

(63) *Baka* (Kilian-Hatz 1995:194–195)
     kɔ̀mbɛ mo ʔɔ bike jɛ̀jɛ   a   mò   a   kà?
     FUT   2s put D.FUT limit POSS   2sPOSS in   where
     'Where would you draw the line?'

Kɔ̀e/kɔ̀mbɛ can also indicate future tense without being supported by any other future marker, as in (64).

(64) *Baka* (Kilian-Hatz 1995:125)
     kɔ̀mbɛ bo   jo ʔèe   tɛ   mòsùkà.
     FUT   person eat thing with   sauce
     'We will eat it with sauce.'

Concerning the category of the future elements, in her introductory treatment of the verbal system in Baka, Kilian-Hatz suggests that they are adverbs (Kilian-Hatz 1995:39). Nevertheless, when she gets to the discussion of individual elements, she claims, both for *là* and *bike*, that they are fully grammaticalized future markers (see Kilian-Hatz 1995:109, 194). As for *bike*, it is clearly related to the adverb *bike* which means 'some day' or 'perhaps'. Kilian-Hatz (1995:193) states that "Als temporales Adverb steht *bike* vor dem Subjekt am Satzanfang. Dies ist die reguläre Position für zeitliche Bestimmungen in Baka." (As a temporal adverb, *bike* precedes the subject at the beginning of the clause. This is the regular position for temporal determiners in Baka.) The example she gives is the following:

(65) *Baka* (Kilian-Hatz 1995:195)
     bike   ʔ-á   gɔ   a   Yàunde.
     some.day 3s.HUM-PERF go   to   Yaunde
     'Some day he will go to Yaunde.'

Concerning constructions like (63), where *bike* follows the verb, Kilian-Hatz
(1995:194) asserts that in this position *bike* is not an adverb. However, other
examples presented in her book show that temporal adverbials can indeed follow
the verb. This holds not only for PP adverbials, but also for bare adverbs like
ngili 'yesterday' and *makàlà* 'today':

(66) *Baka* (Kilian-Hatz 1995:206)
     pàmè   ʔé   wòtò-ngi   ngili.
     wild.pig 3s.HUM pass.by-N.PAST   yesterday
     'A wild pig passed by yesterday.'

Moreover, in (64) the general future marker is in the clause-initial position,
which is claimed to be the position for adverbs. Kilian-Hatz's statements about
the correlation between position and function are therefore not entirely convincing. Rather, it is possible, as far as I can see, that the so-called future markers in
Baka are in fact adverbs, not heads of the verbal extended projection.

Finally, it should be noted that there is also good reason to doubt the
classification of the past tense markers as true tense markers, since two of these
can apparently combine to give one simple tense. In nonverbal clauses the
combination of the remote past marker and the near past marker expresses the
near past ('yesterday'), as in (67), and in (68), we have a double occurrence of
the marker of the immediate past, one suffixed to the verb and one free.

(67) *Baka* (Kilian-Hatz 1995:207)
     bo   kὲ   ʔɔ̀-ngi   nε   ʔé   kà?
     person REL REM.PAST-N.PAST   REL 3s.HUM who
     'Who is that person who was here yesterday?'

(68) *Baka* (Kilian-Hatz 1995:207)
     ndeke ma   à   kpi-ε   wεε.
     almost 1s   PERF die-IMM.PAST IMM.PAST
     'I almost died.'

Should it turn out that the past tense markers of Baka are not really realizations of $T°$ heads at all, then another problem would be resolved which I have
not so far mentioned explicitly: namely, the relative ordering of tense and aspect
markers in this language. If there is a universal order of functional heads, it is
almost certain that tense precedes aspect (see section 5.2). From this order, the
Baka surface pattern could not be derived by ordinary head movement. But if the

suffixed marker—for example, in (57)—does not represent a T° head, this problem of course disappears.

It is possible that a similar argumentation goes through for the other languages in my survey that are claimed to have nonbound tense markers following the verb, without there being any indication that the verb has moved across the tense marker by phrasal movement. In Kriyol the postverbal tense marker shown in (69) may co-occur with tense marking on the verb, as in (70).

(69) *Kriyol* (Kihm 1994:99)
    N   konta u   ba.
    1s   tell   2s   PAST
    'I had told you.'

(70) *Kriyol* (Kihm 1994:35)
    Kil   tera   yera   (ba)   demokrátiku.
    that   country   be.PAST   PAST   democratic
    'That country used to be democratic.'

If the marking of the copula in (70) represents the T° head, *ba* is probably not a real tense marker. Interestingly, although Kihm (1994) analyses *ba* as a tense marker most of the time, he also (Kihm 1994:108) suggests that it is an adverb. If the latter is correct, Kriyol is not a counterexample to the claim that there is no excorporation.

In Maori and in the Karen languages Moulmein Sgaw and Eastern Kayah, there are also postverbal elements that are claimed to be tense or aspect markers. On closer investigation, the postverbal markers in Maori appear to have adverb-like functions (see, e.g., Bauer 1993), while the postverbal markers in Karen look more like the lower verbs in serial verb structures (see Jones 1961 on Moulmein Sgaw and Solnit 1986 on Eastern Kayah). Hence, none of these languages presents indisputable evidence that the verb may head-move across inflectional heads.

It should also be noted that even in isolating languages, the free elements that indisputably are purely grammatical markers of tense and aspect tend to precede the verb, or they follow the verb as a result of VP-movement. In this light, much clearer evidence would be required if we were to conclude that Maori and Karen were exceptions. In the absence of such evidence, I will tentatively conclude that the functional elements related to the verb are always generated to the left of the verb, that they may end up as suffixes on the verb as a result of head movement, and that they may also follow the verb at Spell-Out if the whole VP moves, but they cannot be realized as free postverbal markers as a result of the verb having head-moved through or across them.

2.3.3 Final remarks on excorporation

On the basis of the foregoing discussion, I conclude that there is no such thing as excorporation. If excorporation were an option, we would expect to see clear cases where the surface order of heads is the reverse of the base-generated order, even in the absence of affixation. As the preceding discussion reveals, this is what we do not find, at least not as far as the heads of the extended projection of the verb are concerned. What our theory might have to allow for is the possibility that a moving head may skip another head under very special circumstances, as in Long Head Movement, which was mentioned above.

If excorporation is ruled out, it follows that once a complex head is formed, any further movement operations targeting this complex head must move the head as a whole. It does not automatically follow, however, that a complex head must be spelled out as one word. As Roberts (1997) notes, if movement is copying and there is a choice of spelling out either the higher or the lower copy, then there is also the possibility that when a complex head is the result of movement, some of the elements that make up this head may be spelled out in the position they occupied before the complex head was formed. He then takes this a step further and claims that, under certain circumstances, the constituents of a complex $X°$ *cannot* be spelled out under that same $X°$. More specifically, he proposes that there is a ban on spelling out more than one morphological word under a single $X°$. This is formalized as follows (Roberts 1997:426):

(71) * $[_{X°} W_1 W_2]$ where W_n is a morphological word.

Because of (71), which I will refer to as the OWPHC (One Word Per Head Constraint), in the configuration $[_{X°} W_1 W_2]$ the moved W will have to be spelled out in its base position.

According to Roberts, this is what lies behind the so-called restructuring phenomena in Romance, whereby certain operations that are normally clause-bound are allowed to apply across a clause boundary if the matrix verb is of the right kind.[29] Thus, in Italian there is the contrast between (72) and (73).

(72) *Italian* (Roberts 1997:424)

Le	nuove	case	si	comincer-anno	a	costru-ire.
the	new	houses	*si*	begin-FUT.3p	to	build-INF

'The new houses will start being built.'

(73) *Italian* (Roberts 1997:424)

a.
Si	otterr-à		di	costru-ire	le	nuove	case.
si	get.permission-FUT.3s		to	build-INF	the	new	houses

'One will get permission to build the new houses.'

b.*
Le	nuove	case	si	otterr-anno		di	costru-ire.
the	new	houses	*si*	get.permission-FUT.3p		to	build-INF

In (72), the object of the lower verb has moved to the matrix subject position by a process of Long DP-movement, which is one of the operations associated with restructuring. In (73), by contrast, such movement of the lower object is blocked. On Roberts's (1997) analysis, long movement is allowed in (72) because the lower verb is in fact incorporated into the higher verb. The reason this incorporation is not directly visible is that the highest copy of the lower verb is not spelled out, since spelling it out would violate the OWPHC.

Roberts's proposal has certain weaknesses, however, that might lead one to suspect that the OWPHC does not hold. First, the OWPHC requires that one has a definition of 'morphological word' that is independent of the morpheme configurations formed by the syntax. Unfortunately, it is not at all obvious that such a definition exists. Rather, there is reason to believe that, at least as far as complex heads are concerned, the morphological word must be defined on the basis of the structure provided by syntax, so that if two or more morphemes constitute a complex head, there is nothing to prevent them from being interpreted as one morphological word. Second, Roberts claims that when there is a potential violation of the OWPHC, the incorporee must be spelled out in the highest position it occupied prior to the offending incorporation. Now if Roberts's general idea concerning restructuring is correct, the three verbs in (74) must all ultimately constitute one complex X°; but because of the OWPHC, they are spelled out separately.[30]

(74) *Spanish*

Estos	edifícios	se	acab-an	de	comenz-ar	a	constru-ir.
these	buildings	*se*	just.have-3p	P	begin-INF	to	build-INF

'These buildings have just began being built.'

One might wonder, if each verb is spelled out as high as possible while still respecting the OWPHC, why the lower verb *construir*, for example, is not spelled out together with *a*, or the intermediate verb *comenzar* together with *de*. I see no alternative to assuming that the element *a* and *de*, traditionally analyzed as prepositions, represent heads that intervene between the verbs in (74), so that if the two lower verbs incorporate into the higher verb, there must be movement through *a* and *de*. The only way to explain why *construir* and *a*, for example, are not spelled out as a unit *construir-a* is by saying that *a* is also a morphological word, so that *construir-a* violates the OWPHC. This would be rather surprising, considered that grammatical elements like *a* often end up as affixes, arguably added to the complex word by head movement. A similar argument can be made, by the way, on the basis of Roberts's own example (72).

Moreover, there exist words that apparently are clear-cut violations of the OWPHC. Some examples are given below:

(75) *Northern Saami*

a. máná-id+gárdi
   child-PL.GEN+garden
   'kindergarten'

b. goarru-n+mášiidna
   sew-N-machine
   'sewing machine'

The immediate constituents of the compounds in (75) could themselves appear as separate words. Nevertheless, since the compounds also have the behavior of words, I assume that each compound is a complex head (this is the most plausible analysis in all these cases; see section 6.3). This means that here we see examples of two morphological words being dominated by one single X°. To allow for this, we might say that two or more morphological words may be spelled out under one X° if their combination is also a morphological word, or else that compounds are allowed because they are not formed by movement, so that there is no alternative to spelling them out as one complex head. The first solution renders Roberts's constraint nonfalsifiable and meaningless, and the second solution would imply that the way in which a complex of morphemes is formed has consequences for how it will be dealt with later on. This is a very dubious idea; rather, from what is being said elsewhere in this study about the status of the word, we would assume that what matters is the fact that certain morphemes cling together in certain ways, and how they came to do this is not important. If this is a correct assumption, it follows that compounds where each part can appear as a separate word present counterevidence to Roberts's principle as stated in (71). One might then doubt the validity of this principle altogether and assume, instead, that every complex head can be spelled out as a complex word.

2.4 Merger of adjacent heads

Another mechanism that allows syntactic heads to be combined morphologically is proposed in Halle and Marantz (1993, 1994) under the name of *morphological merger* (see also Marantz 1984, 1988). This is the operation whereby structurally adjacent heads are joined under a zero level node while still remaining separate terminals under this node. More specifically, the structural adjacency requirement is taken to mean that two heads, X° and Y°, can be merged if one head heads the complement of the other, so that the initial structure is as shown in (76).

(76)

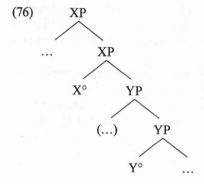

As an illustration of how merger works, Halle and Marantz (1993) offer the example of tensed main verbs in English. As mentioned earlier, it is generally assumed that English main verbs do not move out of VP. Nevertheless, they carry inflectional affixes associated with the functional categories of the clause. According to Halle and Marantz, the surface realization of verb+tense is due to the Tense head having merged with the main verb. The resulting inflected word is located in the base position of the verb; presumably, this reflects a characteristic feature of the merger operation. In (77a) is shown the initial structure proposed by Halle and Marantz (1993:134) for a sentence like *They sleep late*. The structure after merger is shown in (77b).

(77)

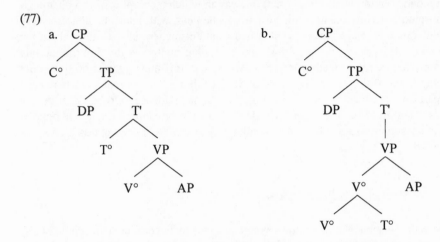

The idea of merger is intended to be an alternative to the somewhat unsatisfactory affix-lowering analysis. It appears however that certain weaknesses of the latter are preserved in the merger approach as formulated by Halle and Marantz. Notice, for example, that TP in (77b) lacks a head; T° is assumed to leave no trace as it merges with V°. If T° *did* leave a trace, on the other hand, that would also be a problem, since the trace would not be c-commanded by T°.

One thing to keep in mind here is that the derivation from (77a) to (77b) is not claimed to take place in syntax proper but instead at a level called Morphological Structure (MS) which is situated between S-structure and PF. The organization of grammar according to Halle and Marantz (1993) is shown in the diagram in (78).

Now if it really is the case that "MS is a level of grammatical representation with its own principles and properties" (Halle & Marantz 1993:115) the structure in (77b) may be well-formed at that level. Nevertheless, Halle and Marantz claim that MS is a *syntactic* representation (see, e.g., Halle & Marantz 1993:114). We would therefore expect the basic principles of syntactic phrase structure to hold also at MS. In this light, the headlessness of (77b) is rather problematic.

(78)

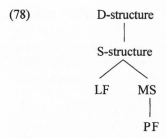

The fact that T° is to the right of V° at PF is also seen as a consequence of MS principles. Halle and Marantz assume that at the syntactic levels of D-structure, S-structure, and LF there is only hierarchical ordering of constituents and that a linear ordering of terminals is imposed at MS. The process of merger in itself is not, as far as I can see, associated with any predictions of linear order. Instead, the actual order of morphemes must presumably be attributed to the properties of individual affixes. This means that the theory of merger as it now stands leaves much to stipulation.

The merger analysis of English main verbs is dealt with in more detail in Bobaljik (1995). In particular, the notion of *adjacency* is clarified. On Bobaljik's account, two heads are adjacent in the sense required for merger to take place even if a trace or an adverbial intervenes between them. An overt DP or the negator *not* will, by contrast, disrupt adjacency and block the merger operation. The examples in (79) are used to illustrate this claim.

(79) *English* (Bobaljik 1995)
   a. Sam likes green eggs and ham.
   b. Sam does not eat horseradish.
   c. Did Sam eat the horseradish?
   d. Who ate my horseradish?
   e. I often eat fish.
   f. An adverb never disrupts adjacency.

The syntactic structure ascribed to (79a) is as in (80) (see Bobaljik 1995:62). Here the adjacency relation is indisputable, so I° and V° can merge.

(80)

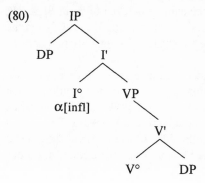

According to Bobaljik, the inflectional affix α will be spelled out as a suffix on the verb as a result of merger, even though it precedes the verb stem in linear (syntactic?) order. Bobaljik (1995:62 n. 8) notes that "the fact that it [the inflectional affix] is regularly realized as a suffix is presumably an idiosyncratic phonological characteristic." Again, the somewhat unsatisfactory lack of general ordering principles of the merger approach is demonstrated.

The example (79b) shows that when *not* intervenes between the inflection and the verb stem, the latter two are not adjacent in the relevant sense and *do*-insertion is necessary. The structure proposed for (79b) is shown in (81) (Bobaljik 1995:63).

(81)

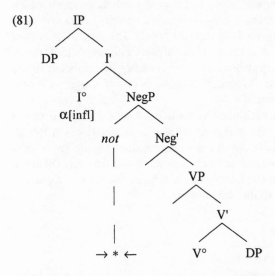

According to Bobaljik, the negator in Spec-NegP blocks the merger of I° and V°, and, consequently, the dummy verb *do* must be inserted in I° to rescue the affix.

By the same token, *do*-support is also triggered if a DP occupies a Spec position between the inflectional affix and the verb stem. A question like (79c) is a case in point. Here I° has presumably raised to C°, so that the subject in Spec-IP intervenes between I° and V°, and *do*-support applies. If the subject has also moved, however, as in (79d), where the subject is taken to be in Spec-CP, only the trace of the subject comes between the inflectional affix (in C°) and the verb stem (in V°). In this configuration the two heads can again merge, and the main verb appears in its inflected form.

Bobaljik goes on to argue that merger can be allowed even if there is phonologically overt material between the merging heads. The only condition is that the intervening material is adverbial. Examples (79e) and (79f) serve to illustrate this. In these cases Bobaljik assumes that the adverb is adjoined to VP, so that the merging heads I° and V° are on opposite sides of the adverb in the linear order. Bobaljik's suggestion is that adjoined material in general does not block the merger operation.

However plausible that might be, let it be noted here that on an alternative conception of adverb placement, like the one advocated by Cinque (1999), the adverbs in (79e,f) may be considered to be generated above the T° head (in Spec-TP or higher), so that there is no overt material between T° and V°. On this analysis, it might even be possible that the verb has actually moved to the site of the inflectional marker (see section 5.4.2).

The main objection to the conception of morphological merger as envisaged by Halle and Marantz and by Bobaljik is nevertheless the absence of ordering principles, which leads to the view mentioned above that the surface order of morphemes must depend on the idiosyncratic properties of individual lexical items. That is, there is no generalization to be made concerning the relation between, on one hand, the underlying order of syntactic terminals that make up a complex word and, on the other hand, the order of morphemes within that word. This is not a very satisfactory conclusion, especially in light of recent developments in syntactic theory, where the search for a more principled explanation of surface order is a recurrent issue. If we adopt the idea that linear order follows from very general principles of grammar, and that all variation in order, both within and across languages, must correlate with some other property in a regular fashion, it would clearly be desirable to have a theory that puts more restrictions on the application of merger than the theories offered so far.

It would be tempting, for example, to propose that no operation applying after syntax can alter the ordering of elements. If this is correct, then if two syntactic heads merge morphologically without head-to-head-movement, the surface (morphological) order must reflect the underlying (syntactic) order. The idea that word formation can operate in this manner is also suggested by Cinque (1999), who points to the verbal morphology of the Bantu languages as a possible example. As is well known, in many Bantu languages the inflectional markers are prefixed to the verb, as in (82).

(82) *Chibemba* (Cinque 1999:70; from Givón 1972)
 n-kà-láá-boomba
 1s-FUT-PROG-work
 'I'll be working tomorrow.'

Since the order of morphemes in the complex verb in (82) exactly matches what is assumed to be the order of corresponding syntactic heads (AgrS/Fin-Tense-Aspect-V), Cinque (1999) proposes that the prefixes are really particles cliticized onto the verb. That is, what has happened in (82) is that the phonological realizations of a sequence of sentential functional heads are glued together phonologically in the absence of operations that change their relative order. This kind of word formation will be dealt with in more detail in chapter 4.

2.5 The word properties of complex heads

In this chapter it has been suggested that grammar places heavy restrictions on the application of head-to-head movement. In head-to-head movement a head must move to the next higher head, and if the movement operation is repeated, the newly formed complex head must move as a whole. Finally, the constituents of a complex head must be spelled out as a continuous string. This means that the shape of a complex head reveals both the original order of the terminals from which the head was built and the derivational history of the head itself. In short, it appears that the Generalized Mirror Principle (see section 2.1) holds universally: from a sequence of syntactic heads X-Y-Z, a complex head containing X and Z must come out as Z+Y+X.

It follows that a complex head has the properties characteristic of words that were discussed in section 1.4.2. It necessarily shows internal cohesion, its subcomponents cannot be moved out, and it cannot be interrupted by material that is not part of the complex head. If the complex head moves, it moves as a whole, so that within the clause, it will be one distributional unit. Further, we do not expect to see heads moving across a complex head. It is possible, though, for phrasal constituents to move around it, so that the complex head may have independent distribution relative to these constituents. The result is that what is contained in a complex X° will always belong to one and the same word; more precisely, it can be no more than one word.

Head movement operations will often join a lexical element with the elements in its functional domain, thereby producing inflected words where the inflectional elements are suffixed to the lexical root. But in addition, head movement may also move a lexical element into another lexical element, as proposed in Baker (1985, 1988a). Some lexical elements always attract the head of their complement. Since a lexical element of this type never occurs on its own, but invariably has its complement attached to it, it will have the appearance of a suffix; that is, it will be what is traditionally viewed as a derivational morpheme. In other cases, the incorporation of a lexical element into another is optional, as in example (49), chapter 1. Then the incorporation host is not regarded as an affix, but as a free element, and the complex head that may be formed is referred to as a compound word.

Notes

1. When no source is given, Northern Saami examples are my own.
2. See Cinque (1999) for an argumentation along these lines in favor of an invariant inventory of syntactic heads. Concerning polarity heads in particular it is interesting to note that whereas the languages of Europe generally lack the affirmative counterpart of the negation, Dutch has developed the affirmative marker *wel*, which has the same distribution as the negative marker *niet*. *Wel* and *niet* are often used contrastively, as the examples in (i) illustrate.

(i) *Dutch*   (Cook 1995:218)

  a.   Jan weet het niet, maar ik wel!
    Jan knows it not, but   I *wel*
    'Jan doesn't know it, but I do.'

  b.   Vandaag niet, morgen wel.
    today not,   tomorrow *wel*
    'Not today, but tomorrow.'

Wel is clearly different from the elements that are used for emphasis in other Germanic languages, in that *wel* cannot be combined with the negation, and, strikingly, 'yes or no' can be expressed in Dutch as *ja of nee* or *wel of niet*. Thus, I see no alternative to treating *wel* as the realization of a polarity head with a [-NEG] feature. But if a language like Dutch can develop an affirmative marker, we have a good indication that affirmative clauses in all languages contain an affirmative or [-NEG] head.

3. A similar proposal for restructuring verbs is made in Roberts (1997).

4. The following example shows that the question marker is located below the complementizer. If the complementizer is in Force° (see Rizzi 1997), the question marker must be in a lower head. The most plausible candidate is Foc°. Alternatively, we might postulate on the basis of (i) that there is a position for pure subordinators over Force° (see Bhatt & Yoon 1991).

(i) *Northern Saami*

 So-n   jeara-i,   ahte ea-t -go mii   vuolgge?
 3s-NOM ask-PAST.3s that NEG-1p -Q we.NOM go
 'She asked if we shouldn't go.'

5. An argument which has sometimes been raised against syntactic word formation is based on the idea that morphological subcategorization is analogous to syntactic subcategorization, so that the Projection Principle applies to both types of subcategorization with the result that both types of subcategorization must be satisfied at all levels. This would require an affix to be base-generated adjacent to its base, and, hence, word formation by syntactic movement operations is ruled out. (See, e.g. , Bok-Bennema & Groos 1988 and Ackema 1995.).

However, in Lieber (1981) morphological subcategorization is explicitly stated as something different from syntactic subcategorization, which Lieber refers to as *insertion frames*. For Baker (1988a) it is essential that the two be kept apart, since in his theory, syntactic subcategorization frames cause affixal lexical items to be base-generated independently of their potential host, whereupon morphological subcategorization frames force measures to be taken so that all affixes are attached to appropriate hosts at S-structure. In short, it is the conflicting requirements imposed by the two kinds of subcategorization frames which provide the driving force behind syntactic word formation.

In Ouhalla (1991:25) all selectional properties are brought together under the Generalized Projection Principle, which reads as follows: "The selectional properties of lexical items must be satisfied at the relevant levels of representation." However, he assumes that morphological selectional properties are specified as having to be satisfied at S-structure, unlike other selectional properties, which must be satisfied at all levels. Thus, his proposal makes little difference as regards the assumed contrast between morphological and syntactic selection.

In a framework like that of the present work, where syntactic movement is seen as a consequence of the need for feature checking, the distinction between syntactic subcategorization and morphological subcategorization can be restated as the distinction between the features that determine the position where an element is merged and the features that cause movement of that element subsequent to the merge operation. That is, the base generation of a morpheme, affixal or not, is the consequence of syntactic selection which applies in a uniform manner to all heads, while the ultimate positioning of the morpheme depends on whether or not the morpheme itself or some constituent of which it is a part contains features that may trigger movement.

On this background, objections like the following, from Ackema (1995:17), is not necessarily to the point: "If syntax and morphology are to be regulated by the same principles, this distinction [between morphological subcategorization and syntactic subcategorization] is very awkward, as it implies that selection works in a different way below zero compared to the way it works above zero." This statement reflects a view where morphology is taken to imitate syntax without being an integrated part of syntax. On the present approach, by contrast, the positioning of bound morphemes is executed in the same subpart of grammar as the positioning of free morphemes, and subject to the same restrictions. Among these restrictions are the constraints imposed by syntactic subcategorization and those related to movement. Although these constraints apply to the same derivation, they take effect in different places, because they are different in content and thus relevant at different stages.

6. A similar point was made by Koopman (1984) in response to Lasnik (1981), where the Stray Affix Filter was originally formulated.

7. This is also pointed out by Svenonius (1994a). I would like to add here that this will be the case unless we assume a relativized minimality condition on head movement as discussed in Roberts (1994). Notably, even in the latter approach morphologically driven head movement is taken to be strictly local, subject to a non-relativized HMC.

8. Since it is not combined with finiteness, T° is then realized as a participial ending. See Julien (forthcoming a).

9. In Holmberg et al. (1993) the -*Vn* that is the final suffix of passive verbs is analyzed as a realization of a finite/subject agreement head. Their reason for assuming this is that -*Vn* is in complementary distribution with the subject agreement suffixes that are found on active verbs and which also appear on the negation in (17b). Note that there is no real subject agreement in (17b); the negation has exactly the same form if the argument is plural, as in (i).

(i) *Finnish*
    Talo-j-a   e-i   maala-ta.
    house-PL-PART   NEG-3s   paint-PASS
    'The houses are not being painted.'

Thus, if -*Vn* is agreement, one must say that the default (non-agreeing) agreement marker is -*Vn* in affirmative passives and -*i* in negated passives. In this light, the claim that -*Vn* is a marker of affirmative polarity, perhaps in combination with default agreement, is no less plausible than the claim that it is a realization of agreement.

10. Taken at face value, Lieber's claim that movement out of non-L-marked categories is impossible would in fact rule out all head movement operations other than noun incorporation, since L-markedness is a property of XPs which have a theta-role or case. Since VP, for example, is not L-marked, VP would always be a barrier for head movement. To allow for verb movement out of VP, Lieber must, following Chomsky (1986), assume that head movement out of VP proceeds in two steps, whereby the moving element first adjoins to VP and then crosses the higher segment of VP. But if the barrierhood of VP can be circumvented in this manner, we would expect the same possibility to exist for other movement operations, such as the movement out of a complex X°.

11. It is worth noting that the alleged case of head excorporation that one is most likely to come across in the literature involves the so-called verb raising construction in Dutch. An example of this is given here:

(i) *Dutch*   (Koopman 1994:265)
    a.   dat   ik   Jan   hier   liet   komen
           that   I   Jan   here   let   come
           'that I let Jan come here'

    b.   Laat   Jan   maar   hier   komen.
           let   Jan   but   here   come
           'Go ahead, let Jan come here.'

On the traditional SOV analysis of Dutch, (i) is taken to be a result of the lower verb *komen* having right-adjoined to *liet*, and (ii) is then analyzed as the excorporation of the higher verb, the host (see, e.g., Roberts 1991, Koopman 1994). But clearly, in a Kaynean framework the traditional analysis is no longer available, and instead, we must assume that the verbs in (i)–(ii) reflect the base-generated order (as pointed out by Roberts 1997; see also Zwart 1993, den Dikken 1996).

12. The example given by Roberts (1991, 1994) of this type of movement is clitic climbing:

(i) *Italian*   (Roberts 1991)
    La$_i$ vole-vo   chiamare   t$_i$ ieri.
    her want-PAST.1s call-INF   yesterday
    'I wanted to call her up yesterday.'

It is possible that this and other alleged cases of non-local head movement will eventually receive a different analysis. For example, in the theory of Sportiche (1996) the clitic *la* in (i) is base-generated in its surface position. See also the previous footnote on Dutch verb raising.

13. The genera are (language in parentheses): Adamawa-Ubangi (Mbum), Platoid (Jukun), Kuliak (Ik), Bongo-Bagirmi (Baka), Moru-Madi (Logbara, Moru), Mangbutu-Efe (Mamvu), Biu-Mandara (Mofu-Gudur), Central Kushitic (Bilin), Indic (Hindi), Karen (Moulmein Sgaw), Miao-Yao (Hmong Njua), Palaung-Khmuic (Khmu), Nicobar Islands (Nicobarese), Central-Eastern Malayo-Polynesian (Maori), Kolopom, Timor-Alor-Pantar (Bunak), Torricelli (Olo), Yele-Solomons (Yele), West Barkly (Wambaya), Daly (Ngankikurungkurr), Athabask-Eyak (Dogrib, Slave), Siouan

(Dakota), Wintun (Wintu), Coahuiltecan (Coahuiltec), Pimic, Taracahitic (Tara-humara), Yanoman (Sanuma), Tucanoan (Guanano), Mondé (Gavião), Tupí-Guaraní (Urubu-Kaapor), Botocudo (Krenak), Ge-Kaingang (Kaingang, Shokleng), Portu-guese-based creoles (Kriyol).

14. Further support is found in the (rather sketchy) treatment of Nicobarese in Das (1977). Das states that in the verb-initial language Nicobarese, indicators of tense follow the subject. Interestingly, in his list of Nicobarese utterances, the only example of a transitive verb is the following, with the verb and both arguments preceding the tense marker, whereas the only element following the tense marker is the adverb meaning 'tomorrow', which presumably is generated higher than VP.

(i) *Nicobarese* (Das 1977:29)
    cuɛl   iskul   cin   min   hu̯reic
    go   school   I   FUT   tomorrow
    'I shall go to school tomorrow.'

Hence, it is possible that the verb precedes the tense marker as a result of VP fronting.

15. At least one language, Yele, can also be ignored on other grounds. Yele, an SOV language, has portmanteau morphemes encoding mood, aspect, tense, and subject/object agreement (for details, see Henderson 1995). The morphemes that express (among other things) object agreement follow the verb, as shown below:

(i) *Yele* (Henderson 1995:15)
    Kaawa   ngê   dê   m:uu   té
    Kaawa   ERG.SG   TMA/SAGR   see   TMA/OAGR
    'Kaawa saw him.'

However, Henderson states (p. 14) that "the morphemes appended to the verb root—prefixes and suffixes in many languages—are in Yele separated from the verb on phonological grounds." But, if the TMA and Agr elements are treated as separate words on purely phonological grounds, we cannot be certain that they do not form a complex X° with the verb after all, and that the order in (i) is derived by ordinary head movement of the verb, without excorporation. We have seen, in section 1.4.1, that a complex X° may contain more than one phonological word—compounds being a typical case in point.

16. Taracahitic, represented in the survey by Tarahumara, should probably also be ignored for independent reasons. The analysis according to which Tarahumara has free tense/aspect markers following the verb is found in Thord-Gray (1955). In Burgess (1979), however, it is claimed that the tense/aspect markers in Tarahumara are verbal suffixes. If Burgess is right, the V+T/A complex may be formed by ordi-nary head movement, or by movement of VP to a higher Spec.

17. Serzisko (1992) gives an example which suggests that the complementizer corresponding to 'that' cannot serve as the host for the tense marker. The example is the following:

(i) *Ik* (Serzisko 1992:84)
    maa   na   en-it-i   toimɛna   tse-ikota   naa   kij'a
    NEG   PAST   see-2p-OPT   that   dry-AND   PAST   world.ABS
    'Don't you see that the world has dried (= that it has dawned)?'

I am not sure how the contrast between (i) and (30) should be explained, but it could be that the complementizers have different positions and that some locality effect is involved.

18. On the position of grammatical mood below tense, see section 5.2.

19. However, the examples he gives suggest that this only holds when the auxiliary includes a phonologically overt speech act marker. When the speech act marker is missing, the auxiliary comes first, as in (i).

(i) *Tohono O'odham*   (Saxton 1982:122)

n-t	hi	wo	m-oi
1sS-CTMP	CONTR	FUT	2sO-accompany.PERF

'As for me, I'd like to accompany you.'

This indicates that it is the speech act marker that attracts an element to the clause-initial position.

20. Marantz (1988), building on Pranka (1983), assumes that in the case where the negation precedes the auxiliary, the auxiliary has moved to the right across the negation. This assumption is based on an analysis where the negation is a sub-component of V' and therefore not available for movement. Clearly, if we assume instead that the negation is generated in the Spec of NegP, the idea that the negation moves to the left across the auxiliary is fully plausible.

21. Object markers, which normally appear to the immediate left of the verb, are also available for fronting, as demonstrated below. This indicates that the object markers are not the realizations of inflectional heads; instead, they must be phrasal of nature.

(i) *Tohono O'odham*   (Saxton 1982:110)

a.	pi	a-ñ	ha	ñɨi-d	g	a-'al
	NEG	NONIMP-1sS	3pO	see-IMPF	ART	children(REDUP)

'I don't see the children.'

b.	ha	a-ñ	ñɨi-d	g	a-'al
	3pO	NONIMP-1sS	see-IMPF	ART	children(REDUP)

'I see the children.'

22. In this example, there is a non-singular marker *-rr-* infixed into the auxiliary, in addition to the suffixed dual marker.

23. A few verb stems precede the auxiliary instead of following it. According to Hoddinott and Kofod (1988:167–168) these elements are "mainly adjectival in function and describe cognitive and emotional states or physical conditions." Here is an example:

(i) *Ngankikurungkurr*   (Hoddinott & Kofod 1988:168)

Dege	lengkirr	ng-agani-m.
stomach	bad	1s-AUX-PRES

'I am ill/upset.'

24. In Hoddinott and Kofod (1988) the elements that represent arguments within the verbal complex are referred to as 'bound pronouns'. However, since these elements do not disappear if a full DP argument is present, I think it is more correct

to see them as agreement markers. Examples (44) and (46) show subject agreement doubled by a DP subject (see also (54b)), and the following example illustrates the same point for object agreement:

(i) *Ngankikurungkurr*   (Hoddinott & Kofod 1988:103)
     Yedi   fagarri   w-arri-ni   n-err   du   wa-weti   e-fengku.
     man   two   3NS.PERF-AUX-PAST   3SMASC.IO-dS   show CLASS-little CLASS-snake
     'The two men showed the little boy the snake.'

25. Reduplication of the main verb expresses continuation or repetition (Hoddinott & Kofod 1988:152).

26. The present tense in Ngankikurungkurr includes the immediate past (Hoddinott & Kofod 1988).

27. Some of the auxiliaries can stand alone, without a main verb, as we see from this example. The meaning of this particular auxiliary is 'bring, take, carry' (see Hoddinott & Kofod 1988:135). Although many of the auxiliaries have a lexical meaning, I have for simplicity glossed them all as AUX.

28. Here the ergative/instrumental marker *ningki* has the meaning 'when' (see Hoddinott & Kofod 1988:179).

29. Cinque (2000) proposes that the operations associated with restructuring do not cross a clause boundary after all; instead, the higher verbs in constructions that allow restructuring are simply inserted in functional heads which belong to the extended projection of the base verb.

30. Thanks to Arantzazu Elordieta for help with this example.

3

Head-Final Languages

3.1 Overview

In the preceding chapter, it was argued that complex words can be formed in syntax by head movement. For example, a verb root may head-move into its functional domain, so that functional morphemes end up as suffixes in a complex verbal word. It follows from this that if a complex verb form is built up by one or more applications of the head movement operation, the surface position of this verb must be at least as high as the head that represents the outermost morpheme in the verb form. Some languages, such as Northern Saami, do indeed conform to this expectation:

(1) *Northern Saami* (= ex. (3), ch. 2)
    Mii   veahkeh-eažža-i-met da-i-d   olbmu-i-d.
    1p.NOM help-POT-PAST-1p   that-PL-ACC person-PL-ACC
    'We might (have) helped those people.'

Here the final morpheme of the complex verb is the subject agreement marker. Presumably, the verb is situated in the position of the Fin° head (see section 2.2). In the neutral word order, the only argument that precedes it is the subject. If this is taken to mean that the subject is located in the Spec of FinP, the Northern Saami clause appears to corroborate the incorporation theory.

The same argumentation will generally hold for most languages that have verbal inflectional suffixes and verb-medial or verb-initial word order. An example of a language with the latter order is Guajira, shown in (2). The incorporation analysis implies that the verb in (2) must have moved at least to the head that hosts subject agreement, which may be TP or some higher head (see section 5.3).

(2) *Guajira* (= ex. (5), ch. 2)
    Ant-irr-e-chi   taya   kattaluota-kalü.
    arrive-CAUS-FUT-MASC.SG   1s.MASC letter-FEM.SG.DEF
    'I will make the letter arrive.'

The fact that not only the object but also the subject follows the verb can be explained in two ways: either, as suggested in Chomsky (1993) for the more well-known VSO language Irish, the subject moves to the subject licensing position only at LF, so that it occupies some lower position at Spell-Out, or, alternatively, the verb has moved to some head, higher than the head that hosts subject agreement, with no morphological effect on the verb form. The latter analysis leaves open the possibility that the subject appears in its designated checking position in surface syntax. (For a more detailed discussion of the VSO order, see, e.g., Bobaljik & Carnie 1996 and McCloskey 1996.)

The problem with the head movement approach is encountered when we look at verb-final languages, such as Turkish and Kobon:

(3)   *Turkish*   (Kornfilt 1997:219)
      Ben   kitab-ı   oku-du-m.
      1s   book-DEF.OBJ   read-PAST-1s
      'I read the book.'

(4)   *Kobon*   (Davies 1989:178)
      Yad   wög   g-ei-nab-in.
      1s   work   do-DUR-FUT-1s
      'I will be working.'

In both of the above examples the final suffix on the verb is the subject agreement marker, which suggests that the verb has moved to the subject licensing head. At the same time, the object intervenes between the verb and the subject. As Kayne (1994) notes, this is particularly problematic if a given head can have only one specifier/adjunct, as required by the antisymmetry theory. Kayne, discussing the Germanic SOV languages in this connection, assumes that the subject has moved higher than the subject licensing position, thus leaving space for the object to also be situated above the verb. This means that both arguments appear in some position higher than the position in which they are presumably licensed. The plausibility of this type of argument raising, as well as the question of what the motivation might be for such movement, will have to be investigated in more detail if an analysis along these lines is to be advocated.

There are languages that present an even harder puzzle in relation to the incorporation analysis of morphologically complex verbs, however. Consider the following Haruai clause:

(5)   *Haruai*   (Comrie 1993:317)
      An   nöbö   dyb   hön   nöy-n-ŋ-a.
      we   man   big   pig   give-FUT-1p-DECL
      'We will give the big man a pig.'

Here the verb root has combined with a tense marker, a subject agreement marker, and, finally, an affirmative declarative marker (see Comrie 1993), which can probably be identified with the SpeechAct° head of Cinque (1999).[1] Since on the incorporation analysis the verb in (5) must be located in the SpeechAct°

head, which is the highest head of IP, the surface positions of the three arguments call for a revision of common assumptions about argument positions. If the Spec of the SpeechAct° head is reserved for speech act adverbials, as claimed by Cinque (1999), it follows that the arguments in (5) must have moved to focus and/or topic positions within the CP-domain (see Rizzi 1997). This is not wholly implausible; for example, Baker (1996) suggests that in polysynthetic languages, DP arguments are always adjoined outside of IP. It will have to be investigated whether there is a connection between the structure found in polysynthetic languages and the constructions under discussion here.

There appears to exist another process, however, not involving head movement at all, which may lie behind a construction like the one in (5). This is the successive movement of a phrase containing both the arguments and the verb into the specifier positions of the functional heads of IP. The relation between the elements of the complex verbal word in (5) is then a Spec-head relation. The idea that the Spec-head relation can participate in word formation is the topic of this chapter.

This proposal is somewhat unorthodox, since unlike head movement, movement of phrases is not generally recognized as a source of word formation. However, in section 3.2 I present some data from nominal morphology that can be taken as evidence that it is indeed possible for a head to form a word with an element in its Spec. In section 3.3 I go on to investigate the correlation between verb-finality and tense suffixes, which so often has been noted. I argue that although there can be OV order in the absence of verbal suffixes and vice versa, the majority of verb-final orders must be formed by a derivation that also gives rise to suffixing verbal morphology.

In section 3.4 I give a more detailed analysis of the syntax of languages that are not only verb-final but consistently head-final, at least as far as their IP is concerned, and I argue that the surface order is derived by moving the complement of every inflectional head H° to the Spec of HP. With the complement in Spec, the head will be the final element of its phrase. At the same time, since the complement in Spec is also head-final, H° will be immediately preceded by the head of its complement in the surface order, and, consequently, the sequence of heads can be perceived as a complex word. In fact, I claim that in head-final languages, phrasal movement is the principal and perhaps the only means of deriving complex words. What lies behind this property is absence of strong head features, which allows the complement-selectional features of the complement-taking heads to take effect.

The proposal is developed mainly on the basis of Lezgian, a head-final language belonging to the Nakho-Dagestanian or Northeast Caucasian family. I have chosen to focus on this language because, as we shall see, it has some interesting properties that can be taken as indications that the surface order of morphemes is derived in the way I have just suggested. In addition, I deal with well-known head-final languages such as Japanese, Turkish, and Hindi, which arguably have the same syntactic structure as Lezgian.

In section 3.5 I sum up the properties that characterize head-final languages, and I point to some problems concerning the syntax of head-final languages that still remain to be solved.

The chapter is rounded off, in section 3.6, with some final considerations of the movement of complements to Spec, which I have claimed to be of paramount importance in the syntax of strictly head-final languages. The questions that are taken up have to do with the distribution of this particular type of movement and with its morphological consequences.

3.2 The specifier-head relation

The claim that a head can form a *phonological* word with material in its Spec is not a very daring one. This is the analysis that suggests itself for constructions with second-position clitics, for example. Presumably, second-position clitics appear in second position because they always attract a phrase to their Spec, a phrase which then serves as the host for the clitic. An example of a second-position clitic is the Greenlandic coordinating particle *-lu*. As was shown in example (37), chapter 1, this particle forms a word with whatever element precedes it. Since the phrase that precedes *-lu* belongs to the second conjunct, whereas logically, *-lu* intervenes between the two conjuncts, we may infer that the phrase preceding *-lu* has raised from the complement of the particle to the specifier position of the particle. Further, the category of the element that *-lu* attaches to is subject to a great deal of variation: it may be adverbial, as in (6a); verbal, as in (6b); or nominal, as in (6c). Because of this variation, the particle is not conceived of as an affix but as a clitic.

(6)   *Greenlandic*   (= ex. (37), ch. 1)
    a. Ippasaq tikip-put   aqagu-lu   ikinnguta-at tiki-ssa-pput.
       yesterday arrive-IND.3p tomorrow-and   friends-3p   arrive-FUT-IND.3p
       'They arrived yesterday and their friends will arrive tomorrow.'

    b. Isir-puq   ingil-lu-ni-lu.
       come.in-IND.3s   sit.down-CTMP-4s-and
       'She came in and sat down.'

    c. Pilirtuttumik irrui-vuq   ini-mi-nul-lu   majuar-lu-ni.
       quickly   wash.up-IND.3s room-4s.REFL-ALL-and go.up-CTMP-4s
       'He washed up quickly and went up to his room.'

If there are cases where the category of the final element of the phrase in Spec is not subject to variation, so that the combination of a certain type of head with a certain type of preceding element in its Spec has some regularity, we might expect these combinations to have the appearance of words.

Here I will look at an instance of nominal word formation where the specifier-head relation seems to play a vital part—namely, the comitative plural suffix in Northern Saami. Unlike other case suffixes in this language, the comitative plural marker is positioned after possessive suffixes, so that it is always the final element of the inflected noun. Formally, it also co-occurs with case marking inside the possessive marker. Compare the comitative plural in (7a) with the comitative singular in (7b) and the illative plural in (7c):

(7) *Northern Saami* (Nickel 1990)

    a. vielja-i-d-an-guin   b.   vielja-in-an
       brother-PL-ACC/GEN-1sPOSS-COM   brother-COM-1sPOSS
       'with my brothers'   'with my brother'

    c. vielja-i-das-an
       brother-PL-ILL-1sPOSS
       'to my brothers'

The comitative plural further differs from other case markings in that it need not be copied on other constituents of the noun phrase, as shown in (8a), whereas for other cases, copying is obligatory—see (8b,c):

(8) *Northern Saami*

    a. da-i-d   vári-i-guin
       DEM-PL-ACC/GEN   mountain-PL-COM
       'with those mountains'

    b. da-i-dda   vári-i-de
       DEM-PL-ILL   mountain-PL-ILL
       'to those mountains'

    c.* da-i-d   vári-i-de
       DEM-PL-ACC/GEN   mountain-PL-ILL
       'to those mountains'

Since the morpheme *-guin* in these and other respects behaves in the same way as Saami postpositions, it is analyzed by Nevis (1988b) as a clitic postposition. For Nevis, an important reason for seeing it as a clitic and not as an affix is that he takes the possessive marker to be a clitic as well. However, if Kanerva's (1987) claim that Finnish possessive markers are true suffixes can be extended to Northern Saami, the motivation for treating *-guin* as a clitic disappears, and this marker too can be viewed as a suffix. The latter view is supported by the fact that the comitative marker is highly selective with respect to the category of the stem it attaches to: it has to be a noun, which may carry one or several inflectional suffixes (cf. Zwicky & Pullum 1983). But in spite of its affixal status, the comitative marker is, as Nevis notes, still syntactically similar to postpositions, the word class from which the suffix has emerged diachronically (see Korhonen 1981).

The proposal I advance here is that the comitative suffix is phonologically attached to a DP that has moved to its Spec, and further, that the syntax of the comitative construction is exactly parallel to that of postpositional phrases. In other words, the transition from postposition to case suffix has not affected the syntactic structure. In order to clarify this, I first make a brief investigation of postpositional phrases.

Traditional grammar has it that postpositional phrases should structurally be the mirror image of prepositional phrases. This view might look plausible as long as only very simple structures are considered, but if one looks at more complex structures, it turns out that the traditional view must be wrong and that Kayne's (1994) asymmetry approach must be essentially correct. See, for example, what happens if a PP is embedded in a DP inside another PP. In a language like English, where complementation is uniformly to the right, we get a rightward branching structure where every constituent comes out as a continuous string:

(9)   [DP a book [PP about [DP historical sites [PP in [DP the former GDR]]]]]

In Northern Saami, PPs follow the noun inside DP, whereas the DP precedes the P inside PP, as the following shows:

(10) *Northern Saami*
    [DP su   odda   girji   [PP [DP syntávssa   ] birra]]
    his/her new   book.NOM.SG   syntax.GEN.SG   about
    'his/her new book on syntax'

On the traditional view, according to which complements of postpositions are generated to the left of P, one would expect multiple embeddings of PPs to yield the structure indicated below, with the postpositions lumped together at the end of the string, as in (11).

(11) [DP ...N... [PP [DP ...N...[PP DP P]] P]]

As (12) shows, this is not what one gets in Northern Saami, however. The construction shown in (12a) corresponds to the structure given in (11). But as indicated, it is ungrammatical. What surfaces instead is the construction in (12b), with a discontinuous embedded DP.

(12) *Northern Saami*
    a.* Lea buorre su   odda   girjji   syntávssa   birra
        is   good   her   new   book.GEN.SG syntax.GEN.SG about
        ektui.
        compared.to

b. Lea buorre su   ođđa girjji   ektui   syntávssa
   is good her new book.GEN.SG compared.to syntax.GEN.SG
   birra.
   about
   'It is good compared to her new book on syntax.'

Similarly, relative clauses, when embedded in a PP complement, will be separated from their correlates, as illustrated in (13):

(13) *Northern Saami*
   a. olbmo-t   gea-t   doppe orr-ot
      person-NOM.PL   who-NOM.PL   there live-PRES.3p
      'people who live there'

   b. olbmu-i-d   gaskkas, gea-t   doppe orr-ot
      person-PL-GEN   among   who-NOM.PL   there live-PRES.3p
      'among (the) people who live there'

These facts suggest that postpositional phrases are not just mirror images of prepositional phrases and that one should instead adopt an analysis along the lines of Kayne (1994). Kayne proposes that "postpositional phrases must be derived by moving the complement of the adposition into the specifier position of that adposition (or of a higher functional head)" (pp. 47-48). But if complements of postpositions have moved to the Spec of the adposition, the material that appears to the right of the postposition in (12a) and (13b) must then have been left behind. As for the double PP construction in (12a), the structure of the higher PP must be as shown in (14).

(14)

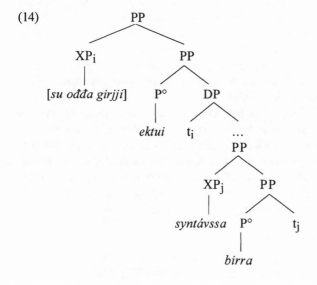

The generalization that can be made, at least for Saami, concerning what moves and what does not, is that the head noun and everything that precedes it will move, whereas all elements following the noun will be stranded.

What remains to be explained is how the noun and all elements preceding it can be moved as one constituent that does not include the postnominal elements of DP. As many details of DP structure are still poorly understood, one can only hope that future advances in syntactic theory will shed more light on this. In any case, the problem will not be related to postpositional phrases exclusively, but it will be the more general one of how to account for, in a Kaynean framework, all constructions that formerly were regarded as instances of right dislocation.[2]

Returning to the comitative plural marker, which has developed from a post-position and is now a suffix, it appears that its syntax is still that of a postposition. This means that its complement will be forced into its specifier position. But just like in other postpositional constructions, phrasal constituents following the nominal head of the complement will not take part in this movement. This is illustrated in (15).

(15) *Northern Saami*

buot	fulkk-i-iddea-met-guin	Suoma	bealde
all	relative-PL-ACC/GEN-1pPOSS-COM	Finland.GEN	side.on

'with all our relatives on the Finnish side'

The only difference between an ordinary postposition and the comitative plural marker is that the latter appears to form a morphological unit with material in its Spec. In this case, the proposal put forward by Kayne (1994), that the movement from complement position to Spec position can be a step in the formation of complex words, seems to be confirmed.

A final point of some interest is the observation that the comitative marker *-guin* does not interact phonologically with the nominal it attaches to. Nevis (1988b:44) sees this as an indication of the marker's status as a clitic. It is also, however, in accordance with Kayne's proposal that a typical feature of this type of word formation is that the morphemes brought together in a Spec-head configuration will never fuse. This is a consequence of the fact that a word derived in this way is not a syntactic constituent.

If we now apply these considerations to the verbal constructions noted to be problematic for a head movement analysis of complex words, we see that if a morphologically complex verbal word can be built by successive movements to specifier positions, the order of elements found, for example, in the Haruai clause in (5) can be readily accounted for. As suggested in (16), one might propose here that an XP (possibly a multi-layered VP) has moved to the Spec of TP. The whole TP in turn ends up in the Spec of SpeechActP.

(16) *Haruai* (cf. ex. (5), ch. 3)

[SpeechActP [TP [VP	an	nöbö	dyb	hön	nöy] -n -ŋ] -a	]
	we	man	big	pig	give-FUT-1p-DECL	

Concerning the subject agreement marker, I will leave the question of its structural location open. In any case, provided that the verb root is the final element in the XP that moves first, the verb and the verbal inflection markers will end up as a sequence of morphemes that may be interpreted as a word. Word formation of this type is the topic of this chapter. But before we go on to deal with this in detail, we will take a look at the connection between verb-final order and verbal suffixes, which can be observed in Haruai and many other languages.

3.3 Tense suffixes and verb-final order

It was noted in section 1.5 that there seems to be a connection between tense suffixes and verb-final order. This connection has been known since Greenberg (1966), who reports that in his sample, 10 out of 12 exclusively suffixing languages have SOV as their basic order. From table 1.8, which shows the worldwide frequency of various combinations of word order and tense marker position, we see that the combination of verb-final order and a tense marker suffixed to the verb is found in 41% of all genera. This combination is twice as frequent as the second most frequent one, verb-medial order and tense suffix, which is found in 19% of all genera. Moreover, verb-final order and suffixed tense marker is the most frequent combination in all geographical areas except Southeast Asia and Oceania, which indicates that the high frequency of this combination is not due to areal factors. In Southeast Asia and Oceania, the combination of verb-medial word order and a free tense marker preceding the verb is by far the most frequent one, found in 64% of all genera. But notably, here verb-final order and tense suffix comes in second, albeit with a frequency of only 18%.

Creole languages, as shown in table 1.7, are rather deviant in this respect— only two of the creole languages represented in my survey have tense suffixes, whereas verb-medial order combined with a free tense marker preceding the verb is found in all creole groups.

So far, we have only stated the observation that verb-final order and tense suffixes are often seen together. It is not at all clear at this point what the explanation might be. Of course, one possibility is that it is simply a coincidence. Since tense markers are more often than not realized as suffixes, while SOV is more frequent than any other order (see the bottom and right margins of table 1.8), it should come as no surprise that the combination of tense suffix and verb-final order is also relatively frequent. It is also conceivable, on the other hand, that there is a causal relation between verb-final order and tense suffixes; either that verb-final order favors suffixes or that tense suffixes favor verb-final order. In other words, it is possible that one or both of the following implications hold:

(17) *Two possible implications*
    a. V-final order   ⇒   tense suffix
    b. tense suffix   ⇒   V-final order

In an attempt to find out whether (17a) or (17b) is a correct generalization, I will now take a closer look at some of the figures that were presented in table 1.8. Recall that in that table, the frequency of each combination was calculated relative to the total number of genera. I did not calculate the frequency of the different tense marker types relative to word order or the frequency of the different word orders relative to tense marker type. This is what I will do here, in order to see which one (if any) of the variables is conditioned by the other.

Before we go on to consider the relation between tense suffixes and verb-final order, however, we might reasonably ask if the high frequency of tense suffixes in verb-final orders reflects a high frequency of postposed tense markers in general in these languages. An answer to this question can be read off from table 3.1. In this table, which is based on the figures given in table 1.8, I show, for each of the three word order types (verb-initial, verb-medial, and verb-final), first the ratio of postposed tense markers relative to the total number of tense markers, and then the ratio of suffixed tense markers relative to the total number of postposed tense markers.

We see that verb-final languages have postposed tense markers more often than other languages, with a frequency of 92% as opposed to 53% in verb-initial languages and 67% in verb-medial languages. As for the affixation rate of postposed tense markers (i.e., the percentage of affixes relative to the total number of grammatical markers), we see that it is rather high in all orders. That is, postposed tense markers are as a rule suffixed. The tendency is not quite as dominant, though, in verb-initial and verb-medial languages as in verb-final languages. It should be borne in mind, however, that for verb-initial languages the absolute numbers are small: only 5 genera in my survey contain languages with verb-initial order and free postposed tense markers.

A conclusion that can be drawn from table 3.1 is that the reason why tense suffixes are often found together with verb-final order is that postposed markers are more frequent in verb-final orders than in other orders, and also that the

TABLE 3.1
Frequency of postposed tense markers and suffixed tense markers in the three main word orders.

Word order	Total no. of genera	Genera with postposed tense markers	Frequency of postposed markers (%)	Genera with tense suffixes	Suffixation ratio of postposed markers (%)
V-initial	36	19	53	14	74
V-medial	100	67	67	54	81
V-final	138	127	92	114	90

TABLE 3.2
Realization of tense marker calculated relative to word order.

Word order	Frequency of prefixes		Frequency of suffixes		Frequency of free preposed markers		Frequency of free postposed markers		Total
	No.	%	No.	%	No.	%	No.	%	
V-initial	16	44	14	39	8	22	5	14	$N = 36$
V-medial	24	24	54	53	44	44	13	13	$N = 101$
V-final	18	13	114	83	12	16	13	9	$N = 138$

affixing tendency of postposed tense markers is slightly stronger in verb-final languages.

As a next step, we try to determine the direction of the correlation between verb-final order and suffixed tense marker. Consider first table 3.2, where the frequencies of the four types of tense marker are calculated for each word order type. (Note that I have calculated on the basis of genera, so that, e.g., a frequency of 44% for prefixes in verb-initial order means that the combination of prefix and verb-initial order is found in 44% of the genera that have languages with verb-initial order. Since more than one combination may be found within one single genus, the percentages often add up to more than 100%.)

We see here that of all the genera that have verb-initial languages, 44% have verb-initial order combined with tense prefixes and the combination of verb-initial order and tense suffixes is nearly equally frequent. There are also quite a few free preposed markers (22%). Finally, free postposed markers (14%) are more frequent in these languages than elsewhere.

In verb-medial languages, suffixes are predominant (53%), closely followed by free preposed markers (44%), whereas prefixes come in third with 24%.

In verb-final languages, the frequency of suffixes is an overwhelming 83%. The other three types of tense markers are all conspicuously infrequent, with percentages ranging from 9% to 13%. Thus, if a language is verb-final, it will also with more than chance frequency have tense suffixes. This means that the implication in (17a), V-final order $\Rightarrow$ tense suffix, seems to hold.

In table 3.3, I deal again with the same combinations that were the basis for table 3.2, but this time the frequencies are calculated in the opposite direction. Instead of calculating tense marker type relative to word order, I now calculate the frequency of each word order type relative to tense marker type (note that the frequencies of "uncertain" word order are not shown).

We see from this table that languages with tense prefixes are most likely to have verb-medial word order (40%), but they also often have verb-final order (30%), and, moreover, 27% of them have verb-initial order.

TABLE 3.3
Word order calculated relative to realization of tense marker.

Tense marker	Frequency of V-initial order		Frequency of V-medial order		Frequency of V-final order		Total
	No.	%	No.	%	No.	%	
Prefix	16	27	24	40	18	30	$N = 60$
Free preposed	8	13	44	70	16	25	$N = 63$
Suffix	14	7	54	27	114	56	$N = 202$
Free postposed	5	15	13	39	13	39	$N = 33$

Among languages with free preposed tense markers there is much less variation: 70% of them have verb-medial order, whereas 25% have verb-final order and 13% have verb-initial order.

Languages with tense suffixes tend to have verb-final order. Tense suffixes combine with verb-final order in 56% of the genera that have suffixes, which is twice as often as they combine with verb-medial order (27%). Moreover, the likelihood of a language with tense suffixes having verb-initial order is only 7%. Also note that several genera contain suffixing languages where the basic word order is not established, which means that the order is said to be free or information is lacking. Table 1.8 showed that such cases are found in 53 genera, which is 26% of the genera that have languages with tense suffixes. In other words, "uncertain" order combines with suffixes just as frequently as verb-medial order.

Finally, languages with free postposed tense markers have either verb-medial or verb-final word order; for any language with a free postposed tense marker, either order has a 39% likelihood of occurring. By comparison, verb-initial order is found in only 15% of the cases.

The conclusion that can be drawn from table 3.3 as far as the combination of tense suffixes and verb-final order is concerned, is that if a language has tense suffixes, the best guess is that it also has verb-final order. However, the chances are just a little more than 50%. Thus, even if verb-final order is clearly more frequent among languages with tense suffixes than among languages with other realizations of the tense markers, the implication tense suffix ⇒ V-final order is not very strong, and certainly not as strong as the converse implication.

Seen in light of the syntactic approach to morphology under investigation in this work, it is expected that tense suffixes should be compatible with any word order. As noted in the introduction to this chapter, if suffixes result from head movement, a verb carrying a tense suffix must have moved at least as high as $T°$. On this view, verb-initial order means that none of the arguments have moved higher than the verb, and verb-medial order means that the subject but not the object has undergone such movement. Finally, in verb-final order all the arguments must have moved higher than the $V°+T°$ complex. As also noted earlier, this is not wholly implausible, although it would have to be worked out in more detail.

If this is all there is to say about verb suffixes in different word orders, however, we would have no explanation for the fact that the vast majority of verb-final languages have tense suffixes. If verb-final order is derived simply by moving the arguments high up in the clause, then there is no direct connection between having verb-final order and having tense suffixes. We would then expect to find not only the configuration SO V+T, with the subject and the object higher than a T° head into which the verb has moved, but also SOTV, with the subject and the object higher than a T° head into which the verb has *not* moved. However, the latter pattern is not very frequent. In my survey, where a total of 280 genera were investigated, the order SOTV, with a free tense marker immediately preceding a clause-final verb, is the basic order in only three of them: in the Central Khoisan language Nama; in the Southern Cushitic language Iraqw; and in Yele, a language of the Yele-Solomons group. In addition, this order is an option in Ngankikurungkurr of the Daly group and in Nevome, which is an older variety of Piman (see appendix 2 for details).

An example of SOTV order, from Nama, is shown in (18).

(18) *Nama* (Hagman 1977)

píli	ke	//nãápá	maríàsà	╪xanísà	kè-rè	màa
Bill	DECL	there	Mary	letter	REM.PAST-IMPF	give

'There Bill gave Mary a letter.'

The declarative marker *ke* could be the spellout of the speech act modality head postulated by Cinque (1999) to be the highest head of the inflectional domain, or of the Force head of Rizzi (1997), which is taken to be the highest head in the CP-domain. It follows that the subject in (18) has moved as least as high as Spec-SpeechActP and possibly to Spec-ForceP. The adverbial and the direct and indirect objects must all be situated between Force°/SpeechAct° and T°, since they follow the declarative marker but precede the tense marker. The tense marker and the aspect marker that follows it are presumably both in their base positions; even if the aspect marker appears to be suffixed to the tense marker, I assume that this is just phonology, since aspect markers are normally generated below tense markers (the morphological properties of heads in their base positions will be discussed in more detail in the next chapter). Neither is there any indication, morphological or syntactic, that the verb has moved in (18). Hence we have here an example of SOV order derived simply by moving all arguments high up in the clause.[3]

In addition, there are 18 genera in my survey with languages where the tense marker is prefixed to a clause-final verb, as in (19). As will become clear in the next chapter, I think there is good reason to assume that the syntactic relation between the verb root and the tense marker is the same in (19) as in (18) above. This means that there are 23 genera in my survey where verb-final order is derived by moving all arguments to the left of the tense marker.

(19) *Rikbaktsa* (Boswood 1978:22)
    Ka-zo   pitsi   pi-boro-ko.
    1s-father cashew   NONPAST-eat-CONT
    'My father is eating cashew nuts.'

Further, 11 of the genera represented in my survey contain languages with the order STOV—that is, with the object situated between the verb and a free preposed tense marker. Two examples of this pattern are given in (20)–(21).

(20) *Koranko* (Kastenholz 1987:109)
    à   yá   kɔlɔmabolɔ   kári
    3s   PAST   tree-branch   break
    'She/he broke a branch.'

(21) *Vata* (Koopman 1984:19)
    à   nĪ-kā   sǎká   lì
    1p   FUT   rice   eat
    'We will eat rice.'

In (22a,b), the object precedes the verb but follows the free aspect marker.

(22) *Supyire* (Carlson 1991:208–209)
    a. U   a   wùù   ɲyà.   b. U   a   Zhyé   ɲyà.
       3s   PERF   us   see   3s   PERF   Zhyé   see
       'She/he saw us.'   'She/he saw Zhyé.'

As far as I am able to tell from the sources I have consulted, languages with S T/A O V allow PPs to follow the verb, as below:[4]

(23) *Koranko* (Kastenholz 1987:107)
    ń   yá   à   kɛ́   màafɛ   rɔ̀
    1s   PAST   3s   put   sauce   in
    'I put it in the sauce.'

(24) *Vata* (Koopman 1984:113)
    à   nĪ-kā   yué   sǎká   nyĒ   slé-ɛ̀   mlÍ
    1p   FUT   children   rice   give   house   in
    'We will give rice to the children in the house.'

(25) *Supyire* (Carlson 1991:206)
    U   a   kàrè   Sukwoo   na.
    3s   PERF   go   Sukwoo   to
    'She/he has gone to Sukwoo.'

Thus, it appears that the order STOV is derived by overt movement of the subject and the object to positions outside of VP, presumably for case reasons, whereas clausal elements not in need of case checking stay in situ. In particular, there is no movement of the verb, so that the tense marker and the verb are separated by the object after the object has moved to its surface position.

Although the derivations that lead to SOTV and STOV orders seem very simple, in that they only manipulate elements with case and leave other constituents in the positions where they originate, verb-final languages with the tense marker preceding the verb are not very numerous, as we just have seen. The five genera with SOTV, the 18 genera with SO T+V, and the 11 genera with STOV make only 34 genera of a total of 280 genera represented in the survey. Compared to this, the combination of verb-final order and tense suffixes is more than three times as frequent, being found in 114 genera altogether. In addition, there are 13 genera with SOV and a free postposed tense marker. These facts suggest that deriving a verb-final order is not always merely a question of getting the complement of the verb away from its base position. Rather, it appears that derivations that produce verb-final order also tend to create verb suffixes. This needs to be explained.

In this connection, it is of particular interest to note that lexicalist approaches to morphology cannot offer a principled explanation of the correlation between tense suffixes and verb-final order. On a lexicalist view, all verb-final orders can be derived by moving the subject and the object to their checking position while leaving the verb in its base position, or at least not moving it across the object. This means that the order SOV+T would have the same structure as the order STOV, the only differences being that in the former case, the T° head is silent and the tense feature of the verb is phonologically realized, whereas in the latter case, it is the other way round. But if the tense marker on the verb is just the spellout of a feature that the verb brings with it from the lexicon, there is no particular reason why it should so often be realized as a suffix in verb-final orders, except for the general tendency for suffixes to be preferred over prefixes, a fact that is itself in need of explanation. The tendency for tense suffixes to be more strongly preferred in verb-final languages than in languages with other word orders would have to be regarded as a mere accident.

The idea I want to pursue is that the implication V-final order $\Rightarrow$ tense suffix is not just accidental; rather, the reason verb-final order so often goes with tense suffixes is that verb-final order often, although not always, is derived by means of a procedure that results in verb-final order and tense suffixes. This procedure consists of successive movements of complements to Spec. This means that most verb-final languages are not only verb-final, they are head-final in a more general sense. In the following sections, my analysis of head-final languages will be developed in some detail.

3.4 Deriving head-final order

Our main objective in the following will be to get a clearer picture of the structure of head-final languages. Notably, by head-final languages I do not refer to languages like Nama, Koranko, Vata, and Supyire (see (18)–(25) above), which have the object in front of the verb but otherwise are head-initial at the clausal level, with a basic order SOTV or STOV. What I have in mind is the much larger class of languages that are consistently head-final in their IP. As it happens, these languages are also generally characterized by suffixing morphology, as we saw in the preceding section. This is the correlation that I am going to investigate.

We start by looking at the Dagestanian language Lezgian, which I take to be a typical representative of this class of languages. The presentation is based on the detailed description of Lezgian found in Haspelmath (1993). As shown in (26)–(28), all arguments and adverbials normally precede the verb in Lezgian, and the tense marker is a suffix on the verb.

(26) *Lezgian* (Haspelmath 1993:299)

Kamalov.a[5]	itim.di-z	stol.di-q^h	čka	q̃alur-na.
Kamalov.ERG	man-DAT	table-POSTESS	place.ABS	show-AOR

'Kamalov showed the man a seat at the table.'

(27) *Lezgian* (Haspelmath 1993:254)

Ada	sa	šumud	sefer.d-a	Nurbala.di-q^h	galaz
she.ERG	one	how.many	time-INESS	Nurbala-POSTESS	with

q'üler-na.
dance-AOR

'She danced with Nurbala several times.'

(28) *Lezgian* (Haspelmath 1993:200)

Čun	pud	hafte.d-a	saki	wiri	ülkwe.d-a	q̃eq̃we-da.
we.ABS	three	week-INESS	almost	all	country-INESS	pass-FUT

'In three weeks we will pass through almost the whole country.'

As already noted, such structures pose a potential problem for any theory of word formation stating that complex words are built up in syntax. Since the verbs in (26)–(28) carry tense suffixes, it follows from the syntactic approach to word formation that the verbs must have moved at least to T°. But then all other constituents of the clause, arguments as well as adverbials, must precede T°. This is discussed in the following subsections.

First, in 3.4.1, I argue that in the clauses shown here, and in similar constructions in other languages, T° has come to be clause-final as a result of its complement, containing the verb and also arguments and adverbials, having moved to Spec-TP. More generally, the reason some languages are characterized by head-finality in their syntax and by agglutination in their morphology is that these languages make extensive use of complement movement to Spec.

In 3.4.2 I focus on the arguments of the verb, and I show how all arguments can be licensed inside (a multi-layered) VP in languages of this type, so that the single operation of moving VP suffices to get all arguments in front of T°.

In 3.4.3 I deal more extensively with the claim that there is no head movement of the verb in head-final languages. The discussion concentrates on Japanese, since the literature on Japanese offers a wealth of data that are relevant to this question. I assume, however, that my conclusions are valid for other head-final languages as well.

The claim that the arguments are licensed inside VP in head-final languages raises the question of how it is possible for these languages to allow all the non-canonical word orders that they are known to also display. This question is taken up in 3.4.4, and I propose that the observed variation is due to movements into the CP-domain—more specifically, to the topic and focus positions that are found there (Rizzi 1997). These movements can have profound consequences for the surface order of clausal constituents, to the effect that a wide range of permutations of the arguments and the verb are possible.

3.4.1 Movement of complement to Spec

There are indications that it is not necessarily the case that every clausal constituent (i.e., every argument and every adverbial) has moved separately to a preverbal position in the Lezgian examples shown in (26)–(28). Instead, it is possible that movement of considerably larger phrases is involved. This is the idea I try to develop further. I begin by considering the following:

(29) *Lezgian* (Martin Haspelmath, personal communication)

Baku.d-a	irid	itim	gülle.di-z	aq̃ud-na	luhu-da.
Baku-INESS	seven	man.ABS	bullet-DAT	take.out-AOR	say-HAB

'They say that in Baku seven men were shot.'[6]

On an LCA-based analysis (Kayne 1994), the complement of the verb 'say' in (29) must have moved to the left across the verb. The verb itself has probably moved at least to T°. Although the suffix -*da* is glossed here as 'habitual', it is formally identical to the future marker (compare (29) to (28)). Haspelmath's (1993:130) explanation of this is that -*da* used to be a general non-past marker, but later the progressive present has come to be expressed by means of the imperfective, so that -*da* has retained only its non-progressive meanings—the future and the simple or habitual present. Hence, one may assume that -*da* in all its uses is a temporal and not an aspectual marker. This means that the embedded clause in (29) must be at least as high as Spec-TP.

Interestingly, in Lezgian there exists an alternative to the construction shown in (29). Instead of embedding the quote under the full verb 'say', a hearsay evidential marker can be suffixed to the verb of the quote, as in (30). The suffix -*lda* has very recently developed from the verb form *luhuda* '(one) says'. The source of the marker is still transparent to the speakers, and there is some degree of variation between the suffix and the full verb (Haspelmath 1993:148).

(30) *Lezgian* (Haspelmath 1993:148)

Baku.d-a　　irid　　itim　　gülle.di-z　　aq̃ud-na-lda.
Baku-INESS　seven　man.ABS　bullet-DAT　take.out-AOR-EVID
'They say that in Baku seven men were shot.'

Again, we have a potential problem for a syntactic theory of word formation, according to which the verb in (30) must have moved all the way to the head that encodes various types of evidence. As argued by Cinque (1999), this head, termed Evidential Mood, is one of the highest heads within the IP-domain, preceded only by the SpeechAct° head mentioned earlier and a head that expresses evaluative modalities, in addition to the heads in the CP-domain (see Rizzi 1997). Hence, the arguments and the locative in (30) must all be situated higher than the evidential head on this analysis. The question is then what positions these constituents occupy.

I would like to propose that the constructions shown in (29) and (30) have largely the same syntactic structure. In particular, just as the embedded clause has moved as a whole to a Spec position which is higher than the Spell-Out position of the matrix verb in (29), so has the corresponding string, which is the complement of Evid°, moved as a whole to a Spec above Evid° in (30), presumably to Spec-EvidP. The clause-initial locative phrase is probably even higher; most likely, it is situated in a Spec-TopP position within the CP-domain. The latter suggestion is based on Haspelmath's (1993) assertions that topics precede non-topics and that adverbials of setting are often placed clause-initially. I take this to indicate that there are topic positions high up in the clause (see Rizzi 1997), and that adverbials of setting tend to be treated as topics.[7]

In short, I propose that the structure of (30) is roughly as shown in (31) (with irrelevant projections omitted).

(31)

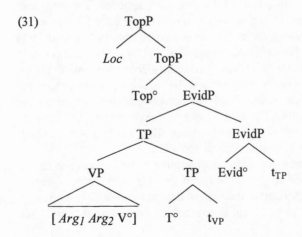

In this structure, the verbal word is made up of a sequence of heads that have become linearly adjacent as a consequence of successive movements of complements to the nearest Spec (as suggested for agglutinating SOV languages in Kayne 1994:52–54). In this way, every phrase within IP is made head-final, and when such a phrase moves to the Spec of the next higher head, the head of the moved phrase will be linearly adjacent to that head, and the two heads together will be perceived as a word.

Note, by the way, that I do not assume that all constituents in Lezgian end up being head-final; for example, the Top° head at the left periphery of (31) probably has its complement in base position, to the right. We will return to the questions concerning the syntax of the left periphery in section 3.4.4.

It follows from the proposed analysis that the verbal word is not a syntactic constituent in Lezgian. That it is nevertheless seen as a word is not unexpected given the criteria for wordhood that were established in section 1.4.2. If movement to Spec occurs without exception, the verbal head will always be adjacent to T° at PF after movement of VP to Spec-TP, and T° will always be adjacent to Evid°. There will never be intervening overt material, although the heads are separated by the traces of the moved phrases. This means that the criterion of internal cohesion is met. Further, since other constituents may move independently of the verb—for example to topic position—the verbal word appears to have independent distribution, even though it cannot move as a constituent itself. Finally, its being perceived as a word is probably facilitated by the phonological lightness of the functional markers inserted in T° and Evid° (neither of them ever bear stress; see Haspelmath 1993:69), and by the semantic connection between the verb and the markers in question.

Interestingly, Lezgian has a particle which also could be seen as a realization of Evid°. This is the particle *man*, shown in (32), which indicates indirect evidence.

(32) *Lezgian* (Haspelmath 1993:241)

Ak'	xalija,	Šafiga	Dewlet.a-n	ruš	ja	man.
hence		Šafiga	Dewlet-GEN	daughter	be.PRES	PRT

'So Šafiga must be Dewlet's daughter.'

If *man* is really a realization of the evidential head, it must be generated higher than most other constituents of the clause. Nevertheless, it is strictly clause-final (Haspelmath 1993:241). This means that in (32) the complement of Evid° has moved to the left of the head. It is therefore a plausible claim that this is also the case in (30).

If we now return to (29), we see that this construction could also be derived without head-to-head movement. We have already noted that there must have been movement of the embedded clause to a higher Spec; this was part of the motivation for postulating a similar operation in (30). In addition, both the higher and the lower verbal word may have been derived in the same way—that is, by movement of VP to Spec-TP. The overall structure of (29) could then be as suggested in (33) (again with intervening empty projections left out).

(33)

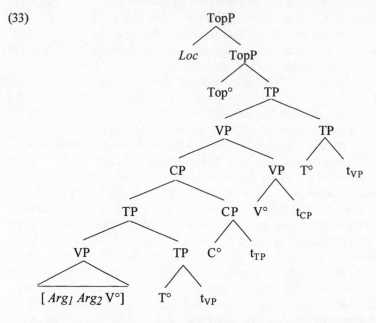

Another interesting phenomenon in Lezgian is the so-called verbal compounds, which are lexicalized (i.e., listed) combinations of a noun or an adjective plus a light verb, either *awun* 'do, make' or *x̂un* 'be, become' (Haspelmath 1993:178). The masdar forms of some *awun*-compounds are given in (34).

(34) *Verbal compounds in Lezgian* (Haspelmath 1993:178)
  a. *k'walax aw-un*   work do-MSD   = 'work'
  b. *fikir aw-un*   thought do-MSD   = 'think'
  c. *ištirak aw-un*   participation do-MSD = 'participate'
  d. *tešwiš aw-un*   confusion do-MSD   = 'confuse'

As an alternative, the verb root in these compounds can be phonologically reduced, so that the verbal suffixes appear to be attached directly to the nouns. This gives *k'walax-un* instead of *k'walax awun*, and so on. Notably, the subject will appear in the ergative case regardless of whether the object is realized as a free nominal or as a part of the verbal word (Haspelmath 1993:284). The following pair illustrates this:

(35) *Lezgian* (Haspelmath 1993:284)
  a. Ada   k'walax   iji-zwa.   b.   Ada   k'walax-zawa.
     she.ERG work.ABS   do-IMPF   she.ERG work-IMPF
     'She is working.'   'She is working.'

The case marking of the subject in (35b) indicates that the object nominal is still syntactically present, even if it is contained in the verbal word morphologically. It must be because the object requires absolutive case marking that this case is not available for the subject. As a rule, if the object is incorporated into the verb by head-to-head movement, it does not have structural case (Baker 1988a). Hence, it appears that the nominal object in (35b) does not form a complex head with the verb, but, rather, it sits in a Spec immediately to the left of the verb, just like the object in (35a).[8] This means that (35b) is another example of a head forming a word with an element in its Spec. Then the difference between (35a) and (35b) is not a structural one; it lies only in the phonological realization of the verbal head, which is null in (35b) but non-null in (35a).

An example which shows even clearer that a complex word is not necessarily also a complex head is the following:

(36) *Lezgian* (Haspelmath 1993:179)
    a. Ama-j-bur.u   sekinwil.e-ldi   čpi-n   kesibwal-da.
       remain-PTC-N.PL.ERG quietness-SUPDIR selves-GEN   poverty-FUT
       'The others will quietly eke out their miserable existence.'

    b. [Amajburu sekinwileldi [$_{TP}$ [$_{VP}$ [$_{DP}$ čpi-n kesibwal] V°] [$_{T°}$ da] t$_{VP}$]

Here the tense morpheme forms a word with the final noun phonologically. Syntactically, the noun is part of a DP that contains the preceding genitive but excludes the (empty) verb and the tense marker. Obviously, syntactic constituency does not coincide with phonological constituency here. Thus, it is again possible that the DP is contained within a head-final VP, with a phonologically empty head, which has moved to Spec-TP. This structure is indicated in (36b).

A similar situation is seen in the following examples from Japanese and Turkish. Like other head-final languages, Japanese and Turkish have nominal and adjectival predicates immediately in front of the copula, and there is a tendency that the copula is perceived as a suffix on the predicate:

(37) *Japanese* (Tsujimura 1996:127)
    a. Taroo-wa   nihonzin-da.
       Taroo-TOP   Japanese-COP
       'Taroo is a Japanese.'

    b. Taroo-wa   doitugo-no   sensei-da.
       Taroo-TOP   German-GEN   teacher-COP
       'Taroo is a German teacher.'

(38) *Turkish* (Kornfilt 1997:444)
    Oya çok kıskanç-tı.[9]
    Oya very jealous-PAST
    'Oya was very jealous.'

(39) *Turkish* (Kornfilt 1997:77, 79)
     a. (Ben) satıcı-y-ım.   b.   (Ben) satıcı-y-dı-m.
       I   seller-COP-1s   I   seller-COP-PAST-1s
       'I am a seller.'   'I was a seller.'

At least in examples (37b) and (38) it seems clear that the copula is combined with a phrase syntactically, even if it attaches to only the last element of that phrase morphologically. Thus, it is again the syntax that creates a morpheme sequence that may be taken to constitute a word. I will assume that the order of predicate and copula is due to movement of the predicate to the Spec of the copula. Because of the internal ordering of elements in nominal and adjectival phrases in these languages, the consequence of this movement is that the copula is always immediately preceded by a noun or an adjective. Accordingly, the conditions are such that the copula can be analyzed as a suffix on the noun or on the adjective.

Concerning the trigger for the movement of complements to Spec positions, I assume that it has to do with c-checking, the notion introduced in section 2.2.2. I proposed there, following Holmberg (2000a), that c-checking may be executed in one of three ways:

(40) *Checking of c-selectional features (c-checking)* (= ex. (16), ch. 2)
     A selectional feature of a head Y selecting a complement XP may be checked
     a. by movement of the X feature to $Y°$
     b. by head movement of $X°$ to $Y°$
     c. by movement of XP to the Spec of YP

I also claimed that c-features cannot trigger head movement on their own. In the case of head movement, c-features can only be checked as 'free riders' if head movement is triggered by some other feature. If such strong features are absent, however, in a language with strong c-features, the c-features must take effect so that a checking relation can be established overtly. I will assume that in this case, the option of XP-movement is invariably chosen. In other words, when the c-features of $X°$ are attracted by a higher head, the whole XP is moved along. For example, if $T°$ has weak V-features but strong c-features, $V°$ will not be incorporated into $T°$; instead, the whole VP will be moved to Spec-TP. In a language where every head of the IP-domain has these characteristics, the result will be structures like those shown in (31) and (33).

That syntactic movement in head-final languages is triggered by c-checking rather than, for example, case checking, at least in clausal syntax, is indicated by the fact that many clausal heads take their complement to the left in the surface order, even if that complement is a verbal projection. For example, aspectual and modal verbs have their complements to the left:

(41) *Lezgian* (Haspelmath 1993:157)
Qurxulu   xar   q̃wa-z   bašlamiš-na.
terrible   hail.ABS   fall-INF   begin-AOR
'A terrible hail began to fall.'

(42) *Lezgian* (Haspelmath 1993:356)
Dide.di-z   šeher.di-z   fi-z   k'an-zawa.
mother-DAT[10]   town-DAT   go-INF   want-IMPF
'Mother wants to go to town.'

(43) *Lezgian* (Haspelmath 1993:100)
Mirg.i-waj   ülen.di-laj   xkadari-z   x̂a-na-č.
deer-ADEL   swamp-SUPEL   jump-INF   can-AOR-NEG
'The deer could not jump across the swamp.'

(44) *Turkish* (Kornfilt 1997:375)
Okú-ya-ma-yabil-ir-im.
read-can-NEG-can-AOR-1s
'I might be unable to read.'

(45) *Japanese* (Tsujimura 1996:130)
Taroo-ga   susi-o   zenbu   tabe-te-simat-ta.
Taroo-NOM   sushi-ACC   all   eat-GER-finish-PAST[11]
'Taroo finished eating all the sushi.'

In example (45), it is also interesting to note that the complex verbal word consists of two inflected verbs. As we see, the base verb *tabe* 'eat' has gerundive marking, which I will take to be the non-finite realization of present tense (see Julien 2001). The higher verb *simat* 'finish' has a finite tense marker. Nevertheless, the two verbs are included in one single word. On my analysis, this illustrates my claim that a sequence of verbal heads built up by successive movements to Spec tends to be treated as one word.

Moreover, in head-final languages CP complements of verbs normally appear to the left of the verb, even if CPs are generally not assumed to have case:

(46) *Lezgian* (Haspelmath 1993:365)
Wiri   ajal-r.i-z   [Musaq'.a-n   dide
all   child-PL-DAT   Musaq'-GEN   mother.ABS
q'e-nwa-j-di   ]   či-zwa-j.
die-PERF-PTC-N.SG.ABS   know-IMPF-PAST
'All the children knew that Musaq's mother had died.'

(47) *Turkish*   (Kornfilt 1997:47)

Herkes   sen   sinema-ya   git-ti-n   san-iyor.
everybody   you.NOM   cinema-DAT   go-PAST-2s   believe-PRES
'Everybody believes that you went to the movies.'

(48) *Japanese* (Oka 1996:377)

John-ga   Mary-ni   kare-o   homeru   yoo-ni[12]   tanon-da.
John-NOM   Mary-DAT   he-ACC   praise   to.do   ask-PAST
'John asked Mary to praise him.'

Presumably, the movement operations that have taken place in these examples are all triggered by c-features. I will therefore conclude that the properties that characterize the head-final languages are the following: (1) there are no strong features to trigger obligatory overt movement of arguments or of heads; and (2) in the absence of argument movement and head movement, the need for c-checking forces every complement XP to move to the Spec of the next higher head. This is then the process that yields verb-final order and, at the same time, suffixal morphology.

3.4.2   Argument licensing

In the foregoing discussion, I glossed over the question of what goes on inside VP in head-final languages. I suggested, though, that the complement-to-Spec movement must begin at the very bottom of the structure if every phrase is to be made head-final. Then VP is a problem. If there were successive movements to Spec inside (a possibly multi-layered) VP, one might expect that the object would move to the lowest Spec and that the lower VP, containing the object and the verb, would then move to a higher Spec inside the extended VP (which for simplicity I refer to as VP and not, e.g., vP). But it is not clear whether there would be enough specifier positions available inside VP to serve as landing sites, or, if there were, what would be the relative ordering of the lower VP and the subject.

My proposal is that a head cannot attract its complement to its Spec if another phrase can be merged in that Spec. That is, I assume that the need to accommodate all relevant items into the phrase marker overrides overt checking of c-features. In other words, merge is preferred over move (see Chomsky 1995). Another possible reason is that all projections of the extended VP are ultimately projections of the verb. It is therefore conceivable that the relation between a v head and its VP complement is not really a complement selection relation and that c-features are not involved. If the higher heads of VP have no c-features to check, there is no trigger for phrasal movement inside VP.[13]

What about the arguments? In (31) and (33) it was suggested that the arguments stay inside VP. Then the question is how they are licensed. In an attempt to give an answer, I start from the account of object licensing found in Chomsky (1995:352), according to which object raising is triggered by a strong nominal feature in v, a higher verbal head in a multi-layered VP. This feature can be checked against the object if the object moves to (the outer) Spec of $v°$. Since Chomsky assumes that $V°$ obligatorily moves to $v°$, it follows that the case and φ-features of the object in Spec-vP can at the same time be checked against $V°$. Suppose now that $v°$ has no strong features, so that it is like the heads of the IP-domain with respect to feature strength (except for the lack of c-features in $v°$). Then we must assume that $V°$ does not move to $v°$ and that the object will not move to the Spec of VP. It may still be necessary for the object to have its case and φ-features checked against $V°$, but this can presumably be done by moving the object to the lower Spec-VP, given that the lower $V°$ stays in its base position.

Alternatively, it is conceivable that the object is simply base-generated in a specifier position (see, e.g., Marantz 1993), so that there is no object movement at all. If this assumption is correct, it paves the way for an analysis of (49) stated solely in terms of c-checking.

(49) *Lezgian* (Haspelmath 1993:98)

Žiraf.di	q̃ib	sa	q'aq'an	tar.ci-n	xil.e-l
giraffe.ERG	frog.ABS	one	high	tree-GEN	twig-SUPESS
ecig-na.					
put-AOR					

'The giraffe put the frog on a twig of a tall tree.'

The locative phrase in (49) is selected by the verb, and therefore generated inside the maximal VP, presumably as the innermost complement (Hale & Keyser 1993). But as we see, the locative precedes the verb in the surface order. This is what we would get if c-checking is executed by movement of the locative to the lower Spec-VP. (As we will see below, the locative phrase is probably a PP, so that it does not need to move for case reasons.) As for the object, it must be situated in a higher Spec. I will assume that the features of $V°$ that are relevant for the licensing of the object can move to the higher $v°$ heads, so that this poses no problem for the checking of the case and φ-features of the object. Further, I assume that the subject occupies the highest Spec in the extended VP. The structure of the VP in (49) is then as shown in (50).

The question is then how the subject in head-final languages can have its case and φ-features checked. Interestingly, in the Kaynean interpretation of phrase structure which I have been assuming throughout this work, the first projection of $X°$ is a segment of XP. This means that the subject in the highest Spec-VP is not dominated by VP. If VP moves to higher Specs—for example, to Spec-TP—the subject will not be dominated by TP, either. Hence, it is conceivable that the features of the subject will be accessible to higher clausal heads, so that checking can take place even if the subject does not move out of VP. The mechanism behind this could be similar to the long-distance agreement discussed in Chomsky (1998).

(50)

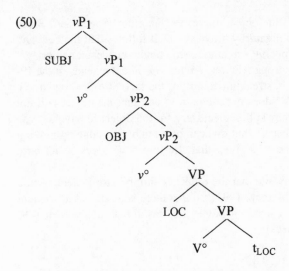

Notably, such long-distance checking is possible only if there is repeated movement of complements to Spec. Thus, it appears that the characteristic properties of head-final languages conspire, as it were, to produce the observed order: first, absence of strong V and N features leaves the verb and its arguments in their base position; next, strong c-features trigger XP-movement, which creates a configuration where the subject is licensed. In this way, the properties in question are interdependent.

As for the indirect object, it is often situated between the subject and the direct object in head-final languages, as in shown in (26) above and in the following examples:

(51) *Lezgian* (Haspelmath 1993:88)

Ruš-ar.i	Zubail.a-z	čpi-n	šeher	q̃alur-zawa.
girl-PL.ERG	Zubail-DAT	self-GEN	town.ABS	show-IMPF

'The girls are showing Zubail their town.'

(52) *Lezgian* (Haspelmath 1993:88)

Za	wa-z	ada-n	wiri	simfoni-jar	ja-da.
I.ERG	you-DAT	he-GEN	all	symphony-PL.ABS	play-FUT

'I will play all his symphonies for you.'

(53) *Japanese* (Tsujimura 1996:177)

Taroo-ga	Hanako-ni	hana-o	age-ta.
Taroo-NOM	Hanako-DAT	flower-ACC	give-PAST

'Taroo gave Hanako flowers.'

On the analysis sketched above, this means that the indirect object also surfaces in a VP-internal position. Then its case might be expected to pose problems: it cannot be in a local relation to V° and have its case checked that way, nor can its case be licensed by higher heads, as I suggested of the subject. However, on closer inspection it appears that there isn't a problem after all, since the indirect object in head-final languages is probably not a DP but a PP—that is, it does not correspond to the dative shifted indirect object in a language like English, but instead, to the prepositional dative. Consequently, there is no need for case checking or licensing of the indirect object.

That the indirect object in head-final languages is a PP is suggested by the fact that directional adverbials have the same realization as indirect objects in these languages. Some examples of directional adverbials are given below:

(54) *Lezgian* (Haspelmath 1993:89)
Ča-z   muhman-ar   ata-na.
we-DAT   guest-PL.ABS   come-AOR
'Some guests came to us.'

(55) *Japanese* (Tsujimura 1996:177)
Taroo-ga   tana-ni   hon-o   oi-ta.
Taroo-NOM   shelf-to   book-ACC   put-PAST
'Taroo put the book on the shelf.'

In Turkish, the direct object precedes the indirect object in the neutral order, according to Kornfilt (1997). Still, the indirect object has the same form as directional adverbials:

(56) *Turkish* (Kornfilt 1997:220)
Hasan   kitab-ı   Ali-ye   ver-di.
Hasan   book-ACC   Ali-DAT   give-PAST
'Hasan gave the book to Ali.'

(57) *Turkish* (Kornfilt 1997:243)
Hasan   Ankara-ya   git-ti.
Hasan   Ankara-DAT   go-PAST
'Hasan went to Ankara.'

Hence, in the languages under discussion here, dative nominals contain an element corresponding to the preposition 'to'. This could be an empty adposition that triggers dative marking on the noun, or it could be the dative suffix itself.

I think there is good reason to take the latter option and claim that the dative marker is a postposition. Consider the following Turkish example:

(58) *Turkish* (Matthews 1991:170)
Ankara   ve   Izmir-e
Ankara   and   Izmir-DAT
'to Ankara and Izmir'

As we see, the dative marker shows up only on the second conjunct. If the dative marker is a P°, the dative phrase in (58) could be derived simply by moving the DP complement of P° to Spec-PP (cf. what was said in section 3.2 about postpositional phrases.)

Thus, it is possible that dative marked nominals in head-final languages is another example of a Spec element and a head which together have the appearance of a word. Given that the noun is always the last constituent of DPs in these languages, the noun and the postposition will always be adjacent after this movement has taken place, which means that the combination of noun and dative marker will have the distribution that is typical of words.

According to Haspelmath (1993:213), postpositions differ from case markers in Lezgian in that postpositions are longer, they often have internal structure, and they are written as separate words. Notably, the latter property is probably a consequence of the two first ones. If an element, such as an adposition, is phonologically heavy, moreover, if it has internal structure, it is not very likely to be seen as an affix. If, on the other hand, it is phonologically light, it will tend to be viewed as an affix if it regularly appears next to a lexical element of one particular class. This does not mean that the light, affixal element cannot be of the same class as the heavier, non-affixal element. As I argue throughout this work, wordhood has more to do with distribution than with the constituting properties of elements. It is therefore quite possible that the case markers in Lezgian are in fact postpositions. It is interesting in this connection to note that only oblique case markers are overt in this language. Both the ergative and the absolutive are zero, the difference being that the ergative requires the oblique stem whereas the absolutive uses the bare stem. In this light, it is even more likely that overt case markers are postpositions.[14]

As for the claim that the arguments in verb-final languages are licensed inside VP, a similar proposal has recently been advanced for Japanese, for example, by Yanagida (1996) and Nakajima (1999). It has also been argued, however, that arguments in Japanese can be licensed outside of VP. This is claimed by Koizumi (1994), who discusses the phenomenon of stative verbs taking nominative objects, as exemplified in (59).

(59) *Japanese* (Koizumi 1994:213)
    a. John-ga   huransugo-ga   deki-ru.
       John-NOM   French-NOM   can-PRES
       'John speaks French.'

    b.* John-ga   huransugo-o deki-ru.
       John-NOM   French-ACC can-PRES
       'John speaks French.'

Koizumi argues that nominative objects are licensed in a higher position than accusative objects. More specifically, he proposes that nominative objects are licensed in Spec-TP, whereas accusative objects are licensed in Spec-AgrOP. He bases his claim on the observation that nominative objects can take higher scope than accusative objects. This is illustrated in (60).

(60) *Japanese* (Koizumi 1994:221–222)
    a. John-ga   migime-dake-o   tumur-e-na-i   (koto)
        John-NOM   right.eye-only-ACC   close-can-NEG-PRES   fact
        '(the fact that) John cannot close only his right eye'
  = '(the fact that) John cannot wink his right eye'
      (Neg > can > only)

    b. John-ga   migime-dake-ga   tumur-e-na-i   (koto)
        John-NOM   right.eye-only-NOM close-can-NEG-PRES   fact
        '(the fact that) it is only his right eye that John cannot close'
      (only > Neg > can)

As we see, when the object has accusative case, it is inside the scope of the modal verb, which is inside the scope of the negation. When the object has nominative case, on the other hand, it takes scope over both the modal and the negation. Hence, at some level the nominative object must be interpreted in a higher position than is possible for the accusative object. This suggests that at least nominative objects are not licensed inside VP.

It is not necessarily the case, however, that the nominative object has moved overtly out of VP in (60b). In fact, Koizumi himself proposes that the relevant licensing relation is established at LF. This view is supported by Ura (1994), who deals with constructions where the subject appears in the dative, as in (61) (note that (61a) is an alternative to (59a)). These examples show that when the subject appears in the dative case, the object cannot appear in the accusative.

(61) *Japanese* (Ura 1994:356)
    a. John-ni   eigo-ga   deki-ru.
        John-DAT   English-NOM   can-PRES
        'John speaks English.'

    b.* John-ni   eigo-o   deki-ru.
        John-DAT   English-ACC   can-PRES
        'John speaks English.'

That is, it cannot do so in root clauses. Apparently, there is no accusative case available in a clause where the subject has dative case. But if a clause containing a dative subject is embedded under an epistemic verb of the right type, the object of that clause may have nominative or accusative case:

(62) *Japanese* (Ura 1994:356)
  a. Boku-wa [John-ni   piano-ga   hik-er-u   to]   omow-u.
      I-TOP   John-DAT   piano-NOM   play-can-PRES   C   think-PRES
      'I think that John can play the piano.'

  b. Boku-wa [John-ni   piano-o   hik-er-u   to]   omow-u.
      I-TOP   John-DAT   piano-ACC   play-can-PRES   C   think-PRES
      'I think that John can play the piano.'

Ura (1994) suggests that the accusative object in (62b) is licensed by the matrix AgrO. Still it remains inside the embedded clause at Spell-Out. Hence, he concludes that the raising of the accusative object to a licensing projection within the matrix clause must take place at LF.

That the accusative object in a clause with a dative subject has a higher position at LF than the accusative object in a clause with a nominative subject is indicated by the semantic contrast between (63a) and (63b).

(63) *Japanese* (Ura 1994:359)
  a. Boku-wa [John-ga   mizu-nashide   seirogan-dake-o
      I-TOP   John-NOM   water-without   seirogan-only-ACC
      nom-er-u   to]   omow-u.
      drink-can-PRES   C   think-PRES
      'I think it is possible for John to swallow only *seirogan* without water.'
      (can > only)

  b. Boku-wa [John-ni   mizu-nashide   seirogan-dake-o
      I-TOP   John-DAT   water-without   seirogan-only-ACC
      nom-er-u   to]   omow-u.
      drink-can-PRES   C   think-PRES
      'I think that it is only *seirogan* that John can swallow without water.'
      (only > can)

When the embedded subject has nominative case, both the subject and the accusative object are presumably licensed within the embedded clause. Accordingly, the object is within the scope of the modal marker, as in (63a). But since an accusative argument cannot be licensed inside a clause where the subject appears in the dative, as demonstrated in (61b), the accusative object in (63b) must be licensed by an element in the matrix clause. Hence, in this case the object takes scope over the modal in the embedded clause, even if it is spelled out in the same position as the object in (63a).

In short, the Japanese data shown in the above examples are compatible with the analysis I have already proposed, according to which the arguments in head-final languages may stay inside VP. The only adjustment that is necessary to account for the special case marking patterns in Japanese is that we must allow for the possibility that certain licensing relations can be established across the

VP boundary. Overt movement might still play a role in this respect, however. If my proposal is correct that the syntax of head-final languages is characterized by successive movements of complements to Spec, the lower VP in (60a,b) must be at least as high as Spec-TP. It is conceivable that it is this raising of the VP that enables an object contained within VP to establish a relation to a licenser outside VP. Similarly, in (62) and (63) the embedded clause has probably moved to a Spec within the higher VP. As a result, a checking relation may be established between the higher V and the object inside the embedded clause.

Ura (1994) discusses an even more striking example of the phenomenon of long-distance licensing. As (64a) shows, an object inside a clause that is embedded under a nominal may optionally be marked with genitive case. The example in (64b) demonstrates that if there is no nominal above the clause, genitive marking of the object is impossible.

(64) *Japanese* (Ura 1994:367)

    a. John-ga   imooto-ga   piano-o/piano-no   hik-er-u
        John-NOM   sister-NOM   piano-ACC/piano-GEN   play-can-PRES
        toyuu   uwasa
        C   rumor
        'the rumor that John's sister can play the piano'

    b. John-ga   imooto-ga   piano-o/*piano-no   hik-er-u.
        John-NOM   sister-NOM   piano-ACC/piano-GEN   play-can-PRES
        'John's sister can play the piano.'

Ura proposes that the genitive case of the object in (64a) is checked by LF-movement of the object to Spec-DP. He further claims that in Japanese, multiple Specs are possible and that the object moves via the outer Spec of AgrSP (the DPs 'John' and 'sister' are assumed to occupy two other Specs of the same head).[15]

However, one might point out here that the position of the clause to the left of the nominal head suggests that the clause as a whole has raised to a Spec inside the nominal projection. In fact, the clause may have moved all the way to Spec-DP. Then it is possible that moving the clause is equivalent to moving the object, as far as the case checking of the object is concerned, and that this is what allows the object to appear in the genitive case, the case that is generally associated with Spec-DP.

Further evidence that the arguments may stay inside VP in Japanese comes from the distribution of numerals associated with the subject. As shown in (65a), the adverbial *kinoo* 'yesterday' may intervene between the subject and the numeral. Internal arguments, on the other hand, cannot do so, as we see from (65bc). They have to follow the numeral, as in (65d).

(65) *Japanese* (Nakayama & Koizumi 1991:305–306)

    a. Gakusei-ga   kinoo   3-nin   hon-o   kat-ta.
       student-NOM   yesterday 3-CLASS book-ACC   buy-PAST
       'Three students bought a book yesterday.'

    b.* Gakusei-ga   niku-o   3-nin   kit-ta.
       student-NOM   meat-ACC   3-CLASS   cut-PAST
       'Three students cut the meat.'

    c.* Gakusei-ga   kono   naihu-de   3-nin   niku-o   kit-ta.
       student-NOM   this   knife-with   3-CLASS meat-ACC   cut-PAST
       'Three students cut the meat with this knife.'

    d. Gakusei-ga   3-nin   kono   naihu-de   niku-o   kit-ta.
       student-NOM   3-CLASS this   knife-with   meat-ACC   cut-PAST
       'Three students cut the meat with this knife.'

If the numerals associated with the subject are still in the base position of the subject, the fact that internal arguments must follow the numeral suggests that the internal arguments in the sentences in (65) are spelled out in a position that is lower than the base position of the subject—in other words, that they are inside VP at Spell-Out. As for the movement of the subject that we see in (65a), I assume that it is triggered by a topic or focus feature. Focus and topic movement can also apply to internal arguments, as we shall see shortly. However, I think there is a solid basis for the conclusion that the formal licensing of an argument that has no topic or focus feature takes place within VP.

This means that even the subject may stay inside VP in head-final languages. Certain facts indicate that this claim is correct. In head-final languages, subjects are not islands, in sharp contrast to subjects in a non-head-final language like English. From the examples in (66) we see that *wh*-extraction is possible out of subjects in Japanese. Although Saito and Fukui (1998) point out that both (66a) and (66b) are slightly degraded because they involve extraction out of a complex DP, the crucial fact is that extraction out of a subject, as in (66a), is no worse than extraction out of an object, as in (66b).

(66) *Japanese* (Saito & Fukui 1998:463)

    a.? Nani-o$_i$ John-ga   [[[Mary-ga t$_i$ kat-ta   ]   koto-ga]
       what-ACC   John-NOM   Mary-NOM buy-PAST   fact-NOM
       mondai-da to] omotte-ru   no?
       problem-is C   think-PRES Q
       'What$_i$, John thinks that [the fact that Mary bought t$_i$] is a problem?'

b.? Nani-o_i   John-ga   [[Mary-ga   t_i kat-ta   ]   koto-o]
what-ACC   John-NOM   Mary-NOM   buy-PAST   fact-ACC
mondai-ni   site-ru   no?
problem-into   make-PRES   Q
'What_i, John is making an issue out of [the fact that Mary bought t_i]?

According to Saito and Fukui, (66a) is possible because, unlike subjects in English, subjects in Japanese are targets for adjunction. They further suggest that the reason for this contrast is that subjects are adjoined to IP in English but fully contained in the projection of I° in Japanese. This is not too different from my proposal that the subject stays in VP in Japanese but moves to a higher Spec in English.

In Turkish, it is OK to relativize out of a subject, as in (67a), but difficult to relativize out of an adverbial, as in (67b).

(67) *Turkish* (Kural 1997:502)

    a. [[Ahmet-in t_i   kır-ma-sı-nın   ]   ben-i   üz-düğ-u   ] bardak
        Ahmet-GEN   break-INF-3s-GEN   I-ACC   sadden-PTC-3s   glass
        'the glass that Ahmet's breaking (it) saddened me'

    b.*? [[Ahmet   t_i kır-dığ-i   için] Ayşe-nin   bağır-dığ-ı] bardak
        Ahmet   break-PTC-3s   for   Ayşe-GEN   yell-PTC-3s   glass
        'the glass that Ayşe yelled because Ahmet broke (it)'

The degraded status of (67b) shows that relativization does not apply freely in Turkish. Rather, it must be the case that subjects are more similar to complements than to adjuncts as far as extraction is concerned. Kural (1997) suggests that extraction out of subjects is possible because subjects are head-governed by the verb. This cannot mean, however, that subjects are complements; since a given verb can have only one complement, it must be the object and not the subject. However, in the analysis I have given of head-final structures, both objects and subjects sit in Spec positions inside VP. Hence, their structural relation to the lexical verb is fairly similar, and I will assume that it is this relation that makes extraction possible out of subjects as well as out of objects. In particular, if the subject in these languages is licensed inside VP, it is in the local domain of a V° head, even though it is not a sister of a V° head. Evidently, this is sufficient to prevent the highest projection of the subject DP from being a barrier.

Another indication that subjects stay relatively low in Turkish, also mentioned by Kural (1997), is the fact that negative polarity items in subject position are licensed by the negation that is suffixed to the verb. As demonstrated in (68), a negative polarity item cannot be A-moved out of the domain of the verb that bears the negation. Hence, the subject cannot have moved very high in (69), either.

(68) *Turkish* (Kural 1997:503)

     a. Kimse$_i$ Ahmet tarafından [t$_i$ uyu-du   ]   san-ıl-mı-yor.
         anyone   Ahmet by   sleep-PAST   think-PASS-NEG-PRES
         'No one is thought by Ahmet to have slept.'

     b.* Kimse$_i$ Ahmet tarafından [t$_i$ uyu-ma-dı   ]   san-ıl-ıyor.
         anyone   Ahmet by   sleep-NEG-PAST   think-PASS-PRES
         'No one is thought by Ahmet to have slept.'

(69) *Turkish* (Kural 1997:502)
     Kimse   uyu-ma-dı.
     anyone   sleep-NEG-PAST
     'No one slept.'

Kural's interpretation is that in the grammatical (68a) and (69) the subject must be c-commanded by the verb that bears the negation. This would not be the case if the complex verb is formed by head movement. The verb would then be at least as high as T°, and the subject would be in Spec-TP or higher.

But note that Benmamoun (1997) argues that a negative polarity item is licensed if it is the structural specifier of the head that hosts the negation or if it is c-commanded by the negation. He bases his argument on data from Moroccan Arabic, where negative polarity items also may precede the negation. On my analysis of head-final languages, the subject is contained in Spec-NegP, and no projection between the subject and NegP dominates the subject:

(70)

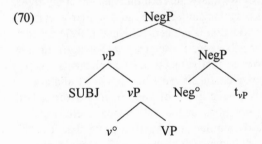

If Benmamoun is right, it is expected that the negation should be able to license a negative polarity subject in this configuration. In English, by contrast, there is always another head between the subject and the negation, so that the subject is never in the local domain of a following negation, hence the contrast between English and the head-final languages.[16]

Returning now to Lezgian, this language has a focus marker *-ni*, with the meaning 'also, too, even' (Haspelmath 1993:328), which can be attached to clausal constituents of various types. Interestingly, when *-ni* is attached to a nominal phrase, it only takes scope over that phrase. This is illustrated in (71).

(71) *Lezgian* (Haspelmath 1993:329)

Ada-n	širin	mec.i	q̃wan-ni	č'al.a-l	ǧi-da.
he-GEN	sweet	tongue.ERG	stone-even	speech-SUPESS	bring-FUT

'His sweet tongue will make even a stone talk.'

But when focus *-ni* is attached to an embedded verb, as in (72), it cannot pick out just the verb. Instead, it takes scope over the whole embedded clause.

(72) *Lezgian* (Haspelmath 1993:328)

Čan bade,	wuna	za-z	[kal-er	aca-z	]-ni
dear grandmother	you.ERG	I-DAT	cow-PL.ABS	milk-INF-too	

čir-da-ni?
teach-FUT-Q
'Dear granny, will you teach me to milk cows too?'

I will assume that when *-ni* is attached to a focused constituent, that constituent has moved to the Spec of *-ni*. In the absence of head movement of the verb, it must be the whole infinitival projection that has moved to Spec-*ni* in (72). If this projection contains all the arguments, it follows that it is the embedded clause as a whole that is focused. In other words, the fact that a verb in Lezgian cannot be picked out by the focus marker *-ni* speaks in favor of the analysis I have proposed of Lezgian clause structure.

The analysis proposed here also enables us to give an account of certain agreement phenomena in Hindi. As (73) illustrates, both nominal and verbal complements appear to the left of their respective selecting heads in Hindi. This suggests that Hindi belongs to the class of head-final languages, where movement may be triggered by c-features and not necessarily by case features.[17]

(73) *Hindi* (Mahajan 1990:90)

Raam-ne	roTii	khaa-nii	caah-ii.
Ram-ERG$_{MASC}$	bread$_{FEM}$	eat-INF.FEM	want-PAST.FEM.SG[18]

'Ram wanted to eat bread.'

The most conspicuous difference between Hindi and the languages we have already looked at has to do with morphology: in Hindi, the long suffix sequences that characterize many head-final languages are absent. This does not mean, however, that the basic structure of Hindi is necessarily very different from that of, say, Turkish or Japanese.

Hindi also differs from the languages discussed above in having object agreement on the verb. That is, object agreement is found with the forms that are usually referred to as 'perfective tenses'. Thus, we have object agreement in (73), where the verb that selects the nominal object is in the infinitive, but the higher verb 'want' is in the past tense, and also in (74a), where both the main verb and the auxiliary 'be' have past marking, but not in (74b), where the main verb has imperfective marking (i.e., non-finite present, according to Julien 2001).

Further, as we see, agreement on the verb covaries with the form of the subject, so that the subject has ergative marking when the verb agrees with the object but no marking when the verb agrees with the subject.

(74) *Hindi* (Mahajan 1990:72–73)

    a. Raam-ne   roTii   khaa-yii   th-ii.
       Ram-ERG$_{MASC}$ bread$_{FEM}$ eat-PAST.FEM.SG be-PAST.FEM.SG
       'Ram had eaten bread.'

    b. Raam   roTii   khaa-taa   th-aa.
       Ram$_{MASC}$ bread$_{FEM}$ eat-PRES.MASC.SG be-PAST.MASC.SG
       'Ram (habitually) ate bread.'

The Hindi agreement pattern is discussed by Mahajan (1990), who proposes that object agreement reflects movement of the object to Spec-AgrOP. The idea is that the past participle verb (which is also the form that passives are based on) is unable to assign structural case to the object, and, accordingly, the object of a verb with past (participle) morphology must move to Spec-AgrOP to receive case. The subject in these constructions has inherent case—the ergative—and may stay inside VP. When the verb has a non-perfective form, on the other hand, it assigns structural case to the object, but the subject must then move to Spec-AgrS and trigger subject agreement on the verb.

As an alternative, the specific object of a past participle may be marked with the dative marker *-ko*. Then the verb does not agree with any of its arguments, but shows up in the default form instead, as in (75).

(75) *Hindi* (Mahajan 1990:87)

    Siita-ne   laRkii-ko dekh-aa.
    Sita-ERG   girl-DAT   see-PAST.MASC.SG
    'Sita saw the girl.'

Mahajan (1990) suggests that a *ko*-marked object has also moved out of VP and that, just like an agreeing object, it is case marked in the Spec of an Agr-projection.

Obviously, Mahajan's analysis leaves a number of problems unaccounted for, such as the availability of inherent subject case only when the object is not case marked by the verb; the fact that both the main verb and the auxiliary show object agreement, even if AgrO is supposed to be lower than the auxiliary; the alternation between *ko*-marking and object agreement; and, finally, the phenomenon of 'long-distance' agreement illustrated in (73), where the object agrees not only with the lower verb but also with the higher verb 'want', of which it is not an argument.

The analysis I tentatively suggest is the following. The constructions in (74) are biclausal, as argued in Julien (2001) for all constructions with so-called aspectual auxiliaries, and both the auxiliary and the main verb are marked for tense. In (74b), both the subject and the object are licensed inside (the lower) VP, as I have claimed to be the normal situation in head-final languages. The lower VP moves to the Spec of the lower TP, so that the verb comes to immediately precede T°. The lower verbal projection then moves to the Spec of the auxiliary for c-checking, and, finally, the auxiliary VP moves to the higher Spec-TP. The result is shown in (76).

(76)

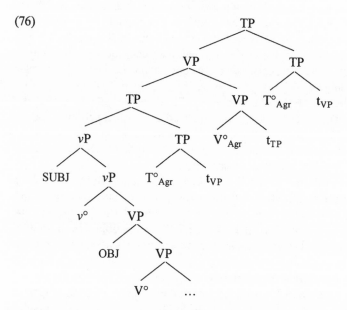

On the assumption that agreement features do not represent projecting syntactic heads (see the discussion of agreement markers in section 5.3), I propose that the agreement features reside in the T° head in Hindi. This means that in the configuration shown in (76), the subject in the highest Spec of VP is not dominated by VP and will thus be able to have its φ-features registered by the agreement features in T°, so that subject agreement is triggered on the base verb. Moreover, the features of the subject are also accessible to the higher T°. Accordingly, the φ-features displayed by the higher T° as well as those of the lower T° will be required to match the φ-features of the subject. The situation is exactly the same if the higher verb is lexical and not an auxiliary, so that we get the long-distance agreement exemplified in (73).

I have already suggested that it is precisely this relation between, on the one hand, the subject in the highest Spec of VP, and, on the other hand, the heads that VP enter into a Spec-head relation with that allows the subject to stay inside VP. In the configuration that is built up in head-final languages when the phrasal projection in the IP-domain move to higher Specs, the subject can stay inside VP and nevertheless be licensed from outside of VP. That is, the licensing of the subject is even in these languages dependent on the properties of the functional heads of the IP-domain. Now this assumption becomes crucial. Combined with the observation that participial (i.e., non-finite) T°s are often unable to license a subject (see Julien 2001 for arguments in favor of the claim that the participial ending represents a T°), it can explain why ergative marking of the subject goes with object agreement in Hindi. When the verb combines with a T° that is realized as a past participle, the subject is no longer licensed in the normal way. It is rescued by insertion of the ergative postposition, which, I assume, is in principle similar to the preposition insertion that gives rise to the auxiliary 'have' in many Indo-European languages (see Kayne 1993). Embedded in a PP, the subject becomes inaccessible to the agreement features in T°. The object, however, is licensed inside VP as usual, and, consequently, it is the φ-features of the *object* that are registered by the agreement features in T°, not the φ-features of the subject.

This means that I take the opposite view of Mahajan (1990), who suggests that object agreement arises because a verb realized as a perfect participle fails to case-mark the object, so that the object must move out of VP and be licensed by AgrO° instead. On my analysis, it is the subject and not the object that is exceptionally licensed in object agreement constructions.

Finally, when both arguments are marked with postpositions, as in (75), neither the φ-features of the subject nor the φ-features of the object are accessible to T, and in this case, what we get is default agreement.[19] Thus, it appears that the case and agreement patterns of Hindi are fully compatible with a view of Hindi as a language that has the same basic syntax as other head-final languages.

3.4.3   On verb movement in Japanese

In the preceding subsection I mentioned two authors who have both suggested that the arguments are normally licensed inside the VP in Japanese: Yanagida (1996) and Nakajima (1999). However, their proposals differ from the analysis I have presented of head-final languages in one important respect: they both claim that while the arguments may stay inside VP, the verb itself moves out. The issue of verb movement is what I investigate in this subsection. I base the discussion on Nakajima (1999), who supports his proposal with some arguments based on Otani and Whitman (1991) and Koizumi (1995), and I try to demonstrate that they are not necessarily convincing, so that my proposal, according to which the verb is contained in VP when the VP moves, is still tenable.

The argumentation in Otani and Whitman (1991) rests on the observation that sentences with object gaps allow both sloppy identity readings and strict identity readings. Consider the example in (77).

(77) *Japanese*   (Otani & Whitman 1991:346–347)
  a. John-wa   zibun-no   tegami-o   sute-ta.
      John-TOP   self-GEN   letter-ACC   discard-PAST
      'John$_i$ threw out self$_i$'s letters.'

   b. Mary-mo   [*e*]   sute-ta.
      Mary-also   discard-PAST
      'Mary$_i$ also threw out self$_i$'s letters'
  or 'Mary also threw out John's letters.'

The empty element in (77b) appears to give the same effect as VP-ellipsis in English, which is exemplified below:

(78) *English*
   a. John$_i$ threw away his$_i$ letters.
   b. Mary did [$_{VP}$ *e*], too.

The reply in (78b) could mean that Mary threw away John's letters (the strict identity reading) or that Mary threw away Mary's letters (the sloppy identity reading). Constructions with subject gaps, however, allow only the strict identity reading.[20] Otani and Whitman (1991) therefore conclude that the presence of an empty DP anaphor alone does not make the sloppy identity reading available. They propose instead that (77b) contains a phonologically empty VP, just like (78b). More precisely, the empty element in (77b) is taken to be a VP anaphor. Then there are two options at LF: either this VP is treated as a copy of the VP in (77a), which gives the strict identity reading, or the variables of the empty VP are taken to be bound within the clause, in which case we get the sloppy identity reading (see Otani & Whitman 1991 for technical details).

If there really is an empty VP in (77b), the verb must have moved overtly out of VP. However, Hoji (1998) argues that Japanese null object constructions of the type in (77b) do not allow sloppy identity readings to the same extent as VP ellipsis in English and, accordingly, that null object constructions do not provide evidence that the verb has moved out of VP. He offers the following example:

(79) *Japanese* (Hoji 1998:131)
   a. John-wa   zibun(zisin)-o   nagusame-ta.
      John-TOP   self-ACC   console-PAST
      'John$_i$ consoled himself$_i$.'

   b. Bill-mo [*e*]   nagusame-ta.
      Bill-also   console-PAST
  # 'Bill$_i$ consoled himself$_i$ too.'

As Hoji (1998) points out, on the empty VP analysis we would expect the sloppy identity reading to be allowed in (79b), which is not the case.

Moreover, Hoji (1998) demonstrates that the locality effect found with VP ellipsis is sometimes absent from Japanese null object constructions. The locality effect of VP ellipsis is demonstrated in (80).

(80) *English* (Hoji 1998:128)

    a. John$_i$ saw his$_i$ mother, and Mary knew that Bill did [$_{VP}$ *e*] too.

    b. Mary knew that Bill saw Bill's mother.

    c.# Mary knew that Bill saw Mary's mother.

The second conjunct in (80a) can get the reading in (80b), but not the reading in (80c). In the following Japanese example, a similar effect obtains:

(81) *Japanese* (Hoji 1998:136)

    a. John-wa   zibun-no gakusei-o   suisensi-ta.

        John-TOP   self-GEN   student-ACC recommend-PAST

        'John$_i$ recommended his$_i$ own student.'

    b. Mary-wa   Bill-mo   [*e*]   suisensi-ta   to   omottei-ta.

        Mary-TOP   Bill-also   recommend-PAST C   think-PAST

   # 'Mary$_i$ thought that Bill recommended her$_i$ student.'

As we see, the non-local sloppy reading is disallowed in (81b). However, if *mo* 'also' is replaced by the nominative marker *ga*, this reading becomes available:

(82) *Japanese* (Hoji 1998:136)

    a. John-wa   zibun-no gakusei-o   suisensi-ta.

        John-TOP   self-GEN   student-ACC recommend-PAST

        'John$_i$ recommended his$_i$ own student.'

    b. Mary-wa Bill-ga   [*e*]   suisensi-ta   to   omottei-ta.

        Mary-TOP   Bill-NOM   recommend-PAST C   think-PAST

        'Mary$_i$ thought that Bill recommended her$_i$ student.'

In this respect, the Japanese null object construction is clearly not comparable to the English VP ellipsis.

    The alternative proposal that Hoji (1998) advances is that the null object in Japanese is an empty element whose content is supplied by the context. This allows sloppy identity readings, as well as strict identity readings. A final observation that supports this analysis is that Japanese null objects also allow an unspecified reading, as in the following example:

(83) *Japanese* (see Hoji 1998:143)

    a. John-wa   zibunzisin-o   suisensi-ta.

        John-TOP   self-ACC   recommend-PAST

        'John recommended himself.'

    b. Bill-mo [*e*]   suisensi-ta,   dare-ka sira-na-i   kedo.

        Bill-also   recommend-PAST who-Q knew-NEG-PRES but

        'Bill also recommended (somebody), but I don't know who.'

In the English VP ellipsis construction, a continuation as in (84b) is clearly not possible:

(84) *English*
    a.   John recommended himself.
    b. # Bill did [$_{VP}$ *e*] too, but I don't know who.

In short, there seems to be plenty of support for Hoji's (1998) claim that null object constructions in Japanese should not be analyzed on a par with VP ellipsis.

    The second argument that Nakajima (1999) adduces in favor of the verb movement hypothesis is taken from Koizumi (1995) and has to do with cleft constructions. The claim is that the cleft construction in (85a) is derived from the non-cleft in (85b):

(85) *Japanese* (Nakajima 1999:90)
    a.

Mary-ga	age-ta	no	wa	John-ni	ringo-o	mittu
Mary-NOM	give-PAST	N	TOP	John-DAT	apple-ACC	three

       da.
       be.PRES
       'What Mary gave is three apples to John.'

    b.

Mary-ga	John-ni	ringo-o	mittu	age-tada.
Mary-NOM	John-DAT	apple-ACC	three	give-PAST

       'Mary gave three apples to John.'

On this analysis, the string made up of the indirect and the direct object is taken to be clefted out of the original clause, leaving the subject and the (inflected) verb behind. It is then argued that the only way in which the two objects can be one constituent, eligible for movement, is if they are contained in a VP that has been vacated by the verb.

    This argumentation would be convincing if it were clear that the cleft construction is derived as suggested. But notably, the construction in (85a) looks similar to English pseudo-clefts, where a copula links a free relative clause and some other constituent. As we see from (86), phrases of various categories can appear as the second conjunct in a pseudo-cleft construction.

(86) *English* (after Heycock & Kroch 1999; Svenonius 1994b)
    a. [What he promised] was [$_{CP}$ to reform himself].
    b. [What Mary was] was [$_{AP}$ proud of herself].
    c. [What Fiona bought] was [$_{DP}$ that ancient dictionary].
    d. [What we want] is [$_{SC}$ the dog fluent in Italian].
    e. [What I really hated] was [$_{SC}$ Zeke on the harmonica].

I will assume that the nominalized topicalized part of the Japanese cleft construction corresponds to the free relatives in (86a–e). Notably, the latter are also clearly nominal, as the following demonstrates:

(87) [What Fiona bought] looked expensive.

The only puzzle that (85a) presents, when compared to English, is the category of the second conjunct. It is possible, though, that it is a small clause. If it were a VP, some additional mechanism must be postulated to account for (88), where the dative argument goes to the topicalized part, instead of being clefted along with the direct object, as in (86a).

(88) *Japanese* (Oka 1996:382)
     John-ga   Mary-ni   tanon-da-no-wa   [PRO Bill-o   hihansuru
     John-NOM   Mary-DAT   ask-PAST-N-TOP   Bill-ACC criticize
     yooni] da.
     to.do   be.PRES
     'What John asked Mary to do was criticize Bill.'

Hence, the analysis suggested by Nakajima (1999) of the Japanese cleft construction is not necessarily correct. Instead, it is likely that Japanese cleft constructions can be subsumed under an analysis like that of Heycock and Kroch (1999), who argue that pseudoclefts are a type of equative constructions. For them, the two constructions in (89) are essentially the same:

(89) *English* (Heycock & Kroch 1999:382)
     a. Fiona's only purchase was that ancient dictionary.
     b. What Fiona bought was that ancient dictionary.

I will not go into the details of the cleft constructions here; I will only note that if they can be analyzed along the lines just suggested, they do not provide clear evidence for a verb movement analysis of Japanese.

     The final argument presented by Nakajima (1999) as support for the verb movement analysis of Japanese is also from Koizumi (1995), and it is based on coordination constructions like the one shown in (90).

(90) *Japanese* (Nakajima 1999:91)
     Mary-ga   ringo-o   2-tu   to   Nancy-ga   banana-o
     Mary-NOM   apple-ACC   2-CLASS   and   Nancy-NOM banana-ACC
     3-bon   tabe-ta.
     3-CLASS   eat-PAST
     'Mary ate two apples, and Nancy three bananas.'

Since the empty verb in the first conjunct is necessarily identical to the overt verb in the second conjunct, Nakajima (1999) claims that (90) is a case of across-the-board extraction. Since it follows from this assumption that the verb must have moved out of the first conjunct altogether, the construction is seen as evidence that the verb does indeed raise out of VP overtly in Japanese.

Notably, there are other ways to analyze the coordination structure in (90). In the terminology of Wilder (1997), it is an example of *backward deletion*, whereby material appearing in the final conjunct is deleted from one or several nonfinal conjuncts. The main proposal of Wilder (1997) is that cases of ellipsis associated with coordination structures should not be analyzed in terms of across-the-board movement or by postulating that conjuncts only consist of what is overt. He points out that the idea of across-the-board movement is developed with the sole purpose of handling cases of shared constituents in coordination structures. One example is given below:

(91) *English* (Wilder 1997:61)
    a. Mary came in and sat down.
    b. Mary$_i$ I° [$_{VP}$ t$_i$ came in] and [$_{VP}$ t$_i$ sat down]

If the sentence in (91a) involves coordination of VPs—what Wilder refers to as the 'small conjunct' hypothesis—the subject must be the head of two chains simultaneously, bearing a relation to one trace inside each VP, as indicated in (91b). Dependencies of this form are not assumed to exist outside of coordination. Because of this, and because they are very problematic for syntactic theory in general, it would be better to do without them.

Wilder's (1997) proposal is that only CPs and DPs can be coordinated, and that seemingly smaller coordinates result from deletion of elements inside one or more of the conjuncts. This approach is able to explain cases that are hard for 'small conjunct' analyses to tackle. For example, Larson (1988) suggested that constructions like (92a) are formed by coordination of two small VPs, out of which the verb has moved so that only the two internal arguments are left behind. This analysis is shown in (92b). For comparison, Wilder's deletion analysis is shown in (92c).

(92) *English* (see Wilder 1997:85)
    a. John offered, and Mary gave, a gold Cadillac to Billy Schwartz.
    b. [$_{IP}$ John [$_{VP}$ offered t$_{VP}$]] and [$_{IP}$ Mary [$_{VP}$ gave t$_{VP}$]] [$_{VP}$ a gold Cadillac [t$_V$ to Billy Schwartz]]
    c. [$_{CP}$ John offered ~~a gold Cadillac to Billy Schwartz~~] and [$_{CP}$ Mary gave a gold Cadillac to Billy Schwartz]

In this particular example, the two analyses do equally well. However, there are cases where the 'small conjunct' analysis gets into serious trouble. Consider (93), where the missing part of the first conjunct consists of the main verb plus the verb and part of the object of a relative clause modifying the object of the main verb.

(93) *German* (Wilder 1997:85)

Er	hat	einen	Mann,	der	drei ___,	und
he	has	a	man	who	three	and
sie	hat	eine	Frau,	die	vier Katzen besitzt,	gekannt.
she	has	a	woman	who	four cats owns	known

'He knew a man who owns three cats, and she knew a woman who owns four cats.'

In no theory can the missing material be claimed to be a constituent. But on the deletion approach, the analysis is straightforward: the relevant material is simply not pronounced in the first conjunct, since it can be recovered from the second conjunct. A similar example involving DP-coordination in English is added in (94). As we see, the same reasoning applies as for the previous example.

(94) *English* (Wilder 1997:86)

[$_{DP}$ a positively ___] and [$_{DP}$ a negatively charged electrode]

Wilder (1997) further argues that backward deletion is a PF operation which is governed by the following conditions:

(95) *Conditions on backward deletion* (see Wilder 1997)
   a. An ellipsis site is right-peripheral in its domain [= its conjunct].
   b. The phonological forms of the deleted item and the licensing item are identical.
   c. The relation of an antecedent to its domain is identical to the relation of the ellipsis site to its domain.

On this analysis, (90) is a coordination of two CPs. Since they have identical final constituents, the conditions for backward deletion are met; accordingly, backward deletion applies at PF, so that only the final conjunct has its verb pronounced. (To be precise, on the Late Insertion approach which I have assumed, this must mean that phonological material is inserted in the second verb but not in the first verb.)[21]

To sum up, we have seen that the arguments that have been advanced in favor of the hypothesis that the verb moves out of VP in Japanese can all be disputed. Hence, I will maintain that the verb does not move in head-final languages, including Japanese. Instead, the whole VP moves to the left of T° and other inflectional markers.

3.4.4 Movement to the CP-domain

The foregoing discussion has given the impression that movement of complements to Spec is the only movement process that operates in the syntax of head-final languages. This is however not the case. The correct generalization is that the *unmarked* word order of head-final languages appears to be derived solely by means of successive movements of complements to Spec. This is what distinguishes head-final languages from other language types. But notably, in most verb-final languages the constituents of the clause may appear in various marked orders, which must result from other movement operations. In particular, it appears that many verb-final languages make extensive use of movement to the topic and focus positions that are found in the CP-domain (Rizzi 1997). Sometimes these movements may blur the head-finality of the language and even lead people to claim that the language has a flat structure. In reality, what is going on is, I think, massive phrasal movement to the CP-domain.

In (96) I show the structure that Rizzi (1997) proposes for the left periphery of the clause—that is, for the CP-domain. We see that according to his proposal, the sequence of clausal heads above IP (where IP is shorthand for the sequence of modal, aspectual, and temporal heads; cf. Cinque 1999) is, from the bottom up, a finite head, one or several topic heads, a focus head, another set of topic heads, and, finally, a head that encodes the illocutionary force of the clause.

(96)

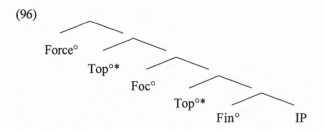

It appears that in head-final languages, smaller or larger constituents may be attracted from the lower part of the clause to the Spec positions within the CP-domain, in particular to the focus position Spec-FocP and the topic positions Spec-TopP. Presumably, this movement is triggered by focus and topic features that may be present on the moved constituents. An example is given in (97).

(97) *Lezgian*   (Haspelmath 1993:303)
    Am$_i$ ni-waj   [t$_i$ aq̃wazar-iz] že-da?
    he.ABS   who-ADEL   stop-INF   can-FUT
    'Who will be able to stop him?'

According to Haspelmath (1993:303), the situation here is that "the argument of the main verb is in the middle of the subordinate clause." However, lowering of the matrix subject into the subordinate clause is not likely to be possible. I therefore assume that it is the embedded object that has moved, as indicated. Since topics (the entity that the sentence is about) represent old information, whereas focused elements represent new or non-presupposed information (see, e.g., Lambrecht 1994, Rizzi 1997), I will assume that the object in (97) is in a topic position. It is the interrogative subject that is the focus in this construction; hence, it is likely that the subject sits in Spec-FocP. This means that the object must be in a higher position, in Spec-TopP.

In the following Turkish example, both the direct and the indirect object have come to precede the subject as a result of topic movement:

(98) *Turkish* (Kornfilt 1997:205)
    Kitab-ı   Ali-ye   Hasan dün   ver-di.
    book-ACC Ali-DAT Hasan yesterday give-PAST
    'As for the book, and as for Ali, Hasan gave it to him yesterday.'

These facts are consistent with Rizzi's (1997) proposal that there are multiple Top° heads immediately below the highest head Force°—each of which provides a landing site for a topicalized constituent in its Spec.

The same ordering of arguments is seen in the following Lezgian example:

(99) *Lezgian* (Haspelmath 1993:151)
    Za-z   axtin juǧ   Allah.di hič   ta-x̂u-raj.[22]
    I-DAT   such   day.ABS Allah.ERG never NEG-give-OPT
    'May God never give me such a day.'

Haspelmath (1993) gives no indication of the discourse-related properties of this sentence. However, he states (Haspelmath 1993:301) that word order in Lezgian is "determined by information structure rather than by grammatical relation." In particular, it is generally the case that given information precedes new information. This suggests that movements to the focus position and to the higher topic positions play an important role in Lezgian syntax. It is precisely these movements that would cause given information (topics) to precede new information (focus), often in such a way that arguments appear in non-canonical order.

Notably, the movements just illustrated cannot have been triggered by c-features: the constituents in Spec-TopP and Spec-FocP are not the complements of the respective heads. I will hypothesize that in head-final languages, a head will not attract its complement to its Spec for c-checking if some other constituent is required to appear in the Spec position. Thus, in the CP-domain the c-features are normally overridden by the topic and focus features, so that only a constituent marked as topic can be attracted to Spec-TopP, and only a constituent marked as focus can be attracted to Spec-FocP. C-checking must then presumably be done by feature movement.

Of all head-final languages, Japanese is perhaps most extensively discussed in the syntactic literature. The various non-canonical word orders in Japanese have also received a fair amount of attention, under the label of 'scrambling'. A classification of 'scrambling' in Japanese is found in Oka (1996). Oka notes, following Tada (1993), that there are three types, which he terms 'short scrambling', 'medium scrambling', and 'long scrambling', respectively. In short scrambling, a clause-internal operation, the moved constituent appears immediately to the right of the subject. In medium scrambling, also a clause-internal operation, the landing site is to the left of the subject. Finally, in long scrambling, an element is moved from an embedded clause into a higher clause.

What has puzzled many researchers is that Japanese scrambling seems to have both A- and A'-properties. I think it can be shown that argument dislocation with A-like properties is topic movement, whereas dislocation showing only A'-properties is focus movement.

The basic order of a double object construction, which is S IO DO V, was shown in (53). The two clause-internal scrambled orders are shown in (100) below, and long scrambling, which operates across clause boundaries, is shown in (101).

(100) *Japanese* (Miyagawa 1997:1)

a. John-ga   piza-o$_i$ Mary-ni   t$_i$ age-ta.
   John-NOM   pizza-ACC   Mary-DAT   give-PAST
   'John gave Mary pizza.'

b. Piza-o$_i$ John-ga   Mary-ni   t$_i$ age-ta.
   pizza-ACC   John-NOM   Mary-DAT   give-PAST
   'John gave Mary pizza.'

(101) *Japanese* (Takahashi 1993:666)

Pizza-o$_i$ John-wa   [Mary-ga   naze [Jennifer-ga t$_i$ tabe-ta   to]
pizza-ACC   John-TOP   Mary-NOM   why Jennifer-NOM eat-PAST   C
it-ta   to]   omotte-ru   no?
say-PAST C   think-PRES   Q
'Why does John think that Mary said that Jennifer ate pizza?'

Oka (1996) further demonstrates that long scrambling has all the characteristics of A'-movement; that is, movement to a position which is not a designated argument position, in contrast with A-movement, which is movement to a designated argument position (these notions largely correspond to L-related and non-L-related; see Chomsky 1993). Long scrambling in Japanese yields Weak Crossover and Strong Crossover effects, it allows reconstruction, and it does not feed anaphor binding. Hence, the A'-nature of long-distance movement in Japanese seems to be unquestionable.[23]

The so-called medium scrambling, by contrast, may display both A- and A'-properties. It yields Strong Crossover effects, it reconstructs, but does not necessarily give Weak Crossover effects, and it can feed anaphor binding. In Tada (1993) it is concluded that medium scrambling has a mixed status. Oka (1996) proposes instead that medium scrambling is a cover term for two types of movement, one with A- and one with A'-properties (as later argued by Miyagawa 1997).

Notably, it was pointed out already by Lasnik and Stowell (1991) that there exist two classes of A'-dependencies: one class induces Weak Crossover effects, and one doesn't. As Lasnik and Stowell showed, the Weak Crossover effect arises whenever a trace or a pronoun is locally A'-bound by a true quantifier phrase. If the A'-binder is not a true quantifier phrase, on the other hand, there is no Weak Crossover effect.

It was also noted by Lasnik and Stowell (1991) that *topicalization* (topic movement) gives the latter type of A'-dependency. This point is also made by Rizzi (1997), who argues that in some languages, like Italian, topic movement does not involve an operator at all. Instead, the topic is co-indexed with a clitic and thereby with a clitic trace, which represents the position with which the topic is ultimately associated:

(102) *Italian*   (Rizzi 1997)
    [Il   tuo   libro]$_i$, lo$_i$ ho   comprato t$_i$.
    the   your   book   it   have.1s bought

In other languages, topic movement does involve an operator, according to Rizzi (1997). For example, for English topic movement constructions Rizzi proposes the analysis shown in (103).

(103) *English*   (Rizzi 1997)
    Your book$_i$, O̶p$_i$ I bought t$_i$.

The empty operator in (103) is taken to be an anaphoric operator binding a null constant. The function of this operator is to connect the null constant to an antecedent. Hence, there is no quantification involved and, accordingly, no Weak Crossover effect.[24]

In fact, it can be shown that topic movement exhibits exactly the set of properties that is found with medium scrambling—that is, movement to clause-initial position—in Japanese. Topic movement gives Strong Crossover effects, but no Weak Crossover effects, and it allows both anaphor binding and reconstruction. Focus movement, on the other hand, is quantificational, as demonstrated by Rizzi (1997), so that it displays all the properties normally associated with A'-movement. The properties of topic and focus movement are illustrated in (104)–(107).[25]

(104) *Weak Crossover*
    a.   John$_i$, his$_i$ mother praised t$_i$.   TOPIC
    b. * JOHN$_i$, his$_i$ mother praised t$_i$.   FOCUS

(105) *Strong Crossover*
    a. * [John$_i$'s mother]$_j$, he$_i$ visited often t$_j$.   TOPIC
    b. * [JOHN$_i$'S MOTHER]$_j$, he$_i$ visited often t$_j$.   FOCUS

(106) *Reconstruction*
    a.   [A picture of himself$_i$]$_j$, John$_i$ was eager to have t$_j$.   TOPIC
    b.   [A PICTURE OF HIMSELF$_i$]$_j$, John$_i$ was eager to have t$_j$.   FOCUS

(107) *Anaphor binding*

    a.   [For John$_i$]$_j$, Mary made a picture of himself$_i$ t$_j$.   TOPIC

    b. * [FOR JOHN$_i$]$_j$, Mary made a picture of himself$_i$ t$_j$.   FOCUS

It is likely that the reason the status of medium scrambling has been hard to pin down is that movement to a clause-initial position can be either topic or focus movement. If it is topic movement, we see certain properties which are normally associated with A-movement, such as anaphor binding and absence of Weak Crossover effects. If it is focus movement, on the other hand, it shows the full range of typical A'-properties.

As for the so-called short scrambling, which moves an element to a position immediately following the subject, Oka (1996) claims that it has only A-properties. It gives no crossover effects, and it does not reconstruct, but it feeds anaphor binding. Hence, it is possible that the order DO IO can be derived by means of A-movement.[26] In some cases, however, short scrambling clearly has A'-properties (see, e.g., Miyagawa 1997). I will assume that in these cases, the 'scrambled' constituent has been focus moved, as suggested by Miyagawa (1997), and that it follows the subject because the subject has moved to Spec-TopP, which is, of course, a natural thing for subjects to do.

The idea that argument movement in Japanese is driven by focus and topic features has already been put forth in Yanagida (1996).[27] As noted above, her proposal differs from mine as far as verb movement is concerned. She assumes that there is movement of T° to C°, followed by raising of VP to Spec-CP; topicalized and focused constituents originating inside VP then move to higher Specs within CP. More precisely, she claims that topics move to the highest Spec, whereas focused constituents move to a Spec between the topic position and the VP.

Except for the question of verb movement, Yanagida's analysis is identical to the claim I have made about head-final languages in general. We will now look at some of the evidence she presents.

First, an adverb like *hayaku* 'quickly' may precede all arguments of the verb, including the subject, as in (108a). Yanagida (1996) concludes from this that the subject, like the other arguments, may stay inside VP. She assumes that the adverb is a VP adverb, which presumably is moved along when the VP raises.

(108) *Japanese* (Yanagida 1996:287)

    a.

Hayaku	Jiroo-ga	sono	tegami-o	yon-da.
quickly	Jiroo-NOM	that	letter-ACC	read-PAST

       'Quickly Jiroo read that letter.'

    b.

Jiroo-ga	hayaku	sono	tegami-o	yon-da.
Jiroo-NOM	quickly	that	letter-ACC	read-PAST

       'Jiroo read that letter quickly.'

As shown in (108b), the celerative adverb may also follow the subject. In the approach I am endorsing here, the adverb in (108ab) is generated in a Spec position in the lower part of IP. Consequently, (108a) is not hard evidence that the subject can be inside VP in surface syntax, but it does not contradict this claim, either. In (108b), the subject must have left at least the lower part of IP.

Interestingly, an object can also follow or precede a celerative adverb, as demonstrated in (109).[28]

(109) *Japanese* (Yanagida 1996:285)
  a. Taroo-wa   hayaku   sono   tegami-o   yon-da.
     Taroo-TOP   quickly   that   letter-ACC   read-PAST
     'Taroo quickly read that letter.'

  b. Taroo-wa   sono   tegami-o   hayaku   yon-da.
     Taroo-TOP   that   letter-ACC   quickly   read-PAST
     'Taroo read that letter quickly.'

If the object has a focus marker, on the other hand, it must precede the celerative adverb, as demonstrated in (110). This would follow if focused elements move to Spec-FocP, as I have claimed. The order in (110b) can then only be derived by topicalizing the adverb, which is relatively bad.

(110) *Japanese* (Yanagida 1996:286)
  a. Taroo-wa   sono   tegami-wa   hayaku   yon-da,   keredo ano
     Taroo-TOP   this   letter-FOC   quickly   read-PAST   but   that
     tegami-wa   hayaku   yoma-na-katta.
     letter-FOC   quickly   read-NEG-PAST
     'Taroo read this letter fast, but he didn't read that letter fast.'

  b.?* Taroo-wa   hayaku   sono   tegami-wa   yon-da,   keredo
       Taroo-TOP   quickly   this   letter-FOC   read-PAST   but
       hayaku   ano   tegami-wa   yoma-na-katta.
       quickly   that   letter-FOC   read-NEG-PAST
       'Taroo read that letter fast, but he didn't read that letter fast.'

Note that the focus marker *wa* is identical to the topic marker. However, it has been known since Kuno (1973) that the marker *wa* in Japanese has two different functions. Hence, the first *wa* in (110) marks the topic, and the second *wa* marks the focus. I assume that these markers are generated in Top° and Foc°, respectively.[29]

Having thus established that clause-internal fronting operations can move an element to focus or topic positions, we will take another look at movement across clause boundaries. As already noted, so-called long-distance scrambling in Japanese appears to be focus movement. More precisely, focused elements, but not topics, can be extracted out of a finite clause. But notably, it is possible to extract *two* constituents from an embedded clause and move them to the front of the matrix clause. Moreover, the fronted constituents can appear in either order, as shown in (111).

(111) *Japanese* (Saito & Fukui 1998:443–444)

a. Bill-ga   [Mary-ga   John-ni   sono   hon-o   watasi-ta
   Bill-NOM   Mary-NOM   John-DAT   that   book-ACC   hand-PAST
   to]   it-ta.
   C   say-PAST
   'Bill said that Mary handed that book to John.'

b. John-ni$_i$ sono hon-o$_j$ Bill-ga   [Mary-ga t_i t_j watasi-ta
   John-DAT   that book-ACC   Bill-NOM   Mary-NOM   hand-PAST
   to]   it-ta.
   C   say-PAST
   'Bill said that Mary handed that book to John.'

c. Sono hon-o$_j$ John-ni$_i$ Bill-ga   [Mary-ga t_i t_j watasi-ta
   that   book-ACC   John-DAT Bill-NOM   Mary-NOM   hand-PAST
   to]   it-ta.
   C   say-PAST
   ''Bill said that Mary handed that book to John.'

The possibility of applying long-distance scrambling to two elements of the embedded clause simultaneously seems to cast doubt on the claim that long-distance scrambling in Japanese is focus movement. If every clause has only one Spec-FocP position (see Rizzi 1997), it follows that there can be only one focused element per clause and that the two fronted phrases in (111b) and (111c) cannot both have been focused.

I still think that my analysis can be defended, however. Recall that in the discussion of the cleft construction in (85a) I suggested that the reason why the direct and the indirect object can be clefted together is that the two objects together can move as one constituent, which I took to be a small clause. It is possible that a similar explanation can be offered for (111b) and (111c). Suppose that one object can somehow be adjoined to the other, so that a constituent is formed which is comparable to a small clause. Then (111b) and (111c) can be formed by focus movement of this constituent. The order variation may have to do with the alternative orders of the objects that was discussed earlier, so that if the adjunction operation applies to the IO DO order, we get a complex constituent [DO [IO]], and if the adjunction operation applies to the DO IO order, we get [IO [DO]].

A piece of data which can be taken as support for this analysis is found in Sakai (1994). He shows first that in a construction with multiple embeddings of finite clauses, it is OK to have a clause-internal fronting in the most deeply embedded clause and at the same time move a phrase from that clause to the front of the matrix clause, as in (112a). It is not possible, by contrast, to extract two phrases out of the most deeply embedded clause in such a way that one phrase ends up in the matrix clause and the other phrase ends up in an intermediate clause. This is shown in (112b).[30]

(112) *Japanese* (Sakai 1994:308–309)

    a. Boston-e$_i$ Masao-ga   [Kumiko-ga   [Tokyo-kara$_j$
        Boston-to   Masao-NOM Kumiko-NOM Tokyo-from
        Takashi-ga   t$_j$ t$_i$ it-ta   to] it-ta   to] omottei-ru.
        Takashi-NOM   go-PAST   C   say-PAST C   think-PRES
        'Masao thinks that Kumiko said that Takashi went from Boston to Tokyo.'

    b.* Boston-e$_i$ Masao-ga   [Tokyo-kara$_j$ Kumiko-ga
        Boston-to   Masao-NOM Tokyo-from   Kumiko-NOM
        [Takashi-ga t$_j$ t$_i$ it-ta   to] it-ta   to] omottei-ru.
        Takashi-NOM   go-PAST C   say-PAST C   think-PRES

According to Sakai, (112b) is blocked because there is only one escape hatch in the lower clause, and the two scrambled phrases cannot both move through this escape hatch. But we saw in (111) that two arguments can move out from an embedded clause if they stay together all the way. This suggests that the fronted phrases in (111b) and (111c) have indeed moved as one constituent. Then (112b) shows that a part of a complex focused constituent cannot be stranded in an intermediate position. This is precisely what we would expect.

If this approach is taken to apparent cases of multiple long-distance fronting, we can maintain that long-distance fronting is focus movement and, further, that not more than one constituent can be focus-moved out of a given finite clause. The latter is a limitation which probably derives from there being only one Foc° head per clause.

As a rounding-off of the discussion of focus and topic movement in Japanese, it is interesting to note that Japanese allows focusing of the VP if the VP is embedded under an auxiliary. This can be seen from (113), where the focus marker *wa*, which I take to be the realization of Foc°, follows immediately after the non-finite verb, and also from (114), where the non-finite VP precedes the subject which in turn precedes the auxiliary, which must mean that the lower VP has been extracted from the projection of the auxiliary.

(113) *Japanese* (McGloin 1987:178)
    Make   wa   shi-na-katta.
    lose   FOC do-NEG-PAST
    'I didn't LOSE.'

(114) *Japanese* (Kikuchi et al. 1994:144)
　　[Mary-o　　　naguri-sae]$_i$　John-ga　　　 t$_i$ si-ta.
　　Mary-ACC　 hit-even　　　John-NOM　　　do-PAST
　　'John even hit Mary.'

Just like in the case of Japanese, the movements that yield alternatives to the unmarked word order in Hindi are traditionally referred to as 'scrambling'. A discussion of scrambling in Hindi is found in Mahajan (1990, 1997). Mahajan (1990) states that scrambling can be movement to an L-related position or to an non-L-related position, where an L-related position is the specifier or comple-ment position of V° or of a head in the IP-domain, so that 'L-related' and 'non-L-related' roughly correspond to A and A', as already noted. There is reason to believe, however, that in the same way as in Japanese, the contrast has to do with topic versus focus. Consider the sentence in (115), which Mahajan gives as an example of movement of an argument to an L-related position (on his proposal, to Spec-TP).

(115) *Hindi* (Mahajan 1990:26)
　　Sab-ko$_i$　　　　unkii$_i$ bahin　pyaar　kar-tii　　　 th-ii.
　　everyone-DAT　 their　　sister　 love　 do-PRES.FEM　 be-PAST.FEM.SG
　　'Their$_i$ sister loved everyone$_i$.'

Mahajan's conclusion is based on the lack of Weak Crossover effects in this construction. But as we have seen, topic movement, which I have assumed, with Rizzi (1997), to be movement to Spec-TopP, has the A-like properties of not inducing Weak Crossover effects and allowing anaphor binding, even though it takes a constituent to a landing site within the CP-domain, so that it must be characterized as A'- or non-L-related movement. Hence, it is possible that the preposed object in (115) is in Spec-TopP.

As shown in (116) and (117), a similar fronting operation can feed anaphor binding, which is another indication that scrambling in Hindi can be movement to Spec-TopP.

(116) *Hindi* (Mahajan 1990:32–33)
a.*?? Apne$_i$　bacoN-ne　　　 Mohan-ko$_i$　ghar　　se　　nikaal
　　self's　 children-ERG　 Mohan-DAT　house　from　 throw
　　di-yaa.
　　give-PAST.MASC.SG
　　'Self's$_i$ children threw Mohan$_i$ out of the house.'

b. ? Mohan-ko$_i$　apne$_i$　bacoN-ne　　　ghar　　se　　nikaal
　　Mohan-DAT　self's　 children-ERG　 house　 from　 throw
　　di-yaa.
　　give-PAST.MASC.SG
　　'Self's$_i$ children threw Mohan$_i$ out of the house.'

(117) *Hindi* (Mahajan 1997:194)
a. ??? Ek duusre¡ ke   parivaarō-ne Siitaa ɔr   Raam-ko¡ bulaa-yaa.
   each other's   family-ERG   Sita   and Ram-DAT call-PAST.MASC.SG
   'Each other's families invited Sita and Ram.'

b.   Siitaa ɔr   Raam-ko¡ ek duusre¡ ke   parivaarō-ne bulaa-yaa.
     Sita   and Ram-DAT each other's   family-ERG   call-PAST.MASC.SG
     'Each other's families invited Sita and Ram.'

Mahajan (1990) also gives examples of fronted arguments that *do* induce
Weak Crossover effects, as in (118), where the fronted complex *wh*-phrase
cannot be coreferential with the pronoun inside the subject relative clause.

(118) *Hindi* (Mahajan 1990:51)
      [Apnii¡   kOn sii   kitaab]ⱼ [us   aadmii-ne¡ jis-ne   use*ⱼ
      self's   which   book$_{FEM}$ that   man-ERG   who-ERG   it
      parh liyaa] tⱼ   pheNk d-ii.
      read   throw give-PAST.FEM.SG
      'The man who read it threw away self's which book.'

Together with the fact that the subject can bind the anaphor inside the fronted
(object) *wh*-phrase, this indicates that the fronting has nothing but typical A'-
properties, which is expected under the present analysis: *wh*-elements cannot be
topics, but they can be focus-moved—that is, fronted to Spec-FocP. As we have
seen, focus movement has all the properties traditionally associated with A'-
movement.[31]

Mahajan (1990) states, on the background of the Hindi data, that contrary to
what was proposed by Webelhuth (1989), there can be no positions with 'mixed'
properties, positions which are not clearly either A-positions (L-positions) or A'-
positions (non-L-positions). Thus, "while an NP can show properties of being in
an L-position or of being in an non-L-position, it cannot simultaneously show
both" (Mahajan 1990:47). This translates into my framework as follows: a
fronted argument can be in Spec-TopP or in Spec-FocP, so that there is variation
among fronted arguments with respect to Weak Crossover and anaphor binding,
but, of course, no argument can be in both positions simultaneously. So when
Dayal (1994) points out that there is a type of scrambling in Hindi which has
some but not all of the properties that are typical of A'-movement, this is then
what I have identified as movement to Spec-TopP, which is A'-movement but
nevertheless different from, for example, focus movement.[32]

In most head-final languages, the preferred position for a focused constituent
is immediately before the verb (see Dezsó 1978, Herring 1990). This may be the
result of non-focused constituents having raised to the higher topic positions to
get out of the scope of the focus feature in Foc°.[33] Thus, a picture emerges of
head-final languages according to which they are heavily discourse configura-

tional (Kiss 1995); that is, in these languages the surface form of a clause will be largely determined by its place in the discourse.

The preverbal position is also where *wh*-phrases are often found in head-final languages, as in the following examples:

(119) *Lezgian* (Haspelmath 1993:421)
    Naq'   park.d-a   Kerim.a-z   tup   ni   ga-na?
    yesterday park-INESS Kerim-DAT ball.ABS who.ERG give-AOR
    'Who gave the ball to Kerim in the park yesterday?'

(120) *Turkish* (Kornfilt 1997:30)
    Dün   sinema-ya   hangi   öğrenci   git-ti?
    yesterday cinema-DAT which   student   go-PAST
    'Which student went to the movies yesterday?'

Alternatively, the *wh*-phrase may appear in initial position:

(121) *Lezgian* (Haspelmath 1993:423)
    [Šumud   lahaj   kurs.un-a   ]   student.di   k'el-zawa?
    how.many ORD   study.year-INESS student.ERG study-IMPF
    'In which year of study is the student?'

(122) *Turkish* (Kornfilt 1997:27)
    ? Ne-yi   Ahmet raf-a   koy-du?
    what-ACC   Ahmet shelf-DAT put-PAST
    'What did Ahmet put on the shelf?'

My proposal is that the difference between focus or *wh*-movement to clause-initial position and focus or *wh*-movement to preverbal position is that in the latter cases, but not in the former, non-focused constituents are moved to topic positions above FocP.

Interestingly, at least in Turkish, a fronted *wh*-phrase cannot co-occur with a focused constituent, as (123) demonstrates.

(123) *Turkish* (Kornfilt 1997:28)
    * Ne-yi   raf-a   AHMET   koy-du?
    what-ACC   shelf-DAT Ahmet   put-PAST
    'What did AHMET put on the shelf?'

This fact suggests that the clause-initial focus position and the preverbal focus position are one and the same and that in (123) the focused phrase and the *wh*-phrase compete for this single position. In other words, interrogative features are located in Foc°. This is not a novel proposal; the parallelism between focused and questioned constituents has been noted by many researchers (see, e.g., Rochemont 1986, Choe 1995, Rizzi 1997).

However, this idea goes against the popular belief that head-final languages lack *wh*-movement. For example, Kayne (1994:54), following Bach (1971), assumes that head-final languages generally have *wh* in situ, and he explains it as a consequence of Spec-CP being occupied by IP. What I have argued in the foregoing is that the movements of complements to Spec for c-checking that we find in head-final languages are restricted to the IP-domain. The specifier positions in the CP-domain are available as landing sites for various elements from within IP. Thus, Kayne's explanation does not go through in my model. But if the generalization that Kayne intends to explain is invalid anyway, there is of course no problem.

Kayne (1994:142 n. 22) points to Imbabura Quechua as being exceptional among head-final languages in having obligatory *wh*-movement to clause-initial position (see Cole 1985:27). A *wh*-question from Imbabura Quechua is shown in (124).

(124) *Imbabura Quechua*	(Cole 1985:17)
　　　Ima　　　alku-ta-taj　　Marya-ka　　chari-n?
　　　what　　dog-ACC-Q　　Maria-TOP　　have-3
　　　'What kind of dog does Maria have?'

Kayne suggests that the question marker *taj* that obligatorily follows the *wh*-phrase might be the realization of C°, so that we have direct evidence that IP has not moved to Spec-CP (only the *wh*-phrase has).

However, with the expanded CP-structure of Rizzi (1997), it is possible for several constituents to appear in the CP-domain simultaneously. In (124), it thus appears that both the *wh*-phrase and the topicalized subject have moved to the CP-domain. If my analysis of head-final languages is correct, what distinguishes Imbabura Quechua from the majority of head-final languages is that in Imbabura Quechua there is no movement to Spec positions above the fronted *wh*-phrase. Judging from (124), one might guess that the reason for this is that the question marker is the realization of Force°, since it precedes the topic. This would mean that the *wh*-phrase occupies the highest Spec within its clause.

If the polarity question marker *chu* is also a realization of Force°, the order in (125a) follows directly. The order in (125b) would then be derived by moving TopP to Spec-ForceP.

(125) *Imbabura Quechua*	(Cole 1985:15)
　　　a. Na-chu　　Juzi-ka　　Agatu-pi　　kawsa-n?
　　　　　NEG-Q　　José-TOP　　Agato-in　　live-3
　　　　　'Doesn't José live in Agato?'

　　　b. Kan-ta-ka　　　ufya-naya-n-chu?
　　　　　you-ACC-TOP　　drink-DESID-3-Q
　　　　　'Do you want to DRINK?'

Evidence against this analysis would be a construction where a topicalized constituent is followed by a *chu*-marked constituent that is not clause final. As far as I can see, no such example is given in Cole (1985).

The more common pattern in polarity questions in head-final languages is to have an interrogative marker which appears as the last element of the verbal word. Examples of run-of-the-mill polarity questions are given in (126)–(128).

(126) *Lezgian* (Haspelmath 1993:417)
    Wi   dust.uni-z   wiči-n   pul   žǧa-na-ni?
    you.GEN friend-DAT self-GEN money.ABS find-AOR-Q
    'Did your friend find his money?'

(127) *Japanese* (Yanagida 1996:284)
    Taroo-wa   Pari-de   tokei-o   kat-ta   ]   no?
    Taroo-TOP Paris-LOC watch-ACC buy-PAST   Q
    'Did Taroo buy a watch in Paris?'

(128) *Turkish* (Kornfilt 1997:5)
    Ahmet sinema-ya   git-ti   mi?
    Ahmet cinema-DAT go-PAST Q
    'Did Ahmet go to the cinema?'

Given what has already been said about the syntax of head-final languages, it is likely that these constructions are derived by moving a large constituent, presumably the whole IP, into the Spec-FocP, and that the interrogative suffix is the realization of a [Q] feature in the Foc° head (see Julien 2000 for more details).

Kornfilt (1997:5) notes that a sentence-final question particle has the whole sentence in its scope. This means, I assume, that in the default case the whole IP is associated with the [Q] feature, and, accordingly, the whole IP is attracted to the Spec of the question marker. But it is also possible to associate the [Q] feature with a smaller constituent. It will then be that constituent and not the whole IP that moves to Spec-FocP, and we get a construction where the question marker is not sentence-final, as in (125a) and below:

(129) *Turkish* (Kornfilt 1997:191)
    Kitab-ı   HASAN   mı Ali-ye   ver-di?
    book-ACC Hasan   Q   Ali-DAT give-PAST
    'Did HASAN give the book to Ali?'

In this polarity question, the questioned argument moves alone to Spec-FocP, leaving the non-questioned elements of IP behind. Further, in the model I am assuming here, the fact that the questioned argument is preceded by a non-questioned argument must mean that the latter has moved to Spec-TopP.

In the following Lezgian examples, it appears that IP has moved to Spec-FocP, so that the question marker is attached to the verb, as usual. However, in each example a phrase has escaped the constituent that ends up in Spec-FocP:

(130) *Lezgian* (Haspelmath 1993:300)
    Amma pul   gwa-ni wa-w?
    but   money.ABS be.at-Q you-ADESS
    'But do you have money?'

(131) *Lezgian* (Haspelmath 1993:300)
    Wa-z   či-da-ni   [zun   jif.i-z   wučiz   elüq'-zawa-t'a]?
    you-DAT know-FUT-Q I.ABS night-DAT why   bark-IMPF-COND
    'Do you know why I bark at night?'

If we assume, as the earlier discussion suggested, that there is obligatory movement of complements to Spec in all IP projections, then the only way to get out of an IP projection is to leave IP altogether. Hence, the postverbal elements in (130) and (131) must be in positions higher than IP but below Spec-FocP. Only a constituent in such a position will be able to stay behind if IP moves to Spec-FocP. The position in question is probably the lower Spec-TopP, as shown in (96). We will see later that this seems to be the position for backgrounded material, as compared to the higher topic position, which contains more salient elements. In any case, it is clear that the Q-marked constituent that has moved to Spec-FocP is not the complement of Foc°. Thus, we see again that the heads in the CP-domain do not always check the c-feature of their complements by moving their complements to their Specs, and, consequently, the projections within the CP-domain are not necessarily head-final.

The analysis I am proposing here is inspired by the analysis given by Kayne and Pollock (1998) for French subject inversion constructions of the type shown in (132). According to Kayne and Pollock (1998), (132a) is derived by movement of the subject to the lower Spec-TopP, followed by movement of the remnant IP to Spec-FocP. The *wh*-phrase is taken to be in the highest Spec of the CP-domain. Kayne and Pollock hypothesize that the *wh*-phrase passes through a Spec position in IP, thereby giving IP a [+FOCUS] feature by Spec-head agreement. This in turn triggers movement of IP to Spec-FocP. They also point out that if the subject in (132a) is in Spec-TopP, the marginal status of (132b) follows, since (non-specific) indefinites are not appropriate as topics.[34]

(132) *French* (Kayne & Pollock 1998)
    a. Qu'a   mangé Pierre?   b. ?? Qu'a   mangé quelqu'un?
       what-has eaten   Pierre   what-has eaten   somebody
       'What has Pierre eaten?'   'What has somebody eaten?'

A similar analysis also seems to go through for constructions like (133) and (134), which are *wh*-questions with a non-questioned argument following the verb.

(133) *Lezgian* (Haspelmath 1993:111)
Hiẋtin televizor k'an-zawa wa-z?
which television-ABS want-IMPF you-DAT
'What kind of TV set do you want?'

(134) *Lezgian* (Haspelmath 1993:150)
Wuč güzlemiš-in za, Širinbala?
what.ABS wait-HORT I.ERG Širinbala
'What shall I wait for, Širinbala?'

I will assume here that the whole IP has been pied-piped to Spec-FocP, thereby crossing the subject, which must have escaped out of IP, presumably to a lower topic position.[35]

We can now also explain why all *wh*-elements tend to line up in front of the verb when there is more than one *wh*-element in one clause, as in (135).

(135) *Turkish* (Kornfilt 1997:31)
a. Manzara-yı kim kim-e göster-di?
landscape-ACC who who-DAT show-PAST
'Who showed the landscape to whom?'

b.? Kim manzara-yı kim-e göster-di?
WHO landscape-ACC who-DAT show-PAST
'Who showed the landscape to whom?'

Kornfilt (1997:31) suggests that in this case, all *wh*-elements move to a preverbal position. This is not possible in the model I am assuming, however. Instead, what we see in (135) is probably that the whole IP is fronted to Spec-FocP and that non-questioned object has raised further to Spec-TopP, whereas the subject and the indirect object stay in their base positions inside VP.[36] The degraded status of (135b) shows, in my model, that non-questioned elements should preferably move to topic position and not stay in IP.

Notably, many languages where the unmarked word order is verb-final allow one or more constituents to appear to the right of the verb even in declarative clauses. Some examples are shown below:

(136) *Lezgian* (Haspelmath 1993:229)
Zun-ni q̃we-da Biliž.di-z q'wan.
I.ABS-also come-FUT Biliž-DAT up.to
'I, too, will come all the way to Biliž.'

(137) *Turkish* (Kornfilt 1997:206–307)

a. Ali-ye   kitab-ı   ver-di   Hasan.
   Ali-DAT   book-ACC   give-PAST   Hasan
   'He gave the book to Ali, Hasan.'

b. Kitab-ı   ver-di   Hasan Ali-ye.
   book-ACC   give-PAST   Hasan Ali-DAT
   'He gave the book to him, Hasan to Ali.'

These constructions could be derived in the same way as (132)–(134); that is, by movement of a constituent to the lower Spec-TopP followed by movement of the remnant IP to Spec-FocP. It is possible that the fronted IPs in (136)–(137) have a focus feature that gives the same effect as the interrogative features in the previous examples of non-verb-final order. That a focused IP can be fronted was shown already in (113) and (114).

As pointed out by Erguvanlí (1984) and Kural (1997), postverbal phrases in Turkish represent the background of the discourse, the context that is assumed by speaker and hearer in a given situation (what Kornfilt 1997:206 refers to as the *shared presuppositions*). I will propose that backgrounded material is located in the lower Specs in the CP-domain—that is, in the positions below Foc°. In Rizzi (1997) these positions are taken to be topic positions. However, the notions 'topic' and 'background' are closely related in that both refer to information that is already known by speaker and listener. Thus, it is conceivable that a slight modification of Rizzi's proposal is in place, and that 'background' is a more accurate term for the material in the lower Specs inside CP.

Postverbal constituents are also found in Japanese. From the account given by Shimojo (1995) it appears that the analysis just given for Turkish also may hold for Japanese. Shimojo states that postverbal elements should represent 'active' information—information that is focused in the consciousness of the discourse participants—and he gives the following example of a context where a postverbal element is acceptable:

(138) *Japanese* (Shimojo 1995:125)

a. Ken   osoi nee.   b. A   kimasi-ta   yo   Ken ga.
   Ken   late PRT   ah   come-PAST   PRT   Ken NOM
   'Ken is late.'   'Ah, there Ken comes.'

He also notes that the sentence in (138b) would be less natural without any foregoing mention of 'Ken'. I take this as an indication that the syntactic and discourse-functional properties of postverbal elements are the same in Japanese as in Turkish.[37]

Kural (1997) notes that postverbal constituents must have moved, since they are islands for overt and covert movement. He argues, against Kayne (1994), that postverbal constituents are right-adjoined to CP. However, the opacity of the postverbal constituent is expected also on my analysis. I argued earlier in this chapter that VP and the V-related projections in IP do not count as barriers, even if they raise to the Spec of the next higher projection, and also that arguments that stay inside VP are not necessarily islands. Thus, extraction is possible from subjects as well as from objects as long as they stay inside VP. But if a phrase moves out of VP to a Spec within the CP-domain, we would expect it to become an island. In addition, moving out of the background position implies moving to a focus or topic position. Since this is incompatible with background status, we have another explanation for the observed opacity of postverbal constituents.

Kural (1997) further claims that postverbal constituents take scope over preverbal constituents. If this were indisputably true, it would suggest that postverbal constituents are situated higher than the elements preceding the verb, and thus be strong support of Kural's analysis. But as Haider (1997) notes, the background status of postverbal elements can explain the scope effect. Belonging to the fixed background of the discourse, the postverbal phrases necessarily get a specific interpretation, which forces them to be outside the nuclear scope of a preverbal quantifier. This, and not the structural relation between the involved phrases, determines the LF-representation of these constructions.

Interestingly, as Kural (1997) also notes, an anaphor or pronoun in the postverbal constituent can be bound from preverbal position, as in the following:

(139) *Turkish* (Kural 1997:506)

a. Herkes$_i$ dün ara-mış [*pro*$_i$ anne-sin-i].
   everyone yesterday call-RP.PAST mother-3s-ACC
   'Everyone$_i$ called his$_i$ mother yesterday.'

b. Herkes$_i$ dün ara-mış birbir-in-i$_i$.
   everyone yesterday call-RP.PAST each.other-3s-ACC
   'Everyone called each other yesterday.'

According to Kural (1997), postverbal constituents reconstruct at LF whenever it is required by binding theory, while reconstruction is blocked elsewhere. We would then expect there to be no reconstruction if appropriate binding relations can be established in the surface structure. This means that if Kural's proposal is correct, a postverbal object should be able to bind into a preverbal subject. But as (140) demonstrates, this is not possible.

(140) *Turkish* (Murat Kural, personal communication)
* Birbir-ler-in-in anne-ler-i ara-dı adam-lar-ı.
  each.other-PL-3-GEN mother-PL-3s call-PAST man-PL-ACC
  'Each other's mothers called the men.'

Whereas the ungrammaticality of (140) requires some additional stipulation if Kural's (1997) analysis is adopted, it follows naturally from the analysis I am proposing. The object in (140) is lower than the subject both before and after movement, and consequently, binding by the object into the subject is impossible whether or not there is reconstruction. My analysis also predicts that a preverbal subject will be able to bind into a postverbal object, as in (139).

To see whether it is the surface positions or the base positions of the arguments that are relevant for the binding relations in (139) and (140) an example with a postverbal subject and a preverbal object must be considered. One such example is given in (141).

(141) *Turkish* (Murat Kural, personal communication)
[*pro*$_i$ anne-sin-i   ]   ara-dı   herkes$_i$/Mehmet$_i$.
his   mother-3s-ACC call-PAST everyone/Mehmet
'Everyone$_i$/Mehmet$_i$ called his$_i$ mother.'

If the postverbal subject in (141) is lower than the preverbal object, as I am assuming, the binding relation must be established before the fronting of the IP containing the object and the complex verb—in other words, there is reconstruction of the object to its base position below the subject. Hence, it is possible that reconstruction also applies in (139) and (140), so that the binding relations in the surface order do not tell us anything about the surface hierarchical relations.

The analysis just suggested also goes through for Hindi. Moreover, it appears that considerations of Hindi constructions with postverbal elements can add some more details to the analysis. Contrary to what Kural (1997) claims for Turkish, Mahajan (1997) argues, on the basis of binding facts, that postverbal constituents in Hindi are situated in a lower position than preverbal constituents. Consider the examples (142)–(143), which show that whereas a preverbal constituent can bind into a postverbal constituent, the converse is not possible.

(142) *Hindi* (Mahajan 1997:192)
Raam-ne harek aadmii-ko$_i$ lotaa-ii   uskii$_i$ kitaab.
Ram-ERG every man-DAT   return-PAST.FEM.SG his   book$_{FEM}$
'Ram returned every man$_i$ his$_i$ book.'

(143) *Hindi* (Mahajan 1997:190)
* Raam-ne uske$_i$ maalik-ko d-ii   harek kitaab$_i$.
Ram-ERG its   owner-DAT give-PAST.FEM.SG every book$_{FEM}$
'Ram gave every book$_i$ to its$_i$ owner.'

The analysis suggested by Mahajan (1997) is that the verb has moved to Agr°$_{IO}$, the indirect object to Spec-AgrP$_{IO}$, and the direct object to Spec-AgrOP, which is lower than Spec-AgrP$_{IO}$. The observed binding possibilities would follow from this configuration. But as Mahajan himself notes, his analysis runs into problems with constructions like (144), where the direct object follows both the main verb and the auxiliary but still agrees with both of them.

(144) *Hindi* (Mahajan 1997:193)

Raam-ne	har ek	admii-ko$_j$	lɔṭaa-ii	th-ii
Ram-ERG	every	man-DAT	return-PAST.FEM.SG	be-PAST.FEM.SG

uskii$_j$ kitaab.

his book$_{FEM}$

'Ram had returned every man$_j$ his$_j$ book.'

His proposal is that in this construction the direct object must have moved to Spec-AuxP since it agrees with the auxiliary. With the auxiliary preceding the direct object, he further assumes that the auxiliary has moved to a higher head, which he refers to as Agr$_{AUX}$. In addition, the Spec of this higher head is occupied by the constituent containing the IO and the agreeing participle.

The problem with Mahajan's analysis is that it involves a number of movement operations that are hard to motivate, such as the movement of the direct object to Spec-AuxP and the movement of AgrP$_{IO}$ to the Spec of AgrP$_{AUX}$. In addition, it is unclear how the subject fits into the picture that he sketches.

On my analysis, the sentence in (144) is derived as follows. The word order with the main verb preceding the auxiliary results from moving the extended projection of the main verb into the Spec of the auxiliary. In addition, the VP headed by the main verb, as well as the VP headed by the auxiliary, moves to the Spec of the nearest TP, so that the respective tense markers come to follow their associated verbs. Thus, at one stage the object is contained in the constituent in the Spec of the higher TP, and this relation is reflected in the agreement. Subsequently, there is raising of the object to a lower Spec-TopP and of the higher IP, that of the auxiliary, to Spec-FocP.

As Mahajan (1997) demonstrates, in Hindi a preverbal constituent will bind all postverbal constituents—see (145). This is also expected on my analysis.

(145) *Hindi* (Mahajan 1997:203)

Har ek	kitaab$_i$	dikhaa-ii	uske$_j$	maalik-ko	uske$_j$	lekhak-ne.
every	book	show-PAST.FEM.SG	its	owner-DAT	its	writer-ERG

'Its$_j$ author showed its$_j$ owner every book$_i$.'

Mahajan (1997) further shows that it is possible in Hindi to have more than one postverbal element and that, in this case, the first postverbal element can bind into the second postverbal element, but not the other way around:

(146) *Hindi* (Mahajan 1997:202)

a.
Raam-ne	dikhaa-ii	har ek	kittab$_i$	uske$_i$
Ram-ERG	show-PAST.FEM.SG	every	book$_{FEM}$	its

maalik-ko.

owner-DAT

'Ram showed every book to its owner.'

b. Raam-ne   dikhaa-ii   har ek aadmii-ko$_i$ uskii$_i$ kitaab.
   Ram-ERG   show-PAST.FEM.SG every man-DAT his   book$_{FEM}$
   'Ram showed every man his book.'

c.* Raam-ne   dikhaa-ii   uske$_i$ maalik-ko   har ek kittab$_i$.
    Ram-ERG   show-PAST.FEM.SG its   owner-DAT   every book$_{FEM}$
    'Ram showed its owner every book.'

d.* Raam-ne   dikhaa-ii   uskii$_i$ kitaab   har ek
    Ram-ERG   show-PAST.FEM.SG his   book$_{FEM}$ every
    aadmii-ko$_i$.
    man-DAT
    'Ram showed his book to every man.'

As we see, a postverbal direct object can bind into a postverbal indirect object, as in (146a), but it is also possible for a postverbal indirect object to bind into a postverbal direct object, as in (146b). This suggests that it is the surface configuration and not the underlying structural relation that is of importance. In other words, unlike Turkish, Hindi has no reconstruction of postverbal elements. Then (146) is support for my analysis: if each of the postverbal constituents occupies a Spec position in the CP-domain, the first postverbal constituent is necessarily higher than the second one; accordingly, the first will be able to bind into the second. As we see, this is borne out: regardless of which object comes first, it will bind into the object that comes second in the postverbal domain.

For Turkish, Kural (1992) demonstrates that the first of two postverbal constituents can bind the second, but the opposite is also possible. However, Kural's examples all involve a direct object binding an indirect object. Hence, it could be that the binding relations simply reflect the hierarchical relations between the arguments before movement, as suggested above.

In my model, an account can also be readily offered of the fact that *wh*-phrases are uncomfortable in postverbal position, which Mahajan (1997:209 n. 9) notes as somewhat surprising, given that *wh*-phrases in Hindu can stay in situ or "scramble quite freely," as he puts it. If postverbal elements are located in the designated position for backgrounded material, it is not surprising at all that *wh*-elements are disfavored in postverbal position: a *wh*-phrase can of course never represent information that is presupposed in the discourse.[38]

A similar line of reasoning applies in the case of the following example, whose slightly marked status is left unexplained in Mahajan (1997).

(147) *Hindi* (Mahajan 1997:204)
   ? ε-ne   dikh-aa   di-yaa   [[tumhaara
     I-ERG   show-PAST.MASC.SG   give-PAST.MASC.SG   your
     Raam-ko$_i$ likh-aa   hua] pətr]   se$_i$.
     Raam-DAT   write-PAST.MASC.SG   be   letter   him
     'I show the letter you had written to Ram$_i$ to him$_i$.'

One might reasonably assume that the postverbal constituents in (147) contain too much information to easily be treated as background.

Another possibility in Hindi complex tense constructions is to have postverbal elements between the main verb and the auxiliary. Mahajan (1997) gives an example of the appropriate context for this order, shown here as (148).

(148) *Hindi* (Mahajan 1997:208)

Sitaa-ne	kitaab	bhej-ii	Raam-ko	th-ii,
Sita-ERG	book$_{FEM}$	send-PAST.FEM.SG	Ram-DAT	be-PAST.FEM.SG

par	mil	vo	Mohan-ko	ga-yii.
but	receive	it	Mohan-DAT	go-PAST.FEM.SG

'Sita had sent the book to Ram, but it got to Mohan instead.'

In this construction, the postverbal element appears to be focused instead of backgrounded. Hence, it is likely that the postverbal element is in Spec-FocP. The lower IP, headed by the main verb, must then be in Spec-TopP.

That it is possible for postverbal elements to be situated either in a lower Spec-TopP or in Spec-FocP is suggested by the discussion of Tamil in Herring (1994). She argues that, in Tamil, postverbal constituents can be backgrounded or emphasized (in addition to being afterthoughts). This indicates that both derivations are possible in this language and that postverbal constituents in Spec-FocP are emphasized while postverbal constituents in the lower Spec-TopP are backgrounded.

One might in fact suspect that constructions with a focused constituent in Spec-FocP preceded by IP in Spec-TopP are widespread also outside of the head-final languages. It could be that this is what lies behind clause-final focus in general. For example, Kayne and Pollock (1998) note that in the following type of inversion in French, which is not dependent on *wh*-fronting but on PP-preposing, the inverted subject is not in Spec-TopP:

(149) *French* (Kayne & Pollock 1998)

a.	Dans	la	forêt	vivait	un	vieil	ermite.
	in	the	forest	lived	an	old	hermit

b.	Dans	cette	forêt	vivait	quelqu'un.
	in	this	forest	lived	somebody

This conclusion is based on the fact that (149b) is grammatical. As noted earlier, non-specific indefinites cannot be topics.

They may however well be focused, as demonstrated below:

(150) *English*
  a. SOMEBODY must know it.
  b. A PLUMBER could have fixed it.

This contrast is also noted by Rizzi (1997), who gives the following Italian examples:

(151) *Italian* (Rizzi 1997)
    a.* Nessuno,   lo ho   visto.
        nobody   him have.1s seen

    b. NESSUNO ho   visto.
       nobody   have.1s seen

The construction in (151a), with an indefinite quantifier as topic, is ungrammatical, whereas (151b), with a focused indefinite quantifier, is perfectly normal.

As pointed out by Kayne and Pollock (1998), the subject of an inverted construction is never in its canonical position. This is indicated by the fact that clitic subjects cannot be inverted:

(152) *French* (Kayne & Pollock 1998)
    a. * Qu'a   mangé il?
       what-has eaten he
       'What has he eaten?'

    b. * Dans cette   forêt vivait il.
       in   this   forest lived he

Hence, the postverbal subject in (149) must have moved—for example, to Spec-FocP, as my analysis suggests.

Furthermore, Zubizarreta (1998) notes, for Spanish, that the only acceptable full sentence answer to (153a) is (153b).

(153) *Spanish* (Zubizarreta 1998:125–126)
    a. Quién te   regaló la   botella de   vino?
      who you.DAT gave   the bottle of   wine
      'Who gave you the bottle of wine?'

    b. Me   regaló la   botella de   vino   María.
      me.DAT gave   the bottle of   wine   Maria
      'MARÍA gave me the bottle of wine'

This suggests that the postverbal subject in (153b) is focused. The material preceding the subject is arguably the topic. The order in (153b) could then be seen as the result of movement of the subject to Spec-FocP and the remainder of IP to Spec-TopP. In other words, on this account Zubizarreta's "P-movement" is syntactically driven movement into the CP-domain. Whether a similar analysis goes through for all other cases of apparent movement to clause-final position is clearly an interesting topic for further investigation.

3.5 The properties of head-final languages

I will now summarize my proposals concerning head-final languages, and then point to some questions of head-final syntax that remain to be dealt with. One question has to do with adverbial placement, while another one, of a more technical nature, has to do with the cyclicity of the syntactic operations that I am proposing.

The defining property of a head-final language is that complements of all categories appear to the left of their selecting heads. This easily detectable property suggests that there is leftward XP-movement which is not driven by case. For example, when a main verb precedes an auxiliary, the order cannot have been derived by head movement, since head movement would never allow the main verb to cross the auxiliary (see section 2.3). Hence, there must have been movement of VP or of a larger verbal projection to the left of the auxiliary (I assume that auxiliaries universally take their complements to their right). Case or other features which are generally assumed to trigger movement of arguments cannot possibly be relevant to this movement. Rather, there must be a trigger that is special to this particular movement type. On this background, I have proposed that in head-final languages, c-features are checked by overt XP-movement.

If this is correct, there is a particular set of properties that we would expect all head-final languages to share. These properties are listed in (154).

(154) *Characteristic properties of head-final languages*
   a. Complements appear to the left of their selecting heads.
   b. The morphology is suffixing and agglutinating.
   c. Indirect objects have the same realization as directional PPs.
   d. Arguments are licensed inside VP.
   e. Movement of arguments is triggered by focus and topic features.

First, the morphology of a language where complex words are made up of a head plus elements in its Spec must be exclusively suffixing, and probably also agglutinating, in the sense that there is no fusion of morphemes in the syntax. Next, since it is VP and the phrasal projections of IP that move to higher Spec positions, the arguments must be licensed inside VP, as I have claimed to be the case in Lezgian, Japanese, Turkish, and Hindi. Further, it is conceivable that for this to be possible, the indirect object must be realized as a PP. Finally, if there is syntactic movement of arguments at all, it must be triggered by discourse-related features such as topic and focus.

Although the proposals presented in the preceding subsections seem to have some success in accounting for the data, there are still some problems that remain unresolved. One problem has to do with the positions of adverbs. In the theory of Cinque (1999), adverbs are generated in specifier positions within the IP-domain. But if in head-final languages the specifier position of every head in the IP-domain is occupied by the complement of that head, as I have proposed, it is hard to see how adverbs could be accommodated. Nevertheless, of course there are also adverbs in these languages. We will take a brief look at how they can be positioned.

In the first two examples below, (155) and (156), an adverb from the higher part of IP (see Cinque 1999) appears at the left edge of the sentence. According to the analysis I have already given of Lezgian syntax, there has been movement of a verbal projection to Spec-TP in (155) and to the Spec of a Mood head in (156). The adverbs could still be in their base positions, which are higher than the Spec to which the verbal projection has moved (see Cinque's hierarchy of heads which is given in ex. (75) ch. 5).

(155) *Lezgian*   (Haspelmath 1993:307)

Bažahat	[q̃we-da-j	jis.a-n	beher]
hardly	come-FUT-PTC	year-GEN	crop.ABS
c'inin-da-laj		qʰsa-n-di	že-da.
this.year-GEN-N.SG-REL		good-N.SG.ABS	be-FUT

'Next year's crop will hardly be better than this year's.'

(156) *Lezgian*   (Haspelmath 1993:151)

Belki	za-z	anaj	wun	akwa-n.
perhaps	I-DAT	there	you.ABS	see-HORT

'Perhaps I will see you there.'

The example (157) could be analyzed in a parallel fashion to (155) and (156), with the minor modification that in (157) the subject has been moved to a position preceding the adverb—to a focus or topic position in the CP-domain.

(157) *Lezgian*   (Haspelmath 1993:308)

Evelin.a-kaj	sa	šak-ni	ala-z	xudoxžnik	že-da.
Evelin-SUBEL	one	doubt-even	be.on-INF	artist.ABS	become-FUT

'Evelin will no doubt become an artist.'

The analysis could even be extended to (158), although this order is compatible with Cinque's (1999) hierarchy of heads only if the adverb has also been fronted. According to that hierarchy, the base position of an aspectual adverb like *immediately* (termed 'proximative' in Cinque 1999) is lower than the T°(future) head, which presumably has the VP in its Spec in this construction. However, fronting of adverbs is an option that is widely attested in other languages (see Cinque 1999), so that there is no reason to exclude the possibility that it has also taken place here.

(158) *Lezgian*   (Haspelmath 1993:275)

Il'ič.a	hasätda	q̃ün.ü-qʰaj	tfeng	galud-na.
Il'ič.ERG	immediately	shoulder-POSTESS	rifle.ABS	take.off-AOR

'Il'ič immediately took the rifle off his shoulders.'

An alternative explanation for (158) is that the position of the temporal heads is lower than suggested in Cinque (1999), in fact lower than proximative adverbs.

Examples (159)–(161) show other adverbs which, according to Cinque (1999), are also generated in the lower part of IP—celerative adverbs in (159) and (160), and a manner adverbial in (161).

(159) *Lezgian*   (Haspelmath 1993:89)
Čimi   č'aw.u-z   weq'-er   fad   q'ura-da.
hot   time-DAT   grass-PL quickly   dry-HAB
'In the hot season grass dries quickly.'

(160) *Lezgian*   (Haspelmath 1993:301)
Zun   tadi-z   xür.ü-z   qʰfi-da.
I.ABS quick-ADV   village-DAT   return-FUT
'I will quickly return to the village.'

(161) *Lezgian*   (Haspelmath 1993:324)
Bade   axwar.i-k   ku-ma-z,
grandmother.ABS   sleep-SUBESS   be.under-still-INF
ada   jawaš-diz   partal-ar   aluk'-na.
she.ERG   quiet-ADV   cloth-PL   put.on-AOR
'While grandmother was still asleep, she quietly put on her clothes.'

Even though the subject precedes the adverb in these examples, the constructions are not necessarily problematic for my claim that arguments are normally licensed inside VP. It is possible that the order subject > adverb is derived by raising the subject—for example, to a topic position.

A similar explanation could perhaps also be called upon in the case of (162), where both the subject and the object precede the manner adverbial.

(162) *Lezgian*   (Haspelmath 1993:115)
Ruš-ar.i-z   urus   č'al   lap   zajif   či-zwa-j.
girl-PL-DAT   Russian   language.ABS   very weak   know-IMPF-PAST
'The girls knew Russian very poorly.'

It is conceivable that both the subject and the object are located in Spec positions within the CP-domain in this example; for example, the subject could be in Spec-TopP and the object in Spec-FocP.

Alternatively, it could be that the manner adverbial is generated in one of the lower Spec positions inside VP, as proposed by Adger and Tsoulas (2001). The basis of Adger and Tsoulas's analysis of manner adverbials, and also of locative and temporal adverbials, is the observation that these adverbials are somehow connected to the lexical aspect of the verb and to the ability of the verb to license arguments—that is, to the properties which in Borer (1998), for example, are taken to be associated with the heads of the extended VP.

Strikingly, manner adverbials are not too infrequently found between the object and the verb in head-final languages. The following examples are from Turkish, Punjabi, Tamil, and Kobon, all of which are evidently head-final (see the respective references):

(163) *Turkish* (Kornfilt 1997:92)
    Hasan   gömleğ-i   iyi-ce   yıka-dı.
    Hasan   shirt-ACC good-ADV   wash-PAST
    'Hasan washed the shirt well.'

(164) *Punjabi* (Bhatia 1993:92)
    ó   ne   kamm xushii   xushii   kiit-aa.
    he   ERG work   happiness happiness do-PAST.MASC
    'He did the work very happily.'

(165) *Tamil* (Asher 1985:89)
    nii   inta veeley-e   koɲcam nallaa ceyya-ɳum
    you this work-ACC   a.little well   do-DEB
    'You must do this work rather better.'

(166) *Kobon* (Davies 1989:115)
    Yad nöŋ-bin   Kaunsol   nipe manö nöŋö   hag-ep bɨ.
    1s   perceive-PERF.1s councillor 3s   talk   truthfully say-N man
    'I know that the councillor [is a man who] speaks truthfully.'

The idea of Adger and Tsoulas (2001) that there is a close structural relation between manner adverbials and V° can be incorporated into my model of head-final languages—for example, by taking manner adverbials to occupy the innermost Spec of VP. This would give a very simple explanation of the order shown in the above examples, since it would allow for the proposal that the arguments and the adverbial are in their base positions inside VP. Locatives, as in example (49), might then be generated in the next higher Spec inside VP, and not in complement position, as suggested in (50).

The problem that specifically concerns adverbials in head-final languages is, however, that when an adverbial appears in the Spec of one of the heads in IP, the complement of that head cannot move to the Spec for c-checking. Thus, the presence of IP adverbs seems to be in conflict with the claim that complements in Lezgian regularly move to the nearest Spec.

However, in the discussion of the VP in head-final languages, I proposed that merge overrides movement. That is, the complement of a given head cannot move to the Spec of that head if some other constituent is a candidate for merger in the Spec position. On this account, the movement of the complement to Spec for c-checking is seen as the default operation, which only takes place when the Spec position would otherwise be empty. Hence, when a head has an adverb in its Spec, movement of the complement to Spec is blocked.

Another problem of a more theoretical character has to do with the cyclicity of the movement operations that I have proposed. Recall that I have assumed that the arguments are licensed inside VP and that they can be moved from VP to a position in the CP-domain. At the same time, I have proposed that the VP itself raises to a higher Spec. If the arguments move out of VP before the VP raises, the raising of VP is countercyclic. Countercyclic operations are not assumed to be allowed (see, e.g., Chomsky 1995, Collins 1997). If syntactic operations apply in a cyclic fashion, the arguments must move out of VP after VP has raised to a higher Spec. The problem is now that phrases in specifier positions are normally considered to be islands for extraction. In particular, this idea has been used in the literature to explain why subjects are islands. Technically, islandhood has been formulated as a consequence of not being L-marked (Chomsky 1986) or of not being sister of a head (Manzini 1992). We would therefore expect the VP to become an island as soon as it has moved from its base position.

If the analysis I have given of head-final languages is essentially correct, it must nevertheless be the case that elements can move out of constituents in Spec positions. Hence, the existing theories of locality will have to be revised so as to allow for these operations. However, it is beyond the limits of the present work to develop a new locality theory. I will only give a few suggestions about the direction that the necessary revisions might take.

It should be noted that current locality theories make reference to extraction out of subjects and not out of Spec elements in general. There are several differences between subjects and VPs that might cause extraction out of VPs to be less restricted than extraction out of subjects. For one thing, subjects are arguments whereas VPs are not. In the theory of Manzini (1992), arguments enter into dependencies that are different from the dependencies that are relevant for other syntactic elements. Hence, extracting an argument out of a subject will establish a dependency that crosses a dependency of the same kind. Moving an argument out of VP will not cause interference problems in the same way. It is conceivable that similar considerations apply in the case of extraction of adverbials out of verbally related projections.

Moreover, the successive movements to Spec that I have postulated for the IP-domain in head-final languages all involve movement of a phrase to the Spec of another phrase that belongs to the same extended projection. Crucially, the heads that belong to one and the same extended projection have no conflicting features, rather, the features of one head supplement those of another. For example, the heads in the extended projection of VP supply the verbally related features that are not generated in $V°$ itself. In this sense, VP can be said to be non-distinct from the other IP projections. Consequently, when VP has raised to Spec-TP, the Spec of TP is non-distinct from TP. It is conceivable that, because of this, extraction out of VP is treated like extraction out of TP. If this line of thought can be defended, it follows that movement out of VP is no more problematic in a head-final language than in a language where VP stays in its base position.

3.6   Final remarks on movement to Spec

The starting point of the discussion of head-final languages was the idea that there must exist a syntactic operation that creates head-final structures and, at the same time, complex words where grammatical markers follow a lexical root. In the preceding sections, I tried to justify the claim that this operation is movement of complements to the Spec of their selecting heads. I further argued that this type of movement normally applies to every category within IP if it applies at all. It is these successive movement operations that give the strictly head-final languages their characteristic properties. In addition, I suggested that movement of various constituents to positions in the CP-domain can give rise to ordering variations in these languages, which otherwise would be rigidly SOV.

In this section, we deal with certain aspects of movement to Spec which deserve some more attention in the present context. In 3.6.1 we see that movement of IP to the CP-domain may take place also in languages that do not make use of complement-to-Spec movement within IP. In 3.6.2 I turn to the morphological consequences of movement to Spec, and I claim that whether or not this process gives a complex word as output depends on the overall distribution in the language in question of the resulting morpheme strings. In addition, prosodic properties may also come into play.

3.6.1   Movement of complement to Spec in IP and CP

Holmberg (1998b) presents some proposals that are similar in two important respects to what I have suggested here. He assumes, first, that complement movement to Spec can be a word-forming process and, second, that this word-forming operation must apply uniformly in languages where it is employed. However, he does not distinguish between IP-internal complement movement to Spec and complement movement to Spec in the CP-domain. Because of this, certain constructions appear problematic for his analysis. But we will see that if one draws a distinction between movement triggered by c-features and movement triggered by other features, the constructions that Holmberg points to as problematic are not problematic after all.

As Holmberg notes, many VO languages have a sentence-final question particle, so that the surface order is SVOQ or VSOQ. Among the examples he gives are the following:

(167) *Copala Trique*   (Holmberg 1998b; after Hollenbach 1992)

    a. Oh   zoh sahanx man   gwaa nah
         give   he   money body John   Q
         'Is he giving money to John?'

    b. Me   ra   weh   ne   zoh ga
         which inside house sit   he   WH
         'In which house does he live?'

c. Uchrah   zoh   cruun   a
   split   he   wood   DECL
   'He splits wood.'

According to Holmberg (1998b), if the question particles are realizations of C°, these structures are problematic for the proposal that movement to Spec must apply uniformly throughout a derivation: the complement of C° has apparently moved to Spec-CP even if the same type of operation has not applied within that complement.

However, it follows from what I have proposed in this chapter that while movement of a complement to Spec within IP will be triggered by a head that has strong c-features but weak N- and V-features, movement of a complement to Spec in the CP-domain will be triggered by discourse-related features. That is, when a constituent is attracted to a specifier position in the CP-domain, it will be the discourse-related features of the attracting head that are responsible, regardless of whether the attracted constituent is the complement of that very head or a phrase generated further away from that head.

If we now consider the Copala Trique examples in this light, we see that in every case, the verb and its arguments appear to the left of a marker which presumably is a realization of Foc° (the question markers) or of Force° (the declarative marker). Hence, FocP/ForceP is head-final although the projections in IP are not. I assume that this order results from movement of IP to the relevant Spec. In (167a), what has moved to the Spec of the question marker is exactly the phrase that the question marker takes scope over. Thus, this could be movement to check the Q-feature. Similarly, the movement in (167b) could be triggered by the *wh*-features of the question marker and of the question word. The only thing that is exceptional with this construction is that the *wh*-phrase does not move alone but pied-pipes the whole IP. Still, it is not inconceivable that the movement counts as *wh*-movement. Also note that the unmarked word order in Copala Trique is VSO (Holmberg 1998b), which means that the *wh*-phrase seems to have moved to a position in front of the verb before the whole IP moved to the Spec of the question marker. Finally, in (167c) IP precedes a declarative marker. Again, this could be a case of movement, to the Spec of the marker, of the phrase that the marker takes scope over. In other words, what we see in (167c) is the declarative counterpart of the Q-movement in (167a).

Thus, the fact that Copala Trique can move the IP to Spec positions within the CP-domain even if the language shows no sign of movement of complements to Spec within IP is not a problem for my theory. If movement of complements to Spec within the CP-domain is essentially different from movement to Spec in IP, we would expect that languages can have one without the other.

For the sake of illustration, I add below some more examples from languages that evidently move IP to the CP-domain but show no sign of having the complement-to-Spec movements in IP that were postulated above for the head-final languages.

(168) *Mandarin Chinese* (Li & Thompson 1981:547)
    Ni   neng   xie   Zhongguo   zi   ma?
    you   can   write   Chinese   character   Q
    'Can you write Chinese characters?'

(169) *Sre* (Manley 1972)
    a. Khay lɔt   hə   Səgòn   ʔə?
       he   go   to   Saigon Q
       'Is he going to Saigon?'

    b. Kɔ̀n nɛ   ləh   nchi   (tayh)?
       child that do   what   WH
       'What is that child doing?'

(170) *Mon* (Guillon 1976:415, 417)
    a. Ko   'ai   ā   wa   baña   ra.
       elder.brother 1   go   open.space   ricefields   DECL
       'My elder brother went to the farm.'

    b. Rai   tamṅa   ā   padai   hlā   hā?
       COLL fisherman   go   to   lake   Q
       'Are the fishermen going to the lake?'

All three languages shown above have SVO order, and they may have tense, mood, or aspect markers between the subject and the verb (see appendix 2 for details). This suggests that the subject moves out of VP to the Spec of one of the projections of IP. As for the verb, it is possible that it stays in VP in Sre and Mon, where it follows all IP elements. In Mandarin Chinese there is probably verb movement, since there may be aspectual markers following the verb (see the discussion of Mandarin Chinese aspectual markers in sec. 1.4.2), but the verb does not move to the head that has the subject in its Spec. The object follows the verb in all three languages. Thus, these languages obviously do not have the syntax that is typical of head-final languages. Nevertheless, they have clause-final markers of illocutionary force. Hence, the argumentation that was put forth for Copala Trique probably also holds for Mandarin Chinese, Sre, and Mon: the movements that give clause-final force markers are not triggered by c-features but by the features that are specific to the CP-domain.

    In particular, note (169b), where the *wh*-element is in the position that objects normally occupy in Sre. As the whole IP precedes the [+WH] question marker, it seems likely that IP is pied-piped to the Spec of the question marker without any foregoing IP-internal movement of the *wh*-phrase. Thus, although *wh*-questions in Sre are slightly different from their Copala Trique counterparts, exemplified in (167b), it could the same mechanism that lies behind the ultimate order.

The conclusion to be drawn from this subsection is that if, in a given derivation, there is movement of complements to Spec triggered by c-features, these movements will affect every projection of IP. However, as we have just seen, the projections in the CP-domain may be head-final even in languages that do not have head-final syntax in IP. This shows that movement of complements to Spec in IP is different from movement of complements to Spec in the CP-domain. Hence, it is possible, as I have claimed in this chapter, that the former is triggered by the need for c-checking while the latter is triggered by the discourse-related features of the CP-domain.

3.6.2 The word-forming power of movement to Spec

A leading idea of the present work is that if two morphemes are linearly adjacent, there is always the possibility that they may be perceived as constituting a word. Whether this will actually happen does not depend on the syntactic configuration but on other factors such as the regularity of that particular morpheme combination in the language in question, its distribution relative to other elements, and the direction of phonological word formation. This means that movement to Spec always has the potential of creating a complex word, but it does not always actually do so, not even in strictly head-final languages.

First, there are numerous cases where a head that attracts a phrase to its Spec forms a word with that phrase phonologically, but because the category of the phrase itself or of its final element is not fixed, the attracting head is not conceived of as an affix but as a clitic. We have seen several examples of clitics in the preceding chapters, such as the Zoque ergative marker - *'is*, which was shown in example (16), chapter 1; the Greenlandic coordinator -*lu*, shown in example (37), chapter 1 and in example (6) in the present chapter; and the Northern Saami question marker -*go*, which was shown in example (11), chapter 2.

The Zoque ergative marker - *'is* is always preceded by a DP. I will take this to mean that the ergative marker attracts the DP to its Spec. The ergative marker then forms a phonological word with the last lexical element of the DP. As the following examples show, this can be a noun, as in (171a); an adjective, as in (171b); or the verb of a relative clause, as in (171c). Also note that in the latter case, the object of the relative clause follows the ergative marker. This is an indication that the suggestion is correct that what precedes the ergative marker originates below it.

(171) *Zoque* (= ex. (16), ch. 1)

    a.   te'   che'-bü   xha'e-'is   mya'ü-bya   tüp
         DET   little-REL   girl-ERG   sell-INCMPL   fruit
         'The little girl is selling fruit.'

    b.   te'   xha'e   che'-bü-'is   mya'ü-bya   tüp
         DET   girl   little-REL-ERG   sell-INCMPL   fruit
         'The little girl is selling fruit.'

c. te'   püt   kyud-u-bü-'is   te'   tüp   ka'-u
   DET   man   eat-COMPL-REL-ERG   DET   fruit die-COMPL
   'The man who ate the fruit died.'

Because the ergative marker thus forms a phonological word with elements of various categories, it is analyzed as a clitic. But consider now what would be the situation if there were no variation with respect to the final element in DPs in Zoque, if, for example, they were consistently noun-final. Then the ergative marker would always follow immediately after a noun. Most likely, it would then be regarded as a case suffix and not as a clitic. Thus, it is the internal organization of DPs in Zoque which gives the ergative marker the appearance of a clitic.

This is a neat illustration of my claim that, contrary to popular belief which states that because the elements *-lu*, *-go*, and *-'is* are clitics they attach to elements of any category, the fact that they attach to elements of various types is what causes them to be perceived as clitics and not as affixes. Apart from the distributional properties that we have just seen, there is nothing to give clitics any special status in the system of grammar. A clitic is simply a phonologically light element that, for reasons that are only indirectly related to the properties of that element itself, happens to appear adjacent to elements of various categories.

By the same token, an affix can be seen as a phonologically light element that, for reasons that are only indirectly related to the properties of that element itself, happens to appear adjacent to elements of one particular category, or at least adjacent to morphemes that are associated with one particular lexical class. This is what lies behind the word-forming power of the movement-to-Spec operation. Consider again the Lezgian example repeated below as (172).

(172) *Lezgian* (= ex. (29), ch. 3)

    Baku.d-a   irid   itim   gülle.di-z   aq̃ud-na   luhu-da.
    Baku-INESS   seven   man.ABS   bullet-DAT   take.out-AOR   say-HAB
    'They say that in Baku seven men were shot.'

I proposed in section 3.4.1 that this construction is the result of repeated movements of complements to Spec. The lower VP is in the Spec of the embedded tense marker, the lower TP is in the Spec of the higher verb, and the higher VP is in the Spec of the higher tense marker.

But notably, although this means that each of the morphemes that make up the sequence of verbs is in a Spec-Head relation with one of the others, only two of these relations are taken to establish a complex word. The lower verb, which is the final element of the phrase in the Spec of the aorist marker, is included in a word with that marker; similarly, the higher verb and the habitual marker also form a word. The aorist marker, however, is not in the same word as the higher verb, even though the lower IP, of which the aorist marker is the last element, is in the Spec of the higher verb. This indicates that it is not the structural relation between two morphemes that determines whether or not they will be seen as parts of one and the same word. The structural relation between the lower verb and the aorist marker is identical to the structural relation between the aorist marker and the higher verb. Still, the former relation but not the latter is seen as a word-forming one. This contrast is due to the distributional properties of the morphemes. The aorist marker is always adjacent to a verbal stem. It is thus the combination of verbal stem + aorist marker that has independent distribution and internal cohesion, which are the properties that characterize words (see sec. 1.4.2). The combination of the inflected verb *aq̃ud-na* and the following verb *luhun* 'say' has none of these properties. The verbal root *luhu-* is not necessarily preceded by verbal material; it could also be preceded by a noun, as in (173). Thus, although the verb *aq̃ud-na* is linearly adjacent to the verb *luhu-da* in (172), the sequence does not have sufficient regularity in the language to be conceived of as a word.

(173) *Lezgian* (Haspelmath 1993:299)

"Bedel,	sa	mani	lah,"	teklif-na	Abil.a.
Bedel	one	song.ABS	say.IMP	propose-AOR	Abil.ERG

'"Bedel, sing a song," proposed Abil.'

One will remember from the discussion in section 3.4.1 that the inflected verb form *luhuda* 'they say', in the environment exemplified in (172), has developed into the hearsay evidential marker *-lda*. The example that was given is repeated below as (174).

(174) *Lezgian* (= ex. (30), ch. 3)

Baku.d-a	irid	itim	gülle.di-z	aq̃ud-na-lda.
Baku-INESS	seven	man.ABS	bullet-DAT	take.out-AOR-EVID

'They say that in Baku seven men were shot.'

Unlike its source *luhuda*, the evidential marker *-lda* is an affix. In the model I am assuming here, all that is required for this development to take place is that the contracted form *-lda* is restricted to the hearsay reportive function. If the short form *-lda* only appears in this function, it will always immediately follow an inflected verb: it will be preceded by the quote, and the quote will always be verb-final. This means that *-lda* no longer has the distribution of a full verb. Instead, the distribution of the combination verb+tense+*lda* will be such that the criteria for wordhood are met, and, accordingly, the contracted form *-lda* is reanalyzed as an inflectional marker. But importantly, the structural relation between *-lda* and the preceding morpheme in (174) is exactly the same as the structural relation between *luhuda* and the preceding morpheme in (172). Thus, we have here another illustration of the suggestion I made in chapter 1 that word formation is dependent on distributional properties and not on structural relations.

Having the appropriate distribution is not always enough to cause two morphemes to be conceived of as a complex word, however. Prosodic properties may also play a part. This can be seen in the New Guinean language Sanio-Hiowe, which, according to the data given in Lewis (1972), has SOV order with verbal inflectional markers following the verb. An example is given in (175).

(175) *Sanio-Hiowe* (Lewis 1972:16)

ta	ate	haiye	homai	yei	ariari	se
some	this	leaves	break	FUT	lie	V

'Some lied (and said) they were going to break off leaves.'

We see here that the order of elements within the clause is exactly as in the head-final languages that have been discussed in this chapter. The embedded clause precedes the higher verb, the object of the embedded clause precedes the embedded verb, and the verb precedes the tense marker. In addition, the noun *ariari* 'lie' precedes the verbalizer *se*, forming a complex which is similar to compound verbs in, say, Lezgian.

In the examples in (176), the verb is followed by an aspect marker and then by a past tense marker. Since the tense marker is probably generated higher than the aspect marker (see Cinque 1999), this is the order we would get if there is movement of VP to Spec-AspP and then of AspP to Spec-TP.

(176) *Sanio-Hiowe* (Lewis 1972:16–17)

a. kanakana sato tei na   we
    bushman here stay CONT PAST
    'The bushman stayed here.'

b. onu   tei   ye
    sit   PERF   PAST
    'We sat down.'

The difference between these Sanio-Hiowe constructions and Lezgian is that the Sanio-Hiowe tense and aspect markers are not considered to be suffixes on the verb, at least not by Lewis (1972), even if they bear the same relation to the verb linearly, and possibly also structurally, as tense and aspect markers in Lezgian. The reason for this contrast is probably found in prosody. Lewis (1972:12), who refers to the tense and aspect markers of Sanio-Hiowe as 'auxiliaries', reports that "each verb, auxiliary, or auxiliary compound within the verb phrase is accented." That is, because the tense and aspect markers in the above examples are stressed independently of the verb root, the verbal roots and inflectional markers are seen as separate words.

Lewis (1972) also claims, however, that verbs in Sanio-Hiowe can carry suffixed markers of past tense and of aspect. She states that the suffixes "are homophonous with the tense and aspect auxiliaries [but as] suffixes they do not have their own accent" (Lewis 1972:18). Some examples of suffixed markers are given below:

(177) *Sanio-Hiowe* (Lewis 1972:18–19)

    a. isau-we   au   fu   we
        grab-PAST   DIR   put   PAST
        'He grabbed it and put it up.'

    b. toti-nau   tapa'asi   ro   wo
        think-CONT finish   DUR   CONJ
        'Thought, then finished.'

Finally, there can also be what Lewis calls 'compound auxiliaries', which are combinations of two verbal markers where only the first one is stressed. This is illustrated in (178). Presumably, these forms also result from moving AspP to Spec-TP.

(178) *Sanio-Hiowe* (Lewis 1972)

    a. ai   atu   te   na-we   b.   ani nehi ti   na-wei
       cross fight   PL   CONT-PAST   get find go   CONT-FUT
       'The men were fighting cross.'   'I will find him and go.'

The facts of Sanio-Hiowe suggest that whether or not a given verbal marker will be seen as a separate word or as forming a complex word with a verb or with another verbal marker is not so much dependent on structure as on prosody. As I see it, having separate stress is not a consequence of being a word; instead, the fact that an element has separate stress causes it to be perceived as a word. This is in accordance with the claim put forward in chapter 1 that a word is not defined as such in the grammar; words only come into being in the perception of the string of morphemes that is eventually spelled out.

As noted by Kayne (1994:53), we would expect the Spec-head relation to give rise to purely agglutinative word forms. If individual morphemes correspond to syntactic terminal nodes, then portmanteau markers—markers that are the realization of more than one inflectional category—must be the result of two or more terminal nodes having fused syntactically into one single node. The conditions under which fusion may take place still remain to be investigated. However, as a first guess we would assume that fusion is more likely to occur in complex heads than across phrasal boundaries; see Halle and Marantz (1993, 1994) where fusion is seen as an operation that can apply to sister nodes.[39] Hence, if a word is made up of a head and an element that sits in the Spec of that head, we would expect each underlying morpheme of that word to be spelled out separately.

The head-final languages that have been discussed above conform to this expectation to a considerable degree. There are cases, though, where the morphology can be seen as agglutinating only if phonologically empty markers are recognized. Of course, if empty markers can be freely postulated, anything can be made to fit into an agglutinative pattern. To keep the theory more restrictive,

I will assume that an empty inflectional marker must share the distribution of at least one overt marker. Consider the Lezgian example in (179).

(179) *Lezgian* (= ex. (46), ch. 3)
    Wiri   ajal-r.i-z   [Musaq'.a-n   dide-Ø-Ø
    all   child-PL-DAT   Musaq'-GEN   mother-SG-ABS
    q'e-nwa-j-di-Ø-Ø   ]   či-zwa-j.
    die-PERF-PTC-N-SG-ABS   know-IMPF-PAST
    'All the children knew that Musaq's mother had died.'

As indicated, I propose that absolutive case and singular number are represented by phonologically empty markers (zero markers). We also see that these markers contrast with the non-zero markers of plural number and of dative case. Thus, there seems to be good reason to assume that the case and number features of *dide* 'mother', for example, are not expressed directly by the root form *dide* itself but by the absence of overt case and number markers. Accordingly, it can be stated that each inflectional category in *dide* is expressed by a separate marker.

The agglutinative nature of Lezgian morphology is also seen in the following examples, which nevertheless exhibit a couple of exceptions to the general pattern. These exceptions are the first person singular ergative pronoun *za* in (180) and the present tense copula *ja* in (181).

(180) *Lezgian* (= ex. (52), ch. 3)
    Za   wa-z   ada-n   wiri simfoni-jar   ja-da.
    I.ERG you-DAT he-GEN   all symphony-PL.ABS play-FUT
    'I will play all his symphonies for you.'

(181) *Lezgian* (Haspelmath 1993:313)
    Ruš-ar q'eleč' jak'-ar.i-n-bur   ja.
    girl-PL thin   flesh-PL-GEN-N.PL be.PRES
    'The girls are lean.'

Still, it is not necessarily the case that these forms are the result of fusion. As noted in n. 5, the ergative in Lezgian can be analyzed as a zero marker, just like the absolutive. The difference between ergative and absolutive is that the ergative attaches to the so-called oblique stem which also combines with overt case markers. This means that the ergative case is manifested only indirectly in the pronominal form *za*, which contrasts with the absolutive *zun* (Haspelmath 1993:184).

As for the verbal form *ja*, which appears to represent a verb root and a tense marker simultaneously, it should be observed that the verb in question is 'be', which is the semantically least contentful of all verbs. Even as a main verb, 'be' has very little content, as can be seen from the fact that it is phonologically empty in many languages, which is very unusual for a lexical root. Hence, it is possible that *ja*, which appears to be a single morpheme, is the realization of the present tense, whereas the verb root itself is not spelled out. This is all the more plausible as the ordinary marker of the simple present in Lezgian is -*da*, which is not too different from *ja*.[40] The past tense form of the copula, *tir*, could be analyzed as an allomorph of past tense or of the copula itself. Whichever one chooses the actual form has to be considered as the result of conditioned allomorphy, since *tir* is neither a regular tense marker or a regular realization of the copula.[41]

Notably, the present tense copulas in Japanese and Hindi are also not segmentable. In Japanese, the present form of the copula, *da* (see (37) and (85a)) contrasts with the segmentable past form *dat-ta*; thus, the present form apparently consists of only the root. In Hindi, the present third singular form *hε* contrasts with the past forms *th-aa* (masculine) and *th-ii* (feminine), which carry the regular past tense markers.

I will hypothesize on the basis of these facts that if a head-final language has a verb form where the tense marker is not formally separate from the verbal root, this will be a form of the copula. The form in question can be taken to represent only the tense marker or only the root, and we are not forced to assume that there has been fusion of the terminal nodes V° and T°.

As for the Hindi past tense forms just mentioned, the suffixes -*aa* and -*ii* are glossed in the examples in this chapter as 'PAST.MASC.SG' and 'PAST.FEM.SG', respectively. This glossing indicates that the markers are the combined spellout of tense and agreement. This is a little misleading, however, as will be clear from the paradigm given in (182).

(182) *Hindi tense and agreement suffixes* (from McGregor 1972)

	Present (Imperfect)		Past (Perfect)	
	Masculine	Feminine	Masculine	Feminine
Singular	-taa	-tii	-aa	-ii
Plural	-te	-tii	-e	-iiṁ

As we see, if *t*- is added to the past tense suffixes, the present (traditionally: imperfect) markers result (with the proviso that the past feminine plural has a suffix -*ṁ* which is absent in the corresponding present form). Hence, it could be postulated that past tense is represented by a zero marker and that the suffixes that are found in past tense forms represent only agreement (either subject or object agreement, as shown above).

Thus, it appears that the concept of zero markers combined with conditioned allomorphy will take us a long way toward explaining the realization of morphosyntactic features in head-final languages. In languages of this type, it is generally the case that each underlying morpheme is spelled out separately, by an empty or a non-empty marker, and any process which makes reference to more than one morpheme in the surface string must be purely phonological by nature, applying to morphemes that are linearly adjacent without paying attention to their structural relationship. This is what we would expect if complex words in languages of this type are normally made up of elements that have become adjacent as a consequence of movement into specifier positions.

Notes

1. The universal hierarchy of clausal functional heads (below the CP-domain) posited in Cinque (1999:106) is given in example (75), chapter 5.

2. One such phenomenon—namely, stranding of relative clauses—is discussed by Kayne (1994:124–125). On Kayne's analysis, the structure of a relative construction like *the book that I read* is as shown in (i):

(i) $[_{DP} [_{D^\circ}$ the] $[_{CP}$ book$_i$ $[_{C'} [_{C^\circ}$ that] I read t$_i$]]]

Here one would not expect *the book* to move as a constituent, leaving behind the relative clause. According to Kayne, this is in fact borne out—the D° in a structure like (i) cannot move along with the material in Spec-CP. Consequently, the English article *a*, unlike *the*, should not be associated with this D°; rather, it must be included in Spec-CP along with the relative correlate. Hence, we get the grammatical (ii) contrasting with the marginal (iii).

(ii)   A man walked in who we knew in high school.
(iii) ?? The man walked in who we knew in high school.

According to Kayne, the reason (iii) is not absolutely ungrammatical is that *the* does not necessarily reflect the D° of (i).

But even if certain cases of complement stranding could be accounted for as suggested, it is not clear how the explanation could be extended to (13b), or how it would follow that the Dutch counterpart of (iii) is fully grammatical, as shown in (iv) (similarly in German, see Büring & Hartmann 1997):

(iv)   *Dutch* (de Vries 1999:299)
       Ik   heb   de   man gesignaleerd die   en   rode koffer   draagt.
       I   have the   man noticed   who   a   red   suitcase carries
       'I have noticed the man who carries a red suitcase.'

An interesting alternative analysis of 'extraposed' relatives has been proposed by de Vries (1999). According to him, there is a coordination relation between an 'extraposed' relative clause and its antecedent, such that the second conjunct denotes a subset of the first. The coordinative head is phonologically empty, and any material within the second conjunct which also appears in the first conjunct is deleted. On this analysis, the structure of (iv) is (v). Now the constituency problem disappears, of course.

(v)   Ik heb [de man gesignaleerd] &: [de man die en rode koffer draagt gesignaleerd]

3. Another fact about Nama which is relevant in this connection is that whereas full pronominal objects appear in the same position as nominal objects, light pronominal objects follow the verb:

(i) *Nama*   (Hagman 1977)

a. //'ũku ke   //'ĩĩpà kè   mũũ
    they DECL   him REM.PAST   see
    'They saw him.'

b. //'ũku ke   kè   muu-pi
    they DECL   REM.PAST   see-him
    'They saw him.'

We would assume the constructions in (ia) and (ib) to be related by movement and that the light pronominal object in (ib) stays in its base position inside VP, whereas DPs and full pronouns move out. Thus, Nama is a counterexample to Greenberg's (1966) Universal 25, which states that "if a pronominal object follows the verb, so does the nominal object."

4. According to Koopman (1984), in Vata this is an option only for PPs that are not subcategorized by the verb.

5. The ergative in Lezgian is formed from the absolutive by adding an oblique stem suffix. Thus, the ergative form *Kamalova* is made up of the absolutive form *Kamalov* plus the oblique suffix *-a*. However, the oblique stem suffixes should probably not be treated as the realization of ergative case, since all other oblique cases are formed by adding a case suffix to the oblique stem (see Haspelmath 1993). Therefore the ergative is more plausibly analyzed as a zero suffix. I follow Haspelmath's practice and separate the oblique suffixes, which show considerable variation in form (see Haspelmath 1993:74–77), from the absolutive stem with a period, without representing them in the glosses.

6. See Haspelmath (1993:287–288) on the interpretation of omitted subjects in Lezgian.

7. According to Benincà and Poletto (1999), 'scene setting' adverbials appear in a position preceding nominal topics.

8. Note, by the way, that the Lezgian compound verbs shown in (34) and (35) can be seen as support for the hypothesis put forward by Hale and Keyser (1993) that unergatives are underlyingly transitives.

9. Here the tense marker is in reality followed by the agreement marker, just like we see in (39). However, since the verbal agreement marker for the third person singular is phonologically zero, I have not indicated it in the examples.

10. In Lezgian, 'want' and other verbs denoting affection and perception take a dative subject (see Haspelmath 1993:280–283).

11. I will use the glosses PAST and PRESENT for the tense markers in Japanese, although in the literature one may also encounter PAST/NONPAST or PERFECT/IMPERFECT.

12. Literally, *yoo-ni* is the dative form of *yoo* 'manner, way'. It can be used to form adverbs, as in *kono-yoo-ni* (this-way-DAT) 'like this'. When it marks a clausal complement, it is interpreted as 'to do' (Kaori Takamine, personal communication).

13. If serial verb constructions involve two or more verbs appearing inside one single extended VP, such that both/all verbs share one set of inflectional heads, we can explain why inflection appears on the first verb in SVO-languages but on the second verb in SOV-languages (Baker 1989). In SVO-languages, the higher verb head-moves to the inflectional heads, while in SOV-languages, the whole VP moves to the Spec of the lowest inflectional head.

14. The parallel between case markers and postpositions in Lezgian is also illustrated in the following examples. In (i), a clause with a masdar verb appears in the dative; in (ii), a masdar clause is combined with a postposition. As we see, the only difference between the two constructions is that the dative marker is seen as a suffix on the verb, which is the last element of the clause, whereas the postposition is seen as a separate word. This does not mean that the two constructions cannot have the same syntactic structure.

(i) *Lezgian* (Haspelmath 1993:363)

Wiči-n	ümür.di-n	exirimži	jis-ar	Mehamed.a	[lezgi
self-GEN	life-GEN	last	year-PL.ABS	Mehamed.ERG	Lezgian
č'al.a-n-ni		urus	č'al.a-n	slovar'	tük'ür-un.i]-z
language-GEN-and		Russian	language-GEN	dictionary	create-MSD-DAT
baxš-nawa-j.					
dedicate-PERF-PAST					

'Mehamed had dedicated the last years of his life to writing a Lezgian-Russian dictionary.'

(ii) *Lezgian* (Haspelmath 1993:214)

Či	asker-r.i	[Berlin.di-n	winel	jaru	pajdax	ak'ur-un]
our	soldier-PL.ERG	Berlin-GEN	above	red	flag.ABS	hoist-MSD
patal	exirimži	hužum	awu-na.			
for	last	attack.ABS	do-AOR			

'Our soldiers made the last attack to hoist the red flag over Berlin.'

15. See n. 29 for a counterargument to the claim that two nominative DPs are specifiers of one and the same head.

16. Negative polarity items are also reported to appear in subject position in West Greenlandic (Michael Fortesque, personal communication, Acquaviva 1997), which probably also is a head-final language. See also Laka (1993) on Basque and Yoon (1994) on Korean.

17. Kayne (1994:54) also suggests that Hindi belongs to the class of languages that make use of successive movements of complements to Spec.

18. In accordance with my argumentation in Julien (2001), I have glossed as PAST the suffix that Mahajan (1990, 1997) glosses as PERF(ECT). Strikingly, even when it appears on a non-finite verb it is formally identical to the marking on the finite verb. Similarly, I use PRES(ENT) instead of IMPERFECT.

19. This does not explain why agreeing objects and objects marked with -*ko* are necessarily specific, while non-agreeing objects are non-specific, as noted by Mahajan (1990). I assume, though, that an account of this contrast can be provided which is compatible with the analysis outlined here. Presumably, it has to do with the aspectual properties of the predicate.

20. The example they give is the following:

(i) *Japanese*   (Otani & Whitman 1991:347)

    a.   Zibun-no hatake-no   ninzin-ga   Makuguregaa   ozisan-no
        self-GEN   garden-GEN   carrot-NOM   McGregor   Mr.-GEN
        daikoobutu desi-ta.
        big.favorite be-PERF
        'The carrots from his own garden were Mr. McGregor's big favorite.'

    b.   Piita-mo [*e*]   daisuki   desi-ta.
        Peter-also   very.fond.of be-PERF
        'Peter was also very fond of the carrots from Mr. McGregor's garden.'
   #   'Peter was also very fond of the carrots from his own garden.'

21. It has been noted that in SVO languages, the second verb is phonologically empty in constructions corresponding to (90). In other words, SVO languages have *forward deletion* and not *backward* deletion of a shared verb (see Ross 1970). The following examples demonstrate that this is the case in English:

(i)   Mary ate two apples and Nancy, three bananas.
(ii) * Mary two apples and Nancy ate three bananas.

This can be explained if one considers the analysis of forward deletion given by Wilder (1997). According to him, backward deletion is not just a PF operation; it has to be licensed at LF. This can be seen from the fact that the deleted material need not be phonologically identical to the antecedent; what counts is that there is identity at LF. For example, a deleted verb may have an antecedent that has a different surface form. More precisely, agreement can vary, but tense may not, as (iii)–(iv) show:

(iii)   John drinks wine and his kids ~~drink~~ cola.
(iv) * John arrived yesterday and Mary ~~arrives~~ tomorrow.

Wilder relates this to the claim of Chomsky (1993) that tense features are visible at LF whereas agreement features are not. Hence, forward deletion is allowed as long as the deleted material is not different from the antecedent at LF.

It can also be shown that forward deletion does not require that the deleted part has the same position within its conjunct, in surface syntax, as the antecedent. Wilder (1997) illustrates this with the following German example:

(v) *German*   (Wilder 1997:96)
    Es stand gestern ein Mann vor der Tür und ___ bat mich um eine Zigarette.
    it stood yesterday a man before the door and asked me for a cigarette
    'Yesterday, a man stood at the door and asked me for a cigarette.'

On the assumption that the postverbal subject in the first conjunct raises covertly, we have another indication that LF is the relevant level for licensing of forward deletion.

It follows from the conditions listed in (95) that backward deletion applies to the verb in SVO languages only if any material following the verb is also deleted, as in (vi) (Wilder 1997:68).

(vi)   I think John ~~likes Beethoven~~ and you think Mary likes Beethoven.

In all other cases, forward deletion, as in (i)–(ii), is the only option. Since forward deletion involves LF as well as PF, it is more complex than backward deletion. Because of this, I assume that backward deletion is preferred over forward deletion. It would follow that backward deletion of the verb is chosen in Japanese. In English, by contrast, the more costly forward deletion is forced whenever there is an object which is not also deleted. This explains why the verb appears in the second conjunct in the Japanese construction in (90) but in the first conjunct in the corresponding English construction.

Also note that some languages allow both forward and backward deletion (Ross 1970). Since these languages are all SOV, we would expect them to have backward deletion, which is unavailable in SVO languages. But even if forward deletion is more costly, it is apparently not ruled out in every language that also has backward deletion.

22. The prefixed negation shown here combines with non-finite forms of a small class of verbs. It is possible that it does not represent the sentential negation but, instead, is more like derivational negators such as the English *un-*.

23. Saito and Fukui (1998:443 n. 7) claim that the impossibility of anaphor binding by a phrase which is moved long-distance has to do with locality and is no indication that long-distance scrambling is of a different type than medium scrambling. However, an analysis along these lines would not explain why long-distance scrambling yields Weak Crossover effects while medium scrambling does not.

24. Lasnik and Stowell (1991) characterize the empty categories in topic structures as null epithets, since they are similar to overt epithets in their ability to be A'-bound without giving rise to Weak Crossover effects. An example showing the absence of Weak Crossover effect with overt epithets is the following (from Lasnik & Stowell 1991):

(i) I went to visit John$_i$ last week, but his$_i$ secretary told me the man$_i$ was unavailable.

25. Focused constituents give the same effects even when they do not appear in clause-initial position—compare (i) and (ii) below.

(i)   His$_i$ mother praised John$_i$.
(ii) * His$_i$ mother praised JOHN$_i$.

This suggests that there is movement, overt or covert, even when the focused element is not clause-initial (Rochemont 1986, Rizzi 1997).

26. In Turkish, the order IO DO is fully acceptable alongside the order DO IO, shown in (56) (see, e.g., Kornfilt 1997). Further, as Kornfilt (1997) shows, the first object can always bind the second. Hence, it is possible that Turkish, like Japanese, has an optional A-movement operation which alters the ordering of the objects.

27. See also Karimi (1999) on scrambling in Persian.

28. Yanagida (1996) reports that there is a semantic contrast between (109a) and (109b). In (109a) one can have a reading where the adverb modifies the event as a whole. This reading is absent from (109b), which can only mean that Taroo's manner of reading was quick (see also Nakajima 1999:177). The same contrast is observed by Cinque (1999) in languages such as Italian and English. The two positions are prob-

ably not related by movement, since one can have a higher and a lower adverb in one clause, as in (i).

(i) Mary quickly read the letter quickly.

As we see, the higher adverb modifies the event as a whole, whereas the lower adverb modifies the verbal action only. Accordingly, Cinque (1999) proposes that there are two positions inside IP for celerative adverbs. Hence, it is likely that the adverb is in the higher position in (109a) and in the lower position in (109b). What we need then is some explanation of how the object has come to precede the adverb, which presumably is generated outside of VP.

29. It appears, by the way, that just like there are two different *wa* particles, constituents with the nominative marker *ga* can appear in two different projections with different functions. Yanagida (1996) notes that in clauses with two constituents that are marked as nominative subject, the second subject may follow an IP adverb like *mattaku* 'completely', but the first subject must precede the adverb:

(i) *Japanese* (Yanagida 1996:288)
  a. Nihon-ga   mattaku   kokumin-ga seijika-o   sinyoo-sitei-nai.
     Japan-NOM   completely people-NOM politician-ACC trust-DO-NEG
     'It is Japan where completely people distrust politicians.'

  b. * Mattaku   Nihon-ga   kokumin-ga seijika-o   sinyoo-sitei-nai.
       completely Japan-NOM   people-NOM politician-ACC trust-DO-NEG

The two nominative constituents also get different readings. In the terms of Kuno (1973), the first of them will get an 'exhaustive listing' reading, whereas the second will get a 'neutral description' reading.

On Ura's (1994) analysis of (64a,b), the two constituents marked with nominative are both specifiers of AgrSP. This analysis leaves us without an explanation of why they get different readings and why only one of them can follow an IP adverb. It seems more likely that the two *ga*-marked constituents are specifiers of two different heads.

As Yanagida (1996) points out, the adverb placement suggests that the 'neutral description' subject is in VP, whereas the 'exhaustive listing' subject is outside of VP. This gets support from the fact that there is a position for moved constituents between the two 'subjects', as shown in Sakai (1994):

(ii) *Japanese* (Sakai 1994:301)
  a. Masao-ga   yuujin-ga   Boston-ni   sundei-ru.
     Masao-NOM   friend-NOM   Boston-LOC   live-PRES
     'Masao's friend lives in Boston.'

  b. Masao-ga   Boston-ni$_i$ yuujin-ga   t$_i$ sundei-ru.
     Masao-NOM   Boston-LOC   friend-NOM   live-PRES
     'Masao's friend lives in Boston.'

Moreover, Sakai (1994) shows that movement to the position between two nominative phrases can reconstruct:

(iii) *Japanese* (Sakai 1994:302)
    a.   Masao-ga   kodomo-tachi-ga$_i$ otagai-o$_i$ kirattei-ru.
        Masao-NOM   children-PL-NOM   each.other-ACC   dislike-PRES
        'Masao's children dislike each other.'

    b.   Masao-ga   otagai-o$_i$ kodomo-tachi-ga$_i$ kirattei-ru.
        Masao-NOM   each.other-ACC   children-PL-NOM   dislike-PRES
        'Masao's children dislike each other.'

This suggests that the moved constituent in (iib) and (iiib) is in a focus or topic position. But then the first nominative constituent must also be in a focus or topic position, unlike the second one, which is probably inside VP.

30. Thus, there are modifications to the claim made by Saito and Fukui (1998:443) that "multiple scrambling is freely allowed in Japanese."

31. Mahajan (1990) indicates that the *wh*-phrase in (118) and similar examples could be replaced by an indefinite DP without any change of judgments. This corroborates my claim that the fronting in question is focus movement, since indefinites are like *wh*-elements in that they are not felicitous as topics.

32. Kural (1992) also argues that fronting in Turkish is always to an A'-position.

33. The cases where an element appears in the immediate preverbal position as a consequence of movement to the focus position should be distinguished, I believe, from cases where an element is frozen in the lower Spec-VP. For example, Kural (1992) gives some examples of verb-object idioms where the idiomatic reading is lost if the object is moved away from the immediate preverbal position:

(i) *Turkish* (Kural 1992:44)
    a.   Ahmet-in   umut-lar-ı   su-ya   düş-tü.
        Ahmet-GEN   hope-PL-3s   water-DAT   fall-PAST
        'Ahmet lost his hopes.'

    b.   Su-ya   Ahmet-in   umut-lar-ı   düş-tü.
        water-DAT   Ahmet-GEN   hope-PL-3s   fall-PAST
        'Ahmet's hopes fell into water.'

Presumably, the idiomatic reading is lost in (ib) because of the familiar property of objects in idioms that they are non-referential and cannot normally be moved. Hence, there is no need to postulate movement in (ia); most likely, the object is sitting in the lower Spec-VP.

In the case of indefinite DPs, on the other hand, which also normally show up in preverbal position (Kural 1992), a movement analysis is probably the correct one, given that indefinites normally represent new information and would therefore be expected to move to the focus position.

34. More generally, non-specific quantifier phrases cannot be topics; see Cinque (1990), Lasnik and Stowell (1991).

35. It is possible that the *wh*-feature ultimately ends up in Force°, so that the whole clause gets type-marked by it. Evidence for this movement is the fact that a *wh*-phrase unambiguously takes scope over a preceding quantifier, as in (i):

(i) *Turkish* (Kural 1997:508)
Herkes   kim-i   ara-dı?
everyone who-ACC call-PAST
'Who did everyone call?'
(which y, y a person, $\forall$x [x called y]; * $\forall$x which y, y a person, [x called y])

If the subject in (i) is in Spec-TopP, as I assume in my analysis, it follows that the *wh*-feature must have moved to Force° to scope over it.

36. The effect is also seen in the following:

(i) *Turkish* (Kural 1992:40)
  a. Ahmet kim-i   nerde gör-muş?
     Ahmet who-ACC where see-RP.PAST
     Who did Ahmet see where?'

  b. * Ahmet nerede kim-i   gör-muş?
      Ahmet where who-ACC see-RP.PAST
      'Where did Ahmet see who?'

If the direct object is higher than the locative in base structure, it is not surprising that when both the direct object and the locative are questioned, the direct object must precede the locative.

Further, if indefinite DPs are like *wh*-elements in that they trigger movement to Spec-FocP, the following contrast could be explained along the same lines, if the base order of the objects is IO DO (contra Kornfilt 1997):

(ii) *Turkish* (Kural 1992:41)
  a. Ahmet bir ögrenci-ye   bir kitap ver-miş.
     Ahmet a   student-DAT a   book give-RP.PAST
     'Ahmet gave a book to a student.'

  b. * Ahmet bir kitap bir ögrenci-ye   ver-miş.
      Ahmet a   book a   student-DAT give-RP.PAST
      'Ahmet gave a book to a student.'

37. See also the description of the Californian language Central Pomo in Mithun (1993).

38. Postverbal *wh*-phrases are excluded in Turkish as well, except if they are echoed (Kural 1992).

39. Spencer (1991) uses the terms 'fusion', 'multiple exponence', and 'cumulation' to speak of cases where one single formative expresses more than one underlying morpheme. Matthews (1991), on the other hand, makes a distinction between 'cumulation', where a single marker expresses several underlying morphemes, and 'fused marking', which in his terminology refers to cases where two or more markers are realized as one as a result of sandhi processes. Clearly, the way in which 'fusion' is used in the present work is closer to Spencer (1991).

40. Nash (1994) makes a similar proposal for Georgian.

41. The verb form *ze-da* 'be-FUT' in (155) is based on the verb *xun* 'be, become' and not on the standard copula (see Haspelmath 1993:136).

4

Prefixes

4.1 Overview

In the preceding chapters, the word-forming properties of head movement and phrasal movement have been the topic of discussion. What these movement operations have in common is that as a rule they give rise to suffixes. More precisely, if head movement or phrasal movement creates a complex word out of a lexical element and one or more elements from the functional domain of that lexical element, the functional elements will end up as suffixes on the lexical stem.

Needless to say, there are also prefixes to be found in the languages of the world, even though they are not as frequent as suffixes, and they will have to be accounted for. In the LCA-based syntactic model I am assuming throughout this work, there are two logically possible ways to derive a complex word consisting of a lexical stem and a prefix: either the prefix originates in the complement of the lexical element and moves to the left of the lexical element (by head movement or XP-movement) or the prefix originates to the left of the lexical element and there is no subsequent movement operation that alters the relative order of the two items.

The first possibility is illustrated by the Nadëb clauses shown in (1). In (1a), the verb *asooh* 'sit' is combined with the postpositional phrase *bxaah yó* 'tree on'. In (1b), by contrast, the postposition appears as a prefix on the verb, whereas the nominal complement of the postposition is now the object of the verb and moves to the front of the clause, as Nadëb is one of the few languages with OSV as the basic order (Weir 1986).[1]

(1) *Nadëb* (Weir 1986:299–300)
   a. Kalapéé asooh bxaah yó.
      child sit tree on
      'The child is sitting on the tree.'

   b. Bxaah kalapéé y-asooh.
      tree child on-sit
      'The child is sitting on the tree.'

Weir (1986) further demonstrates that when the prefix appears on the verb, it is ungrammatical to have the postposition in the same clause. She concludes that in (1b), it is indeed the postposition that has become a part of the verbal word.

In more current terms, (1b) could be described as the result of the P° having head-moved and left-adjoined to V°, so that a complex head P°+V° is formed.[2] If this is possible, the PP in (1a) must be the complement of the verb; otherwise, the incorporation operation would violate the HMC. When the postposition is incorporated, Spec-PP and Spec-VP are in the same minimal domain; this is what allows the complement of the postposition to raise and become the structural object of the verb.[3]

Analyses along these lines have been suggested for more familiar cases of prefixation as well. For example, it is what Hoekstra (1992) proposes for the Dutch verb prefixes *be-* and *ver-*, shown in (2) and (3).

(2) *Dutch* (see Hoekstra 1992:165)
    a. Ik   woon   *(in)   dit   huis.
        I   live   in   this   house
        'I live in this house.'

    b. Ik   be-woon   dit   huis.
        I   BE-live   this   house
        'I live in this house.'

(3) *Dutch* (Hoekstra 1992:166)
    a. Jan   drinkt   z'n   problemen   *(weg).
        Jan   drinks   his   problems   away
        'Jan drinks his problems away.'

    b. Jan   ver-drinkt   z'n   problemen.
        Jan   VER-drinks   his   problems
        'Jan drinks his problems away.'

In (2) and (3), the prefixes *be-* and *ver-* create verbs whose direct objects cannot be the direct objects of the corresponding non-prefixed verbs, as demonstrated in the (a) examples. When the verb appears without the prefix, the presence of the DP that was the direct object of the prefixed verb requires that the construction also contains a preposition or a particle, in which case the DP is arguably selected by the preposition or the particle and not by the verb. Hoekstra (1992) proposes that the relation between the prefix and the DP object in the (b) examples is similar to the relation between the DP and the particle in (3a); that is, the prefix is underlyingly a particle, which on Hoekstra's analysis means that it is the predicate of a small clause (the subject of the small clause is of course the DP that surfaces in object position). Note that the fact that the prefix appears on the second position verb in (2b) and (3b) indicates that the prefix and the verb constitute a complex head. The difference between the prefixes *be-* and *ver-*

on one hand and particles like *weg* on the other is then that the prefixes but not the particles obligatorily incorporate into the verb.[4]

In a similar vein, Horvath (1978) claims that the preverbal particles in Hungarian, as exemplified in (4a), are in fact intransitive postpositions.

(4) *Hungarian* (Horvath 1978:143)

    a. János ki-ment.   b. János   a   könyvtár-ba ment.
       Janos out-went   Janos the library-ILL   went
       'Janos went out.'   'Janos went to the library.'

By comparing (4a) and (4b), we see that the prefix in (4a) has the same function as the illative phrase in (4b). This is one reason why Horvath (1978) assumes that the prefix is a syntactic element in its own right. She further makes the reasonable assumption that the illative marker and other markers of non-structural case in Hungarian are postpositions (Horvath 1978:158 n. 2), and so the illative phrase in (4b) must be a PP. She then shows that directional prefixes in Hungarian have the same distribution as directional PPs, and she concludes that the 'prefixes' are PPs that consist of the P° alone.

From the example in (4a) one might be led to think that the P° is prefixed to the verb as a result of head incorporation. However, the prefix is not always adjacent to the verb that selects it. If a modal verb is present, the prefix will appear to the left of the modal, as shown in (5a,b).

(5) *Hungarian* (Horvath 1978:150–152)

    a. János ki   akar   men-ni.
       János out wants go-INF
       'Janos wants to go out.'

    b.* János akar   ki-men-ni.
        János wants out-go-INF

    c. János a   könyvtár-ba akar   men-ni.
       János the library-ILL   wants go-INF
       'Janos wants to go to the library.'

    d.* János akar   a   könyvtár-ba men-ni.
        János wants the library-ILL go-INF

As shown in (5c–d), a directional PP has the same distribution as the prefix also in this case. The operation responsible for placing the PP to the left of the modal in (5c) cannot be head movement; it must clearly be phrasal movement. Accordingly, it is possible that the prefix ends up to the left of the modal in (5a) as a result of phrasal movement and that phrasal movement puts the prefix in front of the verb in (4a). This means that in neither case are the prefix and the verb one syntactic constituent. Rather, the verb in (4a) forms a word with an element in a preceding Spec position. On the background of the discussion in the preceding chapter, this should not be seen as an outrageous claim.

More generally, whenever a lexical root has a prefix which does not obviously belong to the functional domain of the lexical element, one should investigate the possibility that the prefix originates inside the complement of the lexical element. There is nothing remarkable about such complex words: just as suffixing patterns can be created by head movement or phrasal movement of lexical roots to the left of the heads of the functional domain, we would expect that prefixing patterns can be created by head movement or phrasal movement of elements from the complements of lexical elements to the left of those lexical elements.

However, given the assumptions about syntax that are the basis of the present investigation, neither the head movement analysis nor the movement-to-Spec analysis can be extended to prefixed tense markers. If a tense marker is prefixed to its associated verb, the verb cannot have moved to or past T°, because it would then have to precede the tense marker instead of following it. The pattern could not have been produced by moving T° to V°, either, since this would be a lowering operation, which has no place in the framework I am assuming.

The only possibility open to us is to claim that if a complex word contains a tense marker preceding a verb root, the tense marker and the verb root must represent syntactic heads that have not been moved with respect to each other. It is still in principle possible that both the tense head and the verb may have moved, but their relative order must be the same in the surface structure as in the base structure. It follows that in such cases the two elements do not constitute a complex head.

It was argued in the preceding chapter that a sequence of two or more elements that are not contained in a single complex head may be perceived as constituting one word if the distribution of that sequence meets the criteria for wordhood: that is, if the sequence has independent distribution externally and shows cohesion and regularity internally. It is conceivable that this does not apply only to elements that have become adjacent after movement of one element to the Spec of the other but also to elements that are adjacent for other reasons. For example, it is possible that if Y° heads the complement of X°, and Spec-YP is empty, the sequence XY can be a word, as suggested in section 1.4.3. This word will then simply consist of the two heads in their base positions. If such cases really exist, it means that words may come into existence even in the absence of any non-phonological process that can possibly be characterized as a word-forming one.

In the remainder of this chapter I pursue the idea that a prefix can be simply the spellout of a head that is in a higher position than the root it combines with distributionally and in many cases also phonologically.

First, in section 4.2, I present the analysis of complex words in Shona given in Myers (1990). According to Myers, many of the morpheme sequences that are customarily treated as words in Shona and other Bantu languages are just phonological words and not syntactic constituents. As we will see, it is prefixes in particular that are attached to stems by purely phonological means. Thus, Myers's conclusions considering Shona words lend support to my claim about temporal and other inflectional prefixes.

In section 4.3 I deal with the contrast between inflectional prefixes and free preposed markers. I show that for some preposed inflectional markers, there are either distributional or phonological reasons, or both, for not treating them as prefixes on the verb: these markers are phonologically heavy or separated from the verb by word-like elements. By contrast, preposed inflectional markers which are phonologically light and always adjacent to the verb tend to be perceived as prefixes on the verb. That is, it appears that this holds for verb-initial and verb-final languages. In verb-medial languages, preposed inflectional markers are more often seen as free elements. The explanation I suggest for this is that in SVO languages, which are clearly in the majority among verb-medial languages, preposed verbal markers could potentially be seen as prefixes on the verb or as suffixes on the subject. This tension is resolved by treating the preposed markers as free elements, so that they go with neither the subject nor the verb.

Finally, the discussion of prefixes is rounded off in section 4.4 with some concluding remarks.

4.2 Complex words in Shona

A way to start thinking about the question of whether a word can be just a sequence of heads in their base positions is to consider the relation between syntactic heads that belong to the same extended projection, where an extended projection consists of a lexical element and the functional categories associated with it. Whereas a lexical element often may have various types of complements, there is no such variation to be found with respect to the functional projections that are generated on top of a lexical element. A lexical element of a given category will always occur with the same set of functional heads, and the base order of these heads is also fixed, I will assume, both within and across languages. This means that the sequence of heads which make up an extended projection has, to a certain degree, the internal cohesion that characterize words. The only way the string can be broken up linearly is by intervening phrases in Spec-positions. If no such intervening phrases are allowed, the sequence will always be a continuous string and thus have the appearance of a single word, consisting of a lexical stem and one or more inflectional prefixes.

Recall that this was the analysis suggested in section 2.4 for the prefix pattern of Bantu verbs. The following example was given:

(6) *Chibemba* (= ex. (82), ch. 2)
     n-kà-láá-boomba
     1s-FUT-PROG-work
     'I'll be working tomorrow.'

Here we have a word consisting of a verb root preceded by an aspect marker, a tense marker, and a subject agreement marker. My proposal is that these are simply heads that are spelled out in their base-generated order. That is, the structural relation between the morphemes that make up the complex word in (6) is as shown schematically in (7). This is then the analysis that I argue for here.

(7)

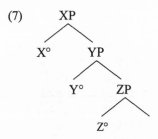

An important work in connection with the analysis of inflectional prefixes is Myers (1990), which presents a detailed study of Shona. Like most Bantu languages, Shona has inflectional prefixes on the verb, whereas derivational markers are normally suffixed. An example of a complex Shona verb is shown in (8).

(8)   *Shona*   (see Myers 1990:27)
      á-cha-rí-téng-és-á
      3sS-FUT-3sO-buy-CAUS-FV
      'He/she will sell it.'

Strings of the type exemplified in (8) have since Doke (1929) been interpreted as words, in Shona as well as in other Bantu languages. A significant fact is that the original motivation for this division was purely phonological: the domain of stress placement and of certain tone alternations was defined as a word. Myers argues that several of the units that are thus traditionally regarded as words are just phonological units and not morphological or syntactic constituents. We will consider some examples.

First, we look briefly at the so-called associative markers in Shona, which are variously referred to as 'prefixes' or as 'inflections', but clearly have the syntactic behavior of prepositions (Myers 1990:81–82). They enter into constructions like the following:

(9)   *Shona*   (Myers 1990:84)
      a. né-va-ná   v-ósé   ava
          ASSOC-2-child   2-all   2.this
          'with all these children'

b. na-áva   va-ná v-ósé
   ASSOC-2.this 2-child 2-all
   'with all these children'

c.? né-v-ose   va-ná   ava
    ASSOC-2-all   2-child 2.this
    'with all these children'

In (9a,b,c), what follows the associative marker is a DP. Interestingly, the grammaticality of the construction as a whole exactly mirrors the grammaticality of that DP. As can be seen from the orthography, the associative marker is traditionally taken to form a word with whatever happens to be the initial element of the following DP. Myers emphasizes that this is merely a phonological fact—note that there are no morphological or syntactic restrictions on this word-forming process—and that from a syntactic point of view, what we have is a preposition with a DP complement. Together the associative marker and the DP have the distribution of a PP:

(10) *Shona* (Myers 1990:85)
     mwaná wo-kú-mushá   kw-édú
     child   ASSOC-17-village 17-our
     'a child of our village'

A DP, on the other hand, would be ungrammatical in the position following the noun in (10) (see Myers 1990:85). All in all, analyzing the associative marker as a preposition is a far more elegant solution than seeing it as nominal inflection.

Other elements in Shona also form a phonological word with elements that follow in linear order. Among these are the copula, as in (11), and the so-called auxiliaries, exemplified by the morphemes immediately preceding the verb root in (12):

(11) *Shona* (Myers 1990:86–87)
     a. íye ndí-babá   wángu   b. ndo-upi   mwana
        he COP-father my   COP-which child
        'He is my father.'   'Which one is the child?'

(12) *Shona* (Myers 1990:90)
     a. sviko-báta   húkú   b. ndi-no-fúmó-end-a
        upon.arrival-catch fowl   1s-HAB-early-go-FV
        'Upon arrival, catch the fowl!'   'I go first thing in the morning.'

All the words shown above share certain phonological characteristics. Each word bears one single main stress, which falls on the penultimate syllable. In this respect, each unit is a phonological word. This does not entail that each unit must also be a constituent in a morphological or syntactic sense, however. It is well known that functional elements do not necessarily map into phonological words; they are often prosodically dependent on full words (see, e.g., Selkirk 1986, Inkelas & Zec 1995, Kager 1995). It appears that in Shona, every phonological word must contain at least one lexical element (see Myers 1990:122–123), which provides the head foot of the phonological word. The head foot, which must be trochaic, is aligned with the right edge of the phonological word (see, e.g., McCarthy & Prince 1993a). As a result, the phonological word in Shona has penultimate stress and consists of a lexical stem with a maximal sequence of functional elements attached to its left (see Myers 1990:121). That is, the formation of phonological words in Shona is comparable to what we saw in section 1.4.1 from Shanghai Chinese; the only difference being that whereas phonological words are formed from left to right in Shanghai Chinese, they are formed from right to left in Shona.

We will now consider in more detail the verbal word given in (8) and repeated here for convenience as (13a). In (13b) I indicate what Myers (1990:116) takes to be the immediate constituents of this string.

(13) *Shona* (= ex. (8), ch. 4)
    a. á-cha-rí-téng-és-a
        3sS-FUT-3sO-buy-CAUS-FV
        'He/she will sell it.'

    b. [[á-cha   ] [rí-téng-és-a   ]]
        3sS-FUT   3sO-buy-CAUS-FV

The second constituent in (13b), minus the object marker, is called the verbal stem. Shona has several processes which appear to make reference to the verbal stem. For example, it is the stem which is reduplicated to form the repetitive, as demonstrated in (14):

(14) *Shona* (Myers 1990:30)
    a. ku-téng-és-á   b. ku-téng-és-á-tengesa
        INF-buy-CAUS-FV   INF-buy-CAUS-FV-REDUP
        'to sell'   'to go all around selling'

Further, Myers argues that the verbal stem is cyclically right-headed, so that each suffix takes scope over the elements to its left. Concerning the object marker, which is the initial element of the second main constituent in (13b), Myers suggests that it is a proclitic on the verb. (See Myers 1990 for details.)

Myers also holds that the cluster of prefixed inflection markers constitutes the other part of the word in (13) and that, within this constituent, the tense marker is suffixed on the subject agreement marker. His reason for saying this is that whereas the subject agreement marker is obligatory with all finite verbs, the tense marker is dependent on the presence of the subject marker.

An important feature of Myers's analysis is the fact that it is based on the assumption that word structure is binary branching throughout. However, if the string in (13) is merely a phonological word this is not necessarily so. I would like to propose instead that the verbal word in (13) has the structure shown in (15), with irrelevant projections left out.

(15)

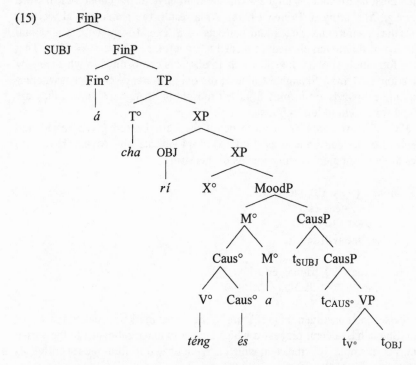

As one can see from (15), I agree with Myers that the so-called verbal stem, which consists of the verbal root together with the suffixes, is a constituent; more precisely, I assume that these elements are contained within one complex head, formed by successive head movement. Since phonological words are built from right to left in Shona, phonological processes would not suffice to include the suffixes in a word with the verb root. Still, the suffixes are fully integrated into the verbal word phonologically. Although each phonological word must contain a lexical root, the main stress need not fall on this root; it may well fall on a suffix—recall that Shona has penultimate stress, so that, for example, in (14a), it is the causative morpheme that bears the main stress. This means that the head foot is always final in the complex made up of a lexical head and its suffixes; in other words, for stress assignment the suffixes count as part of the lexical element. This suggests that the suffixes form a constituent with the verb also outside of phonology. This would be the case if the suffixes are contained in a complex head with the verb stem itself, as indicated in (15). This would also account for Myers's claim that the verbal stem is cyclically right-headed, so that each suffix takes scope over the elements to its left—in a complex head, each element is generated above the elements to its left. The complex head must be located in the position of the rightmost and underlyingly highest head, which happens to be the so-called final vowel (FV in the glosses). Myers (1990:29) states of the final vowels that *-e* marks subjunctive, potential, or negative, and *-a* marks all other verb forms. From this one might guess that the final vowel is a mood marker with the features [±REALIS] and that it represents a mood head into which the verb obligatory moves.[5]

The object marker, which is analyzed by Myers as a proclitic on the verb, does not seem to be a part of this complex head. For example, the object marker is never included in the reduplicated verb stem, as (16) shows. On the other hand, the distribution of the object marker is completely different from that of free object pronouns, which appear in the normal object position following the verb, as in (17).

(16) *Shona* (Myers 1990:48)
   ndi-nó-mu-kúmbir-a-kumbira
   1sS-HAB-3sO-ask-REAL-REDUP
   'I keep asking him.'

(17) *Shona* (Myers 1990:51)
   ku-endes-a   íye
   INF-send-REAL   him
   'to send him'

Myers also notes that the object marker is not obligatory, but it can nevertheless co-occur with a DP object, which then gets a definite reading. In other words, the object marker in Shona is similar to the object marker in Chichewa, which, according to the description in Bresnan and Mchombo (1987), is an incorporated pronoun and not a realization of object agreement.

My proposal is that the incorporated object marker is a *weak* pronoun, which climbs to a Spec position immediately above MoodP. Since it is a widespread phenomenon that weak pronouns raise higher than strong pronouns (and full DPs), we have then to some degree accounted for the distribution of the object marker.

On an alternative analysis that one might want to entertain, the object marker is incorporated into V° before V° moves. This would mean that the object marker is the lowest component of the complex verbal head. However, this analysis runs into problems when applicative constructions are taken into consideration. As shown in (18), an applicative object may be referred to by the prefixed object marker:

(18) *Shona* (Myers 1990:50)
   ku-mú-véréng-er-a
   INF-3sO-read-APPL-REAL
   'to read to him/her'

The applicative morpheme has been analyzed (e.g., in Pylkkänen 2000) as a head in the extended VP. The applied object is then taken to originate in the Spec of the applicative head. According to Pylkkänen, the lower part of the base structure of (18) is as shown in (19).

(19)

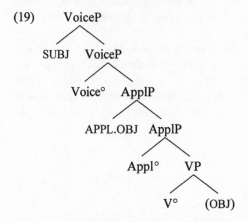

From this initial configuration, it is not possible for the applied object to head-move into V°. On the other hand, if the applied object is realized as a light pronominal, and there is a head higher up in the structure which attracts light pronouns, the applied object would be expected to show up in that higher position. Thus, the analysis suggested above of the object marker in Shona appears to get some support from applicative constructions.

If the weak pronoun in Shona is situated above the complex head which makes up the stem, it can only be included in a word with the stem by phonological means, in the manner already suggested. This would to some extent explain the ambiguities that surround the attempts at giving a morphological analysis of the object marker in Bantu, by the way. For example, Barrett-Keach (1986) argues that the object marker in Swahili is not constituent-final and that it must be grouped with the verb root and not with the preceding inflectional markers. For Myers (1990), as we have just noted, the object marker is attached to the stem without being an integrated part of the stem. Now if the object marker is situated in a Spec between the verb root and the cluster of inflectional markers, it is expected that it shows no clear signs of belonging structurally with either of them.

As for the sequence of prefixed inflectional markers, which Myers takes to be a constituent alongside the stem, one sees from (15) that I assume that these markers represent functional heads which are spelled out in their base positions. Because of the prosodic characteristics of Shona, with phonological words being built from right to left, these heads are attached phonologically to the verb root, to which they bear no particular non-phonological relation.

The whole morpheme string in (13a) is perceived as a grammatical word because it has the distributional properties that are characteristic of words. It has freedom of position relative to other constituents of the clause, and it cannot be interrupted by phrases. Phrasal arguments and adverbials either precede or follow the verbal word, as in (20)–(22).

(20) *Shona* (Myers 1990:65)
sángo rí-no-p-á   anéta
bush   5(SUBJ)-HAB-give-REAL   him-who-is-tired
'The wilderness gives to him who is tired.'

(21) *Shona* (Myers 1990:211)
Vá-cha-téng-a   bángá
3pS-FUT-buy-REAL   knife
'They will buy a knife.'

(22) *Shona* (Myers 1990:90)
ndi-chá-tó-dzok-a   mangwáná   zvekáre
1sS-FUT-must-return-REAL   tomorrow   again
'I'll have to come back again tomorrow.'

The only elements that may intervene between the verb root and the prefixes are the so-called auxiliaries, which have already been presented in (12) above. Another auxiliary is the modal element *tó* in (22), and some further examples are given in (23). As is evident from all these cases, the auxiliaries are seen as part of the verbal word.

(23) *Shona* (Myers 1990:90, 92)
a. ndi-no-fúmó-end-a
   1sS-HAB-early-go-REAL
   'I go first thing in the morning.'

b. ndi-chá-to-chimbidzó-dzok-a
   1sS-FUT-must-quickly-return-REAL
   'I'll have to come back quickly.'

c. v-á-ká-swéro-nyatso-támb-á
   3pS-PAST-REM-all.day-carefully-dance-REAL
   'They danced carefully all day.'

d. v-á-raro-támb-á   ngoma ku-bira
   3pS-PAST-all.night-dance-REAL drums LOC-ceremony
   'They danced all night to the drums at the ceremony.'

Myers's analysis of the auxiliaries is that they are verbs taking the base VP as their complement. The motivation for this analysis is that most of the auxiliaries are formed from verbal roots, with a final vowel *-o* instead of *-a*. Thus, the source of the auxiliary *sviko* in (12a), glossed as 'upon arrival', is transparently the verb *svika* 'arrive'; *chimbidzó* 'quickly' in (23b) is based on *chímbídza* 'hurry'; and *raro* 'all night' in (23d) is based on *rárá* 'sleep' (Myers 1990). The auxiliaries are also subject to certain tone alternations that are otherwise found on verbs (see Myers 1990:91–92). In addition, Myers takes into account the distributional fact that auxiliaries are like verbs in that they immediately follow the verbal inflectional markers.

If Myers is right, the auxiliaries represent verbal heads that are positioned between the inflectional markers and the complex head containing the base verb. In this case, a verbal word of which an auxiliary is a part can still be characterized as a sequence of heads that is spelled out as one phonological word.

The head analysis is probably the correct one, at least for the habitual marker which is included in the class of auxiliaries by Myers (1990) but which presumably represents a functional head between the tense marker and the verb:[6]

(24) *Shona* (Myers 1990:90)
        nd-a-í-end-a
        1s-PAST-HAB-go-REAL
        'I used to go.'

Concerning the other 'auxiliaries', it is also possible that they are in fact adverbs. The final vowel *-o* that appears on the auxiliaries is otherwise used to derive nouns from verbs, as in the following example:

(25) *Shona* (Myers 1990:28)
        mu-chat-o
        3-marry-N
        'marriage'

One might therefore guess that 'auxiliaries' with a final *-o* are deverbal adverbs. If this is really the case, these elements cannot occupy head positions in the verbal projection line; they must be situated in Spec positions instead. The crucial thing about these elements then is that just like IP adverbs in general, they do not expand into complex phrases and because of this, they can be accommodated into the verbal word.

Regardless of which analysis will eventually prove to be the correct one, it is very improbable that the auxiliaries form a complex syntactic head together with the inflectional markers and the base verb. Thus, the verbal word in Shona is not a syntactic constituent. In spite of this, it has several properties that contribute to its status as a word. First, there is the fact pointed out by Myers (1990) that the string consisting of the verbal inflectional markers, the 'auxiliaries', and the verb stem is a phonological word. In addition, it is also probably a minimal utterance. Admittedly, Myers (1990) does not explicitly discuss what the minimal utterances of Shona are, but it is apparent from his many examples that a verbal stem must minimally be combined with a final vowel—that is, with a suffixed mood marker—and with some inflectional marker, which may be either a subject agreement marker combined with a tense marker (of which the finite present tense is phonologically zero) and possibly with aspectual markers, modal markers, and/or object markers, or, alternatively, just the infinitive marker *ku-*. Some examples are given in (26).

(26) *Shona* (Myers 1990)

    a. á-ngá-véreng-e   b. ndí-téng-é
        3s-POT-read-IRR   1s.SUBJC-buy-IRR
        'She/he could read.'   '(that) I might buy'

    c. ku-rí-téng-á   d. ndi-chí-p-á
        INF-5(OBJ)-buy-REAL   1s-PRES.PTC-give-REAL
        'to buy it (a class 5 thing)'   'me giving'

Interestingly, Taylor (1985) gives some examples of possible answers to questions in Nkore-Kiga, another Bantu language. One of his examples is given below:

(27) *Nkore-Kiga* (Taylor 1985:11)

    a. W-aa-twara   amate?   b. N-aa-ga-twara.
        2s-TD.PAST-take   milk   1s-TD.PAST-3s-take
        'Did you take the milk?'   'I did'

As we see, the verbal root is not used as an answer on its own; it is accompanied by a tense marker and a subject marker. This state of facts clearly favors an analysis where the preverbal markers are part of the verbal word. Presumably, this also holds for Shona.

As discussed in section 1.4.2, the distributional properties of freedom of position and internal cohesion, together with the ability to appear as a free form, constitute the only criteria which can be used to pick out the (non-phonological) words in any string of speech. Other properties that have been claimed to distinguish words from other linguistic units can only be ascribed to morpheme strings that have already been identified as words. Hence, I believe that it is the distributional criteria that native speakers and linguists alike rely on in the identification of the words in a given language.

In the case under discussion, the fact that the morpheme string in question also is a phonological word facilitates its being analyzed as a word in a non-phonological sense. However, being a phonological word is not the decisive criterion for wordhood. As we saw in section 1.4.1, a phonological word may comprise elements that are distributed independently of each other in syntax, and, conversely, a grammatical word may consist of more than one phonological word. Hence, it is mainly the distributional properties of the morpheme string made up of the verbal root and verbal markers in Shona which bring about its status as a grammatical word.

4.3 Prefixes and free preposed markers

In the preceding section I argued that the preposed verbal grammatical markers in Shona are taken to form a word with the verb root because a verb root always appears with one or more inflectional markers in front of it. It is clear, however, that not every such string in every language is interpreted as one single word. In (28)–(30) we see examples of languages where the ordering of elements in the clause is similar to that in Shona, but where the preverbal inflectional elements are seen as free elements and not as part of the verbal word.

(28) *Makaa* (Heath 1991:11)
    mə́   á   ŋgə   wííŋg   òmpyə̂
    1s   REM.PAST   PROG   chase.away   dogs
    'I was chasing the dogs away.'

(29) *Sre* (Manley 1972)
    khay   nɛh   rəp   lɔt
    he   PERF   INCH   go
    'He has started to go.'

(30) *Ndyuka* (Huttar & Huttar 1994:495)
    Ofu a   be   pasa mi be   o   sutu   en.
    if   3s   PAST   pass 1s PAST FUT shoot 3sOBL
    'If it had passed by, I would have shot it.'

The relation between inflectional prefixes on one hand and preposed free inflectional morphemes on the other is the topic of this section. I start with some general remarks in 4.3.1, where I also present some facts concerning the frequency of prefixes and free preposed markers in different word orders. The patterns that we find in each main word order type are then discussed in more detail in subsequent subsections: in 4.3.2 I deal with verb-initial languages, in 4.3.3, with verb-final languages and, finally, verb-medial languages are taken up in 4.3.4.

4.3.1 The affixation of preposed markers

The decision to represent the inflectional markers as free elements or as prefixes on the verb is apparently not always based on well-defined criteria. Thus, it sometimes happens that one linguist chooses the prefix analysis while another prefers the particle analysis for one and the same language. For example, Sylvain (1936:79) states that the markers of tense, aspect, and modality in Haitian Creole are prefixed to the verb, as shown in (31). In Spears (1990), on the other hand, all preverbal markers are analyzed as auxiliaries, and they are written as separate words, as in (32).

(31) *Haitian Creole*   (Sylvain 1936:87)
n´   té-kwè   u   t´-a-vini
1p   PAST-think   2s   PAST-FUT-come
'We thought that you would come.'

(32) *Haitian Creole*   (Spears 1990:124)
m   te   di   m   t   a   pati
1s   ANT say   1s   ANT IRR leave.
'I said that I would leave.'

Another language which has caused confusion of this kind is Ewe. In Wester-mann (1907) the verb root is taken to form a unit with preceding grammatical markers and also with the habitual marker, which is positioned after the verb:[7]

(33) *Ewe*   (Westermann 1907)

a. me-ga-gi
   1s-REP-go
   'I went again.'

b. mí-a-yì
   1p-FUT-go
   'We will go.'

c. nye-mé-yì   o
   1s-NEG-go   NEG
   'I do not/did not go.'

d. me-yi-a   agble
   1s-go-HAB   field
   'I usually go to the field.'

By contrast, in Schadeberg (1985) the preverbal markers are viewed as free particles, as the following examples show:

(34) *Ewe*   (Schadeberg 1985)

a. Yàwò áa   wù   dà   lá   ná   m̀
   Yawo   FUT kill   snake DEF for   me
   'Yawo will kill the snake for me.'

b. màmi   ga   kpɔ́   àdzè.
   mother   REP see   witch
   'Again, mother saw a witch.'

There is one exception to this pattern: if the future marker is immediately preceded by a subject pronoun or a negative marker, it fuses with the preceding element. The non-fused form of the future marker, given in (34a), can be compared to the fused forms shown in (35a) and (35b). The non-fused form of the first person plural is shown in (35b), and the non-fused form of the negative marker is shown in (35c).

From these data, it appears that the future marker simply interacts phonologically with certain other markers. For example, we see from (35b) that the future marker is generated below the subject pronoun (which might turn out to be a subject agreement marker). Hence, if right adjunction is out, it cannot be head movement that has combined the two elements in (35a). Instead, the fusion at hand is probably of a purely phonological nature.

(35) *Ewe* (Schadeberg 1985)

    a. mí-a   ga   kpé   ètsɔ̀
        1p-FUT REP meet   tomorrow
        'We shall meet again tomorrow.'

    b. mí m-á   ga   yi   o
        1p NEG-FUT REP go   NEG
        'We should not go.'

    c. àtí lá   mé   kɔ́   ò
        tree DEF NEG tall NEG
        'The tree is not tall.'

An interesting property of Schadeberg's examples is that although none of the preverbal markers is seen as a prefix on the verb, the habitual marker is nevertheless still treated as a suffix, just like in Westermann (1907):

(36) *Ewe* (Schadeberg 1985)

    mè yì-na   àsì   mè   gbèsíàgbè
    1s go-HAB   market to   every.day
    'I go to the market every day.'

In the theory of complex words that has been developed here, this is exactly what one would expect. Since the habitual marker in Ewes is postverbal but not clause-final, the verbal head must have moved and adjoined to the head that hosts the habitual marker. This means that the verb and the habitual marker constitute a complex head, and, accordingly, there is no alternative to seeing the combination of these elements as one complex word.

Preverbal inflectional markers, by contrast, are not included in a complex head with the verb root, and so the analysis according to which these markers belong to the verbal word must be based on distributional and phonological factors. But it should be clear from the discussion in chapter 1 that these criteria do not always unambiguously identify the words of a given string of morphemes. It is therefore no big surprise that we see some variation in the analysis of preposed grammatical elements.

Although distributional criteria do not always suffice to choose between a prefix analysis and a free marker analysis, there still seems to be a certain correlation between the ability of the verb root to appear in isolation and its status as a separate word. We have already seen, in the foregoing section, that in Shona and Nkore-Kiga the verb root must be accompanied by preverbal inflectional markers, and accordingly, the sequence consisting of the preverbal markers and the verb root is taken to be one word. Ndyuka, on the other hand, is a language where the preverbal markers are analyzed as free particles, as shown in (30) above. Strikingly, it turns out that in Ndyuka, an answer may consist of only the verb root. This is demonstrated in the following example:

(37) *Ndyuka* (Huttar & Huttar 1994:45)

    a. San   i   e   du?   b.   (Mi e   ) nyan.
       What 2s PRES do   1s   PRES eat
       'What are you doing?'   'I am eating.'

Moreover, the tense markers in Ndyuka can be left out in other contexts as well. The present tense marker is optional in generic statements, as in (38), and it is disallowed with stative verbs and in copula constructions, as in (39a,b).[8]

(38) *Ndyuka* (Huttar & Huttar 1994:489)

    Te   yu (e)   deen, yu yeye   (e)   waka.
    when 2s PRES dream 2s spirit PRES walk
    'When you are dreaming, your spirit is walking.'

(39) *Ndyuka* (Huttar & Huttar 1994:490)

    a. Mi dda   langa.
       1s father long
       'My father is tall.'

    b. Babun   de   a   Kwata   baka   namo.
       howler.monkey COP LOC spider.monkey back   only
       'Howler monkey is always behind spider monkey.'

A verb unmarked for tense may however also refer to the past, as in (40) and (41). That is, the past tense marker can be omitted, given that the past tense reference has been established earlier in the discourse (Huttar & Huttar 1994).

(40) *Ndyuka* (Huttar & Huttar 1994:490)

    A   busi   lai   anga   meti.
    the jungle load with   animal
    'The jungle was full of animals then.'

(41) *Ndyuka* (Huttar & Huttar 1994:492)

    A   taki,   "Mi á   poi teke a   pina   ya   moo."
    3s   say   1s NEG can take DEF.SG poor   here more
    'He said, "I can't stand this poverty any longer." '

These facts do not force an analysis of the Ndyuka verb as a separate word from the preverbal markers, but they clearly open up the possibility.

    Finally, in some languages not only the verb root but also the preverbal markers have word-like properties. This is the case in Indonesian, for example.

Some of the preverbal markers of tense, aspect, and mood/modality are shown in (42)–(44). The glosses are provided by me after Sneddon's (1996) description of the markers.

(42) *Indonesian* (Sneddon 1996:202)
   Kamu   sudah   harus   di   sini jam   lima.
   2s   COMPL   must   at   here hour   five
   'You must be here by five o'clock.'

(43) *Indonesian* (Sneddon 1996:204)
   Partai itu   tidak akan   bisa membentuk pemerintahan.
   party   that NEG   FUT   can form   government
   'That party will never be able to form a government.'

(44) *Indonesian* (Sneddon 1996:204)
   Dia   bakal   mampu   menaklukkan   mereka.
   3s   DIST.FUT   be.able   defeat   them
   'He will be able to defeat them.'

The preverbal markers are not obligatory; the verb may well appear without any preceding inflectional markers, as in (45).

(45) *Indonesian* (Sneddon 1996:197)
   Dia pergi ke   kantor.
   3s   go   to   office
   'She goes/went/will go to the office.'

Notably, the preverbal markers can also appear on their own, without any verb to follow. For example, a perfectly normal answer to a question like (46a) would be (46b).

(46) *Indonesian* (Sneddon 1996:313)
   a. Anda   sudah   makan?   b.   Sudah.
      2s   COMPL   eat   COMPL
      'Have you eaten?'   'I have.'

Thus, to native speakers as well as to linguists the Indonesian preverbal markers stand out as separate words.

Also contributing to this analysis is the fact that the relative order of the preverbal markers is not entirely fixed. To give an example, alongside (42) the order in (47) is also possible. The meaning of the construction remains the same (Sneddon 1996:202).

(47) *Indonesian* (Sneddon 1996:202)
      Kamu   harus   sudah   di   sini jam   lima.
      2s   must   COMPL   at   here hour   five
      'You must be here by five o'clock.'

In short, because of their ability to appear in isolation and their independent distribution, the preverbal markers in Indonesian are viewed as separate words.

It should be noted at this point that the order variation illustrated by (42) and (47) indicates that the preverbal markers in Indonesian differ structurally from the preverbal markers in Bantu languages, for example. While I have just claimed that the latter represent inflectional heads, the former are probably sitting in the Specs of such heads. Otherwise, the observed order variation would not be expected. That is, the preverbal markers in Indonesian, or at least some of them, must be comparable to adverbs in other languages. As Cinque (1999) shows, there are designated preverbal positions for many classes of IP-adverbs. These adverbs may still display certain alternations in their ordering, which then must be due to syntactic movement operations. As we have just seen, these distributional characteristics are also found with certain Indonesian preverbal markers. Hence, subsuming these markers under the class of IP-adverbs seems to be justified.

So far, the question of whether a preverbal inflectional marker will be viewed as a part of the verbal word has not been related to word order. But as we see from the following tables, the affixation rate of preposed verbal markers varies considerably across word order types. The figures in table 4.1 are taken from Bybee et al. (1990) and show the affixation rate of preposed verbal markers of all classes in the three major word order types.

As we see, preverbal inflectional markers are nearly always affixed in verb-initial languages, and in verb-final languages, they are affixed in two out of three cases. That is, both verb-initial and verb-final languages have prefixes more often than they have free preposed inflectional markers. In verb-medial languages, by contrast, only 40% of all preposed inflectional markers are affixed.

TABLE 4.1
Affixation rate of preposed markers in different word orders (figures from tables 1 and 2 of Bybee et al. 1990).

Word order	Affixation rate of preposed markers (%)	Total number of preposed markers (N)
V-initial	84	81
V-medial	40	498
V-final	68	233
Total	52	812

TABLE 4.2
Affixation rate (in percent) of preposed tense/aspect markers, sorted by word order and geographical area.

Geographical area	Word order		
	V-initial	V-medial	V-final
Africa	83	46	36
Eurasia	none	100	100
SE Asia & Oceania	60	13	100
Australia & New Guinea	none	25	25
North America	57	60	83
South America	none	100	50
Creoles	none	10	0
Total	67	35	53

If we look at tense markers separately, a similar picture emerges. Consider table 4.2, which shows the affixation rate of preposed tense markers—or, for some languages, aspect markers—in different word orders in the language sample that I have surveyed (see appendix 2). The affixation rates are given for the sample as a whole and for each of the geographical areas that were introduced in section 1.5.

We see here that the affixation rates of preposed tense (or aspect) markers are a little lower than the affixation rates of all preposed verbal markers. The pattern with respect to word order is nevertheless the same on a world basis: the affixation rate is highest in verb-initial languages, somewhat lower in verb-final languages, and at its lowest in verb-medial languages.

There are striking differences between geographical areas, however. For example, in North America the normal pattern is reversed: here preposed markers are least frequently affixed in verb-initial languages, while the highest affixation rate is found in verb-final languages. In Africa, on the other hand, verb-final languages have the lowest affixation rate of all word order types. In Southeast Asia and Oceania, the affixation rate of preposed tense markers in verb-medial languages is only 13%, which is much lower than the world average of 35% but close to the corresponding figure for creole languages, 10%. Thus, it appears that certain areal effects come into play. I do not try to account for these effects here; what I do in the following is suggest an explanation for the occurrence of inflectional prefixes and free preposed inflectional markers in the different word orders worldwide.

4.3.2   Verb-initial languages
If we concentrate first on preposed markers in verb-initial languages, it is clear that for these elements there is normally no alternative to being included in a word with the verb if they do not form words of their own, in the distributional or in the phonological sense. This is what Bybee et al. (1990:30) observe when

they say that "with no other lexical material before it in a typical clause, it [i.e., the preposed grammatical marker] must prefix to the verb if it is to become an affix." Thus, we expect to find constructions like the one in (48), with inflectional markers prefixed to the verb, which is the first lexical element of the clause.

(48) *Jacaltec* (Craig 1977:9)

x-Ø-in-mak		metx	tx'i	yu	hune'	te'
COMPL-3ABS-1ERG-hit		CLASS	dog	with	a	stick

'I hit the dog with a stick.'

We would also expect that when preposed inflectional markers in verb-initial languages are *not* affixed to the verb, there must be some phonological or distributional reason for this. Indeed, this appears to be borne out to some extent.

As we see from table 4.2, the pattern exemplified in (48), with prefixed tense or aspect markers and verb-initial order, is found in 16 of the genera represented in my survey. By contrast, free preposed tense or aspect markers occur with verb-initial order in only 8 genera. These are the African genus Biu-Mandara; the genera Atayalic and Central-Eastern Malayo-Polynesian from Southeast Asia and Oceania; and the North American genera Tsamosan, Tsimshian, Mayan, Pimic, and Mixtecan. We will look at some of these cases and see that the absence of affixation is relatively easy to explain as a consequence either of phonology or of distributional facts.

Let us start with another example from Jacaltec, which belongs to the Mayan genus. In (49), there is a phonologically overt object marker, which is situated between the completive marker and the subject agreement marker. Now the completive marker is not included in the verbal word; instead, the completive marker and the object marker together constitute a separate word preceding the verbal word. The subject marker is still prefixed to the verb, just as in (48).

(49) *Jacaltec* (Craig 1977:90)

xc-ach	w-il-a.
COMPL-2ABS	1ERG-see-TRANS

'I saw you.'

There is no obvious reason to assume different syntactic structures for the pre-verbal areas in (48) and (49). Hence, when Craig (1977:121) states that "there is a word boundary between the compound [aspect+absolutive] and the compound [(ergative+) verb stem (+stem final V)]" I take this word boundary to be a phonological one. This must mean that the grouping of morphemes that we see in the above examples reflects the phonological constituency of the language and has nothing to do with syntactic constituency. Probably, when the completive marker *x(c)-* is followed by the absolutive agreement marker *-ach*, the two elements together attain the minimal size that is required of a phonological word; accordingly, the inflectional markers form a preverbal word in (49). In

(48), by contrast, the completive marker cannot possibly form a phonological word on its own, so it is included in the verbal word instead.

The phonology also appears to be responsible for the alternation between prefixes and free preposed markers in the Tsamosan language Upper Chehalis. Kinkade (1964a) classifies some of the preverbal tense and aspect markers of this language as prefixes and others as particles (see also Kinkade 1963b). The prefixes are the continuative marker *s-* and the stative marker *ʔac-*. The particles are the past marker *ta*, the completive marker *ʔet ~ tet*, and the future marker *tɬ'a*.[9] In addition, there is the future marker *ɬ*, which is said to be "a clitic— sometimes it is a free morpheme, sometimes a prefix" (Kinkade 1964a:35).

The past, continuative, stative, and completive markers are shown in (50)– (52). Note that there are two sets of subject agreement markers, one used in the continuative aspect and another used with non-continuative aspects (Kinkade 1964a:34), and that ['] indicates primary stress (see Kinkade 1963a:182). As for the word order, Kinkade (1964b:260) states that although VSO order is found quite commonly in Upper Chehalis, the subject may also precede the verb, but then the uninflected copula *we* appears after the subject. I take this to mean that VSO is the unmarked order and that the order S *we* VO, which we see in all the examples below, results from clefting or focus/topic movement of the subject.

(50) *Upper Chehalis* (Kinkade 1964a:33)
    ʔə́nca   we   ta   s-ʔéɬn-anš
    1s   COP PAST CONT-eat-1sS
    'I was eating.'

(51) *Upper Chehalis* (Kinkade 1964a:36)
    ʔeném   we   ta   ʔac-mósm-čɬ
    1p   COP PAST STAT-sleep-1pS
    'We were sleeping.'

(52) *Upper Chehalis* (Kinkade 1964a:34)
    ʔə́nca   we ʔet   ɬón-n-čn   tet   cə́ne
    1s   COP COMPL push-3sO-1sS ART 3s
    'I pushed him.'

The non-bound future marker *tɬ'a* is used in subordinate clauses, as in the example given in (53).

(53) *Upper Chehalis* (Kinkade 1964a:35)
    ʔet   wáqs-čn tɬ'a-s   ʔax̣-ə́n
    COMPL   go-1sS   FUT-SUFF see-3sO
    'I went to see it.'

The other future marker *ɬ* appears in matrix contexts. If it immediately precedes the verb, it is attached to the verb, as below.

(54) *Upper Chehalis* (Kinkade 1964a:35)
  ʔə́nca   we   ɬ-wáqs-anš
  1s   COP FUT-go-1sS
  'I will go.'

In (55), on the other hand, the future marker is separated from the verb by the completive particle *tet*. Accordingly, the former is not seen as a prefix on the verb.

(55) *Upper Chehalis* (Kinkade 1964a:36)
  ʔə́nca   we   ɬ   tet   ʔax-ə́n-čn
  1s   COP FUT   COMPL   see-3sO-1sS
  'I will see him again.'

However, in this case the future marker may fuse with the completive particle, as shown in (56). According to Kinkade (1964a:36) this is the more common form.

(56) *Upper Chehalis* (Kinkade 1964a:36)
  ʔə́nca   we   ɬ-et   ʔéɬn-čn
  1s   COP FUT-COMPL eat-1sS
  'I am going to eat.'[10]

Notably, the contrast between (55), where the future marker and the completive marker are separate, and (56), where they combine into a 'word', is probably only a phonological contrast. There is no reason to assume that there is also a non-phonological difference between the two expressions. In fact, it turns out that the identification of 'words' in all the Upper Chehalis constructions shown above is based on purely phonological criteria. In Kinkade (1963a:182) the following definition of 'word' is given: "A word may be defined in relation to juncture. Any sequence of phonemes that may both follow and precede juncture (although not necessarily at the same time) is a word." The junctures Kinkade refers to are the phonological phrase boundary and the sentence boundary. His statement means that a 'word' is a morpheme string that can be phonologically grouped either with preceding or with following morphemes, while an 'affix' is a morpheme for which only one of these options is available.

If we look at the tense and aspect markers of Upper Chehalis in this light, we see that the reason some of them are characterized as particles must be that they can attach phonologically to preceding or to following material, depending on what other preverbal elements are present in the construction. Others, which only combine phonologically with the verb, are seen as prefixes. This does not necessarily mean that the free markers must differ from the prefixes as regards their non-phonological status. Instead, whether an element is seen as a prefix or as a particle depends on its position in the string of preverbal markers and on its phonological shape. Phonologically light elements close to the verb are more prone to be seen as prefixes than are heavier elements farther from the verb in the linear order. As for the future marker ɬ, it goes with the verb if it is adjacent to the verb; otherwise it doesn't. That is, its morphological status clearly depends on what other markers are present and has nothing to do with the inherent properties of the element itself. (Note that Kinkade's statement that it is sometimes a free morpheme and sometimes a prefix seems rather meaningless in light of the definition given above: if it can behave as a free morpheme at all, it must be a free morpheme, even if it is not always separated phonologically from preceding and following elements.)

In the model of grammar that I am assuming, the ordering of the preverbal morphemes in Upper Chehalis is determined by syntax. Since the ordering has consequences for how the morphemes are grouped into words, it is correct to say that syntax conditions word formation to a certain extent. The rest, as we have just seen, is phonology.

In the next verb-initial language we will look at, Cou, which belongs to the Atayalic genus, there are also distributional reasons for not treating the preposed inflectional markers as prefixes on the verb. Although the simplest clauses in Cou have the structure shown in (57) and (58), with a short sequence of light markers preceding the verb, in other cases there can be relatively heavy elements intervening between the cluster of inflectional markers and the verb itself, as in (59) and (60).[11]

(57) *Cou* (Szakos 1994:163)
      m-o   b-ait-o   to   tposɨ
      AFOC-PAST AFOC-see-AFOC   ART book
      'He read the book.'

(58) *Cou* (Szakos 1994:168)
      m-i-'o   maine'e   nechuma
      AFOC-PRES-1s return.home.AFOC   yesterday
      'I returned home yesterday.'

(59) *Cou* (Szakos 1994:137)
      o'a   Ø-i-he   h'unano   p-eelɨ-i
      NEG UFOC-PRES-3   neither   UFOC-be.able-LFOC
      'They could not do it either.'

(60) *Cou* (Szakos 1994:163)
      la   huhucmasi   euhŋusu   'e   Eaŋui
      HAB   every.day   swim.AFOC ART Eaŋui
      'Eaŋui swims every day.'

Because of this, it is hard to conceive of the preverbal markers as belonging to the verbal word. Moreover, Szakos (1994:37) states that 'particles', a term which includes tense and aspect markers, are cliticized to the preceding word. This must mean that when some constituent precedes the inflectional cluster, as in

(61), the inflectional cluster goes with this constituent phonologically. This prevents the cluster from being analyzed as a prefix sequence.

(61) *Cou* (Szakos 1994:128)
    nechuma   m-i-'o   mi-mio
    yesterday AFOC-PRES-1s DUR-walk(REDUP)
    'Yesterday I was walking.'

In the Pimic language Tohono O'odham, distribution must be the decisive factor. We will recall from the presentation of this language in section 2.3.2 that it has several preverbal inflectional markers. One of the examples given in that section is repeated in (62).

(62) *Tohono O'odham* (= ex. (36), ch. 2)
    čum   o   pi   mɨḍ g   čɨoj
    CONA NONIMP NEG run ART man
    'The man is trying not to run'

The markers preceding the verb in (62) are all seen as non-affixed. There are apparently a number of reasons for this. First, various elements with considerable phonological weight may separate the preposed markers from the verb. This is exemplified in (63).[12]

(63) *Tohono O'odham* (Saxton 1982:131)
    t   hibab čikp   tako   k   a-t-ki
    CTMP CONC work-PERF yesterday CONJ NONIMP-CTMP-EVID
    hɨmu pi   wo čikp
    now   NEG FUT work-PERF
    'Even though he worked yesterday, today he evidently won't work.'

Furthermore, while the marker of non-imperative mood precedes the negation in (62), the reverse order is also possible, as in (64). This of course invites an analysis where the negation and the non-imperative marker are morphologically free elements.

(64) *Tohono O'odham* (= ex. (37), ch. 2)
    pi   o   mɨḍ g   čɨoj
    NEG NONIMP run ART man
    'The man isn't running.'

However, we see from (63) that the sequence consisting of the non-imperative marker, the tense marker, and the evidential marker is taken to be one word, termed 'auxiliary' in Saxton (1982). This must have to do with the fact that these elements, when present, always appear in a fixed order. More examples of auxiliaries, one of them also including a subject agreement marker, are shown in (65)–(67).

(65) *Tohono O'odham*   (= ex. (38), ch. 2)
am   a-ḍ   kii   g   kɨ-kɨl
LOC NONIMP-REM.PAST live ART old.men(REDUP)
'The oldtimers used to live there.'

(66) *Tohono O'odham*   (= ex. (39), ch. 2)
hɨg a-n-t   wa'i   ñɨi
that NONIMP-1sS-CTMP only see-PERF
'That's the only one I saw.'

(67) *Tohono O'odham*   (Saxton 1982:129)
ku-ṣ-p   am   ɟuuk
and-QUOT-ASS LOC rain
'Presumably it's reportedly raining there.'

The following discussion is based on information given by Saxton (1982). The overall morpheme order in the auxiliary is Mood-SAgr-Tense-Modal$_1$-Modal$_2$. The initial mood marker, which distinguishes between imperative and non-imperative, is probably the realization of the Speech Act head. Thus, it is possible that the order of the mood, subject agreement, and tense markers reflects the base order of the corresponding heads. Modal$_2$ is either the assumptive -*p* or the dubitative -*s*. If this can be associated with root modality, which, according to Cinque (1999), is located below tense, the position of Modal$_2$ after tense is also the base-generated order. Modal$_1$ is more problematic, though. The markers in this position indicate the source of information; the alternates are -*ki* 'evidential', -*ṣ* 'quotative', and -Ø 'experiential'. This suggests that Modal$_1$ represents the evidential head. Since the evidential head precedes the tense head in the base order (Cinque 1999), there must have been movement of the tense head across the evidential head. In the absence of excorporation (see chapter 2), this can only mean that the tense head has adjoined to the evidential head.

As for the subject agreement marker, I will remain agnostic about its precise position in the structure. In chapter 5, I argue that there do not exist syntactic heads which only contain agreement features. Instead, agreement features reside in heads that also have some other content. In section 2.2 I suggested that subject agreement, at least in some languages, resides in the Fin° head (or possibly, in accordance with the proposal put forth by Halle & Marantz 1993, the agreement morpheme is added to the Fin° head). If this is also true for Tohono O'odham, and if the Fin° head is the lowest head in the CP-domain (Rizzi 1997), whereas the Speech Act head is the highest head in the IP-domain (Cinque 1999), the non-imperative marker in (66) can precede the subject marker only if there has been movement of the Speech Act head (realized by the non-imperative marker) to the left of the Finite head (realized by the subject marker).

Alternatively, one might want to guess that the subject agreement marker in Tohono O'odham is situated below Speech Act (see the discussion of agreement markers in section 5.3).

Whatever the internal structure of the so-called auxiliary, it is a salient fact that it is preceded by a maximum of one constituent, as noted in section 2.3.2. If no element above the verb is available for fronting, the verb itself is attracted to the initial position, giving the order in (68).

(68) *Tohono O'odham* (= ex. (40), ch. 2)

maak	a-ñ	g	gogs	g	čuukhug
give	NONIMP-1sS	ART	dog	ART	meat

'I'm giving the dog meat.'

The possibility of placing the verb in front of (as well as after) the auxiliary effectively prevents the auxiliary elements from being analyzed as affixes on the verbal word.

Turning now to Polynesian, it may be somewhat unexpected that the preverbal inflectional markers in these languages are not seen as prefixes on the verb. In clauses like (69) and (70), the preverbal markers, which are unstressed, necessarily combine with the verb prosodically, as the stress placement shows (stress is indicated by accent marks in these examples).[13]

(69) *Samoan* (Mosel & Hovdhaugen 1992:40)

Sā	va'ái loa	le	táma	i	le	tagata	lenéi.
PAST.IMPF	see then	SPCF.SG	boy	to	SPCF.SG	person	this

'The boy looked at this man.'

(70) *Rapanui* (Du Feu 1996:188)

I	tú'u	mai	ái	a	Núa.
PAST	come	DIR	PRON[14]	PERS	Nua

'Nua arrived.'

One would perhaps expect the adjacency and the close phonological relation between the tense markers and the verbs in these cases to suffice to make the combination of tense marker and verb stand out as one word. However, at least in some Polynesian languages—for instance, in Samoan—there can be adverbs intervening in various positions in front of the verb, as shown in (71) and (72).

(71) *Samoan* (Mosel & Hovdhaugen 1992:381)

Na	faatoa	ou	toe	asi-a	ai	laufanua
PAST.PERF	just	1s	again	visit-TRANS	PRON	field.SPCF.PL[15]
o	Salafai.					
POSS	Salafai					

'I visited the fields of Salafai for the first time.'

(72) *Samoan* (Mosel & Hovdhaugen 1992:382)

Sā	matua	le	malamalama	i	le	uiga	moni.
PAST.IMPF	very	NEG	understand	LOC	SPCF.SG	meaning	true.

'(They) did not understand the real meaning at all.'

This fact can be viewed as a reason for not treating the preverbal tense and aspect markers as prefixes on the verb (cf. Mosel & Hovdhaugen 1992:168).

In other Polynesian languages, such as Maori and Rapanui, adverbs normally follow the verb (see Bauer 1993:92, Du Feu 1996:71). But even here, certain adverb-like elements appear in front of the verb, as in the following examples:

(73) *Maori* (Bauer 1993:92)

Ka	aahua	pukuriri	a	Tamahae	ki	a	Rewi.
CTMP	somewhat	(be)angry	PERS	Tamahae	to	PERS	Rewi

'Tamahae was somewhat angry with Rewi.'

(74) *Rapanui* (Du Feu 1996:162)

Pura	vara	tu'u	mai	a	Nua.
HAB	FREQ	come	DIR	PERS	Nua

'Nua usually comes here.'

Note that *vara*, which is translated as 'often' by Du Feu (1996:71) but glossed as 'frequentative' in the above example, could be the realization of an aspectual head.

Regardless of the syntactic status of the elements that intervene between the verb and the initial tense/aspect marker in (73) and (74), one could expect these elements to be seen as part of the verbal word, in the same way as preverbal adverbial elements are included in the verbal word in Shona (see the examples in (23) above). When the preverbal inflectional markers are seen instead as free elements in the Polynesian languages, it is apparently due to the linguistic tradition more than it is the result of thorough considerations. Thus, Capell (1933:418), sketching the history of linguistic investigation in the Pacific, notes that "Malay, being the first well-known language of this family [i.e., Malayo-Polynesian], was naturally made the standard of reference." This means that a language with clearly word-like preverbal markers—Malay is very close to Indonesian, which was discussed above—came to provide the blueprint after which later analyses of other Malayo-Polynesian languages were modeled.[16]

The role of the linguists' hunches can also be seen in other cases, such as in the Mixtec languages. Bradley (1970) states that Jicaltepec Mixtec has free pre-verbal inflectional markers, as shown in (75).

(75) *Jicaltepec Mixtec* (Bradley 1970)

ča	ní	čákuda	rá
T	ASP	sit.down	he

'He has already sat down.'

But in her paper on the very closely related language Chalcatongo Mixtec, Macaulay (1993) treats what seem to be essentially the same markers as prefixes on the verb—see (76).

(76) *Chalcatongo Mixtec* (Macaulay 1993:73)
      a-ni-ndatu-rí   uù   órá
      T-COMPL-wait-I   two   hour
      'I've already been waiting for two hours.'

One might suspect that the alternation that we see between prefixes and free markers in Mixtecan is comparable to the cases where two different analyses have been applied to one single language, as discussed in the introduction to this section: it has more to do with the taste of the analyst than with the actual shape of the language. I assume that in both varieties of Mixtec the preverbal markers are the realizations of inflectional heads that are situated above the position where the verb surfaces, so that the only relation between the inflectional markers and the verb that could be relevant for the conception of the combination of inflection and verb as one word is the linear adjacency.

In Gude and Podoko, which both belong to the Biu-Mandara genus, there are preverbal tense and aspect markers which are represented as free elements even though they are phonologically light and adjacent to the verb:

(77) *Gude* (Hoskison 1983:82)
      kə   kii   Musa   faara
      COMPL   throw   Musa   stone
      'Musa threw/has thrown a stone.'

(78) *Podoko* (Jarvis 1991:217)
      Sa   gəl-i   udzəra.
      PAST   grow-IMPF   child
      'The child was growing up.'

(79) *Podoko* (Jarvis 1991:226)
      A   da   də   yá   da   dá-təka.
      FOC FUT go   1s   to   house-2sPOSS
      'I will go to your house.'

Thus, it is likely that the morphological status of the preverbal markers in Gude and Podoko has been determined on a rather weak basis, just as in some of the languages we have looked at previously.[17]

To sum up, we have seen in this subsection that preposed inflectional markers in verb-initial languages tend to be perceived as prefixes on the verb, and that if they are not, this may be for phonological or distributional reasons, or because a different analysis is dictated by tradition, or for no clear reason at all.

4.3.3   Verb-final languages

Tables 4.1 and 4.2 showed that affixation of preposed inflectional markers is relatively frequent in verb-final languages. For example, we see from table 4.2 that in my survey, 18 genera contain verb-final languages with prefixed tense or aspect markers, while 16 genera contain verb-final languages with free preposed tense or aspect markers. This gives an affixation rate of 53%, which is significantly higher than the corresponding rate in verb-medial languages. Given my claims about the affixation of preposed markers, this might seem somewhat surprising at first: we would not necessarily expect preposed markers to be more frequently affixed in verb-final languages than in verb-medial languages. One would rather assume the possibility for preverbal inflectional markers to attach distributionally and phonologically to the verb to be the same in both word order types.

However, the contrast between verb-final languages and verb-medial languages is even stronger than the overall figures suggest. To see this, we must distinguish between two classes of verb-final languages: languages where the inflectional markers immediately precede the verb and languages where the object intervenes. In the latter group, where the order of elements in the clause is STOV, there is no way the tense marker can be seen as a prefix on the verb or on any other element. Some examples of STOV order are given below.

(80) *Bambara* (Kastenholz 1989:67)
    ń   fà   yé   báara   kɛ
    1s   father   PAST   work   do
    'My father worked.'

(81) *Koranko* (= ex. (20), ch. 3)
    à   yá   kɔlɔmabolɔ   kári
    3s   PAST   tree-branch   break
    'He broke a branch.'

(82) *Vata* (= ex. (21), ch. 3)
    à   nĪ-kā   såká   lì
    1p   FUT   rice   eat
    'We will eat rice.'

In the transitive clauses shown here, the tense marker is followed by the object. In intransitive clauses, by contrast, the tense marker will be followed by the verb. Hence, there is no pattern stable enough for the tense marker to be seen as a prefix. It is conceivable, though, that since the tense marker always immediately follows the subject, it could be seen as a suffix on the subject. However, since DPs in other positions are not followed by tense markers, the pattern DP+T is not a stable one, either; consequently, the tense markers and the subject are not seen as one word. Instead, the tense marker and other inflectional markers are taken to be free elements in languages with STOV order.

In 11 of the 16 genera in my survey that contain verb-final languages with free preposed tense or aspect markers the order is STOV. This leaves only 5 genera with the order SOTV (the order TSOV is not represented at all in my survey and very probably does not exist). As already mentioned in chapter 3, these 5 genera are Central Khoisan, Southern Cushitic, Yele-Solomons, Daly, and Pimic; the languages in question are Nama, Iraqw, Yele, Ngankikurungkurr, and Nevome. An example of Nama clause structure was given in example (18), chapter 3; it is repeated below together with examples from Iraqw, Yele, and Nevome (see section 2.3.2 for examples of Ngankikurungkurr clause structure).

(83) *Nama* (= ex. (18), ch. 3)

píli	ke	//nãápá	maríàsà	‡xanísà	kè-rè	màa
Bill	DECL	there	Mary	letter	REM.PAST-IMPF	give

'There Bill gave Mary a letter.'

(84) *Iraqw* (Tucker & Bryan 1966:587)

àtén	kùŋgá	nùn-à	àr-án
1p	2pMASC	2pO-PAST	see-1pS

'We saw you.'

(85) *Yele* (Henderson 1995:15)

M:aa	ngê	Kaawa	dê	m:uu.
dad	ERG.SG	Kaawa	IND.PUNC.IMM.PAST.3S	see

'Dad saw Kaawa.'

(86) *Nevome* (Shaul 1986)

Pedoro	ohana	pare	a-t'-io	vanna.
Pedro	write	priest	3s-PERF-FUT	erase

'The priest will erase Pedro's writing.'

Since the preposed inflectional markers are always located immediately in front of the verb in these languages, if there is any reason at all to treat them as separate from the verb, it must have to do with phonology.

Interestingly, in Henderson (1995:14) the reliance on phonology in the identification of Yele words is stated explicitly (as also noted in chapter 2 n. 15). Thus, in (87) both the preverbal and the postverbal inflectional marker are separate from the verb phonologically and therefore are rendered as separate words orthographically. (MFS is short for *monofocal subject*—that is, a subject that is either first person or singular. See Henderson 1995:39.)[18]

(87) *Yele* (Henderson 1995:62)

Kaawa	ngê	dê	m:uu	té.
Kaawa	ERG.SG	IND.PUNC.IMM.PAST.3S	see	PROX.3pO.MFS

'Kaawa saw them.'

On purely distributional criteria, the inflectional markers in Yele could just as well be taken to belong to the verbal word, since the inflectional markers do not appear without the verb and there can never be elements intervening.[19] Thus, the fact that the inflectional markers in Yele are still not seen as affixes is just another indication of the fuzziness of the concept 'word'.

However, in the majority of languages where tense and aspect markers immediately precede a clause-final verb, the markers are seen as prefixes of the verb. In my survey, the pattern S O T+V is found in 18 genera, as compared to the 5 genera with SOTV. That is, for verb-final languages with preposed tense markers and no object intervening between the verb and the tense marker, the affixation rate is 78%, which is even higher than the affixation rate of preposed tense markers in verb-initial languages.

More generally, it appears that if a language has verbal grammatical markers that are positioned between the arguments and a clause-final verb, these markers are nearly always perceived as prefixes on the verb. In addition to the 5 genera containing languages with SOTV order, there are another 7 genera in my survey that contain verb-final languages with free verbal markers located between the arguments and the verb. By comparison, there are 49 genera that contain languages with verb-final order and grammatical markers prefixed to the verb, in addition to the 18 genera that contain languages with verb-final order and prefixed tense markers. That is, in 67 out of 79 cases where verb-final order is combined with one or more verbal markers immediately in front of the verb, all the markers are prefixed to the verb. In other words, a verbal marker X in the sequence SOXV is a prefix in 85% of the genera.

These figures may not be entirely correct, though. In the compilation of data for my survey, I concentrated on tense markers and on the morpheme ordering in complex verbs. Hence, all bound markers, as well as all tense markers, were carefully registered, but a few free non-temporal markers may have been overlooked, and it is possible that the affixation percentage is somewhat lower than 85%. Still, I assume that the tendency I have found is real and that the affixation rate of markers immediately preceding a clause-final verb is relatively high.

The ultimate reason for the affixing tendency just noted is not so easy to point out. I would nevertheless like to make a guess along the following lines. A grammatical marker in front of the verb in a verb-final language can be preceded by a number of different constituents: by the subject, as in (88); by the object, as in (89); or, since many verb-final languages tend to move not only arguments but also adverbial phrases high up in the clause, by an adverbial, as in (90).

(88) *Kabardian* (Colarusso 1989:294)
    ɬ'ə   Ø-y-a-ś'ə-f
    man 3-3-PRES-do-able
    'A/any man can do it.'

(89) *Rembarnga* (McKay 1976:495)
ŋinta-yiʔ ŋanapparu pa-ŋa-na
1s-ERG buffalo 3pO-1sS-see.PAST.PUNC
'I saw some buffaloes.'

(90) *Mojave* (Munro 1976a:25)
ʔ-nʸəmora: ʔavu:mak-lʸ ʔ-ədu:lʸ-pč
1-doll back.of.house-LOC 1-hide-TENSE
'I hid my doll behind the house.'

On the other hand, these markers are always followed by the verb, which means that the combination of grammatical marker and verb forms a stable pattern. Thus, if the markers are related to the verb semantically and appear in a fixed order, which will be the case if the markers are the realizations of heads in the extended projection of the verb, they will easily be perceived as prefixes on the verb.

4.3.4 Verb-medial languages
In verb-medial languages, preposed verbal inflectional markers are normally located between the subject and the verb. The only grammatical markers that regularly appear in front of the subject in these languages are markers of illocutionary force. The exceptions in my survey are the tense markers in !Kung and the future marker in Igbo, which may precede or follow the subject, and the negation in Mon, which regularly precedes the subject (see appendix 2).[20]

The markers that precede the subject in SVO order cannot of course be perceived as affixes on the verb. The surprising fact, which has already been noted, is that inflectional markers situated between the subject and the verb in a verb-medial order also tend to be viewed as free morphemes. We see from the calculation made by Bybee et al. (1990) in table 4.1 that the affixation rate of all preposed verbal markers in verb-medial languages is 40%, and table 4.2 shows that the corresponding figure for preposed tense markers in verb-medial languages in my survey is only 35%. More precisely, the pattern S T+V O is found in 24 genera, whereas the pattern STVO is found in 44 genera.

If adjacency between the inflectional marker and the verb were the decisive factor, we would expect preposed markers in verb-medial languages to be affixed to the verb just as often as preposed markers in verb-final languages. Furthermore, we would expect the properties that point toward an analysis of inflectional markers as free elements, such as the portability of the markers and the ability of the verb to be an utterance all by itself, without any inflectional markers, to be evenly distributed over languages of all word orders. In this light, the low affixing tendency of preposed markers in verb-medial languages seems to be rather puzzling.

There are at least two factors which may be part of the solution to this puzzle. First, while there is a tendency in verb-final languages that adverbials as well as arguments are moved high up in the clause, so that they come to precede all verbal inflectional markers, many verb-medial languages allow certain adverbs to interrupt the sequence of heads in the verbal projection (although adpositional phrases normally appear in clause-initial or clause-final position). Indonesian has already been mentioned; another example, from Mokilese, is given below:

(91) *Mokilese* (Harrison 1976:180)
    Ih   ne   pwen   pirin   ken alu.
    he   already only   FUT   then walk
    'He's only about to leave.'

According to Harrison (1976), *pwen* 'only' and *ken* 'then' may precede or follow the future marker. Because of their relative freedom of position, these two elements will be seen as separate words—that is, as adverbs. In turn, the presence of free words between the future marker and the verb stem forces the conclusion that the future marker and the verb root are also separate words. It is conceivable, although it will have to be investigated in more detail, that the appearance of adverbs between the verb root and the preposed inflectional markers and also in between the preposed inflectional markers is more frequent in verb-medial languages than in verb-final languages and that, because of this, the analysis of preposed markers as prefixes on the verb is more often excluded in verb-medial languages.

Second, it should be kept in mind that preposed markers in verb-medial languages are not only regularly adjacent to the verb, they are also regularly adjacent to the subject. In some cases, their distribution causes preposed verbal inflectional markers to be viewed as suffixes on the subject. Consider the following examples from Nɔmaándɛ́:

(92) *Nɔmaándɛ́* (Wilkendorf 1991:110)
    U-ŋɔ-ɔ́   tɔ́lí-ák-a   tu-áyɛ́   tú-koli.
    3s-REM.PAST-3s   set-DUR-FV   13-3sPOSS   13-string
    'He had set his snares.'

(93) *Nɔmaándɛ́* (Wilkendorf 1991:131)
    Tu-ŋe-bul-asɔ́   lɔ́ŋ-ɔ
    1p-IMM.FUT-HAB-1p   call-FV
    'We will call (them) (habitually, today).'

An important fact is that the initial element of the inflectional clusters in (92) and (93) disappears in the presence of a full nominal subject (Wilkendorf 1991:110)—compare (92) and (94).

(94) *Nɔmaándɛ́* (Wilkendorf 1991:110)

ɔ-ɔcɔ	ŋɔ-ɔ́	tɔ́lí-ák-a	tu-áyɛ́	tú-koli.
1-man	REM.PAST-3s	set-DUR-FV	13-3sPOSS	13-string

'The man had set his snares.'

This suggests that the element to which the markers of tense, aspect, and subject agreement are suffixed in (92) and (93) is really a pronominal subject.

The subject together with the verbal inflectional markers cannot possibly be a constituent in any non-phonological sense. Thus, the combination of these elements into one word that we see in Nɔmaándɛ́ must be a matter of either distribution or phonology, or both. But if the regularity of the adjacency between the subject and the cluster of verbal inflectional markers allows the inflectional markers to be perceived as suffixes on the (pronominal) subject in Nɔmaándɛ́, we would expect the same option to exist in other SVO languages with preposed verbal inflectional markers as well. This means that in languages of this type there are two conflicting tendencies as far as the prosodic treatment of the preposed verbal inflectional markers is concerned: the markers could be taken to belong with the subject or with the verb. A way to resolve this conflict is to have them go with neither—that is, to see the inflectional markers as words in their own right. This may be one reason why the affixation rate of preposed verbal inflectional markers in verb-medial languages is so low.[21]

If the tension between relating to the subject and relating to the verb causes preverbal markers in SVO-languages to be seen as free elements, we would expect preverbal markers to be prefixes in pro-drop SVO languages. In a clause where the subject is phonologically empty, the only lexical element that preverbal markers can attach to is the verb. That is, the situation is very much the same as in verb-initial languages. A language where this expectation is borne out is Mono-Alu. In this language, preverbal inflectional markers are sometimes preceded by the subject, as in (95a), and sometimes not, as in (95b). I assume that the preverbal markers are seen as prefixes because of constructions like (95b).

(95) *Mono-Alu* (Fagan 1986)

a.
Batafa	sa-na	kanega	ua	iri-mate.
woman	thing-3sPOSS	husband	with	3pNONFUT-die

'The woman and her husband died.'

b.
Iri-gagana	kalofo	a.
3pNONFUT-go	meeting.house	LOC

'They went to the meeting house.'

In spite of the nice example shown above, affixed preverbal markers are not always found together with pro-drop cross-linguistically, though. Thus, the relevance of the obligatoriness of the subject in SVO-languages for the affixation rate of preverbal markers is not yet clear. It would be easier to evaluate if there

were more preposed verbal markers in OVS languages. In my survey, OVS as
the basic order is found in three genera: in the Caddoan language Wichita, in
Coos (a Penutian language), and in several Carib languages. In Carib and in
Coos most verbal inflectional markers are suffixed to the verb, but agreement is
expressed by preposed markers, as shown in the following example from the
Carib language Panare. (The inversion marker that is prefixed to the verb of the
relative clause is a signal that the object precedes the verb and is higher on the
person hierarchy than the subject—see Payne 1993 for details):

(96) *Panare*   (Payne 1993:130)

Apoj	t-ompi-chaj	chu	aro	y-új-cha-nëj
man	1s-deceive-PAST.PERF	1s	rice	INV-give-PAST.PERF-REL
tikon	uya.			
child	DAT			

'I deceived the man who gave rice to the child.'

However, in some of the examples from the Carib language Kuikuró given in
Franchetto (1990), certain non-bound elements appear which are glossed as
'aspect' but not commented on in the text:

(97) *Kuikuró*   (Franchetto 1990:410)

Tugá-héke	léca	ate-lâ-ko	léha.
water-ERG	ASP	encircle-PUNC-PL	ASP

'The water encircled them.'

(98) *Kuikuró*   (Franchetto 1990:411)

Áiha	u-ikucé-lâ	léha	e-héke.
ASP	1-paint-PUNC	ASP	2-ERG

'You finished painting me.'

As the above examples show, at least some of these aspectual elements may
precede the verb. It is unclear, however, whether they always appear in preverbal
position, in which case they clearly are exceptions to the generalization that
OVS languages do not have free preposed markers, or whether their distribution
is more free (and thus adverb-like).

The only OVS language in which there regularly are several verbal markers in
front of the verb is Wichita. Apart from the elements which Rood (1976) refers
to as adverbs and which may precede or follow the verb, Wichita has numerous
markers that invariably precede the verb. In Rood (1976) these are all regarded as
prefixes and grouped into no less than 25 position classes. Minimally, a verb
root must be preceded by a tense, aspect, or mood marker and an agreement
marker, and it must be followed by an aspectual or modal marker, of which the
perfective is phonologically zero (Rood 1976:22). Two complex Wichita verbs
can be seen in (99).

(99) *Wichita* (Rood 1976:266)
  wa:cʔarʔa kiya-a:-ki-Riwac-ʔaras-ra-ri-kita-ʔa-hi:riks
  squirrel QUOT-3-AOR-big-meat-PAT.PL-PORT-top-come-ITER
  na-ya:k-ri-wi-hirih
  PTC-wood-PL-stand-LOC
  [wa:cʔarʔa kiyaa:kiriwacʔarasarikitaʔahí:riks niya:hkwírih]
  'Squirrel, going many turns, brought the big quantity of meat up to the top
  of the tree.'

The reason all the preposed elements in (99) are taken to be prefixes on the verb
is probably that the ordering relations between the verb and these elements are
more stable than other ordering relations in Wichita clauses. Whereas the subject
and the object may precede or follow the verb, with OVS and SOV as the most
frequent orders in cases where the object is not incorporated (see Rood 1976:23),
the verbal markers that precede the verbs in (99) always do so; moreover, they
appear in a fixed order. Further, the incorporated roots that are included in the
verbal words also appear in fixed positions. This allows for the sequence made
up of the preposed verbal markers, the incorporated roots, and the verb root to be
perceived as one (very!) complex word. Because either the subject or the object
may immediately precede the sequence of verbal markers, seeing these markers
as suffixes on any of the arguments is out of the question.

It is possible that similar considerations apply to other OVS languages as
well. In an OVS language, preposed verbal markers will be located between the
object and the verb in transitive clauses, but in intransitive clauses, they will be
either clause-initial or preceded by the subject (in some OVS languages the
constituent order is VS in intransitive clauses, while in others it is SV). Hence,
the tension between seeing preposed verbal markers as prefixes on the verb and
as suffixes on the subject that were postulated above for SVO languages is
absent in OVS languages. This may be the reason preposed markers in OVS languages tend to be seen as prefixes on the verb. If this is correct, we have indirect
support for my explanation of the domination of free preposed markers over
prefixes in SVO languages. However, the empirical basis for my conclusions
considering OVS languages is admittedly rather weak, and, accordingly, my
suggestions concerning verb-medial languages in general can only be tentative at
the present moment.

4.4 Final remarks on prefixing

In the preceding sections, it was argued that prefixes do not normally form a
constituent in any non-phonological sense with the root that they attach to.
When grammatical markers are nevertheless often attached to a lexical root that
they precede, it is because the morpheme sequence consisting of a lexical root
and one or more preposed markers can have the distributional properties of a
'grammatical' word even if the sequence is not a syntactic constituent. In

addition, the sequence can be a phonological word, in which case it will more easily be perceived as a word in the non-phonological sense as well.

This means that prefixes are different from suffixes in that a suffix bears a close structural relation to the root that it attaches to: either the root and the suffix are included in one complex head, or the root is contained in a phrase located in the specifier position of the suffix. These configurations do not allow other constituents to intervene. Moreover, as argued in chapter 2 for complex heads and in chapter 3 for the Spec-head relation, movement operations will normally target a constituent that includes both the root and the affix. Hence, in these configurations complex words may arise even from morphemes that can be separate words in other contexts.

By contrast, the structural relation between a prefix and the root it attaches to is less stable. It is only the linear adjacency between the two elements that makes them stand out as one word. But of course, two elements that are linearly adjacent without having a close structural relation to each other are not necessarily perceived as one word. The crucial property of the sequence tense+ verb, for example, is that the tense marker never appears outside of this particular constellation. Because of this, the tense marker can be perceived as an affix.

My analysis of inflectional prefixes goes well with the observation made by Bybee et al. (1990) that prefixes are more strongly grammaticalized than suffixes are—in fact, that prefixes are more grammaticalized than are markers of any other distributional type. Becoming grammaticalized means losing the relative free distribution that is characteristic of lexical elements and ending up instead as a realization of a functional head, which has a fixed position in the extended projection of a lexical element. Since an element preceding a lexical root will normally be seen as a separate word if that element can also appear in other environments, it follows that only fully grammaticalized elements will tend to be seen as prefixes.

I assume that the above considerations can account for the existence of prefixed inflectional markers. In addition, we must allow for the possibility that lexical elements can be prefixed to a root if they originate within the complement of that root and become prefixed as a result of movement. For example, in the following complex Mohawk verb the incorporated object must have moved from complement position. Having adjoined to the verb root, it necessarily appears immediately to the left of that root, and it is included in the complex verbal word and preceded by various grammatical markers:

(100) *Mohawk* (Baker 1996:202)
    ʌ-k-atat-ahy-óhare-'s-e'
    FUT-1s-REFL-fruit-wash-BEN-PUNC
    'I will wash the fruit for myself.'

However, a few languages, most of them in North America, are exceptional in that they have prefix sequences which include elements that cannot straightforwardly be analyzed either as realizations of functional heads or as head-moved elements from the complement of the lexical head.

One relevant case is the Wichita example given in (99). Here the lexical roots *Riwac* 'big' and *ʔaras* 'meat' precede the prefixed marker of plural patients and the portative marker. Since there are inflectional markers intervening between these nominal roots and the verb root, the incorporation of the nominal roots, which must originate inside VP, cannot have come about by head movement—head movement would have rendered the nominals adjacent to the verb root.

Similarly, in the following example from Kabardian, a causative marker intervenes between the verb root and the incorporated nominal roots:

(101) *Kabardian*   (Colarusso 1989:307)

Ø-q'ə-ŝə-s-x̌°ə-w-bǧa-də-ǧa-a-t-r-q'm
3-HOR-DEIX-1s-able-2s-side-flat.space-CAUS-ø-stand-PRES-NEG
'I cannot make him stand there beside you.'
[q'ıŝısx̌°ɛbbǧedəǧetìrq'ɛm]

The causative marker probably represents a head which is generated above VP. That is, the causative marker and the verb have retained their base order. But then the incorporated nominal cannot have head-moved to its surface position.

What appears to be the case in (99) and (101) is that the verbal word includes a phrase which has moved, by phrasal movement, from a position inside VP to a specifier position in the verbal inflectional domain. Since this phrase can appear in positions outside the verb as well, it cannot be its distribution that causes it to be seen as a part of the verbal word. Instead, the relevant factor must be phonology. We see in both (99) and (101) that there is considerable phonological interaction between the morphemes that constitute the verbal word. Hence, it appears that where the distributional properties of a preposed morpheme do not suffice to make that morpheme be perceived as an affix, the morpheme may nevertheless be seen as an affix if its bears a close phonological relation to surrounding morphemes.

Notes

1. In my material (see appendix 2), the other languages which are claimed to have OSV as their basic order are the Central Cushitic language Bilin (Hamde 1986), the Pama-Nyungan language Dyirbal (Dixon 1972), the Arawan language Yamamadí (Derbyshire 1986), and the Maipuran language Apuriña (Derbyshire 1986).

2. There are some complications to this picture in that if the verb is already prefixed with the marker *i-*, which is claimed by Weir (1986) to be an aspect marker, the incorporated postposition appears to the left of *i-*, as shown in (i).

(i) *Nadëb*   (Weir 1986:302–303)
    a. Kad   i-yóóm   gúúw gó.
        uncle ASP-plant field   in
        'My uncle plants in the field.'

    b. Gúúw kad   g-i-yóóm.
        field   uncle in-ASP-plant
        'My uncle plants the field.'

It is not clear from Weir's account exactly what the function of *i-* is. It might be the case that it, too, originates below the verb, so that the complex verb in (ib) is the result of successive cyclic head movement.

As we see from (ii), an incorporated postposition may follow the prefixes that Weir refers to as 'thematic'. This would follow if the thematic prefixes originate above the verb.

(ii) *Nadëb*   (Weir 1986:301–302)
    a. Salãap   k-i-yúk   kalapé   hã.
        measles   thematic-ASP-fall children DAT
        'The children caught measles.'

    b. Kalapé   salãap   ka-h-i-yúk.
        children   measles   thematic-DAT-ASP-fall
        'The children caught measles.'

However, (iii) shows that in other cases, the postposition may even precede the thematic prefixes. This would be problematic for a head movement account if the thematic markers represent heads that originate above V°.

(iii) *Nadëb*   (Weir 1986:300–301)
    a. Kalapéé   ka-m-i-hxãak   bxaah yó.
        child   thematic-thematic-ASP-stop.to.rest tree   on
        'The child stops to rest on the tree.'

    b. Bxaah kalapéé   yó   ka-m-i-hxãak.
        tree   child   on   thematic-thematic-ASP-stop.to.rest
        'The child stops to rest on the tree.'

It is possible, though, that (iiib), which is characterized by Weir (1986) as an instance of 'incorporation into VP' does not involve head movement of the postposition but instead phrasal movement of the whole PP followed by preposition stranding.

3. On a descriptive level, this effect is captured by the Government Transparency Corollary of Baker (1988a:64): "A lexical category which has an item incorporated into it governs everything which the incorporated item governed in its original structural position."

4. Constructions like the following, where a directional preposition co-occurs with a corresponding prefix, would seem to pose a serious problem for the analysis of directional prefixes as incorporated prepositions:

(i)   *Latin*   (Haspelmath 1993:169)
      Lapid-em   ad   introitum   ad-fer-t.
      stone-ACC to   entrance   to-carry-PRES.3s
      'She carries the stone to the entrance.'

(ii) *German*   (Haspelmath 1993:169)
      Als   sie   aus   der   Kutsche   aus-stieg,...
      when she   out.of the   coach   out.of-stepped
      'When she got off the coach...'

However, in light of the existence of constructions like (iii) and (iv), where two (nearly) synonymous adpositions appear in one single adpositional phrase, it appears that the incorporation analysis of directional and similar prefixes can perhaps be defended after all.

(iii) *Dutch*   (Hoekstra 1997:160)
      Hij   heeft   naar   Rotterdam   toe   ge-wild.
      he   has   to   Rotterdam   to   *ge*-wanted
      'He has wanted to go to Rotterdam.'

(iv) *German*   (van Riemsdijk 1990: 233)
      auf   mich   zu
      towards   me.ACC to
      'towards me'

Van Riemsdijk (1990) argues that (iv) is formed by moving the PP *auf mich* to the left of *zu*, which is generated higher than *auf mich*. That *mich* goes with *auf* and not with *zu* can be seen from the case marking—*zu* assigns dative case, not accusative. Extending van Riemsdijk's analysis to (i) and (ii), we could say that these constructions are derived by moving the higher adposition up to the verb, leaving the lower, preposed adposition with the nominal complement..

5. There are also other final vowels, which are used to form various nominalizations (see Myers 1990: 36–37). These endings are left out of the discussion here.

6. According to Cinque (1999), grammatical mood (the contrast between realis and irrealis or between subjunctive and indicative) is encoded in the head that is immediately below T°(future). Cinque's proposal is mainly based on the following examples:

(i)   *Ndyuka*   (Cinque 1999:73; from Huttar & Huttar 1994:519)
      I   ben   o   sa   poi   (fu)   nyan   ete?
      2s   PAST FUT   IRR   can   for   eat   yet
      'Would you have been able to eat already?'

(ii) *Kammu*   (Cinque 1999:73; from Svantesson 1994:268)
      Cɔ̀ə   pɔ̀ɔ   pɨan   pə   màh.
      IRR   NEG   can   eat   food
      '(I) will not be able to eat anything.'

We see here that the irrealis marker is higher than the root modals. But if my analysis of the final vowel in Shona as a marker of grammatical mood is correct, it follows that grammatical mood is situated below the habitual aspect and root modals in this language. Interestingly, a similar pattern is found in Jacaltec, as shown in the following example:

(iii) *Jacaltec* (Craig 1977:89)
       Yilal   y-ul-uj   ha-mam   tinaŋ.
       required   3ERG-arrive-IRR 2ERG-father   today
       'Your father is to arrive today.'

This clause is introduced by the modal marker *yilal*, which in this case expresses root modality (it can also have an epistemic function; see Craig 1977). At the same time, the verb carries the suffix *-uj*, which Craig (1977) tends to gloss as 'future' but which she describes as an irrealis marker. The latter analysis is probably the correct one, since *-uj* also appears with negated statives and in irrealis moods.

The complex verb in (iii) must have been derived by head movement of the verb to the head that hosts the irrealis marker—the grammatical mood head. This means that root modals in Jacaltec, which are always clause-initial, are situated higher than the grammatical mood head—which is what I also am claiming to be the case in Shona.

In Loniu, a language with several preposed verbal markers (see Hamel 1994), only one of them, the marker of potential mood, is an affix. This means that the potential mood marker is situated lower than all other verbal markers, including the aspect markers, as the following illustrates:

(iv) *Loniu* (Hamel 1994:113)
      sɛh ma   k-a-la
      they INCH POT-NS-go
      'They were about to go.'

Thus, it appears that Loniu displays the order of inflectional heads, with mood below aspect, that I am proposing for Shona.

On the other hand, in some languages grammatical mood is encoded in an element that precedes even the tense markers. Consider the following example from Yagua:

(v) *Yagua* (Payne & Payne 1990:320)
     ray-niy jṳtay-siy-tya [rạ   jántyuuy-siy   yi-íva]
     1s-MAL   say-PAST-NEG   IRR have.mercy-PAST   2s-DAT
     'I didn't intend to show you mercy.'

We see here that the irrealis marker precedes the verb which has a past tense suffix. Also note that the irrealis marker invariably precedes its clausemate verb, so that we must conclude that it belongs to the embedded clause in this example. This suggests that the irrealis marker is located higher than the tense marker.

To sum up, there seems to be some cross-linguistic variation as regards the position of grammatical mood markers. Given the variation that we have seen above, my analysis of the final vowels in Shona is apparently not wholly implausible. More detailed investigations of the languages just mentioned and of other languages would be required to settle the question.

7. We see from (33c) that Ewe has double marking of the negative. This is not an unusual phenomenon in the languages of the world. One possible analysis, proposed by Pollock (1989) for French, is that one element is generated in the Neg° head while the other is generated in Spec-NegP. But note that the second negative element in Ewe is clause-final, so that objects and adverbials intervene between the verb and this marker. This suggests that what precedes the second negative marker in (33c) is its base structure complement which has moved to its Spec. But then the first negative marker cannot be generated in that very same Spec. A more promising idea is that the first part of the negation represents a Neg° head, generated somewhere above VP, whereas the second part represents a Pol(arity) head, generated higher up than Neg° (the existence and position of these two heads are proposed in Zanuttini 1994), and that the surface word order is derived by moving the complement of PolP, containing the negation in Neg°, to the Spec of PolP. This could be one way to establish a local relation between the Neg° and the Pol° heads, so that the polarity features can be checked (see Zanuttini 1994). A similar proposal has been put forth for Nweh in Nkemnji (1995), as cited in Koopman (1996).

8. I take *e* to be a marker of present tense and *be* to be a past marker even though Huttar and Huttar (1994) gloss them as CONTINUOUS and ANTERIOR, respectively.

9. I have substituted <tɬ> for the crossed lambda which Kinkade uses to symbolize the voiceless lateral affricate.

10. Kinkade translates this example as 'I am going to sing'. This seems to be an error; *ʔéɬn* is otherwise translated as 'eat', whereas 'sing' is *ʔelan*.

11. According to Szakos (1994:127) the present tense marker in Cou is also used to refer to past events that are directly related to the speech event. This is why we sometimes find the present tense marker in cases where English uses past tense, as in (58), (59), and (61). It is not clear to me whether this means that the present in Cou is also a recent past (as far back as the day before), although the examples given in Szakos (1994) might be taken to suggest that this is the case.

12. The perfective suffix which is indicated in the glossing is a subtractive morph, formally realized as truncation of the verb (Saxton 1982).

13. Mosel and Hovdhaugen (1992:168) state that "particles are usually un- stressed, but may be stressed under emphasis and in very slow and careful speech, provided that they are bisyllabic."

14. *Ai* in this use is referred to as 'phoric' by Du Feu (1996) and as an 'anaphoric pronoun' by Mosel and Hovdhaugen (1992). It can be used to refer to an entity whose identity is known from the discourse. In this example, it probably refers to the location (see Du Feu 1996:93–94 on Rapanui and Mosel & Hovdhaugen 1992:459– 462 on Samoan). It can also be used as a resumptive proform, as in the following:

(i) *Samoan*   (Mosel & Hovdhaugen 1992:381)

a. Sā   nofo   i Apia   le   teine.
    PAST.IMPF   live   in Apia   SPCF.SG   girl
    'The girl lived in Apia.'

b. 'O   Apia   sā   nofo   ai   le   teine.
    PR.P   Apia   PAST.IMPF   live   in.it   SPCF.SG   girl
    'It was in Apia that the girl lived.'

If we compare (ia) to (ib), we see that *ai* in (ib) fills the position from where the fronted phrase has been extracted.

15. This form is really just the nominal stem. However, the absence of any article signals that the noun is specific and plural (see Mosel & Hovdhaugen 1992:268).

16. Mosel and Hovdhaugen (1992:45–46) admit their debt to the tradition when they state that the principle of writing every morpheme as a separate word is inherited from the missionaries that were the first to write in Samoan. It is interesting to note that, even though they claim to adhere to this principle, they explicitly make an exception for 'bound morphemes'. Thus, the criteria they use to distinguish between words and affixes are very obscure; for them, a morpheme is a word as long as it is not an affix. However, as far as I can see from their examples, 'bound morphemes' are morphemes which are strictly adjacent to lexical roots, and I suspect that the identification of some morphemes as words and of others as affixes is based, more or less consciously, on the distributional criteria that I laid out in chapter 1.

Krupa (1966:16) also uses distributional criteria to establish that grammatical markers in Maori are words. After noting that Maori verbs are words on Bloomfield's definition of the word as a minimal free form (see section 1.4.2), he states that word-status must also be granted to the verbal particles, since they can be detached from the verbs.

Thus, while investigators of Bantu languages have traditionally relied heavily on phonology in their identification of words, as we saw in section 4.2, linguists working on Polynesian languages have taken distribution to be the decisive factor. As a consequence, preverbal adverbial elements have been perceived as part of the verbal word in Bantu but not in Polynesian. However, that the two ways of identifying words give different results is just what one would expect given that phonological words are not necessarily coextensive with grammatical words (see section 1.4.1).

17. For Gude, the analysis of the completive marker as a free element may be influenced by the fact that certain prepositions may appear in preverbal position and have the function of aspect markers. This is how the continuous and the potential are formed:

(i) *Gude* (Hoskison 1983:85)

    a.   agi   ka-nə   nə   Musa   faara
        in   throw-N   COP   Musa   stone
        'Musa is/was/will be throwing a stone.'.
    lit. 'Musa is/was/will be in throwing a stone'

    b.   ka   ka-nə   nə   Musa   faara
        to/for throw-N   COP   Musa   stone
        'Musa will/may throw a stone.'
    lit. 'Musa is towards throwing a stone.'

The combination of preposition and nominalized verb in these constructions has the appearance of an ordinary PP, and the prepositions defy being analyzed as prefixes on the verb. If the completive marker is seen as a parallel to the aspectual preposi-tions, it, too, will be regarded as a free element. (The element *nə*, which I have inter-preted as a copula in the above examples, is referred to by Hoskison as a 'subject marker'. However, this marker appears between the predicate and the subject in nonverbal clauses, which generally conform to the pattern 'DP/AP predicate *nə* subject', but it does not appear in verbal clauses. I therefore guess that *nə* is a copula.

18. Crucially, since phonological constituency does not necessary coincide with syntactic constituency (see chapter 1), this does not tell us anything about the syntactic relation between the verb and the inflectional markers in Yele. I would nevertheless like to advance the following proposal.

In chapter 2 n.15 I suggested that the postverbal markers in Yele may after all form a complex head with the verb. If this is the case, the operation that puts the verb between the two inflectional markers is head movement of the verb and not movement of a phrase that includes the verb and the preverbal marker. Certain facts suggest that this is correct and that the preverbal marker in Yele is generated higher than the postverbal marker. In Henderson's words (Henderson 1995:14, 36), the preverbal marker, which appears to be a fusion of several inflectional heads, *expresses* tense, aspect, mood, and the person and number of the subject, whereas the postverbal marker *expresses* the person and number of the object but *reflects* the tense, aspect, and mood of the preverbal marker and also the number of the subject. Note, for example, that the tense of the preverbal markers is not *doubled* by the postverbal marker: while six tenses are distinguished in the preverbal marker (future, immediate future, present, immediate past, near past, remote past), the postverbal marker only has a distinction between proximate and remote tense. This means, I assume, that the postverbal element is primarily an object agreement marker, whose actual shape is conditioned by the features of the preverbal marker. Hence, the postverbal marker probably originates below all elements that are included in the preverbal marker. Now if the verb has head-moved to the postverbal marker, it must the postverbal marker that heads the complement of the preverbal marker in the base order. The conditioning of the postverbal marker by the preverbal marker then boils down to the requirement that the preverbal marker must be compatible with the head of its complement.

19. Adverbials are normally located in front of the subject or between the object and the preverbal inflectional marker (see Henderson 1995:59).

20. According to Snyman (1970) the temporal markers in !Kung are adverbs. This makes their conspicuous freedom of position understandable.

21. Bybee et al. (1990) make a similar suggestion. A problem for this argument is that verbal markers located between the subject and the object in SOV languages are not seen as suffixes on the subject, as noted in the preceding subsection.

5

The Distribution of Verbal Markers

5.1 Overview

In the preceding chapters I have claimed that postposed grammatical markers result from movement of heads or phrases, while preposed grammatical markers are the consequence of not moving. These claims might have left the impression that there are no limits to the morphological patterns that can be derived in the system I have sketched. If every marker can surface as a prefix or as a suffix if the necessary movement operations are executed, anything seems to be possible.

As far as individual markers are concerned, they must be allowed by any theory to appear before or after the root, given the variation in morpheme positioning that we see in the languages of the world. However, if the clause as a whole is considered, there are certain patterns of morpheme ordering which we would expect to see, while others are predicted by my theory not to exist.

First, my proposals entail that the morpheme order in sequences of preposed markers should be the converse of the morpheme order in sequences of postposed markers and that, if a root has both preposed markers and postposed markers, the preposed markers will represent heads in relatively high positions and the postposed markers will represent heads in relatively low positions. The reason for this is that the root must have moved past the heads that are realized as postposed markers but not as high as the heads that are realized as preposed markers.

Deviations from this pattern must result from phrasal movement, which may take a lower projection of IP to the Spec of a higher projection of IP and thus create constructions where the verb root and a possibly preposed inflectional marker both precede a higher inflectional marker. But then it should be clear that there really is phrasal movement. For example, the order SAVOT could be derived by movement of the AspP, containing the aspect marker, the verb, and the object, to a Spec somewhere above T°. However, we would not expect to see languages with the order *SAVTO. If the aspect marker and the verb precede the tense marker as a result of movement of AspP to a higher Spec, we would expect the object to be included in the moved phrase, the higher marker thereby ending up in clause-final position.

More generally, on the assumption that tense is generated above aspect, we would expect to see languages with the morpheme orders listed in (1), but not languages with the morpheme orders given in (2).

(1)   *Possible morpheme orders*
   a. (S) T A V (O)
   b. (S) T V+A (O)
   c. (S) (O) V+A+T (O)
   d. S A V O T

(2)   *Impossible morpheme orders*
   a. * (S) A T V (O)
   b. * (S) A V+T (O)
   c. * (S) V+T+A (O)
   d. * S A V T O

In this chapter, I show that these predications are borne out to a considerable degree in the languages represented in my survey (see section 1.5 and appendix 2), and that apparent counterexamples tend to comply with my theory when they are made subject to closer scrutiny.

The notable exception is agreement markers, which are found in so many different positions cross-linguistically that it seems impossible to relate subject agreement or object agreement to one particular syntactic head. Therefore, my conclusion is that agreement features do not head phrases; instead, they are added to syntactic heads that also have some other content.

I start the discussion, in section 5.2, by looking at how verbal markers can be arranged in the three main word orders. In that section, I also try to show how the observed morpheme arrangements can all be derived in syntax.

In section 5.3, I deal with agreement markers. It appears that the agreement markers show so much variation in their distribution that it is impossible to identify them directly with argument-licensing heads.

In section 5.4 I discuss some data which have been presented as evidence against the syntactic approach to word formation. What I intend to show is that the alleged counterexamples are not necessarily convincing and that alternative analyses are possible which retain the view that word formation is syntactic.

In section 5.5 I deal with some of the already existing theories concerned with the distribution of inflectional morphemes. These theories are then compared to the theory presented in this work. I try to demonstrate that my theory is at least as adequate as other theories, as the observed patterns can be argued to follow directly from the syntax of the verbal inflectional domain. Some final remarks follow in section 5.6.

5.2 Word order and the positioning of verbal markers

I now provide an overview of the different arrangements of verbal inflectional markers that are found in the languages of the world, and I indicate how the syntax would be able to produce the different orders. Let us first consider table 5.1, which shows the numbers of preposed and postposed verbal markers in each of the major word order types, as given by Bybee et al. (1990). I ignore the distinction between free and bound markers, since, as explained in earlier chapters, I do not believe that this distinction necessarily reflects a structural contrast.

We see that in verb-initial languages there are more postposed verbal markers than preposed verbal markers, whereas in verb-medial languages there are more preposed verbal markers than postposed verbal markers. Still, the difference between the two orderings is relatively small in both language types. In verb-final languages, by contrast, postposed markers clearly outnumber preposed markers.

If we relate these facts to the proposals I have made concerning the question of how the placement of grammatical markers is effectuated, we see that my proposals seem to make some sense. If postposed markers in verb-initial and verb-medial languages result from head movement of the verb, the observed contrast between the two word order types is expected. In a verb-initial language, the verb must have moved across the subject. If the subject moves to a Spec position in IP, the verb must move even higher. In a verb-medial language, on the other hand, the verb does not move higher than the subject. Hence, it is not surprising that verbs in verb-initial languages cross more inflectional heads and end up with more postposed markers than verbs in verb-medial languages. For verb-final languages, I have proposed that the majority of them are also head-final, which means that there is repeated XP-movement from the VP upward. This process necessarily produces suffixes, which means that my analysis predicts exactly the patterns that we see in verb-final languages.

We now go on to take a closer look at the IP syntax of a number of languages. I deal first with verb-medial languages in 5.2.1; then I turn to verb-initial languages in 5.2.2 and to verb-final languages in 5.2.3.

TABLE 5.1
Positioning of verbal grammatical marker relative to word order. The figures refer to individual markers and are taken from tables 1 and 2 of Bybee et al. (1990).

Word order	Preposed markers		Postposed markers		Total number of markers
	No.	%	No.	%	
V-initial	81	42	111	58	192
V-medial	498	54	423	46	921
V-final	233	19	1018	81	1251

5.2.1   Verb-medial languages

In a verb-medial order, it is possible that the verb has not moved at all, provided that the object does not move overtly, either. Thus, it may be the case that in example (3), the two verbs and the object are in the positions where they are base-generated. Consequently, all grammatical markers precede the verbs, and they appear in their base-generated order. The only element that has moved is the subject, which has raised to a position above all the verbal markers in the inflectional domain.

(3)   *Mauritian Creole* (Adone 1994:103)
      Nu   pa   ti   pu   vin   get   twa.
      we   NEG PAST FUT come see   you
      'We would not have come to see you.'

The same analysis probably applies to examples (4)–(7), where the subject also precedes a series of preverbal markers. Note that the tense markers invariably precede the aspect markers. This indicates that temporal heads are generated above aspectual heads, as proposed by Cinque (1999).

(4)   *Mauritian Creole* (Adone 1994:44)
      Lapli   ti   pe   toñbe.
      rain   PAST IMPF fall
      'Rain was falling.'

(5)   *Makaa* (Heath 1991:11)
      Mə   á   dù   ŋgùl   məlwòg   mə   ləndú.
      1s   REM.PAST HAB drink drink   of   palm
      'I used to drink palm wine.'

(6)   *Guyanese Creole* (K. Gibson 1992:61)
      Shi   bin   a   sing.
      she   PAST PROG sing
      'She was singing.'

(7)   *Papiamentu* (Andersen 1990:67)
      Wan   ta   bai   kome   bonchi.
      John   IMPF INCH eat   beans
      'John is going to eat beans.'

In some verb-medial languages, the verb moves high up in the inflectional domain, thereby picking up all overt inflectional markers. The result is a complex word where the inflectional markers are suffixed to the verb root. In this case, the order of inflectional markers will be the opposite of what we see when there is no head movement in IP. Some examples are given in (8)–(11). Notice that in Macushi, an OVS language, the verbal word is preceded by the object, while a pronominal postverbal subject is cliticized to the verb (see Abbott 1991). In the other examples below, it is the subject that has moved to the front of the verbal word. Other arguments and adverbials follow the verbal word, which indicates that the verbal word is a result of head movement and not of phrasal movement.

(8) *Fulfulde* (Fagerli 1994:54)
     Mi   yah-r-id-i   be'i   fuu haa maayo.
     I   go-TRANS-COMPL-VAP goats   all at   river
     'I took all the goats to the river.'

(9) *Northern Saami*
     Mii   oidni-i-met   Bireh-a   TV-as   ikte.
     we-NOM see-PAST-1p Biret-ACC   TV-LOC   yesterday
     'We saw Biret on TV yesterday.'

(10) *Kashmiri* (Wali & Koul 1997:155)
     bɨ   vuch-a-n   su
     I.ABS   see-FUT.1s-3s   he.ABS
     'I will see him.'

(11) *Macushi* (Abbott 1991:121)
     yei   ya'tî-aretî'ka-'pî-i-ya
     wood   cut-TERM-PAST-3-ERG
     'He finished cutting the wood.'

It also sometimes happens that the verb in a verb-medial language moves halfway up in the inflectional domain, so that in the surface structure, some verbal inflectional markers are suffixed to the verb while others precede it. Berbice Dutch, for example, is a language of this type:

(12) *Berbice Dutch* (Robertson 1990:180–181)
     a. a   wa   kap-a   tun   b. ɛk   wa   mo-tɛ   ɔɪti
        he PAST cut-IMPF field   I   PAST go-PERF   out
        'He was cutting a field.'   'I had gone out.'

The morpheme ordering in (12) can be derived by moving the verb and adjoining it to the aspectual head. This operation will place the verb root to the immediate left of the aspect marker. As for the tense marker, it will still precede the complex head consisting of the verb and the aspect marker. Consequently, it is the tense marker that is preposed while the aspect marker is suffixed to the verb. A simplified sketch of the syntactic structure of (12) is shown in (13).

(13)

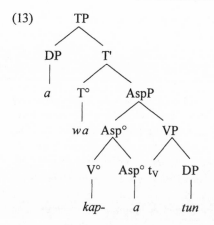

In this configuration, the surface order of morphemes is tense-verb-aspect. Moreover, since the postposed aspect marker is included in a complex head with the verb, while the preposed tense marker is not, the aspect marker is a bound morpheme and the tense marker is free.

The same pattern is found in Nɔmaándέ, as shown in (14). But in Onondaga, shown in (15), where the tense marker probably also precedes the complex head containing the verb root and the aspect marker, the tense marker is nevertheless included in the verbal word. From what was said in chapter 4, we would expect this to be an option alongside the pattern shown in (12) and (14): markers that regularly precede a lexical element can, because of their distribution, be taken to form a word with that element.

(14) *Nɔmaándέ* (= ex. (94), ch. 4)
ɔ-ɔcɔ ŋɔ-ɔ́   tɔ́lí-ák-a   tu-áyέ   tú-koli.
1-man REM.PAST-3s set-DUR-FV   13-3sPOSS   13-string
'The man had set his snares.'

(15) *Onondaga* (Baker 1988a:77; from Woodbury 1975)
Pet waʔ-ha-htu-ʔt-aʔ   neʔ ohwist-aʔ
Pat PAST-3MASC/3NEUT-lose-CAUS-ASP   the money
'Pat lost the money.'

However, we also sometimes find verb-medial languages where a relatively low marker precedes the root and a relatively high marker follows the root. But then it is normally clear that there has been phrasal movement, as my theory predicts. In (16), for example, it appears that the whole IP, including the preposed aspect marker, has moved to a position in front of the affirmative marker. As a result, the aspect marker retains its base-generated position in front of the verb, while the affirmative marker, which originates above IP, comes to follow the verb in the surface structure.

(16) *Jukun* (Shimizu 1980:265)
     ku   na   bi   ra
     he   CONT   come   AFF
     'He is coming.'

That is, (16) is an example of movement of an IP projection in a language that does not belong to the class of head-final languages. Several similar cases were presented in section 3.6.1, and I argued there that in all these cases, the head that attracts the IP to its Spec belongs to the CP-domain. Hence, if a lower marker precedes the verbal root and a higher marker follows the verbal root, the higher marker will represent one of the heads of the CP-domain. In my material, there is no clear counterexample to this generalization.

To conclude this brief discussion of verb-medial languages, we have seen that there are many ways to derive a verb-medial order. The verb moves very high up in IP in some languages, while in others it apparently does not move at all. It then comes as no surprise that preposed and postposed markers are approximately equally frequent in this group and the position of tense markers varies considerably—they become preposed or postposed depending on exactly how high the verb moves.

5.2.2   Verb-initial languages

In a verb-initial language, on the other hand, the verb must necessarily have moved, otherwise it would not precede the subject. But note that VSO order may be the outcome of a very short verb movement. Thus, it may still be the case that the verb follows the inflectional markers, as in (17) and (18). In both these examples, the verb follows the tense and aspect markers, and in (18), there is also an adverbial between the aspect marker and the verb. This indicates that the verb is positioned rather low down in IP. The subject, which follows the verb, must then be even lower; perhaps in its base position inside the extended VP.[1]

(17) *Jicaltepec Mixtec* (Bradley 1970)
     ča   nú   čákuda   rá
     PAST   PERF   sit.down   he
     'He has already sat down.'

(18) *Cou* (Szakos 1994:72)
     moso   la   aok-o   sueum-o   no   mocmo ci   cou
     PAST.AFOC   HAB   constantly-AFOC   attack-AFOC   ART   other   PRT   Cou
     'They constantly attacked other Cou.'

Berber is another verb-initial language with preposed inflectional markers, as illustrated in (19). According to Ouali (1999), the 'aorist' form of the verb is simply the unmarked form, which results from not moving the verb to T°. As

(20) shows, pronominal clitics may appear between the tense marker and the verb. As Ouali points out, this indicates that the verb has not moved to T°.

(19) *Berber* (Ouali 1999:11)
 da-daghex   aghroum
 FUT-buy.1s.AOR   bread
 'I will buy bread.'

(20) *Berber* (Ouali 1999:17)
 da-as-t   wshex
 FUT-him-it   give.1s
 'I will give it to him.'

Another interesting fact about Berber is that postverbal subjects have genitive case, while preverbal subjects have nominative case (Ouhalla 1997):

(21) *Berber* (Ouhalla 1997:205)
 Y-zra   ufrux   Hamish
 3sMASC-see   boy.GEN   Hamish
 'The boy has seen Hamish.'

(22) *Berber* (Ouhalla 1997:208)
 Afrux   y-ssn   tamghart
 boy.NOM   3sMASC-know   woman
 'The boy knows the woman.'

Ouhalla's explanation is that postverbal subjects in Berber have not moved to the position where nominative case is licensed. Rather, postverbal subjects are located immediately above VP. In fact, one might want to suggest that post-verbal subjects are in the position where they originate. In any case, they have not moved very high in IP, and, accordingly, it is possible that the verb has not moved very high, either. Thus, we see that Berber seems to support my claims about inflectional prefixes: they are preposed because the verb has not moved high enough to pick them up as suffixes.

In other verb-initial languages, however, the verb moves high up in IP, so that the verbal inflectional markers end up as suffixes. Some examples of this are given in (23)–(25).

(23) *Turkana* (Dimmendaal 1982:70)
 è-dàk-a-sì   ŋaàtùk   ŋɪ-ɲà
 3-graze-STAT-PL   cows   grass
 'The cows are eating grass.'

(24) *Yagua* (Payne & Payne 1990:389)
      rá-jupatya-y-muuy-siy   níínu
      INAN-fall-INTR-COMPL-PAST   tree
      'The trees all fell down a few weeks ago.'

(25) *Irish* (McCloskey 1996:269)
      Deire-ann siad i gnónaí paidir roimh   am   lui.
      say-PRES they always   prayer before time lie
      'They always say a prayer before bedtime.'

Note that in (24), the aspect suffix precedes the tense suffix, as expected. Also note that in (25), an adverbial intervenes between the subject and the object. This shows that the subject has moved out of VP and crossed some of the projections of the IP-domain. Since the verb precedes the subject in this construction, the verb must have moved even higher. Thus, the syntax of this construction allows us to interpret the fact that the verb carries a tense suffix as a result of the verb having moved to a tense head.

In short, a language with verb-initial order can have preposed or postposed verbal inflectional markers, depending on how high the verb moves. It can also have a combination of pre- and postposed markers, as in (26) and (27).

(26) *Podoko* (= ex. (78), ch. 4)
      Sa   gəl-i   udzəra.
      PAST   grow-IMPF   child
      'The child was growing up.'

(27) *Rukai* (Li 1973)
      wa-kani-ŋa
      PAST-eat-COMPL
      'He/she ate.'

Strikingly, again it is the tense marker that precedes the verb root and the aspect marker that follows it. Thus, the complex word in (27), for example, is perfectly in line with my claim that prefixes represent heads that sit higher than the surface position of the root, while suffixes represent heads that the root has moved to or across. That is, the structure of the word in (27) is again as shown in (13). The same structure also underlies (26), but here the morphological effect is different, presumably for phonological reasons.

A verb-initial language where the syntactic contrast between prefixes and suffixes can be observed directly is Jacaltec. As we saw in section 4.3.2, Jacaltec is a VSO language with preposed aspect markers. It also has a suffixed marker of irrealis mood (see chapter 4 n.6), which is spelled out as -*oj* on intransitive verb and as -*a* on transitive verbs. In example (28) we see a verb that has both a prefixed aspect marker and a suffixed irrealis marker.

(28) *Jacaltec* (Craig 1977:87)
    tita'   ch-Ø-aw-il-a   naj   txoŋbal   tinaŋ
    maybe INCMPL-3ABS-2ERG-see-IRR him market   today
    'Maybe you will see him in the market today.'

In addition, Jacaltec has certain modal markers that appear in second position
in the clause (Craig 1977). From the data given in Craig (1977), it appears that
the second position modal elements are generated higher than any other element
of the clause and that they attract the nearest head, which then left-adjoins to the
modal element. One of the second-position elements is the probability marker
m(i); another is the exhortative marker *ab*. In (29) I show an example where the
negation precedes the exhortative marker, while the incompletive marker is
prefixed to the verb, which follows the exhortative marker. In (30), the probability marker is preceded by the completive aspect marker. In (31), on the other
hand, the probability marker is preceded by the negation.

(29) *Jacaltec* (Craig 1977:73)
    maj-ab   ch-ach   s-mak   naj
    NEG-EXH INCMPL-2ABS 3ERG-hit he
    'May he not hit you!'

(30) *Jacaltec* (Craig 1977:91)
    xma-m   to   naj
    COMPL-PROB go   he
    'Maybe he went.'

(31) *Jacaltec* (Craig 1977:87)
    mat-mi   yel-oj   [ch-al   naj]
    NEG-PROB true-IRR INCMPL-say he
    'What he is saying may not be true.'

My interpretation of these examples is that they are all derived from the
structure shown in (32). Here the modal head precedes the negation, which in
turn precedes the aspectual head. Below the aspectual head is the head that hosts
the irrealis marker. I have termed it Irr° for convenience. I assume that the verb
always moves and adjoins to the Irr° head, so that a complex head V°+Irr° is
formed. This is what lies behind the ordering INCOMPL-V-IRR, shown in (28). I
have no specific proposals concerning the positions of the agreement markers
that intervene between the aspect marker and the verb, so I will ignore them for
the present purpose.

(32)   ModalP

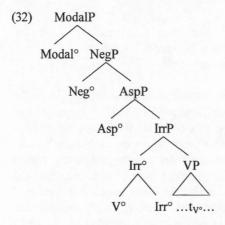

V°   Irr° ...t$_{V°}$...

Concerning the probability and exhortative modals, I take them to be generated in the Modal° head. (In reality, they might be generated in separate heads,
but for each of them, (32) is still an adequate model.) Now it appears to be the
case that these modals need to be preceded by a phonologically overt element. In
this respect, they are rather similar to Icelandic finite verbs, as discussed by
Holmberg (2000b). In (29), where the negation is overt, it is the negation which
is attracted to the Modal° head, so that it comes to precede the modal marker in
the surface order. The aspect marker stays in its normal position right in front of
the verb, and it is perceived as a prefix on the verb. But in (30), the Neg° head
has no phonological realization. It is then the next lower head, the Asp° head,
which is attracted to Modal°. The result is that the aspect marker, which otherwise is prefixed to the verb, becomes separated from the verb by the probability
marker, and it forms a word with the probability marker instead of with the
verb. In my theory, it is predicted that prefixes should be able to behave in this
way. Since inflectional prefixes are not included in the head that contains the
lexical root, it is in principle always possible to move the prefix without
moving the root.

Example (31) serves to show that when the negation is present in a clause
with a probability marker, the negation will be attracted to that marker in the
same way it is attracted to the exhortative modal in (29). It is also interesting to
note that the semantics of (31) indicates that there is movement. Semantically,
the probability marker takes scope over the negation; the reading we get is
PROBABLE > NOT. From the surface order of markers, with the negation
preceding the probability marker, we would expect the reading to be NOT >
PROBABLE. But if the negation originates below Modal°, as I have suggested,
the actual reading is explained: apparently, LF reads off the lower copy of the
negation (i.e., the copy that follows Modal°). PF, on the other hand, targets the
higher copy (i.e., the one that is adjoined to Modal°).

The last Jacaltec example that I present here is (33). Interestingly, here the
exhortative marker is preceded by the verb root and the irrealis marker.

(33) *Jacaltec* (Craig 1977:73)
    way-oj   ab   hoŋ
    sleep-IRR EXH 1pABS
    'Would that we sleep!'

We have already seen that the exhortative marker attracts exactly one constituent to a position in front of it. Hence, the verb and the irrealis marker must be one constituent. Most likely, the two elements together form a complex head, as indicated in (32). This means that the structural difference that I have postulated between prefixes and suffixes has visible consequences in Jacaltec in that a prefix may move without the verb while a suffix moves together with the verb. This is another indication that the syntactic approach to morphology is on the right track.

    The above examples thus conform to the expectation that whenever a root has both preposed and postposed inflectional markers, markers that precede the root should originate high up in the syntactic structure while markers that follow the root should originate in lower positions. But as pointed out in the discussion of verb-medial languages, it sometimes happens that a relatively low marker precedes the root and a relatively high marker follows the root as a result of phrasal movement. Such cases are also found in verb-initial languages. For example, we saw in (26) above that Podoko is a verb-initial language and that the verb moves to an Asp° head. There is thus no question of the Podoko IP being characterized by movement of complements to Spec. Nevertheless, question markers in Podoko are clause-final, as (34) illustrates.

(34) *Podoko* (Jarvis 1991:232)
    A   ɓakavadə̀ kə̀nə   ka   na?
    FOC do.PERF how   2s   Q
    'How did you do that?'

I take this to mean that the question marker is generated high up in the clause, somewhere in the CP-domain, and it attracts the remainder of the clause to its Spec, so that the question marker itself ends up in clause-final position, while all inflectional markers come to precede the question marker in the surface order.[2]

    A conclusion that can be drawn from the preceding discussion is that the range of possible orderings of verb and verbal markers is very much the same in verb-initial and verb-medial languages. The differences between the two orders probably stem from the fact that the verb must move across the subject in verb-initial languages while it does not do so in verb-medial languages. That is, in the average case the verb moves higher in a verb-initial language than in a verb-medial language. Because of this, verb-initial languages as a group have a relatively higher number of postposed markers than verb-medial languages, as table 5.1 shows.

5.2.3 Verb-final languages

Table 5.1 also shows very clearly that verb-final languages have fewer preposed verbal markers than verb-initial and verb-medial languages. As pointed out in chapter 3, this is not what we would expect if verb-final order simply results from moving the arguments to preverbal positions. It this were all that characterized verb-final languages, we would expect to see at least as many preposed markers in verb-final orders as in other orders. The low frequency of preposed markers in verb-final languages suggests that the complement movement theory developed in chapter 3 is on the right track. If strict head-finality is derived by successive movements of complements to Spec, it follows that all verbal heads end up stacked at the end of the clause as suffixes on the verb, and there will be no room for preposed markers. Further, the order of elements in the suffix sequences that we find in head-final languages should be the converse of the base-generated order. For example, aspect markers should precede tense markers. In the following examples, this is borne out.

(35) *Even* (Malchukov 1993:369)
     Huličan   bödele-n   ene-l-re-n.
     fox   feet-3sPOSS   hurt-INCH-NONFUT-3s
     'The fox's paws began to hurt.'

(36) *Magi* (Thomson 1975)
     oni-lo-si-a
     go-IMPF-REM.PAST-2/3s
     'You/he/she were/was going.'

(37) *Atka Aleut* (Bergsland & Dirks 1981:91)
     Anĝaĝina-s   tana-s-xan   slu-za-na-s.
     person-PL   camp-PL-REFL.POSS   spend.summer-HAB-PAST-PL
     'People used to spend the summer at their camps.'

For the few preposed markers that are found in verb-final languages, there are two explanations that could be considered. Either these markers have some exceptional property that prevents them from attracting their complement to their Spec,[3] or they belong to languages where complement-to-Spec movement does not apply. Consider the following examples:

(38) *Rikbaktsa* (= ex. (19), ch. 3)
     Ka-zo   pitsi   pi-boro-ko.
     1s-father cashew   NONPAST-eat-CONT
     'My father is eating cashew nuts.'

(39) *Koranko* (Kastenholz 1987:108)
ànu bé ɲòi tùu-la lùyɛ mà
3p PRES millet stamp-PROG yard in
'They are stamping millet in the yard.'

As discussed in 3.3, the SOV order of languages like Rikbaktsa and Koranko must be derived by separate movements of verb and object. The morphology indicates that the verb has moved to an aspectual head. In Koranko, the object must then minimally have moved to the Spec of this head. However, the postpositional phrase in (39) still follows the verb, in what is presumably its base position, and there appears to be no movement of VP as a whole. The movements that take place have no consequences for the tense marker, which is realized in its base position, above the object and the verb, as a separate word. In Rikbaktsa, the object has moved to a position above tense. With nothing intervening between the tense marker and the verb, the tense marker can be interpreted as a prefix on the verbal root.

In verb-final languages of the head-final type, all grammatical markers normally follow the verbal root. In other verb-final languages we find preverbal inflectional markers, as we have just seen. But just like in verb-medial and verb-initial languages, there are cases here where a marker generated in the CP-domain appears in clause-final position, as in the following examples:

(40) *Koranko* (Kastenholz 1987:314)
kélaye ára ké fɔlɔ wà?
messenger PERF arrive just Q
'Has the messenger already arrived?'

(41) *Slave* (Rice 1989:409)
ledí e-h-dǫ lǫ
tea ASP-1sS-drank EVID
'I drank my tea by mistake.'

Since the base-generated order of verb and aspect marker is retained in these constructions, the verb cannot have come to end up to the left of the higher marker as a result of head movement. Rather, it must be the whole IP that has moved—to the front of the question marker in (40) and to the front of the evidential marker in (41). As a result, in both examples a marker which presumably is generated relatively high up in the clause (see Cinque 1999) is preceded by a sequence of elements, including the verb and an aspect marker, that originate in the complement of that marker. Thus, the morpheme ordering in (40) and (41) is not counterevidence to my proposals concerning word formation.

5.3 Agreement markers

We have seen in the foregoing that the syntactic approach to word formation can be used rather successfully to account for the distribution of verbal inflectional markers. However, there is one inflectional category which does not so easily fit into the relatively rigid framework that syntactic analyses provide. This category is agreement. The variation that we find in the positioning of agreement markers is such that we have to give up the idea put forth in Chomsky (1993) that clauses contain a subject agreement head and an object agreement head which are located in fixed positions universally. Thus, even if it seems clear that there are more heads in the IP-domain than just T°, my claim is that projecting Agr heads are absent from all languages, not only from languages with weak Agr, as proposed by Chomsky (1995). Instead, as mentioned in chapter 3, I assume that agreement features are added to heads that also have some other content.

A similar idea was expressed earlier by Iatridou (1990), Speas (1991), Spencer (1992), Mitchell (1994), and Holmberg and Platzack (1995), among others; see also Rouveret (1991). It is also put forth by Halle and Marantz (1993), who assume that subject agreement features are added to tense heads.[4] I suggested in sections 2.2 and 3.1 that the subject agreement features can alternatively be hosted by the Fin° head. This move was motivated by a rather limited range of data, however. To get a fuller picture of the distribution of agreement markers in the world's languages, I now present some more data from my survey (see section 1.5). Note, by the way, that I have tried, to the extent that my data sources allow it, to distinguish between true agreement markers, which may co-occur with a DP argument, and incorporated pronouns, which may not. It has been my intention to leave argument markers of the latter type out of the discussion.

We first look at the relative ordering of subject agreement markers, tense/aspect markers, and verb roots. The relevant data are given in table 5.2. First, note that several genera contain languages where subject agreement and tense (or aspect in languages that have no tense marker) are regularly expressed by one single marker. If we assume with Halle and Marantz (1993) that the agreement features reside in a separate terminal node that is adjoined to the temporal head, this must be the result of fusion of the agreement node and the tense node, which is assumed by Halle and Marantz to be a process that may apply to sister nodes. Alternatively, one might suggest that the subject agreement features are generated in the tense head, so that all the relevant features are contained in one node from the very beginning. A third possibility is that the tense head has moved to the head that hosts the agreement features and that the two heads have then fused. These analyses are equally plausible for languages where head movement can be assumed to play a role, but not for strictly head-final languages, which do not have head movement, as argued in chapter 3.

TABLE 5.2
Relative order of verb root, tense marker, and subject agreement marker, by word order. Intervening markers of other categories are ignored. The figures refer to genera (see section 1.5).

Morpheme order	Word order				Total
	V-initial	V-medial	V-final	Uncertain	
SAgr/T V			2		2
SAgr/T+V	1	4	3	1	7
V+SAgr/T	3	4	17	2	26
V+T+SAgr	4	17	42	8	64
V+SAgr+T	3		10	3	16
V+SAgr T	1		2		3
SAgr+T+V	4	7	5		14
SAgr T V		6			6
SAgr+T V		5	1		5
SAgr+V+T	4	29	28	7	57
T+V+SAgr	4	2	2	1	9
T V+SAgr		1			1
T+SAgr+V	5	5	3	1	9
T+SAgr V	1	2	1		3
T Sagr+V		3			3
SAgr+V T		1	5		5

An empty cell means that there is no language of the relevant type in my material.

We see from the first three lines of table 5.2 that portmanteau markers of subject agreement and tense tend to be suffixed, and they appear most frequently in verb-final languages; in fact, about half of all occurrences of portmanteau subject agreement and tense markers are as suffixes in verb-final languages. All the relevant languages appear to be of the strictly head-final type, which means that agreement is a notable exception from the strictly agglutinative pattern that otherwise characterize head-final languages.

If fusion across phrase boundaries is not allowed, we must assume that portmanteau markers of subject agreement and tense in head-final languages are the consequence of generating agreement features in the tense head. Also note that if the portmanteau subject agreement and tense marker is not affixed to the verb, it precedes the verb, and the language is verb-final.

In languages where subject agreement and tense are spelled out separately, there are two morpheme arrangements which are far more frequent than the others. V+T+SAgr is found in 64 genera, often in combination with verb-final order but also in languages with other word orders, while SAgr+V+T is found in 57 genera, and it is relatively more frequent in verb-medial order than in other orders. Both these orders would be expected if subject agreement is located in a head which is higher than the tense head, possibly in the Fin° head, as I have suggested. V+T+SAgr could then be the result of moving V° to T° and Fin° or of moving VP to Spec-TP and TP to Spec-FinP. SAgr+V+T could be derived by moving V° to T°, so that the complex V+T became linearly adjacent to the preceding Fin° head. This suggestion goes well with the fact that SAgr+V+T is a frequent pattern in verb-medial languages; it is found in nearly one-third of the 101 genera in my survey that contain verb-medial languages.

Further, SAgr T V, the order that would be the base-generated one if subject agreement is located in the Fin° head, is also found rather frequently, sometimes with and sometimes without affixation. Again, verb-medial languages are dominant, a fact which is in accordance with the observation that verb-medial order is often derived by moving the subject to the front and leaving other elements in their base positions.

In three out of four cases where a verb is combined with a tense marker and a subject marker, we find one of the orders just mentioned, which all allow an analysis where subject agreement is located in a head above tense, such as Fin°. This means that subject agreement markers show a great deal of regularity in their distribution.

Only in one out of four cases do we encounter one of the more deviant patterns. In the majority of these patterns the subject agreement marker is located between the verb root and the tense marker.

In three genera we find the pattern V+SAgr T. One of these genera is Kuliak, represented in my survey by Ik, a language which was discussed in some detail in section 2.3.2. One will recall that Ik is a VSO language where the tense marker is a second position clitic. If no other element precedes the tense marker, a movement operation of the LHM-type moves the verb (with the subject marker) to the front of the tense marker, as in (42).

(42) *Ik* (= ex. (28), ch. 2)
    en-ata   be   ceki-a   saatso
    see-3p PAST   woman-ACC yesterday
    'They saw the woman yesterday.'

In (43), by contrast, the tense marker is preceded by the negation, and the verb stays below the tense marker.

(43) *Ik* (=(i) in ch. 2 n.16)
    maa na   en-it-i   toimɛna tse-ikota naa   kij'a
    NEG PAST see-2p-OPT that   dry-and   PAST world.ABS
    'Don't you see that the world has dried (= that it has dawned)?'

We see that the verb nevertheless carries subject agreement. Hence, it is clear that subject agreement in Ik is generated below tense and also below the optative mood marker.

In the other two genera with V+SAgr T, Indic and Central Cushitic, it appears on closer inspection that the alleged tense marker, which is a postverbal free element, is in fact an auxiliary. The Hindi example given below illustrates this:

(44) *Hindi* (= ex. (74b), ch. 3)
Raam roTii khaa-taa th-aa.
Ram$_{MASC}$ bread$_{FEM}$ eat-PRES.MASC.SG be-PAST.MASC.SG
'Ram (habitually) ate bread.'

Since we thus have two verbs and two verbal projections, the appearance of subject agreement on the main verb, on the auxiliary, or on both does not give any indications about the exact positioning of the agreement features in these languages.

In languages with the patterns T+SAgr+V, T+SAgr V, or T Sagr+V, it also appears that subject agreement must be located below T. Consider the following example, where subject agreement follows not only tense but also the potential marker:

(45) *Loniu* (Hamel 1994:113)
sɛh ya k-ɛ-mɛ ɛtɛ u
3p FUT POT-NONSG-come ANIM.GOAL 1dEXCL
'They will come to (visit) us.'

It is possible that the subject agreement features in Loniu are generated in the same head as subject agreement features in Ik, shown in (43). The difference between the two languages then is that the verb moves to this head (and to the modal head above it) in Ik but stays low in Loniu. One might further assume that the localization of subject agreement in the 16 genera where V+SAgr+T is found, mainly in verb-final languages, is the same as in Ik and Loniu.[5]

The subject agreement features are also probably located in a relatively low head in the languages that have T+V+SAgr or T V+SAgr. The surface order of morphemes can then be derived by moving the verb to the head that hosts subject agreement.[6] One can also note that the arrangements T V+SAgr and T SAgr+V, where a free tense marker precedes a verb that carries the subject agreement marker, are only found in verb-medial languages. Languages that have SAgr+V T, on the other hand, are verb-final. Further, the tense marker then follows the whole VP, so that there must have been movement of a constituent that contains both the head with subject agreement features and the whole verbal phrase to a higher specifier position, for example to Spec-TP.[7] As we have seen in chapter 3, phrasal movement of this type is typical of verb-final languages.

To sum up, the data we have looked at so far suggest that a language has at least three options regarding the positioning of subject agreement: the subject agreement features can be generated in a tense head, in a head above tense, or in a head below tense. The following examples, where both a preverbal inflectional marker and the verb itself is marked for subject agreement, indicate that it is also possible to have subject agreement in two heads simultaneously:

(46) *Mbay* (Keegan 1997:70)
ḿ-ā   ḿ-ndə̄gō
1s-FUT 1s-buy
'I will buy.'

(47) *Lango* (Noonan 1992:142)
án   à-pé   à-wótò   kàmpálà
I   1s-NEG   1s-go.PERF Kampala
'I didn't go to Kampala.'

Moreover, in Sengoi, shown in (48), it appears that the lower option is chosen in the past tense but the higher one in the future tense.

(48) *Sengoi* (Means et al. 1986)
a. Ke ki-ha muit.   b. Guru ajeh ya   ki-lei.
   3s 3s-FUT enter   teacher that PAST 3s-come
   'She will enter.'   'The teacher came.'

Alternatively, it could be that in this language, the subject agreement morpheme is adjoined to the T°(future) head, which is lower than the T°(past) head—see Cinque (1999) and Julien (2001). It would then precede the future marker, as in (48a), but follow the past tense marker, as in (48b).[8]

Another interesting generalization is that if a subject agreement marker follows the verb, it is suffixed to the verb, unless the subject agreement marker is (contained in) a second position clitic. In the latter case, the operation that has moved the verb to the left of the subject agreement marker is LHM, the movement operation of exceptional type that can move a verb across the heads of its extended projection. Some examples of this were given in section 2.3.2. In other words, whereas a free tense marker preceding the verb may carry subject agreement, as in (46) and (48b), a free tense marker which follows the verb without being a second-position clitic does not show agreement. If there is subject agreement in the language in question, it will be attached to the verb.

I am not sure what to make of this, but it could be that in languages where the VP moves as a whole, so that the VP comes to precede the tense marker in the surface order, the arguments are contained within VP and agreement is marked on that head inside the multi-layered VP which is preceded by the subject (see the discussion of the VP in head-final languages in 3.4.2).

If object agreement is also taken into consideration, the distributional facts are as shown in table 5.3. Note that in addition to bound markers, which clearly constitute the majority, I have also included non-bound markers in this table.[9]

There are many points here that could be commented on. I will mention only a few. First, of the 24 theoretically possible orderings of verb root, tense marker, subject agreement, and object agreement, only 4 are not attested; these are OAgr-T-SAgr-V, T-OAgr-V-SAgr, OAgr-T-V-SAgr, and SAgr-V-OAgr-T. The 20 other orderings can all be found in one or more languages.

TABLE 5.3
Relative order of verb root, tense marker, subject agreement marker, and object agreement marker, by word order. Intervening markers of other categories are ignored. The figures refer to genera (see section 1.5).

Morpheme order	Word order				
	V-initial	V-medial	V-final	Uncertain	Total
S/OAgr-V-T[a]		8	11	2	19
T-V-S/OAgr		3			3
V-T-S/OAgr	1	4	3		7
V-S/OAgr-T	1		1		2
T-SAgr-OAgr-V	1	2	1	1	3
SAgr-T-OAgr-V	1	1	2		4
SAgr-OAgr-T-V		1	1		1
SAgr-OAgr-V-T	1	3	7	1	11
T-OAgr-SAgr-V	1	1	1		2
OAgr-SAgr-T-V		2			2
OAgr-SAgr-V-T		1	6	1	8
T-V-SAgr-OAgr		1		1	2
V-T-SAgr-OAgr	1	4	6		9
V-SAgr-T-OAgr		1	1		2
V-SAgr-OAgr-T				1	1
T-V-OAgr-SAgr	1	2			3
V-T-OAgr-SAgr		2	6	1	9
V-OAgr-T-SAgr			5	1	6
V-OAgr-SAgr-T	1		2	1	4
V-OAgr-T/SAgr			1		1
T-SAgr-V-OAgr	2	2	1	1	4
SAgr/T-V-OAgr		2	2		2
SAgr-T-V-OAgr	2	2			3
SAgr-V-T-OAgr	3	3	2		6
OAgr-V-T-SAgr			7		7
OAgr-V-SAgr-T			4		4
OAgr-V-T/SAgr		1		1	2

[a] The notation S/OAgr means that subject and object agreement are combined in a portmanteau marker.
An empty cell means that there is no language of the relevant type in my material.

But notably, the order SAgr-T-OAgr-V, which would be expected if the clause structure is as proposed in Chomsky (1993) and the agreement markers spell out the argument-licensing heads, is not very frequent at all. Rather, when subject marker and object marker are prefixed, the tense marker is often suffixed (and the language is probably verb-final). Further, if a combined subject and object marker is prefixed to the verb, the tense marker is always a suffix. If, on the other hand, a combined subject and object marker is suffixed to the verb, the tense marker can be in any position. It also happens that subject agreement is fused with tense, but only if the resulting marker is word-initial or word-final.

If the subject agreement marker and the object agreement marker are both suffixed, the tense marker often intervenes between the verb stem and the agreement markers. Again, the preferred ordering is not in accordance with Chomsky (1993), on the interpretation mentioned above. The expected ordering V-OAgr-T-SAgr is found in only a few genera, and mostly, perhaps exclusively, in verb-final languages.[10]

The great variation in the positioning of agreement markers has been noted earlier, and it has provoked various reactions. Mitchell (1994) discusses a number of Finno-Ugric SVO languages which exhibit the morpheme order V+T+OAgr+SAgr, so that subject agreement is adjacent to object agreement, while the surface positions of the arguments themselves are not adjacent. She concludes that it cannot be the case that the agreement markers actually spell out the argument-licensing heads. She also points out that agreement is not a meaningful category: it does not contribute anything that was not already present in the derivation, it just repeats the features of the arguments. Thus, agreement is radically different from inflectional categories such as tense and aspect, and, accordingly, one should not necessarily expect agreement to have the same syntactic reality as these other categories. Hence, the distribution of agreement markers is not conclusive evidence that the idea that affix ordering is a consequence of syntax is fundamentally flawed. As far as I can see, this is a very reasonable way of thinking.

In van de Kerke (1996), on the other hand, the distribution of agreement markers is used as a basis for rejecting the syntactic approach to word formation, in particular the theory of Halle and Marantz (1993). One of van de Kerke's examples, which are all taken from southern varieties of Quechua, is shown below:

(49) *Cuzco Quechua*   (van de Kerke 1996:124)
    ñoqa-yku-ta qam maylla-wa-rqa-nki-ku
    1-1PL-ACC   you wash-1O-PAST-2S-PL
    'You washed us.'

Here the relative order of object agreement, tense, and subject agreement does in fact mirror the relative order of syntactic heads as proposed in Chomsky (1993). The exception is the plural marker, which comes last in the suffix sequence but nevertheless reflects the number of the object. Van de Kerke claims that this is impossible to account for in a theory where the complex word is built up in the syntax.

However, if agreement features are added to already existing syntactic heads, as I have suggested above, (49) is not necessarily devastating to the syntactic approach.[11] It is then conceivable that the agreement features associated with one particular argument need not all be added to the same head. One might propose that person features can be inserted separately from number features and that in

Cuzco Quechua all number features, regardless of which argument they refer to, are inserted in a head which is higher than the head that is endowed with the subject person features (see Dechaine 1999 and Manzini & Savoia 2002 for arguments that number agreement is structurally separate from person agreement).

In Noyer (1992), Halle and Marantz (1993), McGinnis (1995), and Halle (1997), similar cases of split agreement are analyzed as the result of fission, an operation whereby a morpheme—that is, a terminal node of syntax—is split up, so that a new node emerges which carries one or more of the features that were present in the original node. The ultimate position of the new node is taken to be determined by the lexical item that is eventually inserted in that node. For a case like (49), it means that the plural marker shows up in word-final position since it is specified as a suffix. It is a main thesis of the present work, however, that the position of an element in the surface order is never directly encoded in its lexical entry. For this reason, I think that the account I have given is the preferable one.

Contrary to van de Kerke's assumption, the relation between the plural morpheme and the person morpheme is local in a certain sense. Quechua apparently belongs to the class of strictly head-final languages discussed in chapter 3, which means that the verbal words are built up by successive movements of complements to Spec. Hence, the structure of (49) is as shown in (50), with AgrS, AgrO, and Num as convenient labels for the heads that host agreement features.

(50)

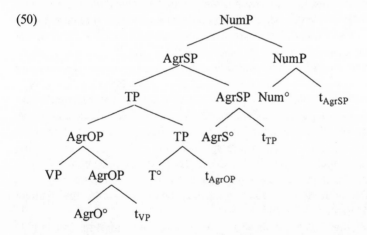

In this structure, the VP, which contains the arguments even in surface structure, is not dominated by the projections that intervene between it and the head that hosts the number feature. The same holds true of the head that hosts the object person feature. Thus, regardless of whether the plural marker reflects a feature of an argument directly or a feature that is also present in the lower agreement marker (where it is not in any case spelled out), the triggering feature sits in the Spec of the head where plural number is realized, and it is not dominated by intervening projections (if VP does not count). Hence, the number feature in the higher head is able to be matched against any plural feature that is present in its Spec, and so a plural subject or a plural object will trigger [+PL] marking of the Num° head.

Van de Kerke goes on to consider the following example from Cochabamba Quechua, which he takes to provide strong evidence against the syntactic approach:[12]

(51) *Cochabamba Quechua* (van de Kerke 1996:125)
      maylla-wa-rqa-yku
      wash-1O-PAST-1PL
      'He/they/you(sg)/you(pl) washed us.'

The problem here is how to account for the matching of the features of the first person plural object with the markers -*wa*- '1obj' and -*yku*- '1pl', and for the absence of any subject marker.

It is an obvious fact that a given morphosyntactic feature or feature combination is not necessarily always spelled out in the same way in one single language. In many cases, it appears that the realization of a particular morpheme depends not only on the content of that morpheme itself but also on the content of other morphemes that are present in the construction. Hence, any theory that aspires to explain the shape of words must have a place for allomorphy and even for conditioned allomorphy. As pointed out in Halle and Marantz (1993, 1994), a theory which assumes Late Insertion is well equipped to deal with allomorphy and other deviations from the strict one-to-one relation between a feature and its exponent. Late Insertion is also a part of my theory (see section 1.3)—I do not assume that the syntactic nodes are matched with lexical items from the very beginning of the derivation, but instead lexical items are inserted into syntactic nodes after the syntactic structure is built and also after certain modifications of that structure have had a chance to take place. This means that at the point where the terminal nodes are paired with appropriate lexical items, information on the feature content of all terminal nodes in the structure is available. For some nodes, the candidates for insertion are specified not only with respect to the features that they spell out but also with respect to the environment that they may appear in. The item that is actually inserted will then be the item which is most compatible with the feature content of the node and with the environment (see Halle & Marantz 1993, 1994).

We see now that it is not necessary to assume that the plural marker in (51) represents the feature combination [+1,+PL]. It is instead possible that -*yku*- is the realization of [+PL] in the environment [+1]. In (49) and (51) it spells out the number of a first person plural object, while in (52) it spells out the number of a first person plural subject.

(52) *Cochabamba Quechua* (see van de Kerke 1996:129)
maylla-yku
wash-(1)PL
'We wash 2s/2p/3s/3p.'

Further, overt subject agreement is absent in (51), and in (52), both subject person agreement and object agreement are missing, if the suffix spells out only number, as suggested. To explain this, we might propose that the [1 plural] subject marker is phonologically zero, and that if one argument is [1 plural], the other argument marker is always phonologically zero or, alternatively, that the features of the other argument marker are simply deleted in the presence of a [1 plural] argument. The latter operation is an example of *impoverishment*— the deletion of certain features in certain environments, as described by Halle and Marantz (1994), Halle (1997), and Noyer (1998). Thus, the morphology of the varieties of Quechua discussed by van de Kerke (1996) is no real stumbling block for the syntactic approach to complex words.

My last illustration of the variability of agreement markers is from the Australian genus Gunwinyguan. Two languages from this genus are shown in (53) and (54).

(53) *Ngandi* (Heath 1978)
ŋa-nu-wo-ni   ma-nič-uŋ   ni-ñara-ŋ-gič
1sS-3sO-give-PAST.CONT CLASS-food-ABS MASC.SG-father-1s-ALL
'I gave the food to my father.'

(54) *Rembarnga* (= ex. (89), ch. 4)
ŋinta-yi   ŋanapparu pa-ŋa-na
1s-ERG   buffalo   3pO-1sS-see.PAST.PUNC
'I saw some buffaloes.'

As we see, both Ngandi and Rembarnga have prefixed subject and object agreement markers that co-occur with argument DPs. In Ngandi, the subject marker precedes the object marker, but in Rembarnga, it is the other way around. Also note that the marker of a [1 singular] subject has the same form in both languages, which suggests that the two languages are closely related. Nevertheless, they have developed different orderings of agreement markers.

From what we have seen earlier in this chapter of the distribution of the markers that represent other verbal inflectional categories such as tense, mood, and aspect, it is clear that a similar development of the ordering of these markers is very unlikely—I would even claim that it is impossible. But as far as agreement markers are concerned, almost anything goes. Thus, either in Ngandi or in Rembarnga the agreement markers must have switched positions. This indicates that agreement markers are of a different nature than other verbal inflectional markers. The proposal adopted here that agreement markers do not in themselves represent syntactic heads, while markers of other categories do, seems to have considerable support both conceptually and empirically.

It is still possible that there are principles that put restrictions on the positioning of agreement markers. Precisely which those principles are is yet to be discovered, however.

5.4 Potential counterexamples

I now turn to some cases of verbal inflection that have been or can be taken as counterevidence to the syntactic approach to word formation. First, in 5.4.1, I discuss Wambaya, a language which has been claimed to have doubly marked tense, so that one single tense is represented by two markers simultaneously. Even in light of the proposals put forth in Cinque (1999) and Julien (2001) that every clause contains more than one temporal head, this should not be possible if every tense marker represents a temporal head. What I argue is that the Wambaya data do allow an alternative analysis which is perfectly in line with the assumption that in fact every marker spells out a syntactic head.

The topic of 5.4.2 is the position of the finite verb in English. As noted in 1.2, the word order in English was the original motivation for the checking approach to inflectional morphology. With the help of the checking theory one could explain how it was possible for the finite verb in English to carry tense morphology and still remain inside VP in the surface structure. But the idea that the verb stays in VP in English is not such a well-established truth as it is often assumed to be. Arguments that the English verb does move have been put forth by several authors. If these arguments are accepted, the question remains as to exactly how far the verb moves. For my theory to go through, the verb in English must move at least to the T°(past) head. As we will see, it is not entirely clear that this is the case. On the other hand, it is not convincingly refuted, either. To settle the question once and for all, more detailed investigations of clause structure and in particular of the positioning of adverbials would be necessary.

In 5.4.3 I look at some languages where the ordering of morphemes within the clause is seemingly not in accordance with the predictions that follow from the conception of complex words defended in this work. But as we shall see, when these languages are analyzed in more detail, it appears that they do not necessarily pose problems for my model after all.

5.4.1 Tense marking in Wambaya
Nordlinger (1995) argues that tense is doubly marked in Wambaya clauses and that the properties of this double tense marking are such that one cannot associate the category of tense with one single syntactic head. As mentioned in section 2.3.2, Wambaya clauses obligatorily contain a second position clitic, which encodes subject and object agreement together with tense, mood, aspect, and directionality. On Nordlinger's analysis, the main verb is also marked for tense,

so that in every tense-marked clause there will be two tense markers. An example of this is shown in (55).

(55) *Wambaya* (Nordlinger 1995:228)
    Ngaj-ba   ngu-ny-u.
    see-FUT   1sS-2O-FUT
    'I will see you.'

The tense marking of the clitic, or, in Nordlinger's terms, of the auxiliary, follows a rather intricate pattern. If the auxiliary is marked for both subject agreement and object agreement, as in (55), the tense distinction is [±FUTURE]. If the auxiliary shows subject agreement only, the tense distinction is either [PAST/PRESENT/FUTURE] (with a singular subject) or [±PAST] (with a non-singular subject).[13] The main verb, by contrast, has two alternating suffixes which are interpreted by Nordlinger as [+FUTURE] and [–FUTURE], respectively. Since there is no indication that (55) is biclausal, the double occurrence of future marking in this construction apparently presents a problem for my model of word formation.

I try to show here that another plausible analysis is available for the markers found on main verbs in Wambaya; namely, that these markers encode a modal value and not tense. This analysis allows us to maintain the idea that each morpheme is the realization of some syntactic head.

The first thing that should be noted about (55) is that the two 'future' markers do not have the same form. This could of course be due to the fact that the final suffix of the auxiliary is a fused marker of tense, aspect, mood, and directionality (Nordlinger 1995), whereas the marker on the verb is not fused with other categories. We might then assume that the Wambaya lexicon contains a set of pure tense markers, which are combined with the main verb, and a set of portmanteau markers containing tense and other features, which appear on the auxiliary.

It is also clear, however, that there are cases where the two alleged tense markers do not have the same temporal value. Some examples of this are given in (56).

(56) *Wambaya* (Nordlinger 1995:228)

  a. Bard-bi   irr-a.   b. Gulug-bi   ngi-Ø.
      run-NONFUT 3p-PAST   sleep-NONFUT 1s-PRES
      'They ran.'   'I am sleeping.'

  c. Bard-ba   irri-Ø.
      run-FUT   3p-NONPAST
      'They will run.'

As already noted, the auxiliary can be marked for future, non-future, present, past, or non-past. In the examples in (56) what we see seems to be the following: since the main verb can only be marked for future or non-future, in each case a marker is chosen that is compatible with the marking of the auxiliary. The most specified marker then determines the interpretation of the construction as a whole. In (56a) and (56b) it is the auxiliary that carries the more specified marker, and in (56c) it is the main verb.

The state of facts just described becomes more complicated when *mood* is taken into consideration. As already mentioned, in Wambaya the final morpheme of the auxiliary encodes both tense and mood. Thus, the auxiliary tense markers shown above must be taken to represent the unmarked or indicative mood. They can be replaced by markers which encode other mood categories such as irrealis and hypothetical:

(57) *Wambaya* (Nordlinger 1995:229)
    a. Guyala   gunu-ny-udi   ngaj-bi.
       NEG   3MASC.SGS-2O-IRR.PRES   see-NONFUT
       'He isn't looking at you.'

    b. Nawu-Ø   ngiyi-ny-agba   narunguji-ni.
       step.on-NONFUT   3FEM.SG.S-2O-HYP car-ERG
       'A car might run you over.'

There is no marker that is specialized to represent the imperative mood, however. Instead, imperative interpretation arises when a 'future' marker on the main verb is combined with a non-future or non-past marker on the auxiliary. This is shown in (58).

(58) *Wambaya* (Nordlinger 1995:229)
    a. Jiyaj-ba   girri-ng-a   manganyma!
       give-FUT 2pS-1O-NONFUT   food
       'Give me some food!'

    b. Jiyaj-ba   girri-Ø   manganyma!
       give-FUT 2pS-NONPAST food
       'Give him/her some food!'
    or 'You will give him/her some food.'

Nordlinger's analysis of these data, formulated within a LFG-based framework, is based on the idea that the interpretation of tense and imperative results from unification of the two relevant markers. She further assumes that the suffix -*ba* is specified in the lexicon as representing [FUTURE] *or* [IMPERATIVE]. When -*ba* co-occurs with the non-future marker on the auxiliary, as in (58a), the imperative reading is forced because otherwise the features of the two markers would not be compatible and unification could not take place. In (58b) either the future or the imperative reading of -*ba* is possible, and the construction is ambiguous.

Nordlinger presents another construction, however, which reveals that the adequacy of her analysis is questionable:

(59) *Wambaya* (Nordlinger 1995:228)
      Ngaj-bi   ngu-ny-u.
      see-NONFUT 1sS-2O-FUT
      'I will see you'

Nordlinger does not discuss (59) in terms of unification, and indeed it is hard to see how this example could be accounted for in her framework. Here the 'non-future' marker *-bi* on the main verb is combined with the future marker on the auxiliary. One would expect these two markers to be incompatible, but according to Nordlinger, (59) is semantically equivalent to (55), which differs from (59) only with respect to the marking of the main verb. Thus, it appears that instead of being the outcome of unification of the two markers, the tense reading one gets stems from the auxiliary alone: regardless of whether the main verb has 'future' or 'non-future' marking, the clause is interpreted as future, in accordance with the marking on the auxiliary.

I propose that the markers *-ba* and *-bi* which appear on the main verb in Wambaya do not signal tense at all. Rather, these markers express a category which I will refer to as *anticipative mood*, with *-ba* as the realization of [+ANTICIPATIVE] and *-bi* as the realization of [−ANTICIPATIVE].[14] On this analysis, there is no need to postulate that *-ba* is ambiguous between a future and an imperative reading, and it also follows that the two markers in (59) are not in conflict. Further, the occurrence of the non-anticipative *-bi* with the irrealis and hypothetical, as in (57a) and (57b), is as expected.

The combinations of the different tenses with the [±ANTICIPATIVE] markers on the verb are shown in table 5.4, which is identical to the table given in Nordlinger (1995) except that 'anticipative' and 'non-anticipative' are substituted for 'future' and 'non-future'. I will argue that the interpretations listed in the last column follow from the assumption that the marker found on the auxiliary is the real tense marker, whereas the marker on the verb encodes [±ANTICIPATIVE].

As one might expect, the past and present tenses can only be combined with non-anticipative (lines 1–2 and 7–8), whereas the future tense can be combined with either anticipative or non-anticipative (lines 3–4). As already noted, the meaning difference between the two combinations is not very significant to speakers of Wambaya; this is understandable since an utterance in the future tense is a predication about the future whether or not the anticipative element is added. Non-future combined with non-anticipative gives a non-future reading (line 5), and non-past combined with a non-anticipative is interpreted as non-past (line 9). All this is rather trivial.

TABLE 5.4
Combinations of tense and mood markers in Wambaya (see Nordlinger 1995).

Marking of auxiliary	Marking of verb	Resulting reading
Present	Non-anticipative	Present
Present	Anticipative	*not acceptable*
Future	Non-anticipative	Future
Future	Anticipative	Future
Non-future	Non-anticipative	Present/Past
Non-future	Anticipative	Imperative
Past	Non-anticipative	Past
Past	Anticipative	*not acceptable*
Non-past	Non-anticipative	Present/Future
Non-past	Anticipative	Future/Imperative

Then in line 6 something more interesting happens. Here non-future is combined with anticipative. Because of the non-future tense, a clause with this combination cannot be interpreted as a predication about the future. Because of the anticipative, it cannot be interpreted as being about the actual state of facts either; it refers to something which is yet to happen. But if a clause refers to something which is yet to happen without being a predication about the future, it is not very surprising that the interpretation one gets is equivalent to an imperative. This interpretation is of course facilitated by the second person subject marking (see (58a)). In line 10, where the anticipative is combined with the non-past marker, ambiguity arises because the non-past can be interpreted either as present or future. In the latter case what we get is again a future reading, whereas in the former case the present tense in combination with the anticipative will force an imperative reading.

Not only the semantics of the different combinations of verbal markers but also the ordering of verbal morphemes follows from the analysis I have just sketched. Consider the clause in (60), which displays what I take to be the basic order of verbal elements in Wambaya.

(60) *Wambaya* (= ex. (34), ch. 2)
     Alanga g-a   yarru-Ø.
     girl   3sS-PAST go-NONANTICIPATIVE
     'The girl went.'

Here the main verb carries the [–ANTICIPATIVE] marking. Both the position and the morphology of the main verb is compatible with the assumption that the anticipative mood is encoded in a head that is located below the temporal heads and that the verb has moved to this head. The auxiliary, which precedes the main verb, is made up of the subject agreement marker and the tense marker, plus the neutral value of directionality (this category has the values 'motion towards speaker', 'motion away from speaker', and 'neutral'; see Green 1995). Since tense and subject agreement originate above anticipative mood, it follows that tense and subject agreement must precede the verb if the verb has only moved to the anticipative mood head.

As for the question of why the auxiliary in Wambaya is not included in a word with the verb root, there are at least a couple of answers to this which both corroborate my claim that the formation of complex words is the consequence of distributional and to a certain degree of phonological factors. As we saw in section 2.3.2, the distribution of verb and auxiliary in Wambaya is such that seeing these two elements as one single word is not possible. The verb may follow the auxiliary, as in (60), or precede it, as below—where the latter alternative probably results from a Long Head Movement operation:

(61) *Wambaya* (= ex. (33), ch. 2)
      Ngaj-ba   ngu-ny-u.
      see-FUT   1sS-2O-ANTICIPATIVE
      'I will see you.'

Since the two morpheme strings referred to as the auxiliary and the verb, respectively, have freedom of position relative to each other, they are necessarily seen as two separate words.

Moreover, phonological word formation in Wambaya does not facilitate the analysis of the auxiliary as a part of the verbal word. Green (1995:416) states that if the auxiliary in Wambaya is monosyllabic, it behaves as a suffix, and if it is polysyllabic, it behaves phonologically as a separate word. This must mean that a monosyllabic auxiliary is included in a phonological word with the lexical word that precedes it. In (60), this has the consequence that the auxiliary is included in a phonological word with the subject, not with the verb. On the other hand, in (61), where the element preceding the auxiliary is the verb itself, the auxiliary is a separate phonological word. Hence, neither in (60) nor in (61) is the auxiliary included in a phonological word with the verb. Of the examples shown here, the verb and the auxiliary belong to the same phonological word only in (56b). Thus, having the verb and the auxiliary in one phonological word is a sporadic phenomenon in Wambaya, and seeing the two elements as one word gets no support from phonology, either.

The main purpose of the preceding discussion of Wambaya was to show that Nordlinger's (1995) claim that Wambaya clauses feature two tense markers is not necessarily correct. It is possible that the markers appearing on the main verb represent mood instead of tense. If this is correct, the idea that tense markers represent syntactic heads can still be maintained.

5.4.2   The position of the finite verb in English
The discussion in the preceding chapters developed the idea that suffixation is directly related to syntactic movement operations, so that a lexical base cannot carry suffixes in the absence of movement. Accordingly, a language without

head movement of the verb or XP-movement which affects the verb will typically have verbal grammatical markers preceding the verb, whereas a language where the verb or the VP moves has verbal suffixes. One would also expect there to be a close correlation between the surface position of a word and the suffixes, if any, that the word contains: if a given element can be a suffix on the lexical base it belongs with only if the lexical base has moved to that element, or alternatively to the Spec of that element, then in the surface order, the lexical base must be at least as high up as the head that the suffix represents.

However, as mentioned in section 1.2 there exist constructions where, on a standard analysis, the verb stays inside VP even if it carries suffixes. The most famous case is English, where the inflected verb obligatorily follows sentence medial adverbs like *never* and *often*:

(62) *English*
    a.   Marie never/often smokes/smoked cigars.
    b. * Marie smokes/smoked often/never cigars.

The adverbs in (62) are traditionally taken to be adjoined to VP, which means that they indicate the left edge of VP; consequently, the required order of adverb and verb in this construction is seen as evidence that the verb is still inside VP. If this is correct, and if lowering operations are ruled out—a view I will accept without further discussion—it cannot be the case that the inflectional markers that appear on the verb in English are generated under a functional head above VP. Instead, the most plausible analysis available is the one presented in Chomsky (1993, 1995), according to which word formation is completed before lexical insertion takes place, and subsequent head movement only serves to ensure that the inserted word has the right combination of features. On this analysis, a tensed verb will always move to $T°$ at some stage of the derivation to have its tense feature checked, but if the relevant feature is weak, there is no need for this movement to take place in the overt syntax. Hence, Chomsky's model is compatible with the view that the surface position of the English verb is inside VP.

The question of whether English has overt verb movement is closely connected to the question of adverbial positions. Therefore I now go through Chomsky's (1995) treatment of adverbial positions and point to some weaknesses of his argumentation. I then suggest an alternative analysis of adverbial placement, based on Cinque (1999), which opens up the possibility that finite verbs in English move out of VP and become inflected by adjoining to inflectional heads.

Chomsky (1995:329–334) starts the discussion of adverbial placement by considering the paradigm shown in (63). On the traditional view that the adverb *often* is adjoined to VP, the verb in (63a) must be inside VP, while in (63b) it has moved out of VP, leaving its complement behind. The reason this operation is not an option in (63c) would then be assumed to have something to do with the need for the DP argument to get case. Either the verb has to stay adjacent to the DP object in order to assign case to it, as proposed by Pesetsky (1989), or else the DP object must also move, as in the proposals of Johnson (1991), Koizumi (1993), and Costa (1996).

(63) *English*
    a.   John often reads to his children.
    b.   John reads often to his children.
    c.   John often reads books.
    d. * John reads often books.

Chomsky has several objections to proposals of this kind. First, he assumes that adverbials cannot be adjoined by Merge to phrases that are θ-related—that is, predicates and arguments—which rules out adjunction of adverbials to VP. Next, he points out that if the adverb *often* is replaced by an adverbial phrase, the order corresponding to the alleged source construction does not exist, as demonstrated in (64a).

(64) *English*
    a. * John every day reads to his children.
    b.   John reads every day to his children.
    c. * John every day reads books.
    d. * John reads every day books.

Still, with the verb preceding the adverbial the construction becomes grammatical, except when there is a DP argument following the adverbial. Thus, we find the same contrast between (64b) and (64d) as between (63b) and (63d). But clearly, the analyses just suggested of (63) cannot be extended to (64). So something must have gone wrong.

Chomsky's proposal is that the underlying structure of (63b) and (64b) is as shown in (65), with the adverbial sitting in the Spec of the lower VP in a VP-shell structure.

(65)

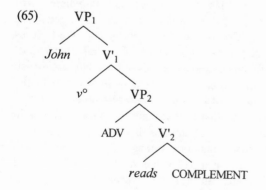

The verb, which is base-generated in the lower $V°$ position, moves to the higher verbal head $v°$ so that it ends up to the left of the adverbial but does not leave VP. This gives the surface order verb-adverb-complement.[15]

But notably, the structure shown above is postulated to be ruled out if the complement is a case-marked DP, because if both the subject and the adverbial intervene between the complement and its checking position in Spec-AgrOP, the complement cannot raise to Spec-AgrOP at LF. Not even verb movement to v and then to AgrO can create the equidistance effects that would be necessary for this movement to take place; the adverbial will always be closer to Spec-AgrOP and be attracted instead of the complement. If the complement is a PP, on the other hand, the structure in (65) does not lead to any problems since the PP needs not and will not move anywhere. This will suffice to explain the contrast between (63b) and (63d), and also between (64b) and (64d). As for the alternative order shown in (63a) and (63c), Chomsky (1995) suggests that in these constructions the adverb is situated in some position above VP, so that the structure in (65) is not relevant at all.

To some extent, Chomsky's analysis can explain the obligatory adjacency between verbs and DP objects in English, which has so often been observed, but it also leaves a number of problems unaccounted for. First, there is the assumption that adverbials can block the movement of an object. Concerning this, Chomsky himself (1995:390 n.104) notes that "the adverb will be relevant only if it has features that the [Agr,V] complex can attract, which is plausible though not obvious." Since a simple adverb like *often* has the same effect as the DP *every day* in this respect, it is far from clear what the relevant features might be. One possibility is that simple adverbs have V-features which can be attracted by AgrO°, whereas a DP adverbial like *every day* has D- or N-features. Even if the offending features of adverbials could be accounted for along these lines, a serious problem remains. If adverbials have features that will be attracted by AgrO° when the adverbial is in an appropriate position, it must be that these features are checked by AgrO°. But if an adverbial has features that can be checked, we would expect that these features *must* be checked. One might then ask what happens when the adverbial is inserted in a position from where it will not be attracted by an Agr complex—for example, if the adverb is generated higher than VP, as in *John often reads books*, so that AgrS° checks the features of the subject and AgrO° checks the features of the object. We would then expect the derivation to crash because of the unchecked features of the adverbial, which it does not. In short, the suggestion that adverbials may interfere with the movement of the object to AgrO° does not seem to be very plausible.

Next, Chomsky's (1995) suggestion that in (63a) and (63c) the adverb is in some higher position, presumably above VP, implies that an adverb like *often* may in principle appear in one of two positions, either inside or outside VP, whereas a DP adverbial like *every day* must be located inside VP. This contrast requires an explanation. Further, whereas in (65), the adverbial sits in the lower Spec-VP and the argument is in complement position, it must be the argument that occupies the Spec of the lower VP in (66). The adverbial must be the complement of VP or be supported by a head even deeper down in the VP-shell structure (see Chomsky 1995:332–333).

(66) John reads to his children every day.

Either of these assumptions leads to certain problems, however, in addition to the somewhat dubious conjecture that arguments and adverbials have no fixed base positions. If the adverbial in (66) is in the most deeply embedded position, we would expect that if more than one adverbial follows the arguments of V, the first of these adverbials should be higher than and take scope over the second. But as noted already by Andrews (1983), it is the second adverbial which takes scope over the first:

(67) *English*
    a. John knocked on the door intentionally twice.
    b. John knocked on the door twice intentionally.

As Andrews points out, the sentence in (67a) involves two instances of intentional knocking, whereas the sentence in (67b) involves one intentional instance of knocking twice. These scope facts do not seem to be compatible with the approach to adverbials suggested in Chomsky (1995).

Another problem has to do with adverbs like *well*, which, as demonstrated in (68)–(69), obligatory follow DP objects but preferably precede PPs.[16]

(68) *English*
    a. * The boys well read the book.
    b. * The boys read well the book.
    c.   The boys read the book well.

(69) *English*
    a. * Mary well told Bill the story.
    b. * Mary told well Bill the story.
    c. * Mary told Bill well the story.
    d.   Mary told Bill the story well.

(70) *English*
    a. * Mary well told the story to Bill.
    b. * Mary told well the story to Bill.
    c.   Mary told the story well to Bill.
    d. ? Mary told the story to Bill well.

In Chomsky's model the fact that *well* must follow all DP objects must mean that both direct and indirect objects move to a checking position at LF. If *well* intervenes between the checking positions and any of the DP arguments, *well* will be attracted to a checking position and block checking of the argument.

The fact that *well* is preferred to precede the goal argument if the goal argument is realized as a PP is harder to understand in this model. Notably, PP-Adv is the neutral order in (71), which is similar to (70) except that *often* has replaced *well* ((71a) requires that *often* is stressed—Peter Svenonius, personal communication).

(71) *English*
    a. Mary told the story OFTEN to Bill.
    b. Mary told the story to Bill often.

    One way to capture the behavior of *well* is by saying that *well* is, for some reason, disfavored in complement position. Nevertheless, in Chomsky's model *well* must be in complement position in (69d), which is perfectly fine. Apparently, the only solution left is to simply state the fact: *well* should precede PP arguments. Obviously, this is highly stipulative and has no explanatory force.

    An alternative to Chomsky's approach is to assume, with Pesetsky (1989), Ouhalla (1990), Johnson (1991), Koizumi (1993), and Costa (1996), that the verb moves out of VP in English. It can then be argued that the reason DP objects are strictly adjacent to the verb is that DP objects raise overtly to the Spec position immediately below the verb (see Johnson 1991, Koizumi 1993, Costa 1996). One could then also claim that manner adverbs like *well* are situated below the position that the object moves to.

    Obviously, we also need a theory of adverbial placement in order to explain the paradigms in (63)–(64). The most promising theory so far of adverbial placement seems to be that of Cinque (1999), according to which adverbials are base-generated in the Spec of clausal functional heads, such that for each class of adverbials there is a functional head which provides the unique position where adverbials of that particular class will be inserted.

    Concerning adverbials like those in (63) and (64), Cinque (1999:26) notes that the fact that adverbials expressing frequency are seen in various positions within clauses does not necessarily mean that the positioning of frequentative adverbials is free. Rather, it appears that there are two positions for adverbials of this type and that each position is associated with one particular reading: the higher position quantifies over the entire event, whereas the lower position indicates how many repetitions are involved in a single event. As we now would expect, the two positions can be filled simultaneously (Cinque 1999:27):

(72) John twice/often knocked three times/often on the door.

    Of course it is also possible to add another frequentative adverbial to constructions like those in (63) and (64). We then get the paradigm in (73), which shows that both the higher and the lower adverb positions are available with PP arguments, as well as with DP arguments. There is a contrast, though, between PPs and DPs in that PPs may precede or follow the lower adverbial, whereas DPs invariably precede it and are adjacent to the verb. If all frequentative adverbials are generated in the Spec of a functional head, this means that both the verb and the DP object invariably move out of VP in English. We see from (63d) that landing sites for the verb and the DP object are found between the higher and the lower positions for frequentative adverbs.

(73) *English*
    a.   Fathers often read every day to their children.
    b.   Fathers often read to their children every day.
    c. * Fathers often read every day books.
    d.   Fathers often read books every day.

In this light, (63d) is ungrammatical because when the verb precedes *often*, *often* is in the lower position, in which case it must be preceded by the DP object as well: *John reads books often*. The same reasoning applies to (64d). The alternation in (63ab) simply means that *often* is in the higher position in (63a) but in the lower position in (63b). In (63c) *often* is again in the higher position, and in (64b) it is in the lower position. As for the ungrammaticality of (64ac), it appears that adverbial phrases like *every day* are disfavored in the higher position for frequentative adverbs, where they would quantify over the event as a whole. Since the repetitive, lower position reading of *every day* is preferred, and since there is nothing in (64a,c) to prevent this reading, it follows that *every day* in (64a,c) is taken to be in the lower position, and accordingly, the word order is wrong: the adverbial must follow the verb and, in (64c), the DP object.[17]

If another frequentative adverb is added, however, so that the higher reading of *every day* is forced, we get some improvement , as indicated in (74a) (Peter Svenonius, personal communication). Still, it is even better to move *every day* to a topic position at the left periphery, from where it can take scope over the entire clause, as in (74b).[18]

(74) *English*
    a. ?? John every day speaks often to his children.
    b.   Every day, John speaks often to his children.

Thus, the paradigms in (63)–(64) can be accounted for by the analysis which involves overt movement of the verb and of DP objects out of VP. Confronted with more complex data, it appears that the overt movement analysis is in fact superior to the one suggested in Chomsky (1995). The overt movement analysis yields an explanation of various patterns of adverbial placement, not only of the fact that adverbials may not intervene between a verb and a DP object. It also has a conceptual advantage in that it allows us to assume that arguments and adverbials are base-generated in fixed positions.[19]

If we now try to establish the exact position of the finite verb in English relative to the hierarchy of functional heads postulated by Cinque (1999), the idea that the tense marker is the realization of the $T°$(past) head appears to face serious problems. In (75), the hierarchy as given by Cinque is shown. For each head, one of the associated adverbs is also given.

(75) *Functional heads and adverbials in the IP domain   (Cinque 1999:106)*
       (Mod = modality, A = aspect, T = tense)

[*frankly* Mood$_{speech\ act}$ [*fortunately* Mood$_{evaluative}$ [*allegedly* Mood$_{evidential}$

[*probably* Mod$_{epistemic}$ [*once* T$_{past}$ [*then* T$_{future}$ [*perhaps* Mood$_{irrealis}$

[*necessarily* Mod$_{necessity}$ [*possibly* Mod$_{possibility}$ [*usually* A$_{habitual}$

[*again* A$_{repetitive1}$ [*often* A$_{frequentative1}$ [*intentionally* Mod$_{volitional}$

[*quickly* A$_{celerative1}$ [*already* T$_{anterior}$ [*no longer* A$_{terminative}$ [*still* A$_{continuative}$

[*always* A$_{perfect(?)}$ [*just* A$_{retrospective}$ [*soon* A$_{proximative}$ [*briefly* A$_{durative}$

[*characteristically* A$_{generic/progressive}$ [*almost* A$_{prospective}$ [*completely* A$_{SgCompletive1}$

[*tutto* A$_{PlCompletive}$ [*well* Voice [*fast/early* A$_{celerative2}$ [*again* A$_{repetitive2}$

[*often* A$_{frequentative2}$ [*completely* A$_{SgCompletive2}$

Even though there might be reasons to suggest certain modifications of this hierarchy of heads (see, e.g., Julien 2001), I see no reason to doubt that the restrictions of adverbial ordering observed by Cinque in general hold. Thus, it seems clear that *almost*, for example, is situated relatively low in IP. As the following example serves to demonstrate, the finite verb must follow *almost* and, by extension, all higher adverbs.

(76) *English*
       a.   Mary probably/willingly/almost killed John.
       b. * Mary killed probably/willingly/almost John.
       c. * Mary killed John probably/willingly/almost.

It can also be shown that the finite verb follows the higher occurrence of *completely*. As noted by Cinque (1999:178 n.57), the two occurrences of *completely* have different semantics. Compare (77a) to (77b).

(77) *English*
       a. John completely forgot her instructions.
       b. John forgot her instructions completely.

In (77a), the instructions did not occur to John at the appropriate moment. Example (77b) is ambiguous; it can have the reading that is also conveyed by (77a), or it can mean that every part of each of her instructions was lost to him. Again, we have a contrast reminiscent of the one shown with frequentials, of modification over the whole event versus modification inside the event. Cinque suggests that modification over the event should be associated with the higher position of *completely* and modification inside the event with the lower position of *completely*. In (77a), *completely* must be in the higher position, so that only the first reading is available. In (77b), *completely* is either in the lower position or in the higher position. If it is in the higher position, the phrase [forgot her instructions] has raised over it. Because of these two possibilities the sentence is ambiguous.

The fact that the verb follows *completely* in (77a) can be taken as an indication that the verb cannot move above $A°_{SgCompletive1}$. On the other hand, we have already seen that the verb must precede *well* and the lower occurrences of frequentative adverbials.[20] This indicates that the finite verb in English is situated between $A°_{SgCompletive1}$ and Voice°.

Even if we can now conclude that the verb moves out of VP in English, the idea that tense morphemes are generated in temporal heads seems to be in serious trouble. If the verb moves only to the completive aspect head, while the temporal heads are situated much higher up, then it cannot possibly be the case that the verb combines with the tense suffix by moving into the head that hosts that suffix.

There is no clear evidence, however, of the position of the temporal head(s) in English. In particular, there appears not to exist any adverbials that unambiguously are located in the Spec of the temporal heads. Cinque (1999:87) observes that in Italian, the only temporal adverbs that can appear sentence medially—that is, in the area where tense heads are supposedly located—are purely deictic adverbs like *ora* 'now' and *allora* 'then'. But notably, in English the adverbs *now* and *then* have a distribution which is not expected if Cinque's proposal is correct. Consider (78) and (79).

(78) *English*
    a.   Now Mary smokes cigars.
    b.   Mary now smokes cigars.
    c. * Mary smokes now cigars.
    d.   Mary smokes cigars now.

(79) *English*
    a.   Then Mary smoked cigars.
    b.   Mary then smoked cigars.
    c. * Mary smoked then cigars.
    d.   Mary smoked cigars then.

The temporal adverbials *now* and *then* may appear clause-initially, after the subject, or clause-finally, in each case without any marked intonation. This fact is not directly compatible with the assumption that *now* and *then* are situated in the Spec of temporal heads. The data we have just seen point more in the direction of Nilsen (2000), who proposes that *now* and *then* are proforms for full PP adverbials, which, as we know, typically appear at the periphery of the clause. The distribution of temporal PP adverbials, illustrated in (80), provides some support for Nilsen's claim. As we see, PP adverbials are clause-initial or clause-final, sharing both these positions with *now* and *then*. But in addition, *now* and *then* may appear between the subject and the verb, a position where PP adverbials can appear only with difficulty. This does not necessarily mean that we are dealing with two essentially different classes of adverbials, however. It is a well-known fact that the distribution of pronouns is often different from that of full DPs. It is possible that the contrast between *now* and *then* on one hand and full PPs on the other hand is comparable to the contrast between pronouns and full DPs.

(80) *English*
    a.   In the seventies Mary smoked cigars.
    b.?* Mary in the seventies smoked cigars.
    c. * Mary smoked in the seventies cigars.
    d.   Mary smoked cigars in the seventies.

Thus, the only evidence we have for the position of temporal heads in English is the position of the finite verb itself. More precisely, the position of the verb shows the position of the tense marker if it really is the case that the tense marking on the verb is the realization of a temporal head. But this takes us back to the question that started the preceding discussion: Does the verb in English move to $T°$(past), or does it not? So we have apparently reached an impasse. If the question is going to be answered at all, it will have to be by means of indirect evidence.

One such piece of evidence is the fact that the position of the finite verb in English has parallels in other languages. In Norwegian, in clauses that are embedded under non-bridge verbs so that the V2-effect is absent (see Vikner 1994), we can also find the verb between the adverbs *helt* 'completely' and *godt* 'well', as in (81a) (this is noted by Cinque 1999:215 n.7). In this example, *helt* must represent the higher completive, since the example (81b) shows that the verb precedes the *lower* completive. Hence, it appears that the verb in Norwegian embedded clauses moves to a position immediately below the higher completive adverb.[21]

(81) *Norwegian*

a. Hun	beklaget	at	hun	ikke	alltid	helt		sov	godt.
she	regretted	that	she	not	always	completely		slept	well

b. Hun	beklaget	at	hun	ikke	lukket	dør-a		helt.
she	regretted	that	she	not	closed	door-DEF.SG		completely

In Italian the verb must move minimally to a position between *completamente* and *bene* (Cinque 1999:214–215 n.7). That is, even if the finite verb in Italian often appears higher in the clause than its English counterpart, the position that it is required to move to is the same as the position it occupies in English and in Norwegian embedded clauses. That is, in all three languages the basic position of the finite verb is the same. At the same time, the finite verb is marked for only one of the inflectional categories that, in the present model, necessarily represent sentential heads. This category is tense. In Italian, the verb is also marked for subject agreement, but as argued in the preceding section, agreement markers do not represent separate sentential heads. Thus, the appearance of an agreement suffix on the verb cannot be taken as an indication of the position of the verb. One might guess, though, that the fact that the finite verb in all three languages moves to the same position outside VP is closely connected to the fact that the verb is marked for tense. It is possible, although it will have to investigated in more detail, that the finite verb in English, Italian, and Norwegian does indeed acquire the tense suffix by moving to a temporal head.

5.4.3 Other problems

There are also languages that pose problems of another type for the theory of word formation that I have been arguing for throughout this work, in that the orderings of verbal inflectional markers that these languages have been claimed to display are not derivable in my model. However, if we look more closely at these apparent counterexamples, it turns out that the inflectional markers that show up in positions where they should not be according to my theory have probably been misanalyzed and that they allow an alternative analysis according to which their surface position is not a problem for the syntactic approach after all. Some of these cases were discussed in 2.3.2. For example, I argued there that in Baka, which is claimed by Kilian-Hatz (1995) to have the order SAVTO, the alleged tense marker does not represent a temporal head, and, consequently, the positioning of this marker is not really a problem for my theory. In the following, I deal with some other apparent counterexamples.

We start with the New Guinean language Hua. Hua has a verbal prefix *u'-* which according to Haiman (1980) is a perfective marker. A verb form with this prefix is shown in (82).

(82) *Hua* (Haiman 1980:200)
   u'-'a'-d-mi-e
   PERF-NEG-1sO-give-IND.3s [22]
   'He did not already give it to me.'

We see here that the negation and the object marker are also prefixed to the verb. All other verbal markers in Hua are suffixed. As for tense, the aorist or non-future is unmarked, while future tense is expressed by the suffix *-gu*, as exemplified in (83).

(83) *Hua* (Haiman 1980:236)
   Kamani'-Ki'   pasi   kzo-gu-e.
   Kamani-COM   letter   write-FUT-IND.1s
   'I'll have Kamani write a letter.'

Although Haiman gives no example of the perfective prefix in combination with the future suffix, his statement that "the perfective prefix may occur before any verb in any tense, aspect, or mood" (Haiman 1980:196) must be taken to mean that the morpheme order PERF+V+FUT is possible in Hua. Since Hua is a verb-final language, so that the verbal suffixes are in fact clause-final, one might think of proposing that this morpheme order could be derived by moving AspP to Spec-TP. However, it appears that proposals along this line are unnecessary after all. For one thing, Hua has another perfective marker as well, which is suffixed to the verb, as shown in (84).

(84) *Hua* (Haiman 1980:151)
     ri   fi'a-ro'   bro-ro-'da   igari'   fera   na   Ko-e
     firewood rack-LOC   put-PERF-1s.SS   spider   big   thing   see-IND.1s
     'I put some firewood on the rack and saw a big spider.'

From (85) we see that the suffixed perfective marker may be followed by the future marker, which is well in accordance with the model I am proposing.

(85) *Hua* (Haiman 1980:155)
     Kosa-K   hau-ro-Ki-e-Ke
     fall-2sO   happen-PERF-FUT-IND.2s-so
     'You'll fall, so—(be careful!).'

I therefore assume that the suffixed perfective marker represents the aspectual head where perfective/imperfective is encoded. Then it cannot be the case that the prefixed perfective marker also represents this head. This is further demonstrated in (86), where both 'perfective' markers appear on one single verb.

(86) *Hua* (Haiman 1980:272)
     u'-bre-ra-ma'   Ke-mo   ne-ma'   borava   ito   ru'a
     already-put-PERF-REL.3s   talk-ARG   be-REL.3s   but   but   again
     bro-ne
     put-IND.1p
     'It was a speech that had already been put (in the tape recorder) but we put it again.'

Interestingly, in this case Haiman glosses the prefixed marker as 'already' and not as 'perfective'. This suggests that the 'perfective' prefix *u'-* is really the Hua counterpart of the English adverb *already*.

The adverbial nature of *u'-* is seen more clearly in (87), where *u'-* combines with the word for 'yesterday'. Although tense markers sometimes combine with nouns, thereby giving meanings as 'the former N' or 'the N to be', it seems that the combination in (87) is of a different kind. As Haiman's translation indicates, this is not a perfective form of 'yesterday'; it is simply a combination of adverbial meanings.

(87) *Hua* (Haiman 1980:196)
    u'-ega
    already-yesterday
    'already yesterday'

Thus, we can conclude that the positioning of the prefix *u'-* in Hua is not a problem after all since this prefix is an adverb. In Julien (2001) it is suggested that 'already' is a modifier of temporal heads. Hence, it is probably generated in a specifier position above the temporal heads. Its position relative to the aspect markers in Hua is therefore not counterevidence to my claims about the order of inflectional markers.

Similar cases are found in a number of other languages. For example, Andamanese is claimed by Manoharan (1989:100) to have a perfect marker which is "prefixed to a sentence of past tense." At the same time, the tense marker is suffixed, as demonstrated in (88a).

(88) *Andamanese* (Manoharan 1989:100–101)
    a. ḍexo   mu-utthu:w-bo   b.   ḍexo   ṭu-ijo-ke
         PERF   1pEXCL-come.out-PAST   PERF   1s-eat-PRES
         'We have come out.'   'I have eaten.'

Note, by the way, that the perfect marker can obviously also combine with the present tense, as in (88b). In any case, one could again propose that there has been movement of AspP to Spec-TP. However, I suspect that *ḍexo* is an adverb with a meaning that can be understood as perfect. It appears in the designated position for adverbs, which is in front of the subject (Manoharan 1989:106). An example of adverb positioning in Andamanese is shown in (89).[23]

(89) *Andamanese* (Manoharan 1989:105)
    itta:xe ṭa-jiyo-bom
    now   1s-eat-NONPAST.CONT
    'I am eating now.'

In this construction, the adverb *itta:xe* 'now' co-occurs with the non-past continuous tense. In (88b), by contrast, we have *ḍexo* in combination with the simple present, which apparently is perfective, since it contrasts with the non-past continuous (Manoharan 1989). It is conceivable that relation between the tense/aspect suffix and *ḍexo* in (88) is parallel to the relation between the adverb and the tense/aspect suffix in (89), so that in both cases, there is a preverbal adverb which adds some nuance to the meaning of the tense/aspect suffix.

We will now turn to North Puebla Nahuatl, a language which, according to Brockway (1979), has a prefixed perfective marker and a suffixed past marker, as shown in (90).

(90) *North Puebla Nahuatl*   (Brockway 1979:167)
     o-ki-paka-k   ika   toton-ki   a-tl
     PERF-3sO-wash-PAST   INSTR heat-ADJ water-ABS
     'He washed it with hot water.'

Since the unmarked word order in this variety of Nahuatl is SVO, the morpheme order PERF-V-PAST cannot be derived by moving AspP across TP; such movement would also place the object in front of the tense marker. So it seems that we have now encountered a real problem.

However, Brockway (1979) also gives examples of the perfective prefix co-occurring with an imperfective suffix, as in (91a,b).

(91) *North Puebla Nahuatl*   (Brockway 1979:179)
    a. o-tla-k^{w}a-yaya   b. o-ki-tek-ta-ya
       PERF-UNSP.O-eat-IMPF   PERF-3sO-cut-PUNC-IMPF
       'He was eating.'   'He had been picking.'

This fact, together with the readings that result from the morpheme combinations shown above, suggests that the prefix *o-* is not the realization of an aspectual head. We see that in (91a), we get continuous aspect even in the presence of the alleged perfective marker. In (91b), the action is completed, which is compatible with the perfective but which might also be a consequence of the punctual marking. Brockway (1979) does not discuss the prefix *o-* in any detail, so it is hard to say what its semantic content might be, but at any rate, I think it can be concluded that it is not really a perfective aspect marker.

In Tepetotutla Chinantec, a prefix interpreted as a perfective marker by Westley (1991) precedes the past tense prefix, as illustrated in (92) (note that I follow Westley and mark the tone of each syllable with an H for high, an M for middle, or an L for low tone).

(92) *Tepetotutla Chinantec*   (Westley 1991)
     ca^L-ma^M-ka^M-gë́?^{L}
     NEG-PERF-PAST-eat.COMPL.3
     'She/he has not yet eaten.'

The morpheme order in (92) is not what we would expect if inflectional prefixes are just heads in their base order. But once more, there is reason to doubt the analysis of a marker that is taken to represent the perfect aspect. For one thing, note that the verb root is marked for completive aspect. In Tepetotutla Chinantec verb roots, tones distinguish between three aspects: progressive/ habitual, intentional, and completive (see Westley 1991). Thus, it is possible that the perfectivity of the construction in (92), which is reflected in the English translation, stems from the completive marking of the verb root and that the adverb *yet* is included in the translation because of presence of the 'perfective' marker in the Tepetotutla Chinantec construction. In other words, the prefix ma^M- is probably an adverb with the meaning 'yet, already'.

This analysis gets some support from the following example, where a verb root in the progressive aspect is combined with the alleged perfective marker:

(93) *Tepetotutla Chinantec* (Westley 1991)
  ma^M-uïg^M za^M co^{MH}
  PERF-climb.PROG.3   3   incline
  'He/she/they is/are already climbing the hill.'

As we see, the resulting reading is imperfective rather than perfective. Hence, the aspectual properties of the predicate seem to be determined by the marking of the verb root. The semantic contribution of the prefix in this case must be what is reflected by the adverb 'already' in the English translation. If this is correct, the position of the prefix ma^M- in Tepetotutla Chinantec is not a problem for my theory after all.

In Walapai (or Hualapai), a mainly suffixing language, there are two pairs of mutually excluding aspectual markers that follow the tense suffixes in the linear order, according to the analysis given in Redden (1966). Some of Redden's examples are given below:

(94) *Walapai* (Redden 1966)
  a. θá-č   kwè   má-hì-wi   b.   ú-hì-yu
     he-NOM   thing   eat-NONPAST-ASP   see-NONPAST-ASP
     'He is eating; he is going to eat.'   'I will see him.'

  c. ɲá-č   ólò   mák-wi-ɲ   d.   smá-k-yu-ɲ
     I-NOM   horse   rent-ASP-PERF   sleep-3-ASP-PERF
     'I'm renting a horse.'   'He slept; he has slept.'

We see from these examples that in the first position following the tense marker one finds the suffix -*wi*, which Redden (1966) characterizes as a marker of 'continuation without interruption', or -*yu*, whose content he takes to be 'continuation with interruption'. These markers can in turn be followed by the perfective marker -*ɲ*, shown above, or by the imperfective marker -*t*. But if aspectual heads are generated below temporal heads, as numerous of our previous examples have indicated, the only way to derive this order syntactically is by moving the verb across the tense marker and the aspect marker and leave the tense and aspect markers in place. If the conclusions that were reached in chapter 2 concerning head movement are correct, this movement on the part of the verb must be phrasal movement. In other words, the morpheme order shown in (94) can only be derived by moving VP directly to a specifier position above T°.

This would mean that Walapai has a kind of LHM (see 2.3.2) which does not move the verb to the front of the clause. If this is true, Walapai is really exceptional, given that such movement has not been encountered in any of the other languages we have looked at so far. It appears that an alternative analysis is available, however. As also mentioned by Redden (1966), the suffixes -*wi* and -*yu* are in fact weakly stressed forms of the verbs *wi* 'do' and *yu* 'be'. Hence, it can be argued that the suffixes are not realizations of aspectual heads but instead of auxiliary verbs. This is how these elements are analyzed by Bender and Yamamoto (1992), who give examples like the following:

(95) *Walapai* (Bender & Yamamoto 1992:300)
      Ma-ch   'ha: mun   ma-thi:-ng-wi-ny.
      2-SUBJ   water   cold   2S/3O-drink-2.SS-do-PERF
      'You drank cold water.'

(96) *Walapai* (Bender & Yamamoto 1992:301)
      Meri-ch   bes   jiwád-k-yu-ny.
      Mary-SUBJ money lack-SS-be-PERF
      'Mary didn't have enough money.'

We see that the complex verbal words in these examples are now taken to contain two verb roots. The main verb, which comes first, carries a prefixed agreement marker and is followed by a marker of clausal embedding, whereas the auxiliary, which follows the main verb, is marked for aspect.

On this analysis, according to which the suffixes -*wi* and -*yu* are V°s and not aspectual markers, the appearance of temporal and other inflectional markers between the main verb and -*wi* or -*yu* is no longer a problem. One such marker, shown in (94a,b) above, is the suffix -*hi*, which was analyzed by Redden (1966) as a non-past marker. This marker also appears in some of the examples in Bender and Yamamoto (1992), but it is now seen as a marker of irrealis mood:

(97) *Walapai* (Bender & Yamamoto 1992:300)
      Ma-ch   mi-sma:-hi-ng-yu.
      2-SUBJ   2-sleep-IRR-2.SS-be
      'You are going to sleep.'

Regardless of the exact content of -*hi*, the order of morphemes shown in (94) is not necessarily a counterexample to the claims I have made about word formation. The crucial fact is that the verbal word in Walapai may contain two verbs—a main verb and an auxiliary. The markers that appear inside the auxiliary must belong to the inflectional domain of the main verb, and when the main verb (or VP) moves so that a complex word is formed where all verbally related heads are suffixed to the main verb, the observed morpheme order follows.[24]

As for Supyire, the order of clausal elements in this language is given in appendix 2 as S Perf Past O V XP. If tense markers are universally generated above aspect markers, this morpheme order must be the outcome of movement. It would be possible to get the aspect marker in front of the tense marker by moving the whole AspP, but then AspP would necessarily include the verb, so that the resulting order would be Perf V Past. In a structure where only the aspect marker and not the verb precedes the tense marker, one would have to say, if the syntactic approach is to be maintained, that the aspectual head has moved on its own across the temporal head. Then if it holds, as claimed in chapter 2, that there can be no skipping of heads and no excorporation, it would follow that the aspectual head must be adjoined to the temporal head, so that aspect and tense form a complex head.

In the absence of examples where other elements intervene between the aspect marker and the past tense marker, the latter analysis might be defendable, even though the two markers are seen as separate words. However, if we look more closely at the Supyire data, it appears once more that the facts are not quite as they appear at first. As (98) shows, the element identified as a past marker has a non-finite verbal suffix:

(98) *Supyire* (Carlson 1991:203)
    U   à   pyi-a   kàrè.
    3s   PERF   PAST-NONFIN go
    'She/he had gone.'

The explanation for this is that *pyi* is not the realization of a temporal head; instead, according to Carlson (1991), it is a verb which is about to acquire the function of a past tense marker. As a full verb, *pyi* means 'do' or 'be', and it may appear as the only verb of its clause, as illustrated in (99).

(99) *Supyire* (Carlson 1991:203)
    U   à   lì pyi.
    3s   PERF   it do
    'She/he did it.'

The fact that *pyi* appears with a non-finite suffix when it is combined with another verb and serves to indicate past tense is a clear indication that even in this function, *pyi* is not yet fully grammaticalized. It is still a verb, inflected in the same way as any other verb that appears in non-final position in serial verb constructions. This can be seen by comparing (98) with (100), which is an example of an ordinary serial verb construction.

(100) *Supyire* (Carlson 1991:204)
     U   à   pa-a   kù   lw.
     3s   PERF   come-NONFIN it   take
     'She/he came and took it.'

We can conclude that in (98), *pyi* is not the realization of the T°(past) head; instead, it is the higher verb in a serial verb construction, and its position after the perfective marker is as expected. However, we would predict that if *pyi* eventually develops into a fully grammaticalized past tense marker, it will begin to appear in front of the perfect marker. Being a realization of a temporal head, it will then also lack the non-finite suffix. Thus, it would be very interesting to follow the development of the past marker in Supyire to see if these expectations are borne out.

In Persian, there is a verbal prefix marking durative aspect. At the same time, tense is apparently indicated in the verb stem itself: a verb stem always appears in either the present tense form or the past tense form (the past stem is identical to the infinitive form minus the infinitival suffix, whereas the formation of the present stem involves further deletion and/or modification—see, e.g., Mahootian 1997). This gives the impression that tense is fused with the verb root, while aspect precedes the fused verb root/tense marker. The examples in (101)–(102) illustrate this.

(101) *Persian*   (Mahootian 1997:228)
    šiva   dærs   mi-xun-e
    Shiva   lesson   DUR-read(PRES)-3s
    'Shiva is studying.'

(102) *Persian*   (Mahootian 1997:241)
    hær   ruz   berenj   mi-xord-im
    every   day   rice   DUR-eat(PAST)-1p
    'We used to eat rice every day.'

But if aspectual heads are generated between the temporal heads and the verb stem, and if two heads can fuse only if they first are combined into one complex head, as suggested in section 3.6.2, then the configuration with an aspect marker preceding a head consisting of the verb root and tense cannot be derived in my model.

However, the so-called past and present stems in Persian probably do not really contain tense features. Each stem form has uses where the tense associated with it would be inappropriate: the past stem also appears in the future tense, while the imperative/subjunctive mood, represented by the marker *be-*, requires the verb stem to have the present form (see, e.g., Mahootian 1997):

(103) *Persian*   (Mahootian 1997:247)
    be-xab-id
    IMP-sleep(PRES)-2p
    'Sleep!'

(104) *Persian*   (Mahootian 1997:249)
    bayæd   dærs   be-xun-æm
    must   lesson   SUBJC-read(PRES)-1s
    'I have to study.'

I conclude from this that the present tense itself is not phonologically realized in Persian. To be sure, most verbs in the present tense include the durative marker *-mi*, as in (101), but since *-mi* also combines with past tense, as in (102), it cannot be analyzed as a marker of present tense. Hence, the present tense morpheme in Persian must be phonologically zero. This must also be the case with the past tense morpheme. Thus, although the only indication of the tense of a given verb is the form of the stem, the stem does not directly spell out the tense morpheme. Rather, the choice of stem form is *conditioned* by the tense or mood morphemes that are included in the construction, without the stem forms actually spelling out tense or mood morphemes. On this analysis, the ordering of elements in Persian verbs do not constitute a serious problem for the syntactic approach to word formation that I am endorsing.

5.5 Syntax and affixation rate

We now look at some of the explanations that have been proposed by other researchers for the ordering of morphemes and for their affixation rate. The explanations under consideration are the historical explanation of Givón (1971), the psycholinguistic explanation of Hawkins and colleagues (Cutler et al. 1985, Hawkins & Cutler 1988, Hawkins & Gilligan 1988), and the relevance theory of Bybee (1985). They are here compared to the theory that I am proposing in this work, and I show that the order of morphemes, as well as the tendency of any given category of verbal markers to be affixed to the verb, can be a consequence of the syntactic order of inflectional heads.

The investigations of the ordering of elements within words that have been conducted so far for the most part belong to the typological tradition and concentrate on the distribution of prefixes and suffixes. Many researchers have noted that there is a statistical predominance of suffixes over prefixes. An early statement of this fact is found in Sapir (1921), where it is pointed out that whereas many languages have only suffixes and no prefixes, exclusively prefixing languages hardly exist. Since then, many attempts have been made to explain the dominance of suffixes.

The first scholar to try to give an explanation for the general tendency to have suffixes rather than prefixes was Greenberg (1963), who argued that not only are prefixes, for psycholinguistic reasons, less likely to develop in the first place, but also they are more prone to being eroded by phonological processes in the course of time.

Psycholinguistic factors are also called upon in several articles by John A. Hawkins and colleagues (Cutler et al. 1985, Hawkins & Cutler 1988, Hawkins & Gilligan 1988). In these works, statistical material is presented which indicates that verb-final languages tend to be suffixing, whereas languages with the object following the verb (VSO and SVO) have both prefixes and suffixes. This is shown in table 5.5, which gives the percentages for the distribution of tense affixes in VO and OV languages, calculated on the base of approximately

TABLE 5.5
Realization of tense affixes in head-initial and head-final word order (Hawkins & Cutler 1988).

Word order	Prefixes (%)	Suffixes (%)
VO or prepositions	26	24
OV or postpositions	1	49

200 languages drawn from three different samples (for details, see Hawkins & Gilligan 1988):

Hawkins and his colleagues assume that there is a Head Ordering Principle (HOP) which plays an important part in determining the order of elements within words as well as within phrases. Given that affixes are generally heads of their words, the HOP can be used to account for the suffixing preference in OV languages and the occurrence of prefixes in VO languages.

But notably, head-initial languages also employ suffixes to a considerable extent, so that prefixes and suffixes are equally frequent in these languages. In order to explain this finding, which is unexpected in light of the HOP, Hawkins and his colleagues propose that another factor in addition to the HOP is involved in the positioning of affixes. This second factor is a psycholinguistic one, having to do with the way in which the process of word recognition works. It is argued that stems are processed before affixes and that the beginning of a word is its most salient part psychologically. Because of this, word structures where the stem is placed before the affix are generally favored.

The psycholinguistic constraints thus reinforce the effect of the HOP in verb-final languages, but in head-initial languages they impose an opposing force of nearly equal strength.

A different type of explanation for the position of affixes was introduced by Givón (1971), who claimed that, since affixes regularly develop from full words, the relative order of affix and stem corresponds to the ordering of the two elements at the latest stage when both were words. It follows that the present morpheme ordering is direct evidence of an earlier syntactic ordering.

In response to this, Comrie (1980) has pointed out that the scenario presented by Givón is to some degree oversimplified. Comrie demonstrates that the syntactic order which has been preserved as morphology is not necessarily the basic word order at the time of reanalysis. It might well be that the present morpheme order reflects an atypical word order from an earlier period. Further, if the present affix has gone through a stage of (special) cliticization, it is even possible that the synchronic morpheme order does not correspond to any earlier word order at all. Today's morphology is therefore not a reliable clue to yesterday's syntax.

In spite of these objections concerning order, it is nevertheless a fact that many affixes have started out as words. The question that needs to be answered is then: What causes these words to end up as suffixes rather than prefixes? One can think of several possible reasons for this: either (1) most of the words that are actual or potential grammatical markers are positioned after the lexical word that they modify (as Givón's article would lead one to believe); or (2) postposed material is more likely to affix than preposed material (as suggested by Hall 1988 and Hawkins & Cutler 1988); or finally, but perhaps less likely, (3) when a preposed element has started the process that will eventually turn it into an affix, it will often switch to a position following the stem it is going to be affixed to.

Hypotheses (1) and (2) above have been investigated by Bybee et al. (1990), who start by noting the following:

> In most cases the position of affixal material is directly traceable to the original position of the lexical material from which it developed. . . . This consideration leads us to ask whether the phenomenon [the predominance of suffixes] is really a 'suffixing preference' or is just part of a more general 'postposing preference' for grammatical material. If it is the latter, then we must seek an explanation for the general ordering of grammatical material, not just for the ordering of affixes. On the other hand, if it is true that postposed material is more frequently affixed than preposed material, then we should seek an explanation in the nature of the affixation process itself. (Bybee et al. 1990:2)

In order to acquire a correct understanding of the questions related to affix positioning, Bybee et al. choose to examine the position of free and bound verbal grammatical markers in a stratified probability sample of 71 languages. In this database, the total numbers of free and bound, proposed and preposed markers are as shown in table 5.6.

We see here that the number of postposed markers is twice as high as the number of preposed markers (1,552 vs. 812). Further, whereas there is a clear tendency that postposed markers are bound—the ratio of free postposed markers to bound postposed markers is 1:4—a preposed marker has an approximately even chance of being free. The combined outcome of these two tendencies is that of a total of 2,364 markers, 1,236 markers (or 52%) are suffixes.

TABLE 5.6
Affixation rate and the position of grammatical morphemes relative to the verb (see Table 1 of Bybee et al. 1990).

Position of marker	Free markers		Bound markers		Total number of markers
	No.	%	No.	%	
Preposed	386	48	426	52	812
Postposed	316	20	1236	80	1552

TABLE 5.7
The distribution of verbal markers in three word order types (data from Table 2 of Bybee et al. 1990.)

Word order	Preposed markers				Postposed markers				Total number of markers
	Free		Bound		Free		Bound		
	No.	%	No.	%	No.	%	No.	%	
V-initial	13	7	68	35	29	15	82	43	192
V-medial	298	32	200	22	82	9	341	37	921
V-final	75	6	158	13	205	16	813	65	1251

If the languages are split up according to basic word order, the result is as shown in table 5.7. Several facts can be read from this table. If we look at postposed markers, we see that the ratio of free markers to bound markers is about 1:3 or 1:4 in all word orders (note that I have calculated the percentages differently from Bybee et al.). That is, all types of languages have suffixes rather than free postposed markers. (As one might recall, table 3.1 showed that the tendency is the same for tense markers.)

Further, suffixes is the most frequent type of marker in all word orders. In verb-final languages the preference for suffixes is overwhelming, but note also that of the few preposed markers in this group, two out of three are bound. In verb-initial languages, prefixes are almost as numerous as suffixes and there are very few free preposed markers. But in verb-medial languages, postposed markers tend to be bound, whereas preposed markers are free in the majority of cases and the number of free preposed markers is nearly as high as the number of suffixes. Hence, the percentages shown in table 5.5, which indicate that prefixes and suffixes are equally frequent in head-initial languages, are valid only for VSO languages and not for SVO languages. (But again, the figures in table 5.7 are in line with the figures for tense markers in table 3.2.)

If we now try to evaluate the two first hypotheses formulated above in light of the findings presented in tables 5.6 and 5.7, we see there is some support for hypothesis (1): the majority of grammatical markers are indeed postposed. As for hypothesis (2), however, it appears that preposed markers affix just as readily as postposed markers except in verb-medial languages. Hypothesis (2) is thus not confirmed; it expresses a tendency that is found in verb-medial languages only.

Bybee et al. (1990) then go on to discuss possible explanations for the patterns shown in table 5.7. As far as verb-final languages are concerned, the suffixing tendency is largely consistent with the diachronic hypothesis of Givón (1971).[25] But in addition to this, they notice that since postposed markers in SOV languages appear between the verb and the clause boundary, they will naturally grow dependent of the verb if they are reduced phonologically. This line of reasoning also applies to preposed markers in VSO languages, and it is an explanation of why the highest rate of affixation is seen at clause boundaries.

For clause-internal markers, on the other hand, they suggest that the factor which determines whether they affix or not is their semantic relevance to the verb stem.

The notion of *relevance* was introduced and treated in much detail in Bybee (1985). Let it therefore suffice to say here that it has to do with the degree to which a grammatical marker alters the basic meaning of the lexical item it is construed with. Bybee's ranking of verbal markers with respect to relevance is shown in (105).

(105) *The relevance hierarchy of verbal markers (Bybee 1985)*
   Valence/voice > aspect > tense > mood/modality

In the morphological theory of Bybee (1985) it is predicted that the higher the relevance of a marker is, the greater is also its tendency to fuse with the lexical stem. This is then the principle that Bybee et al. (1990) use to explain the behavior of grammatical markers in SVO languages. They assume that the verbal markers in these languages, which are typically situated between subject and verb or between verb and object, are not forced to affix to the verb even if they should become reduced. Therefore, it is expected that relevance will be the decisive factor, with the result that highly relevant markers will be affixes more often than will less relevant markers.

As far as preposed markers in SVO languages are concerned, the relevance hypothesis appears to be confirmed. Bybee et al. (1990) show that the frequency of bound markers correlates with the relevance hierarchy given in (105), such that the highest frequency of bounding is found among valence and voice markers, then follow aspect markers, tense markers, and, finally, mood and modality markers. Postposed markers in verb-medial languages do not corroborate the relevance hypothesis, however; postposed tense and mood markers are suffixed more often than expected. The relative frequencies of affixation of verbal markers in verb-medial languages are shown in table 5.8.

We see here that the general tendency for postposed markers in verb-medial languages to be suffixes, which was evident from table 5.7, holds for all types of markers. Bybee et al. admit that this is a problem for their hypothesis but assume that it can be solved by studying the genesis of each individual suffix.

TABLE 5.8
Affixation rate of verbal grammatical markers in verb-medial languages, sorted by position and content of marker. The table combines data from tables 19 and 21 of Bybee et al. (1990).

Content of marker	Preposed markers, affixation rate (%)	Postposed markers, affixation rate (%)
Valence/voice	73	94
Aspect	41	59
Tense	23	80
Mood/modality	10	75

TABLE 5.9
Affixation rate of preposed verbal grammatical markers in verb-final languages, sorted by content of marker (figures from table 20 of Bybee et al. 1990).

Content of marker	Percentage of bound markers
Valence/voice	83
Aspect	67
Tense	25
Mood/modality	29
Negation	17

Two other distributional classes of verbal markers will also have to be accounted for, namely, preposed markers in verb-final languages and postposed markers in verb-initial languages. Concerning the latter, Bybee et al. (1990) note that the relevance hypothesis is difficult to test on these markers, because very few verb-initial languages have postposed markers of all the categories listed in the relevance hierarchy. As for the former type of markers, it is concluded that their realization indicates that relevance is of importance, as predicted. The bounding percentages are given in table 5.9.

Let us now try to summarize the plausibility of each of the proposed explanations of the preponderance of suffixes. First, it seems clear that the diachronic approach of Givón (1971) cannot adequately account for all the relevant data. For example, his theory requires that verbal suffixes in VO languages, insofar as they correspond to earlier verbs, must have arisen at a time when the languages had OV order. This is quite unsupported, however (see, e.g., Comrie 1980); further, Bybee et al. (1990) show that suffixes in verb-medial languages are not necessarily older than suffixes in verb-final languages and that suffixation may take place in VO languages as well as in OV languages.

We must further conclude that it has been demonstrated beyond doubt that the Head Ordering Principle, be it in a synchronic or in a diachronic interpretation, cannot alone be responsible for the observed facts. In combination with the principle suggested by Cutler et al. (1985), Hawkins and Cutler (1988), and Hawkins and Gilligan (1988), which dictates that stems should be placed before affixes for processing reasons, it appears to fare somewhat better as long as overall figures are considered. Thus, table 5.5 above indicates that when the two principles are in conflict, each principle has a 50% chance to win out. However, this approach cannot explain why the effect of the suffixing preference differs from category to category. In the database of Hawkins and Cutler (1988) the ratio of prefixes to suffixes in VO languages is approximately 1:1 for gender, definiteness, tense, mood, and aspect markers; it is closer to 1:3 for plural markers; and case and valence markers are always suffixed (Hawkins & Cutler 1988:293, table 11.5). They do not attempt to explain this variation. Further, if we keep verb-initial languages apart from verb-medial languages, it also appears that at least for the category of tense the suffixing preference is stronger in verb-medial languages than in verb-initial languages (see table 3.2). Hawkins and his colleagues treat all VO languages as one type, so differences between verb-initial and verb-medial languages cannot be captured.

Recall that table 3.2 showed that tense suffixes are found more frequently in verb-medial languages than in verb-initial languages. In addition, it turns out that if all VO languages were treated together, my data would be even less favorable for the HOP than the data of Hawkins and Cutler (1988), showing more suffixing in VO languages and more prefixing in OV languages. However, the suffixing rate in VO languages that can be calculated from my data is very close to the rate given by Dryer (1992). In table 5.10, the figures from Hawkins and Cutler (1988) are compared to those of Dryer (1992) and to those arrived at in this work.

While the HOP predicts that VO languages should have prefixes and OV languages should have suffixes, we see here that the majority of affixes in VO languages are in fact suffixes, according to Dryer (1992) and also according to my survey. At the same time, there are too many prefixes in OV languages for them to be ignored.

Finally, as pointed out by Bybee et al. (1990), another weakness of the theory of Hawkins and his colleagues is that free markers are not taken into consideration, so that one misses the fact that not only the suffixing tendency but also the affixation rate varies with grammatical category and word order.

Unlike the other theories considered here, the relevance theory of Bybee et al. has the potential to explain the variation across categories of the degree of affixation. What it is not able to account for is the position of a marker relative to the stem, although Bybee et al. (1990) suggest that there may be diachronic reasons for the choice of preposed or postposed markers. It is still unclear, on their analysis, why there are so many suffixes in verb-initial languages and why subject agreement is often suffixed in verb-final languages and, in many cases, in verb-medial languages. Moreover, as they admit, it is a serious problem for the relevance theory that postposed markers in verb-medial languages tend to affix regardless of their category.

I now argue that the syntactic approach to word formation is in fact able to offer an explanation for this: if a verbal marker follows the verb but precedes the object, it is probably the case that the verb has head-moved to the marker in question, so that the two form a complex syntactic head. A complex syntactic head will necessarily have the behavior of a word; consequently, the marker will be seen as a suffix on the verb. Because of this, postposed markers in SVO-languages are normally suffixes.

TABLE 5.10
The percentage of tense/aspect suffixes relative to the total number of tense/aspect affixes, in VO and OV languages.

Word order	Hawkins & Cutler	Dryer	Julien
VO	48	64	63
OV	98	92	86

Alternatively, a postposed marker may result from complement-to-Spec movement, which also creates a tight relation between roots and grammatical markers (see chapter 3). In this case, the postposed marker will also tend to be affixed regardless of its category.

As for preposed markers in verb-initial languages, it was shown in chapter 4 that they will often be seen as affixes for phonological reasons—which is very close to the explanation given by Bybee et al. (1990).

Concerning the success of the relevance theory in accounting for the affixation rates of preposed markers in verb-medial and verb-final languages, recall that in the relevance hierarchy the order of categories is valence/voice > aspect > tense > mood/modality, with the more relevant ones listed first. The relevance theory of Bybee (1985) predicts that the higher the relevance of a marker is, the greater is also its tendency to fuse with the lexical stem. Bybee et al. (1990) show that the frequency of bound markers correlates with the relevance hierarchy, such that the highest frequency of bounding is found among valence and voice markers, then follow aspect markers, tense markers, and, finally, mood and modality markers (see tables 5.8 and 5.9).

Strikingly, the relevance hierarchy also corresponds to the order of sentential heads from the verb upward. In the preceding paragraphs we have seen that tense heads precede aspectual heads, which of course precede the V° head itself. Moreover, there is ample evidence that a valence or voice head is situated below tense and aspect. This can be seen from the order of affixes in (106)–(110).

(106) *Northern Saami*
  Vuoiti   almmuh-uvv-o   golggotmánu-s.
  winner.NOM announce-PASS-PRES.3s   October-LOC
  'The winner is [i.e. will be] announced in October.'

(107) *Turkish* (Kornfilt 1997:326)
  Bahçe-de   dans   ed-il-iyor.
  garden-LOC dance   do-PASS-PROG
  'There is dancing in the garden.'

(108) *Boro* (Bhattacharya 1977)
  be   bahtra   mithi-ho-za-bay
  this information know-CAUS-PASS-COMPL
  'This information has been made known.'

(109) *Seri* (Marlett 1990:515)
  i?p-yo-p-ášt
  1sS-REM.REAL-PASS-tattoo
  'I was tattooed'

(110) *Huallaga Quechua* (Weber 1989)
yanapa-ka-sha
help-PASS-3.PERF
'He/she was helped.'

As for mood/modality markers, Bybee et al. (1990) put them in the lowest position of the relevance hierarchy. If our interpretation of the hierarchy is correct, this would mean that mood markers would be the realizations of the highest heads of the clause, farthest away from the base position of the verb. Accordingly, when mood markers are included in complex verbal words, we would expect them to appear outside all other verbal markers. In the examples shown below, this is borne out:

(111) *Nama* (= ex. (18), ch. 3)

píli	ke	//nããpá	maríàsà	ǂxanísà	kè-rè	màa
Bill	DECL	there	Mary	letter	REM.PAST-IMPF	give

'There Bill gave Mary a letter.'

(112) *Lezgian* (= ex. (30), ch. 3)

Baku.d-a	irid	itim	gülle.di-z	aǧud-na-lda.
Baku-INESS	seven	man.ABS	bullet-DAT	take.out-AOR-EVID

'They say that in Baku seven men were shot.'

(113) *Haruai* (= ex. (5), ch. 3)

An	nöbö	dyb	hön	nöy-n-ŋ-a.
1p	man	big	pig	give-FUT-1p-DECL

'We will give the big man a pig.'

(114) *Greenlandic* (= ex. (37a), ch. 1)

Ippasaq	tikip-put	aqagu-lu	ikinnguta-at	tiki-ssa-pput.
yesterday	arrive-IND.3p	tomorrow-and	friends-3p	arrive-FUT-IND.3p

'They arrived yesterday and their friends will arrive tomorrow.'

(115) *Wichita* (Rood 1976:267)
khiʔas-kiya-iy-ki-hirahr-teʔerʔa-s
poor-QUOT-INDEF.S-AOR-ground-lick-IMPF
'The poor ones were licking the ground.'

(116) *Warao* (Romero-Figueroa 1985:129)

Warao-tuma	atuhe-bitu	nahamutu	arai	kahu-ya-yama.
Warao-PL	before-SUPERL	sky	OBL	live-PRES-HEARSAY

'They say that the Warao, long, long ago, lived in the sky.'

(117) *Sranan*   (Seuren 1983:227)
    A   kan ben   e   nyan.
    he can PAST PRES eat
    'He may have been eating.'

However, in the following examples, mood or modality markers intervene between the verb and the tense marker. This indicates that there are also mood and modality heads below the temporal heads.

(118) *Northern Saami*   (= ex. (3), ch. 2)
    Mii   veahkeh-eažža-i-met da-i-d   olbmu-i-d.
    1p.NOM help-POT-PAST-1p   that-PL-ACC person-PL-ACC
    'We might (have) helped those people.'

(119) *Turkish*   (see Brendemoen & Hovdhaugen 1992:168)
    Gör-üş-tür-ül-ebil-ir-ler.
    see-RECIP-CAUS-PASS-POT-AOR-3p
    'They might be made to see each other.'
  = 'They might be confronted with each other.'

(120) *Japanese*   (= ex. (62a), ch. 3)
    Boku-wa [John-ni   piano-ga   hik-er-u   to] omow-u.
    I-TOP   John-DAT   piano-NOM play-can-PRES C   think-PRES
    'I think that John can play the piano.'

(121) *Kamoro*   (Voorhoeve 1975:371)
    apa-kem-ako-ma-n-em
    PREF-give-COND-TENSE-1sO-2sS
    'You would give it to me.'

(122) *Lower Grand Valley Dani*   (Bromley 1981)
    wat-h-ik-i
    kill-FACT-REM.PAST-1s
    'I killed (it) a long time ago.'

(123) *Gooniyandi*   (McGregor 1990:223)
    ngab-ja-wi-la
    eat-SUBJC-FUT-1s
    'I want to eat.'

(124) *Iñupiaq*   (adapted from MacLean 1986:213)
    Spinach-tu-llatu-ru-a-ŋa.
    spinach-eat-like-IND-PAST-1s
    'I liked to eat spinach.'

(125) *Huave*   (Stairs & Erickson 1969:39)
    ap-ko-ma-rang
    FUT-DUB-3-do
    'Maybe he will do.'

(126) *Haitian Creole*   (= ex. (32), ch. 4)
    m   te   di   m   t   a   pati
    1s   ANT   say   1s   ANT   IRR leave.
    'I said that I would leave.'

(127) *Sranan*   (Seuren 1983:227)
    A   ben   o   kan nyan.
    he   PAST   FUT can   eat
    'He would be able to eat / he was going to be able to eat.'

On closer investigation it appears that there are several mood positions in a clause and that speaker oriented modals such as evidentials and epistemic markers are situated relatively high up, whereas the indicators of root modality and of grammatical mood (i.e., realis/irrealis or subjunctive/indicative) are found in lower positions (see Cinque 1999 and chapter 4 n.6). The examples from Sranan in (117) and (127) provide a good illustration of this: when the modal marker *kan* precedes the tense markers, as in (117), it is necessarily epistemic, whereas when it follows the tense markers, as in (127), it has the agent-oriented reading that is typical of root modals.

If we identify the modal markers registered by Bybee et al. (1990) with the higher modal elements, the relevance hierarchy does indeed reflect the base order of verbally related heads in the clause. The effect of relevance can now be restated in structural terms: in a sequence of inflectional heads preceding the verb, the heads that are closer to the verb will have a greater tendency to be included in a word with the verb than will the heads that are farther away from the verb. This is an obvious consequence of imposing a linear ordering on syntactic terminals. If a verb forms a word with one or more of the heads that precede it, it must minimally combine with the closest head. Higher heads can be included in the verbal word only if all intervening heads are also included.

5.6 Final remarks

In this chapter I concentrated on the distribution of verbal inflectional markers relative to their associated verbs and on the relative order of various verbal markers. Although the cross-linguistic variation in this area is considerable, for most categories it nevertheless falls within certain limits. What I have tried to demonstrate is that if we assume that the minimal syntactic elements are individual morphemes, the observed patterns can be derived from the same syntactic base even in a syntax where movement, as well as adjunction, is always to the left and head-movement is strictly local so that excorporation is ruled out.

The only deviant category is agreement: agreement markers appear to have a much freer distribution than markers of other categories have. My proposal is therefore that agreement features do not head phrases but, instead, are added to various verbally related syntactic heads as a signal of the relation between the arguments and those heads.

Concerning the verb in English and in Scandinavian embedded clauses, my results are still somewhat inconclusive. There is obviously more work to be done in this area. However, I think it would be premature to reject the syntactic approach solely on the basis of the English and Scandinavian facts, which are surrounded by so much uncertainty, as long as data from numerous languages are in accordance with the syntactic approach to an overwhelming degree.

Notes

1. Rackowski and Travis (2000) propose for Niuean, a Polynesian VSO language, that there is repeated phrasal movement in the lower part of IP, in much the same way as I have suggested for head-final languages, They also propose that the arguments move out of TP and that TP then moves to a Spec position very high up in the clause, across the positions where the arguments are licensed. It is possible that their analysis goes through for some verb-initial languages. Still, tense markers precede the verb in Niuean. Hence, it must be correct even for this language that the verb does not move across T°.

2. The focus marker *a* in (34) just shows that the clause contains a focused element; it does not indicate the focus position. The actual focus position in Podoko is immediately after the verb (Jarvis 1991).

3. In Julien (forthcoming b) it is argued that certain operators have the relevant property, in that their operator features are stronger than their c-features. As a result, the phrase that is attracted to the Spec of the operator is not necessarily the complement of the operator; instead, it is the target of the operator feature. In this way, we have an explanation of why some head-final languages, such as Hindi, have preverbal negation, as illustrated in (i).

(i) *Hindi*   (Mahajan 1989:224)
    Raam   roTii   nahiiN   khaa-taa.
    Ram   bread   NEG   eat-PRES.MASC.SG
    "Ram does not eat bread."

Here the arguments but not the VP have moved to positions in front of the negation. In the analysis of Julien (2001), the object has moved to Spec-NegP, because it is the target of the negation. The VP then stays below NegP. In other words, because of its operator nature, the negation in Hindi is different from other IP heads in this language in that it does not attract its complement to its Spec.

4. This is also related to the proposal in Baker (1996) that at least in polysynthetic languages, subject agreement markers are adjoined to I° and object agreement markers are adjoined to Asp°.

5. As for the question of the identity of the lower subject agreement head, the best hint I have found so far is the fact that in Bella Coola, subject agreement is fused with voice, as the following shows (see Newman 1969a, 1969b).

(i) *Bella Coola*   (Newman 1969a:177)
knix-tim-ċ
eat-PASS.3p-now
'They are now being eaten.'

This could mean that subject agreement is in fact added here to the voice head, which presumably has the subject generated in its Spec (Kratzer 1996). This suggests that subject agreement features can be added where the subject originates or where the subject is eventually licensed. The only complication is that the subject agreement in (i) actually refers to the derived subject of the passive, which is an underlying object.

6. For Basque, which is recorded in my survey as having prefixed tense and suffixed (ergative) subject agreement, Laka (1993) presents an alternative analysis according to which the real tense marker comes last in the sequence of suffixes.

7. For Olo, a language of the Torricelli phylum, I have insufficient information on the position of the tense marker relative to the object. Laycock (1975) says that "tense/aspect is marked by particles following the verb" and that SOV is the preferred word order. That is, in most Olo clauses the order is SOVT. According to Laycock, SVO also occurs, but he gives no hint as to the position of the tense marker in this order.

8. The first person marker in Huave has the same distribution—see Noyer (1994).

9. If we ignore the tense markers and all non-bound agreement markers, the data in table 5.4 can be directly compared to the data in table 17 in Siewierska and Bakker (1996). The result is shown in the table below. As we see, my findings are quite close to those of Siewierska and Bakker (1996), except for the orders SAgr+V+OAgr and V+OAgr+SAgr. I have no explanation for the difference as regards the order SAgr+V+ OAgr, but the higher frequency of V+OAgr+SAgr in my sample could have to do with the fact that my sample contains more languages from New Guinea and the Americas than did the sample used by Siewierska and Bakker: in my sample, there are 53 languages from New Guinea and 210 American languages (these terms refer to geographic areas and not necessarily to genetic groupings), while the corresponding figures for Siewierska and Bakker's sample are 28 and 69. It is precisely in these areas that I have found most of the occurrences of the pattern V+OAgr+SAgr (in 9 New Guinean genera and 13 American genera).

Occurrences of various morpheme orders. Absolute numbers.

Morpheme order	Siewierska &Bakker	My survey
SAgr+OAgr+V	17	15
OAgr+SAgr+V	8	11
SAgr+V+OAgr	24	12
OAgr+V+SAgr	13	12
V+SAgr+OAgr	11	13
V+OAgr+SAgr	10	25

10. The entry in the 'uncertain' column is Finisterre-Huon, a genus with several languages for which my sources do not give information on the unmarked word order.

11. As mentioned already, Halle and Marantz (1993) also assume that agreement morphemes do not head phrases. When van de Kerke (1996) ascribes to them the view that agreement morphemes are separate syntactic heads, it is clearly a misrepresentation.

12. As far as I can see, it must be the case that (51) can also mean 'She washed us' in addition to the meanings that van de Kerke (1996) gives.

13. An auxiliary that is only marked for subject and not for object may appear in combination with intransitive or transitive verbs, as the agreement for third person objects is zero. An example of an auxiliary with only subject marking combining with a transitive verb is shown in (58b). As we see, the tense marking on the auxiliary represents [NONPAST].

14. The term 'anticipative' is also found in Kastenholz (1987).

15. Chomsky (1995) further argues that in certain cases where an adverbial intervenes between a head and its complement, the separation of head and complement cannot be explained as a result of head movement. The examples he gives of this have the following form:

(i) John made a decision last night to leave town.

In (i) the adverb may have matrix scope even though it is situated lower than the nominal that belongs with the infinitival clause. Since both the nominal head and the determiner precede the adverbial, the nominal cannot have head moved across the adverbial in the manner suggested by Chomsky for the verb in (63b). One might want to propose, though, that there has been phrasal movement of the object to a licensing position outside VP.

16. According to Costa (1996) the order PP-*well* in (70d) is ungrammatical; according to Peter Svenonius (personal communication) it is acceptable but not as good as *well*-PP.

17. It has been argued, however, that bare DP adverbials like *every day* do not occur within the IP domain (see Cinque 1999:202 n.29). If this is correct, *every day* in (73) and in the previous examples does not indicate the position of the lower frequentative head. Instead, *every day* must be taken to pattern with the circumstantial adverbials. (Cf. Nilsen 2000, who suggests that bare DP adverbials are PPs with an empty P. If this is correct, it follows without further stipulation that bare DP adverbials will have the same distribution as other PP adverbials and occur at the end of the clause.) But if we replace *every day* in (73) with a frequential adverb, which must belong within the IP space, we see that we get the same pattern:

(i) *English*
   a.   Fathers often read frequently to their children.
   b.   Fathers often read to their children frequently.
   c. * Fathers often read frequently books.
   d.   Fathers often read books frequently.

Again we must conclude that verbs and DP objects move to a position above the lower frequential head, whereas such movement is optional for PP arguments.

18. As Peter Svenonius points out to me, phrasal adverbials are much worse in preverbal position than simple adverbs with the same meaning:

(i)   John annually donates half of his income to the Salvation Army.
(ii) * John every year donates half of his income to the Salvation Army.

This might have to do with 'every day' being a PP—see the previous note.

19. It is of some interest to consider Pollock's (1997:272 n.11) comments on the examples in (i), which were given by Pesetsky (1989) (and Ouhalla 1990) as evidence that the verb in English can move out of VP:

(i) *English*
   a.   Bill knocked recently on it.
   b.   Sue looked carefully at him.
   c.   Harry relies frequently on it.

Apparently, the verbs in (i) have moved leftward across the adverbs, leaving the PP complements behind. Pollock then points to the following examples, where the verbs may not precede the adverbs:

(ii) *English*
   a. * Bill knocked hardly on it.
   b. * Sue looked hardly at him.
   c. * Harry relies surely on it.

Pollock's explanation for the grammaticality of the constructions in (i) is that the adverbs represented here can be VP-final,and that the word order we see must be derived by rightward movement of the PPs or base generation of adverbs inside a Larsonian VP shell. He further assumes that the constructions in (ii) are out because these adverbs are always higher than VP. On this account, English verbs do not leave VP.

However, if we adopt an analysis of adverbs along the lines of Cinque (1999), according to which adverbs are located within the IP-domain, the verbs in (i) must have moved out of VP. The ungrammaticality of (ii) then simply means that these adverbs originate above the position that the verb moves to.

20. Note that Cinque's (1999) proposal that manner adverbs are generated in the Spec of the voice head is incompatible with the analysis mentioned in n. 5 according to which external arguments are generated in this position. However, this does not invalidate the observation that the verb must precede manner adverbs.

21. Cinque (1999) gives the following example as evidence that the verb in Norwegian precedes the lower completive:

(i) *Norwegian*   (Cinque 1999:215 n.7)
    ...at   han   ikke   lenger   alltid   sov   helt   godt
    that   he   not   longer   always   slept   completely   well

However, the reading I get here is one where *helt* 'completely' modifies *godt* 'well'. That is, *helt* must belong to the adverbial phrase headed by *godt*, and the fact that the verb precedes *helt* in this example does not mean that the verb has moved past the completive aspect phrase.

22. The person and number of the subject in Hua is actually expressed by the form of the final suffix together with the vowel of the preceding morpheme, which alternates according to a system of ablaut (see Haiman 1980). To keep things simple, I indicate the subject agreement only in the final suffix in the Hua examples.

23. The prefixed subject marker shown in (88) and (89) is termed 'subject pronoun' by Manoharan (1989). He gives an example which shows that if the clause contains an object, the object will intervene between the subject pronoun and the verb:

(i) *Andamanese*   (Manoharan 1989:105)
    tɔ   ta:jiyo berulu:-bom
    1s   fish   catch-NONPAST.CONT
    'I am catching fish.'

But unfortunately, he does not give any examples of clauses with full DP subjects, so we cannot tell if the subject marker disappears when a subject DP is present, in which case it is probably an agreement marker.

24. The data suggest that Walapai might belong to the class of head-final languages discussed in chapter 3, so that the complex verbs are formed by successive movments of complements to Spec.

25. The exceptional markers in this respect are person/number agreement markers, which also tend to be suffixed in SOV languages. Bybee et al. (1990) suggest that either this is due to developments involving unstressed pronouns, as described in Comrie (1980), or else the suffixed agreement markers stem from inflected auxiliaries following the verb.

6

On the Morphology Module

6.1 Overview

In this work I argue that morphologically complex words are the outcome of the manipulation of morphemes that takes place in syntax and that wordhood cannot be associated with any particular structural morpheme configuration. If this is all there is to say about complex words, it must be true that grammar does not have at its disposal any specifically word-forming devices. That is, in the theory of word formation I present there is apparently no room for a separate morphological component. The existence and content of a possible morphological component is the question that I take up in this chapter.

It should be noted in this connection that the terms 'component' and 'module' can refer either to a set of rules or operations that act as a block or to a set of rules or principles which apply to the derivation as a whole (see Grimshaw 1986, Baker 1988b, Booij 1997). As emphasized in Baker (1988a, 1988b), for example, it is of course perfectly possible to see morphology as a module or component, in the 'set of principles' sense, without committing oneself to the belief that it is also a component in the 'rule block' sense. Thus, even though it should be clear from the foregoing that I do not assume that the grammar contains a specifically word-forming box, it might still be necessary to postulate rules that deal specifically with the shape of words.

In my model, word formation proceeds through two clearly distinguishable stages: at stage I the syntax puts the morphemes in a certain order, and at stage II appropriate lexical entries are inserted to spell out those morphemes. Ideally, we would expect to find a one-to-one correspondence between the meaningful elements of a word and the underlying syntactic heads. However, it is well known that languages display many deviations from the ideal pattern. Some deviations have to do with the ordering of morphemes (with the syntagmatic dimension) which means that they arise at stage I, while other deviations have to do with the realization of morphemes (with the paradigmatic dimension), and these latter deviations must be introduced at stage II.

In the preceding chapters I mainly concentrated on the linear ordering of morphemes. It is still conceivable that certain other aspects of words, in particular in the paradigmatic dimension, may only be explained with reference to purely morphological principles. This is what I discuss in section 6.2. The

conclusion is that indeed certain aspects of the realization of individual morphemes cannot be explained with reference to phonology or syntax. Hence, this
must be where the morphology module of grammar comes into play. But
notably, while it may be correct to say that the shape of morphemes is
determined by morphology, on this conception of morphology it does not deal
only with word-internal material but with individual morphemes that may or
may not belong to morphologically complex words. Hence, the idea that the
word-building processes are all located in syntax is still maintained.

Whereas section 6.2 concentrates on inflectional morphology, which has also
been the focus of all the preceding chapters, I turn in section 6.3 to the two other
classes of word formation: derivation and compounding. My proposal concerning the difference between inflection and derivation is that inflectional affixes
represent functional heads while derivational affixes represent lexical heads. This
means that derivation is very similar to compounding except for the fact that
derivation involves a lexical element that always co-occurs with at least one
other lexical element. As for the word-forming mechanisms as such, I adopt the
view that derivation and compounding are executed in syntax, just as I have
argued to be the case with inflection.

6.2 Deviations from the agglutinative pattern

Carstairs (1987) gives an overview of the ways in which a word form may fail to
conform to perfect agglutination—that is, to the pattern where every underlying
morpheme has exactly one realization and, conversely, every marker realizes
exactly one underlying morpheme. He notes first that deviations may have to do
with the syntagmatic dimension or with the paradigmatic dimension and,
second, that the situation may be that one morpheme is spelled out by more
than one marker, or else that one single marker is the realization of more than
one morpheme.[1]

We start by considering the syntagmatic dimension, where the 'one morpheme to many markers' deviation means that the content of one and the same
underlying morpheme shows up in two or more places (discontinuous marking),
and the 'many morphemes to one marker' deviation means that what we would
take to be the content of separate morphemes underlyingly are expressed by
means of one single marker (fused marking). These two deviations are discussed
in 6.2.1 and 6.2.2, respectively.

In the paradigmatic dimension, the 'one morpheme to many markers' deviation is the phenomenon of allomorphy, which is taken up in 6.2.3, while the
'many morphemes to one marker' deviation is manifested as systematic homonymi or syncretism. This is the topic of 6.2.4.

6.2.1 Discontinuous marking
Concerning discontinuous marking, also known as extended exponence
(Matthews 1991, Spencer 1991), it would clearly be a problem for a theory like

the one I am advocating, according to which the position of a marker is determined by the syntactic position of the morpheme that it spells out, if one single morpheme can be spelled out by two non-adjacent markers. I suspect, however, that apparent discontinuous markers are really combinations of two different morphemes that for some reason tend to co-occur.

To take an example, Harrell (1962) states that the verbal negation in Moroccan Arabic consists of a prefix *ma-* and a suffix *-š*, as shown in (1).

(1) *Moroccan Arabic* (Harrell 1962:154)
     ma-žber-t-š   le-flus
     NEG-find-PERF.1S-NEG   DEF-money
     'I didn't find the money.'

However, when the object is a negative polarity item or an indefinite noun, the suffix *-š* disappears:

(2) *Moroccan Arabic* (Harrell 1962:154)
     a. ma-šef-na   hedd
         NEG-see-PERF.1p   anyone
         'We didn't see anyone.'

     b. ma-žber-t   flus
         NEG-find-PERF.1s   money
         'I didn't find (any) money.'

This fact indicates that the real negation is the prefix *ma-*. The presence of the suffix *-š* in (1) can be explained as follows. The negation is an operator which needs to bind a polarity variable. Negative polarity items are polarity variables, which must be bound by an appropriate operator (see, e.g., Acquaviva 1997). Further, indefinite nouns can also be bound by similar operators. Hence, in (2a,b) the properties of the negation and of the object are all satisfied. But in (1), the object does not give the negation a variable to bind. Then a polarity variable is inserted, probably in the polarity head, and this variable is spelled out as *-š*. The negation itself could be generated as the specifier of the polarity head, or as the specifier of a Neg° head which is located lower down in the structure (Zanuttini 1994). In either case, the negation, being an operator, must move to the front of the clause to take scope over the variable.

Aymara is another language which has been claimed to have discontinuous negation, as the following example illustrates:

(3) *Aymara* (Adelaar 1998)
     jani-w   jisk^hi-ᶜt'a-ᶜka-sma-ti
     NEG-EVID   ask-MOM-ASP-1S/2O-NEG
     'I did not ask you.'

One possibility is that one of the two elements glossed as NEG in (3) represents a Neg° head while the other represents a polarity head (Zanuttini 1994; see here chapter 4 n.7). However, the suffix *-ti* is also the marker of polarity questions (see, e.g., Hardman et al. 1988). This indicates that *-ti* is a polarity variable, in principle similar to negative polarity items, just like the Moroccan Arabic *-ši*. In negative statements, it is bound by the negation, which is the preverbal *jani*. In polarity questions, we could assume that it is bound by a question operator which is phonologically null—such operators are already well known from the literature.[2]

A rather different case of discontinuous marking is found in Dutch, where some collective nouns are derived by means of the prefix *ge-* in combination with the suffix *-te*. Two examples are given in (4).

(4)   *Dutch*   (Bauer 1988:20)
      a.   het been   'the bone'   >   het   ge-been-te   'the skeleton'
      b.   de berg   'the mountain'   >   het   ge-berg-te   'the mountains'

Bauer (1988) claims that we are dealing here with two affixes which together realize one single morpheme. He notes, though, that each of the two affixes can appear independently of the other. The prefix *ge-* derives (neuter) nouns from verbs and the suffix *-te* derives (non-neuter) nouns from verbs and adjectives. In (5) and (6) I give some examples of derived words formed with these affixes.

(5)   *Dutch*
      a.   bouw-en   'build'   >   het ge-bouw   'the building'
      b.   fluister-en   'whisper'   >   het ge-fluister   'the whispering'
      c.   jammer-en   'complain'   >   het ge-jammer   'the complaint'
      d.   schenk-en   'give'   >   het ge-schenk   'the gift'

(6)   *Dutch*
      a.   belov-en   'promise$_V$'   >   de belof-te   'the promise'
      b.   kalm   'calm'   >   de kalm-te   'the calm'
      c.   sterk   'strong'   >   de sterk-te   'the strength'
      d.   ziek   'sick'   >   de ziek-te   'the disease'

For Bauer, the fact that *ge-...-te* combines with other bases than those that go with the individual affixes plus the apparently non-compositional meaning of *ge-...-te* is evidence that *ge-...-te* is one morpheme. In my theory, it would mean that *ge-...-te* spells out one syntactic terminal node.

However, it does not follow from its properties that the combination *ge-...-te* represents one single morpheme and one single syntactic terminal. It is fully possible for a combination of two morphemes, representing two different syntactic elements, to have a non-compositional meaning and also a distribution which is different from the distribution of its constituting parts. Non-compositional meaning is typical of idioms, which, in the theories like those of

Di Sciullo and Williams (1987) and Jackendoff (1997), are phrasal lexical items with exceptional semantics.

Jackendoff (1997) in particular stresses that idioms have a normal phrasal structure. The English idiom *kick the bucket*, for example, is structurally a normal VP, which is listed in the lexicon with the non-compositional meaning 'die'. He further assumes late insertion of lexical items, so that the matching of lexical items with the larger syntactic structure takes place after those larger structures have been built (see section 1.3). At the point of lexical insertion, a VP idiom must be matched with a VP that is generated by the syntactic component in the normal fashion. Hence, the verb *kick* in *kick the bucket* must be inserted in a V° node, just like any other verb, and *the* and *bucket* must be matched with the D° and N° of the DP that is generated as the object of that verb. More generally, the elements that an idiom consists of are matched individually with appropriate syntactic terminals. There is thus no question of an idiom being a single morpheme in the sense that it should correspond to a single syntactic head. Also note that, on this view, a morpheme can have multiple occurrences in the lexicon in that it may appear as a part of one or more complex lexical entries in addition to being listed as a separate item.

We see now that the Dutch combination *ge-...-te* can be analyzed along similar lines. We might propose that in addition to being listed as separate lexical items, the affixes *ge-* and *-te* are also listed as a unit, with the non-compositional meaning 'collective'. Since both *ge-* and *-te* are of the category N, as (5)–(6) demonstrate, *ge-...-te* can only be inserted in a complex N°, each affix being matched with a different N° inside that complex head. At the same time, these two N°s together are matched with the meaning 'collective'.[3]

Notably, analogous examples can be found where the elements involved are clearly separate in syntax. In Norwegian, the two adpositions *for* 'for' and *siden* 'since' are used together to express 'ago', as illustrated in (7).

(7) *Norwegian*
Det skje-dde   for to uke-r   siden.
it happen-PAST *for* two week-PL *siden*
'It happened two weeks ago.'

In this construction, the individual adpositions have no discernible meaning. Rather, it appears that the combination *for. . .siden* must be listed as an idiom. Also note that the distribution of this idiom is different from the distribution of the individual adpositions. In (7), *for* precedes and *siden* follows the DP, but when they are used separately, both *for* and *siden* are prepositions, as illustrated in (8a,b).

(8) *Norwegian*
a. Jeg lån-te   den for to uke-r.
   I   borrow-PAST it for two week-PL
   'I borrowed it for two weeks.'

    b. Det ha-r   regn-et   siden begynnelse-n av juli.
       it have-PRES rain-PTC since beginning-DEF of July
       'It has been raining since the beginning of July.'

Further, while *siden* 'since' must combine with an expression denoting a time point, the combination *for . . . siden* must combine with an expression denoting a time period, just like *for* does when it appears on its own. Thus, the subcategorizational properties of *siden* are apparently violated in constructions with *for . . . siden*. But in this respect, *siden* is similar to the Dutch affixes *ge-* and *-te*—these elements too have one distribution when they are combined and another when they are not. Since one would probably not want to claim that *for . . . siden* is the realization of one single morpheme, there is no need to make this assumption for the combination *ge-...-te* either.

These few examples illustrate my point that when two or more markers apparently serve to express one meaning, it can often be shown that the markers are in principle separate and have different functions. In other cases, the function of each marker is not so easy to pin down, as in the *ge-...-te* example. But notably, this has to do with the collocation being listed as a lexical item, and it does not prove that we are dealing with a truly discontinuous morpheme.

While the cases that we have considered so far have involved two markers that are taken to jointly express one and the same morpheme, another type of multiple exponence is seen where a given feature is not only represented by its principal marker but is also apparently present in other markers whose main function is to spell out some other feature. In such cases, what we really have is conditioned allomorphy, which causes the conditioned marker to reflect the features of the conditioning marker.[4] This is clearly different from a situation where the same feature is spelled out by two or more markers simultaneously.

An example of conditioned allomorphy is found in the verbal inflection of Island Kiwai, a language where, according to Wurm (1975b), tense is signaled several times within each verb form. Consider now the Island Kiwai verbal paradigm shown in (9).

(9)   *The verbal paradigm of Island Kiwai* (Wurm 1975b:338)

	Present	Near past	Definite past	Imm. future	Indef. future
1s	n-V	n-V	n-V	n-V-ri	ni-do-V-ri
1d	n-V-duru-do	n-V-do	n-V-ru-do	ni-do-V-ri	ni-du-do-V-ri
1t	n-V-bi-duru-mo	n-V-bi-mo	n-V-bi-ru-mo	ni-bi-mo-V-ri	ni-bi-du-mo-V-ri
1p	n-V-duru-mo	n-V-mo	n-V-ru-mo	ni-mo-V-ri	ni-du-mo-V-ri
2/3s	r-V	w-V	g-V	w-V-ri	wi-do-V-ri
2/3d	r-V-duru-do	w-V-do	g-V-ru-do	wi-do-V-ri	wi-du-do-V-ri
2/3t	r-V-bi-duru-mo	w-V-bi-mo	g-V-bi-ru-mo	wi-bi-mo-V-ri	wi-bi-du-mo-V-ri
2/3p	r-V-duru-mo	w-V-mo	g-V-ru-mo	wi-mo-V-ri	wi-du-mo-V-ri

Starting with the person markers, one will notice that the first person subject marker is always *n-* or *ni-*. The marker of subjects that are not first person, on the other hand, has different shapes in different tenses. It appears that *w(i)-* is the basic form and that the alternants *r-* and *g-* are conditioned by the present tense and by the definite past tense, respectively. Thus, even if certain tenses are *reflected* in the form of the non-first person marker, there is no need to say that the person markers are *realizations* of tense.

Further, in the indefinite future forms there are two elements that seem to represent the tense. However, the basic future marker must be the suffix *-ri*. As we see, it also appears in the immediate future tense. The prefix *du- ~ do-* must have some other content, since it combines with *-ri* to give the indefinite future.

An overview of the lexical entries that are involved in the verbal inflection of Island Kiwai is given in (10) and (11).

(10) *Person and number markers in Island Kiwai*

a.	[+1]	↔	/n(i)/		e.	[+SG]	↔	Ø
b.	[−1]	↔	/r/ / ___ [PRES]		f.	[−SG -PL]	↔	/do/
c.	[−1]	↔	/g/ / ___ [DEF.PAST]		g.	[+PL]	↔	/mo/
d.	[−1]	↔	/w(i)/		h.	[TRIAL]	↔	/bi/

(11) *Tense markers in Island Kiwai*

a.	[PRES]	↔	Ø / [+SG]___		e.	[DEF.PAST]	↔	/ru/
b.	[PRES]	↔	/duru/		f.	[FUT]	↔	/ri/
c.	[NEAR PAST]	↔	Ø		g.	[INDEF(FUT)]	↔	/du/
d.	[DEF.PAST]	↔	Ø / [+SG]___				

As one can see from (10) I assume that the principal number distinctions are given by the features [±SINGULAR] and [±PLURAL]. In addition, there is a marker for trial number, but since this marker is never used to mark number on its own, it appears that trial is treated as a subset of plural, so that the trial is expressed by the feature [+PLURAL] in combination with [TRIAL], each realized by a separate marker.

Another example of alleged double marking of tense is shown in (12). As suggested in the glosses, it can be claimed that in these Huave verb forms, the category tense is expressed by the tense markers as well as by the subject person markers.

(12) *Huave* (Stairs & Erickson 1969:39–40)

    a. ap-ko-ma-mong-ïw   b. t-a-kweat-ay-eh
        FUT-DUB-3.FUT-pass-3p   PAST-3.PAST-leave-REFL-3p
        'Maybe they will pass.'   'They left each other.'

However, as Stairs and Erickson (1969) note, the verbal morphology of Huave is characterized by progressive conditioning in the morpheme sequences. Thus, in the complex verbs in (12) the tense marker, which comes first in the morpheme sequence, determines the realization of the third person marker; likewise, the third person marker can determine the shape of the plural marker, which is the last morpheme in the sequence. But if a reflexive marker intervenes between the third person marker and the plural marker, it is the reflexive marker that determines the shape of the plural marker (Stairs & Erickson 1969).

This means that the glosses in (12a,b) are misleading. For example, *-ma-* in (12a) is not a marker of third person *and* future; it is a third person marker which appears in that particular form because it is preceded by a future tense morpheme. Hence, there is no question of tense or any other feature being doubly marked.

Accordingly, for Huave as well as for Island Kiwai, the conclusion is that a complex verb form is a sequence of markers where each marker is the unique realization of some inflectional feature or combination of features.

More generally, I suspect that every case of 'extended exponence' will also allow an alternative analysis: either we have an instance of conditioned allomorphy, or we have two morphemes that for some reason tend to co-occur.[5] Sometimes the content of each marker can be relatively easily identified, as when the trial number in Island Kiwai is marked by the plural marker *-mo-* together with the trial marker *-bi-*. In other cases the exact contribution of each marker is more obscure. But notably, even where two markers apparently serve some specific function together, as in the case of the Dutch collocation *ge-...-te* shown in (4), we are not forced to say that the two markers realize one single morpheme. This point is nicely illustrated, I think, by the Norwegian prepositions shown in (7), which together function as the equivalent of 'ago'.

Moreover, this example also demonstrates that there is nothing specifically morphological about 'extended exponence'. That is, the behavior of *ge-...-te* is not one that distinguishes the constituents of words from the constituents of phrases. Two or more morphemes may act together to express a certain meaning non-compositionally even if the distribution of the morphemes in question is clearly syntactic. When free morphemes belonging to the major lexical categories are involved, such morpheme combinations are called idioms. But importantly, morpheme combinations consisting of two prepositions, as in the *for . . . siden* case, or of two affixal elements, as in the *ge-...-te* case, can be semantically similar to idioms, and the possibility that they are similar to idioms also syntactically cannot be excluded.

6.2.2 Fused marking

The other type of deviation from the agglutinative pattern to be found in the syntagmatic dimension is characterized by one single formative expressing more than one underlying morpheme. This phenomenon has been labeled 'fused marking', 'portmanteau marking', 'cumulation', or 'multiple exponence' (see, e.g., Matthews 1991, Spencer 1991, but see also ch. 3 n. 39 here). Here I will stick to the term 'fused marking', but it should be noted that I will not use it to refer to all cases where "more than one morphosyntactic property is realized in one unsegmentable morph or morphological process," which is Carstairs's (1987) definition of 'cumulative exponence'. Expressing more than one morpho-syntactic property is not necessarily equal to expressing more than one underlying morpheme or one syntactic terminal node. Agreement markers in particular often express more than one morphosyntactic property. I assume, although nothing in the following hinges on it, that an agreement marker represents a single node even if it expresses more than one property. That is, I assume that a feature bundle realized by one single agreement marker is one single morpheme underlyingly and not the result of fusion (see Halle & Marantz 1993).

However, as noted in 6.2.4, we often find markers that apparently express agreement plus something else. We will start by considering the tense and agreement paradigm of Kobon, which is given in (13).

(13) *Kobon tense and subject agreement suffixes* (Davies 1989:166)

	Present	Future	Past	Rem.past	Perfect
1s	-ab-in	-nab-in	-ɨn/-in	-nö	-b-in
2s	-ab-ön	-nab-ön	-an	-na	-b-an
3s	-ab	-nab	-ɨp	-a	-öp
1d	-ab-ul	-nab-ul	-ul	-lo	-b-ul
2/3d	-ab-il	-nab-il	-ɨl	-lö	-b-il
1p	-ab-un	-nab-un	-un	-no	-b-un
2p	-ab-im	-nab-im	-im	-be/-pe	-b-im
3p	-ab-öl	-nab-öl	-al	-la	-b-al

As we see, in the present and future tenses the only irregularity is that the marker of third person singular is phonologically zero. For all other person/number combinations there is an agreement marker which is separate from and follows the tense marker. In the perfect, which evidently belongs to the temporal system (the perfect markers are in complementary distribution with tense markers, whereas other aspect markers must be followed by a tense or perfect marker; moreover, the perfect can often be substituted for the simple past, and vice versa—see Davies 1989:167–170), a similar analysis goes through: the third person singular perfect marker *-öp* can be seen as the result of inserting an epenthetic vowel in front of the perfect marker to facilitate syllabification (/ö/ is a central vowel and hence the least specified of all vowels in Kobon; see Davies 1989:219). Thus, the perfect marker (*-b-* or *-p-*) is always separate from the agreement marker, which is zero in the third person singular.

Concerning the simple past tense, it seems that the markers suffixed to the verb in this tense represent only agreement, so that the past tense marker itself must be analyzed as zero. As for the marker that shows up in the third person singular of the simple past, it could be seen as an allomorph of the past marker or of the third person singular marker. Since both these markers are normally realized as zero, the decision could go either way.

The remaining issue now is the remote past tense. As we see, the suffixes that appear in the remote past cannot easily be segmented into tense markers and agreement markers. To be sure, the consonantal part of these suffixes is probably taken from the agreement markers. However, an analysis where the consonants are taken to be the realization of agreement while the vowels spell out the remote past is burdened with several problems. First, we would have to explain why the tense markers follow the agreement markers in the remote past even though the other tenses have the opposite order. Further, since the agreement markers in the remote past differ from the agreement markers used elsewhere, and there is also great variation in the quality of the vowel, the following lexical entries must be postulated which only appear in the remote past paradigm:

(14) *Kobon subject agreement markers*
    a. {[+1][+SG -PL], [+1][–SG +PL], [+2][+SG -PL]} ↔ /n/ / __[REM.PAST]
    b. {[+2], [–SG +PL]}   ↔ /p/ / __[REM.PAST]
    c. [–SG]   ↔ /l/ / __[REM.PAST]

(15) *Kobon remote past markers*
    a. [REM.PAST] ↔ /ö/ / {[+1] [+SG -PL], [–1] [–SG -PL]}__
    b. [REM.PAST] ↔ /o/ / [+1] __
    c. [REM.PAST] ↔ /e/ / {[+2] [–SG +PL]}
    d. [REM.PAST] ↔ /a/ / {[+2], [+SG -PL], [–SG +PL]}__

The entries given in (14) and (15) do not look very economic. Most of the markers are highly specified; moreover, they are specified to appear in several alternative environments. In addition, there is a large amount of reciprocal conditioning between the remote tense markers and the agreement markers. In this situation, the total amount of information that needs to be stored would not be any larger if the suffixes of the remote past were analyzed as fused markers—markers that spell out remote past tense and subject agreement simultaneously. The lexical entries that would be required by the latter analysis are given in (16). Note that the alternation between -*be* and -*pe* in the second person plural appears to be conditioned by phonology; according to Davies (1989:166), -*be* appears after obstruents and -*pe* elsewhere. Hence, I list here only the base form -*pe*.

(16) *Kobon remote past and subject agreement*
    a. [REM.PAST], [+1], [+SG -PL] ↔ /nö/
    b. [REM.PAST], [+2], [+SG -PL] ↔ /na/
    c. [REM.PAST], [+SG -PL]   ↔ /a/
    d. [REM.PAST], [+1], [–SG -PL] ↔ /lo/
    e. [REM.PAST], [–SG -PL]   ↔ /lö/
    f. [REM.PAST], [+1], [–SG +PL] ↔ /no/
    g. [REM.PAST], [+2], [–SG +PL] ↔ /pe/
    h. [REM.PAST], [–SG +PL]   ↔ /la/

In (16) there are eight entries, whereas in (14) and (15) there are seven altogether. If economy principles are relevant for the contents of the lexicon, it is still likely that (16) would be favored over (14)–(15), since the entries in (16) are relatively simple in that each of them is specified for only one environment. Even if there is an extra entry in (16) compared to (14)–(15), this is probably more than outweighed by the greater complexity of the entries in (14)–(15). It is tempting to conclude that (16) is the correct analysis of the markers that appear in the remote past in Kobon.

It should be noted that even if Kobon is a head-final language, according to the description in Davies (1989), so that we would not expect to see fusion of inflectional heads, postulating fused marking of subject agreement and tense is unproblematic. In preceding chapters I have argued that agreement features do not head phrases; agreement features, when present, are added to heads whose basic content is something else. Suppose now that subject agreement is located in a temporal head in Kobon, at least in the remote past. The result would be a terminal node whose feature content allows for the insertion of lexical entries like those listed in (16). As noted in section 6.2.3, many head-final languages have similar fused markers.[6]

Although fused marking often involves agreement, one can also find cases where a fused marker is the realization of two or more categories that we would assume to be generated in separate syntactic heads. An example is given in (17).

(17) *Bambara* (Kastenholz 1989:67)

    a. ń   mùso má   jέgε fèere
       1s   wife NEG.PAST fish buy
       'My wife did not buy fish.'

    b. dúnan yé   dɔlɔ   mìn
       guest AFF.PAST millet.beer drink
       'The guest drank millet beer.'

In Bambara, tense and polarity are expressed by one single marker (which can be preverbal or suffixed, see example (18), chapter 2. That is, there is no particular property of this marker that can be taken to represent only polarity or only tense (the past markers shown here contrast with the affirmative present *bέ* and the negative present *tέ*). Now if tense and polarity are base-generated in separate syntactic heads, there must have been some subsequent operation that has caused tense and polarity to end up in one single terminal node. In the terminology of Halle and Marantz (1993) this operation is fusion. But notably, Halle and Marantz assume that two nodes can only fuse if they are in the right structural relationship—more precisely, if they are sister nodes. Hence, in a case like (17) fusion must be preceded by head movement, either of the Pol° head to the T°(past) head or of the T°(past) head to the Pol° head, depending on which head is the higher one (it has been claimed that there is some cross-linguistic variation in the position of the Pol° head; see Cinque 1999). After the head movement operation, the Pol° head and the T°(past) head are sisters inside a complex head. The two heads can now fuse, so that a terminal node is created which contains both a tense feature and a polarity feature. In this terminal node a lexical item can be inserted which also is specified for polarity, as well as for tense.

In the theory of Halle and Marantz (1993, 1994), the concept of underspecification plays a vital part. That is, it is assumed that a lexical item can be inserted in a given node even if it contains only a subset of the features that are present in that node. Lexical items may not, on the other hand, be overspecified; that is, they may not contain substantial features that are not present in the node where they are to be inserted. This is clearly seen if we consider the role of impoverishment in the theory. An example of impoverishment discussed by Halle and Marantz (1994) is the absence of a second person plural clitic in Latin American Spanish, where a third person plural clitic is used to spell out the second person plural. If only underspecification were at play, we would expect the second person clitic *te* to be inserted in a node containing the features [+2 +PLURAL]. Since this is not what we get, Halle and Marantz propose that the feature [+2] is deleted in the context [+PLURAL], which is then an example of impoverishment. Since the result is a node that is unspecified for person, a marker which *is* specified for person, such as the [+2] clitic, cannot be inserted. Instead, a clitic appears which has no person features and which normally spells out nodes that are not [+1] or [+2].

This means that in a theory like that of Halle and Marantz (1993) the application of fusion must be determined by the content of the lexicon. To take Bambara as an example, it appears to be the case in this language that every lexical item with the specification [+PAST] also contains a polarity feature. Since overspecification is not possible, these items can only be inserted in terminal nodes that contain both a [+PAST] feature and a polarity feature. That is, unless the Pol° head fuses with T°(past), neither polarity nor tense can be spelled out, and the derivation will presumably crash.

But notably, it can be argued that fusion is a syntactic process: it operates on syntactic terminal nodes and has syntactic terminal nodes as its output. The elements that the fused nodes are matched with, on the other hand, are simply listed in the lexicon. Hence, it is not necessarily the case that there are any specifically morphological aspects to the phenomenon of fusion.

Another point which should be mentioned in this connection is that in all alleged instances of fused marking, an alternative analysis is also possible, according to which the apparently fused marking is really zero marking in combination with conditioned allomorphy in the overt marker. In some cases, the latter analysis will even be the preferred one, as we saw in the discussion of Persian in section 6.2.2. In other cases, it is harder to find the evidence to tip the scales. Consider once again the tense and subject agreement paradigm in Kobon listed in (13). We see that one could argue that the suffixes that appear in the remote past tense in Kobon only spell out agreement and the remote past tense is realized by a zero marker, just like the general past. That is, instead of being included in the content of the marker, as in (15), the feature [REMOTE

PAST] should be given as the contextual feature which conditions the insertion of this particular set of agreement markers.

On the latter analysis, the cases under investigation have even less to do with morphology in the traditional sense. Zero markers can clearly have a syntactic distribution. For example, in many languages the head that hosts the [+Q] feature in questions is realized as zero, while in other languages it is spelled out as a particle. Similarly, positively marked polarity heads are often phonologically empty, in contrast with phonologically non-null negatively marked polarity heads. The other side of the coin, the conditioned allomorphy, is also not restricted to word-internal environments, as we will see below.

As for the question of which analysis is the preferable one, it seems that the two analyses are equivalent as far as descriptive adequacy is concerned. In Kobon, for example, the observed forms could clearly be generated either way. It may be possible, though, to make a choice between the two analyses with reference to their explanatory adequacy: that is, on the basis of considerations of the analyses from the point of view of the language learner. In other words, one should ask if a child acquiring Kobon would postulate that the language has two phonologically empty tense markers, one for the general past and one for the remote past, and that the general past marker triggers insertion of the default subject agreement markers, whereas the remote past marker requires that the subject agreement marker must be chosen from a special set of allomorphs. Alternatively, would the evidence in (13) lead to the conclusion that the remote past tense fuses with subject agreement? But as long as we do not know if there are restrictions on the appearance of zero markers in a structure (apart, perhaps, from the requirement that a zero marker must share the distribution of at least one overt marker, as suggested in section 3.6.2), or if fusion is really an option, such questions cannot be answered conclusively, and I will leave them open.[7]

6.2.3   Allomorphy

We now turn to the paradigmatic dimension. As noted in the introduction, in the paradigmatic dimension the 'one morpheme to many markers' deviation is manifested as allomorphy. In addition to what Halle and Marantz (1993) refer to as context-free allomorphy, which means that different lexical items are chosen as the realization of a given node depending on the feature content of that node, and which will not concern us here, there is also context-dependent or conditioned allomorphy, where the realization of a given node is determined by other morphemes that are present in the structure.

In some cases of conditioned allomorphy, the conditioning factor is phonological. In other cases, however, the alternation between two or more realizations cannot be explained as a consequence of phonology. Rather, the feature content of the surrounding morphemes must also be taken into consideration. We have already seen some examples of such grammatically conditioned allomorphy, in the [–1] markers of Island Kiwai, shown in (11), and in the Huave third person markers, shown in (12).

Booij (1997) argues that allomorphy of this type is evidence that grammar contains a separate morphological module, since the distributional patterns of allomorphs cannot be deduced from phonological or syntactic principles. But I must point out that allomorphic variation does not have relevance only inside words. The conditioning factor is not always contained in the same word as the morpheme that undergoes the alternation. The Spanish spurious *se*, which appears instead of an ordinary third person dative clitic if followed by a third person accusative clitic, is a case in point (see Halle & Marantz 1994 for an analysis in terms of impoverishment). Moreover, as discussed by Odden (1987, 1990, 1996), allomorphic rules may be sensitive to syntactic structure. One example is the Shortening rule in Kimatuumbi, which shortens long vowels under certain syntactic conditions. As demonstrated in (18), the long stem vowel in *kịkóloombe* 'cleaning shell' is shortened if the noun is followed by an adjective which belongs to the same DP. This should be compared to (18c), where *kịkóloombe* is followed by the same adjective, but this time the adjective belongs to a different DP. Then there is no shortening, as we see. Shortening is also absent in a subject nominal that is followed by a verb, as in (18d), or by the negation, as in (18e).

(18) *Kimatuumbi* (Odden 1996:219)

    a. kịkóloombe
       'cleaning shell'

    b. n-aa-m-pé-ị   kịkólombe   kịkúlú
        1sS-REM-3sO-give-PAST   shell   large
        'I gave him a large shell.'

    c. n-aa-m-pé-ị   kịkóloombe   kịkúlú
        1sS-REM-3sO-give-PAST   shell   large
        'I gave the large one a shell.'

    d. kịkóloombe   chaapúwaanjịke
        shell   broken
        'The shell is broken.'

    e. n-aa-kị-bwén-ị   kịkóloombe   lịịlị
        1sS-REM-7(Obj)-see-PAST   shell   NEG
        'I didn't see the shell.'

Hence, the rule of shortening is evidently sensitive to the syntactic relation between the trigger and the target. Since it can also be shown that Shortening interacts with certain phonological rules that are lexical on the traditional criteria, Odden (1987, 1990, 1996) concludes that phonology applies after syntax, so that syntactic information is available to all phonological rules. This is in effect another formulation of the Late Insertion approach adopted in this work (see chapter 1).

Hayes (1990), on the other hand, argues that it is not necessary the case that phonological rules have direct access to syntactic information. Instead, he proposes that the alternants are fully formed without reference to syntax but each alternant is specified to appear in a frame that may be syntactically defined.

However, regardless of which analysis one chooses, that of Odden or that of Hayes (which, as Odden 1990 points out, are empirically very similar), the fact remains that the allomorphy shown in (18) is conditioned by the syntactic environment of the alternating morpheme.[8] Hence, if one of the main responsibilities of the morphology module is to take care of allomorphy that is not phonologically conditioned, as Booij (1997) suggests, it does not follow that the morphology module deals with word formation. Rather, it deals with the realization of individual morphemes in various environments, where the relevant environmental factors may be found inside or outside the word that the alternating morpheme belongs to.

If it is nevertheless more often the case that the trigger for an allomorphic alternation belongs to the same word as the target, this has to do with the properties that constitute words. As argued in chapter 1 and elsewhere in this work, 'word' is a label for a string of morphemes that regularly appear adjacent to each other and in a certain order. This means that if the conditioning factor is contained in the same word as the element that undergoes alternation, each alternant will probably occur relatively frequently, and the alternation has a good chance of surviving. If, on the other hand, a morpheme has an allomorph whose appearance is dependent on some other morpheme which is not part of the same word, one can imagine a situation where the alternation is seen relatively infrequently, and where it will easily get lost.

6.2.4 Homonymi

The last deviation we look at here is the 'many morphemes to one marker' deviation in the paradigmatic dimension, which manifests itself as homonymi. It should first be noted that there can be homonymi between lexical roots, as well as between inflectional elements. Examples of the former are easy to find in English, such as the triple *right*, *rite*, and *write*. However, this type of homonymi is purely accidental; it is the outcome of the phonological developments that have shaped individual lexical elements over time. Because it has nothing to do with grammar there is not much to say about it in the present context.

Accidental homonymi can also be found with affixes. For example, in English the suffix -*(e)s* marks the plural of nouns but also the third singular present of verbs. These two markers are probably not in any way directly related, and the homonymi is probably purely accidental.

A quite different type of affixal homonymi is shown in (19). As indicated, Finnish nouns have distinct forms for singular and plural in the majority of cases. The exceptional cases are the comitative and the instructive, where the singular form is identical to the plural form. As this is a pervasive fact of

(19) *Finnish* (Carstairs 1987:120)
    A partial paradigm of pöytä *'table'*

Case	Singular	Plural
Nominative	pöytä	pöydät
Genitive	pöydän	pöytien
Partitive	pöytää	pöytiä
Essive	pöytänä	pöytinä
Comitative	pöytine	pöytine
Instructive	pöydin	pöydin

Finnish nominal inflection, we are clearly dealing with an example of *systematic homonymi* or *syncretism*, where a contrast between two values of a morphosyntactic feature is neutralized in the context of some other feature, so that the underlying contrast is not reflected in the realization of the morphemes that are involved.

Various proposals have been put forth concerning the analysis of syncretism. In Zwicky (1985b) and Stump (1993) syncretism is handled by means of so-called rules of referral; and in Halle and Marantz (1993, 1994), Halle (1997), and Noyer (1998) it is analyzed as a consequence of impoverishment. I will not go into the details of these analyses here, I will merely note that syncretism must evidently be represented in the grammar. But just like allomorphy, syncretism is not reducible to phonology or syntax. That is, it appears that syncretism is another phenomenon which is genuinely morphological. However, it is also similar to allomorphy in that it does not deal exclusively with the construction of morphologically complex words but, rather, with the shape of morphemes which may or may not be words in their own right.

As already mentioned, syncretism is *systematic* homonymi, which means that syncretism is only possible in paradigms—in matrixes of lexical items where one item differs from its neighbor only in the value of one (morphosyntactic) feature. Further, paradigmatic homonymi must have some regularity in order to be termed systematic. For example, according to Carstairs (1987) inflectional homonymi is systematic only if it generalizes to the paradigm of every member of a given lexical class. Consider now the paradigm of English personal pronouns given in (20).

As we see, in the first and third person there is a formally expressed distinction between nominative and accusative case and between singular and plural number. In the third person singular, there is also a distinction between masculine and feminine gender. In the second person, however, all contrasts other than that of person are neutralized, so that there is only one form of the second person pronoun. This is arguably a case of systematic homonymi. It generalizes not only to the class of personal pronouns but to the whole language—nowhere in English is there a formal case or number distinction in the second person. Moreover, this systematic homonymi meets Carstairs's (1987:116) definition of syncretism: the homonymous forms are simultaneous exponents of more than

(20) *English personal pronouns*

Case, gender, and number	Person		
	1	2	3
Nominative, feminine, singular	I	you	she
Nominative, masculine, singular	I	you	he
Accusative, feminine, singular	me	you	her
Accusative, masculine, singular	me	you	him
Nominative, feminine, plural	we	you	they
Nominative, masculine, plural	we	you	they
Accusative, feminine, plural	us	you	them
Accusative, masculine, plural	us	you	them

one morphosyntactic property, and the context of the homonymi can be stated entirely in terms of these properties. That is, being an instance of syncretism, the homonymi in the second person pronouns in English is an example of what Carstairs takes to be the most common and most stable type of systematic homonymi.

But obviously, the case at hand has nothing to do with the formation of morphologically complex words. This indicates that just like allomorphy, systematic homonymi or syncretism is a question of the form of individual morphemes. This is then as far as morphology goes. It can delete features from terminal nodes, in the process of impoverishment, and it serves to pick out from the lexicon the form that will realize each of the terminal nodes in the syntactic structure. But whether or not these nodes are included in complex words is outside the domain of morphology proper; as argued throughout this work, this is something that should be attributed to the syntactic component of grammar.

6.3 Derivation and compounding

The argumentation in the preceding chapters, which led to the conclusion that morphologically complex words are formed in syntax, only took inflectional elements into consideration. But according to a view that has been advocated by Chomsky (1970), Anderson (1982, 1992), Perlmutter (1988), and others, word-building operations are performed in two separate components, such that derivation and compounding are pre-syntactic while inflection is post-syntactic. This means that the claim that inflection is executed in syntax has no direct bearing on the analysis of derivation and compounding. Thus, at this point some comments on derivation and compounding are clearly in place. I start by looking briefly at the relation between inflection and derivation.

It has often been noted that inflection and derivation are similar in that the same formal devices are used in both types of word formation. Further, even if in most cases it is derivation that feeds inflection, it can also be the other way around, as in (21).

(21) *Central Alaskan Yupik*   (Woodbury & Sadock 1986:235)
       Liisaq   u-na   tai-gu-ur-tuq.
       Lisa-ABS   this.one-ABS   come-IND.3s-utter-IND.3s
       'Lisa uttered: "This one is coming."'

Here *-ur-* 'utter' is an affixal verb which combines with a proposition syntactically and forms a word with the verb of that proposition morphologically. The verb inside the complement of *-ur-* is fully inflected before it is combined with the matrix verb, with the result that the inflectional marker that belongs with the lower verb appears inside the affixal higher verb in the complex word.

More cases of complex words with inflectional markers appearing inside derivational markers are discussed by Pulleyblank and Akinlabi (1988), Booij (1993), and Rainer (1995), among others. Notably, if inflection is syntactic, as I have argued in this study, and if inflection can appear inside derivation, then derivation must also be syntactic. Similarly, since inflection can also appear inside compounds (Booij 1993, 1995), compounding must also be a syntactic operation.

For some derivations, it is possible to find arguments that point directly to a syntactic analysis. Consider the Hindi morphological causative shown in (22a,b).

(22) *Hindi*   (Kulikov 1993:147)
       a. Ādmī-ne   dhīre   mātā-se   bacce-ko   hil-vā-yā.
           man-ERG   slowly   mother-INSTR   child-DAT   eat-CAUS-PAST
           'The man slowly had the mother feed the child.'

       b. Ādmī-ne   mātā-se   bacce-ko   dhīre   hil-vā-yā.
           man-ERG   mother-INSTR   child-dat   slowly   eat-CAUS-PAST
           'The man had the mother feed the child slowly.'

As we see, the adverbial that is combined with the morphological causative can modify the causing event or the caused event, depending on the syntactic position of that adverb. This effect indicates that the two events must at some stage of the derivation be represented in separate syntactic positions, so that the underlying structure of the construction is biclausal. When the adverbial is situated in a relatively low position, it takes scope over the base verb only (the caused event); when it occupies a position higher up, it takes scope over the causative verb (the causing event). Since the verbal elements appear ultimately as one verb form, they must have been joined by movement taking place in syntax.

And certainly, a distinction like that of Anderson (1982, 1992), where inflection is defined as "what is relevant to the syntax" is hard to maintain if one considers the degree to which causatives and other types of derivations interact with syntax. All in all, there seems to be little reason to have inflection and derivation in separate blocks.

For some linguists, this insight has led to the view that both inflection and derivation are executed in the lexicon, in a pre-syntactic word-formation component. If one's theoretical framework opens no way of giving a syntactically based account for all complex words, this is of course the logical conclusion. Witness, for example, the following statement in Lieber (1981:3): "Since derivation and compounding have been counted as lexical processes within all theories of word formation to date, I will argue that inflectional stem allomorphs must be available in the lexicon to feed those processes." It is evident that in this case lexicalism was not chosen for any principled reason but was resorted to because plausible alternatives were lacking at that time. But in light of such investigations into derivational word formation as Baker (1988a) and Hale and Keyser (1993), one might just as well choose a syntacticist position. As pointed out in Drijkoningen (1994), the syntacticist hypothesis is more in agreement with the spirit of minimalism, since it assumes only one computation which generalizes over all types of affixation and only two levels of representation where well-formedness can be evaluated, namely PF and LF. Further arguments in favor of the syntactic view are found in Marantz (1997, 2001).

Notably, as far as their phonological representations are concerned it is not possible to draw a sharp line between inflectional and derivational morphemes. In other words, they are not different at PF. The intuitive distinction between inflection and derivation must therefore be captured with reference to LF. The solution I propose is very simple: derivational morphemes belong to one of the lexical categories, whereas inflectional morphemes are functional elements. This is relevant at LF, since at this interface, lexical morphemes are interpreted as denoting events, properties, and referents (for V, A, and N, respectively),[9] while functional morphemes contribute in other ways to the formation of propositions; for example, a tense morpheme serves to relate the speech event to other events (see, e.g., Giorgi & Pianesi 1997, Julien 2001) and determiners make arguments out of nominals (Longobardi 1994).[10]

It follows that derivation is similar to compounding in that both operations involve combination of lexical elements. The difference between these two types of word formation is that derivation involves one bound lexical element—that is, an element which always co-occurs with some other lexical element—whereas in compounds, either element can also appear independently of the other.

As already noted, some derivations, such as the causative in (22a,b), are arguably formed by syntactic movement. A similar analysis has been put forward for one particular type of compounding—namely, of noun incorporation, the process whereby a verb forms a word with an argument nominal (see, e.g., Baker 1988a). For other derivations and compounds, a movement analysis is not as readily available. However, this does not necessarily mean that the complex words in question are not formed in syntax. Josefsson (1997) and Marantz (1997) propose that words may be formed by Merge as well as by Move. That is, some complex words are base-generated complex heads. As Anders Holmberg (personal communicartion) points out to me, it often happens that phrases are built to a certain complexity before they are inserted into a larger syntactic structure. The idea that a similar procedure is possible for complex heads is therefore rather plausible.

The tendency for derivational affixes to appear inside inflectional ones, if both types are present, is a consequence of different semantic functions of lexical and functional categories. In this respect, there is no difference between affixal lexical elements, appearing in derivations, and non-affixal lexical elements, appearing in compounds. When two lexical categories are combined, either by Merge or by Move, only one of them projects, and the complex as a whole will belong to the lexical category of the projecting element—the head. In other words, the category of the head will override the category of the non-head and prevent non-heads from having their own propositional function. For example, if the noun *child* is combined with the adjective *-ish*, the result *childish* is syntactically an adjective and semantically a property. The syntactic realization of the referent variable of *child* as an argument is blocked, so *child* is not going to be combined with functional elements; only the adjectival element *-ish* will.

Thus, functional categories are normally added only when a (possibly complex) lexical category is ready to be given its syntactic function. The projecting category then determines which functional categories must be added to complete the derivation. Hence, in the normal case, lexical categories (into which roots and derivational affixes are finally inserted) are introduced into the derivation before functional categories (into which inflectional morphemes are inserted).

As for the question of why some lexical elements are affixal whereas others are not, I think that the discussion of derivation in Josefsson (1997) gives us a hint. Josefsson argues that derivational affixes perform certain functions with respect to their host. Either the derivational affix is an operator or it binds and controls the θ-roles related to the host.

As an example of a derivational affix that is an operator, Josefsson gives the Swedish negative prefix *o-* 'un-'. She shows that *o-* can be characterized as negating a scalar feature of its host. That is why we find adjectives like *o-viss* 'un-certain' and *o-sound* 'un-sound' but not *o-grön 'un-green' and *o-oval 'un-oval'.[11]

In fact, the term *derivational* may be inappropriate for an element like *o-*. Being a negation, it is functional rather than lexical. If the difference between derivation and inflection is that derivational affixes represent lexical elements while inflectional affixes represent functional elements, as I have claimed above, it follows that *o-* is an inflectional affix. However, it differs from inflectional affixes in its optionality, and because of this, it is traditionally referred to as a derivational affix.[12]

In any case, it is much more common for derivational affixes to interact with the argument structure of their host. This is what Josefsson (1997) refers to as binding and controlling of θ-roles. For example, she argues that the suffix *-ning*, exemplified in (23), binds the event role of its host. Hence, the derived word as a whole refers to this event.

(23) *Swedish*   (Josefsson 1997:86)
    Jan-s   mål-ning   av   staket-et
    Jan-POSS paint-*ning* of   fence-DEF.SG
    'Jan's painting of the fence'

In Josefsson's terminology, the θ-roles associated with the root which are not bound by the affix are said to be *controlled* by the affix. As we see, these θ-roles may still be available outside the derived word. In (23), both the agent and the patient role of the verb *måla* 'paint' are assigned to arguments outside the derived word. (Actually, Josefsson assumes that the non-head of a complex word is not assigned a lexical category, only a semantic category, but I will abstract away from this here.)

Another example of binding and control of θ-roles is given in (24). As (24b) shows, the adverbial suffix *-bar* '-able' does not allow the agent role of its verbal host to be overtly expressed. Josefsson suggests that this is because *-bar* binds the agent role. The patient role, by contrast, is *controlled* by the suffix *-bar*, and it may be assigned to a constituent outside of the derived adjective, as shown in (24a).

(24) *Swedish*   (Josefsson 1997:115)
    a. en tvätt-bar skjorta   b. * en av   mig tvätt-bar skjorta
        a   wash-able shirt   a by   me   wash-able shirt
        'a washable shirt'

What the affixes shown above have in common is that they must stand in a local relation to some lexical element. The prefix *o-* needs to combine with a predicate denoting a scalar property, and the suffixes *-ning* and *-bar* need to combine with a telic predicate that assigns an agent role (see Josefsson 1997:89, 102). It is these intrinsic properties, I believe, that are responsible for the bound appearance of derivational affixes. The meaning and function of derivational affixes is such that they must co-occur with some other lexical element; they can never appear in isolation or in combination with only inflectional elements.

Concerning compounding, Josefsson (1997) shows that in Swedish, restrictions on compounding can be deduced from the principles that apply when the resulting complex words are inserted into larger syntactic structures. For example, while the noun-verb compound *ving-klippa* 'wing-cut' is OK, the superficially rather similar *gräs-klippa* 'grass-cut' is not. According to Josefsson, the reason for this is that in Swedish, an incorporated nominal cannot serve to check the telicity of the verb (in the sense of Tenny 1987, 1994; Borer 1993; Arad 1998). Only an argument that can move to the Spec of the appropriate functional projection can perform this function. Hence, a complex word consisting of a verb and one of its arguments is only possible if another nominal can be generated as the structural object of the verb. So, while (25a) is OK, (25b) is out.[13]

(25) *Swedish* (Josefsson 1997:69)
 a. Bond-en   ving-klipp-te gås-en.
  farmer-DEF.SG wing-cut-PAST goose-DEF.SG
  'The farmer cut the wings of the goose.'

 b.*Grann-en   gräs-klipp-te hela dag-en.
  neighbor-DEF.SG grass-cut-PAST whole day-DEF.SG

The ungrammaticality of (25b) indicates that Swedish is somehow different from languages where an incorporated object is able to check the telicity of the verb in the same way as non-incorporated objects. Josefsson argues that in Swedish, referentiality is associated with determiners. An incorporated nominal in Swedish is combined with the verb by Merge and necessarily lacks a determiner. Hence, it is non-referential and therefore not able to check the telicity of the verb. In a language where nominals can be incorporated by means of syntactic movement, by contrast, the presence of a determiner is not required to make an expression referential (Baker 1988a, 1996).[14] Thus, in polysynthetic languages a bare incorporated noun stem can have the syntactic function of the object, whereas in Swedish and other non-polysynthetic languages, it may not.

It can be concluded from this brief discussion of derivation and compounding that there is no need to postulate specific, possibly lexical, rules for the combination of lexical categories, or rules that specifically restrict the combination of such elements. It can be maintained that lexical elements can in principle be freely combined, either by merge or by move. The observed restrictions arguably follow from more general syntactic and semantic principles. We would expect this to be the case in all languages; where derivation and compounding is more restricted than in the Scandinavian languages, the reason for this probably lies outside the word-forming operations themselves.

Notes

1. In addition, there are apparently superfluous markers and semantically empty markers. These fall outside of Carstairs's classification, which only takes meaningful elements into consideration.

2. This analysis was suggested to me by Anders Holmberg. See also Muysken (1995) on Quechua.

3. The similarity between complex words with unpredictable meanings on one hand and phrasal idioms on the other is also stressed by Marantz (1997).

4. Booij (1997) also notes that conditioned allomorphy can have the effect of 'extended exponence'.

5. Cf. Matthews (1991:181), who states that "in most instances of extended exponence it is possible to identify one formative as the main exponent."

6. Carstairs (1987) suggests that in Turkish, negation is fused with aorist tense and also, in the third person singular, with subject agreement. This analysis is clearly problematic for the proposals I put forth in chapter 3 concerning the syntax of

Turkish and other head-final languages. However, in Kornfilt (1997) the negative aorist verb forms are described as essentially agglutinating, which differ from other forms only in the realization of the aorist, which is *-z/-y/-Ø* in the negative but *-(A)r* elsewhere.

7. Booij (1997) notes that the Dutch strong verb form *liep* 'walked' can be analyzed either as a past tense stem allomorph which is followed by a phonologically empty past tense suffix, or as the direct expression of 'walk'+[PAST]. The first analysis is reflected in the form *liep-te*, which children tend to produce. Here it is clear that *liep* is seen as an allomorph of the verb stem. Booij also points out that the fact that in the adult language, *liep* blocks the formation of *liep-te*, indicates that *liep* is already specified for past tense; in other words, in the adult language the second analysis takes effect.

Halle and Marantz (1993), by contrast, see ablauted, suffixless past tense forms as the combination of a ablauted stem allomorph with a zero allomorph of the past marker. Each allomorph must then be specified to co-occur with the other. One might speculate if this does not make the system unnecessary complex.

8. Cowper and Rice (1987) argue that the domain of Shortening is the phonological phrase, so that there is no direct reference to syntactic structure. For a discussion of the problems that arise from a prosodic approach to the Kimatuumbi data, see Odden (1987).

9. The categorial status of P appears to be indeterminate between that of a lexical element and that of a functional one—see, for example, Emonds (1985).

10. The lexical/functional distinction is probably at the heart of the split between inflection and derivation noted by Badecker and Caramazza (1989), who describe a patient whose inflection is impaired but whose derivation is intact. It is likely that this observed difference is due to problems with functional categories.

Drijkoningen (1994) has a somewhat different analysis of the LF-distinction between derivation and inflection. He proposes that derivational processes are characterized by a simultaneous change of syntactic category and semantic category, where the syntactic categories are V, N, and A and the corresponding semantic categories are Event, Referent, and Property. Inflection, on the other hand, is said to change only the syntactic category. This is connected to the idea that inflectional affixes are operators semantically, so that they bind the semantic variable of the base without changing its semantic category. While this system allows for an explanation of inheritance phenomena it also has some odd consequences as it stands. For one thing, the definition of inflection appears to exclude such categories as tense, which do not change the syntactic category of the base (it is stated explicitly in a note that tense is of the syntactic category V). Derivational processes that do not change the syntactic category could also not be recognized in Drijkoningen's system. On the other hand, the gerundive nominals in English, for example, would have to be viewed as inflection since there is no change of semantic category.

11. Haegeman (1995) assumes that constituent negation does not involve an operator. However, although a constituent negation obviously does not take sentential scope, it can still be maintained that it is an operator, but with a scope that is more limited than that of sentential negations. For example, in the case of *o-* 'un-', one can argue that it forms a complex head with its host and only takes scope over its sister within that complex head. As Josefsson (1997) points out, the verb *o-fred-a* 'un-peace+V-INF' means 'disturb'; it is not the negative of *fred-a* 'peace+V-INF', which

means 'protect'. Hence, it appears that *o-* in *o-fred-a* only negates the element *fred* 'peace'.

12. Strikingly, the sentential negator *icke* 'not' can also appear inside complex words, as in *icke-verbal* 'non-verbal'. Since *icke* is normally a non-bound element, the form *icke-verbal* may be viewed as a compound, in spite of the functional nature of the negator. This shows that the boundaries between different types of word-formation are not always very sharp.

13. Object-verb compounds are also fine inside nominalizations. For example, *gräs-klipp-are* 'grass-cut-er' is perfectly well formed. This fact is noted by Josefsson (1997), who points out that when a verb is nominalized, there is no need to check the telicity or other features associated with the verb. This is expected, since no verbal functional projections are generated over a nominalized verb. Thus, incorporating the object does not create problems in such cases.

14. In the following Southern Tiwa example, we see that the incorporated nominal can be definite or indefinite even if no determiner is present:

(i) *Southern Tiwa*   (Allen et al. 1984:293)
    Ti-shut-pe-ban.
    1s-shirt-make-PAST
    'I made the/a shirt.'

However, although it is only the noun that incorporates, the object DP may still contain a determiner, which is left behind when the noun incorporates, as in (ii).

(ii) *Southern Tiwa*   (Allen et al. 1984:294)
     Yede   ti-shut-pe-ban.
     that   1s-shirt-make-PAST
     'I made that shirt.'

The point is that in a polysynthetic language like Southern Tiwa, nominal objects do not obligatorily occur with determiners.

Conclusion: The Nature of Words

In this work I have claimed that a word is a morpheme sequence that shows internal cohesion and has independent distribution relative to other morphemes. I have argued that these properties stem from the syntax: although each morpheme is inserted separately into syntactic structure, syntax may cause some groups of morphemes to show the behavior that is characteristic of words. More precisely, as a consequence of the syntactic configurations that they appear in, it often happens that two or more morphemes together can be moved around relatively to other morphemes, or that two or more morphemes form a sequence that cannot freely be interrupted. If two given morphemes form a distributional unit of this kind every time they appear together, the two morphemes in question will be perceived as one word.

This means that 'word' in the non-phonological sense is a distributional concept. That is, what all words have in common is their distributional properties. But crucially, there is not one single syntactic configuration that underlies all complex words. I have suggested that there are at least three configurations that may cause two or more morphemes to be perceived as one word. Morphemes that constitute one word may be included in one complex syntactic head, such that one morpheme is adjoined to another; alternatively, they may be in a Spec-Head relation structurally, or else they may be just a sequence of syntactic heads that are spelled out in the base-generated order. It is possible that other configrations may also have words as their output, but I take the three configurations just mentioned to be the more important ones.

On this approach, words are not necessarily syntactic constituents. A word is a syntactic constituent only if it is also a complex syntactic head. In all other cases, the word does not correspond to any syntactic unit. And as for the idea that the true nature of words is to be found in a component of grammar that is separate from syntax and deals exclusively with the shape of words—in a morphology component—my answer is that the morphology component does not deal with word formation but with the shape of individual morphemes, whether or not these morphemes are included in morphologically complex words.

The consequence of these claims is that words do not really have a place in grammar at all. From the point of view of grammar, 'word' is an epiphenomenon and not a basic concept.

Still, there seems to be no doubt that words do somehow exist. Notably, the term 'word' is perfectly meaningful even to those who have no linguistic training. That is, words are psychologically real, as pointed out by Sapir (1921) and by numerous researchers after him. A typical statement in this respect is the following, from McGregor (1990). Note that 'd-word' is short for 'distributional word', a term which is conceptually identical to 'grammatical word' as defined in section 1.4.2.

> Although single d-words could be elicited and discussed in isolation—native speakers of Gooniyandi were willing to explain their meaning to me— smaller items could not be. Smaller items such as bound morphemes did not seem to have psychological reality, and were not identified on the few occasions when, for one reason or another, I cited them in isolation. (They were, however, immediately identified in retrospect once I provided an example in a d-word.) (McGregor 1990:135)

However, the psychological reality of words and the lack of awareness of word-internal morphemes should not be taken to mean that the elements that are commonly termed words are grammatical constituents or that they form a homogeneous class in any theoretically interesting way. The psychological reality of words is probably a consequence of their distributional properties: since words are the minimal morpheme strings that can be used as utterances and are also the minimal morpheme strings which may be permuted more or less freely, words are the minimal linguistic units that speakers consciously can manipulate. It is then no surprise that words are something that speakers are generally aware of. Word-internal morphemes, on the other hand, cannot be consciously manipulated the way words can, and, because of this, word-internal morphemes are less salient than words in the awareness of speakers.

Not only is the existence of words firmly established in speakers' minds, it is also usually clear which morpheme sequences are words and which are not. Whether as linguists or as speakers of one or more languages, we normally have no problems in identifying the words of the languages that we are familiar with. That is, although I have pointed to a number of examples in the foregoing chapters of morpheme sequences with an ambiguous word status, such cases are the exception rather than the rule. Now since in the majority of cases we are quite confident about the word status of any given morpheme sequence—we can tell without hesitation whether it is one word or several words—one can easily get the impression that there is something special about words: being a word means having some deep property which is the cause of the observable distributional properties of the word. If this is correct, grammar must include one or more components specialized in the formation of words, so that at some point in the derivation of a linguistic expression, certain morpheme combinations can acquire the property that turns them into words.

What I have claimed in the foregoing is that there is no such component. I have not said that there are several structural configurations of morphemes that allow words to be *formed* from the morphemes that are involved. I have said that several structural configurations allow two or more morphemes to be *perceived* as one word. This means that there are no word-forming processes applying to morphemes in certain configurations. Grammar does not contain a device that takes morphemes as input and gives words as output. There is no black box that morpheme sequences must pass through in order to become words. It is the configurations themselves that give us the words. That is all there is to 'word formation'.

On this view, words are rather like constellations of stars: in many cases, there is no particular bond or relation between individual stars belonging to one and the same constellation. Rather, the constellations that we see are a consequence of our point of view. Seen from Earth, some stars form striking patterns that we cannot help but recognize, even if these patterns have no existence outside of our cognition. Still, in some cases stars that seem to be related to each other from our point of view are in fact also close to each other physically. But the point is that this is not decisive. If two stars are close to each other seen from here, we take them to be related whether or not there is any real physical relation between them.

In the same way, words are entities that we cannot help but perceive. When morphemes regularly appear together and in a certain order, we recognize the pattern that they form, and we label it a 'word'. On the basis of this pattern, we assume that there is a particular relation between the morphemes.

Although there are several morpheme configurations that can give rise to words, the closest syntactic relation is found between morphemes that form a complex syntactic head. In this configuration, morphemes will necessarily form a tight sequence; moreover, they may fuse (a *morpheme*-forming process), so that what is more than one morpheme underlyingly may be spelled out by one single lexical item. Because of this, complex syntactic heads sometimes appear to be more word-like than other configurations. Still, the intuition that there is a word can be just as strong for morphemes in other configurations. Whenever syntax causes a sequence of morphemes to show internal cohesion and independent distribution, the sequence is a word from our point of view.

This means that in the many cases where we, as speakers and as linguists, are quite confident that a given morpheme sequence is a word, this is a consequence of the distributional properties of the sequence, which in turn derive from the syntax. Compare, for example, the Japanese construction in (1) to the Northern Saami construction in (2). In (1), the verbal word contains both a main verb and an auxiliary with their respective inflectional markers. In (2), the main verb is in a separate word from the auxiliary.

(1) *Japanese* (= ex. (45), ch. 3)
     Taroo-ga   susi-o   zenbu   tabe-te-simat-ta.
     Taroo-NOM   sushi-ACC   all   eat-GER-finish-PAST
     'Taroo finished eating all the sushi.'

(2) *Northern Saami*
    Biret   geargga-i   borad-eam-es.
    Biret.NOM   finish-PAST.3s eat-PROG-LOC
    'Biret finished eating'

As argued in chapter 3, Japanese has the head-final syntax that is character-ized by movement of VP and of every IP-projection to the next higher Spec. Arguments are either inside VP or in Spec positions in the CP-domain. This means that all verbally related elements always form a tight sequence: as sketched in (3), each of them will be immediately preceded by the head of its complement.

(3) $[_{CP} (\text{Arg}^*) [_{IP} [[[(\text{Arg}^*) \mathbf{V}^\circ] \mathbf{Ger}^\circ t_{VP}] \mathbf{Aux}^\circ t_{Ger^\circ}] \mathbf{T}^\circ t_{Aux^\circ}]]$

As long as the verbal elements do not normally appear in other environments as well—see the discussion of Lezgian in section 3.6.2—they will all be taken to belong to one complex word in this configuration.

In Northern Saami, complex verbal words are formed by head movement—see the discussion in section 2.2. However, the head movement does not necessarily operate all the way from the bottom to the top of the derivation. In (2), the verb *borad-* 'eat' moves to the head that hosts the progressive marker and then to the head that hosts the locative marker. The verb *gearga-* 'finish' moves to the head that hosts tense and then to the head that hosts subject agreement. This means that there are two verbal complex heads in this construc-tion. As we see, there are also two complex verbal words. The reason we have two verbal words here instead of just one is that the two heads are not always strictly adjacent in the linear order. For example, they may be separated by the object of the lower verb, as in (4).

(4) *Northern Saami*
    Biret   geargga-i   guoli   borad-eam-es.
    Biret.NOM   finish-PAST.3s fish-ACC eat-PROG-LOC
    'Biret finished eating (the) fish.'

And in the corresponding question, the higher complex head moves to the front of the question marker, while the lower complex head is not affected. This is shown in (5a). Moreover, a natural answer to this question consists of just the higher complex head—see (5b).

(5) *Northern Saami*
    a. Geargga-i-go   Biret   (guoli)   borad-eam-es?
        finish-PAST.3s-Q Biret.NOM   fish-ACC eat-PROG-LOC
        'Did Biret finish eating (the fish)?'

b. Geargga-i.
   finish-PAST.3s
   'Yes, (she did).'

Hence, it is clear that the verb 'finish' must be in a separate word from the verb 'eat'. It is also clear, however, that each verb forms a word with its inflectional markers, since the inflectional markers always immediately follow the verb root in the linear order. On my analysis, the reason for this is that the verb has head-moved to the inflectional heads, so that the verb and the inflectional markers are included in one complex head. The *consequence* is that the verb plus inflectional markers are taken to constitute one single word.

Thus, we see that while the distribution of the verbal morphemes in (1) causes the whole sequence to stand out as one word, the distribution of the verbal morphemes in (2) is such that the sequence is seen as *two* words. In either case, the distribution is determined by syntax, but notably, there is no strict correspondence between the syntactic configuration of a morpheme sequence and its word status. For example, while each of the morphemes of the sequence in (1) sits in the Spec of the following morpheme, according to my analysis, a similar morpheme sequence produced by head movement would also be seen as a word. Conversely, the morphemes in (2) could have been combined into two words without being combined into complex heads—what is required is that there are morpheme sequences with the right distributional properties.

As I have stressed repeatedly in this work, the relevant properties are internal cohesion and independent distribution. For any sequence of morphemes, having these properties is a necessary and sufficient condition for being seen as a word. Any syntactic configuration that can produce such morpheme sequences can also give rise to words. In the end, it is the distributional properties that determine whether or not a given morpheme sequence is perceived as a word—that is, whether or not it *is* a word.

Symbols and Abbreviations

±	with positive or negative feature value	ANIM	animate
		ANT	anterior
?	(in survey): uncertain	AOR	aorist
(…)	optional element or alternative position	AP	adjectival phrase
		Apass	antipassive
X/Y	X and Y are fused or in the same position	APPL	applicative
		ARG	argument
1	first person	ART	article
2	second person	ASP	aspect
3	third person	AspP	aspect phrase
4	fourth person	ASS	assumptive
	(In glosses of Bantu languages, numbers also refer to noun classes.)	ASSOC	associative
		AUG	augmentative
		AUX	auxiliary
		BEN	benefactive
A	adjective; aspect		
ABL	ablative	C	complementizer
ABS	absolutive	CAUS	causative
AbsAgr	absolutive agreement	CEL	celerative
ACT	active	CL	clitic
ADEL	adelative	CLASS	classifier
ADESS	adessive	COLL	collective
ADJ	adjective	COM	comitative
AdPl	addressee plural	COMPL	completive
Adv	adverb	CONA	conative
AFF	affirmative	CONC	concessive
AFOC	actor focus	COND	conditional
Ag	agent	CONJ	conjunction
Agr	agreement	CONJC	conjunctive
AgrO	object agreement	CONJG	conjugation marker
AgrOP	object agreement phrase	CONN	connective
AgrS	subject agreement	CONT	continuous
AgrSP	subject agreement phrase	CONTR	contrastive
		COP	copula
ALL	allative	CP	complementizer phrase
AND	andative		

CRS	Currently Relevant State	FIN	finite
CTMP	contemporative	FOC	focus
		FocP	focus phrase
d	dual	FREQ	frequentative
DAT	dative	FRUST	frustrative
DEB	debitive	FUT	future
DECL	declarative	FV	final vowel
DEF	definite	GEN	genitive
DEIX	deixis	GER	gerund
DEM	demonstrative	GMP	Generalized Mirror Principle
DEP	dependent		
DEPL	deplacement		
DESID	desiderative	H	high tone
DET	determiner	HAB	habitual
D.FUT	distant future	HMC	Head Movement Constraint
DIM	diminutive		
DIR	directional	HON	honorific
DISABL	disability	HOP	Head Ordering Principle
DISTL	distantial		
DISTR	distributive	HOR	Horizon of Interest
DO	direct object	HORT	hortative
DP	determiner phrase	HUM	human
DeSubj	deictic subject	HYP	hypothetical
DU	dual		
DUB	dubitative	ILL	illative
DUPL	duplicative	IMM	immediate
DUR	durative	IMP	imperative
		IMPF	imperfective
ECP	Empty Category Principle	INAN	inanimate
		INCH	inchoative
EMPH	emphatic	INCMPL	incompletive
EPP	Extended Projection Principle	INCP	inceptive
		Incorp	incorporated root
ERG	ergative	IND	indicative
EVID	evidential	INDEF	indefinite
EXCL	exclusive	INEL	inelative
EXH	exhortative	INESS	inessive
EXP	experiential	INF	infinitive
EXT	extension	INFL	inflection
		INST	instrumental
FACT	factual	INT	intentional
FEM	feminine	INTERR	interrogative

INTR	intransitive	Obj	object
INTS	intensive	OBL	oblique
INV	inversion marker	OBV	obviative
IO	indirect object	OCl	object clitic
IP	inflection phrase	OPers	object person
IRR	irrealis	OPl	plural object
ITER	iterative	OPron	object pronoun
		OPT	optative
L	low tone	ORD	ordinal
LCA	Linear Correspondence Axiom		
		p	plural
LF	Logical Form	P	adposition
LFG	Lexical-Functional Grammar	PART	partitive
		PASS	passive
LFOC	locative focus	PAST	past tense
LOC	locative	Pat	patient
		PEJ	pejorative
M	mood; middle tone	PERF	perfective
MAL	malefactive	Pers	person
MAN	manner	PERS	personal marker
MASC	masculine	PF	Phonological Form
MFS	monofocal subject	PL	plural
MOM	momentaneous	Pol	polarity
MoodP	mood phrase	PolP	polarity phrase
MPass	mediopassive	PORT	portative
MSD	masdar	pos.	position
		POSS	possessive
N	noun	POSTESS	postessive
NEG	negation	POSTP	postposition
NEUT	neuter	POT	potential
N.FUT	near future	PP	adpositional phrase
NOM	nominative	PREF	prefix
NONFIN	non-finite	PRES	present tense
NONFUT	non-future	PreV	preverb
NONIMP	non-imperative	PROB	probable
NP	noun phrase	PROG	progressive
N.PAST	near past	Pron	pronoun
NS	non-singular	PROX	proximate
Num	number	PR.P	presentative preposition
		PRT	particle
O	object	PTC	participle
OAgr	object agreement (marker)	PUNC	punctual

Q	question marker	SUBJC	subjunctive
QUANT	quantifier	Subord	subordination
QUOT	quotative	SUFF	suffix
		SUPDIR	superdirective
REAL	realis	SUPEL	superelative
RECIP	reciprocal	SUPERL	superlative
REDUP	reduplication	SUPESS	superessive
REFL	reflexive		
REL	relative	t	trial
REM	remote	T	tense
REP	repetitive	TERM	terminative
RES	resultative	Th	theme
REV	reversive	TMA	tense, mood, aspect
RP.PAST	reported past	TD.PAST	today's past
		TOP	topic
s	singular	TopP	topic phrase
S	subject	TP	tense phrase
SAgr	subject agreement (marker)	TRANS	transitive
		TSA	toward speaker or action
SC	small clause		
SCl	subject clitic	UFOC	undergoer focus
SClass	subject classifier	UG	Universal Grammar
SG	singular	Unsp.	unspecified
SIM	simultaneous		
SNum	subject number	v	higher verb in VP shell
SPCF	specific	V	verb
Spec	specifier (position)	VAP	voice+aspect+polarity
SPers	subject person	Vo	voice
SPl	plural subject	VOL	volitional
SPron	subject pronoun	VP	verb phrase
SS	same subject		
STAT	stative	ω	phonological word
SUBEL	subelative		
SUBESS	subessive	X°	syntactic head
Subj	subject	XP	phrasal constituent

A Survey of Word Order
and Verb Morphology

The table that follows is a schematic representation of word order and morpheme order in 530 languages. These data were the basis for the tables presented in 1.5. The languages are grouped into 280 genera, as described in 1.5, and also into six geographical areas and a creole group. The names of the genera are given in the leftmost column, then follow the names of the languages, the unmarked order of the main constituents of the clause, and finally, the order of (mainly inflectional) morphemes within the verb or within the clause.[1]

The symbol "=" in the language column indicates that the given data apply to the genus as a whole. Genera marked * are not listed in Dryer (1992); their inclusion here is based on Ruhlen (1987) and Asher and Moseley (1994). For the identification of New Guinean genera I have also used Wurm (1975a).

All abbreviations are explained in appendix 1, except N, W, S, E, and C for North, West, South, East, and Central. The use of capitals as opposed to lower case letters is not significant, except in a few cases where a category is marked twice in one single word form. The marker that appears to be the principal exponence of the category is then written in capitals.

GENUS	LANGUAGE	WORD ORDER	MORPHEME ORDER
Africa			
N. Khoisan	!Kung	SVO	(T) (Q) S (Q) (T) Neg (T) Adv (T) Caus+V O
C. Khoisan	Nama	SOV; S V+OPron	T+A V Caus = *redup*
Kadugli	Katcha	S (Aux) VO	SAgr+T+V+(SPron) SPron+Neg SAgr+T+V
	Krongo	VSO	SAgr+(±)Past+(±)Perf+Freq/ Punc+V+Recip/Refl+Apass/ Dir/Ben+Pass+Trans
Kordofanian	Katla	S Fut V O; S Neg V O Neg	SAgr+V+Caus+Past
	Masakin	SVO; VSO	SAgr/A+V+Appl/Caus
	Rashad	SOV	S(O)Agr+T+V+Caus+OPl+Ind

GENUS	LANGUAGE	WORD ORDER	MORPHEME ORDER
Kordofanian (cont.)	Utoro	SVO	SAgr+V+Appl/Caus+A+ (OPron); V+SAgr
Mande	Bambara	SOV	S T/A/Pol O V (XP) Q
	Koranko	SOV	S T/M/A O V+(A) (XP) Q
	Mende	SOV	S Neg O V+T/A (XP)
N. Atlantic	Fulfulde	SVO	V+Caus+Vo/A/Pol
	Diola	SVO	(Fut+)SAgr+V+T S+V+IOPron+DOPron
Ijoid	Defaka	SOV	V+T
Kru	=	SVO; S T/A/Pol O V	V+Caus
*Dogon**	Dogon	SOV	V+Caus+T+SAgr
Gur	Dagaare	SVO	S T Neg A V+(±)Perf Aff IO DO
	Kuusal	S T/Pol VO	V+(±)Perf
	Supyire	SOV	S Perf Past O V (XP)
	Waama	SVO; S OPron V	V+Caus+A
Adamawa-Ubangi	Amadi	SVO;	V+Caus+T/A
	Gbaya	SVO	SPron+T+V+A
	Linda	SVO	S Cond V/A Irr/Hyp O Neg Q A = *tone*
	Mba	SVO	SAgr+T+V/A
	Mbum	SVO	S (A) V O (Pol/Perf)
	Ngbandi	SVO	SAgr+V+T/A; also A = *tone*
Kwa	Ewe	SVO	SAgr+Fut+V+Hab+O [2] SAgr+Aux V SAgr+Fut Rep T V+Hab O [3]
	Lelemi	SVO	S SAgr (Neg/Modal/T) V O V+Caus
Defoid	Yoruba	SVO	S Neg Fut A V O
Edoid	Edo (Bini)	SVO	SAgr+V+T/A Caus = *tone*
Igboid	Igbo	SVO	(Fut) S Fut/Prog/Hab V+Past/Perf+Appl O Emph

GENUS	LANGUAGE	WORD ORDER	MORPHEME ORDER
Platoid	Jukun	SVO	S Past/Cond Cont Pot/Hab M V Aux SPron IO DO Adv Perf/Modal Neg Q
Cross River	Obolo	SVO	(Fut)+SAgr+(T/Cont)+V
Kainji	Birom	SVO	T/M/A+V
Bantoid	Babungo	SVO	S Neg/T A V O Neg A = *tone*
	Chichewa	SVO	SAgr+T+V+Caus+A
	Kinyarwanda	SVO	SAgr+T+V+Caus+A
	Makaa	SVO	S T A V O
	Nɔmaándé	SVO	S Neg+T+Hab+SAgr V+Dur+FV O; SPron+Neg+T+Hab+SAgr V+Dur+FV O
	Swahili	SVO	(IndNeg)+SAgr+(-IndNeg)+ T/A+(OAgr)+V+Caus/Appl+ M+AdPl
Songhai	Songhai	SVO	S T/M V O
Saharan	Kanuri	SOV	V+(O)+T/SAgr
	Tubu	SOV	Fut+V+SPers+SNum+A/Pol
Maban	Maba	SOV Neg	S/OAgr+Caus+V+T/Pol
	Masalit	SOV (Aux)	SAgr+Caus+V+T+M
Fur	Fur	SOV	S O (Neg) Fut SAgr+V+T/A (Neg)
Nubian	Dongolese Nubian	SOV	Fut+SPron+V+Caus+Perf+ Neg+Cond+T/SAgr+Q
	Hill Nubian	SOV	V+A+T/SAgr
Surma	Murle	Neg VSO	SPers+M/A+V+Appl/Pass+ SNum+SPers
	Mursi	SVO	(T)+(SAgr)+V+A/SAgr (+SPers)
Nera	Nera	SOV	V+Caus/ONum+T/A+ SAgr/M/Q
Nyimang	Nyimang	S (Ind) OV	V/A(+Caus/A)+Num+T±Dep

GENUS	LANGUAGE	WORD ORDER	MORPHEME ORDER
Temein	Temein	SVO	S Fut/Hab/Prog/Neg V O Neg SAgr+Past+V+Appl+Pl+Ind
Tama	Merarit	SOV	SPers+Neg+V+SNum+A Neg+V+SPers+SNum+A
Daju	Shatt	SVO	S (Aux) VO Neg SAgr/A+V
	Sila	SO Neg V	SAgr+V+Caus(+SAgr)
Nilotic	Anywa[4]	SVO	S (Hab) VO; SPron+T V/A$_1$; (SPron)+T+V/A$_1$; SO V/A$_2$+SPron
	Bor[5]	SVO; S T/A/Pol OV	Appl = *tone*
	Kalenjin	VSO	Past+Neg+Perf+SAgr+V+Dir+ Appl+A
	Karimojong	VSO	M/Agr+Caus+V+Freq+ Dir/Ben+Voice/T/SAgr
	Luo	S T/M/Neg VO	(SAgr)+V/Perf+(OAgr) V+Caus Perf = *tone*
	Maasai	VSO	Neg+SAgr+T+V
	Shilluk	SVO	S Neg T/A+V O
	Turkana	VSO	Neg+SPers+T+Caus+V+A+ SNum
Kuliak	Ik	V (T) SO	V+Caus+SAgr
Kresh	Kresh	SOV (Q)	SAgr+V+T
Bongo- *Bagirmi*	Baka	SVO	S (M/A) V+T (T) O
	Mbay	SVO	S (Sagr)+T/A SAgr+V O Neg Q
	Sar	SVO	SAgr+V
*Moru-Madi**	Logbara	SVO	S SPron+V O T/A/Pol
	Lulubo	SVO	SAgr+V/±Perf
	Madi	SVO	S SAgr+V O Compl S SAgr/Impf O Nonfin+V
	Moru	SVO	SVO Compl S SAgr/Impf O Nonfin+V S SAgr+V+Fut O
Mangbetu- *Asua**	Mangbetu	SVO	SAgr+V+T
Mangbutu-Efe	Mamvu	SVO	S SPron+Neg+V O T/A

GENUS	LANGUAGE	WORD ORDER	MORPHEME ORDER
Balendru	Ngiti	SVO	SAgr+V+T; also T/A = *tone*
Berta	Berta	S (Neg) VO	(SPron)+V+Caus+T/A Perf = V+SAgr
Kunama	Kunama	SOV	V+SAgr+T/Pol/Q S/OAgr+OPl+V+T/Pol/Q
Berber	Tamazight	VSO	Q+Neg+T+O+(SAgr)+Pass+ Caus+V+(SAgr) SAgr+V+(O)
Biu-Mandara	Gude	A VSO; Neg SVO; A used-to SVO	V+Caus
	Mofu-Gudur	SVO	S SAgr Prog/Hab T V O Perf Compl
	Podoko	VSO	(Foc) (T) V+Perf SO Q
	Tera	SVO	S T/A/Distl V O
W. Chadic	Hausa	SVO	S Neg SAgr+A/Fut V O Neg Q
	Tangale	S (T/A) VO	V+A/Neg
Omotic	Dizi	SOV	V+T+SAgr Neg+SAgr V+T+(Neg)
	Hamar	SOV	V+Caus/Prog+T/A+Neg+M/Q
	Kullo	SOV	V+T/Pol+SAgr V+Fut
	Ometo	SOV	V+Caus+Perf+Neg+M/SAgr
Beja	Beja	SOV	Neg+SAgr/T+Caus+V+Pl+ (OPron)+Q Neg+V+Caus+SAgr+T+Pl+ (OPron)+Q
C. Cushitic	Bilin	OSV (T)	V+Caus+SAgr
	Kemant	SOV	V+Caus+A/Neg/SAgr+Q
E. Cushitic	Afar	SOV (Aux)	Neg+V+Caus+SPers+T/A+ SNum+M/Conj SAgr+Caus+V+T/A
	Arbore	S Aux OV	Aux=M/A/Pol+SAgr V+SAgr+Perf
	Ba´iso	SOV	V+T+SAgr (?)

GENUS	LANGUAGE	WORD ORDER	MORPHEME ORDER
E. Cushitic (cont.)	Dasenech	SOV	SAgr/A+Neg+Dir/Loc+V+ M/A
	Hadiyya	SOV	V+Caus+T/A/SAgr+Neg/Q
	Oromo	SOV (Q)	Neg+Freq/V+Caus+Pass+ SAgr+T+Ben/Inst (Freq = *redup*)
	Sidamo	SOV	Neg+V+Caus+T/A/SAgr+Q
	Somali	SOV	S O M Neg SAgr OAgr V V+Caus/Ben/Pass+SAgr+T
S. Cushitic	Dahalo	S (Aux) OV	V+Caus+SAgr+T
	Iraqw	S (O) Aux (O) V	Aux=S/OAgr+T/M/A+ Appl/Dir/Instr/Voice V+Caus+Cont+Hab+SAgr+ Neg
	Ma'a	SOV	Neg+SAgr+T+OAgr+V
Semitic	Amharic	SOV (Aux)	Neg+(SAgr)+Caus+V/T/M+ (SAgr)+(OAgr)+Neg+Q
	Gulf Arabic	S Neg VO	Fut+(SAgr)+V/T/Caus+ (SAgr)+OPron
	Modern-Hebrew	VSO; S Neg VO	(SAgr)+(Caus)+V/T/Caus/ (±)Perf+(SAgr)+OPron

Eurasia

GENUS	LANGUAGE	WORD ORDER	MORPHEME ORDER
Basque	Basque	SOV (Aux) (XP)	AbsAgr+DatAgr+T+ Aux/V+AbsPl+DatPl+ErgAgr
Armenian	Armenian	SVO	V+T/SAgr
Indic	Dumaki	SOV (Aux)	V+Caus+T/SAgr Aux+SAgr+M/A
	Hindi	SOV (Aux)	V+Caus+Fut/±Perf+Agr
	Kashmiri	SVO	V+Caus+T+Agr
Iranian	Persian	SOV (Aux)	(Neg)+(Dur)+V/T+SAgr+(OCl)
	Pashto	SOV (Aux)	V+T+SAgr
Albanian	Albanian	S (Aux) VO	Caus+V+T/SAgr
Greek	Greek	SVO	V+T/M+SAgr

GENUS	LANGUAGE	WORD ORDER	MORPHEME ORDER
Italic	Rumanian	S (Aux) VO	V+T+SAgr
	Spanish	S (Aux) VO	V+T/A+SAgr
Celtic	Breton	(XP) Pol VSO; V Pol Aux SO	V+T/M+SAgr
	Irish	VSO	V+T/A+(SAgr)
	Scottish-Gaelic	VSO; Aux SVO	V+T/A
	Welsh	VSO	V+T/SAgr
Germanic	English	S (Aux) VO	V+T
	German	SVO/S Aux OV	V+T+SAgr
	Icelandic	S (Aux) VO	V+T+SAgr
Baltic	Lithuanian	(Q) SVO	V+Caus+Freq+T/M+SAgr+ Refl
Slavic	Croatian	S (Aux) VO; S V+Aux	V+(Impf/)SAgr
	Russian	SVO	(A)+V+(A)+T/SAgr
Samoyedic	Forest Nenets	SOV	V+Caus+T/M+SAgr V+Caus+SAgr+Past
Finnic	Finnish	SVO	V+Caus+T/M+SAgr
	Mari	SOV	V+Caus+T/SAgr
	N. Saami	SVO	V+Caus+M+T+SAgr
Ugric	Hungarian	SVO	V+Caus+Past/Cond+S/OAgr
	Khanty	SOV	V+Caus+T/M+Pass+OAgr+ SAgr
Mongolian	Mongolian	SOV; SVO	V+Caus+T/M
	Buryat	SOV	V+T+SAgr
Tungus	Even	SOV	V+Caus/A+T+SAgr
	Manchu	SOV	V+M/A
Turkic	Chuvash	SOV	V+Caus+Neg+T+SAgr
	Turkish	SOV	V+Refl+Recip+Caus+Pass+ Neg/Pot+A+T+Cond+SAgr
	Tuva	SOV	V+Caus+T
	Uzbek	SOV	V+T/A+SAgr
Japanese	Japanese	SOV Q	V+Caus+T

GENUS	LANGUAGE	WORD ORDER	MORPHEME ORDER
Korean	Korean	SOV (Aux)	V+Caus+Hon+T+Vol+M
Chukchi-Kamchatkan	Alutor	SVO; SOV	(S)Agr/M+(Incorp)+Caus+ (Incorp)+V+caus+T+(O)Agr
	Chukchi	SOV	1+Fut/Irr+(1sO)+Caus+ Incorp+V+caus+1pO+A+ OAgr+SAgr
	Itelmen	SVO (?)	SAgr/M+V+A+T+Conjg+ OAgr+Pl
Nivkh	Nivkh	SOV	OAgr/Refl/Recip+V+Trans+ Neg+(±)Perf/(±)Fut+Caus/Res+ Modal+Evid+Fin+Num+Q
Yukaghir	Yukaghir	SOV	Neg/Subjc+V+Caus+T/M/A+ SAgr
Ket	Ket	SVO	Pers+V+Num; Agr+T+V; T+Agr+V; V+Agr+T; V+T+Agr
Kartvelian	Georgian	SOV	SAgr+OAgr+V+Caus+A+T+ SAgr+Pl
	Laz	SO Neg V	Aff+PreV+Agr+caus+V+ Caus+Impf+Conjc+Agr+Pl+ Fut+Cond/Evid+Q+Quot+ Conj
N.W. Cau-casian	Abkhaz	SOV	Poss+OAgr+Adv+Interr+ PreV+IOAgr+Appl+Loc/Dir+ SAgr+(Neg)+Caus+V+Excess+ Iter+Emph+T/A+M/Neg/ Subord
	Kabardian	SOV	AbsAgr+Hor/Dir+Adv+Deix+ Ben+Com+IO/PreV+Incorp+ ErgAgr+Ag+Disabl+Pres/ Prog+Neg+Caus+V+Postp+ Iter+Able+Emph+Past+Adv+ Pl+T+M+C+Conj
Nax	Chechen	SOV	SAgr+V+Caus+T/M+Q
Avaro-Andi-	Avar	SOV	SClass+V+T
Dido	Tsez	SOV	V+Caus+T

GENUS	LANGUAGE	WORD ORDER	MORPHEME ORDER
Lak-Dargwa	Kubachi	SVO (?)	AbsAgr+V+Caus+T/SAgr AbsAgr+V+Ger/T+Aux+ T/SAgr
	Lak	S (O)V(Aux)(O)	(SAgr)+V+T/A+SAgr
Lezgian	Lezgian	SOV	V+Caus+T/A+(Past)+(Mood)
Burushaski	Burushaski	SOV	(AbsAgr)+Caus+V+T+SAgr
N.W. Dravid-ian	Brahui	SOV; S V+OCl	V+Caus+Neg+T/A+SAgr
Dravidian	Kolami	SOV	V+Caus+T/A+SAgr
proper	Koya	SOV(Aux)	V+T/Mood+SAgr
	Tamil	SOV(Aux/Caus)	V+T/Mood+SAgr
Munda	Santali	SOV	V+Caus+T/A+OAgr+ Fin+SAgr Iter = *redup*

Southeast Asia & Oceania

GENUS	LANGUAGE	WORD ORDER	MORPHEME ORDER
Chinese	Mandarin	SVO	S (A) V+A O Q
Karen	E. Kayah	SVO	S (M/A) V (M/A) O M/Neg
	Moulmein Sgaw	SVO	S Fut/Neg Modal V A O Neg Q
Tibetic	Dumi	SOV (Aux)	(3pS)+NegPast+V+Refl+1+ T+PersAgr+NumAgr+Neg
	Lhasa Tibetan	SOV	Neg+V+Modal+(Neg)+Hon+ T/SAgr+Q
	Newari	SOV	V+T/A
	Classical Tibetan	SOV	SO Neg V (Aux) Perf/Fut+V A/Tense = *root alternation*
Baric	Bodo (Boro)	SOV	V+Caus+Pass+T/A/Neg
	Garo	SOV	V+A+Neg+T
Burmic	Burmese	SOV	Neg+V+Caus/Modal/A+ T/M/A+Evid/Q
	Mikir	SOV (Q)	Caus+V+Neg+A+T
Miao-Yao	Hmong Njua	SVO	S Q Prog Fut Neg A/Modal V (Neg) Modal O Compl

GENUS	LANGUAGE	WORD ORDER	MORPHEME ORDER
Khasi	Khasi	SVO	S SAgr+(Fut)+(Pot) Neg Past Dur (Caus)+V O
Palaung-Khmuic	Khmu	SVO	S Irr Neg Modal V O Perf
	Palaung	SVO	S (Fut) (Neg) V (Emph) O S Perf VO
	Pale	SVO	S T/M/A/Pol V O
Viet-Muong	Vietnamese	SVO	S T (Neg) V O
Katuic	Katu	SVO	S (Caus+)V (Causee) O
Bahnaric	Sre	SVO	S (Perf) (Mood) Caus+V O (Q)
Khmer	Khmer	SVO	S Neg T/A/Modal V O
*Monic**	Mon	SVO	Neg S Modal A V O Q/Decl
Aslian	Sengoi	SV	S (T) SAgr+V S SAgr+Fut V
	Temiar	S VO	Neg T/A SAgr+(Desid)+(A)+ Caus+V A = *redup*
Nicobar Islands	Nicobarese	VOS	V SPron Fut/Cont O
Kam-Tai	Thai	SVO	S (Neg) T/M (Neg) V O
Atayalic	Rukai	VSO	T+V+A+(SPron) *but* Neg+T+(SPron) V Caus+V
	Cou	VOS	Foc+T/A+SAgr Caus+V
Paiwanic	Paiwan	VSO; VOS	T+V Caus+V
W. Malayo-Polynesian	Chamorro	VSO; SVO	Num+(Impf)+V; ErgAgr+Caus+V
	Ilokano	VSO	ActTop/T+Caus+V+ OTop+Agr
	Palauan	S (T/A) VO	also: T/A+V; Caus+V
	Tagalog	VSO	A+Caus+V
	Yapese	(T) S (T) VO	V+Num/Vo+O
Sundic	Indonesian	SVO	S (T/A/Neg/M) V+Caus O

GENUS	LANGUAGE	WORD ORDER	MORPHEME ORDER
C.-E. Malayo-Polynesian	Balawaia	SOV	SAgr/T/M+A+V+(OAgr)+(A)
	Kiliwila	SVO	A+SAgr+V+(O)+(Pl)
	Loniu	SVO	S Fut SPron Int/Inch Perf A O Pot+SAgr+V Neg
	Maori	VSO	T/A V (T/A) SO
	Mokilese	SVO	S M Hab Foc/Ints Mod/Pol Prog+Caus+V+Incorp+Perf O
	Mono-Alu	SOV/SVO	SAgr/T+Caus+V+Ben+OAgr
	Niuean	VSO	T/A Neg Mod V (O) Dir Man A Emph Perf Q S O
	Port Sandwich	S (Mood) VO	SAgr+(A)+V+OAgr
	Pulo Annian	SVO	S SAgr (T/A) (Neg) Caus+V+(OAgr) O (XP)
	Rapanui	VSO	(Q) T/A (Caus) VSO
	Tokelau	T/M/A V O S; T/M/A V S O	
	Woleaian	SVO	S SAgr A/Neg Caus+V O
Andamanese	Andamanese	Perf SOV	V+T/A

Australia & New Guinea

Finisterre-Huon	Kate	?	V+(OAgr)+(A)+T+SAgr
	Nabak	?	OAgr+V+SAgr; V+Modal Aux+T/SAgr
	Selepet	?	V+(OAgr)+(A)+T/SAgr
	Wantoat	SOV (?)	OAgr+V+A/SAgr
E. New Guinea Highlands	Awa	SOV	V+(OAgr)+T+SAgr
	Hua	SOV	Perf+Neg+OAgr+V+Prog+ Perf+Fut/Subjc+M/SAgr
	Kobon	SOV	V+Neg+Dur+T/SAgr
C. and S. New Guinea	Asmat	SOV	(T/A)+V+Caus/Ben+M/A+T+ Q+OAgr+SAgr
	Bainapi	S (T) OV	V+T+(Neg)+(O)+(A)
	Kamoro	SOV	V+M/A+T+OAgr+SAgr
	Kamula	SOV	V+T

GENUS	LANGUAGE	WORD ORDER	MORPHEME ORDER
C. and S New Guinea (cont.)	Pisa	SOV	(Fut)+V+T+SAgr; V+SAgr+NearPast
	Siagha	SOV	V+T+Agr
	S. Kathi	SOV	(OAgr)+V+OAgr+T/M/A+ SAgr+Perf/Opt
Kutubuan*	=	?	V+Caus+T+(SAgr)
Angan	Baruya	SOV	V+T+SAgr IO+V+Ben+SAgr
Gogodala-Suki*	Gogodala	SOV	V+OAgr+Trans+T+SAgr
	Suki	SOV	V+Caus+OAgr+Trans+T+ SAgr
Marind	Marind	SVO; SOV	T+SAgr+IOAgr (+) V+OAgr
Sentani	Sentani	SOV	V+T/A+SAgr+OAgr+(Mode)
Dani-Kwerba	Lower Grand Valley Dani	SOV (Aux)	(OAgr)+V+Fact+(T)+SAgr+ (A); V+OAgr+Aux+Fact+SAgr
Wissel Lakes-Kemandoga	Ekagi	SOV; OSV	Du+DO+IO+V+A+T+SAgr
	Moni	SOV	(O)+V+A+T+SAgr+M
	Uhunduni	SOV	V+(OAgr)+M+T/A+SAgr
W. Bomberai*	Iha	SOV	V+T+SAgr
Binanderean	Binandere	SOV	V+T+SAgr
	Korafe	SOV	V+T/M/SAgr
C. and S-E. New Guinea	Barai	S+(M) O V	V+OAgr+A+(T)
	Mountain Koiari	SOV	V+SPl+OPl+Man+Neg+ SNum+T
	Koita	S (T/A) OV	V+Num+T/Neg
	Magi	SOV	Caus+V+A+M+T+S/OAgr
	Yareba	SOV (?)	Dir+V+A+T+Agr+M Caus V
	Ömie	SOV (?)	V+OAgr+A+M+SAgr+Aux
Madang	Amele	SOV	V+OAgr+Ben(Agr)+SAgr+T
	Haruai	SOV (XP)	V+A+Neg+T+SAgr+M

GENUS	LANGUAGE	WORD ORDER	MORPHEME ORDER
Adelbert Range	Tauya	SOV	OAgr+V+Perf+SAgr+M; V OAgr+Caus+SAgr+M
Teberan- *Pawaian**	Daribi	SOV	V+T/A
	Pawaian	?	V+A/SAgr+M
Eleman*	Toaripi	SOV (?)	V+T (Aux)
Inland Gulf*	Tao	SOV	V+T/SAgr
Trans-Fly- *Bulaka River*	Island Kiwai	SO (Neg) V	Q+SPers+V+ONum+A+T+ SNum
Mek*	Kosarek	SOV	V+(T/A)+(OAgr)+T/SAgr
Border*	Imonda	SOV	SNum+ComNum+Class+V+ S/ONum+Emph+Ben+Irr+ T/A+M+Neg/Q/Top/Ints+ Distl/Emph/Conj
Kolopom	=	SOV T/A	
Timor-Alor- *Pantar**	Bunak	? V T/A	
Torricelli	Olo	SOV; SVO	SAgr+V+(Trans/Ben)+(O) T/A
Sepik-Ramu	Alamblak	SOV; SVO	Caus+V+T+SAgr+OAgr
	Yimas	SOV; OSV	Neg/Pot+OAgr+SAgr+Adv+ Caus/Appl/Com+V+T/A/Irr+ Num
Yele-Solomons	Anêm	SVO Neg	M/SAgr+V+OAgr
	Yele	SOV	SO T/A/SAgr V (TMA/ AbsAgr)
Bougainville	Buin	?	V+OAgr+SAgr
	W. Bougain- ville	?	(OAgr) V+S+T
Reef Islands- *Santa Cruz**	=	?	T/M/A+V+SAgr+OAgr
Mangarayi	Mangarayi	SOV (Aux) ?	Agr+V+Aux+T/A
Nunggubuyu	Nunggubuyu	SVO (?)	SAgr/OAgr+V+T
Tiwi	Tiwi	SVO Q	SAgr/T+Loc+M+O+A+V+ Caus+Rep
Murrinh- *Patha**	Murrinh- Patha	SOV	SAgr+OAgr/BenAgr+V+T

GENUS	LANGUAGE	WORD ORDER	MORPHEME ORDER
Yiwaidjan	Maung	SVO	(OAgr)+SAgr+V+Caus+(T)
Gunwinyguan	Ngalakan	?	S/OAgr(+O)+V+Aux+T/A+Neg/M
	Ngandi	SVO	SAgr+OAgr+Ben+V+Caus+T/A
	Rembarnga	SOV	OAgr+SAgr+Incorp+V+T/A
	Wardaman	SVO; SOV	(M/A)+S/OAgr+V+Caus+T/M V+Suff S/OAgr+Aux+T/M
Maran	Alawa	SVO (?)	Agr+V+A+T+Agr(3s) V Agr+Aux+A+T+Agr(3s)
	Warndarang	SVO	(M/Neg)+S/OAgr+V+T/M/A (Neg)+V+S/OAgr+Aux+T/M/A
W. Barkly	Djingili	?	V+SAgr+OAgr+T/M/A/Dir
	Wambaya	?	V+(±Fut) Aux in 2nd pos. = (Past)+SAgr+(Fut)+(OAgr)+T/M/A/Dir
Djamindjungan* 6 =		SVO; SOV (Aux)	(NegIrr)+SAgr+OAgr+Fut/Irr+V+T
Garawan	Garawa	VOS; VSO (?)	V+T
Daly	Malakmalak	SOV (?)	V+Caus+A SAgr/T/A+OAgr
	Ngankiku-rungkurr	SV*O/SOV*	V*=Neg SAgr/±Perf+Pl+Aux+T+dS+pS OAgr Caus+Incorp+V T/M/A
Djeragan*	Miriwung	SVO (?)	SAgr+OAgr+V+T+M+IO; V SAgr+OAgr+Aux+T+IO
Bunaban*	Gooniyandi	SOV	V+Prog+Mood+T+S/OAgr+Aux+Mode+Obl+Num
Wororan	Wunambal	SVO (XP) (?)	SAgr+V+T+O+Dual/Trial; V SAgr+Aux+T+O+Dual/Trial
Pama-Nyungan	Arabana	SOV	V+Caus+A+T/M/A
	Biri	SVO	V+T+(SAgr) (SAgr if no O)
	Dhirari	Neg SOV	V+Refl/Rec+Ptc Aux+T/M/A
	Diyari	SOV (Aux)	V+Caus+T/M; V+Ptc Aux+T

GENUS	LANGUAGE	WORD ORDER	MORPHEME ORDER
Pama-Nyungan (cont.)	Dyirbal	OS Neg V	V+Voice/Recip+Cel/Rep+ Distr+Refl+T/M
	Gumbainggir	SVO (?)	V+Caus+T S V DO(ABS) IO(ABS)
	Gunya	SVO (?)	V+Caus+A+T+SAgr+O(Agr)
	Lardil	SVO	V+Vo+T
	Margany	SOV; S V OPron; O SPron V	V+Caus+T
	Martuthunia	SVO	V+T/M/A
	Muruwari	SVO; SOV	V+T+SAgr
	Ngamini	SOV (?)	V+Caus+A+T
	Ngiyambaa	SOV (?)	V+Caus+T/A
	Pitta-Pitta	SOV (?); V SPron OPron	V+Caus+T/M/A
	Walmadjarri	SOV	V+A+T Aux in 2nd pos. = T+SPers+OPers+SNum+ ONum
	Warrgamay	SOV (?)	V+Com/Instr+A
	Yidiɲ	SOV (XP)	V+Apass+A+Com+(Apass+) T/M
	Yir Yoront	SOV (?)	V+T+(SAgr)+(OAgr)
	Yukulta	SVO	V+Caus+M Aux in 2nd pos. = OAgr+S/OAgr+Trans+T/±Irr

North America

Eskimo-Aleut	Atka Aleut	SOV	V+Caus+Hab+T+S/OAgr
	Greenlandic	SOV	V+Caus+T/A+M+SAgr+OAgr
	Iñupiaq	?	V+Caus+M+T+S/OAgr
Haida	Masset Haida	SOV	V+Caus+A+T
Tlingit	Tlingit	SOV (?); VS	O+Incorp+Caus/A+S+A+V+A
Athabask-Eyak	Chilcotin	SOV	Cona+Inch+Conjg+Perf/Opt/ Prog+S+Class+V

GENUS	LANGUAGE	WORD ORDER	MORPHEME ORDER
Athabask-Eyak (cont.)	Dogrib	XP Q SOV Fut	OAgr+SAgr+A+V
	Navajo	S Neg OV Neg	PP+Refl+Rev+Iter+Distr+ OAgr+DeSubj+Adv+Th+A+ Perf/Prog/Opt/Fut+SAgr+ Class+V
	Sekani	SOV (?)	(A)+(OAgr)+(SAgr)+ Theme/A+T/A+(SAgr)+Class+ V+M/A
	Slave	Q SOV T Evid	Neg+PP+Adv+Distr+Hab+ Incorp+Num+OAgr+Num+ Th+A+Conjg+Perf/Opt+ SAgr+Class+V
	Tututni	?	Dir/Loc+OAgr/Pl+Compl/ Incp/Iter+Prog/Perf+SAgr+ Class+V+T/Q/Evid
Kutenai	Kutenai	SVO	SAgr+T+V+OAgr+Obv+Pl
Wiyot	Wiyot	S M/A/Neg VO	V+Caus+OAgr+SAgr
Yurok	Yurok	S Prt VO	(S+)V+OAgr+SAgr Prt=Pol/T/A/Modal/Loc Q in 2nd pos.
Algonquian	Blackfoot	VSO; SVO	SAgr+Fut/Perf+Dur+V+Caus+ Trans+OAgr+Num+(OPron)
	Delaware	SVO (?)	SAgr+V+Theme+Dim/Pej+ Obv/Pl+Neg+(S)Agr+A+ (O)Agr+M
	Fox	SVO (?)	1/2Agr+Fut+V+Mood+ S/OAgr
	Ojibwa	VOS	Pers+T+V+Pers+A+Num+ (Obv)
	Passama- quoddy	SVO	SAgr+V+Trans+OAgr SAgr+T V+Trans+OAgr
	Potawatomi	SVO	Agr+M+T+A+Incorp+A+V+ M/Agr
Chimakuan	Quileute	VSO	V+Caus+Pass+Trans+Dir/Fut/ Compl+SFem/SNum+SPers
Wakashan	Kʷakʷ'ala	VSO	V+Caus+T+SAgr+OAgr+Instr
	Nitinat	SVO (?)	V+Caus+M/A+Fut+S+O V+A+Modal+S

GENUS	LANGUAGE	WORD ORDER	MORPHEME ORDER
Bella Coola	Bella Coola	VSO	V+Caus+Pass+S/OAgr+A/Fut+M
Coast Salish	Comox	VSO	V+Intr+OAgr+SAgr+T
	Halkomelem	(Loc) (SCl) VSO	V/A+Ben+Trans/Caus+OAgr+3ErgAgr
	Squamish	VSO	V+Trans+OAgr+SAgr
	Tillamook	SVO (?)	T+V+Caus+IO+DO+S
Tsamosan*	Upper Chehalis	(T/A) VSO; S we (T/A) VO	Neg+T/A+M+V+Inch+Trans+OAgr+SAgr+Adverb
Interior Salish	Shuswap	VSO	V+Trans+Cond+OAgr+SAgr+Pass
Keresan	Acoma	SOV (Aux)	S/OAgr/M+ONum+V+A+SNum
Yuchi	Yuchi	SOV (?)	S/OAgr+V+T/A
Siouan	Catawba	SOV	V+NegImp/Cont/Subord; V+Mom/Aug/Neg+M; V+(±Fut±Perf)/SAgr+M; V+M
	Dakota	SOV (Fut)	S/OAgr+V+Caus+Pl
	Hidatsa	SOV	Instr+Indef+Fut+OAgr+SAgr+Compl+V+Appr+Caus+Iter+Refl+Dur/Mom+Neg+Caus+Desid+Modal+Pl+Mood
	Mandan	SOV	Loc+S/OAgr+Instr+V+Pl+T/M/A; Instr+V+S/OAgr+Caus+T/M/A
Caddoan	Caddo	SOV (?)	S/OAgr/M+Num+Ben+V+T/A
	Pawnee	?	Adv+Dem+Du+Refl+Neg/Q+Evid+M+S+Evid+O+Ben+Aor+Adv+Pl+Iter+Incorp+Adj+Port/Com+Loc+Distr+V+Caus+Perf+Int/Inch/Hab
	Wichita	OVS; SOV	NS+Quot+T/M/A+SPers+PreV/Poss+OPers+M/A+Dat+PreV+Past+Pl+M/A+NS+Coll+OAgr+Incorp+Loc+V+Distr+Iter+Caus+A

GENUS	LANGUAGE	WORD ORDER	MORPHEME ORDER
Iroquoian	Mohawk	?	Sim+Fact+Agr+Incorp+V+ Caus+A+T
	Seneca	?	Adv+Loc+Neg+Dupl+Fut+ Loc/Rep+Ind/Opt+SAgr+ OAgr+Incorp/Refl/Recip+V+ Caus/Dir/Rev+Inch+Distr+ Instr+Appl+*go/walk*+Adv+A+ Cont/Past
	W. Cherokee	SOV; SVO	T/A+SAgr+V+Mood+T/A
Tsimshian	Gitksan	(AbsAgr) VSO	V+Trans+SAgr
	Coast Tsimshian	Neg T/A VSO	
Chinookan	Lower- Chinook	VSO	T/M/A+SAgr+OAgr+IOAgr+ Dir+V+A+T
	Wasco	SVO	T+SAgr+OAgr+IOAgr+Pol+ Dir+V+Caus/Pass+Cont/ Distr+A+Deixis
Takelma	Takelma	SOV	V+Caus+Appl+OAgr+ T/M/A/SAgr
Coos	Coos	OVS; VOS; SV	(SAgr+)V+Trans+A+S/OAgr; V+Caus
Alsea	Alsea	SVO (?)	V+A+O+(A)
Siuslawan	Siuslawan	?	V+Caus+T/A+OCl+SCl; Neg+OCl+SCl V
Klamath	Klamath	SOV	Caus+V+Compl+Incp+*back*+ Dur/Perf+A+Ben+Modal+Fut+ Mood
Sahaptian	Nez Perce	SVO; SOV	S/OAgr+V+SNum+T/M; [7] SAgr+OPl+V+Appl+A [8]
	Sahaptin	?	SAgr+Conn+Trans/Agr+Caus+ V+Dir+Appl+Modal+ SNum+M
Wintun	Wintu	?	Loc/Dir+Dir+V+Distr+Evid+ Dub/Compl/SAgr (Neg) V (Neg) T/M/A
Maidu	Maidu	SOV	V+Caus+T/M+SNum+SPers
Yokuts	Yokuts	Q/Pol SVO	V+Caus+M/A+T

GENUS	LANGUAGE	WORD ORDER	MORPHEME ORDER
Costanoan	=	SVO; OSV	V+T V+Caus
	Mutsun	SVO; VSO; S OPron V; V S OPron	V+MPass/Caus+Ben+Cont+ Dir+T/Perf/Pass/Imp
Miwok	Sierra Miwok	SOV	V+Caus+T/A+OAgr+SAgr
Zuni	Zuni	SOV	OPl+Appl+SPl+V+Neg+ A+Caus+A+SPl+T/M
Chitimacha	Chitimacha	SOV	V+Caus+Pl+Ben+1sO+A+ T/SAgr
Tunica-Atakapa	Atakapa	SOV (?)	(O)Agr+V+Pl+A+SAgr+ Neg+T
	Tunica	SOV	OAgr+V+M/A/SAgr
Muskogean	Alabama	SOV	Instr+Distr+OAgr+(SAgr)+ V+Trans+Caus/Appl+(SAgr)+ Neg+Modal+Dur+T/A
	Choctaw	SOV (Neg)	Agr+V+Caus+Agr+A+T/M
Yuki-Wappo	Wappo	SOV	V+Caus+T
Huave	Huave	VOS ? [9]	T+Dub+(SPers)+V+Dim+ Rep+Refl+(SPers)+SNum
Totonacan	Totonac	VSO (?)	T+V+A
Mixe-Zoquean	Sierra Popoluca	S (Neg)VO; (Neg)VS	S/OAgr+Caus+V+Instr/Ben+A
	Sayula Popoluca	SVO (?)	S/OAgr+Neg/Caus+V+A+ Aug+Pl+*now*+T/M/A+(A)
	Zoque	?	S/OAgr+Caus+V+Compl+ Ben+Pl+Compl+Past+SAgr
Mayan	Cakchiquel	SVO	A+AbsAgr+ErgAgr+V+Caus
	Jacaltec	VSO	Modal Neg (A) VSO (A)+AbsAgr+ErgAgr+V+ Caus+Irr
	K'echi	VOS	T(A)+AbsAgr+ErgAgr+V+Fut
	Toholabal	VSO	A+ErgAgr+V+AbsAgr
	Tzotzil	(A) VOS	Aux+Agr+V+Caus+M/A+Agr
Karok	Karok	SVO (?)	S/OAgr/M+V+Caus+A+T

GENUS	LANGUAGE	WORD ORDER	MORPHEME ORDER
Chimariko	Chimariko	SVO	S+V+T/A
Shasta	Shasta	?	SAgr/T/M+V+Trans+Ben/ Refl+Recip+Compl/Iter+ Pl+Distr+A+Dir
Palaihnan	Achumawi	SOV; SVO (?)	SAgr/M+V+Dir/Caus/Ben/ A/T+Agr(Num?)/M
Yanan*	Yana	SVO	V+T+Agr V+Caus
Pomo	C. Pomo	SOV Neg	V+Caus+A
	E. Pomo	SOV	Instr+Rep+V+Caus+A+T+ Pl+M
	S.-E. Pomo	SOV (?)	Dir+Instr+V+Iter+Dir+(Caus)+ Recip+Refl+(Caus)+Neg+Du+ M+M/A+Q/Evid/Opt
Washo	Washo	SOV	S/OAgr+V+T (?)
Chumash	Chumash	(Adv) VSO	SPers+SNum+Neg/Modal/ Fut/A+Caus+V+OAgr+A
Salinan	Salinan	?	V+Caus+T+S
Esselen	Esselen	SOV; SVO (?)	OAgr+V+Act/Caus+T/A
Seri	Seri	SOV (Decl)	OAgr+SAgr+T/M+Caus+ V(+T?); OAgr+SAgr+T/M+Neg+ Pass+V
Yuman	Diegueño	?	Prog+S/OAgr+V; S/OAgr+V+Fut
	Mojave	SOV (A)	OAgr+SAgr+Caus/Ben+V+T
	Walapai	SOV (?)	SAgr+Caus+V+Distr+Adv+ Neg+Adv+T+Modal+SPl+ SAgr+(±)Cont+(±)Perf+Adv+ Subord
	Yuma	?	N+Loc+Cond+Pl+Imp/ S/OAgr+Caus+V+Dir/Ben/ Modal/Neg/Ints+Hab/Compl+ Adv+T+M
Tonkawa	Tonkawa	SOV	OAgr+Caus+Adv+V+Neg+ Fut+2sO+SNum+Cont+T/M+ SPron

GENUS	LANGUAGE	WORD ORDER	MORPHEME ORDER
Coahuiltecan	Coahuiltec	SOV Caus T Q	SAgr+OAgr+Subord+V
Tequistlatecan	Tequistlateco	SVO	SAgr+V+T
S. Hokan*	Tlapanec	SVO (?)	T/A+2S+Caus+V+S/OAgr
Tanoan	Kiowa	SOV (?)	S/OAgr+V+T
	Tewa	SOV	Neg+S/OAgr+Incorp+V+T/A+ Neg
	S. Tiwa	SOV	S/OAgr+Incorp+V+Caus+T
Numic	Kawaiisu	SVO	V+(Realized)+(Perf)+(*have*)+ (Impf)[10] V+T+(SAgr)+(OAgr)[11] Neg S(ACC) V O(ACC)
	N. Paiute	SOV	Instr+Caus+V+Ben+A
	Shoshone	SOV	V+T/M/A
	S. Paiute	?	V+Caus+T/A+OAgr+SAgr
Tübatulabal*	Tübatulabal	SVO (?)	V+Caus+T+SCl+OCl
Takic	Cahuilla	?	OAgr+SAgr+V+Caus+M/A
	Luiseño	SVO	S M+SAgr+T/A Neg V+Caus+(T/A) O
Hopi	Hopi	S (Neg/M) OV	V+Caus+A+Cont+SPl+M+ Subord
Pimic	Nevome	SO (Aux) V	(O)+V/Perf+Caus+(T)+(S) Aux=(M)+S+Perf+(Fut)+ (Modal)
	N. Tepehuan	VSO	OAgr+V+Caus+T Aux in 2nd pos. = Base+(SAgr)+(Neg)+(T/M/A)
	S.E. Tepe- huan	VSO	(M/A)+(O)+V+Caus+Appl+ A+T+(S)
	Tohono O'odham	VSO	Q Neg Modal VSO Aux in 2nd pos. = M+(SAgr)+(T)+(Modal) Aff+OAgr+V+Distr+Asp+ Conj
Taracahitic	Opata	O S Neg V (?); SOV (?)	V+A+T

GENUS	LANGUAGE	WORD ORDER	MORPHEME ORDER
Taracahitic (cont.)	Tarahumara	SV T/A ?	also: V+T [12] V+Caus V+T/M/A [13]
	Yaqui	Q S Neg OV	V+Caus+Modal+A+Appl
Corachol	Cora	Q Neg SOV	S+O+V+Caus+Modal/Inch/ Dur+Prog+Fut
	Huichol	SVO	Ext+S+Neg+M+O+Dir+V+A; V+Caus
Aztecan	Classical Nahuatl	VSO	(Order)+S+(O)+(Dir)+V+T+ Num; Caus+V; V+Caus
	Huasteca Nahuatl	Neg VSO	SAgr+OAgr+Dim+Dir+ Unsp.O+Incorp+V+Caus+ Appl+A+T+SPl
	Michoacán Nahuatl	SVO; VS	SAgr+OAgr+V+Caus+Appl+ Conn+A+T/Pl
	N. Puebla Nahuatl	Q S Neg VO	Compl+Perf+SAgr+OAgr+ Unsp.O/Hon+V+Caus+Appl+ Hon+A+T+SPl
	Pajapan	?	M/Neg+SAgr+OAgr+V+Caus/ Ben+M+T/A+Num
	Tetelcingo Nahuatl	S Neg VO	(Past+)SAgr+OAgr+Dir+ Unsp.O/Refl+V+Caus+Appl+ Hon+T/A+SPl
*Amuzgo**	Amuzgo	VSO	Emph Neg Modal T+Pl+V+ SPers S O
Otomian	Chichimeco	SOV	SAgr/T/A+V+SNum+Neg+O
	Otomi	Neg VSO	
Mixtecan	Chalcatongo Mixtec	VSO; SVO	T/M/Pol+SPron+Pl+V
	Jicaltepec Mixtec	VSO	Neg T A V S O
Popolocan	Mazatec	?	A+Incmpl/SAgr+V+SAgr
	Popoloc	SVO	M/A+T+V+Loc+Appl/Instr+ Neg+SAgr+OAgr
Chinantecan	Chinantec	VSO	Neg+A+T+V/A/Trans/SAgr; Caus+V

GENUS	LANGUAGE	WORD ORDER	MORPHEME ORDER
Zapotecan	Isthmus Zapotec	SVO (?)	A+Caus+V+(S)+(O)
Tarascan	Tarascan	SVO (?)	V+T+M+OAgr+SAgr

South America

Yanoman	Sanuma	SOV Neg Prt	V+Dur/Punc/Iter+Rep+Ints+ Ext+Spcf+Caus+Cont/Foc+ Dir/Loc Prt=T/Evid/Loc
Cuna*	Cuna	SOV	SAgr+Incorp+V+Inch/Caus+ T/A+Pl
Misumalpan	Miskito	SOV Q	V+T/M/SAgr (Neg); V+Prog/Neg *be*+T/M/SAgr
	Sumu	SOV Decl/Q	V+T/A/Pol/SAgr
Rama*	Rama	SOV	SO Neg V (Aux) (PreV)+(SPron)+V+(A)+T; (PreV)+(SPron)+V+M/Modal
Talamanca	Bribri	SOV	V+T
Guaymí	Ngäbére	SOV; OVS	S Neg (Aux) OV (XP) Q V+A+T+M
Itonama	Itonama	Q SVO	S(O)Agr+Neg+Inter+Rep/ Inch+A+Ben+Caus+Loc/ Incorp+Neg+V+Cont+Dir+ A/Pol+O(S)Agr+Refl+Rep
Timucua*	Timucua	SOV	SPers(+OPers)+V+Trans/ Caus+ActionEmph+SPl+Dur+ Perf+Hab+T+M
Warao	Warao	OSV; SOV	Caus+Dir+V+Motion+Num+ Desid+M/Modal+A+T+Neg+Q
Mura	Pirahã	SOV	V+Dur/Punc+(±)Telic+(±)Perf+ Desid+Neg+Cont+Q+Stat/ Distl/Iter/Certainty+Frust+ Ints+Emph+Cond/Temporal+ Source+Result
Barbacoan	Cayapa	SOV	V+Caus+T+M/Pol/SAgr; V+Fut *be*+M/Pol/SAgr

GENUS	LANGUAGE	WORD ORDER	MORPHEME ORDER
Cahuapanan	Jebero	SVO (?)	Caus+V+Neg/Dir/A+T+SAgr+OAgr
Zaparoan	Huao	SOV	V+T/M/SAgr
Quechua	Ecuadorian Q.	SOV	V+Caus+OAgr+T+SAgr
	Huallaga Q.	SOV	V+Caus+A+OAgr+T+SAgr
	Imbabura Q.	SOV	V+Caus+OAgr+Perf+T/SAgr+Cond/Q
	Tarma Q.	SVO; SOV	V+Caus+OAgr+T+SAgr
Aymara	Aymara	SOV	V+Caus+Refl/Recip+Dir+Ben/Mal+Cont+Pl+(±)Compl+T/M+SAgr+OAgr+Pol
Jaqaru	Jaqaru	SVO	V+Dir+Stat/Caus/Refl+SPl+Modal+Rep+T+S/OAgr
Mapudungu	Mapuche	S Modal VO; SOV, VOS	V+Appl+Neg+T+ODir+Inv+M+SPers+SNum+OInv
Patagonian	Tehuelche	SVO; SOV (?)	(Pron)+V+T/M+(Pron)
Qawescar	Yamana	SVO	SAgr+Appl/Caus/Ben+V+T/M/A
Iranxe	Iranxe	SOV	V+Rev+Caus+Ints/Cont+Fut/Compl+Neg+Compl?
Ticuna	Ticuna	SOV (?)	Cont+Q/Prog/SAgr+Int+O+V+OPl+SPl+Cont/Rep+Caus+Ints+Desid+Adv+Cond
Nambikuaran	Nambikuara	SOV	Cont/Refl/Instr+V+Ben/Caus+OAgr+SAgr+T/Pol+Evid+M
Puinave	Nadëb	OSV (XP)	Theme/A+V; Caus+V
Tucanoan	Cubeo	?	V+T+SAgr
	Guanano	SV; VSO (?)	V+Pl+T/M; V A+T
Cayuvava	Cayuvava	SVO; VOS	M+T/A+Loc/M+SAgr+Class+Pass/Refl/M+V+Class+T/A+Neg+Modal+OAgr+Loc
Trumai	Trumai	SVO; OV SErg	V+Modal Neg; V+A

GENUS	LANGUAGE	WORD ORDER	MORPHEME ORDER
Salivan	Saliva	?	(SAgr)+V+(SAgr)+Neg+T/A+M
Candoshi	Candoshi	?	V+Loc/Ints+T/A+SAgr+Neg/Pot/Emph/Q
Jivaro	Aguaruna	?	V+Caus+OAgr+A+Neg+Pl+S(O)Pers+T+Decl/Opt+Q
Cariri	Kirirí	VOS (?)	SAgr+V+T/A
Mondé*	Gavião	SOV	S (T) O V (M/T) (?)
Tupí-Guaraní	Guajajara	(Q) VSO (Q)	Agr+V
	Guaraní	SVO Q	Neg/Imp+Desid+S(O)Agr+Refl/Recip+Com+V+Caus+Modal+Neg+(A)+T+(A)+Pl
	Kamaiurá	Q SOV	Neg+Agr+V+Neg T/A in 2nd pos.
	Urubu-Kaapor	SOV	SAgr+Caus+V A/Neg/Fut; V SAgr+A
Guahiban	Guahibo	SVO (?)	(Agr?)+Neg+V+Modal+Perf (+Agr?)
Arawan*	Dení	SOV	SAgr+Caus+V+A
	Paumarí	SVO; VS	SAgr+Caus+V+A+Theme/O
	Yamamadí	OSV	SAgr+Caus+V
Chipayan	Chipaya	SOV	V+A/T
Maipuran	Apuriña	OSV	SAgr+Caus+V; V+Caus+OAgr
	Asheninca	S Neg VO	SAgr+(Caus)+V+Caus/Ben+A+T+OAgr
	Guajira	VSO	V+A+T/SAgr (or +T+SAgr); V+SAgr+T/Perf; S+V+T/OAgr; V+Caus+T/Agr
	Island Carib	VSO (?)	Agr+V+Caus+T/A+Agr
	Palikur	SVO	(OAgr+)V+Caus+A+OAgr
	Parecis	SOV	SAgr+V+Caus+A+OAgr
	Terêna	VOS	SAgr+Caus+V+A+OAgr

GENUS	LANGUAGE	WORD ORDER	MORPHEME ORDER
Maipuran (cont.)	Wapishana	SVO	SAgr+V+Refl+Caus+A+M+T+OPron
	Waurá	SVO	SAgr+(Caus+)V+Caus+A+O
	Yucuna	SVO (?)	(Agr)+V+Caus+T/A(+Agr)
Andoke	Andoke	SOV (?)	Dir+Agr+Depl+V+Caus/Ben+M+T/M/SAgr
Peba-Yaguan	Yagua	VSO	Neg (SAgr+M) VSO SAgr+V+Caus+A+T+(OAgr)
Boran	Muinane	SOV (XP) Q	V+Recip+Caus+Pass+Refl+Dir+Desid+Hab+(Mood)+Cont+(Mood)+Past+Mom+(Mood)+Neg+Frust+Mood+SPron
Witotoan	Murui	SOV	V+Caus+A(T/M)+SPl+Neg+Fut+T/SAgr
Carib	Apalai	OVS; SOV	S/OAgr+V+Caus+T/A
	Carib	SOV (?)	S/OAgr+V+Caus+T/A
	Hixkaryana	OVS	S/OAgr+V+T/A/Pl
	Kuikúro	OVS	SPers+V+T/A+Pl
	Macushi	OVS	OPron+V+Caus+A+T+SPron+Num
	Panare	OVS; VSO	S(O)Agr+V+T/A+Trans
	Wayana	?	S/OAgr+V+Caus+Pl+T+Pl
Guaicuruan	Toba	SOV (?)	Agr+V+A+Dir+ONum
Mataco	Mataco	SVO	SAgr+V+T/A
Panoan	Cashibo	SOV	S O Modal+SPers V+Caus+T/A+SAgr
Tacanan	Cavineña	?	V+Caus+T
Rikbaktsa	Rikbaktsa	S Q OV	SAgr+T+OAgr+V+A+SPl V+T/SAgr+Cont+SPl
Iatê	Iatê	SOV (XP)	SAgr+OAgr+Incorp+V+Caus+Neg+T/A+M+Q
Bororoan	Bororo	SVO	SAgr+V+Neg+T
*Botocudo**	Krenak	SOV T/A	Caus+V

GENUS	LANGUAGE	WORD ORDER	MORPHEME ORDER
Chiquito	Chiquito	(S) VO	SAgr+V+Fut+M+OPron+Neg
Ge-Kaingang	Canela	SOV	Q S T/A O V Neg
	Kaingang	SOV	S SAgr O Pl+V Neg Act?
	Shokleng	SOV Stat/Act	V/±Stat/AbsNum

Creoles

English-based, Caribbean	Guyanese Creole	SVO	S T Hab Dur Prog V O
	Saramaccan	SVO	S T/A V O Perf
	Sranan	SVO	S Neg ±A+V O [14]
			S Neg M T A M V O [15]
English-based, West African	Krio	SVO	S Neg T A/Modal V O
English-based, Oceanic	Australian Creole	SVO	S SAgr+T V+Trans+A O
	Bislama	SVO	S SAgr Neg T/M/A VO Compl
	Tok Pisin	SVO	S SAgr Neg T/M/A (Caus) V+Trans O
French-based, Caribbean	Haitian Creole	SVO	S Neg A SAgr+Modal A V O [16]
			S Neg Past+Fut+A+V O [17]
French-based, Indian Ocean	Mauritian Creole	SVO	S Neg T/M/A V O
Dutch-based	Afrikaans	SVO; SOV	S V (Neg) O (Neg); S Past (Neg) O (*ge-*)V (Neg)
	Berbice Dutch	SVO	S (Neg) T/A (Modal) V+ (±Perf) O (Compl) Neg
Portuguese-based	Cape Verdean	SVO	S T/A+(Ant) V O; S V+(Ant) O
	Kriyol	SVO	S Neg A V+Caus Past O; S Neg A V+Caus+OPron Past
Spanish-based	Palenquero	SVO	S T/M/A V O Neg
	Papiamentu	SVO	S Neg Modal T/A VO Compl
Others	Kituba	SVO	S T/A+(Ant) (Inf)+V+(Ant) O

Notes

1. The markers of some derivational categories, such as causative and benefactive, are also included whenever the source provides information about their position. However, the registration of derivational markers is far from complete.

2. According to Westermann (1907).

3. According to Schadeberg (1985).

4. Anywa belongs to the Shilluk cluster of Northern Nilotic (Lusted 1976).

5. The data here are from the language named Bor which belongs to the Dinka group. Another Nilotic language with this name belongs to Northern Luo.

6. The Djamindjungan group is also known as Western Mindi (see Green 1995).

7. Aoki (1970).

8. Rude (1986).

9. See Pullum (1981).

10. Booth (1979).

11. Munro (1976b).

12. Thord-Gray (1955).

13. Burgess (1979).

14. Voorhoeve (1957).

15. Seuren (1983).

16. Spears (1990).

17. Sylvain (1936).

References

Abbott, Miriam. 1991. "Macushi." In Desmond C. Derbyshire and Geoffrey K. Pullum (eds.) *Handbook of Amazonian languages*, Vol. 3, pp. 23–160. De Gruyter, Berlin.

Ackema, Peter 1995. *Syntax below zero.* OTS Dissertation Series, Utrecht University.

Acquaviva, Paolo. 1997. *The logical form of negation.* Garland, New York.

Adelaar, Willem. 1998. Class lectures, LOT Winter School at HIL, Leiden University. [AYMARA, GUARANÍ, QUECHUA]

Adger, David, and George Tsoulas. 2001. "Aspect and lower VP adverbials." *Linguistics in Potsdam* 6, 1–18.

Adone, Danny. 1994. *The acquisition of Mauritian Creole.* John Benjamins, Amsterdam.

Aissen, Judith. 1979. *The syntax of causative constructions.* Garland, New York.

Allen, Barbara J., Donna B. Gardiner, and Donald G. Frantz. 1984. "Noun incorporation in Southern Tiwa." *International Journal of American Linguistics* 50, 292–311.

Andersen, Roger W. 1990. "Papiamentu tense-aspect, with special attention to discourse." In Jon Victor Singler (ed.) *Pidgin and creole tense-mood-aspect systems*, pp. 59–96. John Benjamins, Amsterdam.

Anderson, Stephen R. 1982. "Where's morphology?" *Linguistic Inquiry* 13, 571–612.

Anderson, Stephen R. 1992. *A-morphous morphology.* Cambridge University Press.

Anderson, Stephen R. 1996. "How to put your clitics in their place." *Linguistic Review* 13, 165–191.

Andrews, Avery. 1983. "A note on the constituent structure of modifiers." *Linguistic Inquiry* 14, 695–697.

Aoki, Haruo. 1970. *Nez Perce grammar.* University of California Press, Berkeley.

Arad, Maya. 1998. *VP-structure and the syntax-lexicon interface.* MIT Occasional Papers in Linguistics 16. MIT Working Papers in Linguistics, Cambridge, Massachusetts.

Aronoff, Mark. 1994. *Morphology by itself.* MIT Press, Cambridge, Massachusetts.

Asher, R. E. 1985. *Tamil.* Croom Helm, London.

Asher, R. E., and Christopher Moseley (eds.). 1994. *Atlas of the world's languages.* Routledge, London.

Bach, Emmon. 1971. "Questions." *Linguistic Inquiry* 2, 153–166.

Badecker, William, and Alfonso Caramazza. 1989. "A lexical distinction between inflection and derivation." *Linguistic Inquiry* 20, 108–116.

Baker, Mark C. 1985. "The Mirror Principle and morphosyntactic explanation." *Linguistic Inquiry* 16, 373–415.

Baker, Mark C. 1988a. *Incorporation: A theory of grammatical function changing.* University of Chicago Press.

Baker, Mark C. 1988b. "Morphology and syntax: An interlocking independence." In Martin Eveaert, Arnold Evers, Riny Huybregts, and Mieke Trommelen (eds.) *Morphology and modularity*, pp. 9–32. Foris, Dordrecht.

Baker, Mark C. 1989. "Object sharing and projection in serial verb constructions." *Linguistic Inquiry* 20, 513–553.

Baker, Mark C. 1996. *The polysynthesis parameter.* Oxford University Press.

Barrett-Keach, Camillia N. 1986. "Word-internal evidence from Swahili for Aux/Infl." *Linguistic Inquiry* 17, 559–564.

Bauer, Laurie. 1988. "A descriptive gap in morphology." *Yearbook of Morphology* 1, 17–27.

Bauer, Winifred. 1993. *Maori*. Routledge, London.

Bender, Jorigine, and Akira Y. Yamamoto. 1992. "Hualapai verbs of being, doing, and saying: Transitivity and auxiliaries." *Anthropological Linguistics* 34, 293–310.

Benincá, Paola, and Cecilia Poletto. 1999. "Topic, focus and V2: Defining the CP sublayers." Talk given at the University of Siena, November 1999.

Benmamoun, Elabbas. 1997. "Licensing of negative polarity items in Moroccan Arabic." *Natural Language and Linguistic Theory* 15, 263–287.

Bergsland, Knut, and Moses Dirks. 1981. *Atkan Aleut school grammar*. National Bilingual Materials Development Center, University of Alaska, Anchorage.

Berthelsen, Christian, Inge Kleivan, Frederik Nielsen, Robert Petersen, and Jørgen Rischel (eds.). 1977. *Ordbogi*. Ministeriet for Grønland, Copenhagen.

Beyer, Stephan V. 1992. *The Classical Tibetan language*. State University of New York Press, Albany.

Bhatia, Tej K. 1993. *Punjabi*. Routledge, London.

Bhatt, Rakesh, and James Yoon. 1991. "On the composition of Comp and parameters of V2." In D. Bates (ed.) *Proceedings of the 10th West Coast Conference on Formal Linguistics*, pp. 41–52. Linguistics Dept., Stanford University, California.

Bhattacharya, Pramod Chandra. 1977. *A descriptive analysis of the Boro language*. Department of Publication, Gauhati University, India.

Bickerton, Derek. 1981. *Roots of language*. Karoma, Ann Arbor, Michigan.

Bickerton, Derek. 1984. "The language bioprogram hypothesis." *Behavioral and Brain Sciences* 7, 173–221.

Bickerton, Derek. 1990. *Language and species*. University of Chicago Press.

Blake, Barry J. 1979. "Pitta-Pitta." In R. M. W. Dixon and Barry J. Blake (eds.) *Handbook of Australian languages*, Vol. 1, pp. 182–242. John Benjamins, Amsterdam.

Bloomfield, Leonard. 1933. *Language*. Holt, New York.

Boas, Franz. 1911 (1969). "Introduction." In Franz Boas (ed.) *Handbook of American Indian languages 1*, pp. 1–83. Smithsonian Institution. Bureau of American ethnology, Bulletin 40. Reprinted by Anthropological Publications, Oosterhout.

Bobaljik, Jonathan David. 1995. "Morphosyntax: The syntax of verbal inflection." Doctoral dissertation, MIT.

Bobaljik, Jonathan David, and Andrew Carnie. 1996. "A minimalist approach to some problems of Irish word order." In Robert D. Borsley and Ian Roberts (eds.) *The syntax of the Celtic languages*, pp. 223–240. Cambridge University Press.

Bok-Bennema, Reineke, and Anneke Groos. 1988. "Adjacency and incorporation." In Martin Eveaert, Arnold Evers, Riny Huybregts, and Mieke Trommelen (eds.) *Morphology and modularity*, pp. 33–56. Foris, Dordrecht.

Booij, Geert. 1983. "Principles and parameters in prosodic phonology." *Linguistics* 21, 249–279.

Booij, Geert. 1993. "Against split morphology." *Yearbook of Morphology* 6, 27–49.

Booij, Geert. 1995. "Inherent versus contextual inflection and the split morphology hypothesis." *Yearbook of Morphology* 8, 1–16.

Booij, Geert. 1996. "Cliticization as prosodic integration: The case of Dutch." *Linguistic Review* 13, 219–242.

Booij, Geert. 1997. "Allomorphy and the autonomy of morphology." *Folia Linguistica* 31, 25–56.

Booth, Curtis G. 1979. "Postpositions as verbs in Kawaiisu." *International Journal of American Linguistics* 45, 245–250.

Borer, Hagit. 1993. "The projection of arguments." In Elena Benedicto and Jeffrey Runner (eds.) *Functional projections. University of Massachusetts Occasional Papers* 17, 19–47.

Borer, Hagit. 1998. "Deriving passive without theta roles." In Steven G. Lapointe, Diane Brentari, and Patrick Farrell (eds.) *Morphology and its relation to phonology and syntax*, pp. 60–99. CSLI Publications, Stanford, California.

Borsley, Robert D., Maria Luisa Rivero, and Janig Stephens. 1996. "Long head movement in Breton." In Robert D. Borsley and Ian Roberts (eds.) *The syntax of the Celtic languages*, pp. 53–74. Cambridge University Press.

Boswood, Joan. 1978. *Quer falar a língua dos Canoeiros? Rikbaktsa em 26 lições.* Summer Institute of Linguistics, Brasília.

Bradley, C. Henry. 1970. *A linguistic sketch of Jicaltepec Mixtec.* Summer Institute of Linguistics of the University of Oklahoma, Norman.

Brendemoen, Bernt, and Even Hovdhaugen. 1992. *Tyrkisk grammatikk.* Universitetsforlaget, Oslo.

Bresnan, Joan, and Sam A. Mchombo. 1987. "Topic, pronoun and agreement in Chichewa." *Language* 63, 741–782.

Brockway, Earl. 1979. "North Puebla Nahuatl." In Ronald W. Langacker (ed.) *Studies in Uto-Aztecan grammar.* Vol. 2. Summer Institute of Linguistics/ University of Texas, Arlington.

Burgess, Don. 1979. "Verbal suffixes of prominence in Western Tarahumara narrative discourse." In Linda K. Jones (ed.) *Discourse studies in Mesoamerican languages*, Vol. 1: *Discussion*, pp. 85–94. Summer Institute of Linguistics/University of Texas, Arlington.

Büring, Daniel, and Katarina Hartmann. 1997. "Doing the right thing." *Linguistic Review* 14, 1–42.

Bussmann, Hadumod. 1996. *Routledge dictionary of language and linguistics.* Routledge, London.

Bybee, Joan L. 1985. *Morphology.* John Benjamins, Amsterdam.

Bybee, Joan L., William Pagliuca, and Revere D. Perkins. 1990. "On the asymmetries in the affixation of grammatical material." In William Croft, Suzanne Kemmer, and Keith Denning (eds.) *Studies in typology and diachrony*, pp. 1–39. John Benjamins, Amsterdam.

Capell, A. 1933. "The structure of the Oceanic languages." *Oceania* 3, 418–434.

Carlson, Robert. 1991. "Grammaticalisation of postpositions and word order in Senufo languages." In Elizabeth Closs Traugott and Bernd Heine (eds.) *Approaches to grammaticalization.* Vol. 2: *Focus on types of grammatical markers*, pp. 201–223. John Benjamins, Amsterdam.

Carstairs, Andrew. 1987. *Allomorphy in inflexion.* Croom Helm, London.

Choe, Hyon Sook. 1995. "Focus and topic movement in Korean and licensing." In Katalin É. Kiss (ed.) *Discourse configurational languages*, pp. 269–334. Oxford University Press.

Chomsky, Noam. 1957. *Syntactic structures.* Mouton, The Hague.

Chomsky, Noam. 1970. "Remarks on nominalization." In Roderick A. Jacobs and Peter S. Rosenbaum (eds.) *Readings in English transformational grammar*, pp. 184–221. Ginn and Co., Waltham, Massachusetts.

Chomsky, Noam. 1981. *Lectures on government and binding*. Foris, Dordrecht.

Chomsky, Noam. 1986. *Barriers*. MIT Press, Cambridge, Massachusetts.

Chomsky, Noam. 1991. "Some notes on economy of derivation and representation." In Robert Freidin (ed.) *Principles and parameters in comparative grammar*, pp. 417–454. MIT Press, Cambridge, Massachusetts. [Also in Chomsky 1995.]

Chomsky, Noam. 1993. "A minimalist program for linguistic theory." In Kenneth Hale and Samuel Jay Keyser (eds.) *The view from Building 20*, pp. 1–52. MIT Press, Cambridge, Massachusetts. [Also in Chomsky 1995.]

Chomsky, Noam. 1995. *The minimalist program*. MIT Press, Cambridge, Massachusetts.

Chomsky, Noam. 1998. *Minimalist inquiries: The framework*. MIT Occasional Papers in Linguistics 15. [Also in Roger Martin, David Michaels, and Juan Uriagereka (eds.) 2000. *Step by Step*. MIT Press, Cambridge, Massachusetts.]

Cinque, Guglielmo. 1990. Types of A'-dependencies. MIT Press, Cambridge, Massachusetts.

Cinque, Guglielmo. 1999. *Adverbs and functional heads*. Oxford University Press.

Cinque, Guglielmo. 2000. "'Restructuring' and functional structure." Ms., University of Venice.

Cloarec, France. 1972. *Le verbe Banda*. Langues et civilisations a tradition orale 3. Société d'Ètudes Linguistiques et Anthropologiques de France, Paris.

Colarusso, John. 1989. "East Circassian (Kabardian dialect)." In B. George Hewitt (ed.) *The indigenous languages of the Caucasus*. Vol. 2: *The North West Caucasian languages*, pp. 262–355. Caravan Books, Delmar, New York.

Cole, Peter. 1985. *Imbabura Quechua*. Croom Helm, London.

Collins, Chris. 1997. *Local economy*. MIT Press, Cambridge, Massachusetts.

Comrie, Bernard. 1980. "Morphology and word order reconstruction: Problems and prospects." In Jacek Fisiak (ed.) *Historical morphology*, pp. 83–96. Mouton, The Hague.

Comrie, Bernard. 1993. "Some remarks on causatives and transitivity in Haruai." In Bernard Comrie and Maria Polinsky (eds.) *Causatives and transitivity*, pp. 315–325. John Benjamins, Amsterdam.

Cook, Kevin. 1995. *Dubbel Dutch*. BoekWerk, Groningen, Netherlands.

Costa, João. 1996. "Adverb positioning and V-movement in English: Some more evidence." *Studia Linguistica* 50, 22–34.

Cowper, Elizabeth A., and Keren D. Rice. 1987. "Are phonosyntactic rules necessary?" *Phonology Yearbook* 4, 185–194.

Craig, Colette Grinevald. 1977. *The structure of Jacaltec*. University of Texas Press, Austin.

Cutler, Anne, John A. Hawkins, and Gary Gilligan. 1985. "The suffixing preference: A processing explanation." *Linguistics* 23, 723–758.

Das, A. R. 1977. *A study of the Nicobarese language*. Anthropological Survey of India, Government of India, Calcutta.

Davies, John. 1989. *Kobon*. Routledge, London.

Dayal, Veneeta Srivastav. 1994. "Binding facts in Hindi and the scrambling phenomenon." In Miriam Butt, Tracy Holloway King, and Gillian Ramchand (eds.)

Theoretical perspectives on word order in South Asian languages, pp. 237–261. CSLI Publications, Stanford, California.

Dechaine, Rose-Marie. 1999. "What Algonquian morphology is really like: Hockett revisited." *MIT Occasional Papers in Linguistics* 17, 25–72.

Delsing, Lars-Olof. 1993. "The internal structure of noun phrases in the Scandinavian languages." Doctoral dissertation, Lund university.

Denny, J. Peter. 1989. "The nature of polysynthesis in Algonquian and Eskimo." In Donna B. Gerdts and Karin Michelson (eds.) *Theoretical perspectives on Native American languages*, pp. 230–258. SUNY Press, Albany, New York.

Derbyshire, Desmond C. 1986. "Comparative survey of morphology and syntax in Brazilian Arawakan." In Desmond C. Derbyshire and Geoffrey K. Pullum (eds.) *Handbook of Amazonian languages*, Vol. 1, pp. 469–566. De Gruyter, Berlin.

Dikken, Marcel den. 1996. "The minimal links of Verb (Projection) Raising." In Werner Abraham, Samuel David Epstein, Höskuldur Thráinsson, and C. Jan-Wouter Zwart (eds.) *Minimal ideas*, pp. 67–96. John Benjamins, Amsterdam.

Dezsó, László. 1978. "Towards a typology of theme and rheme: SOV languages." *Linguistisches Kolloquim 12*, pp. 3–11. Niemeyer, Tübingen.

Dimmendaal, Gerrit J. 1982. "The Turkana language." Doctoral dissertation, University of Leiden.

Di Sciullo, Anna Maria, and Edwin Williams. 1987. *On the definition of word*. MIT Press, Cambridge, Massachusetts.

Dixon, R. M. W. 1972. *The Dyirbal language of North Queensland*. Cambridge University Press.

Doke, Clement M. 1929. *The problem of word-division in Bantu, with special reference to the languages of Mashonaland*. Occasional Paper 2, Dept. of Native Development, Southern Rhodesia.

Drijkoningen, Frank. 1994. "Affixation and Logical Form." In Reineke Bok-Bennema and Crit Cremers (eds.) *Linguistics in the Netherlands 1994*, pp. 25–36. John Benjamins, Amsterdam.

Dryer, Matthew S. 1989. "Large linguistic areas and language sampling." *Studies in Language* 13, 257–292.

Dryer, Matthew S. 1992. "The Greenbergian word order correlations." *Language* 68, 81–138.

Du Feu, Veronica. 1996. *Rapanui*. Routledge, London.

Emonds, Joseph E. 1985. *A unified theory of syntactic categories*. Foris, Dordrecht.

Erguvanlí, Eser Ermine. 1984. *The function of word order in Turkish grammar*. University of California Press, Berkeley.

Faarlund, Jan Terje. 1997. "Syntax and morphology in a polysynthetic language: The Zoque noun phrase." Lecture given as part of the course "Forholdet morfologi/syntaks i formell grammatikk." Norwegian University of Science and Technology, Trondheim.

Fagan, Joel L. 1986. *A grammatical analysis of Mono-Alu*. Pacific Linguistics, Series B, 0078-754X 96. Dept. of Linguistics, Research School of Pacific Studies, Australian National University, Canberra.

Fagerli, Ole T. 1994. *Verbal derivations in Fulfulde*. (University of Trondheim) Working Papers in Linguistics 21.

Fortescue, Michael. 1984. *West Greenlandic*. Croom Helm, London.

Franchetto, Bruna. 1990. "Ergativity and nominativity in Kuikúro and other Carib languages." In Doris L. Payne (ed.) *Amazonian linguistics,* pp. 407–427. University of Texas Press, Austin.

Gibson, Kean. 1992. "Tense and aspect in Guyanese Creole with reference to Jamaican and Carriacouan." *International Journal of American Linguistics* 58, 49–95.

Giorgi, Alessandra, and Fabio Pianesi. 1997. *Tense and aspect: From semantics to morphosyntax.* Oxford University Press.

Givón, Talmy. 1971. "Historical syntax and synchronic morphology: An archaeologist's field trip." *Chicago Linguistic Society* 7, 394–415.

Givón, Talmy. 1972. *Studies in Chibemba and Bantu grammar.* Studies in African Linguistics, Vol. 3, Suppl. 3. Dept. of Linguistics and the African Studies Center, University of California, Los Angeles.

Goldsmith, John A. 1990. *Autosegmental and metrical phonology.* Blackwell, Oxford.

Goldstein, Melvyn C., and Nawang Nornang. 1970. *Modern spoken Tibetan: Lhasa dialect.* University of Washington Press, Seattle.

Green, Ian. 1995. "The death of 'prefixing': Contact induced typological change in northern Australia." *Berkeley Linguistics Society* 21, 414–425.

Greenberg, Joseph H. 1963. *Essays in linguistics.* Phoenix Books, University of Chicago Press.

Greenberg, Joseph H. 1966. "Some universals of grammar with particular reference to the order of meaningful elements." In Joseph H. Greenberg (ed.) *Universals of language,* pp. 73–113. MIT Press, Cambridge, Massachusetts.

Grimshaw, Jane. 1986. "A morphosyntactic explanation for the Mirror Principle." *Linguistic Inquiry* 17, 745–750.

Grimshaw, Jane. 1991. "Extended projections." Ms., Rutgers University, New Brunswick, New Jersey.

Grimshaw, Jane. 1997. "Projections, heads, and optimality." *Linguistic Inquiry* 28, 373–422.

Groat, Erich, and John O'Neil. 1996. "Spell-Out at the LF interface." In Werner Abraham, Samuel David Epstein, Höskuldur Thráinsson, and C. Jan-Wouter Zwart (eds.) *Minimal ideas,* pp. 113–139. John Benjamins, Amsterdam.

Guillon, Emmanuel. 1976. "Some aspects of Mon syntax." In Philip N. Jenner, Laurence C. Thompson, and Stanley Starosta (eds.) *Austroasiatic studies, Part 1,* pp. 407–421. University Press of Hawai'i, Honolulu.

Haegeman, Liliane. 1995. *The syntax of negation.* Cambridge University Press.

Hagman, Roy S. 1977. *Nama Hottentot grammar.* Research Center for Language and Semiotic Studies, Indiana University, Bloomington, Indiana.

Haider, Hubert. 1997. "Extraposition." In Dorothee Beerman, David LeBlanc, and Henk van Riemsdijk (eds.) *Rightward movement,* pp. 115–151. John Benjamins, Amsterdam.

Haiman, John. 1980. *Hua: A Papuan language of the eastern highlands of New Guinea.* John Benjamins, Amsterdam.

Hale, Kenneth, and Samuel Jay Keyser. 1993. "On argument structure and the lexical expression of syntactic relations." In Kenneth Hale and Samuel Jay Keyser (eds.) *The view from Building 20,* pp. 53–109. MIT Press, Cambridge, Massachusetts.

Hall, Christopher J. 1988. "Integrating diachronic and processing principles in explaining the suffixing preference." In John A. Hawkins (ed.) *Explaining language universals,* pp. 321–349. Blackwell, Oxford.

Halle, Morris. 1997. "Distributed Morphology: Impoverishment and fission." In Benjamin Bruening, Yoonjung Kang, and Martha McGinnis (eds.) *PF: Papers at the Interface. MIT Working Papers in Linguistics* 30, 425–449.

Halle, Morris, and Alec Marantz. 1993. "Distributed Morphology and the pieces of inflection." In Kenneth Hale and Samuel Jay Keyser (eds.) *The view from Building 20*, pp. 111–176. MIT Press, Cambridge, Massachusetts.

Halle, Morris, and Alec Marantz. 1994. "Some key features of Distributed Morphology." In Andrew Carnie, Heidi Harley, and Tony Bures (eds.) *Papers on phonology and morphology. MIT Working Papers in Linguistics* 21, 275–288.

Hamde, Kiflemariam. 1986. *The origin and development of Bilin.* Bilin Language Project, Asmara University, Eritrea.

Hamel, Patricia J. 1994. *A grammar and lexicon of Loniu, Papua New Guinea.* Pacific Linguistics, Series C, 103. Dept. of Linguistics, Research School of Pacific and Asian Studies, Australian National University, Canberra.

Hardman, M. J., Juana Vásquez, and Juan de Dios Yapita. 1988. *Aymara: Compendia de estructura fonologica y gramatical.* Gramma Impresión, La Paz.

Harrell, Richard S. 1962. *A short reference grammar of Moroccan Arabic.* Georgetown University Press, Washington, D.C.

Harrison, Sheldon P. 1976. *Mokilese reference grammar.* PALI language texts, Micronesia. University Press of Hawai'i, Honolulu.

Haspelmath, Martin. 1993. *A grammar of Lezgian.* Mouton de Gruyter, Berlin.

Hawkins, John A., and Anne Cutler. 1988. "Psycholinguistic factors in morphological asymmetry." In John A. Hawkins (ed.) *Explaining language universals*, 280–317. Blackwell, Oxford.

Hawkins, John A., and Gary Gilligan, 1988. "Prefixing and suffixing universals in relation to basic word order." *Lingua* 74, 219–259.

Hayes, Bruce. 1989. "The prosodic hierarchy in meter." In Paul Kiparsky and Gilbert Youmans (eds.) *Phonetics and phonology 1: Rhythm and meter*, pp. 201–260. Academic Press, San Diego, California.

Hayes, Bruce. 1990. "Precompiled phrasal phonology." In Sharon Inkelas and Draga Zec (eds.) *The phonology-syntax connection*, pp. 85–108. University of Chicago Press.

Heath, Daniel. 1991. "Tense and aspect in Makaa." In Stephen Anderson and Bernard Comrie (eds.) *Tense and aspect in eight languages of Cameroon*, pp. 3–15. Summer Institute of Linguistics/University of Texas, Arlington.

Heath, Jeffrey. 1978. *Ngandi grammar, texts, and dictionary.* Australian Institute of Aboriginal Studies. Humanities Press, Canberra.

Henderson, James. 1995. *Phonology and grammar of Yele, Papua New Guinea.* Pacific Linguistics, Series B, 0078-754X 112. Dept. of Linguistics, Research School of Pacific and Asian Studies, Australian National University, Canberra.

Herring, Susan C. 1990. "Information structure as a consequence of word order type." *General session and parasession on the legacy of Grice. Berkeley Linguistics Society* 16, 163–174.

Herring, Susan C. 1994. "Afterthoughts, antitopics, and emphasis: The syntacticization of postverbal position in Tamil." In Miriam Butt, Tracy Holloway King, and Gillian Ramchand (eds.) *Theoretical perspectives on word order in South Asian languages*, pp. 119–152. CSLI Publications, Stanford, California.

Heycock, Caroline, and Anthony Kroch. 1999. "Pseudocleft connectedness: Implications for the LF interface level." *Linguistic Inquiry* 30, 365–397.

Hoddinott, William G., and Frances M. Kofod. 1988. *The Ngankikurungkurr language*. Pacific Linguistics, Series D, 77. Dept. of Linguistics, Research School of Pacific Studies, Australian National University, Canberra.

Hodge, Stephen. 1990. *An introduction to classical Tibetan*. Aris and Phillips, Warminster.

Hoekstra, Eric. 1997. "Analysing linear asymmetries in the verb clusters of Dutch and Frisian and their dialects." In Dorothee Beerman, David LeBlanc, and Henk van Riemsdijk (eds.) *Rightward movement*, pp. 153–169. John Benjamins, Amsterdam.

Hoekstra, Teun. 1992. "Aspect and theta theory." In Iggy M. Roca (ed.) *Thematic structure: Its role in grammar*, pp. 145–174. Foris, Berlin.

Hoji, Hajime. 1998. "Null object and sloppy identity in Japanese." *Linguistic Inquiry* 29, 127–152.

Holmberg, Anders. 1998a. "Word order variation in some European SVO languages: A parametric approach." In Anna Siewierska (ed.) *Constituent order in the languages of Europe*, pp. 553–598. Mouton de Gruyter, Berlin.

Holmberg, Anders. 1998b. "Basic word order." Talk given at ConSOLE 7, University of Bergen, December 1998.

Holmberg, Anders. 2000a. "OV order in Finnish." In Peter Svenonius (ed.) *The derivation of VO and OV*, pp. 123–152. John Benjamins, Amsterdam.

Holmberg, Anders. 2000b. "Scandinavian Stylistic Fronting: How any category can become an expletive." *Linguistic Inquiry* 31, 445–483.

Holmberg, Anders, Urpo Nikanne, Irmeli Oraviita, Hannu Reime, and Trond Trosterud. 1993. "The structure of INFL and the finite clause in Finnish." In Anders Holmberg and Urpo Nikanne (eds.) *Case and other functional categories in Finnish*, pp. 177–206. Mouton de Gruyter, Berlin.

Holmberg, Anders, and Christer Platzack. 1995. *The role of inflection in Scandinavian syntax*. Oxford University Press.

Horvath, Julia. 1978. "Verbal prefixes: A non-category in Hungarian." *Glossa* 12(2), 137–162.

Hoskison, James Taylor. 1983. "A grammar and dictionary of the Gude language." Doctoral dissertation, Ohio State University.

Huttar, George L., and Mary L. Huttar. 1994. *Ndyuka*. Routledge, London.

Iatridou, Sabine. 1990. "About AgrP." *Linguistic Inquiry* 21, 551–577.

Inkelas, Sharon, and Draga Zec. 1995. "Syntax-phonology interface." In John A. Goldsmith (ed.) *The handbook of phonological theory*, pp. 535–549. Blackwell, Oxford.

Jackendoff, Ray. 1997. *The architecture of the language faculty*. MIT Press, Cambridge, Massachusetts.

Jarvis, Elizabeth. 1991. "Tense and aspect in Podoko narrative and procedural discourse." In Stephen Anderson and Bernard Comrie (eds.) *Tense and aspect in eight languages of Cameroon*, pp. 213–237. Summer Institute of Linguistics/ University of Texas, Arlington.

Jäschke, H. A. 1954. *Tibetan grammar*. Frederick Ungar, New York.

Johnson, Kyle. 1991. "Object positions." *Natural Language and Linguistic Theory* 9, 577–636.

Jones, Robert B. Jr. 1961. *Karen linguistic studies*. University of California Press, Berkeley.

Josefsson, Gunlög. 1997. *On the principles of word formation in Swedish*. Lund University Press. [Published 1998 as *Minimal words in a minimal syntax*. John Benjamins, Amsterdam.]

Juilland, Alphonse, and Alexandra Roceric. 1972. *The linguistic concept of word*. Mouton, The Hague.

Julien, Marit. 2000. "Syntactic heads and word formation: A study of verbal inflection." Doctoral dissertation, University of Tromsø.

Julien, Marit. 2001. "The syntax of complex tenses." *Linguistic Review* 18, 123–165.

Julien, Marit. (Forthcoming a). "On the negated past in Finnic and Saami." In Satu Manninen and Diane Nelson (eds.) *Generative approaches to Finnic linguistics: Case, features and constraints*. CSLI, Stanford, California.

Julien, Marit. (Forthcoming b). "Word order type and syntactic structure." In Johann Roorych and Pierre Pica (eds.) *Language Variation Yearbook*.

Kager, René. 1995. "The metrical theory of word stress." In John A. Goldsmith (ed.) *The handbook of phonological theory*, pp. 367–402. Blackwell, Oxford.

Kanerva, Jonni M. 1987. "Morphological integrity and syntax: The evidence from Finnish possessive suffixes." *Language* 63, 498–521.

Karimi, Simin. 1999. "Is scrambling as strange as we think it is?" In Karlos Arregi, Benjamin Bruening, Cornelia Krause, and Vivian Lin (eds.) *Papers on morphology and syntax, Cycle one. MIT Working Papers in Linguistics 33*, 159–190.

Karlsson, Fred. 1991. *Finsk grammatik*. Suomalaisen Kirjallisuuden Seura, Helsinki.

Kastenholz, Raimund. 1987. "Das Koranko." Doctoral dissertation, Universität zu Köln.

Kastenholz, Raimund. 1989. *Grundkurs Bambara (Manding) mit Texten*. Rüdiger Köppe, Cologne.

Kayne, Richard S. 1991. "Romance clitics, verb movement, and PRO." *Linguistic Inquiry* 22, 647–686.

Kayne, Richard S. 1993. "Toward a modular theory of auxiliary selection." *Studia Linguistica* 47, 3–31.

Kayne, Richard S. 1994. *The antisymmetry of syntax*. MIT Press, Cambridge, Massachusetts.

Kayne, Richard S. 1998. "Overt vs. covert movement." *Syntax* 1, 128–191.

Kayne, Richard S., and Jean-Yves Pollock. 1998. "New thoughts on Stylistic Inversion." Talk given at the conference "Inversion in Romance," University of Amsterdam, May 1998.

Keegan, John M. 1997. *A reference grammar of Mbay*. Lincom Europa, Munich.

Kerke, Simon van de. 1996. "Agreement in Quechua: Evidence against Distributed Morphology." In Crit Cremers and Marcel den Dikken (eds.) *Linguistics in the Netherlands 1996*, pp. 121–131. John Benjamins, Amsterdam.

Kihm, Alain. 1994. *Kriyol syntax*. John Benjamins, Amsterdam.

Kikuchi, Akira, Masayuki Oishi, and Noriaki Yusa. 1994. "Scrambling and Relativized L-relatedness." In Masatoshi Koizumi and Hiroyuki Ura (eds.) *Formal approaches to Japanese linguistics I. MIT Working Papers in Linguistics 24*, 141–158.

Kilian-Hatz, Christa. 1995. *Das Baka*. Institut für Afrikanistik, Universität zu Köln.

Kinkade, M. Dale. 1963a. "Phonology and morphology of Upper Chehalis I." *International Journal of American Linguistics* 29, 181–195.

Kinkade, M. Dale. 1963b. "Phonology and morphology of Upper Chehalis II." *International Journal of American Linguistics* 29, 345–356.

Kinkade, M. Dale. 1964a. "Phonology and morphology of Upper Chehalis III." *International Journal of American Linguistics* 30, 32–61.

Kinkade, M. Dale. 1964b. "Phonology and morphology of Upper Chehalis IV." *International Journal of American Linguistics* 30, 251–260.

Kiss, Katalin É. 1995. "Introduction." In Katalin É. Kiss (ed.) *Discourse configurational languages*, pp. 3–27. Oxford University Press.

Klavans, Judith L. 1985. "The independence of syntax and phonology in cliticization." *Language* 61, 95–120.

Koizumi, Masatoshi. 1993. "Object agreement phrases and the Split VP hypothesis." In Jonathan D. Bobaljik and Colin Phillips (eds.) *Papers on case and agreement I. MIT Working Papers in Linguistics* 18, 99–148.

Koizumi, Masatoshi. 1994. "Nominative objects: The role of TP in Japanese." In Masatoshi Koizumi and Hiroyuki Ura (eds.) *Formal approaches to Japanese linguistics I. MIT Working Papers in Linguistics* 24, 211–230.

Koizumi, Masatoshi. 1995. "Phrase structure in minimalist syntax." Doctoral dissertation, MIT.

Koopman, Hilda. 1984. *The syntax of verbs*. Foris, Dordrecht.

Koopman, Hilda. 1994. "Licensing heads." In David Lightfoot and Norbert Hornstein (eds.) *Verb movement*, pp. 261–296. Cambridge University Press.

Koopman, Hilda. 1996. "The Spec head configuration." Ms., UCLA.

Korhonen, Mikko. 1981. *Johdatus lapin kielen historiaan.* Suomalaisen Kirjallisuuden Seura, Helsinki.

Kornfilt, Jaklin. 1997. *Turkish.* Routledge, London.

Kratzer, Angelika. 1996. "Severing the external argument from its verb." In Johan Rooryck and Laurie Zaring (eds.) *Phrase structure and the lexicon*, pp. 109–137. Kluwer, Dordrecht.

Kristoffersen, Gjert. 2000. *The phonology of Norwegian.* Oxford University Press.

Krupa, Viktor. 1966. *Morpheme and word in Maori.* Mouton, The Hague.

Kulikov, Leonid. 1993. "The second causative." In Bernard Comrie and Maria Polinsky (eds.) *Causatives and transitivity*, pp. 121–154. John Benjamins, Amsterdam.

Kuno, Susumu. 1973. *The structure of the Japanese language.* MIT Press, Cambridge, Massachusetts.

Kural, Murat. 1992. "Properties of scrambling in Turkish." Ms., University of California, Los Angeles.

Kural, Murat. 1997. "Postverbal constituents in Turkish and the Linear Correspondence Axiom." *Linguistic Inquiry* 28, 498–519.

Laka, Itziar. 1993. "The structure of inflection: A case study in X° syntax." In José Ignacio Hualde and Jon Ortiz de Urbina (eds.) *Generative studies in Basque linguistics*, pp. 21–70. John Benjamins, Amsterdam.

Lambrecht, Knud. 1994. *Information structure and sentence form.* Cambridge University Press.

Lapointe, Steven. 1980. "A theory of grammatical agreement." Doctoral dissertation, University of Massachusetts. [Published 1985 by Garland, New York.]

Larson, Richard K. 1988. "On the double object construction." *Linguistic Inquiry* 19, 335–391.

Lasnik, Howard. 1981. "Restricting the theory of transformations: A case study." In Norbert Hornstein and David Lightfoot (eds.) *Explanation in linguistics: The logical problem of language acquisition*, pp. 152–173. Longmans, London.

Lasnik, Howard, and Tim Stowell. 1991. "Weakest crossover." *Linguistic Inquiry* 22, 687–720.

Laycock, D. C. 1975. "The Torricelli phylum." In Stephen A. Wurm (ed.) *New Guinea area languages and language study,* Vol. 1: *Papuan languages and the New Guinea linguistic scene,* pp. 767–780. Pacific Linguistics, Series C, 38. Dept. of Linguistics, Research School of Pacific and Asian Studies, Australian National University, Canberra.

Lees, Robert B. 1960. *The grammar of English nominalizations.* Mouton, The Hague.

Lewis, Sandra C. 1972. "Sanio-Hiowe verb phrases." *Papers in New Guinea Linguistics 15,* 11–22. Pacific Linguistics, Series A, 31. Dept. of Linguistics, Research School of Pacific Studies, Australian National University, Canberra.

Li, Charles N., and Sandra A. Thompson. 1981. *Mandarin Chinese.* University of California Press, Berkeley.

Li, Paul Jen-kuei. 1973. *Rukai structure.* Institute of History and Philology, Academia Sinica, Nankang, Taipei.

Lieber, Rochelle. 1981. *On the organization of the lexicon.* Indiana University Linguistics Club, Bloomington, Indiana.

Lieber, Rochelle. 1992. *Deconstructing morphology.* University of Chicago Press.

Longobardi, Giuseppe. 1994. "Reference and proper names: A theory of N-movement in syntax and Logical Form." *Linguistic Inquiry* 25, 609–665.

Lusted, Marie. 1976. "Anywa." In M. Lionel Bender (ed.) *The non-Semitic languages of Ethiopia,* pp. 495–512. African Studies Center, Michigan State University, East Lansing.

Macaulay, Monica. 1993. "Argument status and constituent structure in Chalcatongo Mixtec." *Special session on syntactic issues in Native American languages, Berkeley Linguistics Society* 19, 73–85.

MacLean, Edna Ahgeak. 1986. *North Slope Iñupiaq grammar.* Alaska Native Language Center, University of Alaska, Fairbanks.

Mahajan, Anoop. 1989. "Agreement and Agreement Phrases." In Itziar Laka and Anoop Mahajan (eds.) *Functional heads and clause structure. MIT Working Papers in Linguistics* 10, 217–252.

Mahajan, Anoop. 1990. "The A/A-bar distinction and movement theory." Doctoral dissertation, MIT.

Mahajan, Anoop. 1997. "Rightward scrambling." In Dorothee Beerman, David LeBlanc, and Henk van Riemsdijk (eds.) *Rightward movement,* pp. 186–213. John Benjamins, Amsterdam.

Mahootian, Shahrzad. 1997. *Persian.* Routledge, London.

Malchukov, Andrey L. 1993. "Adversative constructions in Even in relation to passive and permissive." In Bernard Comrie and Maria Polinsky (eds.) *Causatives and transitivity,* 369–384. John Benjamins, Amsterdam.

Manley, Timothy M. 1972. *Outline of Sre structure.* University Press of Hawai'i, Honolulu.

Manoharan, S. 1989. *A descriptive and comparative study of Andamanese language.* Anthropological Survey of India, Government of India, Calcutta.

Manzini, M. Rita. 1992. *Locality.* MIT Press, Cambridge, Massachusetts.

Manzini, M. Rita, and Leonardo M. Savoia. 1998. "Clitics and auxiliary choice in Italian dialects: Their relevance for the person ergativity split." *Recherches Linguistiques de Vincennes* 27, 115–138.

Manzini, M. Rita, and Leonardo M. Savoia. 2002. "Parameters of subject inflection in Italian dialects." In Peter Svenonius (ed.) *Subjects, expletives, and the EPP*, p. 157–199. Oxford University Press.

Marantz, Alec. 1982. "Re reduplication." *Linguistic Inquiry* 13, 435–482.

Marantz, Alec. 1984. *On the nature of grammatical relations*. MIT Press, Cambridge, Massachusetts.

Marantz, Alec. 1988. "Clitics, morphological merger, and the mapping to phonological structure." In Michael Hammond and Michael Noonan (eds.) *Theoretical morphology*, pp. 253–270. Academic Press, San Diego.

Marantz, Alec. 1993. "Implications of asymmetries in double object constructions." In Sam A. Mchombo (ed.) *Theoretical aspects of Bantu grammar*, pp. 113–150. CSLI Publications, Stanford, California.

Marantz, Alec. 1997. "No escape from syntax." *University of Pennsylvania Working Papers in Linguistics* 4(2), 201–225.

Marantz, Alec. 2001. "Words." Talk given at the West Coast Conference of Formal Linguistics 20, University of Southern California, Los Angeles, February 2001.

Marlett, Stephen A. 1990. "Person and number inflection in Seri." *International Journal of American Linguistics* 56, 503–541.

Matthews, Peter H. 1991. *Morphology*. Second edition. Cambridge University Press.

McCarthy, John. 1982. *Formal problems in Semitic phonology and morphology*. Garland, New York.

McCarthy, John and Alan Prince. 1986. "Prosodic morphology." Ms., University of Massachusetts/Brandeis University.

McCarthy, John, and Alan Prince. 1993a. "Generalized alignment." *Yearbook of Morphology* 6, 79–153.

McCarthy, John, and Alan Prince. 1993b. "Prosodic morphology I." Ms., University of Massachusetts/Rutgers University.

McCloskey, James. 1996. "Subjects and subject positions in Irish." In Robert D. Borsley and Ian Roberts (eds.) *The syntax of the Celtic languages*, pp. 241–283. Cambridge University Press.

McGinnis, Martha. 1995. "Fission as feature-movement." In Rob Pensalfini and Hiroyuki Ura (eds.) *Papers on minimalist syntax. MIT Working Papers in Linguistics* 27, 165-187.

McGloin, Naomi Hanaoka. 1987. "The role of *wa* in negation." In John Hinds, Senko K. Maynard, and Shooichi Iwasaki (eds.) *Perspectives on topicalization: The case of Japanese wa*, pp. 165–183. John Benjamins, Amsterdam.

McGregor, William. 1990. *A functional grammar of Gooniyandi*. John Benjamins, Amsterdam.

McKay, G. R. 1976. "Rembarnga." In R. M. W. Dixon (ed.) *Grammatical categories in Australian languages*, pp. 494–505. Linguistic Series 22, Australian Institute of Aboriginal Studies. Humanities Press, [Atlantic Highlands], New Jersey.

Means, Nathalie, Gordon P. Means, and Paul B. Means. 1986. *Sengoi–English, English–Sengoi dictionary*. Joint Centre on Modern East Asia, University of Toronto/York University, Toronto.

Mitchell, Erika. 1991. "Evidence from Finnish for Pollock's theory of IP." *Linguistic Inquiry* 22, 373–379.

Mitchell, Erika. 1994. "When Agr$_O$ is fused to Agr$_S$: What morphology can tell us about the functional categories." In Heidi Harley and Colin Phillips (eds.) *The morphology-syntax connection. MIT Working Papers in Linguistics* 22, 111–130.

Mithun, Marianne. 1993. "Prosodic determinants of syntactic form: Central Pomo constituent order." *Special session on syntactic issues in Native American languages, Berkeley Linguistics Society* 19, 86–106.

Miyagawa, Shigeru. 1997. "Against optional scrambling." *Linguistic Inquiry* 28, 1–25.

Monachesi, Paola. 1995. "A grammar of Italian clitics." Doctoral dissertation, Tilburg University.

Monachesi, Paola. 1996. "On the representation of Italian clitics." In Ursula Kleinhenz (ed.) *Interfaces in phonology*, pp. 83–101. Akademie Verlag, Berlin.

Mosel, Ulrike, and Even Hovdhaugen. 1992. *Samoan reference grammar*. Scandinavian University Press, Oslo.

Munro, Pamela. 1976a. *Mojave syntax*. Garland, New York.

Munro, Pamela. 1976b. " On the form of the negative sentence in Kawaiisu." *Berkeley Linguistics Society* 2, 308–318.

Muysken, Pieter. 1995. "Focus in Quechua." In Katalin É. Kiss (ed.) *Discourse configurational languages*, pp. 375–393. Oxford University Press.

Myers, Scott. 1990. *Tone and the structure of words in Shona*. Garland, New York.

Nakajima, Takashi. 1999. "Word order in the Minimalist Program: A derivational approach." Doctoral dissertation, Cornell University.

Nakayama, Minaharu, and Masatoshi Koizumi. 1991. "Remarks on Japanese subjects." *Lingua* 85, 303–319.

Nash, Léa. 1994. "On BE and HAVE in Georgian." In Heidi Harley and Colin Phillips (eds.) *The morphology-syntax connection. MIT Working Papers in Linguistics* 22, 153–171.

Nespor, Marina, and Irene Vogel. 1986. *Prosodic phonology*. Foris, Dordrecht.

Nevis, Joel Ashmore. 1988a. *Finnish particle clitics and general clitic theory*. Garland, New York.

Nevis, Joel Ashmore. 1988b. "A morphotactic paradox in Northern Saame: Comitative -guim." *Ural-Altaische Jahrbücher, Neue Folge* 8, 38–50.

Newman, Stanley S. 1969a. "Bella Coola grammatical processes and form classes." *International Journal of American Linguistics* 35, 175–179.

Newman, Stanley S. 1969b. "Bella Coola paradigms." *International Journal of American Linguistics* 35, 299–306.

Nichols, Johanna. 1990. "Linguistic diversity and the first settlement of the New World." *Language* 66, 475–521.

Nickel, Klaus Peter. 1990. *Samisk grammatikk*. Universitetsforlaget, Oslo.

Nilsen, Øystein. 2000. *The syntax of circumstantial adverbials*. Novus, Oslo.

Nkemnji, Michael Akamin. 1995. "Heavy pied-piping in Nweh." Doctoral dissertation, University of California, Los Angeles.

Norman, Jerry. 1988. *Chinese*. Cambridge University Press.

Noonan, Michael. 1992. *A grammar of Lango*. Mouton de Gruyter, Berlin.

Nordlinger, Rachel. 1995. "Split tense and mood inflection in Wambaya." *Berkeley Linguistics Society* 21, 226–236.

Noyer, Rolf. 1992. "Features, positions and affixes in autonomous morphological structure." Doctoral dissertation, MIT.

Noyer, Rolf. 1994. "Mobile affixes in Huave: Optimality and morphological well-formedness." In Erin Duncan, Donka Farkas, and Philip Spaelti (eds.) *Proceedings of the Twelfth West Coast Conference on Formal Linguistics*. CSLI/Leland Stanford Junior University.

Noyer, Rolf. 1998. "Impoverishment theory and morphosyntactic markedness." In Steven G. Lapointe, Diane Brentari, and Patrick Farrell (eds.) *Morphology and its relation to phonology and syntax*, pp. 264–285. CSLI Publications, Stanford, California.

Odden, David. 1987. "Kimatuumbi phrasal phonology." *Phonology Yearbook* 4, 13–36.

Odden, David. 1990. "Syntax, lexical rules and postlexical rules in Kimatuumbi." In Sharon Inkelas and Draga Zec (eds.) *The phonology-syntax connection*, pp. 259–277. University of Chicago Press.

Odden, David. 1996. *The phonology and morphology of Kimatuumbi*. Clarendon Press, Oxford.

Oka, Toshifusa. 1996. "Scrambling in Japanese and English." In Masatoshi Koizumi, Masayuki Oishi, and Uli Sauerland (eds.) *Formal approaches to Japanese linguistics II. MIT Working Papers in Linguistics* 29, 361–388.

Olza Zubiri, Jesús, and Miguel Angel Jusay. 1978. *Gramática de la lengua guajira*. Serie Lenguas indígenas de Venezuela, 20. Centro de Lenguas Indígenas, Universidad Católica Andrés Bello, Caracas.

Osborne, C. R. 1974. *The Tiwi language*. Australian Aboriginal Studies 55. Linguistic Series 21. Australian Institute of Aboriginal Studies, Canberra.

Osumi, Midori. 1995. *Tinrin grammar*. Oceanic Linguistics Special Publication 25. University Press of Hawai'i, Honolulu.

Otani, Kazuyo, and John Whitman. 1991. "V-raising and VP-ellipsis." *Linguistic Inquiry* 22, 345–358.

Ouali, Hamid. 1999. "The clause structure and clitics in Berber." MPhil thesis, University of Tromsø.

Ouhalla, Jamal. 1990. "Sentential negation, Relativised Minimality and the aspectual status of auxiliaries." *Linguistic Review* 7, 183–231.

Ouhalla, Jamal. 1991. *Functional categories and parametric variation*. Routledge, London.

Ouhalla, Jamal. 1997. "Genitive subjects and the VSO order." In Artemis Alexiadou and T. Alan Hall (eds.) *Studies on Universal Grammar and typological variation*, pp. 197–218. John Benjamins, Amsterdam.

Parks, Douglas R. 1976. *A grammar of Pawnee*. Garland, New York.

Payne, Doris L. 1993. "Nonconfigurationality and discontinuous expressions in Panare." *Special session on syntactic issues in Native American languages, Berkeley Linguistics Society* 19, 121–138.

Payne, Doris L., and Thomas E. Payne. 1990. "Yagua." In Desmond C. Derbyshire and Geoffrey K. Pullum (eds.) *Handbook of Amazonian languages*, Vol. 2, pp. 249–474. De Gruyter, Berlin.

Pearson, Matthew. 2000. "Two types of VO languages." In Peter Svenonius (ed.) *The derivation of VO and OV*, pp. 327–363. John Benjamins, Amsterdam.

Perlmutter, David M. 1988. "The Split Morphology hypothesis: Evidence from Yiddish." In Michael Hammond and Michael Noonan (eds.) *Theoretical morphology*, pp. 79–100. Academic Press, San Diego.

Pesetsky, David. 1989. "Language-particular processes and the Earliness principle." Ms., MIT.

Platzack, Christer. 1998. "A visibility condition for the C-domain." *Working Papers in Scandinavian Syntax* 61, 53–99.

Pollock, Jean-Yves. 1989. "Verb movement, Universal Grammar, and the structure of IP." *Linguistic Inquiry* 20, 365–424.

Pollock, Jean-Yves. 1997. "Notes on clause structure." In Liliane Haegeman (ed.) *Elements of grammar*, pp. 237–279. Kluwer, Dordrecht.

Pranka, Paula M. 1983. "Syntax and word formation." Doctoral dissertation, MIT.

Pulleyblank, Douglas. 1986. *Tone in Lexical Phonology*. Reidel, Dordrecht.

Pulleyblank, Douglas, and Akinbiyi Akinlabi. 1988. "Phrasal morphology in Yoruba." *Lingua* 74, 141–166.

Pullum, Geoffrey K. 1981. "Languages with object before subject: A comment and a catalogue." *Linguistics* 19, 147–155.

Pylkkänen, Liina. 2000. "What applicative heads apply to." *University of Pennsylvania Working Papers in Linguistics* 7(1), 197–210.

Rackowski, Andrea and Lisa Travis. 2000. "V-initial languages: X or XP movement and adverbial placement." In Andrew Carnie and Eithne Guilfoyle (eds.) *The syntax of verb Initial languages*, pp. 117–141. Oxford University Press.

Rainer, Frantz. 1995. "Inflection inside derivation: Evidence from Spanish and Portuguese." *Yearbook of Morphology* 8, 83–91.

Redden, James E. 1966. "Walapai II: Morphology." *International Journal of American Linguistics* 32, 141–163.

Rice, Keren. 1989. *A grammar of Slave*. Mouton de Gruyter, Berlin.

Riemsdijk, Henk van. 1990. "Functional prepositions." In H. Pinkster & I. Genée (eds.) *Unity in diversity*, pp. 229–241. Foris, Dordrecht.

Rivero, María Luisa. 1994. "Clause structure and V-movement in the languages of the Balkans." *Natural Language and Linguistic Theory* 12, 63–120.

Rizzi, Luigi. 1997. "The fine structure of the left periphery." In Liliane Haegeman (ed.) *Elements of grammar*, pp. 281–337. Kluwer, Dordrecht.

Rizzi, Luigi, and Ian Roberts. 1989. "Complex inversion in French." *Probus* 1, 1–30.

Roberts, Ian. 1991. "Excorporation and minimality." *Linguistic Inquiry* 22, 209–218.

Roberts, Ian. 1993. *Verbs and diachronic syntax*. Kluwer, Dordrecht.

Roberts, Ian. 1994. "Two types of head movement in Romance." In David Lightfoot and Norbert Hornstein (eds.) *Verb movement*, pp. 207–242. Cambridge University Press.

Roberts, Ian. 1997. "Restructuring, head movement, and locality." *Linguistic Inquiry* 28, 423–460.

Roberts, Ian. 1998. "Have/Be raising, Move F, and Procrastinate." *Linguistic Inquiry* 29, 113–125.

Robertson, Ian E. 1990. "The tense-mood-aspect system of Berbice Dutch." In Jon Victor Singler (ed.) *Pidgin and creole tense-mood-aspect systems*, pp. 169–184. John Benjamins, Amsterdam.

Rochemont, Michael S. 1986. *Focus in generative grammar*. John Benjamins, Amsterdam.

Romero-Figueroa, Andrés. 1985. "OSV as the basic word order in Warao." *Lingua* 66, 115–134.

Rood, David S. 1976. *Wichita grammar*. Garland, New York.

Ross, John Robert. 1970. "Gapping and the order of constituents." In Manfred Bierwisch and Karl Erich Heidolph (eds.) *Progress in linguistics*, pp. 249–259. Mouton, The Hague.

Rouveret, Alain. 1991. "Functional categories and agreement." *Linguistic Review* 8, 353–387.

Rude, Noel. 1986. "Topicality, transitivity, and the direct object in Nez Perce." *International Journal of American Linguistics* 52, 124–153.

Ruhlen, Merritt. 1987. *A guide to the world's languages.* Vol. 1: *Classification.* Stanford University Press, Stanford, California.

Sadock, Jerrold M. 1980. "Noun incorporation in Greenlandic." *Language* 56, 300–319.

Sadock, Jerrold M. 1986. "Some notes on noun incorporation." *Language* 62, 19–31.

Saito, Mamoru, and Naoki Fukui. 1998. "Order in phrase structure and movement." *Linguistic Inquiry* 29, 439–474.

Sakai, Hiromu. 1994. "Derivational economy in long distance scrambling." In Masatoshi Koizumi and Hiroyuki Ura (eds.) *Formal approaches to Japanese linguistics I. MIT Working Papers in Linguistics* 24, 295–314.

Sapir, Edward. 1921. *Language.* Oxford University Press.

Saxton, Dean. 1982. "Papago." In Ronald W. Langacker (ed.) *Studies in Uto-Aztecan grammar.* Vol. 3, pp. 93–266. Summer Institute of Linguistics/ University of Texas, Arlington.

Schadeberg, Thilo C. 1985. *A small sketch of Ewe.* Afrikanistische Arbeitspapiere. Sondernummer. Institut für Afrikanistik, Universität zu Köln.

Selkirk, Elisabeth. 1982. *The syntax of words.* MIT Press, Cambridge, Massachusetts.

Selkirk, Elisabeth. 1986. "On derived domains in sentence phonology." *Phonology Yearbook* 3, 371–405.

Selkirk, Elisabeth, and Tong Shen. 1990. "Prosodic domains in Shanghai Chinese." In Sharon Inkelas and Draga Zec (eds.) *The phonology-syntax connection,* pp. 313–337. University of Chicago Press.

Serzisko, Fritz. 1992. *Sprachhandlungen und Pausen: Diskursorientierte Sprachbeschreibung am Beispiel des Ik.* Max Niemeyer, Tübingen.

Seuren, Pieter A. M. 1983. "The auxiliary system in Sranan." In Frank Heny and Barry Richards (eds.) *Linguistic categories.* Vol. 2: *Auxiliaries and related puzzles,* pp. 219–251. Reidel, Dordrecht.

Shaul, David Leedom. 1986. *Topics in Nevome syntax.* University of California Press, Berkeley.

Shimizu, Kiyoshi. 1980. *A Jukun grammar.* Veröffentlichungen der Institut für Afrikanistik und Ägyptologie der Universität Wien 11. Beiträge zur Afrikanistik 9. Institut für Afrikanistik, Vienna.

Shimojo, Mitsuaki. 1995. "Focus structure and morphosyntax in Japanese: *Wa* and *ga,* and word order flexibility." Doctoral dissertation, State University of New York, Buffalo.

Siewierska, Anna, and Dik Bakker. 1996. "The distribution of subject and object agreement and word order type." *Studies in Language* 20, 115–161.

Sneddon, James Neil. 1996. *Indonesian reference grammar.* Allen and Unwin, St. Leonards, New South Wales.

Snyman, J. W. 1970. *The !Xũ (!Kung) language.* A.A. Balkema, Cape Town.

Solnit, David Benedict. 1986. "A grammatical sketch of Eastern Kayah (Red Karen)." Doctoral dissertation, University of California, Berkeley.

Spears, Arthur K. 1990. "Tense, mood, and aspect in the Haitian Creole preverbal marker system." In Jon Victor Singler (ed.) *Pidgin and creole tense-mood-aspect systems,* pp. 119–142. John Benjamins, Amsterdam.

Speas, Margaret. 1991. "Functional heads and inflectional morphemes." *Linguistic Review* 8, 389–417.

Spencer, Andrew. 1991. *Morphological theory*. Blackwell, Oxford.

Spencer, Andrew. 1992. "Nominal inflection and the nature of functional categories." *Journal of Linguistics* 28, 313–341.

Sportiche, Dominique. 1996. "Clitic constructions." In Johan Rooryck and Laurie Zaring (eds.) *Phrase structure and the lexicon*, pp. 213–276. Kluwer, Dordrecht.

Sproat, Richard. 1985. "On deriving the lexicon." Doctoral dissertation, MIT.

Sproat, Richard. 1988. "On anaphoric islandhood." In Michael Hammond and Michael Noonan (eds.) *Theoretical morphology*, pp. 291–301. Academic Press, San Diego.

Stairs, Emily F., and Barbara Erickson. 1969. "Huave verb morphology." *International Journal of American Linguistics* 35, 38–53.

Stump, Gregory. 1993. "On rules of referral." *Language* 69, 449–479.

Svantesson, Jan-Olof. 1994. "Tense, mood and aspect in Kammu." In Carl Bache, Hans Basbøll, and Carl-Erik Lindberg (eds.) *Tense, aspect and action*, pp. 265–278. Mouton de Gruyter, Berlin.

Svenonius, Peter. 1994a. "C-selection as feature checking." *Studia Linguistica* 48, 133–155.

Svenonius, Peter. 1994b. "Dependent nexus." Doctoral dissertation, University of California, Santa Cruz.

Sylvain, Suzanne. 1936. *Le créole haïtien*. Meester, Wetteren, Belgium.

Szakos, József. 1994. "Die Sprache der Cou." Doctoral dissertation, Rheinische Friedrich-Wilhelms-Universität, Bonn.

Tada, Hiroaki. 1993. "A/A-bar partition in derivation." Doctoral dissertation, MIT.

Takahashi, Daiko. 1993. "Movement of *wh*-phrases in Japanese." *Natural Language and Linguistic Theory* 11, 655–678.

Taylor, Charles. 1985. *Nkore-Kiga*. Croom Helm, London.

Tenny, Carol L. 1987. "Grammaticalizing aspect and affectedness." Doctoral dissertation, MIT.

Tenny, Carol L. 1994. *Aspectual roles and the syntax-semantics interface*. Kluwer, Dordrecht.

Thomson, N. P. 1975. "Magi phonology and grammar: Fifty years afterwards." In Thomas Edward Dutton (ed.) *Studies in languages of Central and Southeast Papua*, pp. 599–666. Pacific Linguistics, Series C, 29. Dept. of Linguistics, Research School of Pacific and Asian Studies, Australian National University, Canberra.

Thord-Gray, I. 1955. *Tarahumara–English, English–Tarahumara dictionary and an introduction to Tarahumara grammar*. University of Miami Press, Coral Gables.

Toyoshima, Takashi. 1997. "'Long' head movement, or wrong 'head movement'?" *Chicago Linguistic Society* 33, 401–416.

Travis, Lisa. 1984. "Parameters and effects of word order variation." Doctoral dissertation, MIT.

Troike, Rudolph C. 1981. "Subject–object concord in Coahuilteco." *Language* 57, 658–673.

Trosterud, Trond. 1994. "Auxiliaries, negative verbs and word order in the Sami and Finnic languages." In Ago Künnap (ed.) *Minor Uralic languages: Structure and development*, 173–181. University of Tartu, Estonia.

Tsujimura, Natsuko. 1996. *An introduction to Japanese linguistics*. Blackwell, Oxford.

Tucker, A. N., and M. A. Bryan. 1966. *Linguistic analysis: The non-Bantu languages of north-eastern Africa*. Oxford University Press.

Ura, Hiroyuki. 1994. "Superraising in Japanese." In Masatoshi Koizumi and Hiroyuki Ura (eds.) *Formal Approaches to Japanese Linguistics I. MIT Working Papers in Linguistics* 24, 355–374.

Vikner, Sten. 1994. "Finite verb movement in Scandinavian embedded clauses." In David Lightfoot and Norbert Hornstein (eds.) *Verb movement*, pp. 117–147. Cambridge University Press.

Voorhoeve, C. L. 1975. "Central and Western Trans-New Guinea Phylum languages." In Stephen A. Wurm (ed.) *New Guinea area languages and language study*, Vol. 1: *Papuan languages and the New Guinea linguistic scene*, pp. 345–460. Pacific Linguistics, Series C, 38. Dept. of Linguistics, Research School of Pacific and Asian Studies, Australian National University, Canberra.

Voorhoeve, J. 1957. "The verbal system of Sranan." *Lingua* 6, 374–396.

Vries, Mark de. 1999. "Extraposition of relative clauses as specifying coordination." In Tina Cambier-Langeveld, Anikó Lipták, Michael Redford, and Erik Jan van der Torre (eds.) *Proceedings of ConSole VII*, pp. 293–309. Student Organisation of Linguistics in Europe, Leiden.

Wali, Kashi, and Omkar N. Koul. 1997. *Kashmiri*. Routledge, London.

Webelhuth, Gert. 1989. "Syntactic saturation phenomena and the modern Germanic languages." Doctoral dissertation, University of Massachusetts, Amherst.

Weber, David John. 1989. *A grammar of Huallaga (Huánuco) Quechua*. University of California Press, Berkeley.

Weir, E. M. Helen. 1986. "Footprints of yesterday's syntax." *Lingua* 68, 291–326.

Westermann, Diedrich. 1907. *Grammatik der Ewe-Sprache*. Dietrich Reimer, Berlin.

Westley, David O. 1991. *Tepetotutla Chinantec syntax*. Summer Institute of Linguistics/University of Texas, Arlington.

Wilder, Chris. 1997. "Some properties of ellipsis in coordination." In Artemis Alexiadou and T. Alan Hall (eds.) *Studies on Universal Grammar and typological variation*, pp. 59–107. John Benjamins, Amsterdam.

Wilkendorf, Patricia. 1991. "Le système temporel et aspectuel de la langue nɔmaándɛ." In Stephen Anderson and Bernard Comrie (eds.) *Tense and aspect in eight languages of Cameroon*, pp. 105–146. Summer Institute of Linguistics/University of Texas, Arlington.

Woodbury, Anthony C., and Jerrold M. Sadock. 1986. "Affixial verbs in syntax: A reply to Grimshaw and Mester." *Natural Language and Linguistic Theory* 4, 229–244.

Woodbury, Hanni. 1975. "Noun incorporation in Onondaga." Doctoral dissertation, Yale University.

Wurm, Stephen A. (ed.). 1975a. *New Guinea area languages and language study*, Vol. 1: *Papuan languages and the New Guinea linguistic scene*, pp. 323–344. Pacific Linguistics, Series C, 38. Dept. of Linguistics, Research School of Pacific and Asian Studies, Australian National University, Canberra.

Wurm, Stephen A. 1975b. "The Trans-Fly (sub-phylum level) stock." In Stephen A. Wurm (ed.) *New Guinea area languages and language study*, Vol. 1: *Papuan languages and the New Guinea linguistic scene*, pp. 323–344. Pacific

Linguistics, Series C, 38. Dept. of Linguistics, Research School of Pacific and Asian Studies, Australian National University, Canberra.

Yanagida, Yuko. 1996. "Deriving surface order in discourse configurational languages." In Masatoshi Koizumi, Masayuki Oishi, and Uli Sauerland (eds.) *Formal approaches to Japanese linguistics II. MIT Working Papers in Linguistics* 29, 283–302.

Yoon, James H. 1994. "Korean verbal inflection and checking theory." In Heidi Harley and Colin Phillips (eds.) *The morphology-syntax connection. MIT Working Papers in Linguistics* 22, 251–270.

Zanuttini, Raffaella. 1994. "Re-examining negative clauses." In Guglielmo Cinque, Jan Koster, Jean-Yves Pollock, Luigi Rizzi, and Raffaella Zanuttini (eds.) *Paths towards Universal Grammar*, pp. 427–451. Georgetown University Press, Washington, D.C.

Zheng, Lijun. 1994. "An elementary generative syntax of verbal constructions in Chinese." MPhil thesis, University of Trondheim, Norway.

Zubizarreta, Maria Luisa. 1998. *Prosody, focus, and word order.* MIT Press, Cambridge, Massachusetts.

Zwart, C. Jan-Wouter. 1993. "Dutch syntax: A minimalist approach." Doctoral dissertation, University of Groningen, Netherlands.

Zwicky, Arnold M. 1985a. "Clitics and particles." *Language* 61, 283–305.

Zwicky, Arnold M. 1985b. "How to describe inflection." *Berkeley Linguistics Society* 11, 372–386.

Zwicky, Arnold M., and Geoffrey K. Pullum. 1983. "Cliticization vs. inflection: English n't." *Language* 59, 502–505.

Other Sources Consulted for Language Classification and Language Data

GENERAL

Asher, R. E., and J. M. Y. Simpson (eds.). 1994. *The encyclopaedia of language and linguistics*. Pergamon Press, Oxford.

Campbell, George L. 1991. *Compendium of the world's languages*. Routledge, London.

Klose, Albrecht. 1987. *Sprachen der Welt*. K. G. Saur, Munich.

Voegelin, Charles Frederick, and Florence Marie Robinett Voegelin. 1977. *Classification and index of the world's languages*. Elsevier, New York.

AFRICA

Abdel-Massih, Ernest T. 1971. *A reference grammar of Tamazight*. Center for Near Eastern and North African Studies, University of Michigan, Ann Arbor.

Allan, Edward J. 1976. "Kullo." In M. Lionel Bender (ed.) *The non-Semitic languages of Ethiopia*, pp. 324–350. African Studies Center, Michigan State University, East Lansing.

Allan, Edward J. 1976. "Dizi." In M. Lionel Bender (ed.) *The non-Semitic languages of Ethiopia*, pp. 377–392. African Studies Center, Michigan State University, East Lansing.

Andersen, Torben. 1994. "From aspect to tense in Lulubo: Morphosyntactic and semantic restructuring in a Central Sudanic language." In Carl Bache, Hans Basbøll, and Carl-Erik Lindberg (eds.) *Tense, aspect and action*, pp. 235–263. Mouton de Gruyter, Berlin.

Arensen, Jon. 1982. *Murle grammar*. Occasional papers in the study of Sudanese languages. College of Education, University of Juba/Summer Institute of Linguistics/Institute of Regional Languages, Juba.

Armbruster, Carl Hubert. 1960. *Dongolese Nubian: A grammar*. Cambridge University Press.

Biddulph, Joseph. 1989. *Bornuese for beginners*. Languages Information Centre, Pontypridd, Wales.

Bliese, Loren. 1976. "Afar." In M. Lionel Bender (ed.) *The non-Semitic languages of Ethiopia*, pp. 133–165. African Studies Center, Michigan State University, East Lansing.

Bodomo, Adams B. 1993. *Complex predicates and event structure*. (University of Trondheim) Working Papers in Linguistics 20.

Bodomo, Adams B. 1997. *The structure of Dagaare*. CSLI Publications, Stanford, California.

Böhm, Gerhard. 1984. *Grammatik der Kunama-Sprache*. Veröffentlichungen der Institut für Afrikanistik und Ägyptologie der Universität Wien, 32. Beiträge zur Afrikanistik, 22. Institut für Afrikanistik, Vienna.

Bouquiaux, Luc. 1970. *La langue birom*. Societé d'édition "Les Belles Lettres," Paris.

Bremicker-Peter, Ursula. 1990. "Description systematique du Waama." Thesis, A.N.R.T. Université de Lille III.

Cowan, J. Ronayne, and Russell G. Schuh. 1976. *Spoken Hausa.* Spoken Language Services, Ithaca, New York.

Creider, Chet A. 1989. *The syntax of the Nilotic languages.* Dietrich Reimer, Berlin.

Edgar, John. 1989. *A Masalit grammar.* Dietrich Reimer, Berlin.

Elderkin, E. Derek. 1976. "Southern Cushitic." In M. Lionel Bender (ed.) *The non-Semitic languages of Ethiopia,* pp. 279–297. African Studies Center, Michigan State University, East Lansing.

Fagborun, J. Gbenga. 1994. *Yoruba verbs and their usage.* Virgocap, Bradford, England.

Faraclas, Nicholas. 1984. *A grammar of Obolo.* Indiana University Linguistics Club, Bloomington, Indiana.

Glinert, Lewis. 1989. *The grammar of Modern Hebrew.* Cambridge University Press.

Haberland, Eike, and Marcelli Camberti. 1988. *Ibaaddo ka-Ba'iso: Culture and language of the Ba'iso.* Carl Winter, Heidelberg.

Hacquard, Augustin. 1897. *Manuel de la langue soñgay parlée de Tombouctou à Say dans la boucle du Niger.* J. Maisonneuve, Paris.

Hagège, Claude. 1970. *La langue mbum de Nganha.* Société d'Ètudes Linguistiques et Anthropologiques de France, Paris.

Hartmann, Josef. 1980. *Amharische Grammatik.* Frans Steiner, Wiesbaden.

Hayward, Dick. 1984. *The Arbore language.* Helmut Buske, Hamburg.

Hetzron, Robert 1990. "Hebrew." In Bernard Comrie (ed.) *The major languages of South Asia, the Middle East and Africa,* pp. 192–210. Routledge, London.

Höftmann, Hildegard. 1971. *The structure of Lelemi language.* VEB Verlag Enzyklopädie, Leipzig.

Holes, Clive 1990. *Gulf Arabic.* Routledge, London.

Hollingsworth, Kenneth R. 1991. "Tense and aspect in Mofu-Gudur." In Stephen Anderson and Bernard Comrie (eds.) *Tense and aspect in eight languages of Cameroon,* pp. 239–255. Summer Institute of Linguistics/ University of Texas, Arlington.

Hudson, Grover. 1976. "Highland East Cushitic." In M. Lionel Bender (ed.) *The non-Semitic languages of Ethiopia,* pp. 232–277. African Studies Center, Michigan State University, East Lansing.

Hudson, Richard A. 1964. "A grammatical study of Beja." Doctoral dissertation, School of Oriental and African studies, University of London.

Hudson, Richard A. 1976. "Beja." In M. Lionel Bender (ed.) *The non-Semitic languages of Ethiopia,* pp. 97–132. African Studies Center, Michigan State University, East Lansing.

Innes, Gordon. 1962. *A Mende grammar.* Macmillan, London.

Jenewari, Charles E. W. 1983. *Defaka: Ijo's closest linguistic relative.* Delta series 2. University of Port Harcourt Press.

Jungraitmayr, Hermann. 1991. *A dictionary of the Tangale language.* Dietrich Reimer, Berlin.

Kauczor, Daniel. 1920. *Die Bergnubische Sprache.* A. Hölder, Vienna.

Kaye, Alan S. 1990. "Arabic." In Bernard Comrie (ed.) *The major languages of South Asia, the Middle East and Africa,* pp. 170–191. Routledge, London.

Kutsch-Lojenga, Constance. 1993. *Ngiti: A Central-Sudanic language of Zaire.* Rüdiger Köppe, Cologne.

Ladusaw, William A. 1985. "The category structure of Kuusal." *Berkeley Linguistics Society* 11, 196–206.

Larochette, J. 1958. *Grammaire des dialectes mangbetu et medje.* Annales du Musée Royal du Congo Belge, Tervuren.

Leslau, Wolf. 1995. *Reference grammar of Amharic.* Harassowitz, Wiesbaden.

Lukas, Johannes. 1937. *A study of the Kanuri language, grammar and vocabulary.* Oxford University Press.

Lydall, Jean. 1976. "Hamer." In M. Lionel Bender (ed.) *The non-Semitic languages of Ethiopia,* pp. 393–438. African Studies Center, Michigan State University, East Lansing.

Marchese, Lynell. 1986. *Tense/aspect and the development of auxiliaries in Kru languages.* Summer Institute of Linguistics, Arlington, Texas.

McIntosh, Mary. 1984. *Fulfulde syntax and verbal morphology.* KPI, Boston.

Melzian, Hans Joachim. 1942. *Vergleichende Charakteristik des Verbums in Bini.* Institut für Lautforschung an der Universität Berlin/Otto Harrassowitz, Leipzig.

Moreno, Martino Mario. 1938. *Introduzione alla lingua ometo.* A. Mondadori, Milan.

Newman, Paul. 1970. *A grammar of Tera.* University of California Press, Berkeley.

Nordbustad, Frøydis. 1988. *Iraqw grammar.* Dietrich Reimer, Berlin.

Novelli, Bruno. 1985. *A grammar of the Karimojong language.* Dietrich Reimer, Berlin.

Nwachukwu, P. Akụjụọobi. 1987. *The argument structure of Igbo verbs.* Lexicon Project Working Papers 18. Center for Cognitive Science, MIT, Cambridge, Massachusetts.

Omondi, Lucia Ndong'a. 1982. *The major syntactic structures of Dholuo.* Dietrich Reimer, Berlin.

Owens, Jonathan. 1985. *A grammar of Harar Oromo.* Helmut Buske, Hamburg.

Palayer, Pierre. 1990. "Le langue Sar." Thesis, A.N.R.T. Université de Lille III.

Picard, André. 1958. *Textes berbères dans le parler des Irjen.* Publications de l'institut d'études orientales d'Alger.

Plungian, Vladimir A. 1993. "Three causatives in Dogon and the overlapping of causative and passive markers." In Bernard Comrie and Maria Polinsky (eds.) *Causatives and transitivity,* pp. 391–396. John Benjamins, Amsterdam.

Reh, Mechthild. 1985. *Die Krongo-Sprache.* Dietrich Reimer, Berlin.

Rossini, Carlo Conti. 1912. *La langue des Kemant en Abyssinie.* Schriften der Sprachenkommisison, Band IV. Kaiserliche Akademie der Wissenschaften, Vienna.

Rowlands, E. C. 1993. *Yoruba.* Hodder and Stoughton, London.

Saeed, John Ibrahim. 1993. *Somali reference grammar.* Dunwoody Press, Kensington, Maryland.

Santandrea, Stefano. 1976. *The Kresh Group, Aja and Baka languages (Sudan).* Istituto Universitario Orientale, Naples.

Sapir, J. David. 1965. *A grammar of Diola-Fogny.* Cambridge University Press.

Sasse, Hans-Jürgen. 1976. "Dasenech." In M. Lionel Bender (ed.) *The non-Semitic languages of Ethiopia,* pp. 196–221. African Studies Center, Michigan State University, East Lansing.

Schadeberg, Thilo C. 1984. *A sketch of Swahili morphology.* Second edition. Foris, Dordrecht.

Schaub, Willi. 1985. *Babungo.* Croom Helm, London.

Thalmann, Peter. 1989. "Elements de grammaire Kroumen Tepo." Thesis, A.N.R.T. Université de Lille III.

Thompson, E. David. 1976. "Nera." In M. Lionel Bender (ed.) *The non-Semitic languages of Ethiopia*, pp. 484–494. African Studies Center, Michigan State University, East Lansing.

Tosco, Mauro. 1991. *A grammatical sketch of Dahalo*. Helmut Buske, Hamburg.

Triulzi, A., A. A. Dafallah, and M. L. Bender. 1976. "Berta." In M. Lionel Bender (ed.) *The non-Semitic languages of Ethiopia*, pp. 513–532. African Studies Center, Michigan State University, East Lansing.

Turton, David, and M. Lionel Bender. 1976. "Mursi." In M. Lionel Bender (ed.) *The non-Semitic languages of Ethiopia*, pp. 533–561. African Studies Center, Michigan State University, East Lansing.

Verkens, A. 1928. *La langue des makere, des medje et des mangbetu*. Bibliotheque Congo 25. Editions Dominicaines, Gent, Belgium.

Wald, Benji. 1990. "Swahili and the Bantu languages." In Bernard Comrie (ed.) *The major languages of South Asia, the Middle East and Africa*, pp. 285–308. Routledge, London.

EURASIA

Alhoniemi, Alho. 1985. *Marin kielioppi*. Suomalais–Ugrilainen Seura, Helsinki.

Aronson, Howard I. 1991. "Modern Georgian." Alice C. Harris (ed.) *The indigenous languages of the Caucasus*. Vol. 1: *The Kartvelian languages*, pp. 219–312. Caravan Books, Delmar, New York.

Bobaljik, Jonathan David, and Susi Wurmbrand. 1997. "Preliminary notes on agreement in Itelmen." In Benjamin Bruening, Yoonjung Kang, and Martha McGinnis (eds.) *PF: Papers at the Interface. MIT Working Papers in Linguistics* 30, 395–423.

Bogoras, Waldemar. 1922 (1969). "Chukchee." In Franz Boas (ed.) *Handbook of American Indian languages 2*, pp. 631–903. Smithsonian Institution. Bureau of American Ethnology, Bulletin 40. Reprinted by Anthropological Publications, Oosterhout N.B., The Netherlands.

Bray, Denis de S. 1909. *The Brahui language, Part I: Introduction and grammar*. Superintendent Government Printing, Calcuttta.

Butt, John, and Carmen Benjamin. 1994. *A new reference grammar of Modern Spanish*. Arnold, London.

Camaj, Martin. 1984. *Albanian grammar*. Otto Harrassowitz, Wiesbaden.

Chang, Suk-Jin. 1996. *Korean*. John Benjamins, Amsterdam.

Charachidzé, Georges. 1981. *Grammaire de la langue avar*. Editions Jean Favard, Paris.

Collinder, Björn. 1940. *Jukagirisch und uralisch*. Uppsala universitets årsskrift, 1940:8. Uppsala.

Donner, Kai. 1955. *Ketica*. Suomalais–ugrilaisen seuran toimituksia 108. Suomalais–Ugrilainen Seura, Helsinki.

Emenau, M. B. 1955. *Kolami, a Dravidian language*. University of California Press, Berkeley.

Friedman, Victor A. 1984. "Status in the Lak verbal system and its typological significance." *Folia Slavica* 7, 135–149.

Ghosh, Arun. 1994. *Santali*. Gyan Publishing House, New Delhi.

Gillies, William. 1993. "Scottish Gaelic." In Martin J. Ball and James Fife (eds.) *The Celtic languages*, pp. 145–227. Routledge, London.

Gruzdeva, Ekaterina. 1998. *Nivkh*. Lincom Europa, Munich.

Gulya, János. 1966. *Eastern Ostyak chrestomathy*. Indiana University, Bloomington.

Haenisch, Erich. 1961. *Mandschu-Grammatik*. VEB Verlag Enzyklopödie, Leipzig.

Hewitt, B. George. 1989. "Abkhaz." In B. George Hewitt (ed.) *The indigenous languages of the Caucasus*. Vol. 2: *The North West Caucasian languages*, pp. 37–88. Caravan Books, Delmar, New York.

Hewitt, B. G., and Z. K. Khiba. 1989. *Abkhaz*. Routledge, London.

Holisky, Dee Ann. 1991. "Laz." In Alice C. Harris (ed.) *The indigenous languages of the Caucasus*. Vol. 1: *The Kartvelian languages*, pp. 395–472. Caravan Books, Delmar, New York.

Kachru, Yamuna. 1990. "Hindi–Urdu." In Bernard Comrie (ed.) *The major languages of South Asia, the Middle East and Africa*, pp. 53–72. Routledge, London.

Kämpfe, Hans-Rainer, and Alexander P. Volodin. 1995. *Abriß der Tschuktschischen Grammatik*. Tunguso Siberica 1. Otto Harrassowitz, Wiesbaden.

Kenesei, István, Robert M. Vago, and Anna Fenyvesi. 1998. *Hungarian*. Routledge, London.

Koptjevskaja-Tamm, Maria, and Irina A. Muravyova. 1993. "Alutor causatives and noun incorporation." In Bernard Comrie and Maria Polinsky (eds.) *Causatives and transitivity*, 287–313. John Benjamins, Amsterdam.

Kozinsky, Isaac, and Maria Polinsky. 1993. "Causee and patient in causative of transitive." In Bernard Comrie and Maria Polinsky (eds.) *Causatives and transitivity*, pp. 177–240. John Benjamins, Amsterdam.

Krueger, John R. 1961. *Chuvash manual*. Indiana University Publications. Uralic and Altaic series 7. Bloomington.

Lewis, G. L. 1967. *Turkish grammar*. Clarendon Press, Oxford.

Lorimer, D. L. R. 1935. *The Burushaski language*. Vol. 1: *Introduction and grammar*. Instituttet for Sammenlignende Kulturforskning. Serie B Skrifter, 29. Aschehoug, Oslo.

Lorimer, D. L. R. 1939. *The Dumaki language*. Publications de la Commission d'Enquete Linguistique 4. Dekker & van de Vegt, Nijmegen, Netherlands.

Mac Eoin, Gearóid. 1993. "Irish." In Martin J. Ball and James Fife (eds.) *The Celtic languages*, pp. 101–144. Routledge, London.

Mackenzie, D. N. 1990. "Pashto." In Bernard Comrie (ed.) *The major languages of South Asia, the Middle East and Africa*, pp. 132–150. Routledge, London.

Magner, Thomas F. 1991. *Introduction to the Croatian and Serbian language*. Pennsylvania State University Press, University Park, Pennsylvania/Thomas F. Magner.

Mallinson, Graham. 1986. *Rumanian*. Croom Helm, London.

Manandise, Esméralda. 1988. *Evidence from Basque for a new theory of grammar*. Garland, New York.

Martin, Samuel E. 1992. *A reference grammar of Korean*. Charles E. Tuttle Company, Rutland, Vermont.

Maslova, Elena S. 1993. "The causative in Yukaghir." In Bernard Comrie and Maria Polinsky (eds.) *Causatives and transitivity*, 271–285. John Benjamins, Amsterdam.

Mathiassen, Terje. 1990. *Russisk grammatikk*. Universitetsforlaget, Oslo.

McGregor, Ronald Stuart. 1972. *Outline of Hindi grammar.* Clarendon Press, Oxford.

Nichols, Johanna. 1994. "Chechen." In Rieks Smeets (ed.) *The indigenous languages of the Caucasus.* Vol. 4: *The North East Caucasian languages, Part 2,* 1–77. Caravan Books, Delmar, New York.

Normann, Magne. 1972. *Tysk grammatikk for gymnaset.* Damm, Oslo.

Ó Siadhail, Mícheál. 1989. *Modern Irish.* Cambridge University Press.

Poppe, Nicholas. 1964. *Grammar of written Mongolian.* Otto Harrassowitz, Wiesbaden.

Pulkina, I. M. *A short Russian reference grammar.* Progress Publishers, Moscow.

Saltarelli, Mario. 1988. *Basque.* Croom Helm, London.

Sammallahti, Pekka. 1974. *Material from Forest Nenets.* Castrenianumin toimitteita 2. Suomalais–Ugrilainen Seura, Helsinki.

Sammallahti, Pekka. 1998. *The Saami languages.* Davvi Girji, Kárášjohka, Norway.

Schmitt, Rüdiger. 1981. *Grammatik der Klassisch-Armenischen.* Innsbrücker Beiträge zur Sprachwissenschaft, Institut für Sprachwissenschaft der Universität Innsbrück.

Senn, Alfred. 1966. *Handbuch der litauischen Sprache.* Band 1: *Grammatik.* Carl Winter, Heidelberg.

Smyth, Herbert Weir. 1920. *Greek grammar.* Harvard University Press, Cambridge, Massachusetts.

Sohn, Ho-Min. 1994. *Korean.* Routledge, London.

Steever, Sanford B. 1990. "Tamil and the Dravidian languages." In Bernard Comrie (ed.) *The major languages of South Asia, the Middle East and Africa,* pp. 231–252. Routledge, London.

Stephens, Jannig. 1993. "Breton." In Martin J. Ball and James Fife (eds.) *The Celtic languages,* pp. 349–409. Routledge, London.

Tchekhoff, Claude. 1980. "The organization of a voice-neutral verb: An example in Avar." *International Review of Slavic Linguistics* 5, 219–230.

Thomas, Alan R. 1992. "The Welsh language." In Donald MacAulay (ed.) *The Celtic languages,* pp. 251–370. Cambridge University Press.

Thráinsson, Höskuldur. 1994. "Icelandic." In Ekkehard König and Johan van der Auwera (eds.) *The Germanic languages,* 142–189. Routledge, London.

Timm, Lenora A. 1989. "Word order in 20th century Breton." *Natural Language and Linguistic Theory* 7, 361–378.

Tyler, Stephen A. 1969. *Koya: An outline grammar.* University of California Press, Berkeley.

Vamling, Karina, and Revaz Tchantouria. 1991. *Sketch of the grammar of Kubachi.* Working Papers 38. Department of Linguistics, Lund University.

Vogt, Hans. 1971. *Grammaire de la langue Géorgienne.* Universitetsforlaget, Oslo.

Watkins, T. Arwyn. 1993. "Welsh." In Martin J. Ball and James Fife (eds.) *The Celtic languages,* pp. 289–348. Routledge, London.

Wurm, Stefan. 1945. *Der özbekische Dialekt von Andidschan.* Sitzungsberichte, Akademie der Wissenschaften in Wien. Philosophisch-historische Klasse 224 Band 3. In Kommission bei Rudolf M. Rohrer, Brünn.

SOUTHEAST ASIA AND OCEANIA

Benjamin, Geoffrey. 1976. "An outline of Temiar grammar." In Philip N. Jenner, Laurence C. Thompson, and Stanley Starosta (eds.) *Austroasiatic studies, Part 1*, pp. 129–187. University Press of Hawai'i, Honolulu.

Burling, Robbins. 1961. *A Garo grammar*. Deccan College, Postgraduate and Research Institute, Pune, India.

Charpentier, Jean-Michael. 1979. *La langue de Port-Sandwich*. Société d'Ètudes Linguistiques et Anthropologiques de France, Paris.

Clark, Marybeth. 1981. "Some auxiliary verbs in Hmong." In *The Hmong in the West: Observations and reports. Papers of the 1981 Hmong Research Conference*, pp. 125–141. University of Minnesota, Minneapolis.

Costello, Nancy. 1966. "Affixes in Katu." In *Katu linguistic articles*, pp. 63–86. Summer Institute of Linguistics, Huntington Beach, California.

Driem, George van. 1993. *A grammar of Dumi*. Mouton de Gruyter, Berlin.

Egli, Hans. 1990. *Paiwangrammatik*. Otto Harrassowitz, Wiesbaden.

Gibson, Jeanne D. 1992. *Clause union in Chamorro and in universal grammar*. Garland, New York.

Grüssner, Karl-Heinz. 1978. *Arleng Alam: Die Sprache der Mikir*. Franz Steiner, Wiesbaden.

Hargreaves, David. 1986. "Independent verbs and auxiliary functions in Newari." *Berkeley Linguistics Society* 12, 401–412.

Harriehausen, Bettina. 1990. *Hmong Njua*. Max Niemeyer, Tübingen.

Henderson, Eugénie J. A. 1976. "Vestiges of morphology in Modern Standard Khasi." In Philip N. Jenner, Laurence C. Thompson, and Stanley Starosta (eds.) *Austroasiatic studies, Part 1*, pp. 477–522. University Press of Hawai'i, Honolulu.

Henne, Henry, Ole Bjørn Rongen, and Lars Jul Hansen. 1977. *A handbook on Chinese language structure*. Universitetsforlaget, Oslo.

Hovdhaugen, Even, Ingjerd Hoëm, Consulata Mahina Iosefo, and Arnfinn Muruvik Vonen. 1989. *A handbook of the Tokelau language*. Norwegian University Press, Oslo.

Jacob, Judith M. 1968. *Introduction to Cambodian*. Oxford University Press.

Janzen, Hermann. 1976. "The system of verb-aspect words in Pale." In Philip N. Jenner, Laurence C. Thompson, and Stanley Starosta (eds.) *Austroasiatic studies, Part 1*, pp. 659–667. University Press of Hawai'i, Honolulu.

Jensen, John Thayer. 1977. *Yapese reference grammar*. PALI language texts, Micronesia. University Press of Hawai'i, Honolulu.

Josephs, Lewis S. et al. 1975. *Palauan reference grammar*. PALI language texts, Micronesia. University Press of Hawai'i, Honolulu.

Kolia, J. A. 1975. "A Balawaia grammar sketch and vocabulary." In Thomas Edward Dutton (ed.) *Studies in languages of Central and Southeast Papua*, pp. 107–226. Pacific Linguistics, Series C, 29. Dept. of Linguistics, Research School of Pacific and Asian Studies, Australian National University, Canberra.

Lalou, Marcelle. 1950. *Manuel élémentaire de tibétain classsique*. Adrien Maisonnneuve, Paris.

Lawton, Ralph, Malcolm Ross, and Janet Ezard. 1993. *Topics in the description of Kiriwina*. Pacific Linguistics, Series D, 0078-7531 84. Dept. of Linguistics,

Research School of Pacific and Asian Studies, Australian National University, Canberra.

Li, Charles N. 1991. "The aspectual system of Hmong." *Studies in Language* 15, 25–58.

Lyman, Thomas Amis. 1974. *Dictionary of Mong Njua*. Mouton, The Hague.

Lyman, Thomas Amis. 1979. *Grammar of Mong Njua (Green Miao)*. Blue Oak Press, Sattley, California.

Massam, Diane 2000. "VSO and VOS: Aspects of Niuean word order." In Andrew Carnie and Eithne Guilfoyle (eds.) *The syntax of verb initial languages*, pp. 97–116. Oxford University Press.

Milne, Mary Lewis Harper. 1921. *An elementary Palaung grammar*. Clarendon Press, Oxford.

Moore, John, and Saowalak Rodchue. 1994. *Colloquial Thai*. Routledge, London.

Nagaraja, K. S. 1985. *Khasi, a descriptive analysis*. Deccan College, Postgraduate and Research Institute, Pune, India.

Oda, Sachiko. 1977. "The syntax of Pulo Annian, a Nuclear Micronesian language." Doctoral dissertation, University of Hawai'i, Honolulu.

Okell, John. 1969. *A reference grammar of colloquial Burmese*. Oxford University Press.

Schachter, Paul, and Fe T. Otanes. 1972. *Tagalog reference grammar*. University of California Press, Berkeley.

Silva-Corvalán, Carmen. 1978. "The Ilokano causative in universal grammar." *Berkeley Linguistics Society* 4, 223–237.

Sohn, Ho-Min. 1975. *Woleaian reference grammar*. PALI language texts, Micronesia. University Press of Hawai'i, Honolulu.

Steele, Susan. 1975. "Is it possible?" *(Stanford University) Working Papers on Language Universals* 18, 35–58.

Thompson, Laurence C. 1965. *A Vietnamese grammar*. University of Washington Press, Seattle.

AUSTRALIA AND NEW GUINEA

Alpher, B. 1976. "Yir Yoront." In R. M. W. Dixon (ed.) *Grammatical categories in Australian languages*, pp. 269–281. Linguistic Series 22, Australian Institute of Aboriginal Studies. Humanities Press, [Atlantic Highlands], New Jersey.

Austin, John, and Randolph Upia. 1975. "Highlights of Ömie morphology." In Thomas Edward Dutton (ed.) *Studies in languages of Central and Southeast Papua*, pp. 513–598. Pacific Linguistics, Series C, 29. Dept. of Linguistics, Research School of Pacific and Asian Studies, Australian National University, Canberra.

Austin, Peter. 1976. "Dhirari." In R. M. W. Dixon (ed.) *Grammatical categories in Australian languages*, pp. 757–763. Linguistic Series 22, Australian Institute of Aboriginal Studies. Humanities Press, [Atlantic Highlands], New Jersey.

Austin, Peter. 1981. *A grammar of Diyari, South Australia*. Cambridge University Press.

Beale, Tony. 1976. "Biri." In R. M. W. Dixon (ed.) *Grammatical categories in Australian languages*, pp. 266–268. Linguistic Series 22, Australian Institute of Aboriginal Studies. Humanities Press, [Atlantic Highlands], New Jersey.

Birk, D. B. W. 1976. *The Malakmalak language, Daly River (Western Arnhem Land)*. Pacific Linguistics, Series B. Dept. of Linguistics, Research School of Pacific Studies, Australian National University, Canberra.

Breen, J. G. 1976. "Ngamini, and a note on Midhaga." In R. M. W. Dixon (ed.) *Grammatical categories in Australian languages,* pp. 745–750. Linguistic Series 22, Australian Institute of Aboriginal Studies. Humanities Press, [Atlantic Highlands], New Jersey.

Breen, J. G. 1981. "Margany and Gunya." In R. M. W. Dixon and Barry J. Blake (eds.) *Handbook of Australian languages*, Vol. 2, pp. 274–393. John Benjamins, Amsterdam.

Bromley, H. Myron. 1981. *A grammar of Lower Grand Valley Dani.* Pacific Linguistics, Series C, 63. Dept. of Linguistics, Research School of Pacific Studies, Australian National University, Canberra.

Bruce, Les. 1984. *The Alamblak language of Papua New Guinea (East Sepik).* Pacific Linguistics, Series C, 81. Dept. of Linguistics, Research School of Pacific Studies, Australian National University, Canberra.

Capell, Arthur. 1969. "The structure of the Binandere verb." *Papers in New Guinea Linguistics 9,* pp. 1–32. Pacific Linguistics, Series A, 18. Dept. of Linguistics, Research School of Pacific and Asian Studies, Australian National University, Canberra.

Capell, Arthur. 1975. "The 'West Papuan phylum': General, and Timor and areas further west." In Stephen A. Wurm (ed.) *New Guinea area languages and language study,* Vol. 1: *Papuan languages and the New Guinea linguistic scene,* pp. 667–716. Pacific Linguistics, Series C, 38. Dept. of Linguistics, Research School of Pacific and Asian Studies, Australian National University, Canberra.

Capell, Arthur. 1976. "Dieri." In R. M. W. Dixon (ed.) *Grammatical categories in Australian languages,* pp. 742–745. Linguistic Series 22, Australian Institute of Aboriginal Studies. Humanities Press, [Atlantic Highlands], New Jersey.

Capell, Arthur, and A. J. Hinch. 1970. *Maung grammar.* Mouton, The Hague.

Chadwick, Neil. 1976. "The Western Barkly languages." In R. M. W. Dixon (ed.) *Grammatical categories in Australian languages,* pp. 390–397, 432–437. Linguistic Series 22, Australian Institute of Aboriginal Studies. Humanities Press, [Atlantic Highlands], New Jersey.

Cowan, H. K. J. 1965. *Grammar of the Sentani language: With specimen texts and vocabulary.* M. Nijhoff, The Hague.

Davis, Donald. 1964. "Wantoat stem classes and affixation." In Benjamin F. Elson (ed.) *Verb studies in five New Guinea languages,* pp. 131–138. Summer Institute of Linguistics of the University of Oklahoma, Norman.

Dench, Alan Charles. 1995. *Martuthunira.* Pacific Linguistics, Series C, 125. Dept. of Linguistics, Research School of Pacific and Asian Studies, Australian National University, Canberra.

Dixon, R. M. W. 1977. *A grammar of Yidiɲ.* Cambridge University Press.

Dixon, R. M. W. 1981. "Wargamay." In R. M. W. Dixon and Barry J. Blake (eds.) *Handbook of Australian languages,* Vol. 2, pp. 1–144. John Benjamins, Amsterdam.

Donaldson, Tamsin. 1980. *Ngiyambaa.* Cambridge University Press.

Dutton, Thomas Edward. 1975. "A Koita grammar sketch and vocabulary." In Thomas Edward Dutton (ed.) *Studies in languages of Central and Southeast Papua,* pp.

281–412. Pacific Linguistics, Series C, 29. Dept. of Linguistics, Research School of Pacific and Asian Studies, Australian National University, Canberra.

Eades, Diana. 1979. "Gumbayngir." In R. M. W. Dixon and Barry J. Blake (eds.) *Handbook of Australian languages*, Vol. 1, pp. 244–361. John Benjamins, Amsterdam.

Evans, Nick. 1995. "Current issues in Australian languages." In John A. Goldsmith (ed.) *The handbook of phonological theory*, pp. 723–761. Blackwell, Oxford.

Farr, James, and Cynthia Farr. 1975. "Some features of Korafe morphology." In Thomas Edward Dutton (ed.) *Studies in languages of Central and Southeast Papua*, pp. 731–769. Pacific Linguistics, Series C, 29. Dept. of Linguistics, Research School of Pacific and Asian Studies, Australian National University, Canberra.

Foley, William A. 1991. *The Yimas language of New Guinea*. Stanford University Press.

Furby, E. S. 1977. *A preliminary analysis of Garawa phrases and clauses*. Pacific Linguistics, Series B. Dept. of Linguistics, Research School of Pacific Studies, Australian National University, Canberra.

Garland, Roger, and Susan Garland. 1975. "A grammar sketch of Mountain Koiali." In Thomas Edward Dutton (ed.) *Studies in languages of Central and Southeast Papua*, pp. 413–470. Pacific Linguistics, Series C, 29. Dept. of Linguistics, Research School of Pacific and Asian Studies, Australian National University, Canberra.

Heath, Jeffrey. 1976. "Nunggubuyu." In R. M. W. Dixon (ed.) *Grammatical categories in Australian languages*, pp. 408–411. Linguistic Series 22, Australian Institute of Aboriginal Studies. Humanities Press, [Atlantic Highlands], New Jersey.

Heath, Jeffrey. 1980. *Basic materials in Warndarang*. Pacific Linguistics, Series B, 72. Dept. of Linguistics, Research School of Pacific Studies, Australian National University, Canberra.

Heeschen, Volker. 1992. *A dictionary of the Yale (Kosarek) language*. Dietrich Reimer, Berlin.

Hercus, Luise A. 1994. *A grammar of the Arabana-Wangkangurru language, Lake Eyre Basin, South Australia*. Pacific Linguistics, Series C, 128. Dept. of Linguistics, Research School of Pacific and Asian Studies, Australian National University, Canberra.

Hoddinott, William G., and Frances M. Kofod. 1976a. "Djamindjungan." In R. M. W. Dixon (ed.) *Grammatical categories in Australian languages*, pp. 397–401, 437–441. Linguistic Series 22, Australian Institute of Aboriginal Studies. Humanities Press, [Atlantic Highlands], New Jersey.

Hoddinott, William G., and Frances M. Kofod. 1976b. "Ngangikurungur." In R. M. W. Dixon (ed.) *Grammatical categories in Australian languages*, pp. 401–405, 691–698. Linguistic Series 22, Australian Institute of Aboriginal Studies. Humanities Press, [Atlantic Highlands], New Jersey.

Hudson, Joyce. 1976. "Walmadjari." In R. M. W. Dixon (ed.) *Grammatical categories in Australian languages*, pp. 653–667. Linguistic Series 22, Australian Institute of Aboriginal Studies. Humanities Press, [Atlantic Highlands], New Jersey.

Keen, Sandra. 1983. "Yukulta." In R. M. W. Dixon and Barry J. Blake (eds.) *Handbook of Australian languages*, Vol. 3, pp. 190–304. John Benjamins, Amsterdam.

Klokeid, T. J. 1976. "Lardil." In R. M. W. Dixon (ed.) *Grammatical categories in Australian languages*, pp. 550–584. Linguistic Series 22, Australian Institute of Aboriginal Studies. Humanities Press, [Atlantic Highlands], New Jersey.

Kofod, F. M. 1976. "Miriwung." In R. M. W. Dixon (ed.) *Grammatical categories in Australian languages*, pp. 584–586, 646–653. Linguistic Series 22, Australian Institute of Aboriginal Studies. Humanities Press, [Atlantic Highlands], New Jersey.

Leeding, Velma J. 1976. "Garawa." In R. M. W. Dixon (ed.) *Grammatical categories in Australian languages*, 382–390. Linguistic Series 22, Australian Institute of Aboriginal Studies. Humanities Press, [Atlantic Highlands], New Jersey.

Loving, Richard, and Howard McKaughan. 1964. "Awa verbs part I." In Benjamin F. Elson (ed.) *Verb studies in five New Guinea languages*, pp. 1–30. Summer Institute of Linguistics of the University of Oklahoma, Norman.

McDonald, Lorna. 1990. *A grammar of Tauya*. Mouton de Gruyter, Berlin.

McElhanon, Kenneth Andrew. 1973. *Towards a typology of the Finisterre-Huon languages*. Pacific Linguistics, Series B, 22. Dept. of Linguistics, Research School of Pacific and Asian Studies, Australian National University, Canberra.

Merlan, Francesca. 1983. *Ngalakan grammar, texts and vocabulary*. Pacific Linguistics, Series B, 89. Dept. of Linguistics, Research School of Pacific Studies, Australian National University, Canberra.

Merlan, Francesca. 1989. *Mangarayi*. Routledge, London.

Merlan, Francesca. 1994. *A grammar of Wardaman*. Mouton de Gruyter, Berlin.

Oates, Lynette. 1976. "Muruwari." In R. M. W. Dixon (ed.) *Grammatical categories in Australian languages*, pp. 244–248, 342–347, 472–474. Linguistic Series 22, Australian Institute of Aboriginal Studies. Humanities Press, [Atlantic Highlands], New Jersey.

Olson, Mike. 1975. "Barai grammar highlights." In Thomas Edward Dutton (ed.) *Studies in languages of Central and Southeast Papua*, pp. 471–512. Pacific Linguistics, Series C, 29. Dept. of Linguistics, Research School of Pacific and Asian Studies, Australian National University, Canberra.

Reesink, Ger P. 1976. "Languages of the Aramia River area." In Ger P. Reesink et al. *Papers in New Guinea Linguistics 19*, pp. 1–76. Pacific Linguistics, Series A, 45. Dept. of Linguistics, Research School of Pacific and Asian Studies, Australian National University, Canberra.

Roberts, John R. 1987. *Amele*. Croom Helm, London.

Seiler, Walter. 1985. *Imonda, a Papuan language*. Pacific Linguistics, Series B, 93. Dept. of Linguistics, Research School of Pacific Studies, Australian National University, Canberra.

Sharpe, M. C. 1976. "Alawa." In R. M. W. Dixon (ed.) *Grammatical categories in Australian languages*, pp. 257–262, 505–515, 708–734. Linguistic Series 22, Australian Institute of Aboriginal Studies. Humanities Press, [Atlantic Highlands], New Jersey.

Thurston, William R. 1987. *Processes of change in the languages of north-western New Britain*. Pacific Linguistics, Series B, 0078-745X 99. Dept. of Linguistics, Research School of Pacific Studies, Australian National University, Canberra.

Vászolyi, E. 1976. "Wunambal." In R. M. W. Dixon (ed.) *Grammatical categories in Australian languages*, pp. 424–426, 629–645. Linguistic Series 22, Australian Institute of Aboriginal Studies. Humanities Press, [Atlantic Highlands], New Jersey.

Walsh, Michael. 1976. "Murinjpata." In R. M. W. Dixon (ed.) *Grammatical categories in Australian languages*, pp. 405–408, 441–444. Linguistic Series 22, Australian Institute of Aboriginal Studies.) Humanities Press, [Atlantic Highlands], New Jersey.

Weimer, Harry, and Natalia Weimer. 1975. "A short sketch of Yareba grammar." In Thomas Edward Dutton (ed.) *Studies in languages of Central and Southeast Papua*, pp. 667–729. Pacific Linguistics, Series C, 29. Dept. of Linguistics, Research School of Pacific and Asian Studies, Australian National University, Canberra.

Wurm, Stephen A. 1975c. "Eastern Central Trans-New Guinea languages." In Stephen A. Wurm (ed.) *New Guinea area languages and language study*, Vol. 1: *Papuan languages and the New Guinea linguistic scene*, pp. 461–526. Pacific Linguistics, Series C, 38. Dept. of Linguistics, Research School of Pacific and Asian Studies, Australian National University, Canberra.

Wurm, Stephen A. 1975d. "The East Papuan phylum in general." In Stephen A. Wurm (ed.) *New Guinea area languages and language study*, Vol. 1: *Papuan languages and the New Guinea linguistic scene*, pp. 783–804. Pacific Linguistics, Series C, 38. Dept. of Linguistics, Research School of Pacific and Asian Studies, Australian National University, Canberra.

NORTH AMERICA

Andrews, J. Richard. 1975. *Introduction to Classical Nahuatl*. University of Texas Press, Austin.

Baker, Mark, and Lisa deMena Travis. 1998. "Events, times, and Mohawk verbal inflection." *Canadian Journal of Linguistics* 43, 149–203.

Barker, M. A. R. 1964. *Klamath grammar*. University of California Press, Berkeley.

Bascom, Burton. 1979. "Northern Tepehuan." In Ronald W. Langacker (ed.) *Studies in Uto-Aztecan grammar*, Vol. 3, pp. 267–393. Summer Institute of Linguistics/University of Texas, Arlington.

Beeler, M. S. 1976. "Barbareño Chumash grammar." In Margaret Langdon and Shirley Silver (eds.) *Hokan studies*, pp. 251–269. Mouton, The Hague.

Beller, Richard, and Patricia Beller. 1979. "Huasteca Nahuatl." In Ronald W. Langacker (ed.) *Studies in Uto-Aztecan grammar*, Vol. 2, pp. 199–306. Summer Institute of Linguistics/University of Texas, Arlington.

Berinstein, Ava. 1985. *Evidence for multiattachment in K'echi*. Garland, New York.

Bishop, Ruth G. 1979. "Tense-aspect in Totonac narrative discourse." In Linda K. Jones (ed.) *Discourse studies in Mesoamerican languages*, pp. 31–68. Summer Institute of Linguistics/University of Texas, Arlington.

Bloomfield, Leonard. 1927. "Notes on the Fox language." *International Journal of American Linguistics* 4, 181–219.

Boas, Franz. 1911a (1969). "Chinook." In Franz Boas (ed.) *Handbook of American Indian languages, Part 1*, pp. 559–677. Smithsonian Institution. Bureau of American Ethnology, Bulletin 40. Reprinted by Anthropological Publications, Oosterhout.

Boas, Franz. 1911b (1969). "Kwakiutl." In Franz Boas (ed.) *Handbook of American Indian languages, Part 1*, pp. 423–557. Smithsonian Institution. Bureau of

American Ethnology, Bulletin 40. Reprinted by Anthropological Publications, Oosterhout.

Boas, Franz. 1927. "Additional notes on the Kutenai language." *International Journal of American Linguistics* 4, 85–104.

Boas, Franz. 1947. *Kwakiutl grammar.* American Philosophical Society, Philadelphia.

Boas, Franz, and Ella Deloria. 1941 (1976). *Dakota grammar.* Memoirs of the National Academy of Sciences, Vol. 23. United States Government Printing Office, Washington, D.C. Reprinted by AMS Press, New York.

Bright, William. 1957. *The Karok language.* University of California Press, Berkeley.

Buckley, Eugene. 1988. "Temporal boundaries in Alsea." *Berkeley Linguistics Society* 14, 10–22.

Canestrelli, Philippo. 1927. "Grammar of the Kutenai language." *International Journal of American Linguistics* 4, 1–84.

Chafe, Wallace L. 1960a. "Seneca morphology II." *International Journal of American Linguistics* 26, 123–129.

Chafe, Wallace L. 1960b. "Seneca morphology III." *International Journal of American Linguistics* 26, 224–233.

Chafe, Wallace L. 1960c. "Seneca morphology IV." *International Journal of American Linguistics* 26, 283–289.

Chafe, Wallace L. 1961a. "Seneca morphology VI." *International Journal of American Linguistics* 27, 114–118.

Chafe, Wallace L. 1961b. "Seneca morphology VII." *International Journal of American Linguistics* 27, 223–225.

Chafe, Wallace L. 1961c. "Seneca morphology VIII." *International Journal of American Linguistics* 27, 320–328.

Chafe, Wallace L. 1976. *The Caddoan, Iroquoian, and Siouan languages.* Mouton, The Hague.

Clark, Lawrence E. 1961. *Sayula Popoluca texts, with grammatical outline.* Summer Institute of Linguistics of the University of Oklahoma, Norman.

Cook, Eung-Do. 1989. "Chilcotin tone and verb paradigms." In Eung-Do Cook and Keren D. Rice (eds.) *Athapaskan linguistics,* pp. 145–199. Mouton de Gruyter, Berlin.

Cowan, Marion M. 1969. *Tzotzil grammar.* Summer Institute of Linguistics of the University of Oklahoma, Norman.

Crowell, Edith. 1949. "A preliminary report on Kiowa structure." *International Journal of American Linguistics* 15, 163–167.

Davies, William D. 1986. *Choctaw verb agreement and universal grammar.* Reidel, Dordrecht.

Davis, Philip W., and Ross Saunders. 1997. *A grammar of Bella Coola.* University of Montana Occasional Papers in Linguistics 13. University of Montana, Missoula.

De Angulo, Jaime. 1932. "The Chichimeco language." *International Journal of American Linguistics* 7, 152–194.

De Angulo, Jaime, and L. S. Freeland. 1931. "The Achumawi language." *International Journal of American Linguistics* 6, 77–120.

DeLancey, Scott. 1991. "Chronological strata of suffix classes in the Klamath verb." *International Journal of American Linguistics* 57, 426–445.

Dixon, Roland B. 1910. "The Chimariko Indians and language." *University of California Publications in American Archaeology and Ethnology* 5, 293–380.

Dozier, Edward. 1953. "Tewa II: Verb structure." *International Journal of American Linguistics* 19, 118–127.

Dryer, Matthew S. 1985. "Tlingit: An object-initial language?" *Canadian Journal of Linguistics* 30, 1–13.

Dunn, John Asher. 1979. *A reference grammar for the Coast Tsimshian language.* National Museums of Canada, Ottawa.

Edel, Mary M. 1939. "The Tillamok language (Coast Salish)." *International Journal of American Linguistics* 10, 1–57.

Enrico, John. 1991. *The lexical phonology of Masset Haida.* Alaska Native Language Center, University of Alaska, Fairbanks.

Foley, Lawrence. 1980. *Phonological variation in Western Cherokee.* Garland, New York.

Foster, Mary Le Cron. 1969. *The Tarascan language.* University of California Press, Berkeley.

Foster, Mary Frazer Le Cron, and George McClelland Foster. 1948. *Sierra Popoluca speech.* Smithsonian Institution, Institute of Social Anthropology, Publication 8. U.S. Government Printing Office, Washington, D.C.

Frachtenberg, Leo J. 1922a (1969). "Coos." In Franz Boas (ed.) *Handbook of American Indian languages, Part 2,* pp. 297–429. Smithsonian Institution. Bureau of American Ethnology, Bulletin 40. Reprinted by Anthropological Publications, Oosterhout.

Frachtenberg, Leo J. 1922b (1969). "Siuslawan (Lower Umpqua.)" In Franz Boas (ed.) *Handbook of American Indian languages, Part 2,* pp. 431–629. Smithsonian Institution. Bureau of American Ethnology, Bulletin 40. Reprinted by Anthropological Publications, Oosterhout.

Frantz, Donald G. 1991. *Blackfoot grammar.* University of Toronto Press.

Freeland, Lucy Shepard. 1951. *Language of the Sierra Miwok.* Waverly Press, Baltimore.

Fuchs, Anna. 1970. *Morphologie des Verbs in Cahuilla.* Mouton, The Hague.

García de León, Antonio. 1976. *Pajapan, un dialecto Mexicano del Golfo.* Instituto Nacional de Antropología e Historia, Mexico City.

Gerdts, Donna B. 1988. *Object and absolutive in Halkomelem Salish.* Garland, New York.

Goddard, Ives. 1979. *Delaware verbal morphology.* Garland, New York.

Golla, Victor. 1976. "Tututni (Oregon Athapaskan)." *International Journal of American Linguistics* 42, 217–227.

Grafstein, Ann. 1989. "Disjoint reference in a 'free word order' language." In Donna B.Gerdts and Karin Michelson (eds.) *Theoretical perspectives on Native American languages,* pp. 163–175. State University of New York Press, Albany.

Grimes, Joseph E. 1964. *Huichol syntax.* Mouton, The Hague.

Grune, Dick. 1995. *Hopi.* Joseph Biddulph, Pontypridd, Wales.

Haas, Mary R. 1946 (1963). "A grammatical sketch of Tunica." In *Linguistic structures of Native America,* pp. 337–366. Viking Fund Publications in Anthropology, 6. Viking Fund, New York. Reprinted by Johnson Reprint Corporation, New York.

Haas, Mary R. 1953. *Tunica dictionary.* University of California Press, Berkeley.

Hagège, Claude. 1981. "Le comox lhaamen de Colombie Britannique." *Amérindia (Revue d'Ethnolinguistique Amerindienne Paris),* Special issue 2, 1–187.

Halpern, A. M. 1946 (1963). "Yuma." In *Linguistic structures of Native America,* pp. 249–288. Viking Fund Publications in Anthropology, 6. Viking Fund, New York. Reprinted by Johnson Reprint Corporation, New York.

Hardy, Heather K., and Philip W. Davis. 1988. "Comparatives in Alabama." *International Journal of American Linguistics* 54, 209–231.

Hardy, Heather K., and Philip W. Davis. 1993. "The semantics of agreement in Alabama." *International Journal of American Linguistics* 59, 453–472.

Hargus, Sharon. 1988. *The lexical phonology of Sekani.* Garland, New York.

Harris, Herbert Raymond II. 1981. "A grammatical sketch of Comox." Doctoral dissertation, University of Kansas.

Hart, Helen Long. 1957. "Hierarchical structure of Amuzgo grammar." *International Journal of American Linguistics* 23, 141–164.

Hess, H. Harwood. 1968. *The syntactic structure of Mezquital Otomi.* Mouton, The Hague.

Hoard, James E. 1979. "The semantic representation of oblique complements." *Language* 55, 319–332.

Hockett, Charles F. 1948a. "Potawatomi I." *International Journal of American Linguistics* 14, 1–10.

Hockett, Charles F. 1948b. "Potawatomi II." *International Journal of American Linguistics* 14, 63–73.

Hockett, Charles F. 1948c. "Potawatomi III." *International Journal of American Linguistics* 14, 139–149.

Hockett, Charles F. 1948d. "Potawatomi IV." *International Journal of American Linguistics* 14, 213–225.

Hoijer, Harry. 1933. *Tonkawa: An Indian language of Texas.* Columbia University Press, New York.

Hollenbach, Barbara. 1992. "A syntactic sketch of Copala Trique." In C. Henry Bradley and Barbara Hollenbach (eds.) *Studies in the syntax of Mixtecan languages 4,* pp. 173–431. Summer Institute of Linguistics/University of Texas, Arlington.

Jacobs, Melville. 1931. "A sketch of Northern Sahaptin grammar." *University of Washington Publications in Anthropology* 4, 85–292.

Jacobsen, William H., Jr. 1977. "A glimpse of the pre-Washo pronominal system." *Berkeley Linguistics Society* 3, 55–73.

Jamieson, Carole Ann. 1982. "Conflated subsystems marking person and aspect in Chiquihuitlán Mazatec verbs." *International Journal of American Linguistics* 48, 139–167.

Jones, William. 1911 (1969). "Algonquian (Fox)." In Franz Boas (ed.) *Handbook of American Indian languages, Part 1,* pp. 735–873. Smithsonian Institution. Bureau of American Ethnology, Bulletin 40. Reprinted by Anthropological Publications, Oosterhout N.B., The Netherlands.

Kennard, Edward. 1936. "Mandan grammar." *International Journal of American Linguistics* 9, 1–43.

Kroeber, A. L. 1910. "The Chumash and Costanoan languages." *University of California Publications in American Archaeology and Ethnology* 9, 237–271.

Kroskrity, Paul V. 1984. "Negation and subordination in Arizona Tewa: Discourse pragmatics influencing syntax." *International Journal of American Linguistics* 50, 94–104.

Kuipers, Aert Hendrik. 1967–1969. *The Squamish language. Grammar, texts, dictionary.* Mouton, The Hague.

Kuipers, Aert Hendrik. 1974. *The Shuswap language. Grammar, texts, dictionary.* Mouton, The Hague.

Langdon, Margaret. 1970. *A grammar of Diegueño (the Mesa Grande dialect).* University of California Press, Berkeley.

LeSourd, Philip S. 1993. *Accent and syllable structure in Passamaquoddy.* Garland, New York.

Li, Charles N., and Sandra A. Thompson. 1977. "The causative in Wappo: A special case of doubling." *Berkeley Linguistics Society* 3, 175–181.

Li, Charles N., Sandra A. Thompson, and Jesse O. Sawyer. 1977. "Subject and word order in Wappo." *International Journal of American Linguistics* 43, 85–100.

Lindenfeld, Jacqueline. 1973. *Yaqui syntax.* University of California Press, Berkeley.

Lupardus, Karen Jacque. 1982. "The language of the Alabama Indians." Doctoral dissertation, University of Kansas.

Mason, J. Alden. 1918. "The language of the Salinan Indians." *University of California Publications in American Archaeology and Ethnology* 14, 1–154.

Matthews, G. Hubert, and Red Thunder Cloud. 1967. "Catawba texts." *International Journal of American Linguistics* 33, 7–24.

McLendon, Sally. 1975. *A grammar of Eastern Pomo.* University of California Press, Berkeley.

Merrifield, William R. 1959. "The Kiowa verb prefix." *International Journal of American Linguistics* 25, 168–176.

Meyer, Karen Sundberg. 1992. "Word order in Klamath." In Doris L. Payne (ed.) *Pragmatics of word order flexibility,* pp. 167–191. John Benjamins, Amsterdam.

Miller, Wick R. 1965. *Acoma grammar and texts.* University of California Press, Berkeley.

Moshinsky, Julius. 1974. *A grammar of Southeastern Pomo.* University of California Press, Berkeley.

Nevin, Bruce E. 1976. "Transformational analysis of some 'grammatical morphemes' in Yana." In Margaret Langdon and Shirley Silver (eds.) *Hokan studies,* pp. 237–250. Mouton, The Hague.

Newman, Stanley S. 1944. *Yokuts language of California.* Viking Fund, New York.

Newman, Stanley S. 1965. *Zuni grammar.* University of New Mexico Press, Albuquerque.

Okrand, Marc. 1977. "Mutsun Grammar." Doctoral dissertation, University of California, Berkeley.

Pickett, Velma B. 1989. "Aspect in Isthmus Zapotec." In Mary Ritchie Key and Henry M. Hoenigswald (eds.) *General and Amerindian ethnolinguistics.* Mouton de Gruyter, Berlin.

Piggott, Glyne L. 1989. "Argument structure and the morphology of the Ojibwa verb." In Donna B. Gerdts and Karin Michelson (eds.) *Theoretical perspectives on Native American languages.* State University of New York Press, Albany.

Pitkin, Harvey. 1984. *Wintu grammar.* University of California Press, Berkeley.

Preuss, K. Th. 1932. "Grammatik der Cora-Sprache." *International Journal of American Linguistics* 7, 1–84.

Radin, Paul. 1929. "A grammar of the Wappo language." *University of California Publications in American Archaeology and Ethnology* 27, 1–194.

Radin, Paul. 1935. "Notes on the Tlappanecan language of Guerrero." *International Journal of American Linguistics* 8, 45–72.

Richter, Gregory C. 1982. "Highland Chontal morphology: Some new perspectives." *International Journal of American Linguistics* 48, 472–476.

Riggs, Stephen Return. 1893 (1973). *Dakota grammar, texts, and ethnography.* U.S. Government Printing Office, Washington, D.C. Reprinted as *Contributions to North American ethnology* 9, Ross and Haines, Minneapolis.

Rigsby, Bruce. 1989. "A later view of Gitksan syntax." In Mary Ritchie Key and Henry M. Hoenigswald (eds.) *General and Amerindian ethnolinguistics*, pp. 245–259. Mouton de Gruyter, Berlin.

Robertson, John S. 1980. *The structure of pronoun incorporation in the Mayan verbal complex.* Garland, New York.

Robinett, Florence M. 1955. "Hidatsa II: Affixes." *International Journal of American Linguistics* 21, 160–177.

Robins, R. H. 1958. *The Yurok language.* University of California Press, Berkeley.

Sapir, Edward. 1922 (1969). "The Takelma language of soutwestern Oregon." In Franz Boas (ed.) *Handbook of American Indian languages, Part 2*, pp. 1–296. Smithsonian Institution. Bureau of American Ethnology, Bulletin 40. Reprinted by Anthropological Publications, Oosterhout.

Sapir, Edward. 1990. *The collected works of Edward Sapir.* Vol. 7: *Takelma texts and grammar.* Mouton de Gruyter, Berlin.

Sapir, Edward. 1992. *The collected works of Edward Sapir.* Vol. 10: *Southern Paiute and Ute.* Mouton de Gruyter, Berlin.

Saunders, Ross, and Philip W. Davis. 1975. "The internal syntax of lexical suffixes in Bella Coola." *International Journal of American Linguistics* 41, 106–114.

Saunders, Ross, and Philip W. Davis. 1989. "Lexical morphemes in Bella Coola." In Mary Ritchie Key and Henry M. Hoenigswald (eds.) *General and Amerindian ethnolinguistics*, pp. 289–301. Mouton de Gruyter, Berlin.

Saxon, Leslie. 1989a. "Agreement in Dogrib." In Donna B. Gerdts and Karin Michelson (eds.) *Theoretical perspectives on Native American languages*, pp. 149–162. State University of New York Press, Albany.

Saxon, Leslie. 1989b. "Lexical versus syntactic projection: The configurationality of Slave." In Eung-Do Cook and Keren D. Rice (eds.) *Athapaskan linguistics*, pp. 379–406. Mouton de Gruyter, Berlin.

Saxon, Leslie. 1990. "Reflexive agreement binding." *Special session on general topics in American Indian linguistics, Berkeley Linguistics Society* 16, 116–127.

Shaul, David Leedom. 1990. "Tequima (Opata) inflectional morphology." *International Journal of American Linguistics* 56, 150–162.

Shaul, David Leedom. 1995. "The Huelel (Esselen) language." *International Journal of American Linguistics* 61, 191–239.

Shimkin, D. B. 1949. "Shoshone I: Linguistic sketch and text." *International Journal of American Linguistics* 15, 175–188.

Shipley, William F. 1964. *Maidu grammar.* University of California Press, Berkeley.

Silver, Shirley Kling. 1966. "The Shasta language." Doctoral dissertation, University of California, Berkeley.

Silverstein, Michael. 1976. "Hierarchy of features and ergativity. " In R. M. W. Dixon (ed.) *Grammatical categories in Australian languages*, pp. 112–171. Linguistic Series 22, Australian Institute of Aboriginal Studies. Humanities Press, [Atlantic Highlands], New Jersey.

Silverstein, Michael. 1984. "Wasco-Wishram derivational processes vs. word-internal syntax." *Papers from the parasession on Lexical Semantics, Chicago Linguistic Society* 20, 270–288.

Sischo, William R. 1979. "Michoacán Nahual." In Ronald W. Langacker (ed.) *Studies in Uto-Aztecan grammar*, Vol. 2, pp. 307–380. Summer Institute of Linguistics/University of Texas, Arlington.

Snapp, Allen, John Anderson, and Jay Anderson. 1982. "Northern Paiute." In Ronald W. Langacker (ed.) *Studies in Uto-Aztecan grammar*, Vol. 3, pp. 1–92. Summer Institute of Linguistics/University of Texas, Arlington.

Steele, Susan. 1978. "The category AUX as a language universal." In Joseph H. Greenberg (ed.) *Universals of human language*, Vol. 3: *Word structure*, pp. 7–45. Stanford University Press.

Steele, Susan. 1990. *Agreement and anti-agreement: A syntax of Luiseño*. Kluwer, Dordrecht.

Swadesh, Morris. 1946 (1963). "Chitimacha." In *Linguistic structures of Native America*, pp. 312–336. Viking Fund Publications in Anthropology, 6. Viking Fund, New York. Reprinted by Johnson Reprint Corporation, New York.

Swadesh, Mary Haas, and Morris Swadesh. 1932. "A visit to the other world, a Nitinat text." *International Journal of American Linguistics* 7, 195–208.

Swanton, John R. 1911a (1969). "Haida." In Franz Boas (ed.) *Handbook of American Indian languages, Part 1*, pp. 205–282. Smithsonian Institution. Bureau of American Ethnology, Bulletin 40. Reprinted by Anthropological Publications, Oosterhout.

Swanton, John R. 1911b (1969). "Tlingit." In Franz Boas (ed.) *Handbook of American Indian languages, Part 1*, pp. 159–204. Smithsonian Institution. Bureau of American Ethnology, Bulletin 40. Reprinted by Anthropological Publications, Oosterhout.

Swanton, John R. 1929. "A sketch of the Atakapa language." *International Journal of American Linguistics* 5, 121–149.

Sylestine, Cora. 1993. *Dictionary of the Alabama language*. University of Texas Press, Austin.

Teeter, Karl V. 1964. *The Wiyot language*. University of California Press, Berkeley.

Teeter, Karl V., and Nichols, John D. 1993. *Wiyot handbook*. Algonquian and Iroquoian Linguistics, Winnipeg.

Tomlin, Russ, and Richard Rhodes. 1979. "An introduction to information distribution in Ojibwa." *Chicago Linguistic Society* 15, 307–310.

Tuggy, David H. 1979. "Tetelcingo Nahuatl." In Ronald W. Langacker (ed.) *Studies in Uto-Aztecan grammar*, Vol. 2, pp. 1–140. Summer Institute of Linguistics/University of Texas, Arlington.

Turner, Paul R. 1968. "Highland Chontal clause syntagmemes." *Linguistics* 38, 77–83.

Uhlenbeck, C. C. 1938. *A concise Blackfoot grammar*. Noord-Hollandsche Uitgeversmaatschappij, Amsterdam.

Velten, H. V. 1939. "Three Tlingit stories." *International Journal of American Linguistics* 10, 168–180.

Voegelin, Charles F. 1935. "Tübatulabal grammar." *University of California Publications in American Archaeology and Ethnology* 34, 55–190.

Whorf, Benjamin Lee. 1946 (1963). "The Hopi language, Torewa dialect." In *Linguistic structures of Native America*, pp. 158–183. Viking Fund Publications in Anthropology, 6. Viking Fund, New York. Reprinted by Johnson Reprint Corporation, New York.

Willett, Thomas Leslie. 1991. *A reference grammar of Southeastern Tepehuan.* Summer Institute of Linguistics/University of Texas, Arlington.

Williams, Ann F., and Robert E. Longacre. 1966. "Popoloca clause types." *Acta Linguistica Hafniensia* 10, 161–186.

Wolff, Hans. 1948. "Yuchi phoneme and morphemes, with special reference to person markers." *International Journal of American Linguistics* 14, 240–243.

Wolff, Hans. 1951. "Yuchi text with analysis." *International Journal of American Linguistics* 17, 48–53.

Yegerlehner, John. 1959. "Arizona Tewa II: Person markers." *International Journal of American Linguistics* 25, 75–80.

Young, Robert W. and William Morgan, Sr. 1987. *The Navajo language.* University of New Mexico Press, Albuquerque.

SOUTH AMERICA

Adam, Lucien, and Victor Henry 1880 (1968). *Arte y vocabulario de la lengua chiquita.* Maisonneuve, Paris. Reprinted by Kraus Reprint, Nendeln/Liechtenstein.

Adelaar, Willem. 1977. *Tarma Quechua.* Peter de Ridder Press, Lisse, Netherlands.

Alphonse, Ephraim S. 1956. *Guaymí grammar and dictionary, with some ethnological notes.* Smithsonian Institution, Bureau of American Ethnology, Bulletin 162. U.S. Government Printing Office, Washington, D.C.

Anderson, Lambert. 1966. "The structure and distribution of Ticuna independent clauses." *Linguistics* 20, 5–30.

Arnold, Jennifer. 1994. "Inverse voice marking in Mapudungun." *Berkeley Linguistics Society* 20, 28–41.

Bendor-Samuel, John T. 1961. *The verbal piece in Jebero.* Linguistic Circle of New York. Monograph 4. Supplement to *Word* 17.

Borgman, Donald M. 1990. "Sanuma." In Desmond C. Derbyshire and Geoffrey K. Pullum (eds.) *Handbook of Amazonian languages*, Vol. 2, pp. 15–248. De Gruyter, Berlin.

Burtch, Bryan, and Mary Ruth Wise. 1968. "Murui (Witotoan) clause structures." *Linguistics* 38, 12–29.

Camp, Elizabeth L. 1985. "Split ergativity in Cavineña." *International Journal of American Linguistics* 51, 38–58.

Camp, Elizabeth, and Millicent Liccardi. 1967. "Itonama." In Esther Matteson (ed.) *Bolivian Indian grammars*, Vol. 2, pp. 257–352. Summer Institute of Linguistics, Norman, Oklahoma.

Cardenas, Víctor Hugo, and Javier Albó. 1983. "El aymara." In Bernard Pottier (ed.) *America latina en sus lenguas indigenas*, pp. 283–310. UNESCO/Monte Avila Editores, Paris.

Chapman, Shirley, and Desmond C. Derbyshire. 1991. "Paumarí." In Desmond C. Derbyshire and Geoffrey K. Pullum (eds.) *Handbook of Amazonian languages*, Vol. 3, pp. 161–352. De Gruyter, Berlin.

°

Conzemius, Eduard. 1929. "Notes on the Miskito and Sumu languages of eastern Nicaragua and Honduras." *International Journal of American Linguistics* 5, 57–115.

Cox, Doris. 1957. "Candoshi verb inflection." *International Journal of American Linguistics* 23, 129–140.

Craig, Colette Grinevald. 1991. "Ways to go in Rama: A case study in polygrammaticalization." In Elizabeth Closs Traugott and Bernd Heine (eds.) *Approaches to grammaticalization*, Vol. 2: *Focus on types of grammatical markers*, pp. 455–492. John Benjamins, Amsterdam.

Derbyshire, Desmond C. 1979. *Hixkaryana*. Lingua Descriptive Studies 1. North-Holland, Amsterdam.

Dickeman-Datz, Margaret. 1985. "Transitive in indefinite voice in Bribri." *International Journal of American Linguistics* 51, 388–390.

Everett, Daniel. 1986. "Pirahã." In Desmond C. Derbyshire and Geoffrey K. Pullum (eds.) *Handbook of Amazonian languages*, Vol. 1, pp. 200–325. De Gruyter, Berlin.

Fernandez-Garay, Ana. 1995. "L´ergativité en tehuelche." *Linguistique* 31, 27–47.

Gómez Bacarreza, Donato, and José Condori Cosme. 1992. *Morfologia y gramatica del idioma aymara.* [s. n.], La Paz.

Goodbar, Perla Golbert de. 1985. "Hacía una morfología verbal del Yagan." *International Journal of American Linguistics* 51, 421–424.

Granberry, Julian. 1990. "A grammatical sketch of Timucua." *International Journal of American Linguistics* 56, 60–101.

Gregores, Emma, and Jorge A. Suárez. 1967. *A description of colloquial Guaraní.* Mouton, The Hague.

Hardman, M. J. 1966. *Jaqaru.* Mouton, The Hague.

Harrison, Carl H. 1986. "Verb prominence, verb initialness, ergativity and typological disharmony in Guajajara." In Desmond C. Derbyshire and Geoffrey K. Pullum (eds.) *Handbook of Amazonian languages*, Vol. 1, pp. 407–439. De Gruyter, Berlin.

Henry, Jules. 1935. "A Kaingang text." *International Journal of American Linguistics* 8, 172–218.

Hoff, B. J. 1968. *The Carib language.* Martinus Nijhoff, The Hague.

Holmer, Nils M. 1946. "Outline of Cuna grammar." *International Journal of American Linguistics* 12, 185–197.

Huestis, George. 1963. "Bororo clause structure." *International Journal of American Linguistics* 29, 230–238.

Jackson, Walter S. 1972. "A Wayana grammar." In Joseph E. Grimes (ed.) *Languages of the Guianas*, pp. 47–77. Summer Institute of Linguistics/University of Oklahoma, Norman.

Kakumasu, James. 1986. "Urubu-Kaapor." In Desmond C. Derbyshire and Geoffrey K. Pullum (eds.) *Handbook of Amazonian languages*, Vol. 1, pp. 326–403. De Gruyter, Berlin.

Key, Harold H. 1967. *Morphology of Cayuvava.* Mouton, The Hague.

Klein, Harriet E. Manelis. 1981. "Location and direction in Toba: Verbal morphology." *International Journal of American Linguistics* 47, 227–235.

Koehn, Edward, and Sally Koehn. 1986. "Apalai." In Desmond C. Derbyshire and Geoffrey K. Pullum (eds.) *Handbook of Amazonian languages*, Vol. 1, pp. 33–127. De Gruyter, Berlin.

Kondo, Victor. 1974. "Textos Guahibo." In *Folclor indígena de Colombia*, pp. 199–231. División Operativa de Asuntos Indígenas/Summer Institute of Linguistics/Editorial Townsend, Lomalinda.

Kramer, Marvin. 1993. "Hixkaryana word order." *Special session on syntactic issues in Native American languages, Berkeley Linguistics Society* 19, 57–72.

Krivoshein de Canese, Natalia, and Reinaldo Decoud Larrosa. 1983. *Gramática de la lengua guaraní*. N. Krivoshein de Canese, Asunción.

Kroeker, Barbara. 1982. *Aspectos da língua nambikuára*. Summer Institute of Linguistics, Brasília.

Landaburu, Jon. 1979. *La langue des Andoke (Amazonie colombienne)*. Langues et Cvilisations a Tradition Orale 36. Société d'Ètudes Linguistiques et Anthropologiques de France, Paris.

Lapenda, Geraldo. 1968. *Estrutura da lingua Iatê*. Universidade Federal de Pernambuco, Recife.

Larsen, Thomas W. 1984. "Case marking and subjecthood in Kipeá Kirirí." *Berkeley Linguistics Society* 10, 189–205.

Larson, Mildred L. 1966. *Vocabulario aguaruna de Amazonas*. Instituto Lingüístico de Verano, Yarinacocha.

Lindskoog, John N., and Carrie A. Lindskoog. 1964. *Vocabulario cayapa, compilado*. Serie de vocabularios indígenas Mariano Silva y Aceves, 9. Instituto Lingüístico de Verano/Ministerio de Educación Pública, Quito.

Martín, Eusebia Herminia, and Lucy Therina Briggs. 1981. "Aymara syntactic relations and derivational verb suffixes (revised version)." *International Journal of American Linguistics* 47, 236–242.

Meader, Robert E. 1967. *Iranxe: Notas gramaticais e lista vocabular*. Museo Nacional, Universidade Federal do Rio de Janeiro.

Monod-Becquelin, Aurore. 1975. *La pratique linguistique des Indiens Trumai*. Langues et Civilisations a Tradition Orale 9. Société d'Ètudes Linguistiques et Anthropologiques de France, Paris.

Moore, Denny. 1989. "Gavião nominalizations as relative clause and sentential complement equivalents." *International Journal of American Linguistics* 55, 309–325.

Muysken, Pieter. 1977. *Syntactic developments in the verb phrase of Ecuadorian Quechua*. Peter de Ridder Press, Lisse, Netherlands.

Muysken, Pieter. 1981. "Quechua word structure." In Frank Henry (ed.) *Binding and filtering*, pp. 279–327. Croom Helm, London.

Osborn, Henry A. Jr. 1967. "Warao III: Verbs and suffixes." *International Journal of American Linguistics* 33, 46–64.

Payne, David Lawrence. 1981. *The phonology and morphology of Axininca Campa*. Summer Institute of Linguistics, University of Texas, Arlington.

Payne, Doris L. 1986. "Basic constituent order in Yagua clauses: Implications for word order universals." In Desmond C. Derbyshire and Geoffrey K. Pullum (eds.) *Handbook of Amazonian languages*, Vol. 1, pp. 440–465. De Gruyter, Berlin.

Payne, Thomas E. 1990. "Transitivity and ergativity in Panare." In Doris L. Payne (ed.) *Amazonian linguistics*, pp. 429–453. University of Texas Press, Austin.

Peeke, M. Catherine. 1973. *Preliminary grammar of Auca*. Summer Institute of Linguistics/University of Oklahoma, Norman.

Popjes, Jack, and Jo Popjes. 1986. "Canela-Krahô." In Desmond C. Derbyshire and Geoffrey K. Pullum (eds.) *Handbook of Amazonian languages*, Vol. 1, pp. 128–199. De Gruyter, Berlin.

Porterie-Gutierrez, Liliane. 1990. "Documentos para el estudio de la lengua chipaya." *Amerindia* 15, 157–191.

Romero-Figueroa, Andrés. 1997. *A reference grammar of Warao*. Lincom Europa, München.

Salser, J. K. 1974. "Textos Cubeo." In *Folclor indígena de Colombia*, pp. 91–154. División Operativa de Asuntos Indígenas/Summer Institute of Linguistics/Editorial Townsend, Lomalinda.

Schauer, Stanley. 1974. "Texto Yucuna." In *Folclor indígena de Colombia*, pp. 253–333. División Operativa de Asuntos Indígenas/Summer Institute of Linguistics/Editorial Townsend, Lomalinda.

Seki, Lucy F. 1985. "A note on the last Botocudo language." *International Journal of American Linguistics* 51, 581–583.

Seki, Lucy. 1990. "Kamaiurá (Tupí-Guaraní) as an Active-Stative language." In Doris L. Payne (ed.) *Amazonian linguistics*, pp. 367–391. University of Texas Press, Austin.

Shell, Olive A. 1957. "Cashibo II: Grammemic analysis of transitive and intransitive verb patterns." *International Journal of American Linguistics* 23, 179–218.

Smeets, Ineke. 1989. "A Mapuche grammar." Doctoral dissertation, University of Leiden.

Suárez, María Matilde. 1977. *La lengua sáliva. Serie Lenguas indígenas de Venezuela 19*. Centro de Lenguas Indígenas, Instituto de Investigaciones Históricas, Universidad Católica Andrés Bello, Caracas.

Taylor, Douglas. 1977. *Languages of the West Indies*. John Hopkins University Press, Baltimore.

Tracy, Frances V. 1974. "An introduction to Wapishana verb morphology." *International Journal of American Linguistics* 40, 120–125.

Urban, Greg. 1985. "Ergativity and accusativity in Shokleng (Gê)." *International Journal of American Linguistics* 51, 164–187.

Viñas Urquiza, María Teresa. 1974. *Lengua Mataca*. Centro de estudios lingüisticos, Universidad de Buenos Aires.

Walton, James W., and Janice Walton. 1975. *Una gramática de la lengua muinane*. Instituto Lingüístico de Verano/Ministerio de Gobierno, República de Colombia, Bogotá.

Waltz, Nathan. 1974. "Texto Guanano." In *Folclor indígena de Colombia*, pp. 11–61. División Operativa de Asuntos Indígenas/Summer Institute of Linguistics/Editorial Townsend, Lomalinda.

Weir, E. M. Helen. 1990. "Incorporation in Nadëb." In Doris L. Payne (ed.) *Amazonian linguistics*, pp. 321–363. University of Texas Press, Austin.

Young, Philip D., and Talmy Givón. 1990. "The puzzle of Ngäbére auxiliaries: Grammatical reconstruction in Chibchan and Misumalpan." In William Croft, Suzanne Kemmer, and Keith Denning (eds.) *Studies in typology and diachrony*, pp. 209–243. John Benjamins, Amsterdam.

CREOLES

Byrne, Francis. 1992. "Tense, scope and spreading in Saramaccan." *Journal of Pidgin and Creole Languages* 7, 195–221.

Crowley, Terry. 1990. *Beach-la-Mar to Bislama*. Clarendon Press, Oxford.

Cunningham, Irma A. E. 1992. *A syntactic analysis of Sea Island Creole*. University of Alabama Press, Tuscaloosa.

Donaldson, Bruce C. 1993. *A grammar of Afrikaans*. Mouton de Gruyter, Berlin.

Dutton, Tom, and Dicks Thomas. 1985. *A new course in Tok Pisin*. Pacific Linguistics, Series D, 67. Dept. of Linguistics, Research School of Pacific and Asian Studies, Australian National University, Canberra.

Graber, Philip L. 1991. "Thematic participant in a Kriol story." *Journal of Pidgin and Creole Languages* 6, 209–227.

Jones, Frederick C. V. 1990. "The grammatical items *bin*, *fO*, and *mOs* in Sierra Leone Krio." *Linguistics* 28, 845–866.

Kihm, Alain. 1990. "Aspect in Kriyol and the theory of inflection." *Linguistics* 28, 713–740.

Kouwenberg, Silvia. 1994. *A grammar of Berbice Dutch Creole*. Mouton de Gruyter, Berlin.

Mufwene, Salikoko S. 1990. "Time reference in Kikongo-Kituba." In Jon Victor Singler (ed.) *Pidgin and creole tense-mood-aspect systems*, pp. 97–117. John Benjamins, Amsterdam.

Schwegler, Armin. 1991. "Negation in Palenquero: Syncrony." *Journal of Pidgin and Creole Languages* 6, 165–214.

Silva, Izione S. 1990. "Tense and aspect in Capeverdean Crioulo." In Jon Victor Singler (ed.) *Pidgin and creole tense-mood-aspect systems*, pp. 143–168. John Benjamins, Amsterdam.

Todd, Loreto. 1984. *Modern Englishes*. Blackwell, Oxford.

Language Index

The genus of each language is given in parentheses.

Subject Index